INVESTMENT MIGRATION IN EUROPE AND THE WORLD

Over the past decades a growing number of countries have offered citizenship or residence in return for a donation or investment. Taking a multi-disciplinary approach to the study of this phenomenon, this collection examines its legal, political, and conceptual implications. The volume consists of four parts. The first part documents recent trends in investment migration and seeks to understand its implications for our understanding of the concept of citizenship. The second part provides a legal and normative assessment of investment migration, from the perspective of both EU and international law. The third part presents case studies of investment migration practices in countries from around the world, including from jurisdictions that have so far remained under-researched. The fourth part deals with the specific EU legal-political context and also engages with the case launched by the European Commission against Malta. The book assembles the leading experts in the field and offers a rigorous and balanced analysis of this sometimes controversial field.

Investment Migration in Europe and the World

Current Issues

Edited by
Dimitry V Kochenov
Madeleine Sumption
and
Martijn van den Brink

•HART•
OXFORD • LONDON • NEW YORK • NEW DELHI • SYDNEY

HART PUBLISHING
Bloomsbury Publishing Plc
Kemp House, Chawley Park, Cumnor Hill, Oxford, OX2 9PH, UK
1385 Broadway, New York, NY 10018, USA
Bloomsbury Publishing Ireland Limited, 29 Earlsfort Terrace, Dublin 2, D02 AY28, Ireland

HART PUBLISHING, the Hart/Stag logo, BLOOMSBURY and the Diana logo are trademarks of Bloomsbury Publishing Plc

First published in Great Britain 2025

A catalogue record for this book is available from the British Library.

A catalogue record for this book is available from the Library of Congress.

Library of Congress Control Number: 2025933511

ISBN: HB: 978-1-50995-522-0
ePDF: 978-1-50995-524-4
ePub: 978-1-50995-523-7

Typeset by Compuscript Ltd, Shannon

For product safety related questions contact productsafety@bloomsbury.com

To find out more about our authors and books visit www.hartpublishing.co.uk. Here you will find extracts, author information, details of forthcoming events and the option to sign up for our newsletters.

The tribune answered, 'it cost me a large sum of money to get my citizenship'.
Paul said, 'But I was born a citizen.'

Acts 22:28

Preface

INVESTMENT MIGRATION IS driven by the unequal nature of the world's nationality quality and the speed of global economic development. Over the past decades a growing number of countries have offered residence or citizenship in return for a payment or investment. While residence by investment programmes (RBI) have been common for many years in high-income countries, the recent development of citizenship by investment (CBI) programmes in both the European Union – particularly in Malta – and the wider world has attracted much debate and controversy.

From banal collectors of exotic documents and allegiances to those driven by a pressing need – like the opposition Belarusians abroad without valid documents and cut off from consular services by own government until they return to perish at home, or the simple passport-poor, whose citizenship is of such low quality that it is a liability around the world – the attraction of citizenship or residency for the buyers is compelling.

One does not need to delve into the history of Roman citizenship or turn to the Bible: just visit a Google office in Dubai where well-off passport-poor and exiles show each other newly bought documents of exotic islands they would never visit that make more or less normal life possible. For states offering investment migration the attraction is often less obvious. For those who dare to put a transparent price on citizenship it brings a clear but possibly controversial way to raise revenues. For everyone else, economic benefits are by no means guaranteed.

This book takes a multi-disciplinary approach to investment migration in order to better understand the phenomenon and to examine its legal, political and conceptual implications. The book consists of four parts. The first part documents recent trends in investment migration and seeks to understand its implications for our understanding of the concept of citizenship. The second part provides a legal and normative assessment of investment migration, from the perspective of both EU and international law. The third part presents case studies of investment migration practices in countries from around the world, including from countries that have so far remained under-researched. The fourth part deals with the specific EU legal-political context and also engages with the case launched by the European Commission against Malta.

This volume assembles work from both young scholars and established authorities from law, sociology and politics, and is based, besides chapters solicited specifically for this book project, on a selection of the most significant updated contributions to *Investment Migration Working Papers* – a series which was co-founded by Dimitry Kochenov together with Madeleine Sumption and which they co-edited together with Martijn van den Brink between 2015 and 2020, as well as some revised contributions to the *Citizenship by Investment: Law, Policy and Sociology* seminar, which Madeleine Sumption and Dimitry Kochenov co-convened at the School of Anthropology at Oxford in Hilary term of 2020–21 academic year. This book is a natural companion of *Citizenship and Residence Sales* (Cambridge University Press, 2023) co-edited by Dimitry Kochenov and Kristin Surak of the London School of Economics and Political Science.

The book you are holding in your hands has benefited from expert help from dozens of colleagues on both sides of the Atlantic and in China, who acted as reviewers and to whom we are much indebted – and from the wonderful research assistance of Mariam Begadze and Emma Schulte. Open access publication was made possible by the generous grant from the Provost's Open Access Fund of the Central European University in Vienna and Budapest and the support of the Investment Migration Council (IMC) in Geneva, of which Professor Kochenov has served as the founding chairman. The editors are grateful to Agnes Batory (CEU), Bruno L'ecuyer (IMC), Diane Geraci (CEU Library) and Sinead Moloney (Hart Publishing) for supporting this project.

DVK, MS and MvdB
Shanghai, London, Leiden
September 2024

Contents

Contributors

Odile Ammann, University of Lausanne

Vasiliki Apatzidou, Queen Mary, University of London

Luuk van der Baaren, Copenhagen University

Elena Basheska, Central European University (CEU) Democracy Institute, Budapest

Martijn van den Brink, Leiden University

Miriam Cohen, University of Montreal

Gareth Davies, Vrije Universiteit Amsterdam

Qishi Fu, Investment migration practitioner, China

Sarah Ganty, Yale Law School, New Haven; Université Catholique de Louvain

Oskar J Gstrein, Campus Fryslân, University of Groningen, Leeuwarden

Shah Guido, Senior European Commission official contributing incognito

Guillermo Íñiguez, University of Oxford

Hans Ulrich Jessurun d'Oliveira, European University Institute, Florence and UvA, University of Amsterdam, Emeritus

Dimitry V Kochenov, CEU Democracy Institute, Budapest and CEU Department of Legal Studies, Vienna

Sau Kong Lee, Hong Kong University

Hanwei Li, Yan'an University

Vadim Poleshchuk, Political Advisor, European Parliament, Brussels

Daniel Sarmiento, Complutense University, Madrid

Peter J Spiro, Temple Law School, Philadelphia

Francesca Strumia, City, University of London

Madeleine Sumption, University of Oxford

Matjaž Tratnik, University of Maribor

Niovi Vavoula, University of Luxembourg

Jacquelyn D Veraldi, CEU Democracy Institute, Budapest

JHH Weiler, NYU Law School

Petra Weingerl, University of Maribor

Abbreviations

ACERWC	African Committee of Experts on the Rights and Welfare of the Child
ACHR	American Convention on Human Rights
ACHPR	African Charter on Human and Peoples' Rights
ACRWC	African Charter on the Rights and Welfare of the Child
AEEAΠ	Επενδύσεων σε Ακίνητη Περιουσία [Real Estate Investment Company]
AEOI	automatic exchange of information
AFMP	Agreement on the Free Movement of Persons (Switzerland)
AG	Advocate General (EU)
AICEP	Agência para o Investimento e Comércio Externo de Portugal
AKEΣ	Αμοιβαίο Κεφάλαιο Επιχειρηματικών Συμμετοχών [venture fund]
AML	Anti-money laundering
APEMIP	Associação dos Profissionais e Empresas de Mediação Imobiliária de Portugal [The Association of Real Estate Professionals and Companies of Portugal]
ARI	Autorização de Residência para atividade de Investimento [Golden Residence Permit Program]
BAIIP	Business Assistance-Immigrant Investor Program (Quebec)
BDC	Business Development Bank of Canada
BIVs	business investment visas
BJREECM	*Baltic Journal of Real Estate Economics and Construction Management*
B2B	business-to-business
CAD	Canadian dollar
CAS	Court of Arbitration for Sport
CBI	citizenship by investment
CCDI	Central Commission for Discipline Inspection
CEDAW	Convention on the Elimination of Discrimination Against Women
CEO	chief executive officer

CERD	International Convention on the Elimination of All Forms of Racial Discrimination
CFR	Charter of Fundamental Rights of the European Union
CIC	Citizenship and Immigration Canada
CIES	Capital Investment Entrant Scheme (Hong Kong)
CIPG	Centre for Innovation Policy and Governance
CJEU	Court of Justice of the European Union
CJEL	*Columbia Journal of European Law*
CJRL	*Columbia Journal of Race and Law*
CKJICL	*Chicago-Kent Journal of International and Comparative Law*
CLB	Canadian Language Benchmarks
CMW	International Convention on the Protection of the Rights of All Migrant Workers and Members of Their Families
CPC	Communist Party of China
CR	*The Chinese Repository*, Vol I – XX (1832–1850)
CRC	Convention on the Rights of the Child
CRPD	Convention on the Rights of Persons with Disabilities
CRS	Common Reporting Standard
DAAS	*Diplomatic Archives of the Institute of Modern History*, Academia Sinica
DCIAP	Portuguese Central Department of Investigation and Penal Action
DQHD (GX)	*(Qinding) Da Qing huidian (Guangxu) ((Royal Commissioned) Collected Statutes of Great Qing: Reign of Guangxu)*
DQHD (QL)	*(Qinding) Da Qing huidian (Qianlong) ((Royal Commissioned) Collected Statutes of Great Qing: Reign of Qianlong)*
DQHDZL (QL)	*(Qinding) Da Qing huidian zeli (Qianlong) ((Royal Commissioned) Collected Sub-statutes of Great Qing: Reign of Qianlong)*
EB	employment-based
ECA	Educational Credential Assessment
EComHR	European Commission of Human Rights
ECtHR	European Court of Human Rights
ECJ	European Court of Justice
ECN	European Convention on Nationality

ECRIS-TCN	European Criminal Record Information System for Third-country Nationals (EU)
EDPL	*European Data Protection Law Review*
EEA	European Economic Area
EEC	European Economic Community
EESC	European Economic and Social Committee
EFTA	European Free Trade Association
EJCL	*European Journal of Comparative Law and Governance*
EJIL	*European Journal of International Law*
EJML	*European Journal of Migration and Law*
EJPR	*European Journal of Political Research*
ΕΚΕΣ	Εταιρεία Κεφαλαίου Επιχειρηματικών Συμμετοχών [Venture Capital Company]
ELJ	*European Law Journal*
EPL	*European Public Law*
EPRS	European Parliamentary Research Service
ESTA	Electronic System for Travel Authorization (US)
ETIAS	European Travel Information and Authorization System (EU)
EP	European Parliament
EPPO	European Public Prosecutor's Office
EUDO	The European Union Democracy Observatory
Exam Regs	*Kechang tiaoli (Xianfeng) (Examination Regulations, Xianfeng edn)*
FATF	Financial Action Task Force [Groupe d'action financière]
FIIP	Federal Immigrant Investor Programme (Canada)
FNIA	Federal Act on Foreign Nationals and Integration (Switzerland)
FRONTEX	European Border and Coast Guard Agency (EU)
GC Telegrams	First Historical Archives of China (ed), *Qing dai Junjichu dianbao dang huibian (Compilation of Telegram Records of the Grand Council of the Qing Dynasty)* (China Renmin UP 2005)
GDP	Gross domestic product
GDPR	General Data Protection Regulation (EU)
GLJ	*German Law Journal*

GQ Code	Da Qing lüli (Great Qing Code)
HELP	*Health Economics, Policy & Law*
HJRL	*Hague Journal on the Rule of Law*
HKD	Hong Kong dollar
HKSAR	Hong Kong Special Administrative Region
HRC	Human Rights Committee
HRLJ	*Human Rights Law Journal*
IBR	*International Business Review*
ICCPR	International Covenant on Civil and Political Rights
ICJ	International Court of Justice
ICLQ	*International and Comparative Law Quarterly*
ICON	*International Journal of Constitutional Law*
ICSID	International Centre for Settlement of Investment Disputes
ICT	Information and communication technology
IDA	Identity Documents Act (Estonia)
IGC	inter-governmental conference (EU)
IIVC	Immigrant Investor Venture Capital (Canada)
IJDL	*International Journal of Discrimination and the Law*
IJELP	*International Journal for Education Law and Policy*
IJGLS	*Indiana Journal of Global Legal Studies*
IJSDP	*International Journal of Sustainable Development and Planning*
IJURR	*International Journal of Urban and Regional Research*
ILC	International Law Commission
ILR	indefinite leave to remain (UK)
IMR	*International Migration Review*
IREF	*International Review of Economics and Finance*
IRN	Portuguese Institute for Registries and Notaries
IRPA	Immigration and Refugee Protection Act (Canada)
IIP	Individual Investor Programme (Malta)
IIP	Immigrant Investor Programme (Ireland, Australia, Canada, UK)
IT	Information Technology

JACAR	Japan Centre for Asian Historical Records, National Archives of Japan
JAEH	*Journal of American Ethnic History*
JCER	*Journal of Comparative Effectiveness Research*
JCES	*Journal of Contemporary European Studies*
JCMS	*Journal of Common Market Studies*
JEMS	*Journal of Ethnic and Migration Studies*
JEP	*Journal of Economic Perspectives*
JERL	*Journal of Energy and Natural Resources Law*
JESP	*Journal of European Social Policy*
JHE	*Journal of Higher Education*
JLE	*Journal of Law and Equality*
JOPP	*Journal of Political Philosophy*
LHR	*Law and History Review*
MAC	Migration Advisory Committee (UK)
MCAA	Multilateral Competent Authority Agreement
MEP	Member of the European Parliament
MFN	most-favoured-nation
MJ	*Maastricht Journal of European and Comparative Law*
MLR	*Modern Law Review*
MS	Member State of the European Union
MIPEX	Migrant Integration Policy Index
NAFTA	North American Free Trade Agreement
NILR	*Netherlands International Law Review*
OASA	Federal Ordinance on Admission, Residence, and Gainful Employment (Switzerland)
OECD	The Organisation for Economic Co-operation and Development
OEE	Alternative Investments Schemes
OLAF	European Anti-Fraud Office
PCIJ	Permanent Court of International Justice
PEPs	politically exposed persons
POS	Point of Sale

PRC	People's Republic of China
PRIIME	Employment Integration Program for Immigrants and Visible Minorities (Quebec)
QJ	First Historical Archives of China (ed), 'Qian Jia shiqi keju maoji shiliao (Fraud in Imperial Examinations during the Reigns of Qianlong and Jiaqing)' [2000] *Historical Archives* 13
QWT	*Qing wenxian tongkao (Comprehensive Investigations Based on Literary and Documentary Sources: Qing Dynasty)*
RAISE	Reforming American Immigration for Strong Employment (US)
RBI	residence by investment
ROI	return on investment
SARS	severe acute respiratory syndrome
SCR	*Statelessness and Citizenship Review*
SEF	Serviço de Estrangeiros e Fronteiras [Foreigners and Borders Service, Portugal]
SLTD SSNIP	small but significant and non-transitory increase in price
SRIEL	*Swiss Review for International and European Law*
STEP	Start-up Entrepreneur Programme (Ireland)
STLR	*Stanford Technology Law Review*
TDAWN	Interpol Travel Documents Associated with Notices
TEA	Targeted Employment Area (US)
TEU	Treaty on the European Union
TFEU	Treaty on the Functioning of the European Union
TLCP	*Transnational Law and Contemporary Problems*
TWHM	Wang X (ed), *Rizhi shiqi jimin yu guoji shiliao huibian (Historical materials on Taiwanese registration and Japanese nationality during the Japanese Colonial Era)* (Taiwan Historica 2010)
UNDRIP	Declaration on the Rights of Indigenous Peoples
URM	Underrepresented minority
USCIS	US Citizenship and Immigration Services
USD	United States dollar
VAT	Value Added Tax
VIS	Visa Information System (EU)

XZSL	*Qing mo Min chu xianzheng shiliao jikan (Compilation of Constitutional Materials in the Late Qing to Early Republican Period)* (Beijing Library Press 2006)
YEL	*Yearbook of European Law*
YJIL	*Yale Journal of International Law*
UDHR	Universal Declaration of Human Rights
VUWLR	*Victoria University Wellington Law Review*
1MDB	1Malaysia Development Berhad

Tables, Figures and Maps

Tables

Figures

Maps

Table of Cases

International and Supranational Jurisdictions

Permanent Court of International Justice

International Court of Justice

UN Human Rights Committee

Court of Justice of the European Union

The General Court of the European Union

European Commission of Human Rights

European Court of Human Rights

Inter-American Commission on Human Rights

African Commission on Human and Peoples' Rights

African Committee of Experts on the Rights and Welfare of the Child

National Jurisdictions

Canada (Federal Court)

Italy (Italian Council of State)

Netherlands (Dutch Council of State)

United Kingdom (Supreme Court)

United States (Supreme Court)

Introduction: Advancing Investment Migration Scholarship

DIMITRY V KOCHENOV, MADELEINE SUMPTION AND MARTIJN VAN DEN BRINK

INVESTOR MIGRATION HAS rapidly emerged as one of the most controversial, contested and captivating practices within contemporary migration and citizenship policy. The very idea of putting a price tag on citizenships and residences abhors many. That some investor migration schemes have additionally been riven with corruption,[1] and been used by states to shrug off their responsibilities to their stateless population,[2] has only fuelled and reinforced criticism. Yet, at the same time, well-designed investor migration policies – under some conditions – can provide a welcome financial boost to the local economy, with revenues in smaller island states easily exceeding 10 per cent of the government budget or their GDP.[3] Further to this, investor migration helps people with deep pockets move up the global citizenship hierarchy and acquire the rights, privileges and freedoms of those with sought-after Western passports.[4] Indeed, it helps losers in the so-called 'birthright lottery'[5] to secure a 'super citizenship'[6] of a rich country and benefit from the 'citizenship rents' that come with it.[7] The fact that it provides a selective escape route for the wealthy with 'sub-standard citizenships'[8] explains at once the popularity of investor migration among the most immediate beneficiaries and its critical reception among some politicians and scholars.

Investment migration clearly is a complex and multifaceted phenomenon. Numerous recent studies confirm and augment this understanding.[9] While the initial reaction of political

[1] Nagy, 'Investment Migration and Corruption' in Kochenov and Surak (eds), *Citizenship and Residence Sales* (Cambridge University Press 2023); Corrado and Marsh, 'Investment Migration and the Importance of Due Diligence' in Kochenov and Surak (eds), *Citizenship and Residence Sales* (Cambridge University Press 2023); Van Fossen, 'Passport Sales: How Microstates Use Strategic Management to Organise the New Economic Citizenship Industry' (2018) 13 *Island Studies Journal* 285.

[2] Spiro, 'Investment Citizenship and the Long Leash of International Law' in Kochenov and Surak (eds), *Citizenship and Residence Sales*; Abrahamian, *The Cosmopolites* (Columbia Global Reports 2015).

[3] Surak, 'Investment Migration: Empirical Developments in the Field and Methodological Issues in Its Study' in Kochenov and Surak (eds), *Citizenship and Residence Sales*, 66; Surak, 'Do Passports Pay off?' (2024) *JEMS* (early view).

[4] Harpaz, 'Citizenship and Residence Rights as Vehicles of Global Inequality' in Kochenov and Surak (eds), *Citizenship and Residence Sales*.

[5] Shachar, *The Birthright Lottery* (Harvard University Press 2009).

[6] Kochenov, *Citizenship* (MIT Press 2019) 239.

[7] Milanović, *Capitalism, Alone* (Belknap 2019); Kalm, 'Citizenship Capital' (2020) 34 *Global Society* 528.

[8] Kochenov and Lindeboom, 'Empirical Assessment of the Quality of Nationalities' (2017) 4 *EJCL* 314; Kochenov, 'Victims of Citizenship' in Kochenov and Surak (eds), *Citizenship and Residence Sales*.

[9] See, especially, Kochenov and Surak (eds), *Citizenship and Residence Sales*; Surak, *The Golden Passport* (Harvard University Press 2023); Džankić, *The Global Market for Investor Citizenship* (Palgrave Macmillan 2019); Kälin, Ius Doni *in International Law and EU Law* (Brill-Nijhoff 2019).

theorists was one of moral indignation,[10] they have started offering more nuanced examinations. Some remain critical of the commodification of citizenship,[11] but others argue that investor migration is no more arbitrary or unjust than more traditional ways of allocating legal beloning.[12] Social scientists, meanwhile, have much improved our empirical understanding of the investor migration market, of the actors on the scene, the motivations of states selling passports and visas and of the individuals willing to pay hefty sums to buy them and the possible financial and economic consequences of these policies.[13] Lawyers, in response to ongoing lawsuit against investor migration schemes,[14] have closely examined how norms of international and European Union law apply to these schemes.[15] Add to this historians who show the 'long pedigree' of contemporary investor migration,[16] public policy scholars interested in questions of (successful) policy design[17] and (political) economists inquiring into the economic factors driving investors' choices,[18] and what emerges is a thriving and thoroughly interdisciplinary field of study.

This book contributes to this field. Studies before this one have tried making sense of the curious world of investor migration, but were, as Atossa Abrahamian remarked, 'not afraid to raise more questions still'.[19] With this book, we hope to answer some of these questions, even if the individual contributions will no doubt also raise more still. This book also builds on recent studies in another way. It understands investor migration not as an outlying phenomenon in the field of citizenship and migration, but instead as a practice with direct implications for contemporary understanding of the mechanisms underpinning the essential functions of citizenship and the global distribution of rights and opportunities.[20] Investor migration is part of the wider transformation of citizenship and residence that has been underway for decades.[21]

[10] eg Shachar, 'Citizenship for Sale?' in Shachar et al (eds), *The Oxford Handbook of Citizenship* (Oxford University Press 2017).

[11] Mavelli, 'Citizenship for Sale and the Neoliberal Political Economy of Belonging' (2018) 62 *International Studies Quarterly* 482; Tanasoca, 'Citizenship for Sale: Neomedieval, Not Just Neoliberal?' (2016) 57 *EJS* 169. For critical reflection, see Roy, 'The "Streetlight Effect" in Commentary on Citizenship by Investment' in Kochenov and Surak (eds), *Citizenship and Residence Sales*, 306.

[12] Erez, 'A Blocked Exchange?' in Kochenov and Surak (eds), *Citizenship and Residence Sales*; Kochenov, 'Citizenship for Real: Its Hypocrisy, Its Randomness, Its Price' in Bauböck (ed), *Debating Transformations of National Citizenship* (Springer 2018) 51.

[13] See especially, Surak, *The Golden Passport*. See also Kalm, 'The Business of Citizenship' (2022) 37 *Global Society* 68.

[14] Case C-181/23 *Commission v Malta* OJ C 173/27 pending. Cf. Sarmiento and Íñiquez's as well as Weiler's contributions to this volume and van den Brink, '3½ Myths about EU law on Citizenship for Sale' (VerfBlog 2024).

[15] On international law, Spiro, 'Investment Citizenship and the Long Leash of International Law' in Kochenov and Surak (eds), *Citizenship and Residence Sales*; van der Baaren, 'Investor Citizenship and State Sovereignty in International Law' in Kochenov and Surak (eds), *Citizenship and Residence Sales*. On European Union law, van den Brink, 'Revising Citizenship within the European Union' (2022) 23 *GLJ* 79; Sarmiento and van den Brink, 'EU Competence and Investor Migration' in Kochenov and Surak (eds), *Citizenship and Residence Sales*; Kochenov, 'Genuine Purity of Blood' (2020) LEQS Paper No. 164/2020.

[16] Prak, 'Citizenship for Sale in Pre-Modern Europe' in Kochenov and Surak (eds), *Citizenship and Residence Sales*. See also, Lee's chapter in this volume.

[17] Sumption, 'Can Investor Residence and Citizenship Programmes Be a Policy Success?' in Kochenov and Surak (eds), *Citizenship and Residence Sales*; Gamlen et al, 'Citizenship as Sovereign Wealth: Re-thinking Investor Immigration' (2019) 10 *Global Policy* 527.

[18] Consterdine and Hampshire, 'Buying in? The Political Economy of Investor Migration in Western Europe' (2023) *WEP* 47 (7): 1588–1613; Solimano, 'Why Do Wealthy Individuals Migrate Internationally' in Kochenov and Surak (eds), *Citizenship and Residence Sales*.

[19] Abrahamian, 'Preface' in Kochenov and Surak (eds), *Citizenship and Residence Sales*, xviii.

[20] Spiro, 'Cash-for-Passports and the End of Citizenship' in Bauböck (ed), *Debating Transformations of National Citizenship* (Springer 2018) 17; Kochenov, 'Citizenship for Real', 51.

[21] Bosniak, *The Citizen and the Alien* (Princeton University Press 2006); Tully, *On Global Citizenship* (Bloomsbury 2014); Bloom, *Noncitizenism* (Routledge 2017); Swider, *A Rights-Based Approach to Statelessness*

This transformation is partly characterised by its (supposedly inevitable) lightening and the growing 'instrumentalism and a dissociation of citizenship from nationhood'.[22] States have expanded the reach of citizenship rights following the acceptance that they are not 'container societies'[23] and cannot continue denying the rights and status of citizenship to people with meaningful ties to their societies. For states, however, it has also meant granting membership to people seemingly *without* meaningful social ties to their society, sometimes to remedy past injustices,[24] recognize perceived co-ethnic kin but more so for instrumental reasons: to attract the best, the brightest or simply the (ultra-)rich.[25] For individuals, it means they can acquire what Yossi Harpaz calls 'compensatory citizenship' – a status that makes up 'for deficits in the original citizenship in terms of opportunities, security, rights and travel freedom'.[26] Investor migration may be at the extreme end of this transformation, amounting to 'the marketization of sovereignty'[27] or what Francesca Strumia in this volume calls 'new generation skilled migration policies', but it cannot be seen or studied in isolation from it.[28]

Investor citizenship also cannot be studied in isolation from the other, more exclusionary, side of this transformation: the fact that people's life chances are in large part determined by their place of birth and the vast global inequalities in today's world.[29] Investor migration obviously isn't the great equaliser, but our understanding and evaluation of it can depend on the side from which it is analysed. Investor citizenship is akin to queue jumping for some, but the only way to enter the queue for others. For some, it is a mercantilist practice favouring winners, for others, a (minor) corrective for some structural global inequalities.[30] For some, investor migration is an unjustified meritocratic practice.[31] For others, it is indeed meritocratic, yet preferable over more exclusive anti-meritocratic practices.[32] In other words, our view on investor citizenship depends partly on how the problem is conceived. Is the problem that a small minority of those, who are branded out as 'second rate' by birth can cross national borders too unimpeded, or rather that the vast majority finds it almost impossible to cross those borders at all? Is the solution, to put it provocatively, to bring the wealthy passport poor down or everyone else up?[33] The answer may be neither or both or, quite likely, be more nuanced than the questions posed this way allow, but the questions show that our assessment of investor migration can vary depending on the wider perspective of citizenship and migration we adopt. Some of the chapters in this volume illustrate this tension.

(Doctoral Thesis, University of Amsterdam, 2018); Kochenov, 'Interlegality – Citizenship – Intercitizenship', in Klabbers and Palombella (eds), *The Challenge of Interlegality* (Cambridge University Press 2019) 133; Kochenov, 'Statelessness: A Radical Rethinking of the Dominant Citizenism Paradigm' (2024) 20 *Annual Review of Law and Social Science* 117.

22 Joppke, 'The Inevitable Lightening of Citizenship' (2010) 51 *EJS* 9.

23 Calavita, 'Law, Citizenship, and the Construction of (Some) Immigrant "Others"' (2005) 30 *Law & Social Inquiry* 401, 405.

24 Maatsch, *Ethnic Citizenship Regimes* (Palgrave Macmillan 2011); Jessurun d'Oliveira, 'Iberian Nationality Legislation and Sephardic Jews' (2015) 11 *EUConst* 13.

25 Shachar, 'Picking Winners' (2010) 120 *YLJ* 2088; Džankić, *The Global Market*, ch 6; Surak, 'Global Citizenship 2.0 The Growth of Citizenship by Investment Programs' (2016) IMC Research paper 2016/02.

26 Harpaz, 'Compensatory Citizenship' (2019) 45 *JEMS* 897.

27 Surak, 'Marketizing Sovereign Prerogatives' (2021) 62 (2) *EJS* 275–308.

28 Kochenov and Surak, 'Learning from Investment Migration' in Kochenov and Surak (eds), *Citizenship and Residence Sales*. See also the chapter by Kochenov and van den Brink in this volume.

29 Milanović, *Global Inequality* (Belknap 2018); Boatcă, *Global Inequalities beyond Occidentalism* (Ashgate 2015).

30 Boatcă, *Global Inequalities beyond Occidentalism*.

31 See Ammann's chapter in this volume.

32 See Ganty's chapter in this volume.

33 For discussion of this tension, see, eg van den Brink, 'Revisiting Citizenship within the European Union'; Roy, 'The "Streetlight Effect"'.

Investor migration of course not only raises foundational questions of borders, mobility and membership. The nuts and bolts of investor migration – its design, practical implementation and day-to-day operation in different countries – can raise equally important questions. How do investor migration practices differ from country to country? How can countries design their investor migration policies to be politically or economically successful? How can they address worries about money laundering, tax evasion and other risks potentially associated with the practice? How do countries, with or without investor migration schemes, adjust their citizenship and migration policies in response to investor migration practices elsewhere? Many of this volume's contributions tackle such questions. Some do so directly, such Jacquelyn Veraldi and Oskar Gstrein's chapter discussing what measures countries can take to mitigate the risks of CBI practices; many others do so indirectly. These include single-country studies of Canada, Estonia, Greece and late-Imperial China, chapters discussing the EU's response to investor migration and two comparative studies: one comparing the United Kingdom and the United States and another comparing European naturalisation requirements.

Before continuing, we should address some definitional issues around investor migration. As Kristin Surak reminds us, one definitional issue is that 'neither "investment" nor "migration" accurately captures what goes on under the label'.[34] While many countries award citizenship or residence in return for an investment in, for example, property or the local economy, not all schemes allow a return on the money spent. Maltese citizenship, for example, can be obtained through a non-refundable donation to the state budget.[35] Moreover, while the term migration implies a change of country of residence for a certain duration, many investors do not move their principal place of abode to their new country of residence or citizenship – if they visit at all, that is. The travel and settlement freedoms that come with acquiring a passport or right to reside can be one motivation for investors, but others invest for the business, taxation or educational opportunities a passport or visa provides.[36] That said, it is widely agreed that investor migration includes both citizenship by investment (CBI) and residence by investment (RBI), which, according to the OECD definition, 'allow foreign individuals to obtain citizenship or temporary or permanent residence rights on the basis of local investments or against a flat fee'.[37] A second definitional issue is whether CBI and RBI cover the full spectrum of investor citizenship, or whether the latter also includes business and entrepreneurial visas. Depending on their design, such visas can amount to an 'investor-lite model',[38] illustrating the difficulty of delineating investor migration from other migration practices. Such visas usually fall outside the definition of investor migration, outside our definition too.

Even on this 'narrow' definition, investor migration emerges as a widespread and still growing phenomenon. Although the sale of citizenship dates back to pre-modern times,[39] contemporary CBI practices date back to 1984 when Saint Kitts and Nevis began operating its scheme, followed by Dominica, Cambodia and Mauritius in the 1990s. The 16 other countries with CBI schemes launched them between the late 2000s and 2020, showing the rapid spread of CBI in the last two decades.[40] The popularity of RBI has equally been on the rise. According to the 2019 European Commission report on investor citizenship and residence schemes, 20 EU

[34] Surak, 'Investment Migration', 27. See also Sumption, 'Can Investment Citizenship and Residence Programmes Be a Policy Success?'.

[35] Citizenship Act 1965 (MT), as amended by Acts XV and XXXVIII of 2020.

[36] Surak, 'Investment Migration', 48–52.

[37] As discussed in detail by Surak in this volume.

[38] Sumption, 'Can Investment Citizenship and Residence Programmes Be a Policy Success?'.

[39] Prak, 'Citizenship for Sale'.

[40] Surak, 'Investment Migration', 35–36.

Member States run such schemes. Estimates of the total number of states offering RBI schemes globally range, depending on definitional and methodological choices, between 50 and 70. In other words, no matter how one views investor migration, there is still much to learn about this practice, which allows us to gain valuable insights about the changing nature of citizenship, residence and belonging in the contemporary world.

I. STRUCTURE OF THE VOLUME

The chapters in this volume address many of the issues mentioned above, and others, from various disciplinary perspectives. The book is divided into four parts.

A. Investor Migration: Conceptualisation and Context

The first part, 'Investor Migration: Conceptualisation and Context', enhances our understanding of investor migration by contextualising the phenomenon. How do CBI and RBI practices relate to other, more conventional, citizenship and migration policies? What principles and ideals underlie these practices and what should that mean for our evaluation of them? And how does the fact that we live in a world of global inequality influence the practice of and our view of investor migration? These are some of the questions addressed in Part I.

William Worster's analysis departs from the *Nottebohm* judgment of the International Court of Justice and the principle of 'genuine link' established in that judgment.[41] This principle underlies much national and international criticism of CBI practices and the judgment is therefore often invoked to challenge such practices. Worster, however, highlights the developments in international human rights law that have taken place since *Nottebohm* and argues, in light of these developments, that states may criticise the nationality laws of other states but not easily punish individuals for these laws. Questioning someone's nationality raises human rights issues and must be justified as a necessary and proportionate measure to promote a legitimate governmental interest. Finally, applying this legal framework to the practice of CBI, Worster concludes that non-recognition of nationalities obtained through investment is difficult to justify under international law.

Francesca Strumia compares CBI and RBI with traditional policies for selecting skilled migrants and argues that CBI and RBI, together with policies that seek to attract entrepreneurs or talented athletes, amount to 'new generation skilled migration policies' that differ from traditional skilled migration policies in two ways. First, while traditional policies focus on the input migrants offer in terms of education and experience into the host state's society, new policies are rather geared toward their output in terms of financial capital or employment. Second, new programmes change the state's role in administering immigration and citizenship law, transforming them from 'border guards' into 'headhunters'. These changes, Strumia argues, contribute to the polarisation of the dual approach to border management adopted by states, which is characterised by the simultaneous opening and closure of borders, and have produced two models of membership.

[41] *Nottebohm (Liechtenstein v Guatemala)* [1955] ICJ Rep. 4. For earlier discussions of the judgment see Macklin, 'Is it Time to Retire *Nottebohm*?' (2017) 111 *AJIL* 492; Kunz, 'The *Nottebohm* Judgment' (1960) 54 *AJIL* 536; van den Brink, 'Revisiting Citizenship within the European Union'; Sloane, 'Breaking the Genuine Link' (2009) 50 *Harv Int'l LJ* 1.

Odile Ammann's chapter tells us a similar story but from the perspective of meritocracy. Like Strumia, she perceives CBI and RBI as policies in continuity with other policies to attract desired immigrants and citizens. The premise of her analysis is that we 'live in a world where citizenship and immigration law are justified with reference to "merit"', in which CBI and RBI 'are just the tip of the meritocratic iceberg'. She does not take this line of analysis to justify CBI and RBI schemes but rather uses it to offer a more holistic appraisal of contemporary immigration and citizenship policy. CBI and RBI are the symptoms of a wider problem, namely the use of merit as a crucial selection criterion, a concept used to justify inequality. The takeaway of her argument is, in other words, that CBI and RBI are just as problematic as other citizenship and immigration policies using this criterion.

Sarah Ganty further problematises states' reliance on merit as a way to distinguish between prospective immigrants and citizens. Whereas Ammann objects to merit on the grounds that it can entrench and exacerbate inequalities, Ganty argues that the criterion is problematic as it reproduces 'patterns of "racialisation" or "ethnicisation" of the "other"'. However, she also claims that criticism of meritocratic institutions can be racially and ethnically charged as well. Ganty uses CBI and RBI to illustrate and analyse this tension. On the one hand, CBI and RBI are eminently meritocratic and therefore run the risk of being racially and ethnically loaded, like many other investment and citizenship laws around the world. On the other hand, the fierce criticism of CBI and RBI for departing from traditional modes of obtaining citizenship shows that criticism of meritocratic practices can be just as racially and ethnically charged. If the choice is between these two evils, Ganty encourages us to favour the inclusive meritocratic rationale over the exclusive anti-meritocratic rationale.

B. Legal Regulation: Empirical and Normative Perspectives on Investor Migration

The second part, 'Empirical and Normative Perspectives on Investor Migration', dives into some legal issues surrounding investor migration. What inroads have international and European law made into the domain of citizenship and migration, and do these inroads make investor migration suspect? How do the legal and practical requirements for obtaining citizenship by investment compare with those in other naturalisation procedures? And to what extent is the regulation of investor citizenship subject to other, so far unexplored, legal constraints, such as competition or fundamental rights law? These legal questions are tackled in the second part.

In his chapter, Peter Spiro provides an anatomical analysis of one of the very few inroads international law has made into national sovereignty over the attribution of nationality: the *Nottebohm* judgment of the International Court of Justice and the principle of 'genuine link' – the principle at the heart of the case launched by the European Commission against the Maltese CBI scheme.[42] Spiro shows not only that *Nottebohm* has been fiercely contested since the ruling, but also, looking at the practice of different international courts, that the principle of genuine link has never become an established norm of customary international law. On the contrary, it bears all the hallmarks of a jurisprudential illusion.

Matjaž Tratnik and Petra Weingerl take this analysis further and provide a meticulous analysis of the applicability of the genuine links mentioned in *Nottebohm* in the context of EU law and the different types of naturalisations that the Member States offer. They demonstrate that

[42] *Commission v Malta* pending.

the Commission's invocation of genuine links points in the direction of a potential breach of EU law by the Guardian of the Treaties, as it does not only contravene both horizontal and vertical division of competences in the EU, but also is a frontal assault on the freedom of movement of EU citizens, thereby undermining the achievement of the key objective of the internal market.

In her chapter, Kristin Surak moves beyond the recent analysis by the Organisation for Economic Co-operation and Development (OECD) and Financial Action Task Force (FATF) to investigate whether and how residence and citizenship documents pose risks concerning identity laundering, money laundering and tax evasion. Drawing on nine years of fieldwork and a new dataset on investment migration, she shows that such risks operate through building legible profiles that are acceptable to financial institutions as evidence of a person's relationship to a jurisdiction. The analysis examines the scale of actual problems to show that the biggest risks in these domains are posed by grey-market and black-market options. Therefore, to properly address financial crime threats, attention should be directed to possibilities for acquiring citizenship or residence documents through financial means that are adjacent to investment migration programmes – such as business investor visas or documents gained through corruption. In conclusion, Surak argues for a 'problem-based approach' focused on actual harms instead of a 'programme-based approach' that starts from specific citizenship and residence schemes.

Like other chapters, the chapter by Dimitry Kochenov and Martijn van den Brink also takes the focus on the genuine links as the point of departure. According to the European Commission, the genuine links require that naturalisation be 'residence-based'. Kochenov and van den Brink study the relationship between the two most common legal concepts in European migration and citizenship law – legal residence and physical presence – thereby shedding doubt on the Commission's assumption. Their study has three findings. First, legal residence is an important requirement in ordinary naturalisation procedures, but not in many preferential naturalisation procedures. Second, legal residence does not coincide with physical presence, either in EU law or national law, and the required duration of physical presence is often significantly shorter than the required duration of legal residence. Third, national authorities often do not, and cannot, examine whether naturalisation applicants have been physically present long enough.

The three remaining chapters of the second part discuss various other legal questions that (may) arise in the regulation of investor migration. Gareth Davies examines the possibility of cartelisation in the investor migration market and asks whether this would fall within the scope of EU competition law. While this may seem like an imaginary scenario, there have been price wars between countries offering their citizenship for sale,[43] so Davies is right that it may be interesting for states to put a system in place that prevents the price of passports or visas from being driven too low. If an investor migration cartel is established within the EU, will Member States run into legal trouble? Davies argues that such a cartel could raise issues under EU competition law, although the law is sufficiently ambiguous that a case against cartelisation can go either way.

Jacquelyn Veraldi and Oskar Gstrein's chapter examines the underexplored tension between transparency requirements and the right to privacy in investment migration.[44] Increased transparency is one of the measures proposed to address the security risks associated with investor migration, but what if this compromises the privacy of individuals who naturalise? Veraldi

[43] Nesheim, 'Caribbean CIP "Race to the Bottom"' (Investment Migration Insider, 18 October 2017) www.imidaily.com/caribbean/caribbean-cip-race-bottom-time-form-cartel/.

[44] See also Kochenov, Gstrein and Veraldi, 'On the Privacy – Naturalisation Interface' (2020) 42 *Hous J Int'l L* 237.

and Gstrein argue that greater transparency seems necessary to mitigate risks associated with investor migration but that revealing the identities of individuals participating in these programmes would be bad policy. Better policy would be to introduce clear and transparent governance frameworks that improve oversight of investor migration programmes. This can achieve the transparency required regarding investor migration while respecting the privacy of the individuals involved.

Madeleine Sumption's chapter questions the economic benefits of residence by investment, drawing on a study of the United States and United Kingdom's experience. Commentators and scholars often take it for granted that RBI programmes bring economic benefits, suggesting that governments are selling their souls at a handsome price. But perhaps they are giving away their souls for free? Sumption argues that simply raising revenues is not enough to ensure an economic benefit: the investments must actually stimulate new economic activity, but applicants shy away from higher-risk investments where their money is most needed. At the same time, a financial investment is not a very precise way to identify the types of people policymakers most want to attract. Sumption suggests that policymakers interested in getting an economic benefit from RBI programmes should put more thought to what they really want to achieve and whether an investor programme is the right way to achieve it.

C. Investment Migration Regulation in Europe and the World

The third part, 'Investment Migration Regulation in Europe and the World', consists of individual and comparative case studies. The chapters in this part provide a better understanding of the regulation of investment migration in Europe and the world. They vary in the perspective chosen, from single-country to comparative studies, from contemporary to historical accounts, and from critical to more positive appraisals of investor migration but all of the chapters highlight countries and dynamics that have so far been understudied.

Luuk van der Baaren and Hanwei Li's chapter studies investment migration from China to Portugal from the perspectives of both emigration and immigration when it was at the height of its popularity. It describes how the Portuguese investment programme worked out in practice between 2012 and 2018, a peak period of Chinese interest, and explains that the programme's economic contributions were significant but different from what the government originally intended. The chapter outlines the key drivers of Chinese investor emigration, highlighting, in particular, the attractiveness of the low presence requirements, access to the Schengen Area and the option to invest in real estate. Rather than emigrating instantly, investors mostly participated in the programme as a 'backup plan', allowing them to emigrate at any time, creating a form of 'quasi-migration'. In addition, the chapter shows that the Chinese government mainly perceives investment migration as a risk and has implemented measures to curb the participation of wealthy Chinese in investment programmes.

Niovi Vavoula and Vasiliki Apatzidou's chapter discusses Greece's golden visa programme. They offer an in-depth analysis of the programme and critically assess its benefits and flaws. Despite being a highly sought-after programme by investors, it has not received much attention from scholars. This chapter outlines the legal framework governing the golden visa programme and shows how interest in it has evolved since its creation in 2013. In addition, Vavoula and Apatzidou reflect on why this programme has proved so attractive and highlight some of its flaws. Concerning the latter, they emphasise the programme's impact on the housing market, the inadequate vetting of applicants and money laundering risks.

Miriam Cohen draws our attention to a pioneer in the field of investor migration: the Canadian investor immigration programmes. Cohen provides an overview of the legal regulation of Canadian investor migration over time and an analysis of its shortcomings. Having sketched the outlines of the Canadian immigration legal framework, Cohen reviews the requirements to be met by prospective investors in the three phases of the Canadian investor migration laws. She then discusses the demise of Canadian investor migration – the programme was officially abolished in 2021 – before critically inquiring whether Canadian citizenship should be a commodity traded for an investment.

Qishi Fu's chapter focuses on internal investment migration: the curious case of investor migration from mainland China to Hong Kong. In the years Hong Kong's investor migration programme was running, from 2003–15, people from mainland China constituted the main group of applicants, even though mainland Chinese were not allowed to apply. Fu shows how applicants from mainland China were able to bypass the nationality requirement, shedding light on the interactions between different investor migration schemes around the world and especially the 'South-South connections that are part of the global market'.[45] Since there was an exception for mainland Chinese with permanent residence in a foreign country, those seeking residency rights in Hong Kong resorted to the practice of purchasing third-country permanent residence, taking advantage of convenient RBI programmes of West African and Pacific Island states, before applying for investor residence in Hong Kong. Coincidentally, interest in Hong Kong's programme thus fuelled demand for RBI schemes elsewhere.

In his chapter, Vadim Poleshchuk takes stock of Estonia's e-Residency programme 10 years after it was launched. The programme was the first in the world to offer non-residents a transnational digital identity, with the objective to develop the Estonian economy, science, education and culture. Viewed against that objective, Poleshchuk argues that the programme has been successful: it has proven economically beneficial and strengthened Estonia's image as an advanced technological country. At the same time, and contrary to the hopes of some experts, the programme did not change perceptions of citizenship, migration and belonging. Moreover, new geopolitical realities, especially the Russian invasion into Ukraine, put pressure on the supposed universality of the programme.

The final chapter of Part III takes us back to historical times. Sau Kong Lee studies the acquisition of foreign nationalities – often against a financial investment – by Chinese subjects within China during the last imperial, Qing dynasty. Adding to our growing knowledge of investor migration in pre-contemporary times,[46] the chapter examines the practice of changing subject status during the Qing dynasty to access opportunities, which later turned into a practice of acquiring foreign nationalities to obtain benefits Chinese subjects did not enjoy. Lee shows that since the Qing government treated Chinese subjects less favourably than foreign nationals, acquiring foreign nationality was the way to ensure equality of rights, opportunities and personal security.

D. Investment Migration Conundrums in the European Union

There are few places in the world where investor migration practices are more fiercely contested than in the European Union, especially due to the European Commission's ongoing legal and

[45] Surak, 'Investment Migration', 68–69.
[46] Prak, 'Citizenship for Sale'.

political fight against the sale of national and European citizenship.[47] Part IV, 'Investment Migration Conundrums in the European Union', takes stock of this fight, both through a critical appraisal of the Commission's actions of the Commission and by providing new insights into the construction of the Commission's lawsuit against Malta's CBI scheme.

In his chapter, Hans Ulrich Jessurun d'Oliveira, the doyen of citizenship studies in Europe, analyses two reports and a recommendation by the European Commission and the European Parliament, which seek to outlaw CBI within the EU. More specifically, Jessurun d'Oliveira examines the two main arguments the Commission relies upon in its claim that CBI is contrary to EU law: the principle of genuine link and the principle of sincere cooperation. As regards the first, Jessurun d'Oliveira, echoing Peter Spiro's chapter, argues that the principle of genuine link, as pronounced by the International Court of Justice, was problematic when it was decided and became even more problematic since: the Commission's argument that the principle of sincere cooperation acts as a legal obstacle to CBI programmes is criticised for being incompatible with the primacy of Member States' nationalities over EU citizenship. Ultimately, Jessurun d'Oliveira concludes, the EU should be very reluctant to interfere in the domain of nationality – not just in the context of CBI but in general – given the sensitivity of this domain and its direct connection to the national identity of Member States.[48]

This view is reinforced in the chapter by Daniel Sarmiento and Guillermo Íñiguez, who provide a meticulous *tour d'horizon* of all the ECJ case law of relevance in order to show precisely that: the Commission is in breach of the principle of conferral when it attempts to misrepresent the binding automatic requirement of the mutual recognition of the Member States' nationalities as a ground for intervention in the domain of the essential aspects of their statehood. This is all the more the case, given that flimsy *Nottebohm* logic is used, which directly contradicts the current interpretation of the Treaties offered by the ECJ in *Micheletti*. The authors agree with Advocate General Collins, who offered a very similar reading in his Opinion in *Commission v Malta*, recommending that the case be dismissed, since the Commission failed to demonstrate any breach of EU law by Malta, which sells citizenship – and also recommended that the Commission pay Malta's costs.

Dimitry Kochenov and Elena Basheska come to similar conclusions as other leading commentators engaging with EU citizenship, including Jessurun d'Oliveira, Weiler, Sarmiento and Íñiguez and also Tratnik and Weingerl writing for this volume. While agreeing with them regarding the Commission's actions, they appraise these actions in different terms. For them, the Commission's attack on CBI betrays nationalist ethnocentric thinking, since the genuine links the Commission favours and defends are ultimately those established by the principle of *ius sanguinis*; indeed, as Kochenov and Basheska argue, the principle of blood connection echoes Hans Kundnani's telling 'Eurowhiteness' perspective on the European Integration project.[49] They also argue that the Commission ignores the many ways in which states confer nationality on foreigners, and that many of those do not respect the genuine connections the Commission pushes for. Instead, they advise the Commission to take a more informed approach consistent with the EU's raison d'être of non-discrimination based on nationality, which precludes discrimination on the basis of the grounds of acquisition of that nationality too.

[47] This fight is not limited to the European continent, as the Commission attempts to export its views – the legality of which has been questioned by AG Collins in the recent Opinion in *Commission v Malta* – also to the Caribbean and the Pacific. See eg Kochenov and Worster, 'EU's Neo-Colonialism' (EU Law Live, 8 March 2022).

[48] See also Jessurun d'Oliveira, 'Union Citizenship and Beyond' in Cambien et al (eds), *European Citizenship under Stress* (Brill-Nijhoff 2020) 28.

[49] Kundnani, *Eurowhiteness* (Hurst 2023).

The rich postscriptum by Joseph HH Weiler concludes the discussion on investor citizenship's legality under EU law. In his view, contrary to the Commission's allegations, it is not Malta that is selling European values by offering its citizenship for sale, but rather it is the Commission that does so by seeking to outlaw the Maltese practice. For Professor Weiler, the Commission's case is an attempt to circumvent the correct constitutional procedures laid down in the Treaties and thereby redefine the relationship between EU and national citizenship. He shares with Jessurun d'Oliveira the view that the case against Malta amounts to an unconstitutional power grab, but unlike Jessurun d'Oliveira, Weiler is not opposed to more transnational regulation of national rules on the acquisition and loss of nationality. Rather, he would favour additional regulation but argues this should be left to institutions with the requisite legitimacy to regulate the issue – the EU legislative process or the *Herren der Verträge* amending the Treaties – thereby drawing our attention to the oft-ignored question of institutional choice in EU citizenship law.

The book concludes with an insider's *divertissement* showcasing in Aesopian language how law and identities are framed in contemporary Europe. The tale is a wonderful backdrop for the insightful socio-legal studies, dry black-letter legal analyses and amusing accounts of the workings of citizenship by investment that fill the rest of the book you are holding in your hands.

I.

Investor Migration: Conceptualisation and Context

1

Citizenship by Investment and the Right to Change Nationality

WILLIAM THOMAS WORSTER

I. INTRODUCTION

WHILE NATIONALITY LAW is, in principle, in the exclusive domain of states, increasingly some states are becoming more hostile to that freedom for nationality acquired through citizenship by investment (CBI). So far, this new approach to CBI by some states takes several forms. It can be refusal to tolerate the legislation of other states and pursuing active intervention against those laws, or it can be terminating visa-free access to nationals when the state has a CBI scheme. CBI is an easy target and sits at the forefront of the degradation in freedom for states to make their own nationality laws. However, as these measures gain momentum, they are also putting increased pressure on the human right to nationality and the right to be free from discrimination. This chapter reflects on the current state of nationality law and nationality discrimination law to provide a human rights counter-narrative to this increasing hostility to CBI.

The primary possible argument to defend these measures against CBI stems from the International Court of Justice (ICJ) *Nottebohm* case.[1] In short, the Court concluded that states need not necessarily respect a claim to diplomatic protection on the basis of an individual's nationality, if that nationality does not bear a 'genuine connection' to the state. Aside from the many infirmities of the *Nottebohm* case, this argument omits the important and growing role of human rights in relation to nationality. Since *Nottebohm*, not only has the right to a nationality matured, but so have related rights, such as the rights to renounce nationality, leave any state, acquire nationality and change nationality, with corresponding duties on states to release nationals from their legal bond. These rights exist to facilitate people's movements away from less desirable states with poorer quality rights, yet they also affirm that individuals acquire other rights only by and through the mechanism of nationality as a state-based, international sorting mechanism for people.[2] In addition, human rights protecting individuals from discrimination have begun to permeate nationality law to protect people from discrimination on the basis of national origin, as well as from discrimination on the basis of their naturalisation, multiple nationality and form of naturalisation. These developments in turn raise doubts about the genuine connection argument. Admittedly, these rights are often not fully

[1] *Nottebohm* (Liechtenstein v Guatemala) [1955] ICJ Rep. 4.
[2] On this point, see generally Brubaker, *Citizenship and Nationhood in France and Germany* (Cambridge 1992).

realised and many states retain barriers to nationality that violate these protections de jure or de facto,[3] but as international law develops and human rights evolves, so must states' approach to nationality law. All of these developments demand that the narrative around CBI, and its dubious reliance on *Nottebohm*, be reoriented away from the traditional inter-state discussion to one that centres human rights in relation to nationality and reaffirms rights of individuals to leave states and seek new nationalities.

As one prominent example, after a long history of criticising CBI schemes, the European Commission has taken action to eradicate it within the EU. More than 10 years ago, the Commission began questioning CBI programmes in several EU Member States,[4] supported by a European Parliament resolution.[5] The arguments in those documents have largely focused on alleged connections between CBI and tax evasion, corruption and other criminality.[6] These studies have also argued that, while CBI produces benefits for the state conferring citizenship, it produces burdens on the other EU Member States, in violation of the EU principle of sincere cooperation.[7] Apparently, the Commission believes that once citizenship is acquired by investment, the new citizens rarely live in the state of nationality, and instead exercise their rights as EU citizens to relocate to more attractive locations in other EU Member States. As such, the Commission makes the remarkable submission that, by exercising their fundamental rights as (new) EU citizens to free movement within the Union, these individuals are somehow acting as undesirable citizens abusing the system. Of course, this overlooks the fact that no one raises doubts when other EU citizens also move to those same desirable destinations, provided that they acquired their EU citizenship by birth or other means of naturalisation. In addition, the EU has levelled other arguments against CBI. On 16 September 2020, in the EU State of Union speech, the President of the European Commission, Ursula von der Leyen, announced that 'European values are not for sale' and that CBI schemes would receive the highest scrutiny.[8] While poetic, the substance of the underlying argument is not quite clear and appears to combine notions of opposition to the privileges wealthy people enjoy and the need for European identity to be earned, yet it runs contrary to the widespread, unearned acquisition of EU Member State nationality on ethnic grounds or luck of birth.[9] To buttress these views, the Commission has argued that there is no absolute legal obligation for the EU to tolerate EU Member State nationality laws, citing to *Nottebohm*,[10] and arguing that the only acceptable connections for nationality under EU Member State laws would include descent,

[3] Kochenov, *Citizenship* (MIT Press 2019); Kochenov, 'Abstract Citizenship in the Age of Concrete Human Rights' in Tushnet and Kochenov (eds), *Handbook on the Politics of Constitutional Law* (Elgar 2023).

[4] European Commission, 'Strengthening Citizens' Rights in a Union of Democratic Change: EU Citizenship Report 2017' COM/2017/030final; European Commission, 'On progress towards effective EU citizenship 2013–2016' COM(2017) 32final; European Commission, 'Investor Citizenship and Residence Schemes in the European Union' COM(2019) 12final.

[5] European Parliament resolution on EU citizenship for sale (2013/2995(RSP) [2014] OJ C482/117; European Parliament resolution on a comprehensive Union policy on preventing money laundering and terrorist financing (2020/2686(RSP) OJ C371/92; Also see Jesserun d'Oliveira's chapter in this volume.

[6] Council Decision 2022/2198 on the suspension in the whole of the application of the Agreement between the European Union and the Republic of Vanuatu on the short-stay visa waiver (ST/13631/2022/INIT) OJ L292/47; European Commission, 'Proposal for a Council Decision on the partial suspension of the application of the Agreement between the European Union and the Republic of Vanuatu on the short-stay visa waiver' COM(2022) 6 final.

[7] Brubaker, *Citizenship and Nationhood in France and Germany*.

[8] von der Leyen, 'Building the world we want to live in: A Union of vitality in a world of fragility' (State of the Union Address, 16 September 2020) https://ec.europa.eu/commission/presscorner/detail/ov/SPEECH_20_1655.

[9] Joppke, 'Citizenship between De- and Re-Ethnicization' (2003) 44 *EJS* 429. Also see generally Kundnani, *Eurowhiteness* (Hurst 2023).

[10] European Commission Report COM(2019)12 final.

national origin, marriage, birth in the country or a term of residence.[11] Shortly thereafter, the European Commission began infringement procedures against Cyprus and Malta for their CBI schemes,[12] though it strangely left untouched similar schemes in other EU Member States.[13] Under such scrutiny, Cyprus has terminated its programme.[14]

In addition to this action by the EU against CBI in EU Member States, some states have also been taking other steps to discourage the practice of CBI. Canada abolished its visa-free travel programmes for both St Kitts and Antigua and Barbuda because those states maintained CBI schemes.[15] A bill is currently pending in the US Congress to also revoke visa-free travel for all nationals from any state with a CBI programme.[16] This proposal comes despite the fact that visa overstay rates of nationals from some states with CBI programmes are quite low[17] and overstay rates have always been the standard determining factor for admission to the US visa waiver programme. And the EU has also joined this campaign, terminating visa-free access to the EU for citizens of Vanuatu due to that state's CBI programme.[18] Under such pressures, some states have abolished their CBI programmes.[19] So far, states have largely not undertaken actions specifically targeting individuals with CBI or raising doubts about the validity of CBI nationality, preferring to approach the issue by either demanding changes in other states' nationality laws or by revoking preferential treatment for all nationals of a particular state. That being said, both Cyprus and Malta have revoked the CBI nationality of certain individuals, if those individuals were later placed on sanctions lists or otherwise accused of misconduct.[20] Also, in 2022, the US changed its non-immigrant investor visa

[11] ibid: 'each Member State needs to ensure that nationality is not awarded absent any genuine link to the country or its citizens'. Cf. Džankić, 'Immigrant Investor Programmes in the European Union (EU)' (2018) 26 *JCES* 64.

[12] 'European Commission opens infringements against Cyprus and Malta for "selling" EU citizenship' (*European Commission*, 20 October 2020) https://ec.europa.eu/commission/presscorner/detail/hu/ip_20_1925.

[13] Eg Kälin, Ius Doni *in International Law and EU Law* (Brill-Nijhoff 2019) 176–82.

[14] 'Cyprus to suspend "EU golden passports" scheme' (*BBC*, 13 October 2020) www.bbc.com/news/world-europe-54522299.

[15] 'Notice – St. Kitts and Nevis citizens now need a visa to travel to Canada' (Government of Canada, 22 November 2014) www.canada.ca/en/immigration-refugees-citizenship/news/notices/notice-kitts-nevis-citizens-need-visa-travel-canada.html; 'Notice – Canada imposes a visa requirement on Antigua and Barbuda' (Government of Canada, 26 June 2017) www.canada.ca/en/immigration-refugees-citizenship/news/notices/imposed-visa-antigua-barbuda.html; 'Statement On Canada Issuing New Policy on Visa-Free Travel' (Government of Antigua and Barbuda, 26 June 2017) https://ab.gov.ag/media_page.php?page=186 (although Canada did not explicitly mention the CBI programme in Antigua and Barbuda, the Government of Antigua and Barbuda confirmed that it had been informed by Canada that its CBI programme as the basis for the decision).

[16] Eg H.R. 6911 No Travel for Traffickers Act 2022 (US).

[17] Eg 'Fiscal Year 2022 Entry/Exit Overstay Report' (U.S. Customs and Border Protection 2023) 15–19 www.dhs.gov/sites/default/files/2023-07/23_0707_FY22_FY23_CBP_Integrated_Entry_Exit_Overstay_Report.pdf (reporting overstays). Malta had overstay rates of 1.07 per cent of all business/tourist arrivals under the visa waiver programme, which is comparable to similar rates from Slovakia and New Zealand, and contrasted with 2.12 per cent from Brunei and 2.97 per cent from Chile, whose visa waiver participation was not called into question. Among states that are not visa waiver participating countries and have CBI programmes, Cyprus had an overstay rate of 1.27 per cent, Vanuatu of 6.06 per cent and Antigua and Barbuda of 2.78 per cent. However, the rates for Vanuatu and Antigua and Barbuda have been as low as 0.82 per cent and 1.66 per cent in 2020, far less than other countries participating in the visa waiver programme, see 'Fiscal Year 2020 Entry/Exit Overstay Report' (U.S. Customs and Border Protection 2021) 16–20 www.dhs.gov/sites/default/files/2021-12/CBP%20-%20FY%202020%20Entry%20Exit%20Overstay%20Report_0.pdf.

[18] Council Decision 2022/2198 OJ L292/47; European Commission Proposal COM(2022)6 final; also see Kochenov and Worster, 'EU's Neocolonialism' (EU Law Live, 8 March 2022).

[19] Twomey, 'Citizenship Revocation and the Normalisation of *Ex-post* Conditionality in Investment Migration Law' in Kochenov and Surak (eds), *Citizenship and Residence Sales* (Cambridge 2023) 429 et seq.

[20] See eg 'Malta: Three IIP [CBI] applicants had their citizenship revoked in scheme's lifetime' (*Malta Today*, 16 March 2022) www.maltatoday.com.mt/news/national/115671/three_iip_applicants_had_their_citizenship_revoked_in_schemes_lifetime; 'Malta Revoked Citizenship to Russian national' (*Malta News Agency*, 1 April 2022) www.maltanewsagency.com/2022/04/malta-revoked-citizenship-to-russian-national/; 'Cyprus to revoke 10 more passports

law to require three years of continuous domicile in order to qualify for an investor visa, if the person acquired their nationality by virtue of a CBI programme, thus distinguishing between nationals with CBI nationality and those who acquired nationality through other means.[21] It remains to be seen whether states will take even more aggressive approaches against CBI in the future.

Much of this discussion over anti-CBI measures has focused on the legal relationships between states, their obligations to recognise each other's public acts of granting nationality and the implications of *Nottebohm*. However, this discussion largely avoids any mention of individual human rights, especially the right to change nationality and protections against discrimination, yet the ICJ may be shifting away from *Nottebohm* and towards a stronger appreciation of human rights. In his dissenting opinion in the *Qatar v UAE CERD* case, Judge Robinson noted that human rights have evolved considerably since the *Nottebohm* judgment and that its precedent must be read in light of this evolution.[22] Qatar had specifically invoked the 'genuine connection' test in its argument.[23] In fact, the majority of the ICJ in the *Qatar v UAE CERD* case appeared to want to constrain the application of *Nottebohm*.[24] Accordingly, even in the view of the ICJ, there is a need to bring a refreshed view on human rights to any discussion in the area of nationality law. As human rights obligations have grown, they have sharpened the distinction between state rights opposable to other states and individual rights opposable to states, with *Nottebohm* only relevant for the former. As a result, the impact of the case, if it ever had any, is surely shrinking in favour of an approach more centred on human rights.

This chapter will provide a brief overview of international human rights protections relevant for nationality, covering the right to a nationality and related rights to renounce nationality, change nationality and acquire nationality. It will also briefly review the law on discrimination as it pertains to nationality and overlaps with national origin discrimination, and other relevant grounds for discrimination. This overview will highlight the developments in human rights that have emerged since *Nottebohm*. In addition, this chapter will observe that the development of human rights law not only applies to states in regard to their own nationality laws, but also to third states in recognising the application of nationality law by other states. In light of the application of human rights law, this chapter will argue that, while states may critique other states' nationality laws, they must take care not to infringe on individual human rights pertaining to nationality. Measures that infringe those rights must be justified as necessary and proportionate to promote legitimate governmental interests. In the final section, this chapter will apply this legal framework to the practice of CBI, reaching conclusions on the limits of measures to constrain CBI nationality.

issued under discredited citizenship scheme' (*Reuters*, 12 October 2022) www.reuters.com/world/europe/cyprus-revoke-10-more-passports-issued-under-discredited-citizenship-scheme-2022-10-12/; Januzi, 'Cyprus Has Revoked 222 Passports Granted Through Golden Passport Scheme So Far' (*Schengen News*, 19 January 2023) https://schengen.news/cyprus-has-revoked-222-passports-granted-through-golden-passport-scheme-so-far/; 'Government starts process to deprive man of Maltese citizenship after he appears on US sanction list' (*Malta Independent*, 6 March 2024) www.independent.com.mt/articles/2024-03-06/local-news/Government-starts-process-to-deprive-man-of-Maltese-citizenship-after-he-appears-on-US-sanction-list-6736259177.

[21] Sect 5902(b) of James M. Inhofe National Defense Authorization Act (NDAA) 2022 (US); Balakrishnan, 'Extra scrutiny for non-resident US visa applications' (Citizenship by Investment Journal, 13 April 2023) https://citizenshipbyinvestment.news/index.php/2023/04/13/extra-scrutiny-for-non-resident-us-visa-applications/.

[22] Diss. Opin. of Judge Robinson in *Application of the International Convention on the Elimination of All Forms of Racial Discrimination* (Qatar v UAE) [2021] ICJ Rep. 71, para 9.

[23] eg Written Statement of the State of Qatar in *Qatar v UAE* (2019) https://icj-cij.org/sites/default/files/case-related/172/172-20190830-WRI-01-00-EN.pdf (citing *Nottebohm*, 23 'genuine connection').

[24] Worster, 'Reining in the *Nottebohm* Case' (2023) 41 *B.U. Int'l L.J.* 301, 326.

II. RIGHT TO NATIONALITY

As noted above, states are largely free to set their nationality laws as they wish,[25] within the limited constraint of international law. One constraint is the right to a nationality. The right to a nationality is covered by multiple major human rights treaties and instruments[26] and some have even argued that the right to a nationality constitutes a non-derogable norm.[27] It is certainly the basis for the enjoyment of other rights, what Arendt famously described as the 'right to have rights'.[28] The Universal Declaration on Human Rights (UDHR) provides both that '[e]veryone has the right to a nationality' and that '[n]o one shall be arbitrarily deprived of his nationality nor denied the right to change his nationality'.[29] This right was considered so central to the other rights that it was included in the very first drafts of the UDHR.[30] It appears not to have been contested throughout the discussions.[31] The same right to a nationality was then adopted in various forms in other human rights treaties.[32] Yet at the same time, the right

[25] Art 1 of The Hague Convention on Certain Questions Relating to the Conflict of Nationality Laws (1930) 179 *UNTS* 89, 99; ILC, Kamto (Special Rapporteur), Fourth report on the expulsion of aliens, A/CN.4/594 (2008), para 4; *Nottebohm*, para 20.

[26] Art 5(d)(iii) of International Convention on the Elimination of All Forms of Racial Discrimination (1965) 660 UNTS 195 (CERD); Art 24(3) of International Covenant on Civil and Political Rights (1966) 999 UNTS 171 (ICCPR); Art 9 of Convention on the Elimination of Discrimination Against Women (1979) 1249 UNTS 13 (CEDAW); Art 10(2) of Convention on the Rights of the Child (1990) 1577 UNTS 3 (CRC); Art 29 of International Convention on the Protection of the Rights of All Migrant Workers and Members of Their Families (1990) 2220 UNTS 3 (CMW); Art 18 of Convention on the Rights of Persons with Disabilities 2515 UNTS 3 (CRPD); Art 20(2) of American Convention on Human Rights (1969) 1144 UNTS 123 (ACHR); African Charter on Human and Peoples' Rights (1981) 1520 UNTS 217 (ACHPR); Art 6 of African Charter on the Rights and Welfare of the Child (1990) OAU Doc CAB/LEG/24.9/49 (ACRWC); Arts 3–4 of the European Convention on Nationality (1997) ETS 166 (ECN); also see Art 15(1) of Universal Declaration of Human Rights (1948) UNGA Res. 217 A(III) (UDHR); Art 6 of Declaration on the Rights of Indigenous Peoples (2007) UNGA Res. 61/295 (UNDRIP).

[27] *Case of Expelled Dominicans & Haitians v Dominican Republic*, IACtHR Ser. C No. 282 (2014), para 253; *Case of Girls Yean & Bosico Children v Dominican Republic*, IACtHR Ser. C No 130 (2005), paras 136–38.

[28] Arendt, *The Origins of Totalitarianism* (Harcourt Brace Jovanovich 1973) 292.

[29] Art 15 UDHR.

[30] Art 10 of Draft Outline of International Bill of Rights, UN Doc. E/CN.4/AC.1/3 (1947) ('The rights of emigration and expatriation shall not be denied.'); ibid, Art 32 ('Everyone has a right to a nationality. Everyone is entitled to the nationality of the State where he is born unless and until on attaining majority, he declares for the nationality open to him by virtue of descent.'); Art 9 of Draft Declaration of the International Rights and Duties of Man, Inter-American Juridical Committee, UN Doc. E/CN.4/2 (1947) ('Every person has the right to renounce the nationality of his birth, or a previously acquired nationality, upon acquiring the nationality of another state.').

[31] Statement of Mr Mora, Uruguay (accepted without opposition), UN ESCOR, 1st Sess., 14th mtg., UN Doc. E/CN.4/SR.14 (1947) ('The right to freedom of movement ought also to include the freedom to change one's nationality'); Art 11 of UN CHR, Proposal for a Human Rights Convention Submitted by the Representative of the United States on the Commission on Human Rights, UN Doc. E/CN.4/37 (1947) ('Everyone shall have the right to emigrate'); Nisot (Rapporteur), Report Submitted to Commission on Human Rights, Draft Declaration of Human Rights, UN Doc. E/CN.4/52 (1947), 6–7; Art 10(2) of UN CHR, Comments from Governments on the Draft International Declaration on Human Rights, Draft International Covenant on Human Rights and the Question of Implementation, Communication from the United Kingdom, UN Doc. E/CN.4/82/Add.9 (1948) 4 ('everyone has the right to divest himself of his nationality, if he wishes to do so'); Art 9 of UN CHR, Lauterpacht (Rapporteur), Preliminary Report on Human Rights, the Charter of the United Nations and the International Bill of the Rights of Man, UN Doc. E/CN.4/89 (1948), 38 ('The right of emigration and expatriation shall not be denied'); Statement of Mr Malik, Lebanon, UN ESCOR, 3d Sess., 59th mtg., UN Doc. E/CN.4/SR.59 (1948) 11 ('No one should be arbitrarily deprived of his nationality or of the right to change his nationality'); Art 13 of Draft International Declaration of Human Rights, UN Doc. E/CN.4/148/Add.1, annex A, (1948) ('No one should be arbitrarily deprived of his nationality or denied the right to change his nationality.'). Also see UN CHR, Mubanga-Chipoya (Rapporteur), Final Report on Analysis of the Current Trends and Developments Regarding the Right to Leave any Country Including One's Own, and to Return to One's Own Country, and Some Other Rights or Consideration Arising Therefrom, UN Doc. E/CN.4/Sub.2 (Part 1) (1987), para 60.

[32] As such, it may be supported by other rights. For example, in conjunction with the right to a nationality, their rights must be interpreted and applied to promote their best interests, see Art 3 CRC. On this basis, the African

to a nationality is just that: a right to *a* nationality, and not to any particular nationality.[33] Thus, the acquisition of any nationality will suffice, regardless of the rights and freedoms it entails, or its desirability, and through any means, including CBI, as this chapter argues.

From the text providing a right to nationality in the UDHR, it is clear that the right can be limited, provided the limitations are not arbitrary.[34] Arbitrariness can take several forms. It can be procedural or substantive.[35] It can arise from discrimination on the basis of national origin, gender and other prohibited grounds.[36] It also demands that nationality laws are at least necessary and proportionate to legitimate governmental aims.[37] The prohibition on arbitrary nationality laws applies to laws on the acquisition of nationality at birth and for acquisition of nationality through naturalisation.[38] While, in principle, international law makes no prescriptions on the specific criteria to qualify for naturalisation,[39] it does limit states from imposing arbitrary requirements. To this, we can add that states have obligations under the Refugee Convention and Statelessness Conventions to facilitate the naturalisation of refugees and stateless persons respectively,[40] and, as such, they must refrain from unnecessary naturalisation requirements for persons in those categories in particular.

Committee of Experts on the Rights and Welfare of the Child have opined that being stateless is, in general, not in a child's best interests, see ACERWC, General Comment No. 2 on Article 6 of the ACRWC, ACERWC/GC/02 (2014) ('being stateless as a child is generally an antithesis to the best interests of children'). This view has been implicitly supported by UN HRC: *Denny Zhao v The Netherlands*, U.N. Doc. CCPR/C/130/D/2918/2016(2020), para 8.2. This analysis should not be interpreted to mean that statelessness would never be in the best interests of the child: Swider, 'Why End Statelessness?' in Bloom et al (eds), *Understanding Statelessness* (Routledge 2017) 191.

[33] Worster, 'European Union Citizenship and the Unlawful Denial of Member States Nationality' (2020) 43 *Fordham Int'l. L.J.* 767.

[34] Art 15(2) UDHR; UNHRC, Secretary-General, Annual Report of the United Nations Commissioner for Human Rights and Reports of the Office of High Commissioner and the Secretary-General: Arbitrary Deprivation of Nationality, UN Doc. A/HRC/10/34 (2009); Bialosky, 'Regional Protection of the Right to a Nationality' (2015) 24 *Cardozo J Int'l & Comp L* 153, 189. Also see *K2 v United Kingdom* (dec.), no. 42387/13, 2 February 2017, para 53 et seq; Case C-135/08 *Rottmann* ECLI:EU:C:2010:104, para 53; Worster, 'European Union Citizenship and the Unlawful Denial of Member States Nationality', 767.

[35] eg Eritrea-Ethiopian Claims Commission, *Civilian Claims* (Eritrea v Ethiopia), Partial Award (2004) 44 ILM 601 (*Eritrea-Ethiopian Claims Commission Partial Award*), paras 57–78; *Bronstein v Peru*, IACtHR, Ser. C, No. 74 (2001), para 95; Council of Europe, Explanatory Report to the European Convention on Nationality (1997) ETS no. 166, 36; UNHRC, UN Secretary-General Report, Human Rights and Arbitrary Deprivation of Nationality, UN Doc A/HRC/13/34 (2009), paras 40–46; UNHRC, UN Secretary-General Report, Human Rights and Arbitrary Deprivation of Nationality, UN Doc A/HRC/25/28 (2013), para 40.

[36] Art 15 UDHR; CERD; Art 24(3) ICCPR; Art 9(1) CEDAW; Arts 7, 8 CRC; Art 18 CRPD; HRC, General Comment No. 24 on Issues Relating to Reservations Made upon Ratification or Accession to the Covenant or the Optional Protocols thereto, or in Relation to Declarations under Article 41 of the Covenant, CCPR/C/21/Rev.1/Add.6 (1994); CERD, General Recommendation XXX on Discrimination Against Non-Citizens (2004).

[37] Also see HRC, General Comment No. 27 on Article 12 (Freedom of Movement), CCPR/C/21/Rev.1/Add.9 (1999), para 21; *Borzov v Estonia*, UN Doc. CCPR/C/81/D/1136/2002 (2004) paras 7.3–7.4; *Tsarjov v Estonia*, UN Doc. CCPR/C/91/D/1223/2003 (2007) para 7.6; *Šipin v Estonia*, UN Doc. CCPR/C/93/D/1423/2005 (2008) para 6.2; *Q v Denmark*, UN Doc. CCPR/C/113/D/2001/2010 (2015), paras 7.3, 7.7; UNHRC, Draft Report of the Working Group on the Universal Periodic Review: Myanmar, UN Doc. A/HRC/WG.6/23/L.9 (2015), paras 7.54, 7.55, 7.66; UNHRC, Draft Report of the Working Group on the Universal Periodic Review: Austria, UN Doc. A/HRC/WG.6/23/L.20 (2015), paras 5.4, 5.5; ACERWC, *Institute for Human Rights and Development in Africa ('IHRDA') and Open Society Justice Initiative v Kenya*, No. Com/002/2009 (2011) (*Nubian Children case*), para 57; *Yean & Bosico v Dominican Republic*, paras 136, 139, 141; *Expelled Dominicans & Haitians v Dominican Republic*, para 263; UN SG, Human Rights and Arbitrary Deprivation of Nationality (2009); Kochenov, 'EU Influence on the Citizenship Policies of the Candidate Countries' (2007) 3 *JCER* 124.

[38] *Modise v Botswana*, ACHPR Comm. No. 97/93 (1993); *Yean & Bosico v Dominican Republic*, para 166; *Genovese v Malta*, no. 53124/09, § 30, 11 October 2011.

[39] Worster, 'Reining in the *Nottebohm* Case'.

[40] Art 34 of Convention relating to the Status of Refugees (1951) 189 UNTS 137; Protocol Relating to the Status of Refugees (1967) 606 UNTS 267; 'Global Action Plan to End Statelessness 2014–2020' (UNHCR 2014) 16; 'High-Level Segment on Statelessness: Results and Highlights' (UNHCR 2020).

Alongside the right to a nationality, states must not create situations of statelessness against the will of the individual, which intersects with the right to a nationality. Several treaties prohibit the creation of statelessness.[41] Some authorities, including this author, have attempted to locate an international legal obligation on states to grant nationality in certain cases, arguing that the prohibitions on creation of situations of statelessness are especially robust for children,[42] and that both conventional and customary international law have evolved to indicate the state of birth as the state which bears the primary obligation to grant nationality in such situations.[43] The right to a nationality in conjunction with the obligation to avoid statelessness requires states to restore nationality, if it would lead to statelessness.[44] As such, the creation of statelessness would amount to substantive arbitrariness in nationality law.[45] While in some cases, an individual might prefer statelessness and wish to be released from their nationality, and the prohibition on statelessness acts as a prison with the state duty-bound to contain the person,[46] other individuals may wish to acquire nationality in their state of choosing and will be excluded.[47] Thus, the obligation to prevent statelessness means that states of the undesired nationality must affirm their grip on the individual and not release the individual without guarantees of a substitute nationality,[48] which could be near impossible to acquire. At the same time, the prohibition can buttress acquired nationality whose loss would result in statelessness.

III. RIGHT TO CHANGE NATIONALITY

The right to a nationality includes the right to change nationality.[49] The UDHR expressly states this,[50] but, while the right to a nationality is extensively studied, the right to change nationality has received less attention. Much of the UDHR drafting history, and subsequent scholarly attention, focuses on securing the right to have a nationality and avoidance of statelessness,

[41] Convention on the Reduction of Statelessness (1961) 989 UNTS 175; Convention Relating to the Status of Stateless Persons (1954) 360 UNTS 117.

[42] eg Art 7 CRC; Castilho, 'Article 15 – The Right to a Nationality', in Rivera (ed), *The Universal Declaration of Human Rights* (Brill-Nijhoff 2023) 362.

[43] Worster, 'The Obligation to Grant Nationality to Stateless Children under Customary International Law' (2019) 27 *Mich. St. Int'l. L Rev.* 441; Worster, 'Customary International Law Requiring States to Grant Nationality to Stateless Children Born in Their Territory' (2022) 4 *SCR* 113. See also de Groot, 'Children, Their Right to a Nationality and Child Statelessness' in Edwards and van Waas (eds), *Nationality and Statelessness under International Law* (Cambridge University Press 2014).

[44] UNHRC, Resolution 20/5 on Human Rights and Arbitrary Deprivation of Nationality, UN Doc. A/HRC/RES/20/5 (2012), para 12. Also see generally Prener, *Denationalisation and Its Discontents* (Brill-Nijhoff 2022) 73; Adjami and Harrington, 'Scope and Content of Article 15 of the Universal Declaration of Human Rights' (2008) 27 *Refugee Survey Quarterly* 93, 101.

[45] See *Eritrea-Ethiopian Claims Commission Partial Award*, paras 57–78.

[46] See eg Fraser and Caestecker, 'Jews or Germans?' (2013) 31 *LHR* 391; Lauterpacht, 'The Nationality of Denationalized Persons' (1948) 1 *Jewish Ybk Int'l L.* 164. On the transformation of citizenship from a right to a duty, see Swider, 'Why End Statelessness?'; Bloom, 'Can Citizenship Studies Escape Citizenism?' (2022) 26 Citizenship Studies 372. Also see Worster, 'Respecting the Right to a Nationality in International Sport' in Boillet et al (eds), *Sports and Human Rights* (Springer 2024).

[47] This distinction typically revolves around whether the state's nationality is desirable, including how it treats its nationals and minority groups, see eg Kochenov, 'Statelessness: A Radical Rethinking of the Dominant Citizenism Paradigm' (2024) 20 *Annu. Rev. Law Soc. Sci.* 117.

[48] Kochenov, *Citizenship* (MIT Press 2019) 38–59.

[49] Art 15(2) UDHR. Also see generally Worster, 'Human Rights and the Taxation Consequences for Renouncing Citizenship' (2017) 62 *St. Louis U. LJ.* 85.

[50] Art 15 UDHR.

rather than on the possibility to change nationality from one to another.[51] Yet, the right to change nationality is articulated in the same provision as the right to a nationality and must enjoy the same protections as the right to a nationality. The UDHR serves as a foundation, albeit formally non-binding, on which the structure of human rights law has been built.[52] Its terms on change must be viewed as an inherent part of the right to a nationality. After all, change of nationality involves acquisition of nationality. This is especially the case when the exercise of the right to change involves loss of any and all nationality(ies) as a condition for acquisition of nationality, and the refusal of the change would result in statelessness.[53] Thus, the right to a nationality should be read to include the right to seek, enjoy, retain and change nationality. As a result, some international instruments have explicitly included the right to change nationality as part of the right to a nationality. For example, the American Convention on Human Rights (ACHR) clearly provides a right to change nationality without arbitrary interference.[54] In line with this provision, there is no reason to think that the protection of the right to change nationality is of any lesser importance that the right to nationality generally. Both must be protected with the same vigour.

In addition, the right to change nationality is intertwined with a range of human rights beyond the right to a nationality. Some have linked the right to change nationality to the right to form one's own identity and right to private life.[55] In *Mennesson*, the European Court of Human Rights (ECtHR) held precisely that nationality and identity are linked, so even though the refusal of nationality by France was based on the state's permissible prohibition on in vitro fertilisation, the consequences for the child's nationality resulted in a denial of French social identity.[56] The Court has held similarly for the right to maintain social identity during times of state succession, though it effectively meant that the state must accept change of nationality to the new state.[57]

Also, the right to change nationality follows from the right to renounce nationality. This author has previously argued that everyone has the right to renounce one's nationality,[58] and the right to renounce nationality can be understood as one part of the right to change nationality.[59] It is certainly likely that the right to renounce exists under customary international law.[60] It appears in the European Convention on Nationality (ECN)[61] and in the domestic law of virtually every state.[62] The ECtHR has held that individuals have an implicit right to renounce nationality under the European Convention on Human Rights (ECHR), again following from the right to private life and identity.[63] Yet, at the same time, the right to renounce is dependent

[51] Morsink, *The Universal Declaration of Human Rights* (PennPress 1999) 80; Castilho, 'Article 15', 360 et seq.

[52] Art 15(2) UDHR.

[53] cf Case C-118/20, *JY v Wiener Lanesregierung* ECLI:EU:C:2022:34; Also see Kochenov, 'Double Nationality in the EU' (2011) 17 *ELJ* 323; Kochenov and de Groot, 'Helpful, Convoluted and Ignorant in Principle' (2022) 47 *EL Rev.* 699.

[54] Art 22(3) ACHR. Also see Adjami and Harrington, 'Scope and Content of Article 15 of the Universal Declaration of Human Rights', 99.

[55] *Riener v Bulgaria*, no. 46343/99, §31–32, 23 May 2006 (Maruste J dissenting); UNHRC, Human Rights and Arbitrary Deprivation of Nationality, UN Doc A/HRC/RES/32/5 (2016), para 11; UN SG, Arbitrary Deprivation of Nationality (2009), para 59.

[56] *Genovese v Malta*, paras 30–33; *Mennesson v France*, no. 65192/11, 26 June 2014.

[57] *Fjodorova v Latvia*, no. 69405/01, 9 October 2003.

[58] Worster, 'Human Rights and the Taxation Consequences for Renouncing Citizenship'.

[59] Whelan, 'Citizenship and the Right to Leave' (1981) 75 *Am. Polit. Sci. Rev.* 638.

[60] Moreno-Lax, *Accessing Asylum in Europe* (Oxford University Press 2017) 340–50; Harvey and Barnidge, 'Human Rights, Free Movement, and the Right to Leave in International Law' (2007) 19 *Int'l. J. Refug. L.* 20; Worster, 'Human Rights and the Taxation Consequences'; eg Russia's suspension of nationality renunciations has rightly earned it serious criticism, see Kochenov, 'Statelessness'.

[61] Art 8 ECN.

[62] See generally Worster, 'Human Rights and the Taxation Consequences'.

[63] *Ramadan v Malta*, no. 76136/12, 21 June 2016 (Pinto de Albuquerque J dissenting).

on having a nationality to change to, otherwise states would implicate the prohibition on creating statelessness. Therefore, the near universal expression of the right to renounce nationality, in light of the prohibition of statelessness, results in an obligation to release a national from their bond should they wish to change nationality.

In addition to these rights, the right to change nationality also implicates the right to leave one's own state, in the broadest understanding of 'leave'.[64] Freedom to leave any state is widely understood as essential to personal liberty.[65] Part of the basis for recognising this right so explicitly was that migration was a universal condition of the human experience across millennia.[66] It has been affirmed not only in the UDHR, but also in the International Covenant on Civil and Political Rights (ICCPR),[67] among a range of other human rights treaties,[68] such as the Migrant Workers Convention, Racial Discrimination Convention, Apartheid Convention and Convention on the Rights of the Child.[69] The right to leave has even been affirmed for situations of armed conflict in the Fourth Geneva Convention[70] and various diplomatic treaties for international envoys.[71] The freedom to leave is not tied to any particular purpose for leaving, so no justification is necessary.[72] Temporary travel or permanent migration are both included.[73] But it is critical to recall that the right to leave is not matched by a right to enter any state in particular.[74]

The right to leave any state enjoys similar protection as the right to a nationality in that, while it may be limited, those limitations must be exceptional.[75] Derogations to the right to

[64] Worster, 'Human Rights and the Taxation Consequences'.

[65] HRC, General Comment No. 27; UN Commission on Human Rights, Inglés (Special Rapporteur), Study of Discrimination in Respect of the Right of Everyone to Leave Any Country, Including his Own, and to Return to his Country, UN Doc E/CN. 4/Sub.2/220/Rev.1 (1963) 9; Hannum, *The Right to Leave and Return in International Law and Practice* (Martinus Nijhoff 1987) 4; Cranston, 'The Political and Philosophical Aspects of the Right to Leave and to Return' in Vasak and Liskofsky (eds), *The Right to Leave and to Return* (The American Jewish Committee 1976) 21; Whelan, 'Citizenship and the Right to Leave', 636; McAdam, 'An Intellectual History of Freedom of Movement in International Law' (2011) 12 *Melb. J. Int. Law* 27; Chetail, 'The Transnational Movement of Persons under General International Law' in Chetail and Bauloz (eds), *Research Handbook on International Law and Migration* (Elgar 2014) 10–15.

[66] eg Henkin, *The Age of Rights* (Columbia 1990) 19; Merrills and Robertson, *Human Rights in the World* (4th edn, Manchester 2001) 29; Joseph and Kyriakakis, 'The United Nations and Human Rights' in Joseph and McBeth (eds), *Research Handbook on International Human Rights Law* (Elgar 2010) 2.

[67] Art 12(2) ICCPR.

[68] Art 5(d)(i) CERD; Art 10(2) CRC; Art 18(1)(c) CRPD; Art 8(1) CMW; International Convention on the Suppression and Punishment of the Crime of Apartheid (1973) 1015 UNTS 243; Art 22(2) ACHR; Art 12(2) ACHPR; Art 2(2) of Protocol 4 to the European Convention for the Protection of Human Rights and Fundamental Freedoms (1963) ETS 46; Art 22(2) of Commonwealth of Independent States Convention on Human Rights and Fundamental Freedoms (1996) 3 IHRR 212; Art 27(a) of Arab Charter on Human Rights (2005) 12 IHRR 893.

[69] Art 5(d)(ii) CERD.

[70] Arts 35, 37, 48 of Geneva Convention Relative to the Protection of Civilian Persons in Time of War [Fourth Geneva Convention] (1949) 75 UNTS 287.

[71] Art 44 of Vienna Convention on Diplomatic Relations (1961) 500 UNTS 95; Art 26 of Vienna Convention on Consular Relations (1963) 596 UNTS 261.

[72] HRC, General Comment No. 27, para 8; *Pereira Montera v Uruguay*, UN Doc. CCPR/C/18/D/106/1981 (1983), para 9.4; *Vidal Martins v Uruguay*, CCPR/C/15/D/57/1979 (1982), para 7; *Lichtensztejn v Uruguay*, UN Doc. CCPR/C/18/D/77/1980 (1983), para 8.3; *Varela Nunez v Uruguay*, UN Doc. CCPR/C/19/D/108/1981 (1983), para 9.3.

[73] HRC, General Comment No. 27.

[74] UNGA, Third Committee, Summary Record of the 120th mtg., 3rd sess., UN Doc AC.3/SR.120 (1948), 316; HRC, Summary Record of the 1635th mtg., 61st sess., UN Doc CCPR/C/SR.1635 (1997), para 11; HRC, Summary Record of the 1711th mtg., 64th sess., UN Doc CCPR/C/SR.1711 (1998), para 20; HRC, Summary Record of the 2236th mtg., 82nd sess., UN Doc CCPR/C/SR.2236 (2004), para 50; HRC, Summary Record of the 2835th mtg, 103rd sess. UN Doc CCPR/C/SR.2835 (2012), para 6; Kochenov, 'The Right to Leave any Country Including Your Own in International Law' (2012) 28 *Connecticut J.Int'l L.* 43.

[75] HRC, General Comment No. 27, paras 9, 11, 13.

leave must meet the same standard as other rights in the ICCPR of arbitrariness.[76] The measures must be provided by law, necessary[77] and serve a compelling governmental interest,[78] such as protecting national security, public order, public health or morals and the rights and freedoms of others.[79] The limitations on the right must be the least burdensome means to achieve those ends[80] and cannot otherwise infringe other human rights.[81] On this basis, states may restrict the right to leave because of the need to serve a prison sentence,[82] attend judicial proceedings,[83] render military service,[84] among other justifications.[85] The threshold is high. Thus, a state cannot refuse passports to political dissidents[86] and cannot even refuse to permit a person to leave who might hold state secrets.[87] Even burdensome passport fees are prohibited.[88]

The right to leave overlaps with and supports the right to change nationality. Of course, leaving a state physically is not precisely identical to renouncing nationality and acquiring a new nationality. The right to leave, coupled with the right to a nationality, the right to renounce and the protection against statelessness, constitute parts of the right to change nationality.[89] After all, in order to change, one must be able to leave behind one nationality by renouncing and acquire a new nationality.[90] Otherwise, we do not speak of change, but rather adding an additional nationality. The right to change nationality in the UDHR was consistently framed as part of a right to 'emigrate' and a right to leave any state, including one's own.[91] The discussions at the UN over the UDHR show that the right to leave and change nationality were often intermingled into a generalised 'right to emigrate'.[92]

[76] ibid; HRC, General Comment No. 29 on States of Emergency, CCPR/C/21/Rev.1/Add.11 (2001), para 2; *Vidal Martins v Uruguay*; *Varela Nunez v Uruguay*; *El Ghar v Libya*, CCPR/C/82/D/1107/2002 (2004), para 9.3; *Farag El Dernawi v Libya*, CCPR/C/90/D/1143/2002 (2007), para 6.2; HRC, Belarus, UN Doc CCPR/C/79/Add.5 (1992), para 6; HRC, Gabon, UN Doc CCPR/CO/70/GAB (2000), para 16; HRC, Syrian Arab Republic, UN Doc. UN Doc CCPR/CO/71/SYR, para 21; HRC, Democratic People's Republic of Korea, UN Doc CCPR/CO/72/PRK (2001), para 20; Harvey and Barnidge, 'Human Rights, Free Movement, and the Right to Leave in International Law', 6. Also see *Battista v Italy*, no. 43978/09, § 36, 2 December 2014.

[77] Nowak, *UN Covenant on Civil and Political Rights* 2nd edn (Engel 2005) 274.

[78] HRC, General Comment No. 27, para 16; *Bwalya v Zambia*, CCPR/C/48/D/ 314/1988 (1993), para 6.5.

[79] HRC, General Comment No. 27, para 11; *Hertzberg et al. v Finland*, CCPR/C/15/D/16/1979 (1982), paras 6.3, 10.4; *Bhinder v Canada*, CCPR/C/37/D/208/1986 (1989), paras 4.2, 6.2; *González del Río v Peru*, CCPR/C/46/D/263/1987 (1992) para 5.3; *Celepli v Sweden*, CCPR/C/51/D/456/1991 (1994), para 7.5; *Karker v France*, CCPR/C/70/D/833/1998 (2000), paras 9.2, 9.3, 10.

[80] HRC, General Comment No. 27, paras 14, 16; HRC, General Comment No. 29, paras 2, 4–5.

[81] HRC, General Comment No. 27, para 11.

[82] Nowak, *UN Covenant on Civil and Political Rights*, 270.

[83] HRC, General Comment No. 27, para 16; *González del Río v Peru*, para 5.3; Nowak, *UN Covenant on Civil and Political Rights*, 270.

[84] *Peltonen v Finland*, CCPR/C/51/D/492/1992 (1994) para 8.3; HRC, Russian Federation, UN Doc. CCPR/C/79/Add.54 (1995), para 20.

[85] *González del Río v Peru*, para 5.3; *Peltonen v Finland*, para 8.3; HRC, Russian Federation, para 20; Nowak, *U.N. Covenant on Civil and Political Rights*, 268–70.

[86] HRC, General Comment No. 27, paras 9, 17; *Vidal Martins v Uruguay*, para 7; *Lichtensztejn v Uruguay*, para 8.3; *Pereira Montera v Uruguay*, para 8; *Varela Nunez v Uruguay*, para 9.3; *El Ghar v Libya*, para 8; *El Dernawi v Libya*, para 6.2; HRC, Iraq, UN Doc CCPR/C/79/Add.84 (1997), para 14 (HRC, Iraq); Nowak, *UN Covenant on Civil and Political Rights*, 279.

[87] HRC, General Comment No. 27, para 16; HRC, Gabon, UN Doc. CCPR/C/79/Add.71 (1996), para 16; HRC, Uzbekistan UN Doc. CCPR/C/UZB/CO/3 (2010), para 18; HRC, Turkmenistan, UN Doc. CCPR/C/TKM/CO/1 (2012), para 12; Nowak, *UN Covenant on Civil and Political Rights*, 269–70.

[88] HRC, General Comment No. 27, para 17; HRC, Iraq, para 14.

[89] Whelan, 'Citizenship and the Right to Leave', 638.

[90] ibid.

[91] Kochenov has argued that change can even be understood to mean freedom from the arbitrary state citizenship international regime, see Kochenov, 'Statelessness'.

[92] ibid.

Numerous authorities have concluded that the right to leave directly flowed from the rights expressed in the UDHR.[93] When the ICCPR was adopted, it provided for both a right for every child to a nationality and a right to leave any state.[94] The ICCPR does not expressly cover the right to change nationality as a part of leaving. It says only that '[e]veryone shall be free to leave any country, including his own'.[95] Yet it inherently carried this same meaning as covering change of nationality.[96] The right to leave any state has been consistently understood to be essential to human development[97] and intertwined with the other rights in the ICCPR and UDHR.[98] As Inglés stated, in his capacity as Special Rapporteur, '[t]he right to change one's nationality presupposes the right to leave one's country'.[99] Nowak even seems to view change of nationality as a form of leaving, of emigration.[100] After all, nationality renunciation is a form of leaving a state.[101] As we recall from above, the right to leave is not dependent on any justification, and certainly renunciation and change of nationality is one reason for leaving.[102] Therefore, change of nationality follows from and is part of the right to a nationality and the right to leave any state. Any analysis of measures that impair the right to change nationality must be examined under the same test applied to both the right to a nationality and the right to leave any state.

While the individual has a right to seek, change, retain and enjoy a new nationality,[103] there is no corresponding obligation on the part of states to grant nationality. Some have even argued that the right to change nationality covers the right to choose to seek whichever nationality one wishes,[104] though no naturalisation application is guaranteed. Thus, the right to a nationality, the right to leave and renounce nationality, the right to emigrate and the right to acquire and change nationality grant the individual broad freedom to leave and adhere to different states, should those states offer mechanisms for acquiring nationality.

Therefore, naturalisation procedures and requirements to acquire and change nationality may not be arbitrary. States should not impose burdensome hurdles to naturalisation for long-term residents[105] and decisions on procedural exemptions must have a reasoned basis.[106] In general, the Human Right Committee (HRC) has encouraged states to liberalise their nationality and naturalisation laws, which some states have done.[107]

[93] UN CHR, Inglés, Study of Discrimination, 11; UN CHR, Boutkevitch (Special Rapporteur), Working Paper on the Right to Freedom of Movement and Related Issues, UN Doc. E/CN.4/Sub.2/1997/22 (1997), para 5.

[94] Art 12(2) ICCPR.

[95] ibid.

[96] HRC, General Comment No. 27, para 8; *Pereira Montera v Uruguay*, paras 9.3–9.4; *Vidal Martins v Uruguay*, para 7; *Lichtensztejn v Uruguay*, para 8.4; UN CHR, Boutkevitch, Working Paper, para 5.

[97] HRC, General Comment No. 27, para 1.

[98] UN CHR, Mubanga-Chipoya, Final Report on the Right to Leave any Country; UN CHR, Boutkevitch, Working Paper, para 5.

[99] UN CHR, Inglés, Study of Discrimination, 11.

[100] Nowak, *UN Covenant on Civil and Political Rights*, 267, 274.

[101] Joseph, Schultz and Castan, *The International Covenant on Civil and Political Rights* 2nd edn (Oxford 2005) 355.

[102] ibid. Also see 'The Right to Leave and the Right to Return: A Declaration Adopted by the Uppsala Colloquium, Sweden, June 21, 1972 (1973) 7 IMR 62, 63.

[103] Krūma, *EU Citizenship, Nationality and Migrant Status* (Martinus Nijhoff 2013) 68; Chan, 'The Right to a Nationality as a Human Right' (1992) 12 *HRLJ* 1, 13; Brasington, 'After Alyosha' (2011) 20 *TLCP* 197, 221.

[104] Kolczyńska, 'O treści prawa człowieka do posiadania obywatelstwa' (2021) 13 *Krytyka prawa* 179.

[105] CERD, General Recommendation XXX.

[106] *J.S.K.N. v Denmark*, CCPR/C/136/D/2754/2016 (2022), paras 8.3–8.4.

[107] CERD, Germany, UN Doc. CERD/C/304/Add.115 (2001), para 7; CERD, Estonia, UN Doc. CERD A/57/18(SUPP) (2002), paras 353–54; CERD, Latvia, UN Doc. CERD/C/63/CO/7 (2003), para 13; CERD, Sweden, UN Doc. CERD/C/64/CO/8 (2004), para 4(d).

IV. NATIONALITY AND DISCRIMINATION LAW

Again, there is no international law laying out criteria for naturalisation and states may largely set the criteria for naturalisation as they see fit.[108] Nonetheless, in addition to the limitations mentioned above due to the right to a nationality, there are also limitations on nationality law from the law on discrimination. States must treat all persons as equal before the law and may not discriminate on the basis of 'race, colour, sex, language, religion, political or other opinion, national or social origin, property, birth or other status'.[109] These grounds are not limited to direct, intentional discrimination, but include profiling[110] and facial neutral laws with discriminatory effect.[111] Any discriminatory measures may only be permitted if they are necessary and proportionate to legitimate governmental interests.

These prohibitions on discrimination also apply to naturalisation laws. For example, states may not discriminate on the basis of national origin or other nationality in their naturalisation laws,[112] or on the basis of gender.[113] Now, it is true that some states maintain discriminatory naturalisation laws, and many states have de facto discriminatory nationality regimes.[114] There is still considerable work to be done in this area to fully realise these protections, but some progress has been made. In *Borzov*, for example, the HRC held that discrimination against a person on the ground of his national origin was acceptable, but only in combination with his military participation in the armed forces of the former occupying state, which constituted a legitimate national security risk.[115] In older case law, the Inter-American Court of Human Rights (IACtHR) tolerated a provision that discriminated on the basis of national origin in naturalisation,[116] on the theory that certain national backgrounds would be more likely to

[108] *Borzov v Estonia*, para 7.4; *Toala et al. v New Zealand*, CCPR/C/70/D/675/1995 (2000), paras 11.5–11.6; *J.S.K.N. v Denmark*, para 8.5; Adjami and Harrington, 'Scope and Content of Article 15 of the Universal Declaration of Human Rights', 93.

[109] HRC, General Comment No. 27, para 18; HRC, General Comment No. 28 on Article 3 (2000), para 16; *Gillot v France*, CCPR/C/75/D/932/2000 (2002), para 8.5; HRC, Iraq, para 14; UNHRC, Draft report of the Working Group on the Universal Periodic Review: Austria, UN Doc. A/HRC/WG.6/23/L.10 (2015), paras 5.4, 5.5; UNHRC, Draft report of the Working Group on the Universal Periodic Review: Myanmar, UN Doc. A/HRC/WG.6/23/L.9 (2015) paras 7.54, 7.55, 7.66; *Nubian Children case*, paras 57, 263; *Yean & Bosico v Dominican Republic*, paras 136, 139, 141; *Expelled Dominicans & Haitians v Dominican Republic*, para 263; Adjami and Harrington, 'Scope and Content of Article 15 of the Universal Declaration of Human Rights', 100.

[110] HRC, United States of America, UN Doc. CCPR/C/USA/CO/4 (2014) 7; HRC, Russian Federation, UN Doc. CCPR/C/RUS/CO/7 (2015).

[111] eg *Pjetri v Switzerland*, CERD/C/91/D/53/2013 (2017).

[112] Art 5 ECN; *Karakurt v Austria*, CCPR/C/74/D/965/2000 (2002), para 8.4.

[113] Historically, women were often more likely to change nationality as a result of marriage and, thus, change of nationality has an additional gendered nuance. See eg Convention on the Nationality of Married Women (1957) 309 UNTS 65; CEDAW; CEDAW, General Recommendation No. 32 on the gender-related dimensions of refugee status, asylum, nationality, and statelessness of women, CEDAW/C/GC/32 (2014), paras 54–58; CEDAW, 'Concluding observations on the seventh periodic report of Iraq', UN Doc. CEDAW/C/IRQ/CO/7 (2019), paras 27–28; CEDAW, 'Concluding observations on the sixth periodic report of Eritrea', UN Doc. CEDAW/C/ERI/CO/6 (2020), paras 31–32; Govil and Edwards, 'Women, Nationality and Statelessness' in Edwards and van Waas (eds), *Nationality and Statelessness under International Law* (Cambridge 2014) 180; Knop and Chinkin, 'Remembering Chrystal MacMillan' (2001) 22 *Mich. J. Int'l. L* 523, 561–69.

[114] Foster and Baker, 'Racial Discrimination in Nationality Laws: A Doctrinal Blind Spot of International Law' (2021) 11 *CJRL* 83, 86; Blake, 'Race-based Statelessness in the Dominican Republic' in Bloom et al (eds), *Understanding Statelessness* (Routledge 2017). Also see Ganty and Ammann in this volume on the effective connections between permissible merit-based criteria and impermissible race-based criteria.

[115] *Borzov v Estonia*, para 7.4. This and similar decisions have been criticised as imposing a constructed guilt on all persons deemed ethnically connected to the occupying forces. Eg Ganty and Kochenov, 'Citizenship imposition is the new non-discrimination standard' (VerfBlog, 22 July 2012); Kochenov, 'Statelessness'.

[116] *Advisory Opinion on Proposed Amendments to the Naturalization Provision of the Constitution of Costa Rica*, IACtHR, Ser. A, No. 4 (1984), para 34.

assimilate successfully. It could be doubted that such measures would be acceptable today. Nonetheless, the importance of this holding for this study is that the naturalisation measures were subjected to a proportionality analysis and had to be justified, even if the margin that states enjoy in this area remains wide.

In addition to the more obvious prohibited grounds of national origin and gender, states may also not discriminate on the basis of language or property,[117] which can be particularly important for this chapter. Most distinctions on the basis of language are prohibited,[118] though states may make some limited linguistic distinctions to preserve its majority or minority languages,[119] or generally to enhance national integration,[120] such as by imposing language requirements for naturalisation.[121] That being said, the HRC has concluded that language requirements cannot be absolute and may only be imposed proportionately.[122] In the case of *JSKN*, the Committee concluded that Denmark's inflexible language requirement for naturalisation was impermissible when there were no exemptions for certain situations.[123] As for distinctions on the basis of property, prohibitions on this discrimination are understood broadly.[124] Of course, some discrimination on the basis of property or wealth is permitted, especially in the areas of taxation, where states have wide discretion to adopt proportionate measures.[125] For this reason, the HRC has accepted differential tax assessments based on reciprocal tax treaties.[126] However, in general, distinctions among people on the basis of wealth or property are restricted and must be necessary and in proportion to compelling governmental interests.

The previous paragraphs discussed the application of laws against discrimination to the acquisition of nationality, but the application of laws on discrimination continue to apply to nationality even after the acquisition of nationality.[127] First, states may not distinguish between naturalised nationals and those who acquired nationality by birth. Here, for example, it is quite problematic that some states apply a lower standard to denationalise individuals who have acquired their nationality by naturalisation rather than by birth.[128] Van Waas and Jaghai have compared this form of discrimination in nationality law to the equally odious discrimination on the basis of gender.[129] The Council of Europe Parliamentary Assembly has been clear that this form of discrimination in nationality law is prohibited,[130] as has the IACtHR.[131] The ECN explicitly prohibits discrimination on the basis of how nationality was acquired, for states that are party to that instrument.[132] Often this form of discrimination revives prejudices

[117] HRC, General Comment No. 27, para 18; HRC, General Comment No. 28; Adjami and Harrington, 'Scope and Content of Article 15 of the Universal Declaration of Human Rights', 100.

[118] *Diergaardt et al. v Namibia*, CCPR/C/69/D/760/1997 (2000), para 10.10.

[119] *Ballantyne et al. v Canada*, CCPR/C/47/D/359/1989 and 385/1989/Rev.1 (1993), para 11.5.

[120] *Ignatane v Latvia*, CCPR/C/72/D/884/1999 (2001), para 7.4.

[121] *Q v Denmark*, paras 7.2–7.5.

[122] *J.S.K.N. v Denmark*, paras 8.3–8.4; *HP v Denmark* (dec.), no. 55607/09, 13 December 2016, para 64.

[123] *J.S.K.N. v Denmark*, paras 8.3–8.4.

[124] eg *Haraldsson and Sveinsson v Iceland*, CCPR/C/91/D/1306/2004 (2007), paras 10.3–10.4.

[125] *Gonçalves et al. v Portugal*, CCPR/C/98/D/1565/2007 (2010), para 7.5; *Bartolomeu v Portugal*, CCPR/C/100/D/1783/2008 (2010), para 8.4.

[126] *Van Oord v Netherlands*, CCPR/C/60/D/658/1995 (1997), para 8.5.

[127] van den Brink, 'A Qualified Defence of the Primacy of Nationality of European Union Citizenship' (2020) 69 *ICLQ* 177, 199.

[128] van Waas and Jaghai, 'All Citizens Are Created Equal, but Some Are More Equal Than Others' (2018) 65 *NILR* 422.

[129] ibid.

[130] PACE, Resolution 2263: Withdrawing Nationality as a Measure to Combat Terrorism: A Human Rights-Compatible Approach?, Doc. 14790 (2019). Cf. UN SG, Human Rights and Arbitrary Deprivation of Nationality (2013), para 6.

[131] IACtHR, Proposed Amendments, 116, para 62.

[132] Art 5(2) ECN; Krūma, *EU Citizenship*, 72.

about questions of loyalty to the state or legitimacy of nationality,[133] and can mask issues of discrimination on the basis of national origin or other protected status.[134] After all, persons who naturalise are highly likely in almost all cases to also have a foreign national origin. In *Biao*, the Grand Chamber of the ECtHR held that this form of discrimination had an indirect effect on persons who did not have the typical local national ethnicity.[135] As such, it could not be justified as legitimate or proportionate, and violated article 14 in conjunction with article 8 of the ECHR.[136] Therefore, questioning the connection of naturalised nationals to the state of nationality will, in general, infringe on rules prohibiting national origin discrimination.[137]

In addition, discrimination on the basis of naturalisation raises issues of discrimination on the basis of birth.[138] While on the one hand, states may discriminate on the basis of birth for the specific act of acquiring nationality, on the other hand, they may not discriminate among their nationals on the basis of birth for other considerations. Not only do almost all cases of naturalisation involve foreign national origin, they also almost always involve a failure to have acquired the new nationality already at birth. While certain benefits or advantages by virtue of birth are outside the scope of human rights,[139] nationality, and the right to acquire or change nationality, are certainly protected rights. As is well known, distinctions in nationality laws on the basis of gender violate the Convention on the Elimination of All Forms of Discrimination against Women (CEDAW).[140] As birth is equally protected under the ICCPR as gender, it must enjoy the same standard of protection. Discrimination on the basis of birth is often invoked in situations of birth out of wedlock, descent (eg caste and similar systems) and adoption.[141] But the Committee on Economic, Social and Cultural Rights has concluded that it is equally applicable to birth to stateless parents, meaning that protections from discrimination on the basis of birth apply to nationality and that individuals should not face discrimination on the basis that their parents had no nationality.[142] Both the International Covenant on Economic, Social and Cultural Rights (ICESCPR) and ICCPR prohibit discrimination on the basis of birth and do not make an exception for its application to nationality laws.[143]

That being said, states appear to have a wide margin of appreciation to impose discriminatory rules on acquisition of nationality by birth, despite it being, in principle, prohibited. This apparent contradiction can be resolved by recognising the wide margin of appreciation for states to discriminate in rules on acquisition of nationality, yet a far more limited margin for distinguishing among current nationals on the basis of how they acquired nationality.[144] Said another way, only once an individual is through the door of nationality are states largely

[133] Van Waas and Jaghai, 'All Citizens Are Created Equal, but Some Are More Equal Than Others', 422.

[134] *Tănase v Moldova*, paras 164–80; UN SG, Human Rights and Arbitrary Deprivation of Nationality (2013), para 6; Jennings and Watts, *Oppenheim's International Law* (Longman 1992) 887, note 3.

[135] *Biao v Denmark*, no. 38590/10, 24 May 2016, para 113.

[136] ibid, paras 102, 138–39. Also see *Abdulaziz, Cabales and Balkandali v UK*, no. 9214/80, 9473/81, 9474/81, §87–89, 28 May 1985; Van Waas and Jaghai, 'All Citizens Are Created Equal, but Some Are More Equal Than Others', 418.

[137] Boll, *Multiple Nationality and International Law* (Martinus Nijhoff 2007) 111.

[138] Art 2(1) ICCPR.

[139] *Hoyos Martínez de Irujo v Spain*, CCPR/C/80/D/1008/2001 (2004), para 6.5.

[140] eg 'Discrimination against women in nationality' (OHCHR Working Group on the issue of discrimination against women in law and in practice 2017) www.ohchr.org/sites/default/files/Documents/Issues/Women/WG/DiscriminationAgainstWomenNationality.pdf; also see Art 9 (1) CEDAW.

[141] CESCR, General Comment No. 20: Non-discrimination in economic, social and cultural rights, UN Doc. E/C.12/GC/20 (2009), para 26.

[142] ibid.

[143] Worster, 'Discrimination on the Basis of Nationality under the Convention on the Elimination of Racial Discrimination' (2022) 35 *Pace Int'l. L.Rev.* 41, 49–53. Also see *Gueye et al. v France*, CCPR/C/35/D/196/1985 (1989), para 9.4.

[144] IACtHR, Proposed Amendments, 116, paras 54–59 (1984).

prohibited from discriminating. In the case of naturalisation, the individual has always, by definition, not received nationality of the state of naturalisation at birth. Yet, states appear to be able to adopt nationality acquisition laws that discriminate on the basis of birth, as virtually all states in the world practice some form of *jus soli* and/or *jus sanguinis* nationality acquisition, and do not grant their nationality to all children born in the world. Discriminatory nationality acquisition laws must, therefore, be viewed as legitimate.[145] However, laws other than naturalisation may attempt to discriminate between nationals who acquired nationality by birth and otherwise. For example, the HRC has found that the link of birth within a territory can serve as a valid basis for some distinctions.[146] In *Gillot*, the HRC had to determine whether it was discriminatory to restrict the list of eligible voters in a self-determination referendum in New Caledonia to those with 'sufficiently strong links' partly on the basis of birth in the territory.[147] The Committee determined that the birth criteria was acceptable because it was only one of several 'objective elements for differentiating between residents as regards their relationship with' the territory.[148] The other factors in that case included length of residence, civil status and holding moral and material interests in the territory.[149] Had those other factors not been present, it is doubtful that birth in the territory alone would be sufficient grounds for the discrimination. Another, perhaps implicit, distinction in *Gillot* is that nationality by birth was not a consideration since the territory was not an independent state where nationality followed from birth status.[150] The content of the discrimination (referendum voting in a decolonial context) was far less severe than discrimination between citizens on the basis of where they were born. Making a distinction between naturalised nationals and those who received nationality by birth is therefore inherently a distinction based on birth. But once we move away from laws on the acquisition of nationality to laws on the differential treatment of nationals, the state would no longer have such a wide margin. Thus, states are constrained from making distinctions among their own nationals on the grounds of their place of birth or family descent for rules other than naturalisation.

Second, and following from the first issue, states may also not discriminate among their nationals on the particular qualification for their naturalisation, once they have acquired nationality. Naturalisation can occur due to a variety of acquired connections to a state. The most typical modes of naturalisation include family ties, employment or other forms of vaguely defined value to the state,[151] such as recognition of service,[152] especially military service,[153] or

[145] However, as regards gender, the Working Group on the issue of discrimination against women in law and in practice concluded that protections from gender discrimination also apply to acquisition of nationality, see 'Discrimination against women in nationality' (OHCHR Working Group on the issue of discrimination against women in law and in practice 2017) 138, though this enhanced protection can be attributed to the unique provisions of Art 9(1) CEDAW which specifically demands this result. There is no comparable enhanced protection for birth, and thus states likely still retain discretion to discriminate on nationality acquisition on the basis of birth.

[146] *Gillot v France*, para 13.5.

[147] ibid, para 13.7.

[148] ibid, para 13.8.

[149] ibid, paras 13.7–13.16; cf *Nottebohm*, 22–25.

[150] *Gillot v France*, paras 13.7–13.16.

[151] Jones, 'The *Nottebohm* Case' (1956) 5 *ICLQ* 230, 236.

[152] Magnus (ed), *Tabellen zum internationalen Recht* (Verlag von Franz Vahlen 1926). Of course, the classification of the variety of domestic laws into particular naturalisation categories is itself nearly impossible in line with each state's unique views on its own values and needs within its *domaine reservé*, see Boll, *Multiple Nationality and International Law*, 99, note 19.

[153] eg Decree of the President of the Russian Federation No. 10 2024 (RF) О приеме в гражданство Российской Федерации иностранных граждан, заключивших контракт о прохождении военной службы в Вооруженных Силах Российской Федерации или воинских формированиях, и членов их семей [On the admission to citizenship of the Russian Federation of foreign citizens who have entered into a contract for military service in the Armed

joining a national sporting team.[154] Due to widespread practice noted above, it appears that this discrimination in setting qualifications for naturalisation is permitted. However, once an individual has acquired nationality, states must not discriminate on the basis of the particular legal basis for the person's naturalisation. Discrimination on the basis of how nationality was acquired could also implicate indirect national origin discrimination, if there was disproportionate impact on people with a particular national origin.[155] Recall that discriminatory measures may also violate human rights when they are neutral on their face, but have discriminatory effects.[156] *Biao* is informative in this regard. Mr Biao was from Togo. In the case, the ECtHR found that his treatment constituted indirect national origin discrimination due to differential treatment on the basis that he acquired his nationality by naturalisation,[157] despite the fact that there are existing Danish nationals with Togolese national origin.[158] Thus, the ECtHR distinguished between nationals on the basis of the grounds for their naturalisation would be impermissible when the grounds for naturalisation have some discernible disproportionate impact on persons with a particular national origin(s). This is true even if that national origin is already represented among the state's nationals through other means of naturalisation. For example, if most persons with a particular national origin in the state acquired their nationality by CBI, then discrimination on the basis of CBI could be indirect discrimination against persons with that national origin.

V. MULTIPLE NATIONALITY

In situations of multiple nationality, the same rules as above are relevant, though they may be applied slightly differently. Any tolerance of dual or multiple nationality is a recent arrival in domestic and international law, having been historically opposed by most states with at least as much vigour as statelessness.[159] States retain some flexibility to treat their own nationals as aliens for certain purposes, when they are dual nationals with another state.[160] Also, there does not appear to be a right to hold multiple nationalities[161] (though this position is contested[162]),

Forces of the Russian Federation or military formations, and members of their families] http://publication.pravo.gov.ru/document/0001202401040001.

[154] CAS 94/123, *Fédération Internationale de Basketball v W. & Brandt Hagen* (1994), para 15 (recognising legitimate nationality acquisition on the basis of *jus soli*, *jus sanguinis* and '[s]ome other exceptional legal concept'); CAS 00/001, *United States Olympic Committee and USA Canoe/Kayak/International Olympic Committee* (2000), paras 19–20; Worster, 'Respecting the Right to a Nationality in International Sport'; Baker and Tracy, 'Team China's foreign-born Olympians' (*Axios*, 17 February 2022) www.axios.com/2022/02/17/team-china-olympic-import-athletes.

[155] Also note that discrimination on the basis of naturalisation due to employment connections might implicate the Migrant Workers Convention and various International Labour Organization conventions, see ILO, Discrimination (Employment and Occupation) Convention 1958 (No. 111); ILO, Migrant Workers (Supplementary Provisions) Convention 1975 (No. 143); ILO, Migration for Employment Convention 1949 (No. 97) as revised. This chapter will not explore these possibilities in detail.

[156] eg *Pjetri v Switzerland*.

[157] *Biao v Denmark*, para 113.

[158] 'Statistics Denmark' (Statbank) www.statbank.dk/statbank5a/default.asp?w=1920.

[159] ILC, Kamto, Fourth report, para 6.

[160] ibid, para 8. Also see French-Mexican Claims Commission, *Georges Pinson* (France v Mexico), Decision No. 6 (1928) 5 RIAA 327; Piotrowicz, 'The Australian-Hungarian Consular Treaty of 1988 and the Regulation of Dual Nationality' (1990) 12 *Syd. L.Rev.* 569, 572–76.

[161] UN SG, Human Rights and Arbitrary Deprivation of Nationality (2013), para 6.

[162] See generally Spiro, 'Dual Citizenship as Human Right' (2010) 8 I-CON 111. Also see von Rütte, *The Human Right to Citizenship* (Brill-Nijhoff 2022) 221; Jesserun d'Oliveira, 'Once Again: Plural Nationality' (2018) 25 *MJ* 22, 32 et seq.

and states may prohibit multiple nationality or refuse to recognise it.[163] Thus, while states may not revoke nationality of a national who holds only one nationality,[164] states are not so limited when the person holds more than one,[165] and such nationality revocation is unlikely to be deemed arbitrary.[166] As a result, states wishing to remove nationality will typically assert that the individual holds a claim to a purported alternative nationality, without regard to whether that bond of nationality actually exists.[167]

However, while holding two or more nationalities does not itself appear to be protected, the acquisition and deprivation of nationality, and curtailment of rights of dual nationals, must still comply with other human rights. For example, the rules mentioned above on discrimination and other requirements of arbitrariness and proportionality certainly apply.[168] As the Committee on the Elimination of Racial Discrimination (CERD Committee) has indicated '[d]ifferential treatment based on … the possession of more than one nationality … might consequently violate the principle of non-discrimination', because discrimination on the basis of dual nationality is often a proxy for other forms of prohibited discrimination.[169] Even if withdrawal of nationality in dual nationality situations was not a proxy for prohibited discrimination, prohibitions on dual nationality could still be disproportionate. In *Tănase*, the ECtHR held that Moldovan law prohibiting Members of Parliament from holding an additional nationality was disproportionate.[170] The law only applied to MPs.[171] While there might be some legitimacy in demanding that MPs express more convincing displays of loyalty to the state than other nationals, the Court questioned this claim and, in any event, held that requiring renunciation was far out of proportion to the goal of loyalty.[172] And as for procedural arbitrariness, while the Eritrea-Ethiopian Claims Commission found that withdrawing nationality from a person with multiple nationality was permitted, it only reached this conclusion because the state had a legal mechanism for making determinations on multiple nationality and any relevant security risks.[173]

In addition, other individual rights may also be at issue in situations of dual nationality, such as rights to EU citizenship. In the *Tjebbes* case,[174] the Court of Justice of the EU held that

[163] Worster, 'International Law and the Expulsion of Individuals with More Than One Nationality' (2009) 14 *UCLA J. Int'l L. & Foreign Aff.* 423. *Eritrea-Ethiopian Claims Commission Partial Award*, paras 57–78; *Expelled Dominicans & Haitians v Dominican Republic*, para 263. Even protections for EU citizenship are of little use in this situation, see Case C-221/17 *Tjebbes* ECLI:EU:C:2019:189.

[164] UN SG, 'Arbitrary Deprivation of Nationality'. States attempting to revive denationalisation and the creation of statelessness as a penalty are routinely criticised for committing unlawful acts, see eg Tripkovic, 'No Country for "Bad" Men' (2023) 63 *Brit. J. Criminol.* 1351.

[165] *Eritrea-Ethiopian Claims Commission Partial Award*, paras 57–78; *Expelled Dominicans & Haitians v Dominican Republic*, para 263. Protections of EU citizenship are of little use in this situation: *Tjebbes*; Swider, 'Legitimizing Precarity of EU Citizenship: Tjebbes' (2020) 57 *CMLRev.* 1163.

[166] *Eritrea-Ethiopian Claims Commission Partial Award*, paras 57–78.

[167] *Johansen v Denmark*, no. 27801/19, 3 March 2022, para 38. Also see *R (on the application of Begum) v Secretary of State for the Home Department* [2021] UKSC 7; Riaz, 'Increasing the Powers of the Secretary of State for the Home Department to Strip Individuals of their British Citizenship: *R (on the application of Begum) v SSHD*' (2023) 86 *MLR* 1517.

[168] de Groot and Vonk, *International Standards on Nationality Law* (Wolf 2016) 45; Van Waas and Jaghai, 'All Citizens Are Created Equal, but Some Are More Equal Than Others', 422.

[169] Spiro, 'Dual Citizenship', 126.

[170] *Tănase v Moldova*, no. 7/08, 27 April 2010, paras 164–80.

[171] ibid.

[172] ibid.

[173] *Eritrea-Ethiopian Claims Commission Partial Award*, paras 57–78. There is some possibility to argue that the Commission's award did not support withdrawal of nationality purely on the ground of dual nationality, but required some showing of an additional factor such as dual nationals who were deemed security risks. Also see *Johansen v Denmark*, para 50.

[174] *Tjebbes*; Swider, 'Legitimizing Precarity of EU Citizenship'.

The Netherlands could deprive its nationals of their nationality, if they held another nationality, lived abroad and failed to renew their passports. However, because the loss of Dutch nationality also implicated the loss of EU citizenship, the Court held that such an action had some limitations. First, implicitly, the person had to live abroad outside of the EU, as living outside The Netherlands, though within the EU, was a right protected by EU law. Second, and more importantly, the Court held that The Netherlands had to take an individualised decision due to the impact on EU citizenship, which entailed an examination of the person's continuing connections to the EU. Thus, although multiple nationality could be grounds for removal of nationality, such removal may implicate the individual's other rights, and, strangely, holding multiple nationality made EU citizenship more precarious.[175]

VI. NATIONALITY RIGHTS AND DISCRIMINATION PROTECTIONS APPLY IN RELATION TO THIRD STATES

Clearly, all of the above applies to states in regards to the application of their own nationality and other laws to their own nationals or applicants for their nationality. However, there is no reason to believe that the right to change nationality and protections from discrimination do not apply equally to state recognition of the application of other states' nationality laws. Quite simply, if the human rights rules mentioned above apply to states *vis-à-vis* their own nationals, it only makes sense that they also apply to states *vis-à-vis* foreign nationals. As noted by some authorities, states must not only respect the right to a nationality in relation to their own nationals, but they must respect this right for all people.[176] It would be quite surprising to argue that, while a state cannot discriminate on the basis of race or gender in its nationality laws, other states are permitted to practice that same discrimination in relation to individuals' foreign nationalities. The state refusing recognition of foreign nationality law would be imposing its own discriminatory measures. If a state may not discriminate against its own nationals on the basis of naturalisation due to reclaimed historic descent or any other ground, a foreign state may not invoke protected grounds to question other states grants of nationality. Both states are held to the same law prohibiting discrimination and requiring recognition of the right to change a nationality.

Even though the same human rights apply to recognition of foreign state action as they do to a state's own actions, the application of those rights may differ in the two situations. Any examination of necessity and proportionality would look at different state interests. While it is acceptable for a state to demand that an individual have certain connections in order to receive its nationality,[177] the question in this section is whether it is acceptable for a third state to demand certain specified connections to a foreign state on its own initiative in order to recognise that foreign state's nationality laws. It is quite a significant distinction to say, on the one hand, that state requirements for language or other connections are proportionate for granting nationality, and to say, on the other hand, that other states can refuse to recognise another state's nationality laws that do not impose language requirements or other connections for naturalisation. In the former, the state interest, and proportionality analysis, strongly favours the state and in the latter, the state interest in questioning foreign law is far lower. And even

[175] de Groot, 'Free Movement of Dual EU Citizens' in Cambien et al (eds), *European Citizenship under Stress* (Brill-Nijhoff 2020) 98–99.

[176] Von Rütte, *Human Right to Citizenship*, 228.

[177] *Toala v New Zealand*, paras 11.5–11.6.

for the former, where the state interest is stronger, that interest may still not be sufficient, as was seen in *JSKN*.[178] It is perhaps even more concerning if a state demands that another state violate the human rights of its own citizens by revoking their nationality unjustly.

Nottebohm does not aid in this analysis. As Peter Spiro has convincingly argued, *Nottebohm* is dubious precedent.[179] Setting aside the flaws in the Court's reasoning and the lack of enthusiastic reception afterwards, the Court appears to be backing away, albeit only incrementally, from the judgment.[180] One of the most important reasons for this waning support is the emergence of human rights law since the judgment in 1955, well before the ICCPR and most of the other instruments discussed in this chapter were adopted. In the *Qatar v UAE CERD* case, the Court affirmed that *Nottebohm* supported the contention that nationality was a relatively easily changeable political-legal status[181] and Judge Robinson suggested that *Nottebohm* must be read in light of the development of human rights since the judgment.[182] However, even if *Nottebohm* was still good law, it must at least confirm that sufficient genuine links would mandate recognition of nationality.

However, we can also distinguish *Nottebohm* from most human rights situations. *Nottebohm*, if it has any validity today, only applies to situations of a state applying its own rights, that is, via diplomatic protection. When a state exercises diplomatic protection, it exercises its own rights for injury to itself.[183] Perhaps it is important here to recall that, in *Nottebohm*, the ICJ explicitly stated that it did not seek to make any determination on the validity of Mr Nottebohm's nationality.[184] It was not adjudicating on Mr Nottebohm's rights in the strictest sense. While it is true that the case had a profound impact on Mr Nottebohm's enjoyment of his rights, the case was only focused on whether any international effects *between states* followed from the grant of nationality, specifically whether the harm to one state's national created a right opposable to the other state.[185] In addition, Mr Nottebohm's nationality was only relevant insofar as it supported the secondary rule of diplomatic protection; the claim by Liechtenstein was not based on harm to his rights to nationality. It is far from clear that the rights held by Mr Nottebohm to (change) his nationality, discrimination protections and other human rights protections, apply to the secondary rules for his state to take up his claim.[186]

Now, it is indeed true that the ICJ appears to be partially lifting this distinction between state and individual injury in diplomatic protection. In the *Diallo* case, the ICJ determined that the injury to the state was identical to, or perhaps flowed directly from, the injury to Mr Diallo's rights under the ICCPR.[187] The Court proceeded to assess compensation with reference to the personal injuries to Mr Diallo that formed the basis of his human rights claims.[188]

[178] *J.S.K.N. v Denmark*, paras 8.3–8.4.
[179] Spiro in this volume.
[180] Worster, 'Reining in the *Nottebohm* Case'.
[181] *Qatar v UAE CERD case*, paras 81–82.
[182] Worster, 'Reining in the *Nottebohm* Case', 326; Robinson J, dissenting in *Qatar v UAE CERD case*, para 9.
[183] Art 1 of ILC, Draft Articles on Diplomatic Protection with commentaries, UN Doc. A/61/10 (2006). Also see *Mavrommatis Palestine Concessions* (Greece v UK) [1924] PCIJ Ser. B no. 3, 12; *Panevezys Saldutiskis Railway case* (Estonia v Lithuania) [1939] PCIJ Ser. A/B no. 76, 16.
[184] *Nottebohm*, 30 (Klæstad, Read and Guggenheim (ad hoc) JJ, dissenting).
[185] *Nottebohm*, 20.
[186] The human rights protections from discrimination mentioned above raise doubts about some of the connections that the ICJ suggested in *Nottebohm* that would substantiate his nationality. For example, the Court considered Nottebohm's place of birth, ownership and use of residential property and business/financial interests, see *Nottebohm*, 22–25.
[187] eg *Ahmadou Sadio Diallo* (Guinea v DR Congo) [2010] ICJ Rep. 692, para 165.
[188] *Ahmadou Sadio Diallo* (Guinea v DR Congo) [2012] ICJ Rep. 324, paras 18–55.

Thus, the Court did not appear to make a distinction between injury to the state and injury to the human rights of one of its nationals. But this approach does not necessarily mean that the ICJ has dissolved the distinction between the harm to the individual and the harm suffered by the state. In the ILC *Draft Articles*, the Special Rapporteur did not address this distinction on point, leaving it unclear whether diplomatic protection involved a harm suffered by the state in its own right or whether diplomatic protection was merely a mechanism for assisting nationals make claims for their own rights.[189] And the types of harms to the individual qualifying for diplomatic protection are also not identical to the full scope of human rights. Amerasinghe observes that diplomatic protection is limited to claims by the state for harms suffered by it, which only cover tortious violations of the 'international minimum standard' in regards to a national.[190] In his view, the 'international minimum standard' is not identical to human rights protections, though it is partially informed by human rights.[191] Therefore, it is still possible to distinguish between the claim by Guinea against the DR Congo in *Diallo* from any claim made by Mr Diallo in his personal capacity. The state-to-state claim merely substantiated and measured the damages to the state by reference to the injury to the individual's rights. It did not use individual human rights claims as a basis for the procedural mechanism for establishing diplomatic protection. These distinctions between the rights of states and the rights of individuals, and the substance and procedure of the claim, could explain any divergence between how nationality was addressed in *Nottebohm* compared to how it is addressed in human rights situations. In short, any precedential value of *Nottebohm*, if it has any, would not apply to cases of individual claims to one's own rights to nationality and protection from discrimination under human rights law. Any other result would permit states to refuse to recognise nationality on a wide range of grounds, such as national origin discrimination masquerading as lack of a genuine connection.

This distinction partly helps explain the direct rejection of *Nottebohm* by the European Court of Justice in the *Micheletti* case.[192] Even though *Micheletti* was decided solely on the basis of EU law rather than general international law, the reasoning follows from the argument above. In the case, Spain cited *Nottebohm*, proposing that the Court adopt the 'effective nationality' test into EU law.[193] However, *Micheletti* was not a claim of one state against another, but rather it was a claim by an individual directly against a state for failure to recognise and give effect to his nationality.[194] This refusal to recognise his EU Member State nationality, in turn, resulted in the denial of Mr Micheletti's individual rights because he held nationality in an EU Member State from which he derived EU citizenship and rights.[195] Thus, the case was entirely focused on failure to honour Mr Micheletti's individual rights under EU law, which, in turn, would have seriously degraded rights of free movement in the EU. The EU Court of Justice rejected the application of *Nottebohm*.

In addition to distinguishing between state and individual rights, as well as substance and procedure, international law has also evolved to carve out a '*Namibia*' exception to recognition of state acts. In *Nottebohm*, the ICJ held that states do not need to recognise the public acts of other states, when those acts violate international law, in particular the act of granting

[189] ILC, Draft Articles on Diplomatic Protection, paras 50(2)–(3).
[190] Amerasinghe, *Diplomatic Protection* (Oxford University Press 2008) 37.
[191] ibid 37–38.
[192] Case C-369/90 *Micheletti* ECLI:EU:C:1992:295.
[193] *Micheletti*.
[194] *Micheletti*, para 2.
[195] ibid, para 9.

nationality.[196] In fact, states are actually prohibited from giving effect to the acts of other states, when those acts violate international law.[197] Unlawful acts should be treated as having 'no legal validity … [being] considered null and void'.[198] One possibility is that the acts constitute violations of *jus cogens* norms,[199] but any unlawful act triggers the principle *ex injuria jus non oritur*.[200] In the *Namibia* advisory opinion, the ICJ held that South Africa violated its obligations to the UN Security Council and that, on that basis, other states could not recognise the effects of its unlawful acts.[201] However, individual rights were a different matter. Failure to recognise some of the acts of the state 'may adversely affect the people [of the state]', even if they were unlawful because they emanated from an unlawful occupation.[202] As a result, other states must recognise those public acts and the Court gave examples of 'the registration of births, deaths and marriages'.[203] Surely, the public acts of nationality acquisition and recording of nationality status would fall in this category, which might, in many cases, directly follow from birth and marriage registration. In fact, nationality has been recognised as having this fundamental character and given this form of remedial recognition. States have recognised the functional 'nationality' of individuals, despite their territory of origin not formally constituting a state.[204] 'Nationals' of Taiwan/Chinese Taipei even enjoy visa-free travel to 143 states.[205] The only exception to recognition in *Namibia* would derive from a very narrow argument that refusal to recognise state acts do not adversely affect the individual. Therefore, even in cases where the state is obliged to refuse recognition of another state's acts due to illegality, the state must still respect those acts that avoid adverse effects on individual rights.[206] The reasoning of *Namibia* applies with all the more force if the public act is lawful. If refusal to recognise nationality is of such profound importance that it acts to excuse unlawful acts and demand their recognition, it can only have even more significance when the public act was lawful. Even if CBI were to be viewed as unlawful, which is not correct, under the *Namibia* precedent, states could only refuse to recognise such an 'unlawful act' if it did not adversely affect the individual.

The applicability of the *Namibia* exception and the inapplicability of *Nottebohm* is not to say that a third state could never refuse recognition of nationality laws, due to CBI or another

[196] *Nottebohm*.

[197] *Mavrommatis Palestine Concessions*, 50; *Case Concerning the Factory at Chorzów* (Germany v Poland) [1927] PCIJ Ser. A, no 9, 31; *Gabčíkovo-Nagymaros Project* (Hungary v Slovakia) [1997] ICJ Rep. 7, 76, para 133.

[198] Art 41(2) of ILC, Draft Articles on Responsibility of States for Internationally Wrongful Acts, with commentaries, UN Doc. A/56/10 (2001); Art 42(2) of ILC, Draft Articles on Responsibility of International Organizations, with commentaries, UN Doc. A/66/10 (2011); *East Timor Case* (Portugal v Australia) [1995] ICJ Rep. 60, 103–04; *Cyprus v Turkey*, no. 25781/94, §14–15, 10 May 2001; *Arbitral Tribunal for Dispute over Inter-Entity Boundary in Brčko Area* (Republika Srpska v Federation of Bosnia and Herzegovina) [1997] UN Doc. S/1997/126, paras 77–78; Jennings and Watts, *Oppenheim's International Law*, 183–84.

[199] Art 41(2) of ILC, Draft Articles on State Responsibility; Art 42(2) of ILC, Draft Articles on International Organization Responsibility.

[200] Worster, 'European Union Citizenship and the Unlawful Denial of Member States Nationality', 767.

[201] *Legal Consequences for States of the Continued Presence of South Africa in Namibia (Southwest Africa) Notwithstanding Security Council Resolution 276 (1970)*, Advisory Opinion [1971] ICJ Rep. 16, 54–56, paras 117–27 (*Namibia Advisory Opinion*). Also see *Cyprus v Turkey*, para 90.

[202] *Namibia Advisory Opinion*, para 122. Also see *Cyprus v Turkey*, paras 4–5.

[203] *Namibia Advisory Opinion*, para 125.

[204] United Nations Compensation Commission, Governing Council, Decision, 27th mtg., 6th sess., S/AC.26/1992/10 (1992), art 5.2; US Department of State, *Foreign Affairs Handbook*, vol 8, 403.4-4(D), 403.4-7(C); Crawford, *The Creation of States in International Law* 2nd edn (Oxford University Press 2006) 569–70.

[205] 'Henley Passport Index (Henley & Partners) www.henleyglobal.com/passport-index/ranking; Kochenov and Lindeboom (eds), *Kälin and Kochenov Quality of Nationality Index* (Hart 2020).

[206] This author has previously argued that unlawful denials of nationality by EU Member States in violation of human rights cannot have the result of denying the individual EU citizenship, see Worster, 'European Union Citizenship and the Unlawful Denial of Member States Nationality', 767.

basis. Provided that act complied with the other norms of international law expressed above, such as protections from discrimination, that act could still be non-arbitrary and proportionate to legitimate aims. But it is critical to acknowledge that this assessment would be different from that of a state unlawfully refusing the application of its own nationality laws. The state granting nationality could very well have legitimate aims for withholding nationality and act proportionately in doing so.[207] However, in the situation of recognition, the question would not be whether it was legitimate for the state to have granted nationality. The question is instead whether it is non-arbitrary and a proportionate measure designed to implement a legitimate government objective to refuse recognition of another state's act that would implicate serious human rights considerations. Perhaps fraud in the acquisition of the nationality or other situations could be justifiable. Given the irrelevance of *Nottebohm* and the requirements of *Namibia*, it would seem that states have little space to refuse recognition of foreign nationality law.

VII. CBI AND THE LAWS ON NATIONALITY AND DISCRIMINATION

In this section, this study will summarise the observations above and apply them to CBI. The focus remains on any third state (or EU) action that might impact human rights to nationality. We take as the underlying reason for CBI the uncontroversial fact that some states offer more attractive rights and benefits, and are thus more desirable. These rights could, but do not necessarily, include more national/international mobility, political participation, financial protection, minority protection, religious liberty, and so on.[208] None of these personal motivations are unlawful, nor are states prohibited from facilitating them. And as we have seen, individuals have various human rights to seek and enjoy other nationalities. In fact, by offering various naturalisation pathways to realise rights, states are promoting human rights.

As an initial observation, this chapter takes a broad perspective on CBI schemes, but it is important to note that they do vary. For example, some states with CBI programmes do not give the same rights to nationals who have acquired nationality through investment rather than birth or other bases of naturalisation. Several CBI programmes (Antigua and Barbuda, Dominica, St Kitts and Nevis and Vanuatu) grant nationality but do not include voting rights, though most others do. Or states might restrict residency rights. For example, the large-scale purchase of Comoran nationality for the UAE's Bidoon population did not clearly include right to residence in the Comoros.[209] The low price ($4000 per person) and the lack of involvement (or outright coercion) of the Bidoon persons concerned,[210] suggest that this operation was not a true, wilful acquisition of nationality. In one case, a Bidoon Comoran received asylum in Canada and was not expelled to the Comoros.[211] If this view is correct, then the

[207] *Toala v New Zealand*, paras 11.5–11.6.

[208] eg 'Karmapa now a Dominican citizen' (*The Tribune*, 9 December 2018) www.tribuneindia.com/news/archive/himachal/karmapa-now-a-dominican-citizen-695631 ('The 17th Karmapa, Ogyen Trinley Dorje [leader of the Karma Kagyu school of Tibetan Buddhism] … had applied for the Indian visa [to return to his seat at the Rumtek monastery in Sikkim] but the authorities had yet not obliged him. The Karmapa had admitted to have taken the passport of Dominica in an interview on YouTube. The passport of Dominica allowed Karmapa the visa-free entry into many Commonwealth countries.').

[209] Abrahamian, 'Who Loses When a Country Puts Citizenship Up for Sale?' (*The New York Times*, 5 January 2018) www.nytimes.com/2018/01/05/opinion/sunday/united-arab-emirates-comorans-citizenship.html.

[210] ibid.

[211] ibid.

Comoran nationality acquired for the Bidoon does not appear to be substantively equivalent to the typical Comoran nationality, and therefore may not truly be a nationality. Perhaps it is better to characterise it as a Comoran identity document. Notwithstanding these variations, this section takes a broad approach to CBI generally rather than any specific CBI programme, and it examines whether states violate human rights if they were to refuse to recognise or otherwise infringe on the enjoyment of CBI nationality.

As a second initial observation, we need to identify any infringement of individual rights, not state's rights. Banning visa-free travel for all nationals from a state that offers a CBI programme affects individuals. This includes the EU actions against Ni-Vanuatu nationals, and Canada's actions against nationals of St Kitts and Antigua and Barbuda. US measures discriminating between foreign nationals who must have three years' residence and those who do not, solely on the rounds of CBI, also affects individuals. Though the states (or EU) adopting these measures might view them as countermeasures against states to be resolved between the states, this argument is not entirely accurate. First, CBI is not generally regarded as unlawful in itself. Second, and more importantly, the measures directly implicate individual rights to change nationality to that of a state offering nationality. If a state singles out individuals for differential treatment on the basis of their CBI nationality, then the state must comply with the standards above. If a state takes action against all nationals of a state, then it is taking collective measures against individuals in retaliation for the exercise of human rights regarding nationality. Unlike diplomatic protection, which is a state's claim in its own right against another state, these kinds of measure are either taken directly against an individual or indirectly impact an individual's ability to acquire or change nationality. Of course, foreign nationals do not have a human right to visa-free travel or demand naturalisation in any state they wish, but they do have a right against violations of their human rights and protections from discrimination. Along these lines, it is instructive that the Human Rights Committee has found states to not be in compliance with human rights in the implementation of their naturalisation laws. While no person has a right to naturalise, the implementation of those laws cannot violate human rights. Moreover, in most cases, the state providing for visa-free travel has legislation that governs the administrative decision to permit visa-free travel, generally based on factors such as low rates of visa overstays by nationals of the state in question. Should overstay rates be sufficiently low, the state will permit visa-free travel for all of that other state's nationals. The state might also engage in reciprocity and only grant visa-free travel to nationals of other states that themselves offer visa-free travel. But specifically targeting CBI as the reason for banning visa-free travel, suggests that, in fact, the state is acting out of hostility to that form of naturalisation and perhaps to such changes in nationality. As the analysis below will explain, it is very difficult to see how this infringement of the right to (change) nationality and freedom from discrimination on prohibited grounds can be justified.

In cases of sole (CBI) nationality, the individual has a right to a nationality under the ICCPR and other conventions as well as protections against being rendered stateless under conventional and customary international law. It might also violate the right to leave any state, right to renounce nationality and/or right to change nationality, if the new nationality acquired by CBI resulted in the loss of any and all other nationality(ies). Recall that the individual need not justify the departure, renunciation or change with any explanation. Thus, it is difficult to imagine that measures to discourage states from providing individuals the ability to change from one to another nationality, even if on the basis of CBI, would be proportionate. No genuine connections test could be applied. This conclusion would take on added weight if the individual was a refugee, stateless person, child, person with disabilities or migrant worker, or if the nationality acquired by CBI was actually the restoration of a nationality previously lost, possibly in contravention of international law. In all of these cases, states have weighty obligations to ensure and respect nationality, and it is quite difficult to imagine situations in which a refusal to recognise nationality could ever be justified, even if the mode of acquisition was CBI.

For persons with one or more nationalities in addition to the one acquired by CBI, measures targeting CBI nationality could potentially enjoy a slightly wider margin of appreciation, though they would still be subjected to a proportionality analysis. States are not entirely free to discourage acquisition of nationality or otherwise discriminate. The remainder of this section will focus on situations of multiple nationality, where states might have slightly more discretion to how they treat CBI nationality.

There are a number of considerations based on the diverse obligations from various sources. Starting with the clearest situation under EU law, if the CBI nationality was from an EU Member State and necessarily bestowed EU citizenship, then outright refusal to recognise it by another EU Member State would result in refusal to honour EU citizenship. As such, it would be directly prohibited by *Micheletti*. This is, of course, a different question from whether the EU Member State may discourage CBI as policy by the other EU Member State. But visiting that dispute on an individual would contravene EU law. Other fields of law are significant. From refugee law, if the person who acquired CBI nationality did so as a means of seeking refuge from a state where they might have a well-founded fear of persecution, they might have a strong argument that the state was interfering with the facilitation of refugee naturalisation. And if the person was a child, then the state proposing to discourage CBI would need to conduct a best interests of the child analysis.[212] One could imagine that if the CBI scheme provided for visa-free travel and escape from a state with poorer child welfare conditions, the conclusion would be obvious.

Aside from issues unique to EU law, refugee law and the law on the rights of the child, these interferences with CBI nationality impacting individuals would need a very strong justification as a necessary and proportionate deviation from the obligation not to discriminate against naturalised persons, or persons with multiple nationality or against persons on the basis of the form of naturalisation, measured by both direct and indirect discrimination assessments.[213] For example, states may not claim lack of a genuine connection when it essentially constitutes discrimination on the basis of holding or lacking language skills, or indirectly discriminates on the basis of gender (eg when the CBI nationality was acquired to ensure family and/or marital unity). Also, states may not take measures against CBI nationality where the acquired nationality constitutes an expression of social identity and/or private life, for example, if the person later acquired a strong personal connection to the state of CBI nationality after the acquisition. None of those discriminatory grounds should be permitted for the state granting the nationality and should not be tolerated from other states either. Thus, states taking action against CBI schemes, must provide carve-outs for these situations.

Taking measures to discourage CBI programmes might also indirectly result in discriminating on the basis of national origin, especially if the measures were motivated by targeting persons on the basis of their national origin (or perceived national origin). The European Commission has submitted arguments of state interests that raise doubts about its motivations because it invoked such prohibited grounds. The Commission has asserted that individuals with certain national origins are not meant to enjoy visa waivers merely on the basis of having

[212] Swider, 'Why End Statelessness?', 191.

[213] Kälin, Ius Doni *in International Law and EU Law*, 72: 'there is nothing in the law suggesting that those who acquired their citizenship through investment should be treated differently from other citizens'.

acquired a better nationality.[214] In essence, the Commission argues that individuals from certain disfavoured states will be permanently refused any recognition of naturalisation without any individualised assessment. While national origin discrimination may be theoretically justified in exceptional situations, it is quite difficult to understand how this blatant discrimination can serve as the governmental interest itself.

In addition, anti-CBI measures undertaken out of hostility against persons on the basis of wealth or property are also prohibited. From von der Leyen's 2020 State of the Union Address that 'European values are not for sale',[215] her primary motivation against CBI appears to be animus to the advantages of wealth or, in the words of EU Advocate General Tesauro, the 'romantic' idea that nationality must be insulated from market forces.[216] For this argument, it is completely unclear what the underlying governmental interest could be. Perhaps it is protection of public morals? But the President does not explain what the objective is and whether it would be legitimate under human rights law, and whether it is an appropriate governmental objective of third states to sit in judgment of the nationality laws of other states. Again, all of these situations demand exceptions from any measures to discourage CBI programmes.

All of the above are dubious governmental interests and even if any of these purported justifications could somehow be exceptionally viewed as legitimate governmental interests, these measures would still need to be non-arbitrary and proportionate. The acquisition of a second, multiple or substitute nationality are all protected acquisitions of nationality and this chapter identified the threshold for justification as quite high. A state may have more flexibility to question holding multiple nationality, but if it challenges the acquisition of nationality, then it runs into the human right to do so, and if its approach to multiple nationality has the intention or effect of discrimination on national origin, then it also runs into problems there. And while a state might very well have wider freedom to prohibit its own nationals from acquiring additional nationalities, that same state has little justifiable interest in whether other states permit multiple nationality. In light of nationality's role as the 'right to have rights', measures discouraging CBI or imposing collective punishment on all of a state's nationals are extreme and overbroad steps. Consider that the vast majority of Ni-Vanuatu who lost visa-free travel did not acquire their nationality by CBI. It is difficult to understand how any measures prohibiting the acquisition of nationality, banning visa-free travel or discriminating between CBI and non-CBI nationality would be narrowly tailored.

Looking at the European Commission's measures in particular, they do not survive this test. The Commission has raised doubts about whether CBI-acquired nationality is 'genuine'[217] and insisted that nationality acquisition through – what it understands as – traditional mechanisms are the only genuine nationalities.[218] This view means that nationality acquisition through birth and descent are favoured,[219] but so are grants of nationalities to celebrities and athletes in the national interest.[220] Nationality granted on the basis of, perhaps much needed, investment, is not favoured. Yet, the Commission does not explain why the modes of naturalisations it selected are deemed traditional other than to assert this conclusion and imply that CBI is necessarily not traditional. The Commission also does not explain whether past and current

[214] ibid ('the countries of origin of successful applicants include some that are typically excluded from other citizenship schemes, such as Iran and Afghanistan').
[215] Von der Leyen, State of the Union Address (2020).
[216] Opinion of AG Tesauro, *Micheletti* ECLI:EU:C:1992:47, para 5.
[217] European Commission Report COM(2019) 12 final.
[218] ibid.
[219] ibid.
[220] ibid.

practices of CBI by other EU Member States are part of or contrary to those traditions. But more importantly, the Commission makes no effort to explain what governmental interest it is protecting by designating certain nationality acquisition policies as traditional. It is unclear how concern over other states' choices about the quality of connections sufficient for nationality would qualify as a legitimate governmental interest of a third state.

As a result, even if the Commission could argue that *Nottebohm* gives it permission to inquire in a genuine connection underpinning nationality, many of the factors for a genuine connection analysis are precluded. It could not consider race, gender, national origin, language or wealth (including property ownership), and it could not consider that the nationality was acquired through naturalisation (and specifically through the mode of CBI). Making any distinctions on these bases would violate protections from discrimination on these grounds and must be excluded from the Commission's critique. Obviously, the Commission would remain free to discriminate on any permitted grounds such as risk to national security, criminal record, fraud in obtaining nationality, and so on, but those other grounds are precluded.

Not only would any application of a genuine connections test have to comply with the requirements above, but the very reason for inquiring into the 'genuineness' of nationality grants would need to be justified. What then would be the legitimate government interest in whether a nationality was understood to be genuine? Measures discouraging CBI nationality schemes would need to be legally prescribed, necessary and proportionate to protect an important governmental interest. The European Commission has rightly identified legitimate governmental interests in security, tax evasion, money laundering and governance as motivations for scrutinising CBI nationality.[221] Yet, surely, the Commission and EU Member States have effective state security, tax, financial and governance mechanisms for such ends. Background checks, tax evasion tracking, identity verification and other means are all readily available, before the state needs to take the extreme step of refusing to recognise a person's nationality. Upon completing a joint report on CBI with the Organisation for Economic Co-Operation and Development, the President of the Financial Action Task Force (FATF) noted that the report, which was highly critical of CBI, nonetheless concluded that CBI could be 'designed and administered in a risk-sensitive way, including by implementing safeguards such as those set out in this paper'.[222] Existing criminal, civil and political solutions are far more tailored to these risks than curtailment of a scheme to provide naturalisation for individuals seeking a better life. CBI itself does not appear to inherently pose any such risk.

Based on the above, it is highly unlikely that the European Commission or the states mentioned above could ever justify their actions against CBI by invoking a genuine connections or similar test. Some arguments closely examining suspicious nationality acquisitions might be tenable, for example, scrutinising CBI acquired through fraud which would necessarily result in a fraud on the third state or CBI funded by illicit funds. But, in general, there are few scenarios where the measures discussed in this chapter could ever constitute necessary and proportionate responses to legitimate government interests. As such, these actors are certainly free to take a policy position that CBI is unwise and encourage other states to curtail or wind down their CBI schemes. After all, states are not obliged to offer CBI. But these actors are limited in their ability to impose legal measures infringing on the right to (change) nationality or to discriminate by demanding consideration of unlawful criteria for nationality.

[221] European Commission Proposal COM(2022) 6 final.

[222] 'Misuse of Citizenship and Residency by Investment Programmes' (FATF/OECD 2023), para 11 www.fatf-gafi.org/content/dam/fatf-gafi/reports/Misuse-CBI-RBI-Programmes.pdf.coredownload.pdf; see also Surak's chapter in this volume.

VIII. CONCLUSION

In summary, this chapter has not argued that it would be impossible to challenge CBI nationality. It has not argued that states must necessarily recognise any legislation of other states, nor has it argued for any interpretation of the EU principle of sincere cooperation. However, the current discussion on CBI in many states focuses on inapplicable precedents. They tend to focus on rights of states in their mutual relations, rather than on the human rights of the individuals concerned. The casual application of *Nottebohm* is evidence of this approach.

Instead, this chapter has focused on how measures against CBI impact individuals and infringe on their human rights. Nationality – whether acquired by CBI, sport performance or any other grounds – is highly protected by multiple overlapping and mutual supportive international protections. States may not take measures to discourage acquisition of nationality or distinguish between individuals that potentially violate the right to a nationality, the right to emigrate and change nationality, the right to personal identity, the rights of the child, refugee rights and protections from discrimination on the basis of national origin, naturalisation, form of naturalisation or dual nationality. States bear a demanding burden to justify any efforts to deviate from these protections.

It is certainly very possible that a state might take issue with another state's naturalisation policies, yet at the same time honour human rights. Such an approach would be in line with the spirit of the *Namibia* exception: condemning state policy, yet not prejudicing the individual. This conclusion is all the more critical when a refusal seriously violates the human rights to nationality, emigration, renunciation and change of nationality, as well as rights to be free of discrimination on the basis of national origin, naturalisation and basis for naturalisation. The discussion over CBI needs to re-centre the individual and reflect on the post-*Nottebohm* human rights landscape to ensure that inter-state debates over policy do not make individuals the objects of retaliation.

2

New Generation Skilled Migration Policies

Talent as Output, High Regard Guests and Citizens in Absentia

FRANCESCA STRUMIA

I. INTRODUCTION

SEEN FROM THE air on a crisp day, the Mediterranean Sea is a friendly blue basin, dotted with islands of different sizes that vegetation colours in numerous shades of green. This composition of blues and greens has inspired through the eras poets, novelists and film-makers. Yet, the idyllic vision conceals one of the most puzzling contrasts of contemporary migration. In the first 20 years of the new millennium, among those verdant islands, some have attracted, through tailored visa policies, affluent investors and high net worth individuals.[1] Others have repeatedly collected on their shores the corpses of less lucky migrants who did not survive hazardous sea-crossings in inadequate boats, under the threat of ruthless smugglers.[2] This striking contrast of destinies makes the southern boundary of the European Union a symbol of the inconsistent texture of twenty-first-century national (and supranational) borders, and of the notions of membership that underpin their regulation.[3] As Europe receives, at the time of writing, the largest wave of displaced persons since the Second World War escaping the conflict in Ukraine, this inconsistency is all the more glaring.[4]

On the one hand, the myriad political, military, civil and economic crises of this young new millennium make borders both exposed and guarded. On the other one, eased communications and transports which have made transnational lives a concrete possibility make borders porous, and as life under pandemic restrictions has taught, increasingly virtually porous.

[1] See eg Ch. 188 of Citizenship Law 1964 (MT); Individual Investor Programme of the Republic of Malta Regulations, SL188.03 2014 (MT).

[2] For an overview of the figures and responses, see 'Saving Lives at Sea and Fighting Migrant Smuggling' (Council of the European Union, 10 April 2024) www.consilium.europa.eu/en/policies/eu-migration-policy/saving-lives-sea/.

[3] For an examination of the troubling role of the EU in (at best) failing to enforce a rights-protective system of handling migration and (at worst) in facilitating these tragedies see Grabowska-Moroz and Kochenov, 'The Loss of Face for Everyone Concerned', in Stoyanova and Smet (eds), *Migrants' Rights, Populism and Legal Resilience in Europe* (Cambridge University Press 2022); Urbina, 'The Secretive Prisons That Keep Migrants Out of Europe' (*The New Yorker*, 28 November 2021).

[4] Savino and Gatta, 'On the Brink of a New Refugee Crisis' (VerfBlog, 10 March 2022); 'IOM Ukraine Response' (IOM 2022) https://displacement.iom.int/sites/g/files/tmzbdl1461/files/reports/IOM_DTM_Crossing%20into%20UKR_neighbouring%20countries_as%20of%202022.05.31.pdf.

In part in response to these transformations, sovereign states engage with borders in novel ways, shifting and bending them to the service of their sovereign objectives and reinventing territoriality in the process while maintaining its 'gravitational force'.[5] The new forms of admission to residence and admission to citizenship that are at the heart of the inquiry in this volume and that aim at facilitating the entry and in some cases the naturalisation of high net worth individuals and innovative entrepreneurs have emerged as a result. I refer to these as 'new generation skilled migration policies'.

This chapter focuses on distinguishing these 'new generation skilled migration policies' from traditional policies for the selection of skilled migrants. The chapter evidences two distinguishing features of the 'new generation' schemes: legal requirements for the entry of skilled migrants focus on talent as 'output' rather than as an 'input'; and the state's role in administering immigration and citizenship law becomes, in the context of these policies, the one of a headhunter. These shifts in the notions of talent underpinning the selection of skilled migrants and in the role of the state in performing the relevant selection harbour implications in terms of changing boundaries and bonds of community membership. Through headhunting for migrants that promise an output, states channel the attribution of the privilege of citizenship on a non-birthright basis along a novel regulatory trajectory.[6] This trajectory is parallel but distinct from traditional ones. A dual track non-birthright citizenship model emerges as a result: heavy, culturalised citizenship for the 'traditional' migrants;[7] thin citizenship, possibly independent of any cross-border movement and held even 'in absentia', for the beneficiaries of 'new generation' policies.[8]

The chapter findings provide on the one hand a nuanced understanding of arguments advanced in the burgeoning literature on investment migration that point among others to the commodification of membership,[9] and to the relation between membership and meritocracy.[10] On the other hand the analysis in the chapter adds to debates in the literature on the evolution of citizenship as a concept, its relation to migration and mobility, its strategic and compensatory value, its gradual hollowing out as well as its colonial legacies.[11] In respect to these latter debates, the chapter takes in part a step back, by questioning the very association between citizenship, settlement and mobility that the traditional literature takes as starting point; in part, it goes one step further. It not only focuses on the fact that citizenship has come to compete with a number of contextual and alternative dimensions of membership threatening

[5] Hirschl and Shachar, 'Spatial Statism' (2019) 17 *ICONS* 387, 393; also Shachar, 'Beyond Open and Closed Borders' (2020) 11 *Jurisprudence* 1, 6.

[6] For the conceptualisation of birthright citizenship as a privilege see Shachar, *The Birthright Lottery* (Harvard University Press 2009); Kochenov, *Citizenship* (MIT Press 2019).

[7] On the culturalisation of immigration policy in Europe, see Orgad, *The Cultural Defense of Nations* (Oxford University Press 2017).

[8] For the fact that investment migrants are often not looking for immediate relocation options see Surak, 'Millionaire Mobility and the Sale of Citizenship' (2021) 47 *JEMS* 166.

[9] See eg Shachar and Hirschl, 'Recruiting "Super Talent"' (2013) 20 *IJGLS* 71; Tanasoca, *The Ethics of Multiple Citizenship* (Cambridge University Press 2018); Džankić, *The Global Market for Investor Citizenship* (Palgrave Macmillan 2019); Erez, 'A Blocked Exchange?' in Kochenov and Surak (eds), *Citizenship and Residence Sales* (Cambridge University Press 2023); Roy, 'The "Streetlight Effect' in Commentary on Citizenship by Investment' in Kochenov and Surak (eds), *Citizenship and Residence Sales*.

[10] Ammann, 'Passports for Sale' (2020) 22 EJML 309, 337. See also Ammann's chapter in this volume.

[11] See eg de Hoon, Vink and Schmeets, 'A Ticket to Mobility?' (2020) 46 *JEMS* 1185, 1203. Harpaz, *Citizenship 2.0* (Princeton University Press 2019); Joppke, 'The Inevitable Lightening of Citizenship' (2010) 51 *EJS* 9; Joppke, 'The Instrumental Turn of Citizenship' (2018) 45 *JEMS* 858; Bauböck, 'Genuine Links and Useful Passports' (2019) 45 *JEMS* 1015. For a critique of citizenship as a colonial and racist concept, see Kochenov, *Citizenship*, 96–104; Boatcă, 'The Colonial Institution of Citizenship and Global Capitalist Dynamics' in Kochenov and Surak (eds), *Citizenship and Residence Sales*.

the notion's inner consistency. It rather points to the alteration in the nature of the rights, responsibilities, affiliations that citizenship itself expresses.

Section II introduces new generation skilled migration policies, setting these in regulatory and theoretical context. Section III takes a step back to trace the role of the regulation of immigration and access to citizenship in defining community membership. In the optic of understanding how this role changes with the advent of new generation skilled migration policies, Section IV analyses the way legal requirements of 'talent' are set in these new policies, as well as the role that states take on in their context in designing and implementing immigration and citizenship law. Section V builds on this analysis to reflect on the implications for notions of community membership and ultimately for the very nature of citizenship.

II. NEW GENERATION SKILLED MIGRATION POLICIES IN REGULATORY AND THEORETICAL CONTEXT

Favour for skilled migrants is a long-established element of immigration policy, informing the immigration laws of several countries. Traditional countries of immigrants,[12] such as the United States, Canada and Australia, have long facilitated the admission and integration of skilled migrants. The US Immigration and Nationality Act encompasses a number of categories of immigrant and non-immigrant visas aimed at skilled migrants: not only the renowned non-immigrant H1-B visa for highly qualified professionals, but also visa for investors and intra-company transferees;[13] a non-immigrant 'genius visa' for persons of extraordinary ability in the sciences, culture or sports;[14] and immigrant visa for persons of extraordinary ability who can self-sponsor themselves and do not need to pass the labour certification procedure that applies to most other categories of economic migrants.[15] The US Act also provides for an immigrant visa for investors, labelled as an 'employment creation' visa, the EB-5.[16] Canada pioneered in 1967 a point-based scheme for skilled immigration, awarding points to applicants for various factors such as education, language knowledge, professional experience and adaptability, and providing for several decades the main route to permanent residence in Canada.[17] Current skilled immigration policy relies on an 'Express Entry' system for three distinct classes of skilled workers, distinguished by the type of work experience of the applicants, whether in Canada or abroad, and whether in a skilled trade.[18] The skilled stream of Australia's migration

[12] For the distinction between countries of immigrants and countries of immigration, see Weil, 'Access to Citizenship' in Aleinikoff and Klusmeyer (eds), *Citizenship Today* (Carnegie 2001) 21.

[13] Sect 101 of Immigration and Nationality Act 1942 (US).

[14] ibid; also see 'O-1 Visa: Individuals with Extraordinary Ability or Achievement' (US Citizenship and Immigration Services, 21 January 2022) www.uscis.gov/working-united-states/temporary-workers/o-1-individuals-extraordinary-ability-or-achievement/o-1-visa-individuals-extraordinary-ability-or-achievement.

[15] Sect 203(b)(1) of Immigration and Nationality Act 1942 (US); also see US Citizens and Immigration Services, 'Employment-Based Immigration: First Preference EB-1' (US Citizenship and Immigration Services, 1 March 2022) www.uscis.gov/working-united-states/permanent-workers/employment-based-immigration-first-preference-eb-1. The ability to self-petition is reserved to the sub-category persons of 'extraordinary ability'. For a critique see Schuck and Tyler, 'Making the Case for Changing U.S. Policy Regarding Highly Skilled Immigrants' (2010) 38 *Fordham Urb. LJ* 327.

[16] Sect 203(b)(5) of Immigration and Nationality Act 1942 (US). See 'About the EB-5 Visa' (US Citizenship and Immigration Services, 17 March 2022) www.uscis.gov/working-united-states/permanent-workers/employment-based-immigration-fifth-preference-eb-5/about-eb-5-visa.

[17] Koslowski, 'Selective Migration Policy Models and Changing Realities of Implementation' (2014) 52 *International Migration* 26, 34.

[18] See Sect 72–87 Immigration and Refugee Protection Regulations, SOR/2002-227 (CA); also see 'Immigrate to Canada' (Government of Canada, 9 March 2022) www.canada.ca/en/immigration-refugees-citizenship/services/immigrate-canada.html.

programme relies on a combined list of eligible skilled occupations that is periodically updated and in whose respect skilled independent visa, skill nominated visa and employer nominated visa are available.[19] The award of these visas relies on a point-based system assigning points to applicants on the basis of a range of eligibility factors such as language, age and education.[20]

In European countries, which are not traditionally countries of immigrants, but have experienced varied histories of immigration in the twentieth century,[21] the regulation of skilled migration has a different connotation. The immigration policies of European countries reflect a range of priorities and are in part a result of colonial histories and of de-colonisation. In many cases their citizenship and immigration policies have indeed been used to restrict or control migratory flows from colonial to metropolitan areas.[22] The immigration and nationality laws of these countries recognise in any case privileged categories of skilled migrants or take into account desert or merit as a ground for granting citizenship.[23] In the context of the European Union, in addition to the regulations of individual countries, the EU common immigration policy has also placed an emphasis on the encouragement of skilled migration. The Pact on Migration and Asylum proposed by the European Commission in 2020 envisages the creation of talent partnerships and includes as action points the proposal of a 'Skills and Talent package' and the pondering of options to form a EU talent pool.[24] EU legislation adopted in response to the goal of attracting talents offers 'blue cards' to highly qualified workers,[25] as well as tailored visas to capable third country national researchers.[26] EU measures corroborate the efforts of individual Member States immigration policies in this sense. In general, the EU common immigration and asylum policy is but a complement of national ones.[27] The need to manage a long perimeter of common external borders has increasingly called for commitment to solidarity and shared responsibility as part of that policy.[28] But the concrete pursuit of these commitments has been hampered by the conflicting priorities of Member States that are differently positioned in respect to those shared external borders and in respect to global migration streams.[29]

[19] 'Skilled Migration Program' (Australian Government: Department of Home Affairs, 17 March 2020) https://immi.homeaffairs.gov.au/what-we-do/skilled-migration-program/recent-changes.

[20] Migration Regulations 1994, Compilation No. 218, 2021 (AU). Also see Koslowski, 'Selective Migration Policy' 34–36.

[21] For an overview: Parsons and Smeeding, *Immigration and the Transformation of Europe* (Cambridge University Press 2006).

[22] Boatcă, 'The Colonial Institution of Citizenship', 12,13.

[23] Art 27 of Immigration Law 1998 (IT). Also see Art 9(2) of Citizenship Law 1992 (IT). France also awards a 'passport talent' residence permit to a broad class of talented individuals, including persons of national or international reputation, performers, authors of literary and artistic work, and highly qualified employees. 'International Talents and Economic Attractiveness' (*France-Visas*) https://france-visas.gouv.fr/en/web/france-visas/france-visas/international-talents-and-economic-attractiveness.

[24] European Commission, 'New Pact on Migration and Asylum' COM/2020/609 final.

[25] Directive 2021/1883 on the conditions of entry and residence of third-country nationals for the purpose of highly qualified employment, [2021] OJ L 382/1.

[26] See Directive 2016/801 on the conditions of entry and residence of third-country nationals for the purposes of research, studies, training, voluntary service, pupil exchange schemes or educational projects and au pairing (recast) [2016] OJ L132/21.

[27] See Arts 77–79 TFEU.

[28] See European Commission Communication COM/2020/609final; also 'Video Conference of Home Affairs Ministers' (Council of the European Union, 14 December 2020) www.consilium.europa.eu/en/meetings/jha/2020/12/14/.

[29] The unanimous decision in February 2022 to activate a temporary protection mechanism under Directive 2001/55/EC in response to the humanitarian crisis prompted by the Russian invasion of Ukraine is a first sign of concrete political willingness to make good on this promise of solidarity and shared responsibility, after the debacle in handling the 2015 refugee crisis. See Council Implementing Decision 2022/382 establishing the existence of a mass

When it comes to scouting for talents, however, distinct sovereign interests as well as their supranational projections seem to converge in a common direction. Convergence, when it comes to skilled migration policies, is not limited to the European context. Regardless of different background histories, states strategies to attract skilled migrants have evolved in similar directions in the last decade. All around the globe, states have come to emulate one another in introducing innovative tools for recruitment of skilled migrants. Similar practices have yielded the schemes referred to in this chapter as 'new generation' skilled migration policies. The term is used to refer to two classes of policies aimed at attracting some very specific groups of desirable contributors to a host State economy and job market: investor schemes and entrepreneur programmes.

Under investor schemes, a number of countries offer visa on a fast-track basis, as well as residence permits of varied durations, to high net worth foreigners who commit to invest a qualifying amount of money in a business established in the relevant country, in bonds issued by its government or in ad hoc public interest funds. Australia, the Netherlands, Ireland, Spain and Portugal, among others, have introduced programmes of this type.[30] As mentioned above, the US have long offered to investors a non-immigrant visa as well as an immigrant visa that albeit belonging to a different family of policies shares some features with the investor visa of new generation. Some other countries have pushed the favour for foreign investors as far as to provide for the immediate grant of citizenship to qualifying applicants, without prior residence requirements or with significantly reduced residence requirements in comparison to naturalisation tracks that are considered ordinary.[31]

Entrepreneur programmes have similar features in terms of the facilitations that they grant, however they are aimed at a different class of desirable migrants. These programmes favour entrepreneurs who propose to set up a new business, usually in the form of a start-up,[32] in the host country and who demonstrate availability of funding to support the project and/or the endorsement of a recognised business organisation in the host country, an innovative idea, and a viable business plan. Chile, Canada, the United Kingdom, Ireland, Italy, the Netherlands and South Korea are a few examples of countries that have introduced start-up, or entrepreneur visa policies, in recent years.[33]

influx of displaced persons from Ukraine within the meaning of Article 5 of Directive 2001/55/EC, and having the effect of introducing temporary protection [2022] OJ L71/1. For an overview of the conflict between EU values and the management of migration in European countries, see Stoyanova and Smet (eds), *Migrants' Rights, Populism and Legal Resilience in Europe* (Cambridge University Press 2022).

[30] The UK had introduced a Tier 1 investor visa in 2008. This has been discontinued as of 17 February 2022 over security concerns. Canada also used to run a Canadian Federal Investor programme, terminated in 2014. For a classification of existing programmes see Džankić, *The Global Market for Investor Citizenship*, 91–135. For an empirical analysis of supply and demand dynamics, as well as programme outcomes, see Surak, 'Investment Migration' in Kochenov and Surak (eds), *Citizenship and Residence Sales*. Also see Surak 'Global Citizenship 2.0' (2016) Investment Migration Working Papers IMC-RP 2016/3.

[31] See eg Individual Investor Programme of the Republic of Malta Regulations, SL188.03 2014 (MT). Cyprus had a similar scheme. See Council of Ministers Decision of 19 March 2014, Scheme for Naturalization of Investors in Cyprus by Exception (CY). The scheme has been amended in 2016 and 2018 and has been suspended in 2020. For an overview see Džankić, *The Global Market for Investor Citizenship*, 191–94. For the elusiveness of the idea of an 'ordinary' naturalisation track see Jessurun d'Oliveira's and Kochenov and van den Brink's chapters in this volume.

[32] A start-up has been defined as a 'temporary organization that searches for a scalable and repeatable new business model'. See Blank and Dorf, *The Startup Owner's Manual* (Wiley 2020) 12–14.

[33] For the Start-Up Chile programme, 'Start-Up Chile' (Start-Up Chile) https://startupchile.org/en/; for the Canadian Start-up Visa Program see 'Start-up Visa Program' (Government of Canada, 10 December 2023) www.canada.ca/en/immigration-refugees-citizenship/services/immigrate-canada/start-visa.html; also see Cohen's chapter in this volume; for the Italian Startup Visa, see, 'Italia Startup Visa' (Ministry of Economic Development) https://italiastartupvisa.mise.gov.it/#homepage; the United Kingdom, after discontinuing its Tier 1 Entrepreneur visa now offers both a two-year non-renewable Start-up visa, and a three-year renewable Innovator Visa that also qualifies for settlement

These novel strategies in immigration are part of a quest for economic growth through innovation in which several countries have become entangled.[34] Attracting talent is a fundamental component of relevant recipes for innovation.[35] In quantitative terms these policies may appear insignificant – the figures for migrants taking advantage of these entry routes are small.[36] In conceptual terms they raise however important questions that have shifted the attention in the literature on skilled migration, and prompted novel strands of inquiry.

This literature has been dominated for decades by economic debates questioning the relative merits of brain gain and brain drain arguments, and the contrast between the interests of countries of origin and those of destination countries in the context of skilled migrants policies. Earlier arguments in this sense focused on whether the circulation of talent from low productivity to high productivity areas overall increased global wealth, or rather disproportionately disadvantaged sending countries.[37] In the twenty-first century relevant studies have rather focused on the economic potential of circular migration, as well as on the beneficial effect for sending countries of remittances, technology transfers and diaspora networks.[38]

With the appearance of new generation skilled migration policies the focus has in part shifted from economic analysis to questions on the legal and ethical implications of relevant policies.[39] Attention has been paid to the risk of abuse of these schemes, and to the connected security concerns that they bring along.[40] The 'race for talent' underpinning these policies has raised concerns for the prospects of belonging and political membership ideas that are traditionally linked to citizenship.[41] It has also been seen as threatening to widen and entrench a

in the UK, see 'Start-up Visa' (UK Government) www.gov.uk/start-up-visa; 'Innovator Visa' (UK Government) www.gov.uk/innovator-visa; for Ireland see 'Start-up Entrepreneur Programme (STEP)' (Immigration Service Delivery, 25 September 2023) www.irishimmigration.ie/coming-to-work-in-ireland/what-are-my-options-for-working-in-ireland/coming-to-work-for-more-than-90-days/start-up-entrepreneur-programme-step/; for the Dutch Startup Visa see Government information for Entrepreneurs, 'Startup Visa' (Business.Gov.nl) https://business.gov.nl/coming-to-the-netherlands/permits-and-visa/startup-visa/; for the South Korean Overall Assistance for Startup Immigration System (OASIS) see 'Startup Visa (D-8-4), Corp' (Global Start-up Immigration Center) OASIS (oasisvisa.kr).

[34] The one for innovation and talent has been referred to as a battle in which both countries and firms are involved. See Lobel, *Talent Wants to Be Free* (Yale 2013) 14.

[35] By way of example the Australian Global Talent Visa Program and Global Talent Employer Sponsored Visa Program are labeled by the Australian government 'Visas for Innovation'. See 'Visas for innovation' (Australian Government: Department of Home Affairs) https://immi.homeaffairs.gov.au/visas/working-in-australia/visas-for-innovation.

[36] For instance, the Italia Startup visa has been granted in the five years between its introduction in 2014 and 2019 to 250 applicants (out of 481 applications). See 'Italia Startup Visa' (Ministry of Economic Development). In the year ending March 2020, the UK granted 729 visas under the now closed Tier 1 (investor visa) route, out of a total of 194,557 work-related visa awarded in that year. See 'Why Do People Come to the UK? To Work' (GOV.UK, 14 November 2023) www.gov.uk/government/statistics/immigration-system-statistics-year-ending-june-2023/why-do-people-come-to-the-uk-to-work.

[37] The former was the argument of the internationalists while the latter was the position of the nationalists. See Solimano, 'Causes and Consequences of Talent Mobility' in Solimano (ed), *The International Mobility of Talent* (Oxford University Press 2008) 2–3. More in general on economic approaches to the brain gain vs brain drain debate see Adams, *The Brain Drain* (Collier Macmillan Ltd 1968); Grubel and Scott, *The Brain Drain* (Wilfrid Laurier UP 1977); for a more recent study contrasting the perspectives of recipient countries and sending countries, see Boeri et al, *Brain Drain and Brain Gain* (Oxford University Press 2012).

[38] Solimano, 'Causes and Consequenses', 3. Also see Thorn-Lauritz and Holm-Nielsen, 'International Mobility of Researchers and Scientists' in Solimano (ed), *The International Mobility of Talent* (Oxford University Press 2008); Hercog and Siegel, 'Promoting Return and Circular Migration of the Highly Skilled' (2011) UNU-Merit Working Paper 15/2011; Agrawal et al, 'Brain Drain or Brain Bank?' (2008) NBER Working Paper 14592.

[39] See Shachar and Hirschl, 'Recruiting Super Talent' (2013) 20 *Indiana Journal of Global Legal Studies* 71; also see Koslowski, 'Selective Migration Policy Models and Changing Realities of Implementation', 26.

[40] See Džankić, *The Global Market for Investor Citizenship*, 1–4; Sumption 'Can Investor Residence and Citizenship Programmes be a Policy Success? in Kochenov and Surak (eds), *Citizenship and Residence Sales*, 21–22; Corrado and Marsh, 'Investment Migration and the Importance of Due Diligence' in Kochenov and Surak (eds), *Citizenship and Residence Sales*.

[41] For a canvas of arguments see Bauböck (ed), *Debating Transformations of National Citizenship* (Springer 2018).

distinction between the opportunities for international mobility of the most skilled and well-off and the disentitlement of unskilled migrants.[42]

In particular, Ayelet Shachar, in examining states' attempts to benefit from the glory of promising Olympic athletes through rushed grants of citizenship, identifies issues of freedom, fairness and community in the background to the race for talent.[43] Singling out talented individuals for fast-track membership certainly serves well their freedom to move. However, in the case of Olympic athletes this is arguably unfair to their countries of origin that invested in training them.[44] The highest threat goes, in any case, to community: in the context of relevant policies, citizenship is no longer a proxy for membership but rather becomes a recruiting tool.[45] Market-oriented considerations – the argument goes – replace the collective identity and allegiance notions that used to be at the basis of the bond of citizenship. And as a consequence, membership in the community is commodified and no longer based on a notion of substantial attachment.[46] The commodification argument has had ample resonance in the literature on investment migration, attracting both endorsers and detractors.[47] Some views qualify the scope of the argument. According to Dora Kostakopoulou, for instance, the facilitations granted to the wealthy and talented are only a problem in the context of a rigid, ethnicised system of naturalisation;[48] whilst Peter Spiro, speaking specifically about 'Olympic citizenship', suggests that what is becoming commodified is residence rather than citizenship, and as long as the two levels are kept distinct, citizenship's dilution as a notion is limited.[49] Moreover, as Dimitry Kochenov forcefully reminds, any critique of the commodification or instrumentalisation of citizenship is premised on the idea that citizenship is a just and rational condition. This premise lays a mantel however over the random and in many cases arbitrary nature of citizenship status.[50]

This latter distinction points to a fundamental question that the debate so far has somewhat overlooked. What is the relative role of residence by investment programmes, and of citizenship by investment programmes in altering existing notions of membership? Both types of programmes award to talented or wealthy outsiders a form of membership. In both types of programme membership is a reward for either a promising business plan and the ability to source the necessary funds to realise it, or for a material monetary contribution to the economy of the host state. In the case of citizenship by investment programmes, the award of membership is in the form of a passport. In the case of residence by investment programmes, the award of membership is in the form of a residence permit, initially for a limited time, but typically renewable, and qualifying the holder, subject to compliance with additional requirements, for naturalisation.[51] Does it matter, then, for purposes of

[42] See Harpaz, 'Citizenship and Residence Rights as Vehicles of Global Inequality', in Kochenov and Surak (eds), *Citizenship and Residence Sales*; Ammann, 'Passports for Sale', 309–37.

[43] Shachar, 'Picking Winners' (2011) 120 *YLJ* 2088, 2107–08.

[44] ibid 2121–29.

[45] ibid 2131.

[46] ibid 2106. Also see Shachar and Hirschl, 'Recruiting Super Talent', 90–92.

[47] See eg Džankić, *The Global Market for Investor Citizenship*; Erez, 'A Blocked Exchange?', in Kochenov and Surak (eds), *Citizenship and Residence Sales*.

[48] Kostakopoulou and Schrauwen, 'Olympic Citizenship and the (Un)Specialness of the National Vest' (2014) 10 *Int'l. J. L. in Context* 143, 149.

[49] Spiro, 'The End of Olympic Nationality' in Jenkins et al (eds), *Allegiance and Identity in a Globalized World* (Cambridge Univeresity Press 2012).

[50] Kochenov, 'Citizenship for Real: Its Hypocrisy, Its Randomness, Its Price' in Bauböck (ed), *Debating Transformations of National Citizenship* (Springer 2018).

[51] For further elaboration on this distinction, see Strumia and Kaushal, 'Opening the Ranks of Constitutional Subjects' (2017) 18 *GLJ* 1657, 1674–75.

our understanding of what membership entails, whether this form of membership is a full-fledged citizenship status, as in the citizenship by investment programmes, or whether it is a 'high-regard guests' status, as in the residence by investment programmes?

Answering this latter question requires clearing the ground around an analytical one. This is the question of how new generation skilled migration policies alter the role of immigration and of citizenship law, both individually and in their reciprocal interaction, in selecting community members. This question in turn requires a preliminary reflection on the very role of immigration and citizenship law in drawing the boundaries of community membership.

III. IMMIGRATION AND CITIZENSHIP LAW AND THE DESIGNATION OF COMMUNITY MEMBERS

Albeit in different ways, both immigration and citizenship law contribute to govern the way states select their members. They both say something, thus, about the quality of being a member. Immigration law sets the legal criteria for admission of foreigners to residence within the territorial boundaries of a state's legal and political community. Citizenship law sets the legal criteria for recognition of a person, whether resident or not, as a full member of that same legal and political community.

The state power to select through immigration law is a corollary of the state widely recognised claim to legitimate closure.[52] Joseph Carens, in acknowledging this power of selection, also underlines how certain categories of migrants have a heightened claim to entry, which conversely constrains a state's power of selection in their respect. This is the case for family members of citizens and residents, as states have a moral, if not legal, duty towards the already members of the community to protect family reunification. It is also the case for refugees and asylum seekers, in whose respect humanitarian considerations drive a moral duty of admission.[53] Beyond these categories, however, states are mostly free to select in their discretion.[54] Most common selection criteria in the 'discretionary' band of immigration law include secondary family relationships, language knowledge, other factors of social and economic integration and the potential for economic contribution.[55]

Citizenship law, beyond selecting who has a qualified claim to entry, identifies criteria for national belonging and translates these into rules for citizenship acquisition. These rules mostly rely on criteria that are proxies for affinity and allegiance. Such criteria are taken for granted in the case of the vast majority of birth-right citizens, however they become requirements to be proved when it comes to non-birth-right citizens.[56]

The powers of selection that states exercise respectively through immigration law and through citizenship law are wielded in different ways and different directions, and they express distinct concerns.[57] Nonetheless, those powers overlap in part. As Catherine Dauvergne has

[52] See eg Miller, 'Immigration: the Case for Limits' in Cohen and Wellman (eds), *Contemporary Debates in Applied Ethics* (Blackwell 2014); Also see Carens, 'Who Should Get in?' (2003) 17 *Ethics & International Affairs* 95, 110.

[53] Carens, 'Who Should Get in?', 96–99.

[54] Although some selection criteria would certainly be morally objectionable. See ibid 104–06.

[55] ibid 106–10.

[56] For an argument on the inequality of birthright citizenship, see Shachar, *The Birthright Lottery*; for a fascinating historical account of the role of consent in the making of American federal citizenship, see Kettner, *The Development of American Citizenship* (University of North Carolina Press 1978) 1608–870.

[57] For an example see the discourses surrounding the distinction between '*Italiani non regnicoli*' and 'non-Italian foreigners' in the context of the post-unification Italian State, Donati, *A Political History of National Citizenship and Identity in Italy, 1861–1950* (Stanford University Press 2013).

observed immigration law performs 'the dirty work of citizenship law'.[58] Immigration and citizenship law operate in this sense in a continuum.[59] This continuity is clearly visible in two instances. First, the selection criteria drawn in each set of laws have become in part entangled in several jurisdictions. Relevant legislation in several western countries has witnessed the flourishing, over the last decade, of integration requirements addressed, albeit in slightly different forms, to both immigrants aspiring to entry and residence, and to residents aspiring to naturalisation.[60] Finally, and most importantly for the arguments explored in this article, nationality law governing non-birth right citizenship and immigration law have traditionally drawn from the same pool of people. That is, non-birth right citizens are typically former migrants. There is a sequence between the status of migrant and the status of non-birth right citizen that both immigration law and citizenship law typically take for granted.

New generation skilled migration policies, whether it is residence by investment schemes, or citizenship by investment schemes do not follow this pattern as neatly. Research suggests that several investment citizens are not actually looking to move to the country of their acquired citizenship.[61] Investors and entrepreneurs who benefit from residence by investment schemes, on the other hand, may be looking for a temporary basis of operations rather than for a path to formal citizenship.[62] The sequence that immigration law and citizenship law postulate between the fact of migration and the fact of the acquisition of non-birthright citizenship is thus altered with the advent of new generation skilled migration policies. Immigration law comes to select a pool of high regard guests who are not necessarily meant to become citizens. And citizenship law comes to select a pool of non-birthright citizens who will not necessarily have immigrated to the country. This per se is not an absolute novelty. Guest-worker programmes have been extensively used throughout the twentieth century and still are.[63] Citizenship by ancestry can also be awarded to external members who were neither born citizens nor have ever migrated to the country of their ancestry.[64] However what is different in the context of new generation skilled migration policies is the way these pools of guests and of distant citizens are formed. First, the criteria to be selected into those pools differ from traditional skilled migration policies. Second, the role of the state, and of its agents, in administering relevant policies is transformed in comparison to traditional patterns. The relevance of these policies for existing understandings of membership must be questioned in the context of these combined transformations.

IV. A CLOSER LOOK AT NEW GENERATION SKILLED MIGRATION POLICIES

A. Talent as Output

New generation skilled migration policies search for a new genus of talent. In comparison to traditional policies, they take a novel approach to defining desirable entrants who deserve

[58] Dauvergne, *Making People Illegal* (Cambridge University Press 2012) 96.
[59] See Kaushal, 'The Migration Footprint' (2016) 12 *JLE* 89.
[60] Orgad, *The Cultural Defense of Nations.*
[61] Surak, 'Investment Migration'.
[62] Kochenov and Surak, 'Introduction' in Kochenov and Surak (eds), *Citizenship and Residence Sales.*
[63] A recent example is the UK temporary visa scheme for poultry workers, pork butchers and HGV driver introduced in October 2021. See 'Recruit a poultry worker, pork butcher or HGV food driver with a temporary visa' (Gov.UK, 1 January 2022) www.gov.uk/guidance/recruit-a-poultry-worker-or-hgv-food-driver-with-a-temporary-visa.
[64] For an argument on the use of these programmes in a compensatory fashion see Harpaz, *Citizenship 2:0.*

eased admission, or citizenship, and they correspondingly alter the focus of relevant legal requirements.[65]

Traditional skilled migration policies target human capital factors, such as education and professional experience, as well as adaptability factors, such as language knowledge. These policies rely on employer sponsorship or on cooperation with trade unions and other labour organisations to identify within the broader spectrum of labour market skills, those that are in shortage in the local market, and in whose respect migrant work could make a concrete contribution.[66] Resort to migration policy to fill specific labour market gaps yielded, during the course of the last century, both European guest workers programmes and admission programmes targeted at specific professional profiles, such as nurses or care workers.[67]

New generation skilled migration policies shift the focus from a targeted search for human capital factors to a quest for prestige, capital and innovation. Prestige is at the heart of models of 'Olympic' citizenship that Ayelet Shachar has carefully described in the context of her analysis of contemporary states' races for talent.[68] A talented athlete brings glory to her adoptive community and thereby contributes to bolster national narratives and images that several states are keen on reaffirming.[69] Investor visa and start-up visa schemes aim for more tangible contributions, respectively, capital and innovative ideas and the ability to translate them into revenue and jobs creation.

Investor schemes are addressed at high net worth individuals who can further a national interest of the host State through commitment of a significant amount of capital. The oldest among the programmes of this type are the US E-2 non-immigrant investor visa and the EB-5 immigrant visa. The former does not rely on fixed capital or investment figures. It is addressed to persons who have made, or are about to make, a 'significant investment' in a US business that they intend to develop or manage. Hence the focus is on the establishment of a viable business, through the commitment of material capital. The EB-5 is more specific in its requirements. It offers a green card to persons who contribute USD 1,000,000 into a new commercial enterprise and who create at least 10 new jobs for US workers. Newer schemes beyond the US resemble the EB-5 in level of specificity of the requirement, although they typically do not offer immediate permanent residence.[70] They include instead clear guidelines on capital availability requirements and on the nature and amount of required investments. The 2012-born Irish Immigrant Investor Programme (IIP), for instance, includes both a capital holding requirement (2,000,000 Euro) and a minimum investment requirement. Aspiring visa holders may elect, among others, to invest 1,000,000 Euro into an Irish immigrant investor bond yielding no interest; to invest at least 500,000 Euro in one or more Irish companies, other than listed companies; to invest at least 2,000,000 Euro into a Real Estate Investment Trust; or to effect a philanthropic donation of at least 500,000 Euro to support a public interest project in the sports, culture, education, health or arts sector.[71]

[65] A differentiation among different types of talent for immigration policy purposes has already been attempted from an economics perspective. See Solimano, 'Causes and Consequences of Talent Mobility', 4 (distinguishing directly productive talent, academic talent, social and cultural talent).

[66] Koslowski, 'Selective Migration Policy Models and Changing Realities of Implementation' (distinguishing three ideal types of skilled migration policy, human capital driven, demand driven, and corporatist).

[67] Clemens, 'What do we Know about Skilled Migration and Development' (2013) MPI Policy Brief No. 3; On the guest workers programme in Germany, see Klusmeyer, 'Aliens, Immigrants and Citizens' (1993) 122 *Daedalus* 81.

[68] Shachar, *Picking Winners*.

[69] ibid.

[70] 'About the EB-5 Visa' (US Citizenship and Immigration Services).

[71] 'I Want to Invest in Ireland' (Irish Department of Justice, 19 January 2024) www.irishimmigration.ie/coming-to-live-in-ireland/i-want-to-invest-in-ireland/.

'Talent', intended here in a part-figured sense as the class of requirements warranting the desirability of a migrant in skilled migration policy, is thus defined, in the context of these programmes, as a combination of wealth and ability to commit capital to a project of interest of the host State. Wealth is treated in some of the programmes as a proxy for business acumen or experience. For instance, the US E-2 visa, while requiring a significant investment, seems to focus on the actual establishment and conducting of a business in the US.[72] However, the most salient requirement in these programmes is the candidate's ability to commit capital. This is the immediate benefit that the visa holder brings to the host country.

The focus of entry requirements in entrepreneur programmes suggests a differently oriented definition of 'talent': relevant schemes do not look for capital per se, but rather for innovative business ideas, whose viability is warranted by the willingness of qualifying investors to commit capital towards their realisation. Relevant programmes are similar in their basic structure: applicants need to submit a business plan to set up, or take over, a business in the host country; they also need to provide evidence that they have secured a minimum threshold of funding for their business project through qualified investors such as angel investors, venture capital funds registered with relevant financial authorities, or government-driven seed competitions.[73] Additional requirements, such as residence conditions, language knowledge, income requirements differ from country to country; as do precise requirements as to the nature of the funds entrepreneurs must have secured. The Canadian start-up visa, for instance, rewards with permanent residence entrepreneurs who have secured either 75,000 Canadian dollars from an angel investor or 200,000 Canadian dollars from an approved venture capital fund participating in the programme.[74] Ireland offers a more flexible formula in terms of the origin of the funds that the applicant entrepreneur must have available. These have to be in a minimum amount of EUR 50,000 and may comprise a mixture of own resources, venture capital and angel investors' funding, business loans and funding provided by Irish state agencies. The applicant also needs to present a convincing business plan for the creation of a high potential start-up. In this latter respect the Irish programme is particularly exacting: a high potential start-up is defined as a business which introduces an innovative service or product and has the potential to generate at least EUR 1,000,000 in revenues and 10 new jobs within three to four years of creation.[75] Eligibility conditions for the new UK start-up visa include having a realistic business plan to establish a start-up that is innovative, viable and scalable, and having the endorsement of a qualifying body in the UK.[76] In some countries, selection for admission through an entrepreneur programme entails, in addition to a visa and residence permit, also access to incubation and acceleration schemes, whereby qualified institutions host and mentor the start-up entrepreneur/team during the initial phase of their project. This is the case, for instance, of Chile, which since 2010 has been selecting promising business projects, to which it awards an initial equity-free grant of between USD 30,000 and 100,000 depending on the programme, as well as the opportunity to participate in acceleration and incubation programmes in Chile.[77]

[72] It should be noted that the E-2 visa is not available to all nationalities, which itself drives a secondary market for the passports that qualify for a E-2 visa.

[73] See 'Start-up Entrepreneur Programme (STEP)' (Immigration Service Delivery, 25 September 2023).

[74] See 'How Can I Qualify for the Start-up Visa Program?' (Government of Canada, 29 September 2021) www.cic.gc.ca/english/helpcentre/answer.asp?qnum=645&top=6.

[75] See 'Start-up Entrepreneur Programme: Guidelines' (Irish Naturalization and Immigration Service, January 2018), 4–5 www.irishimmigration.ie/wp-content/uploads/2020/01/STEP-Guidelines.pdf.

[76] See 'Immigration Rules Appendix Start-up' (Gov.UK, 11 April 2024) Immigration Rules Appendix Start-up – Immigration Rules – Guidance – GOV.UK (www.gov.uk).

[77] See the overview of the 'Build', 'Ignite' and 'Growth' Programmes offered by Start-Up Chile, 'Start-Up Chile – We SUPport Founders beyond Businesses', https://startupchile.org/en/.

While availability of capital is thus key also to entrepreneur programmes, it plays in these programmes a different role in comparison to investor programmes. The ability to secure qualified venture or angel investor funding may be a proxy for the validity of the business idea that the entrepreneur advances; and the availability of the entrepreneur's own funding works otherwise as a guarantee of his ability to concretely pursue the relevant idea. It is the latter idea, however, that is at the basis of the notion of talent underpinning these policies. These schemes scout for innovative and creative entrepreneurs whose business ideas may translate into job-creating and growth-fostering businesses. As a corollary, they reward other skills the applicants may have, such as business judgment, fundraising and networking capabilities, however these latter elements seem tangential to the main objective of capturing good ideas. The search for capital as well as innovative ideas in new generation skilled migration policies suggests that notions of talent underpinning these policies have a different focus in comparison to those underpinning traditional skilled migration policies. In traditional policies, the quest for human capital factors betrayed a search for entrants who had the ability to integrate in the host community and succeed as its members.[78] The notions of talent in relevant policies focused, in other words, on the input that the skilled migrant could bring to the host community, and that warranted his ability to fit in.

Traces of talent as input can be found also in new generation skilled migration policies. While investment programmes often forgo requirements of language knowledge or minimum income, entrepreneur programmes tend to associate specific programme requirements to more traditional ones. Applicants for the Canadian start-up visa, for instance, are required to prove language knowledge and the ability to bring enough money to settle.[79] Similarly, applicants for the UK start-up visa need to prove their knowledge of English and their ability to maintain themselves in the UK.[80]

The focus of the definition of talent in new generation skilled migration policies, however, falls not on input elements that the immigrant feeds into the host country's economy and society, such as prior education, professional experience or language knowledge, but rather on a precise output that the immigrant can produce in the host country:[81] the making of a qualifying investment, in the case of investment programmes; or the realisation, through the planning, funding and setting up of a business, of an innovative entrepreneurial idea in the case of entrepreneur programmes. Requirements in relevant policies are tailored to ensure that the applicants will deliver on the promised output. For instance, entrepreneur programmes require not only evidence of availability of funding to pursue an entrepreneurial project, but also a business plan which is reviewed by committees of qualified experts, as well as proofs of income and activity after a first period of enjoyment of the relevant visa.[82]

[78] Adaptability is for instance an explicit requirement in the context of the Canadian point system, 'Federal Skilled Worker Program (Express Entry): Six Selection Factors' (Government of Canada, 4 January 2024) www.canada.ca/en/immigration-refugees-citizenship/services/immigrate-canada/express-entry/eligibility/federal-skilled-workers/six-selection-factors-federal-skilled-workers.html.

[79] See 'Immigrate with a Start-up Visa: Who Can Apply' (Government of Canada, 2 May 2024) Immigrate with a start-up visa: Who can apply – Canada.ca.

[80] See 'Immigration Rules Appendix Start-up' (Gov.UK, 11 April 2024).

[81] Requirements such as prior education and professional experience may be considered proxies for an output to be produced in the host country, such as economic success or more simply employment in the host country. However, per se, they are input elements, they are assets that the immigrant brings with him or her and that are likely to help in producing an economic output.

[82] See eg 'Italia Startup Visa: Guidelines' (Ministry of Economic Development, Ministry of Foreign Affairs, Ministry of the Interior, 20 March 2018), 31–32 https://italiastartupvisa.mise.gov.it/media/documents/Guidelines%20ISV%20ENG%2020_03_2018%20def.pdf.

Talent intended as output drives a part reconfiguration and reinterpretation of recurring legal requirements in immigration and nationality law.[83] And screening and selecting desirable migrants on this basis leads in turn states, and their agents, to take on new roles in the context of the design, management and implementation of immigration law.

B. The State as Headhunter in Immigration Law

While in the context of skilled migration policies, states have always to some extent looked out for desirable entrants, in the context of new generation skilled migration policies, the role of the state changes in at least three respects. First, in the way immigration laws are designed and written; second, in terms of the management and application of these laws; and lastly, with regard to the branches of public authority and external actors that are involved in the process of selecting desirable immigrants.

In the first respect, on the theory that states have a legitimate interest in closure, and are thus entitled to police their borders, states have long designed laws to manage the admission and exclusion of aliens.[84] While, as considered in the previous sections, there are some continuities in requirements for admission and for naturalisation in the laws of different countries, immigration as well as citizenship law tend to be an expression of a state's sovereign power of self-determination.[85] The rules in these laws, and the rationales inspiring these rules, vary in accordance with a state's external commitments and relations,[86] as well as its internal political and economic circumstances.[87] In the context of new generation skilled migration policies, states rather appear to monitor and emulate one another in enacting relevant regulatory requirements.[88] This makes on the one hand for a measure of international convergence in the features of relevant policies, and of the legal reforms that they feed, regardless of background histories of immigration regulation.[89] On the other hand, it provides a novel example of lawmaking in a transnational space.[90]

[83] The most evident is the dispensing with, or reinterpretation in a flexible direction, of residence requirements that typically characterise both immigration and naturalisation laws.

[84] For an overview of the history of early regulation in this sense in US States, see Neuman, 'The Lost Century of American Immigration Law (1776–1875)' (1993) 93 *Columbia LRev.* 1833; Aleinikoff, 'International Legal Norms and Migration' in Aleinikoff and Chetail (eds), *Migration and International Legal Norms* (TMC Asser Press 2003); Martin, 'The Authority and Responsibility of States' in Aleinikoff and Chetail (eds), *Migration and International Legal Norms*, 31–33; Nafziger, 'The General Admission of Aliens under International Law' (1983) *AJIL* 817–22; also see Wellman and Cole, *Debating the Ethics of Immigration* (Oxford University Press 2011).

[85] Anticipating several other supreme domestic courts and international courts, the US Supreme Court held in 1892 that the power to restrict the entrance of foreigners is 'inherent in sovereignty and essential to self-preservation'. *Nishimura Ekiu v US* [1892] 142 US 651. For self-determination as an argument for community closure: Walzer, *Spheres of Justice* (Basic Books 1983).

[86] British law for instance up until 1962 allowed the unrestricted entry and right of abode of Commonwealth citizens; see Karatani, *Defining British Citizenship* (Routledge 2003) 145–65. Along similar lines, Italian nationality law prescribes eased residence requirements for the naturalisation of nationals of EU Member States. See Art 9(d) of Nationality Law 1992 (IT).

[87] Thoughts go for instance to guest-worker programmes in post-war Germany. For an overview, see Castles et al, *The Age of Migration* 5th edn (Palgrave Macmillan 2014) 107.

[88] See Shachar and Hirschl, 'Recruiting Super Talent'.

[89] Example on point are Canada and Italy, whose Start-up visa policies are remarkably similar in spite of a widely different history of immigration and immigration regulation. See Strumia and Kaushal, 'Opening the Ranks of Constitutional Subjects'.

[90] On law-making in a transnational space: Aleinikoff, 'Transnational Spaces' (2008) 33 *YJIL* 479, 485; Tuori 'On Legal Hybrids and Perspectivism' in Maduro et al (eds), *Transnational Law* (Cambridge University Press 2014) 19; Kochenov, 'Interlegality – Citizenship – Intercitizenship' in Klabbers and Palombella (eds), *The Challenge of Inter-Legality* (Cambridge University Press 2019) 133–55.

Beyond lawmaking, the role of the state changes also with regard to the management and application of immigration and citizenship law. In the frame of traditional immigration and citizenship law, the state mostly acts as a passive 'border guard'. It sets the quota of legal entrants that it is willing to admit in a given period of time, and it sets the criteria that qualify an applicant for admission. Most states make entry and settlement of certain desirable immigrants easier than entry and settlement of the generality of immigrants. This is mostly true with regard to classes of highly talented migrants, such as for instance researchers, artists, sports persons. And it is also true of groups of low skilled migrants who are needed to fill specific gaps in the host State's labour market, as was the case of guest worker programmes in Europe and North America in the second half of the twentieth century.[91] In any case, in traditional immigration policies, the state typically waits at the door for somebody to raise a claim for entry, and then decides, ultimately in its discretion, whether to grant leave to enter. In new generation policies, the state, instead, proactively recruits the immigrants it wants.

It can be argued that the state acted as a recruiter also in the context of twentieth-century guest worker programmes. However, there are some important differences. In these programmes, states rather than selecting desirable migrants tendered a place to classes of workers that were both needed in the host country and in need of migrating to escape unemployment. Guest worker programmes relied on bilateral agreements between sending and recipient country, or in any case the country of destination tended to be an obvious choice for the migrant for geographical or historical reasons. As a result host states, because they were meeting a demand for emigration and because they were not competing with a wide range of other possible destinations, could de facto set the terms of the guest worker's status. These terms were often rather restrictive, binding the guest worker to a job, limiting rights to family reunification and overall marking a sharp distinction between the condition of the citizen and the one of the guest worker.[92] In new generation skilled migration policies, host States compete with other states for the talents that they are seeking to recruit, and they need to convince the prospective migrant of the desirability of the opportunities they offer. In this sense, they act in many ways as headhunters.[93]

Like headhunters, the state and its agents invite applications by actively promoting their 'packages'. Governmental guidelines for relevant programmes have the tone of marketing materials. According to the guidelines for the Irish Entrepreneur Programme, for instance,

> Ireland is a small country that has re-invented itself over the last forty years through the combined force of sheer determination and growing, vibrant ambition. Its young, highly educated workforce has seized the opportunity provided by Foreign Direct Investment and continues to transform Ireland into a dynamic, knowledge based economy for the 21st century.[94]

The governmental website on the Canadian start-up visa is even more explicit. Titled 'Canada Wants Entrepreneurs!', it poses a crucial question and suggests an answer: 'Do you want to build a dynamic company that can compete on a global scale? It starts in Canada.' A list of reasons why Canada should be considered the best place to build a business follows.[95]

Beyond the marketing aspect, states also act comparably to headhunters in selecting new generation skilled migrants. They channel the applications to dedicated screening committees and commissions that perform a pre-selection function. This is the same function that

[91] For an overview: Castles et al., *The Age of Migration*, 220–21.
[92] ibid 104–08.
[93] Shachar and Hirschl, 'Recruiting Super Talent', 87.
[94] 'Start-up Entrepreneur Programme: Guidelines' (Irish Naturalization and Immigration Service, January 2018).
[95] 'Start-up Visa Program' (Government of Canada, 10 December 2023).

headhunters play in support of the recruitment arms of companies and multinationals. The selected applicants are then fast-tracked through regular admission and background check procedures.

This pre-selection function introduces the third respect in which the state's role changes in the context of new generation skilled migration policies: new classes of actors intervene in the process of admission and exclusion of migrants. New actors include branches of government that are not traditionally concerned with the regulation of immigration. For instance, the Italia Start-Up visa is managed by the Ministry for Economic Development, while visa are traditionally a competence of the Ministry for Foreign Affairs.[96] They also include ad hoc committees of technical experts tasked with screening and selecting the applications for relevant programmes. In Chile, while the start-up programme is run officially by the government, the Start-Up Chile team relies on an extensive network of volunteer mentors.[97] In Italy, ministerial representatives coordinate an ad hoc committee of national experts tasked with picking promising entrepreneurs for admission to the country.[98] Similarly in Ireland an Evaluation Committee makes recommendation to the Minister for Justice and Equality on promising start-up projects that should be rewarded with a visa.[99]

States also outsource various aspects of the design and management of relevant programmes to private advisors. This has given rise to a new business field. A few global competitor firms specialised in advisory services on business and investment visa, as well as investment citizenship, have rapidly occupied the market in this respect.[100]

Through these novel state roles and outsourced functions, and through the redefinition of talent in skilled migration policies, the regulation of immigration, and relatedly of citizenship, begins to follow two distinct trajectories.

V. TOWARDS DUAL TRACK MEMBERSHIP

A. Two Trajectories for Immigration and Citizenship Regulation

With the advent of new generation skilled migration policies, and the above-described transformations that these bring about, the traditional model of immigration regulation, where the state acts as a border guard and focuses on the control of admission, comes to be flanked by a novel model. In this latter model, the state acts as a recruiter and focuses on selecting desirable migrants. Whilst the border guard state screens applicants for an input, whether in terms of skills or of family connections, the recruiter state screens them for an output. The bifurcation in the regulation of immigration, and relatedly citizenship, begins here.

The distinction between two different tracks of immigration regulation is not entirely new. The role of the state in international migration has been characterised in the twentieth and twenty-first centuries by a quest for control.[101] This has resulted in many cases into rules attracting the highly skilled and contextually restricting the entry of the low skilled.[102] Relatedly it has been observed that the dichotomy between open and closed borders, long discussed in the

[96] 'Italia Start Up Visa: Guidelines', 5.
[97] 'Mentores – Start-Up Chile' (Start-UP Chile) https://startupchile.org/networks/mentores/.
[98] 'Italia Startup Visa: Guidelines', 31–32.
[99] 'Immigration Rules Appendix Start-up' (Gov.UK, 11 April 2024) 5–6.
[100] See Džankić, *The Global Market for Investor Citizenship*, 147–57.
[101] Castles et al, *The Age of Migration*, 238.
[102] ibid.

literature on international migration,[103] has lost traction as most states take a dual approach to the management of their borders, both closing and selectively opening them.[104]

This dual approach is, however, getting more polarised. This can be observed from several different perspectives. From a first discursive and practical perspective, the narrative and practice of attraction and recruitment of desirable migrants stand in stark contrast with the discourse of repression that accompanies the treatment of irregular migration. Government policies in response to the threat of irregular migration vary from the erection of physical anti-immigrant walls along borders;[105] to pushing back at sea boats of asylum seekers;[106] to the revision of the role and status of border control forces, as in Australia, where in July 2015 the government rebranded the Immigration and Custom agencies as a paramilitary Border Force.[107]

From a second regulatory perspective, the dual approach no longer finds expression just in the distinction between the treatment of the claims for entry of the high- and low-skilled. It is rather reflected in the hardening of two different regulatory trajectories. A first trajectory continues and consolidates the rationale of control that has traditionally informed immigration regulation. On the one hand, even for skilled migrants in the traditional track the trend is towards the introduction of more exacting requirements for entry as well as more thorough screening and admission processes. On the other hand, at least in Europe, immigration regulation has become increasingly culturalised.[108] Integration requirements have become a common feature of the legislation on immigration in a large number of European states. In some countries, relevant requirements take the form of an 'integration agreement' that the immigrant is required to sign with the host State upon receiving a residence permit.[109] Failure to fulfil the terms of the integration agreement may lead to revocation of the residence permit and ultimately to expulsion. Other countries have even introduced 'integration from abroad' programmes, whereby prospective entrants are required to attend courses and take an integration test at the diplomatic representation of the prospective host country. This is the case, for instance, in the Netherlands, where for several categories of immigrants, the grant of a visa and residence permit is conditional upon successful completion of the relevant integration programme.[110] Beyond the first admission of an immigrant, in various countries integration requirements are also a key component of the path to permanent settlement, and to citizenship. The United Kingdom, for instance, administers a 'life in the UK test' to applicants for 'settlement' or for citizenship.[111] The Italian Council of State has repeatedly emphasised that

[103] For a sample of a vast debate see Miller, 'Immigration'; Carens, *The Ethics of Immigration* (Oxford University Press 2013).

[104] Shachar and Hirschl, 'Recruiting Super Talent', 100, 101; Shachar and Hirschl, 'Spatial Statism'.

[105] For an overview, see Hasser and Wittenberg, 'Who Builds Barriers to Entry and Why?' (2015) 40 *International Security* 157.

[106] Push-backs to Libya on the part of Italy were at the heart of the European Court of Human Rights judgment in *Hirsi Jamaa and Others v Italy* [GC], no. 27765/09, ECHR 2012.

[107] See 'Who we are' (Australian Border Force) www.abf.gov.au/about-us/who-we-are.

[108] Orgad, *The Cultural Defense of Nations*; van Oers et al, *A Re-definition of Belonging?* (Brill–Nijhoff 2010); Orgad, 'The Citizen-Makers' (2019) 25 *ELJ* 521, 524.

[109] This is the case for instance in France where entrants are required to sign the 'contrat d'intégration républicaine' (CIR), Art. R-413-2-7 of Code de l'entrée et du sejour des etrangers et du droit d'asyle 2005, as amended by Decree 1734/2020 (FR); in Italy: Art. 4-bis of the Immigration Act 1998 (IT); and for Luxembourg, Art. 8 of Loi concernant l'accueil et l'intégration des étrangers au Grand-Duché de Luxembourg 2008 (LU).

[110] See Dutch Ministry of Social Affairs and Employment, 'Basic Civic Integration Examination Abroad' (Ministry of Social Affairs and Employment) https://secure.cdn.vellance.com/naarnederland/website/brochure/Engels.pdf; also see 'Wet Inburgering 2021' (Overheid, 2 February 2021) https://wetten.overheid.nl/BWBR0044770/2022-01-01.

[111] 'Life in the UK Test' (Gov.UK) www.gov.uk/life-in-the-uk-test; also see T Brooks, *Reforming the UK's Citizenship Test* (Policy Press 2022).

the socio-economic integration of the applicant is a fundamental element in the discretionary scrutiny of the administrative authorities tasked with deciding on the grant of Italian citizenship.[112] In a milder form, an idea of subscription to and adhesion to the cultural and constitutional values of the host country is also at the basis of the oaths of loyalty that coronate the naturalisation process in several countries, in primis the United States.[113] The first trajectory to admission and ultimately membership testifies thus to the states' attempt to exercise some sort of 'cultural' control in assessing claims for entry and membership.

A second trajectory is the one illustrated by new generation skilled migration policies. The claims for entry and membership of talented migrants in the relevant categories are typically pre-screened and then fast tracked through the usual checks and procedures. For instance, applicants for the Italian start-up visa, once their application has been approved by the relevant ministerial committee, enjoy several facilitations in other passages of the admission procedure.[114] In all the programmes that grant directly citizenship, qualifying applicants are even exempted from, or subject to significantly reduced durational residence requirements, which in traditional naturalisation law represent the main guarantee of integration.[115] In this second trajectory thus, accommodating the claims for membership of migrants that promise a defined output, regardless of their integration, becomes a leading element of immigration regulation.

One possible explanation for this diversification in the regulation of immigration and access to citizenship relates to the nature of the powers that relevant lawmaking on the part of the state ultimately expresses. Controlling borders and selecting entrants is the ultimate manifestation of a state's sovereignty. This sovereignty is limited on the one hand by the states' moral and legal obligations to admit migrants for humanitarian reasons. On the other hand, it is constrained by obligations in the context of international partnerships and cooperation agreements. These sets of obligations erode the state's power to define the perimeter of its community of members. Hence states channel their sovereignty in the grey area in-between these two sets of obligations, regulating admission and exclusion in the insignia of control. The first trajectory in immigration and citizenship regulation can be seen as a manifestation of this sovereign resilience.[116] The second trajectory is rather the result of the state working as a transnational actor and competing in a global regulatory arena to win to its community investment, innovation and talent. It is an expression of the state as a new type of sovereign actor wielding its power through international engagement. From this perspective the two trajectories can be seen as expressing a tension between two ways of being of the sovereign state, a traditional one inspired to a Westphalian and monolithic conception of sovereignty, that equals sovereign power to the ability to exclude others, whether other sovereigns or other individuals, from one's sovereign sphere; and a novel one rather propelled by a relational idea of sovereignty that interprets sovereign power as the ability to engage in the international arena.[117] These two ways of being coexist increasingly uncomfortably in the DNA of the twenty-first-century

[112] eg Judgment no. 3006/2011 of 20 May 2011.

[113] For an overview see Strumia, *Supranational Citizenship and the Challenge of Diversity* (Brill–Nijhoff 2013) 53–63.

[114] For instance, under the Italian start-up visa procedure, the committee screening applications is also tasked with obtaining on behalf of an applicant the police's certificate of no impediment, a document that an applicant would have to obtain directly from the police under the normal procedure. See 'Italia Start Up Visa: Guidelines' (Ministry of Economic Development, Ministry of Foreign Affairs, Ministry of the Interior, 20 March 2018) 19.

[115] For a typology of these programmes: Džankić, *The Global Market for Investor Citizenship*, 91–132.

[116] On immigration as the 'last bastion of sovereignty', see Dauvergne, *Making People Illegal*, 47–48.

[117] For a relational account of state sovereignty see Cohen, *Globalization and Sovereignty: Rethinking Legality, Legitimacy and Constitutionalism* (Cambridge University Press 2012) 67.

sovereign state, expressing its very own bipolar disorder. The two emerging tracks of immigration regulation can be seen as a sign of that disorder.

A second explanation for this bifurcation in the regulation of immigration pertains rather than to an attitude of the sovereign state, to a fact of international movement. This is the altered sequence between migration and the holding of citizenship that, as suggested earlier, these policies reveal. The traditional regulatory track is addressed to migrants who want to establish themselves as citizens in a host country. The conditions they are asked to meet in order to naturalise treat non-birth right citizenship as a version of birthright citizenship. The emerging regulatory track addresses a different phenomenon: citizenship without movement, or movement without citizenship. It sets admission and belonging requirements for a novel class of members that comprises both present high-regard guests and citizens 'in absentia'.

The double trajectory in the regulation of immigration and citizenship thus ultimately points to a dual track model of membership.

B. Two Models of Membership

A first membership model results of the first trajectory of regulation. It is addressed to the 'standard' entrants, such as, for instance, labour migrants and 'old generation' skilled migrants. As examined in the previous section, these classes of entrants, in order to be admitted first, and then settle or qualify for citizenship, have to comply with legal requirements ranging from completion of integration courses, to passing citizenship tests, to outright assimilation requirements. The membership status that they are asked to earn this way is a heavy-type, hybrid cultural citizenship. This citizenship represents to some extent the third millennium version of cultural-ethnic citizenship.[118] By imposing relevant requirements on new entrants, states broadcast such cultural citizenship as a signpost of their bounded identity. The relevant citizenship is earned through marked integration processes, and it is lost through dis-allegiance.[119]

A second membership model is the one addressed to the new generation high skilled migrants. To them, states are willing to make available citizenship in a lighter touch version, in exchange for talent 'as output', with discounts on the general integration requirements, or simply at a monetary price. This second membership model is oblivious to clear integration and allegiance requirements.

The future well-being of new generation skilled migrants is tied to that of their host polity for reasons different than in the case of traditional migrants and birth-right members. New generation high skilled visa may attract immigrants who plan to be only half invested community members, and for whom residence in a host country is a temporary arrangement rather than a life commitment. This does not necessarily deny, however, that investment visa holders and start-up visa holders may have an interest in the flourishing of their host country and its community. The former will care for the common good of their country of residence at least to the extent that this is tied to return on their investment.[120] The latter will care about

[118] For a classic distinction between a German and a French model of citizenship along these lines see Brubaker, *Citizenship and Nationhood in France and Germany* (Harvard University Press 1992).

[119] Under UK law for instance a naturalized citizen can be deprived of citizenship 'if he has conducted him or herself in a manner which is seriously prejudicial to the vital interests of the United Kingdom'. See Sect 40 of Nationality Act 1981, as amended by Sect 66 of the Immigration Act 2014 (UK). Also, Forcese, 'A Tale of Two Citizenships' (2014) 39 *Queen's LJ* 551.

[120] In this sense Magni-Berton, 'Citizenship for Those Who Invest into the Future of the State Is Not Wrong, the Price Is the Problem' in Bauböck (ed), *Debating Transformations of National Citizenship* (Springer 2018).

nurturing their business and making it profitable. This in turn will require that they develop networks in the local business community. Start-up visa holders will also develop concrete links through benefiting from incubation and acceleration programmes in the host country. In addition whether the concrete management of the start-up requires actual residence in the host country on the part of the founding entrepreneur or not, there is evidence that within start-up eco-systems novel kinds of communities develop: not only proper innovation hubs as seen in California or on the US East Coast, but also networks of entrepreneurs willing to share experiences and mentor new venturers on a volunteer basis.[121]

Migrants following the first membership track are, like birth-right members, members by virtue of personal, family and identity links that qualify their interest in the flourishing of their polity and bind their destiny to the one of the polity. New generation highly skilled migrants are instead members by virtue of their seeking a return on their investment, of their endeavour to realise their innovative idea in the host country, and of their engaging with local networks of entrepreneurs, business angels and the like. Making sense of the ties they respectively have to their community of belonging requires renouncing a certain idea of citizenship as a settled form of membership. It requires embracing the idea that membership, and citizenship as its formal expression, can be based in a settlement paradigm or else in a mobility paradigm: members can be citizens who have always been here and have always been citizens; they can be guests who are just passing by, have never been citizens, and never will be; they can be citizens who have naturalised at the conclusion of an experience of migration; or they can be citizens who have become such without ever properly being here.[122]

The connections that 'high-regard guests' and citizens in absentia have to their host polity may be thinner than membership links that grew through traditional immigration experiences. They are links nonetheless, perhaps of the kind that substantiates the lightened citizenship that Christian Joppke has most forcefully described.[123] These light citizens that new generation skilled migration policies produce represent a novel group of the cosmopolitan high-flyers that Adrian Favell, speaking with regard to intra-EU migrants in the first decade of the new millennium, had described as 'Eurostars'.[124] New generation skilled migration policies enlarge, in this sense, a trend that free movement under the umbrella of European citizenship had inaugurated first.[125] Favell's Eurostars, other than the new generation highly skilled migrants, do not bring a precise output to their host EU country. In Favell's portrait, these are the highly educated, polyglot professionals, who populate the service sector of the European capitals.[126] The new generation high skilled migrants rather belong to two peculiar, and discrete categories: high net worth individuals, and innovative entrepreneurs. However, the Eurostars and the new generation highly skilled migrants have one other aspect in common: they wear their citizenships, whether the ones they bring along in moving to a different EU country, or the ones they leave behind in residing on a highly skilled visa in another country, or yet the ones they acquire 'in absentia' perhaps through an investment in a host country, with a certain casualness. They can fit in without fully belonging, and while they contribute economically and

[121] For an example see 'Mentores – Start-Up Chile' (Start-UP Chile).
[122] On this Strumia, 'The State and the Citizen-as-Migrant' (2021) RSC Working Paper 2021/79.
[123] Joppke, 'The Inevitable Lightening of Citizenship', 12.
[124] Favell, 'Immigration, Migration, and Free Movement in the Making of Europe' in Checkel and Katzenstein (eds), *European Identity* (Cambridge University Press 2009); Favell, *Eurostars and Eurocities* (Blackwell 2011).
[125] Access to a system of free movement, and to enhanced global mobility options more in general, may be the very pull factor for some of the users of European new generation skilled migration policies. See Harpaz, *Citizenship 2.0*; for a perspective on the use of EU citizenship as a 'ticket to mobility', de Hoon et al, 'A Ticket to Mobility?'.
[126] Favell, 'Immigration, Migration and Free Movement in the Making of Europe'.

weave networks, the memberships they potentially gain or lose, or just stretch in the case of the Eurostars, are not proxies either for their long-term settlement or permanent expatriation, let alone for a shift in their national identities.

As a result, communities come to be made up of long-term, life-committed, culturally integrated members, who are either native-born or have gone through the traditional citizenship acquisition track; as well as of a smaller class of transient members, who bring defined outputs to the community and who may not stick forever, and can only belong in a lighter, more cosmopolitan fashion.

This split in the character of membership offers a first answer to the question of how new generation skilled migration policies alter the role of immigration and citizenship law in defining membership. The breaking up of the consistency of citizenship has long been denounced from several sides. Not only it is lightening, it is losing value and turning instrumental.[127] Some of these arguments may have lost some traction at a time when the Covid-19 pandemic has pushed citizens and residents under the protective wings of their own states, and when the spectre of war threatens the liberal international order. Yet the distinction between a settled and a mobile, or unsettled conception of membership to which new generation skilled migration policies point still holds. And the distinction raises one crucial question that theories of membership and citizenship need to address: how do those different classes of members, the traditional settled citizens on the one hand, and the high regard guests or citizens in absentia on the other hand, interact with one another and with the state?

There are two possible perspectives to answer this question. A first perspective focuses on the risks involved in these evolving patterns of membership. Membership is in danger of becoming stratified by wealth. The light citizens and high regard guests that states are intent in attracting may turn into a lobby for their own interests. This would harden the divide with 'ordinary' members, with detrimental effects for the prospects of community and the very role of the state as provider and guarantor of equal membership rights. Through this lens, membership is becoming commodified and citizenship is losing its meaning in terms of equality of rights.

A second potential perspective leads to question the reciprocal responsibilities of these two types of members and rewrite the social contract around their coexistence. Traditionally, citizenship embodies a two-way relation between state and individual, governor and governed. In the wake of the emergence of different citizenship tracks, it should rather be looked at as a web of relations among different classes of members. The circle of members funding citizenship entitlements and the one of those enjoying citizenship entitlements, as well as the circle of members making collective decisions and the one of those being subject to the same collective decisions no longer necessarily coincide. In light of this, the challenge of citizenship is to come to embody a set of responsibilities, rights, and affiliations that cut across the relevant circles. In other words, a way to preserve the unity of citizenship at a novel, different level is seeking ways to ensure that the investments and ideas of the light citizens and high regard guests contribute to the bonds of solidarity and mutual provision that justify the heavy citizenship of the more traditional members. Weaving membership bonds along these lines can be a way for light citizens to be invested in the community despite the lightness of their personal involvement and cultural affiliation; and for the 'heavy citizens' to recognise the high regard guests as fellow

[127] See eg Joppke, 'The Instrumental Turn of Citizenship'; Bauböck, 'Genuine Links and Useful Passports'; Spiro 'Stakeholder Theory Won't Save Citizenship' in Bauböck (ed), *Democratic Inclusion* (Manchester University Press 2018).

members despite their detached participation. As to the role of the state, this novel vision of citizenship potentially carves out a novel function, beyond guarding borders and headhunting for desirable migrants. That is, mediating between different classes of citizen-members, between the static and disaffected, and the cosmopolitan and unattached, whose contrast risks bringing communities to a breaking point.[128]

VI. CONCLUSION

New generation skilled migration policies are quantitatively of little significance and as at the time of writing many of them are already falling out of fashion. Yet the very engagement of the machinery of the state in the context of these policies, regardless of their limited impact in practice, conceptually brings important alterations to existing notions of membership and citizenship. Through these policies states hunt for casual citizens, who bring a defined output to the community, but maintain a degree of detachment from it. This yields on the one hand a novel trajectory of immigration and citizenship regulation, parallel but distinct from the traditional one. On the other hand, it leads to conceive a dual model of membership that challenges the very consistency of citizenship: while national citizenship remains the mantel that most persons wear throughout their lives, the two trajectories of immigration regulation pull on it at the edges and threaten its coherence at the core. The danger, in particular, is that an invisible wall is gradually built between a cosmopolitan minority of people living life as remote or mobile members and a majority of static citizens who are presumed to belong but may well be disaffected.

The rising of this wall marks a fundamental alteration in the scope and fabric of community membership. Arguments about the commodification of citizenship capture in part resulting concerns. Beyond debates on citizenship and membership, this wall also reflects what could be called the twenty-first century state's bipolar disorder' in a global, and increasingly post-global, era: its contextual responding to two conflicting drives, reclaiming predominant and exclusive responsibility for the interests of a bounded national community on the one hand, and embracing on the other hand the role of participant in a global, interdependent system of states. The findings of this chapter on the membership implications of a rather discrete phenomenon – new generation skilled migration and its regulation – invite to rethink citizenship so as to contain the building up of a similar wall and to deal with the state's disorder. The chapter points to the emergence of a dual track membership model. This requires a conception of citizenship refocused on the reciprocal rights and duties of different classes of citizen-members: for instance, the duties owed by external citizens to communities of origin, as well as the duties owed by internal citizens to migrants. It also requires a conception of the state as a mediator between those different classes. Embracing this latter role more openly may help the twenty-first-century state make sense of its own malaise. And it may be the best legacy yet of new generation skilled migration policies and their uncertain fortunes.

Ultimately, through scouting for talent as output new generation skilled migration policies contribute to add two novel profiles to the identikit of the community member: high regard guests and citizens in absentia. It is these two novel classes of members that problematise, and force to interrogate from novel perspectives existing conceptions of citizenship, as well as the role of the state in excluding, admitting and selecting members.

[128] In this sense see F Strumia, 'The Citizen as Other: The Case from within for Cosmopolitan State Duties and Freedom to Migrate' (2024) 87 *Modern Law Review* 670, 695–96.

3

Residency by Investment and Citizenship by Investment: Just the Tip of the Iceberg?

The Pervasiveness of Meritocratic Considerations in Immigration and Citizenship Law

ODILE AMMANN*

> The proper negative aim of egalitarian justice is not to eliminate the impact of brute luck from human affairs, but to end oppression, which by definition is socially imposed. Its proper positive aim is not to ensure that everyone gets what they morally deserve, but to create a community in which people stand in relations of equality to others.[1]

I. INTRODUCTION

RESIDENCY BY INVESTMENT (RBI) and especially citizenship by investment (CBI) schemes, which enable applicants to obtain residency or citizenship status in exchange for a monetary investment, have met with stark public criticism in recent years. This criticism reached a new peak in October 2020, when the European Commission launched infringement proceedings against Cyprus and Malta regarding their CBI programmes. The Commission justified this escalation by arguing that 'the granting by these Member States of their nationality – and thereby EU citizenship – in exchange for a pre-determined payment or investment and without a genuine link with the Member States concerned' violated EU law,[2]

* I am grateful to Vincent Barras, Martijn van den Brink, Anne-Laurence Graf-Brugère, Dimitry Kochenov, Damian Rosset, Stefan Schlegel and the participants in the 'Transformation of Citizenship' Conference (Karl-Franzens-Universität Graz, 20–21 November 2018) for valuable feedback on previous drafts. I am also indebted to the participants in the COMPAS seminar 'Citizenship by Investment: Law, Policy, and Sociology' (University of Oxford, 11 March 2021), especially to its conveners, Dimitry Kochenov and Madeleine Sumption, and to my co-panelist, Ayelet Shachar. The most recent substantive revisions of this chapter were completed in the Spring of 2022.

[1] Anderson, 'What Is the Point of Equality?' (1999) 109 *Ethics* 287ff.

[2] 'Investor citizenship schemes' (*European Commission*, 20 October 2020) https://ec.europa.eu/commission/presscorner/detail/hu/ip_20_1925; see also, European Parliament resolution on EU citizenship for sale (2013/2995(RSP)) [2014] OJ C482/117.

a claim that remains disputed.[3] More specifically, the Commission invoked the principle of sincere cooperation (article 4(3) TEU), while also considering that CBI 'undermines the integrity of the status of EU citizenship' enshrined in article 20 of the Treaty on the Functioning of the European Union. Further concerns highlighted by the Commission pertain to 'security, money laundering, corruption, circumvention of EU rules and tax evasion'.[4] In June 2021, the Commission reiterated its concerns by sending additional letters of formal notice to the two Member States.[5]

RBI has also been criticised for granting residency status to individuals who can afford it, but who would otherwise not be able to fulfil standard immigration criteria, such as a sufficient degree of integration.[6] While even standard requirements are not neutral in that they tend to treat some applicants more favourably, including based on their citizenship,[7] and to disadvantage less privileged would-be immigrants,[8] some scholars argue that in the case of RBI, inequalities are magnified because some individuals are exempted from complying with such requirements altogether.[9]

Regardless of whether the aforementioned arguments against CBI and RBI hold up to normative scrutiny, public condemnations and scholarly critiques of these (comparatively more controversial) schemes should not gloss over the fact that we already live in a world where citizenship and immigration law are justified with reference to 'merit'. Against this backdrop, CBI and RBI are not surprising developments: they are just the tip of the meritocratic iceberg.

While CBI and RBI seem unmeritocratic at first sight,[10] States often use meritocratic rhetoric to legitimise them.[11] This meritocratic discourse has also been endorsed by some scholars and private firms specialising in CBI and RBI.[12] Yet, what is often overlooked is that *even outside CBI and RBI*, 'merit' (however it is defined) is a decisive – and problematic – criterion relied on by States to select prospective immigrants and citizens.[13] Thus, CBI and RBI schemes are symptomatic of a broader meritocratic trend that pervades citizenship and immigration law at large: 'what is wrong with selling citizenship also applies to other instances of citizenship acquisition',[14] and the same can be said, *mutatis mutandis*, about the sale of residency

[3] Berger, 'Staatsbürgerschaft als Ware' (2021) 81 *ZaöRV/HJIL* 1033; Jessurun d'Oliveira in this volume; Kochenov, 'Genuine Purity of Blood' (2020) LEQS Paper No. 164/2020; Sarmiento and van den Brink, 'EU Competence and Investment Migration' in Kochenov and Surak (eds), *Citizenship and Residence Sales* (Cambridge University Press 2023); Weingerl and Tratnik, 'Relevant Links' in Kochenov and Surak (eds), *Citizenship and Residence Sales*.

[4] European Commission, 'Investor Citizenship and Residence Schemes in the European Union' COM(2019)12 final, 23. See also Fernandes et al., 'Avenues for EU Action on Citizenship and Residence by Investment Schemes' (2021) *EPRS* 19.

[5] 'June infringement packages: key decisions' (European Commission 2021) https://ec.europa.eu/commission/presscorner/detail/en/inf_21_2743.

[6] Fernandes et al, 'Avenues for EU Action'. Also, Shachar, 'Unequal Access' (2021) 25 *Citizenship Stud.* 543; Shachar, 'The Marketization of Citizenship in an Age of Restrictionism' (2018) 32 *Ethics Int. Aff.* 3; Häfliger, 'Die Schweiz sollte nicht käuflich sein' (Tages-Anzeiger, 15 February 2021) www.tagesanzeiger.ch/die-schweiz-sollte-nicht-kaeuflich-sein-121416519273.

[7] On this development of 'inter-citizenships': Kochenov, 'Inter-Legality – Citizenship – Inter-Citizenship' in Klabbers and Palombella (eds), *The Challenge of Inter-Legality* (Cambridge University Press 2019).

[8] Ganty, 'Integration Duties in the European Union' (2021) 28 *MJ* 784, 788.

[9] Kochenov, 'Inter-Legality'.

[10] eg Roy, 'The "Streetlight Effect" on Commentary in Citizenship by Investment' in Kochenov and Surak (eds), *Citizenship and Residence Sales*, 10.

[11] I have made this argument in relation to CBI in O Ammann, 'How (Un)Meritocratic Are Citizenship by Investment Programmes?' (2020) 22 *EJML* 309.

[12] On these firms: Kalm, 'The Business of Citizenship' (2023) 37 *Glob. Soc.* 68.

[13] Yet, CBI and RBI are usually considered to be separate cases: ibid 71.

[14] Armstrong, 'The Price of Selling Citizenship' in Bauböck (ed), *Debating Transformations of National Citizenship* (Springer 2018) 26.

permits versus other immigration routes. Some would argue that the concept of citizenship itself builds on a particular conception of 'merit': under this view, citizenship acquisition based on *ius sanguinis*, for instance, implicitly endorses a racialised conception of merit by emphasising blood connections.[15]

This chapter lays bare the mismatch that exists between public criticism of RBI and CBI, on the one hand, and the (much less contested) meritocratic conceptions that influence citizenship and immigration law, on the other hand. Indeed, the explicit or implicit distinction that is usually drawn between investment versus 'standard' residency and citizenship regimes is only a matter of degree. It does not reflect an actual difference in kind, at least not from the perspective of the ideological underpinnings of these various schemes. To illustrate my argument, I rely on a range of provisions in (mostly) domestic immigration and citizenship law, and on how these provisions are applied in practice. While special emphasis is placed on Swiss immigration and citizenship law, I occasionally draw on the law and practice of other Western States and of the European Union.

The chapter begins with a brief reminder of the meaning of meritocracy (Section II), which I have explored extensively in previous work.[16] It then highlights some of the many manifestations of meritocratic thought in contemporary immigration and citizenship law (Section III). The chapter concludes that States (but also scholars) should recognise that RBI and CBI are just the tip of the iceberg: the roots of the problem lie elsewhere, namely in the pervasiveness of meritocratic thought in immigration and citizenship law at large (Section IV). Instead of uncritically endorsing the ideal of meritocracy, States should acknowledge the stark inequalities that are buttressed by meritocratic thought and, most importantly, strive to create greater equality of opportunity in both immigration and citizenship law.

II. THE CONCEPT OF MERITOCRACY

Meritocracy is, of course, not a legal term, but it is connected to the legal (and moral) principle of equality. As I have defined and discussed the concept of meritocracy elsewhere,[17] I will not go back to these aspects in detail in this chapter. Instead, I will briefly recall the main features, strengths and weaknesses of the concept of meritocracy.

The word 'meritocracy' comes from the Latin verb *merere*, to deserve, and from the Greek noun *krátos*, power. Meritocracy thus consists in government by the meritorious.[18] Meritocracy is a neologism that goes back to the 1950s, and more specifically to Michael Young's book, *The Rise of the Meritocracy*, a forceful critique of meritocratic ideals.[19] Of course, these ideals are much older than Young's dystopian vision. One example is Thomas Jefferson's 'natural aristocracy' based on 'virtue and talents', which he opposed to an 'artificial aristocracy founded on wealth and birth, without either virtue or talents'.[20] Meritocratic considerations became particularly prevalent in the course of the liberal revolutions, which rejected birthright

[15] Achiume, 'Racial Borders' (2022) 110 *Georgetown LJ* 445. Kochenov, 'Ending the Passport Apartheid' (2020) 18 *I-CON* 1525; Roy, 'The "Streetlight Effect"'.

[16] Ammann, 'How (Un)Meritocratic Are Citizenship by Investment Programmes?'.

[17] ibid 313ff.

[18] Jaquet, 'Les transclasses ou l'illusion du mérite' (*France Culture*, 2 October 2018) www.franceculture.fr/sociologie/les-transclasses-ou-lillusion-du-merite-par-chantal-jaquet.

[19] Young, *The Rise of the Meritocracy, 1970–2023* (Thames and Hudson 1958); 'The Merits of Revisiting Michael Young' (*The Economist*, 10 February 2018) www.economist.com/britain/2018/02/10/the-merits-of-revisiting-michael-young.

[20] Letter from Thomas Jefferson to John Adams (28 October 1813).

privileges and feudalism. An even older example is the meritocratic Chinese civil service examination system, which was introduced in the seventh century.[21] Yet, the roots of meritocracy run even deeper and can already be found in the writings of Greek philosophers. The ideal of meritocracy was also influenced by religious thought, especially by the idea of salvation and by the Calvinist doctrine of predestination.[22]

A meritocracy is a system of government that treats individuals equally and that rewards them based on 'merit' alone. According to Richard Arneson, a meritocratic society is 'a society in which (a) equality of opportunity obtains and (b) rewards and remuneration gained by individuals are proportional to their individual desert'.[23] Another definition is the one proposed by Norman Daniels, who refers to mechanisms of job allocation and defines meritocracy as

> a society whose basic institutions are governed by a partial theory of distributive justice consisting of principles of the following types:
>
> (1) A principle of job placement that awards jobs to individuals on the basis of merit;
> (2) A principle specifying the conditions of opportunity under which the job placement principle is applied;
> (3) A principle specifying reward schedules for jobs.[24]

Michael Young used meritocracy pejoratively and warned against its negative consequences. Meritocracy, he wrote, would lead to a new form of aristocracy. It would increase the hubris of the elite and engender popular resentment (and hence populism and polarisation). Since the 1950s, however, meritocracy appears to have lost its negative connotation. Today, the concept is usually employed in a positive sense in public discourse to refer to a system that endorses equality of opportunity.[25]

What could possibly be wrong with meritocracy? How could one criticise a system that aims to achieve greater equality of opportunity and to allocate resources and rewards regardless of ascribed characteristics such as race, gender and socioeconomic background? These are certainly reasons why meritocracy is such an appealing concept. Another, more pragmatic reason that makes meritocracy so attractive to decision-makers is that it helps them rationalise how resources are distributed, and that it motivates individuals to work hard to demonstrate their 'merit'.

Yet, many authors have convincingly argued that meritocracy is flawed in several respects. As these authors show, and as I have argued elsewhere, meritocratic thought generates at least three types of problems.[26] First, 'merit' is a highly indeterminate term that leaves room for subjective value judgments and bias. It raises the question of who defines merit, and how. As a matter of fact, one problem with meritocracy is that the underlying conception of merit often reflects subjective of decision-makers.

Second, in practice, meritocracy does not lead to greater equality of opportunity because it tends to ignore that individuals do not actually have equal starting opportunities. Instead,

[21] Ammann, 'How (Un)Meritocratic', 314.
[22] Sandel, *The Tyranny of Merit*, Ch 2.
[23] Arneson, 'Equality of Opportunity' in Zalta and Nodelman (eds), *The Stanford Encyclopedia of Philosophy* (last revised on 25 March 2015) https://plato.stanford.edu/archives/fall2023/entries/equal-opportunity/.
[24] Daniels, 'Merit and Meritocracy' (1978) 7 *Philos Public Aff* 206, 207ff.
[25] Still, see 'Meritocracy and Its Discontents' (*The Economist*, 7 October 2006) www.economist.com/special-report/2006/10/07/meritocracy-and-its-discontents.
[26] Ammann, 'How (Un)Meritocratic', 317ff.

merit is often achieved through capital, as shown in Daniel Markovits' powerful book on the US education system, titled *The Meritocracy Trap*.[27]

Third, meritocracy makes those who are successful believe that their achievements are morally justified, leading to a meritocratic hubris and to a 'politics of humiliation' (which translates into a rhetoric of 'winners' versus 'losers'[28]). This hubris, coupled with the fact that those who are not successful are held individually responsible for their failures, fuels populist discontent. Through its individualistic outlook, meritocracy neglects the structural obstacles some individuals face. It is also worth noting that even those who 'win' do so at a high price, since their success requires them to invest considerable resources.[29]

Meritocracy is regularly relied on in political discourse,[30] serves as a justification for hiring decisions and promotions, and is frequently discussed in relation to educational policies.[31] It drives admissions processes to higher education institutions and, prior to that, influences the way children are taught and prepared for their professional future. The pressure to be successful is sometimes so strong that some individuals are willing to take significant risks to circumvent meritocratic mechanisms. One illustration is the revelation, in 2019, that wealthy parents had bribed college officials to get their children admitted to top US colleges, which flies in the face of meritocratic ideals.[32]

Meritocracy can be applied to any situation in which scarce resources need to be allocated. This makes it a relevant concept for both citizenship and immigration law. To date, however, it does not appear to have been the object of detailed studies in citizenship and immigration scholarship.

Recently, several legal scholars and legal philosophers published important critiques of meritocratic thought[33] and/or of how the law cements inequalities.[34] Yet, the implications of meritocracy have mostly been analysed in connection to education and employment practices, and not to immigration and citizenship law. Similarly, existing work on the law's contribution to inequality does not usually focus on these two areas of law. Meanwhile, in citizenship and migration studies, meritocracy has played a minor role. Scholars have underlined some problematic aspects of skills-based schemes;[35] they have highlighted the 'arbitrary' features of immigration and citizenship acquisition in general, and their role as a vector of inequality.[36] Yet, these studies do not focus on meritocracy as a concept.

[27] Markovits, *The Meritocracy Trap*.

[28] eg Beinart, 'What Trump Reveals by Calling Terrorists "Losers"' (*The Atlantic*, 24 May 2017) www.theatlantic.com/international/archive/2017/05/trump-isis-losers/527925; Colosimo, 'Réussir sans effort et sans talent?' (*France Culture*, 13 December 2018) www.franceculture.fr/emissions/le-journal-de-la-philo/reussir-sans-effort-et-sans-talent.

[29] Sandel, *The Tyranny of Merit*, Ch 6; Markovits, *The Meritocracy Trap*.

[30] Littler, 'Meritocratic Feeling' in *Against Meritocracy* (Routledge 2017).

[31] Markovits, *The Meritocracy Trap*; Beck, *Meritocracy, Citizenship and Education* (CIPG 2008); Mijs, 'The Unfulfillable Promise of Meritocracy' (2016) 29 *Soc. Justice Res.* 14; Allen, 'Michael Young's *The Rise of the Meritocracy*' (2011) 59 *Br. J. Educ. Stud.* 367; Karabel, *The Chosen* (Houghton Mifflin 2005); Hadjar, *Meritokratie als Legitimationsprinzip* (VS Verlag für Sozialwissenschaften 2008).

[32] Robinson, 'Meritocracy Is a Myth Invented by the Rich' (*The Guardian*, 14 March 2019) www.theguardian.com/commentisfree/2019/mar/14/meritocracy-myth-rich-college-admissions; Polikoff, Lucido and Posselt, 'Why Meritocracy Is a Myth in College Admissions' (*The Conversation*, 15 March 2019) https://theconversation.com/why-meritocracy-is-a-myth-in-college-admissions-113620; Sandel, *The Tyranny of* Merit, 8–10.

[33] Markovits, *The Meritocracy Trap*; Sandel, *The Tyranny of Merit*.

[34] Pistor, *The Code of Capital* (Princeton University Press 2019).

[35] Shachar, 'Selecting by Merit' in Fine and Ypi (eds), *Migration in Political Theory* (Oxford University Press 2016); Erez, 'In for a Penny' (2021) 8 *MOPP* 155; Lim, 'The Indirect Gender Discrimination of Skill-Selective Immigration Policies' (2019) 22 *Critical Review of International Social and Political Philosophy* 906.

[36] eg for citizenship, Kochenov, *Citizenship* (MIT Press 2019).

Given the importance of meritocratic considerations in immigration and citizenship law, existing scholarship needs to be complemented by an analysis of meritocracy. This chapter aims to contribute to filling this gap by shedding light on how meritocratic thought permeates these two bodies of law (and not just RBI and CBI).

III. MERITOCRATIC CONSIDERATIONS IN CONTEMPORARY IMMIGRATION AND CITIZENSHIP LAW

Meritocracy is rarely associated with immigration (below, subsection A) and citizenship law (below, subsection B),[37] although some social science literature refers to the notion of 'deservingness' in relation to the policies of welfare states[38] and more specifically in relation to migration.[39] And yet, these two areas of the law are permeated by meritocratic considerations – just like RBI and CBI. This does not mean that every single aspect of immigration and citizenship law is meritocratic. Still, due to the shift away from (explicit[40]) consideration of ascribed characteristics in the context of immigration and citizenship acquisition, meritocratic criteria have become increasingly relevant.

In focusing on immigration *and* citizenship law, I do not intend to suggest that these two bodies of law can be put on the same footing. They differ in their purpose and in terms of the normative questions they raise. Still, the two areas are connected in several ways: some migrants (especially permanent residents) enjoy many of the rights that are available to citizens,[41] and residency is usually a pathway to citizenship. This may explain why, despite their differences, immigration and citizenship are often considered jointly in scholarly research.[42]

The admission of migrants who enjoy specific rights by virtue of international law (especially the admission of refugees, who are protected by the principle of non-refoulement) raises distinct issues that are beyond the scope of this chapter. Instead, I focus on individuals who do not enjoy such protection under international law and who apply for a residency permit or for citizenship in the receiving country.[43]

[37] See however Ganty, 'Integration Duties in the European Union', 794–98; Davies, 'Has the Court Changed, or Have the Cases?' (2018) 25 *JEPP* 1442; Spescha, 'Ausländische Sozialhilfebeziehende im Fokus der Migrationsbehörde' (*Jusletter*, 8 March 2021), especially n. 63ff https://jusletter.weblaw.ch/juslissues/2021/1058/auslandische-sozialh_259ca3b7e5.html__ONCE&login=false.

[38] Eg van Oorschot, 'Who Should Get What, and Why?' (2000) 28 *Policy & Politics* 33; van Oorschot, 'Making the Difference in Social Europe' (2006) 16 *J. Eur. Soc. Policy* 23.

[39] eg Chauvin et al, 'Employment and Migrant Deservingness' (2013) 51 *Int Migr* 80; Chauvin and Garcés-Mascareñas, 'Becoming Less Illegal' (2014) 8 *Race & Ethnicity* 422; Bonizzoni, 'Looking for the Best and Brightest?' (2018) 56 *Int Migr* 47; Lafleur and Mescoli, 'Creating Undocumented EU Migrants through Welfare' (2018) 52 *Sociology* 480.

[40] As several scholars have argued, ascribed characteristics such as race still play a role in this context, at least implicitly. See eg Achiume, 'Migration as Decolonization' (2019) 71 *Stan. LRev.* 1509; Kochenov, 'Victims of Citizenship', in Kochenov and Surak (eds), *Citizenship and Residence Sales*.

[41] Lister, 'Citizenship, in the Immigration Context' (2010) 70 *MLR* 175, 185; Borna and Stearns, 'The Ethics and Efficacy of Selling National Citizenship' (2002) 37 *J. Bus. Ethics* 193, 194ff. See also Kochenov, *Citizenship*, 135ff.

[42] eg Shachar and Hirschl, 'On Citizenship, States, and Markets' (2014) 22 *J. Political Philos* 231, who analyse both talent migration and CBI schemes. Also Hidalgo, 'Selling Citizenship: A Defence' (2016) 33 *J. Appl. Philos.* 223, 225.

[43] Interestingly, meritocratic thought is not absent from asylum law either, as the 'global meritocracy of suffering' established by this body of law demonstrates. See Bob, 'Merchants of Morality' (*Foreign Policy*, 13 November 2009) https://foreignpolicy.com/2009/11/13/merchants-of-morality/; Ticktin, 'Where Ethics and Politics Meet' (2006) 33 *Am. Ethnol.* 33, 34. The legal definition of refugee already contains meritocratic elements, see Art 1 of the Convention relating to the Status of Refugees (1951) 189 UNTS 137.

A. Immigration Law

With the development of international human rights law and especially anti-discrimination law,[44] States have increasingly abandoned the explicit selection of migrants based on race, gender or other ascribed characteristics (although an individual's citizenship remains a crucial – and legal[45] – criterion). Instead, meritocratic conceptions have become more and more relevant. Such conceptions 'reflect [] a vision of an ideal citizen who is creative and contributory, who has been able to maximise her talent and turn herself into a "net benefit" for her new society'.[46] While the move away from ascribed characteristics would be a positive development, meritocratic criteria are not unproblematic (above, Section II).

This subsection highlights some meritocratic tendencies in contemporary immigration law. It first takes the case of Swiss immigration law (subsection i) before briefly discussing selected examples from other jurisdictions (subsection ii).

i. Merit-Based Immigration: The Example of Switzerland

Several reasons make it worthwhile to examine the case of Switzerland. First, as a country with a strong economy that is located at the heart of the European continent, Switzerland makes for a highly attractive country of immigration. As a matter of fact, its share of foreign residents is particularly high (circa 25 per cent in 2020).[47] Second, Switzerland is not a member of, but maintains close ties to, the EU, with which it concluded an Agreement on the Free Movement of Persons (AFMP) in 1999. Third, Switzerland is a semi-direct democracy where immigration law is regularly the object of popular votes.[48] Fourth, racial discrimination remains an issue in Switzerland. The Service for Combating Racism (a federal government body) finds that an increasing number of individuals in Switzerland experience racial discrimination.[49] Under the Migrant Integration Policy Index (MIPEX), which measures States' efforts to integrate migrants based on an assessment of eight policy areas on a scale of 0 to 100, 'Switzerland's integration policies score 7–8 points below the average Western European/OECD country (e.g. below France, Germany, Italy and the UK)'.[50]

One important manifestation of meritocratic thought in immigration law is that many States give preferential treatment to highly qualified migrants. This is also true in Switzerland, at least as regards so-called third-country (ie, non-EU and non-European Free Trade Area (EFTA)) nationals. Swiss immigration law distinguishes between individuals pursuing gainful

[44] eg Art 26 ICCPR, Art 14 ECHR and Art 15 of the Convention on the Elimination of All Forms of Discrimination against Women (1979) 1249 UNTS 13. See also Art 18 ff. TEU.

[45] Under Swiss law, for instance, nationality does not fall under the list of criteria prohibited by the principle of non-discrimination (Art 8(2) of Federal Constitution of the Swiss Confederation 1999). See also Art 1(2) of the International Convention on the Elimination of All Forms of Racial Discrimination (1965) 660 UNTS 195, which excludes the applicability of the Convention to 'distinctions, exclusions, restrictions or preferences made by a State Party to this Convention between citizens and non-citizens'.

[46] Shachar, 'Selecting by Merit', 197 ff.

[47] 'Anteil der ständigen ausländischen Bevölkerung' (Bundesamt für Statistik, 1 September 2021), www.bfs.admin.ch/bfs/de/home/statistiken/bevoelkerung/migration-integration/auslaendische bevoelkerung.assetdetail.18264545.html.

[48] For a recent example, see 'Eidgenössische Volksinitiative "Für eine massvolle Zuwanderung (Begrenzungsinitiative)"' (Bundeskanzlei BK, 22 Febtuary 2024) www.bk.admin.ch/ch/d/pore/vi/vis483.html.

[49] 'Rassistische Diskriminierung in der Schweiz: Bericht der Fachstelle für Rassismusbekämpfung 2019/2020' (Fachstelle für Rassismusbekämpfung 2021) www.newsd.admin.ch/newsd/message/attachments/68111.pdf.

[50] 'Switzerland 2019' (MIPEX 2020) www.mipex.eu/switzerland; see also 'Methodology' (MIPEX 2020) www.mipex.eu/methodology.

employment and individuals without such employment. Regarding the former, the Federal Act on Foreign Nationals and Integration (FNIA),[51] which primarily[52] applies to third-country nationals,[53] provides that 'gainfully employed foreign nationals' are admitted 'in the interests of the economy as a whole'.[54] These economic interests are emphasised in several provisions of the Act.[55] To be admitted, prospective immigrants must also have 'chances of lasting integration in the Swiss employment market as well as in the social environment'.[56] Moreover, to enter Switzerland, foreign nationals must have (among other things) 'the required financial means for the period of stay'.[57] These requirements, the fulfilment of which is assessed by the authorities, convey a logic of desert – that is, of merit – rather than a logic of rights.[58]

Gainfully employed third-country nationals may only be admitted to reside and work in Switzerland if no domestic employees (a term which includes Swiss citizens, but also permanent residents and persons with a residence permit who are entitled to engage in gainful employment) or citizens of States with which Switzerland has concluded an agreement on the free movement of workers can be found to fill the position.[59] This principle of subsidiarity contradicts meritocratic ideals;[60] instead, it expresses what could be called a 'cartel logic', as it restricts competition.[61] Some authors stress that it leaves the door open for biased employment practices (eg because employers give preferential treatment to applicants from specific – especially Western – countries).[62] In derogation from this protectionist subsidiarity scheme, however, third-country nationals with a Swiss university degree may be admitted if their work is 'of high academic or economic interest'.[63] This departure from the aforementioned 'cartel logic' is again in line with Switzerland's preference for elite (and merit-based) immigration.[64]

Another symptom of this elitist[65] and meritocratic approach is that '[s]hort stay and residence permits for work purposes may only be granted to managers, specialists and other qualified workers'.[66] When granting such permits, the authorities must consider applicants' prospects of economic and social integration based on '[their] professional qualifications and … professional and social adaptability, language skills and age'.[67] In practice, however, a person's (elite) professional qualifications are usually taken as a sufficient indication that these criteria are fulfilled.[68] Moreover, some applicants may be admitted in derogation from this rule, that is:

a. investors and entrepreneurs who maintain existing jobs or create new jobs;
b. recognised persons from the world of science, culture and sport;

[51] Foreign Nationals and Integration Act (FNIA) 2005 (CH).
[52] The Act only applies to EU and EFTA nationals to the extent that the relevant international agreements '[do] not contain any different provisions' or that the FNIA 'provides for more advantageous provisions', Art 2(2) and (3) FNIA.
[53] Art 2(2) and (3) FNIA.
[54] Art 3(1) FNIA.
[55] Nguyen, 'Art. 3' in Nguyen and Amarelle (eds), *Code annoté de droit des migrations* (Stämpfli 2017) 15, with further references.
[56] Art 3(1) FNIA; see also Art 4.
[57] Art 5(1)(b) FNIA.
[58] This should not detract from the fact that in some cases, immigrants have the *right* to be admitted if they fulfil the relevant conditions.
[59] Art 21(1) and (2) FNIA.
[60] On this tension, see Swiss Federal Council Decision VPB 59.17 [1994] (pertaining to the position of first hornist of the Zurich Opera Orchestra).
[61] I am indebted to Stefan Schlegel for bringing this point to my attention.
[62] Uebersax, 'Art. 21' in Nguyen and Amarelle (eds), *Code annoté de droit des migrations* (Stämpfli 2017) 174.
[63] Art 21(3) FNIA.
[64] Uebersax, 'Art. 21', 174.
[65] Vianin, 'Art. 23' in Nguyen and Amarelle (eds), *Code annoté de droit des migrations* (Stämpfli 2017) 186 ff.
[66] Art 23(1) FNIA.
[67] Art 23(2) FNIA.
[68] Vianin, 'Art. 23', 191.

c. persons with special professional knowledge or skills, provided there is a need for their admission;
d. persons who are part of an executive transfer between internationally active companies;
e. persons whose activity in Switzerland is indispensable for economically significant international business relationships.[69]

Through these derogations, the Act makes it possible to take into consideration applicants' potential to contribute to the economy (lit. a, d, and e), their 'performance' (lit. b) and their skills (lit. c), based on the idea that 'it is in the interest of the country to admit such persons'.[70]

The admission of applicants without gainful employment is subject to stricter requirements. Admission may only be envisaged for educational or training purposes[71] (which, again, fits the meritocratic narrative), in the case of retired persons with personal ties to Switzerland,[72] and for individuals who need to undergo medical treatment.[73]

Article 30 FNIA, which provides for derogations from these general admission requirements, is particularly interesting for our purposes. Among other things, derogations are possible if 'important public interests' are at stake (article 30(1)(b) FNIA).[74] This includes 'significant cultural interests', 'state policy reasons', 'the necessity that a foreigner be present in the context of criminal proceedings' and, most importantly, 'significant cantonal fiscal interests'.[75]

Article 30(1)(b) FNIA and the notion of 'significant cantonal fiscal interests' are the gateway to RBI under Swiss law.[76] Wealthy foreigners may be granted a residency permit on this basis and are subject to lump-sum taxation.[77] The press reports that between 2008 and 2016, 523 foreigners obtained a residency permit based on article 30(1)(b) FNIA,[78] and that such applications are hardly ever denied by the federal migration authorities.[79] The fact that the

[69] Art 23(3) FNIA.

[70] Vianin, 'Art. 23', 193. In addition to the requirements set out in arts 20–25 FNIA, salaried employees may be admitted if their activity is expected to benefit the Swiss economy and if an employer has submitted a corresponding application (Art 18 FNIA). Self-employed individuals must engage in an activity that benefits the Swiss economy to be admitted, while also complying with 'the necessary financial and operational requirements' (Art 19(c) FNIA) and having 'an adequate and independent source of income' (Art 19(d) FNIA).

[71] Art 27 FNIA.

[72] Art 28 FNIA.

[73] Art 29 FNIA.

[74] Derogations are also possible to 'simplify the transfer of senior management staff and essential specialists within internationally active companies' (lit. h).

[75] Art 32 of the Federal Ordinance on Admission, Residence, and Gainful Employment (OASA) 2007 (CH).

[76] Miehle, 'Golden Visa' (*Domenig & Partner*, 15 December 2021) www.domenig.law/golden-visa; Imboden, 'Goldene Visa spalten die Politik' (*SRF*, 1 November 2018) www.srf.ch/news/schweiz/aufenthaltsrecht-fuer-reiche-goldene-visa-spalten-die-politik; Schumacher, 'Das Geschäft mit den "goldenen Visa"' (*Tagblatt*, 6 January 2019) www.tagblatt.ch/schweiz/44-goldene-visa-im-jahr-2018-ld.1083048; Galichet, 'Ultrareiche bekommen in der Schweiz eine Aufenthaltsbewilligung' (*Swissinfo*, 26 October 2020) www.swissinfo.ch/ger/ultrareiche-bekommen-in-der-schweiz-eine-aufenthaltsbewilligung/46125188; 'Reiche Chinesen lösen russische Oligarchen an der Spitze ab' (*Blue*, 16 February 2021) www.bluewin.ch/de/news/schweiz/immer-mehr-goldene-visa-fuer-superreiche-chinesen-586165.html; Häfliger, 'Reiche Chinesen kaufen Aufenthaltsbewilligung in der Schweiz' (*Tages-Anzeiger*, 15 February 2021) www.tagesanzeiger.ch/reiche-chinesen-kaufen-aufenthaltsbewilligung-in-der-schweiz-907977366147.

[77] Nguyen, 'Art. 30' in Nguyen and Amarelle (eds), *Code annoté de droit des migrations* (Stämpfli 2017) 275. A proposal to abolish lump-sum taxation was rejected by 59.2 per cent of Swiss voters and almost all Swiss cantons in 2014. See 'Volksabstimmung vom 30.11.2014' (Bundeskanzlei BK, 2 February 2024) www.bk.admin.ch/ch/d/pore/va/20141130/index.html.

[78] Schumacher, '523 Ausländer kauften bisher eine Schweizer "B-Bewilligung"' (*Aargauer Zeitung*, 10 February 2017) www.aargauerzeitung.ch/schweiz/523-auslander-kauften-bisher-eine-schweizer-b-bewilligung-ld.1611931. See also 'Reiche in der Schweiz willkommen' (*SRF Radio*, 1 November 2018) www.srf.ch/audio/echo-der-zeit/reiche-in-der-schweiz-willkommen?partId=11432646.

[79] Imboden reports that between 2008 and 2017, the State Secretariat for Migration granted 578 residency permits based on Art 30(1)(b) FNIA, and that only six applications were denied between 2013 and 2017, Imboden, 'Goldene Visa spalten die Politik'.

cantonal[80] and federal authorities are generally keen to admit wealthy individuals contrasts with the restrictive standard requirements applicable to the admission of third-country nationals with and without gainful employment.[81]

To be fair, and as already highlighted, Swiss immigration law is not exclusively based on meritocratic considerations. In the context of the admission of third-country nationals, education, skills, and past performance are not the only features that are taken into account. Moreover, the FNIA explicitly mentions the relevance of 'international law obligations, humanitarian grounds or the unity of the family'.[82] In 2018, the FNIA and its accompanying ordinance were amended to the effect that refugees and provisionally admitted persons now enjoy broader access to the Swiss labour market.[83]

Still, by giving preference to third-country nationals who are high-skilled, contribute to the economy and have good language skills, the Swiss immigration regime rewards what it considers to be meritorious individuals, while penalising those who lack such credentials. These meritocratic considerations make it possible to advance what are predominantly economic and fiscal interests. Meanwhile, Swiss immigration law does not take the applicants' diverse socioeconomic backgrounds into consideration, nor does it account for the fact that unequal opportunities lead to unequal performance and skills. Instead, it implicitly assumes that admitting so-called 'low-skilled' third-country nationals does not serve the interests of the Swiss economy, interests which play a central role in the Swiss immigration system.[84]

By stating that third-country nationals need to show 'willingness'[85] to integrate, the FNIA leaves room for additional bias in favour of high-skilled and/or wealthy immigrants, who are often more readily assumed to be able to establish social connections in the State of immigration.[86] Another instance of this voluntarist (and meritocratic) approach is the requirement that the authorities assess applicants' degree of integration based on their 'participation in working life or efforts to acquire an education',[87] which also tends to advantage high-skilled migrants.[88] The FNIA defines integration as 'the co-existence of the resident Swiss and foreign population on the basis of the values of the Federal Constitution and mutual respect and tolerance',[89] but the criteria based on which integration is assessed remain vague, and the authorities enjoy substantial leeway.[90] What is 'respect for the values of the Federal Constitution',[91] one of the integration criteria set out in the FNIA?

[80] Baur, 'Le Valais attire les contribuables super-riches' (*Le Temps*, 28 October 2018) www.letemps.ch/suisse/valais-attire-contribuables-superriches; 'Reiche in der Schweiz willkommen' (*SRF Radio*, 1 November 2018).

[81] Retired persons for instance must provide evidence of 'special personal relations to Switzerland' to be admitted (Art 28(b) FNIA).

[82] Art 3(2) FNIA.

[83] See Graf and Mahon, 'Art. 121a de la Constitution et accès au marché du travail' (*Jusletter*, 13 August 2018) https://skmr.ch/assets/publications/180830_article_121a_constitution_et_acces_au_marche_du_travail_Jusletter.pdf.

[84] Nguyen, 'Art. 30', 17.

[85] Art 4(3) FNIA.

[86] This risk has also been highlighted in the literature: Achermann, 'Art. 4' in Caroni et al (eds), *Bundesgesetz über die Ausländerinnen und Ausländer* (Stämpfli 2010) 37; Hercog and Sandoz, 'Selecting the Highly Skilled' (2018) 15 *Migrat. Lett.* 503, 508; Hercog, 'The Privileged and Useful Migrant' (2017) NCCR-on the Move Working Paper No. 16, 12.

[87] Art 58a(1)(d) FNIA.

[88] Empirical research shows that such individuals are deemed less likely to rely on social benefits: Hercog and Sandoz, 'Selecting the Highly Skilled', 508.

[89] Art 4(1) FNIA.

[90] Achermann and Amarelle, 'Art. 4' in Nguyen and Amarelle (eds), *Code annoté de droit des migrations* (Stämpfli 2017) 31ff.

[91] Art 58a(1)(b) FNIA.

What does it mean to 'familiarise [oneself] with the social conditions and way of life in Switzerland',[92] as the FNIA requires? Scholars rightly note that such criteria create 'a latent risk of discrimination'.[93]

Contrary to the admission of third-country nationals, which is governed by the FNIA, the admission of EU and EFTA nationals is regulated by the AFMP.[94] The Swiss immigration system is thus two-tiered.[95] It treats applicants differently depending on their nationality and, potentially, their race,[96] though the former is, as already mentioned, deemed compatible with the constitutional principle of non-discrimination.[97]

Interestingly, contrary to what applies to the admission of third-country nationals, the skills of EU/EFTA nationals are not deemed relevant. Some scholars thus consider that in the context of the admission of third-country nationals, non-economic factors, including 'symbolic' ones (ie, criteria that mainly serve the goal of reassuring the local population), are in fact more important than economic considerations.[98] The irrelevance of applicants' skills under the AFMP shows that meritocratic thought is often applied selectively.

Like the FNIA, the AFMP distinguishes between individuals engaged in gainful employment[99] and individuals who lack such employment.[100] The cornerstone of the Agreement is the principle of non-discrimination, which precludes the parties from discriminating[101] against individuals based on their nationality, and which appears in several provisions of the AFMP.[102] To be admitted, EU/EFTA nationals who are not engaged in gainful employment must prove that they can sustain themselves financially.[103] Hence, they may be admitted if they can contribute to the Swiss economy or if they do not represent an economic burden for the State.

To conclude, Swiss immigration law displays many meritocratic traits, at least in relation to the admission of third-country nationals. By contrast, the admission of EU/EFTA nationals is much less strict and does not include skills-based criteria.

[92] Art 4(4) FNIA.

[93] Achermann and Amarelle, 'Art. 4', 36 with reference to Peter Uebersax.

[94] The Bilateral Agreement on the Free Movement of Persons (AFMP) between Switzerland and the EU 1999.

[95] In the past, Switzerland used to apply a three-tiered system that distinguished between i) EU/EFTA States, which benefitted from the free movement of persons; ii) the United States, Canada, Australia, New Zealand and at a later stage Central and Eastern European States, from which a limited number of workers could be admitted; and iii) all other States, the nationals of which could only be admitted in exceptional circumstances, when these nationals were highly qualified workers. This system was especially criticised for arbitrarily distinguishing between countries belonging to the second versus third category and for entrenching distinctions based on race and religion. See 'Stellungnahme der Eidgenössischen Kommission gegen Rassismus zum Drei-Kreise-Modell des Bundesrats über die schweizerische Ausländerpolitik' (German Federal Commission against Racism, 1996) www.ekr.admin.ch/pdf/960506_stellungnahme_3-kreise-modell_de5cd4.pdf; Uebersax, 'Art. 21', 163 ff.

[96] On the (undertheorised) role of race in immigration policies, see Fine, 'Immigration and Discrimination' in Fine and Ypi (eds), *Migration in Political Theory* (Oxford University Press 2016).

[97] Above note 45.

[98] Hercog and Sandoz, 'Selecting the Highly Skilled', 503.

[99] See Sect II–IV AFMP, pertaining to salaried workers, independent workers and service providers.

[100] Sect V AFMP.

[101] Again, while the AFMP relies on the vocabulary of discrimination, differential treatment based on nationality is not a 'discrimination' in the sense of Art 8(2) of Federal Constitution of the Swiss Confederation 1999. Thus, the principle of discrimination has a different meaning in the context of the AFMP than under the FNIA, for example. On this topic, see also Ammann, 'La non-discrimination, principe charnière d'interprétation' in Besson and Ziegler (eds), *Égalité et non-discrimination en droit international et européen* (Schulthess 2014).

[102] See eg Arts 2 and 7; Annex I, Art 3(1), Art 9.

[103] Art 24, Annex I AFMP.

ii. Merit-Based Immigration in Other Jurisdictions

Like Switzerland, many States (eg, the United States, Canada and Australia) show a preference for the admission of 'meritorious', and more specifically of high-skilled immigrants.[104] This also applies to the EU, which facilitates the immigration of highly qualified individuals through the Council's Directive 2009/50/EC and the 'Blue Card' system that this Directive establishes. In November 2023, a revised version, Directive (EU) 2021/1883, repealed the Blue Card Directive. Like Swiss immigration law, these policies are primarily driven by economic considerations and rely on meritocratic discourse.

The Blue Card Directive of 2009 recalls the Lisbon European Council's objective for the EU to become 'the most competitive and dynamic knowledge-based economy in the world, capable of sustainable economic growth with more and better jobs and greater social cohesion'.[105] It also states that the Community must aim to become 'more attractive to such [highly qualified] workers from around the world and sustain its competitiveness and economic growth', a goal that can be achieved by applying a 'fast-track procedure' to those workers and their families.[106] For this purpose, the Directive establishes 'a flexible demand-driven entry system, based on objective criteria … and on professional qualifications'.[107] Similar language can be found in the revised Blue Card Directive.

In line with meritocratic ideals, the entry system established by the Blue Card Directive purports to be objective. De facto, however, it entrenches inequality by focusing on past achievements and by failing to provide applicants with truly equal opportunities (eg by adopting a forward-looking approach and by assessing applicants' potential). The Blue Card Directive of 2009 requires the salary offered to the applicant to amount to at least 1.2 to 1.5 times the average gross annual salary in the receiving Member State.[108] This shows that merit is often conflated with income, which challenges the distinction scholars usually draw between talent-based and wealth-based immigration.

As regards EU citizenship, Eleanor Spaventa notes that it amounts to an 'earned citizenship' that is 'for the wealthy, healthy, and good Union citizens' and not for less privileged ones.[109] Scholars have criticised the EU's conception of citizenship for amounting to a 'market citizenship' at the service of economic considerations, and not of equality.[110]

Income levels are also a common feature of points-based (sometimes called 'merit-based') immigration systems. Such schemes, which offer another telling example of meritocratic thought, exist in States such as Canada, Australia, New Zealand and the United Kingdom.[111] The first State to introduce such a system, Canada, thereby moved away from the admission of migrants based on their origin.[112]

[104] Salt, 'International Movements of the Highly Skilled' (1997) OECD Social, Employment and Migration Working Papers No. 3, 12; Czaika and Parsons, 'The Gravity of High-Skilled Migration Policies' (2017) 54 *Demography* 603, 604.

[105] Council Directive 2009/50/EC on the conditions of entry and residence of third-country nationals for the purposes of highly qualified employment [2009] OJ L 155/17, rec 3.

[106] ibid, rec 7.

[107] ibid, rec 10.

[108] ibid, Art 5. In the revised version, the salary 'shall be at least 1,0 times, but not higher than 1,6 times, the average gross annual salary in the Member State concerned', see Art 5(3).

[109] Spaventa, 'Earned Citizenship' in Kochenov (ed), *EU Citizenship and Federalism* (Cambridge University Press 2017) 220. See further O'Brien, *Unity in Adversity* (Hart 2017).

[110] Kochenov, 'The Oxymoron of "Market Citizenship"' in Amtenbrink et al (eds), *The Internal Market and the Future of European Integration* (Cambridge University Press 2019).

[111] eg Gower, 'The UK's Points-Based System for Immigration' (2018) House of Commons Library Briefing Paper 7662 https://researchbriefings.files.parliament.uk/documents/CBP-7662/CBP-7662.pdf.

[112] Shachar, 'Selecting by Merit', 181.

Just a few days after the United Kingdom had officially left the EU, in February 2020, the UK government stated that it planned to introduce 'a firm and fair points-based system that will attract the high-skilled workers we need to contribute to our economy, our communities and our public services'.[113] The points-based scheme, which entered into force in 2021, does not distinguish between EU and non-EU citizens.[114] In the United States, in 2017 Republican Senators Tom Cotton and David Perdue proposed to introduce a points-based immigration system through the so-called RAISE (Reforming American Immigration for Strong Employment) Act. Donald Trump then proposed a revised version of the Act.[115] However, the bill failed to garner enough political support.

Points-based schemes consist in rating would-be immigrants with reference to a variety of criteria such as language skills, level of education, professional experience, other relevant skills, age and employment situation. Applicants are hence evaluated based on what looks like a transparent and objective procedure. Such systems are endorsed by States because they are considered to provide incentives to applicants to try their best in order to be admitted.[116] Yet, points-based systems are problematic on several counts.

In assessing and rating qualifications that have already been obtained, States prioritise their own economic needs and reward 'integration outcomes'[117] instead of adopting a prospective approach and offering equal opportunities to would-be immigrants. Points-based systems have also been criticised for perpetuating racial and gender bias.[118] Another problem is the indeterminacy of the concept of skill, which also leaves room for bias. Preference is usually given to diplomas and other measurable past achievements, while the skills of less privileged individuals (eg, their ability to perform care work or other domestic work) tend to be overlooked.[119] For instance, skills-based immigration policies like UK's points-based system have a disparate impact on women: 'talent-based selection worsens existing beliefs about the inferiority of female workers' contributions, as well as women's status as passive or helpless dependents who only achieve their ends by leaning on men'.[120] This aligns with the observation that meritocratic thought translates into a 'lack of recognition for work performance at all skill levels'[121] and for what Sandel calls the 'dignity of work'.[122]

Besides these examples, several other meritocratic proposals have been put forward. Some scholars suggest introducing auction systems through which permits would be sold to those individuals willing and able to pay. This proposal was famously formulated in the early 1990s

[113] 'The UK's Points-Based Immigration System: Policy Statement' (UK Government 2020) www.gov.uk/government/publications/the-uks-points-based-immigration-system-policy-statement/the-uks-points-based-immigration-system-policy-statement.

[114] 'The UK's Points-Based Immigration System: An Introduction for Employers (Accessible Version)' (UK Government 2022) www.gov.uk/government/publications/uk-points-based-immigration-system-employer-information/the-uks-points-based-immigration-system-an-introduction-for-employers.

[115] 'US Merit Based Immigration' (Visaguide World) https://visaguide.world/us-visa/merit-based-immigration/.

[116] Jasso, 'Whom Should We Welcome?' (1988) 53 *Am. Soc. Rev.* 919, 921.

[117] Gower, 'The UK's Points-Based System for Immigration', 5.

[118] Eg Gest, 'Points-Based System Was Meant to Reduce Racial Bias. It Doesn't' (*The Guardian*, 19 January 2018) www.theguardian.com/commentisfree/2018/jan/19/points-based-immigration-racism; Kofman, 'Towards a Gendered Evaluation of (Highly) Skilled Immigration Policies in Europe' (2014) 52 *Int Migr* 116, 117.

[119] Kofman 'Towards a Gendered Evaluation', 119 with further references.

[120] Lim, 'The Indirect Gender Discrimination of Skill-Selective Immigration Policies', 907. In the same vein: Briddick, 'Symposium on Undoing Discriminatory Borders' (2021) 115 *AJIL* 356. Anderson, 'What Is the Point of Equality?', 311.

[121] Binswanger, 'Gegen die Meritokratie' (*Republik Magazin*, 6 February 2021) www.republik.ch/2021/02/06/gegen-die-meritokratie.

[122] Sandel, *The Tyranny of Merit*, Ch 7.

by the economist Gary Becker, who criticised States' use of quotas to limit immigration.[123] In 2014, Sheldon Adelson, Warren Buffett and Bill Gates published an op-ed in which they argued for a more flexible immigration policy vis-à-vis talented graduates, as well as for an expansion of the EB-5 visa programme, noting that it had been created with 'foreigners with financial resources or unique abilities' in mind.[124] In Switzerland, the economists Margit Osterloh and Bruno Frey suggested that immigrants should be required to pay an entry fee.[125] Auctions and entry fees are usually defended on the grounds that they would enable States to select the most 'meritorious immigrants', who are deemed more likely to pay this price.[126] Yet, this amounts to 'selling' residency rights, just like RBI.

Another approach worth mentioning because it aims to create more equal opportunities for immigrants is the allocation of residency permits by lot. In Liechtenstein, this process is applied to half of the residency permits granted to citizens of States belonging to the European Economic Area.[127] Such a lottery system has also been used in the United States since the 1990s in the context of the Diversity Immigrant Visa Program which, as its name suggests, aims to increase the diversity of immigrants entering the United States, although this lottery system has been criticised for being biased and selective.[128]

As a matter of fact, the egalitarian character of selection by lot is often overlooked, both in and outside the immigration context. In 2018, Donald Trump suggested abolishing the US lottery system, 'a program that randomly hands out green cards without any regard for skill, merit, or the safety of American people'. Instead, he stressed that the United States should 'begin moving toward a merit-based immigration system, one that admits people who are skilled, who want to work, who will contribute to [US] society, and who will love and respect [the United States]'.[129] This view neglects that the aim of selection by lot is precisely to ensure greater equality of opportunity and to reduce arbitrariness and nepotism (which lead to a disregard for individuals' skills and potential). Skills-based considerations can very well be taken into consideration when drawing lots, namely when constituting the pool of applicants entitled to participate in the lottery.

B. Citizenship Law

i. Citizenship Acquisition in General

The basic modes of citizenship acquisition fall into two categories: acquisition at birth, and acquisition after birth through naturalisation. In the latter case, citizenship is often

[123] Becker, 'An Open Door to Immigrants: The Auction' (*The Wall Street Journal*, 14 October 1992). See also Becker, 'Why Not Let Immigrants Pay for Speedy Entry?' in Becker and Becker (eds), *The Economics of Life* (McGraw-Hill 1997).

[124] Adelson et al., 'Break the Immigration Impasse' (*The New York Times*, 10 July 2014).

[125] Osterloh and Frey, 'Cooperatives Instead of Migration Partnerships' (2018) 40 *Analyse & Kritik* 201; Osterloh and Frey, 'Die Coronakrise erfordert eine neue Migrationspolitik' (2020) 1078 *Schweizer Monat* 57.

[126] Becker, 'An Open Door to Immigrants'; see also Surak, 'Global Citizenship 2.0' (2016), Investment Migration Working Papers IMC-RP2016/3, 4; Becker and Lazear, 'A Market Solution for Immigration Reform' (*The Wall Street Journal*, 1 March 2013); Crettez, 'Is Selling Immigration Rights Politically Sustainable?' (2011) 77 *Recherches économiques de Louvain* 33, 34.

[127] Arts 37–39 of the Free Movement of European Economic Area Nationals and Swiss Nationals Act 2009 (LI); 'Auslosung Aufenthaltsbewilligung (B)' (*Landesverwaltung Fürstentum Liechtenstein*) www.llv.li/inhalt/1863/amtsstellen/auslosung-aufenthaltsbewilligung-b.

[128] See eg Law, 'The Diversity Visa Lottery' (2002) 21 *JAEH* 3.

[129] 'The Full Transcript of Donald Trump's First State of the Union Address' (*The Independent*, 31 January 2018) www.independent.co.uk/news/world/americas/us-politics/donald-trump-state-of-the-union-2018-full-transcript-latest-immigration-fact-check-congress-a8186516.html.

conceptualised as a status which one either does or does not deserve, while in the former, citizenship is considered a right.[130]

As is well known, citizenship largely goes back to fortuitous circumstances:[131] the citizenship we receive at birth derives either from our place of birth or from our parents' citizenship.[132] Yet, not all citizenships are created equal. While a Swiss passport grants visa-free access to 186 countries, an Afghan passport provides such access to 26 States only, that is, less than a seventh.[133] Increasingly often, visa-free access means not only visa-free travel, but also visa-free settlement and work.[134]

Birthright citizenship is everything but meritocratic: it is based on factors that individuals cannot influence. As Joseph Carens puts it, '[c]itizenship in Western liberal democracies is the modern equivalent of feudal privilege – an inherited status that greatly enhances one's life chances'.[135] Shachar also points out that birthright citizenship has a 'wealth-preserving function'[136] and 'locks in structures of privilege worldwide'.[137]

Citizenship acquisition at birth follows the principles of *ius sanguinis* or *ius soli*.[138] Many countries combine both regimes in their legal orders.[139] In practice, however, the relevance of *ius soli* is limited, as in many cases, individuals born in a State with such a regime have at least one local parent. Blood connections – and, hence, racial considerations – thus have a significant practical relevance in citizenship acquisition.

By contrast, the law of naturalisation governs citizenship acquisition after birth. This body of law is like a 'grab bag' that contains 'a little bit of everything',[140] that is, a multiplicity of heterogeneous requirements that States expect aspiring citizens to fulfil. Such requirements typically pertain to language skills, knowledge of the future country of citizenship, the willingness to integrate, good moral character, the ability to sustain oneself financially and a minimal residency period. States implicitly treat many of these criteria as indicators of 'merit'. Yet, these factors are influenced by the milieu into which a person is born and in which she grows up: indeed, 'merit' (or the absence thereof) hinges on features such as inheritance, social and cultural capital, education, luck, marriage and a history of discrimination.[141]

Like immigration laws (above, subsection A), most naturalisation laws (including those of European States[142]) have abandoned explicit selection based on ascribed characteristics such as race, gender and sexual orientation,[143] a practice prohibited by the European Convention on

[130] On these two dimensions, see Joppke, 'Transformation of Citizenship' (2007) 11 *Citizenship Stud.* 37.

[131] Shachar, *The Birthright Lottery* (Harvard University Press 2009).

[132] Shachar, 'The Worth of Citizenship in an Unequal World' (2007) 8 *Theor. Inq. Law.* 366, 369.

[133] Kochenov and Lindeboom (eds), *Quality of Nationality Index* (Hart 2020); 'The Henley Passport Index' (*Henley & Partners*) www.henleyglobal.com/passport-index/ranking. In 2018, Switzerland was ranked 11th, while Afghanistan was ranked 158th.

[134] Kochenov and Lindeboom (eds), *Quality of Nationality Index*, 32ff. See also Kochenov, 'Inter-Legality'.

[135] Carens, 'Aliens and Citizens' (1987) 49 *Rev Polit* 251.

[136] Shachar, 'The Worth of Citizenship', 366.

[137] ibid, 387.

[138] Regimes of *ius sanguinis* exist in most countries today and are common in Central Europe, North Africa, and Asia, for example. By contrast, *ius soli* characterises most North and South American States. For an overview, see Weil, 'L'accès à la citoyenneté', in *Nationalité et citoyenneté, nouvelle donne d'un espace européen* (Service de l'information et des relations publiques 2002) 9–28.

[139] Surak, 'Global Citizenship 2.0', 1ff.

[140] Orgad, 'Naturalization' in Shachar et al (eds), *The Oxford Handbook of Citizenship* (Oxford University Press 2017) 358.

[141] McNamee, *The Meritocracy Myth* 4th edn (Rowman & Littlefield 2018).

[142] Joppke, 'Comparative Citizenship' (2008) 2 *LEHR* 1, 3 ff.

[143] On the liberalisation of citizenship, see Joppke, 'Transformation of Citizenship', 38 ff. See also Lister, 'Citizenship, in the Immigration Context', 176.

Nationality.[144] Instead, they have turned to the aforementioned meritocratic criteria to determine whether an applicant should be granted citizenship. Naturalisation is typically viewed as a reward for successful integration, and not as a way of supporting this integration.[145] Moreover, in the case of applicants with a perceived ethnic proximity to the State of naturalisation, integration requirements tend to be handled more flexibly.

Taking again the example of Swiss law, the applicable legislation distinguishes between ordinary and facilitated naturalisation. Ordinary naturalisation is open to individuals who comply with specific residency and integration requirements.[146] The applicant's degree of integration is assessed based on a variety of criteria, including (but not limited to[147]) good behaviour, language skills, compliance with Swiss constitutional values and participation in economic life.[148] Special circumstances (such as disability or serious illness, and great difficulties with learning, reading and writing) are also taken into account.[149] Facilitated naturalisation makes it possible for applicants to be granted citizenship after a comparatively short period, for instance following marriage with a Swiss citizen.[150] It is also less costly and complex than ordinary naturalisation.[151]

Under Swiss law, the naturalisation decision involves three levels of governance, namely the municipal, cantonal and federal level (except for decisions on facilitated naturalisation, which are made by the federal authorities). The naturalisation practices of cantonal and especially municipal authorities[152] vary significantly, as do the applicable naturalisation fees. It is worth noting that the European Convention on Nationality prohibits excessive naturalisation fees.[153]

In what follows, I discuss various modes of citizenship acquisition that involve meritocratic considerations. As I have argued elsewhere, States and other actors often rely on meritocratic discourse to advertise and defend CBI (subsection ii); yet, CBI is just the tip of the meritocratic iceberg: many other aspects of citizenship law – including citizenship tests (subsection iii) and citizenship granted based on exceptional achievements (subsection iv) – are based on meritocratic thinking.

ii. Citizenship by Investment

CBI, also referred to as *ius pecuniae*,[154] *ius doni*[155] or *ius argenti*,[156] enables individuals to obtain citizenship in exchange for a monetary investment or a donation. As historian Maarten Prak has shown, the sale of municipal citizenship status already existed in pre-modern times, although this practice differs from contemporary CBI on several counts.[157] While some

[144] Art 5(1) of the European Convention on Nationality (1997) *ETS* 166.

[145] Joppke, 'Comparative Citizenship', 16.

[146] Art 9 ff of the Federal Act on Swiss Citizenship (SCA) 2014 (CH).

[147] Sow and Mahon, 'Art. 14' in Amarelle and Nguyen (eds), *Code annoté de droit des migrations: Volume V, Loi sur la nationalité (LN)* (Stämpfli 2014) 48.

[148] Art 12 SCA and Art 2 ff of the Federal Ordinance on Swiss Citizenship (SCO) 2016 (CH).

[149] Art 9 SCO.

[150] Art 21 SCA.

[151] Ousmane, 'Art. 26' in Amarelle and Nguyen (eds), *Code annoté de droit des migrations* (Stämpfli 2014) 95.

[152] On this topic, see Helbling, 'Switzerland' (2010) 36 *JEMS* 793.

[153] Art 13(1) of the European Convention on Nationality.

[154] Stern, 'Ius Pecuniae' in Dahlvik et al (eds), *Migration und Integration* (V&R unipress 2012); Džankić, 'The Pros and Cons of Ius Pecuniae' (2012) EUI Working Papers EUDO/RSCAS 2012/14; Surak, 'Global Citizenship 2.0', 11, who uses *ius pecuniae* as an umbrella term for investor visa programmes, CBI programmes and discretionary grants of citizenship.

[155] Kälin, Ius Doni *in International Law and EU Law* (Brill-Nijhoff 2019).

[156] Berger, 'Staatsbürgerschaft als Ware', 1046.

[157] Prak, 'Citizenship for Sale in Pre-Modern Europe' in Kochenov and Surak (eds), *Citizenship and Residence Sales*.

contemporary CBI programmes date back to the 1980s and 1990s, like those of Saint Kitts and Nevis (1984) and Dominica (1993), most States introduced CBI programmes fairly recently. Some of these countries are Caribbean islands (Antigua and Barbuda (2013), Grenada (2014)), while others are EU Member States, like Malta (2014) and Cyprus (2011, though the Cypriot programme was discontinued in October 2020).

The amounts attached to citizenship rights vary (as do the required fees, which these amounts do not usually include[158]): Dominica for instance asks for a payment of 100,000 USD. Other relatively cheap passports are those delivered by Antigua and Barbuda (100,000 USD) and Grenada (150,000 USD)[159] Malta requires a contribution of at least 600,000 € and proof of residence in Malta for a period of 36 months or, exceptionally, a contribution of at least 750,000 € and proof of residence in Malta for a minimum period of 12 months.[160] In many cases, residency requirements are either non-existent or easy to comply with (e.g., five days within a five-year period in Antigua and Barbuda). In the case of Malta, proof of residence is not equivalent to physical presence.[161]

Prima facie, CBI is everything but meritocratic; yet, States and other actors regularly use meritocratic discourse to advertise and defend CBI. In other work, I have offered a critical evaluation of the meritocratic discourse that is often used to advertise and defend this type of naturalisation.[162] In this subsection, my goal is to show that meritocratic thought is not specific to CBI, but that it also characterises other aspects of citizenship law.

iii. Citizenship Tests

One manifestation of meritocratic thought in the naturalisation context is that States typically require applicants to take citizenship tests to assess whether they are fit to be granted citizenship. This practice aligns with meritocratic conceptions: it purports to evaluate applicants based on objective criteria. As Liav Orgad notes, '[i]n a way, the entire naturalization process is a test – whether one has resided in the country enough, integrated well into society, behaved lawfully, and acquired certain skills and abilities'.[163] Of course, citizenship tests differ from 'the kinds of educational requirements for meeting [skill-based criteria]':[164] they do not screen applicants for the same kind of skills. Still, in both cases, applicants are gauged with reference to specific requirements that States want them to fulfil.

In the aftermath of 9/11, European States increasingly introduced citizenship tests and reinforced integration requirements in the context of naturalisation procedures.[165] Orgad reports that between 2002 and 2010, the percentage of European countries with a compulsory language requirement jumped from 29 per cent to 71 per cent; the number of European States requiring applicants to take a citizenship test increased threefold between 1999 and 2010.[166]

[158] Surak, 'Investment Migration' in Kochenov and Surak (eds), *Citizenship and Residence Sales*.
[159] Figures retrieved from 'Investment Migration Countries' (*Henley & Partners*) www.henleyglobal.com/countries.
[160] Granting of Citizenship for Exceptional Services Regulations 2020 (MT), First Schedule Naturalisation for Exceptional Services Regulations 2020, Schedule of Fees.
[161] On this distinction, see the chapter by Kochenov and van den Brink in this volume.
[162] Ammann, 'How (Un)Meritocratic'.
[163] Orgad, 'Naturalization', 341. On citizenship tests, see also Orgad, 'The Citizen-Makers' (2019) 25 *ELJ* 524.
[164] Erez, 'In for a Penny', 168.
[165] Joppke, 'Transformation of Citizenship', 41; C Joppke, 'The Instrumental Turn on Citizenship' (2019) 45 *JEMS* 858, 859ff.
[166] Orgad, 'Naturalization', 351ff.

Citizenship tests aim at evaluating applicants' knowledge, but also their character.[167] These tests adopt a logic of desert: those who pass have the required qualities and deserve to be granted citizenship, while those who fail do not.[168] While citizenship tests purport to be impartial and objective, they put some categories of individuals at a disadvantage (eg, those who do not speak the local language and lack the means to invest in language training).[169] This is in line with the finding that standardised tests are not value-neutral and have a disparate impact on women and minorities.[170]

iv. Citizenship Honouring Exceptional Services to the State

Another merit-based practice is the grant of citizenship to individuals as a reward for, and in honour of, their exceptional services to the State. This type of citizenship stands on the same footing as other modes of citizenship acquisition.[171] Like 'Olympic citizenship'[172] rewarding exceptional talent or skill, with which it overlaps, citizenship honouring exceptional achievements is tied to merit and is backward looking, that is, it focuses on a person's past achievements and services to the community.[173]

One prominent example is President Macron's decision, in 2018, to grant French citizenship to Mamoudou Gassama, an undocumented Malian immigrant who had climbed up four storeys to rescue a four-year-old child dangling from a balcony.[174] This grant of citizenship was based on article 21-19 of the French Civil Code, which allows citizenship to be granted to foreigners 'who have rendered exceptional services to France or whose naturalization represents an exceptional interest for France'. This practice is not new: already in Greek and Roman Antiquity, citizenship was occasionally granted for honorific reasons.[175]

The Maltese 'Granting of Citizenship for Exceptional Services Regulations'[176] offer an interesting example in this context, but also, more generally, from the perspective of merit-based citizenship acquisition. These Regulations distinguish between 'exceptional contributions', 'exceptional direct investment' and 'exceptional services by merit', three notions which are defined as follows:

> 'exceptional contribution' means manifestly superior and refers primarily to contributions by scientists, researchers, athletes, sports people, artists and cultural performers;
>
> 'exceptional direct investment' means the investment requirement in the Maltese economy as defined in the First Schedule;

[167] ibid 341.

[168] See eg van Oers, *Deserving Citizenship* (Martinus Nijhoff 2014).

[169] Etzioni, 'Citizenship Tests' (2007) 78 *Political Quarterly* 353, 355; Bauböck, 'What Is Wrong with Selling Citizenship?' in R Bauböck (ed), *Debating Transformations of National Citizenship* (Springer 2018) 40.

[170] eg Young, 'Affirmative Action and the Myth of Merit' in *Justice and the Politics of Difference* (Princeton 2011) 206 ff.

[171] This practice must hence be distinguished from honorific grants of 'citizenship' that do not entail the grant of citizenship rights (at least not rights attached to citizenship at the national level), as they exist in Switzerland, for instance.

[172] Shachar, 'Picking Winners' (2011) 120 *YLJ* 2088.

[173] On the distinction between retrospective and prospective models of meritocracy, see DeSario, 'Reconceptualizing Meritocracy' (2003) 38 *Harv. C.R.-C.L. L. Rev.* 479, 485ff.

[174] 'Emmanuel Macron annonce la naturalisation du sans-papiers malien qui a sauvé un enfant du vide' (*Libération*, 27 May 2018) www.liberation.fr/france/2018/05/27/emmanuel-macron-annonce-la-naturalisation-du-sans-papiers-malien-qui-a-sauve-un-enfant-du-vide_1654608/.

[175] Cecchet, 'Greek and Roman Citizenship' in Cecchet and Busetto (eds), *Citizens in the Graeco-Roman World* (Brill-Nijhoff 2017) 8, 15ff. (regarding Ancient Greece), and 12ff, 16 (regarding Ancient Rome).

[176] Granting of Citizenship for Exceptional Services Regulations 2020 (MT).

> 'exceptional services by merit' means exceptional services to the Republic of Malta or to humanity or whose naturalisation is of exceptional interest to the Republic of Malta.[177]

The Regulations thus provide for three grounds of merit-based citizenship acquisition (though 'merit' is explicitly mentioned only in relation to the third category): 'manifestly superior' skills (which amounts to Olympic citizenship); an 'exceptional direct investment' (CBI); and 'exceptional services'. In other words, individuals with outstanding skills, investors, and individuals who have rendered exceptional services to the State are all eligible for citizenship. Once again, this example shows that merit is a pervasive feature of citizenship law.

Grants of citizenship honouring exceptional services exist in other States as well, for example in Austria, Italy and Luxembourg.[178] In Liechtenstein, the Citizenship Act even provides that foreigners may be granted citizenship if they

> have earned merits by promoting the cultural and economic interests of the state or of a municipality, in particular by increasing the earning potential of the population, or if they make a special contribution to increasing the state and municipal revenues.[179]

Thus, in Liechtenstein, merit is explicitly tied to the State's economic interests – like in the case of CBI.

IV. CONCLUSION: OVERCOMING MERITOCRACY IN IMMIGRATION AND CITIZENSHIP LAW

The concept of meritocracy has been neglected in the literature on RBI and CBI, but also in immigration and citizenship law more generally. Yet, meritocratic considerations are pervasive in (public discourse about) these bodies of law. They especially pervade the concept of citizenship itself, which is based on a narrow conception of merit. Meritocracy is an appealing, but deeply problematic ideal: it is used to justify inequality.[180]

Given the problems created by meritocracy, including in immigration and citizenship law, what can be done about it? This final section briefly sketches two ways in which to overcome the problematic meritocratic paradigm without discarding the aspects that make this concept appealing. It is not sufficient to state – as some defenders of investment schemes do[181] – that RBI and CBI are simply a symptom of the broader exclusionary character of immigration and citizenship law. Instead of clinging to the status quo, States must actively avoid the pitfalls of meritocracy.

First, the indeterminate notion of 'merit' needs to be replaced by clearer and more egalitarian criteria. This requires rethinking the way different skills are valued. As Michael Sandel argues, the dignity of labour needs to be restored, and people's diverse contributions to the life of the community need to be acknowledged. Ultimately, immigration and citizenship criteria should be defined democratically instead of being left to the discretion of the political and economic elites, though discriminatory requirements need to be off limits.

[177] ibid, Sect 3 and 5(2).
[178] Džankić, 'Citizenship with a Price Tag' (2014) 65 *NI Legal Quarterly* 387, 398 ff.
[179] Art 16 of the Citizenship Act 1938 (LI).
[180] Sandel, *The Tyranny of Merit*, 122: '[t]he meritocratic ideal is not a remedy for inequality; it is a justification of inequality'.
[181] See references in Kalm, 'The Business of Citizenship', 4.

Second, and relatedly, States should strive to adopt immigration and citizenship laws that provide more equal opportunities to prospective residents and citizens. For one thing, immigration and citizenship procedures should not be biased towards wealth or other forms of privilege. Moreover, they should not be purely backward-looking; instead, they should consider the potential of applicants to make a valuable contribution.

As Sandel puts it, 'sorting for talent and seeking equality are two different projects'.[182] The closer immigration and citizenship law get to egalitarian values, the more they will achieve what makes meritocracy appealing, namely the promise of equal opportunity. This especially requires doing away with immigration and citizenship requirements that are implicitly based on discriminatory considerations. More fundamentally, immigration and citizenship laws must emancipate themselves from meritocratic thinking, of which RBI and CBI are just one particularly visible side effect.

[182] Sandel, *The Tyranny of Merit*, 161.

4

Race and Merit in the Context of Residency and Citizenship by Investment

SARAH GANTY*

I. INTRODUCTION

THIS CHAPTER EXPLORES the role of merit in the legal field as a proxy to allocate public and social goods, as well as legal statuses. I argue that the norm of merit implemented directly or indirectly in immigration and citizenship law reproduces, in many cases, patterns of 'racialisation' or 'ethnicisation' of the 'other' which makes the criterion of merit legally and morally questionable as it reproduces the old 'blood hierarchy'. However, on the basis of the example of residency (RBI) and citizenship by investment programmes (CBI), I explain that critics of meritocracy tread a delicate line, as opposition to meritocratic institutions can itself be influenced by racial and ethnic biases.

RBI and CBI, which imply that a non-citizen will receive a residence permit or citizenship based on some economic contribution (most of the time an investment),[1] are paradigmatic of the tension between merit and race. These programmes have been under virulent attacks for years precisely because they benefit *only* those who can afford them: the meritorious. If these programmes are meritorious *par excellence*, I argue that they are also racially and ethnically loaded to the point that it is impossible to disentangle merit from race and ethnic origin, as can be observed in many current immigration and citizenship policies around the world. However, the virulent attacks against such programmes, especially CBI, show that rejecting merit as a means of distributing public and social goods, as well as legal statuses, can also be racially and/or ethnically charged. In other words, RBI and CBI programmes reveal a conflict between an inclusive meritocratic rationale – the RBI and CBI programmes – and an exclusive anti-meritocratic rationale – suppressing CBI in favour of 'traditional' means of obtaining citizenship – which reproduce racial and ethnic hierarchies. In this context and based on the example of the European Union, I argue that the former should prevail as it constitutes the lesser evil within a system of citizenship apartheid – a global unequal system based on

* I am grateful to the participants in the workshop on 'What's (in) Nationality? Citizenship-by-investment (CBI) and Beyond' organised by the University of Luxembourg and Maastricht University in April 2022, the American Society of International Law seminar on 'Citizenship and Residence Sales: Any Role for International Law?' in May 2023 and the Yale Graduate seminar in April 2024. Special thank you to Monica Bell, Adi Gal, Dimitry Kochenov and Harry Panagopulos for helpful comments on the previous versions of the chapter.

[1] Surak, *The Golden Passport* (Harvard University Press 2023); Surak, 'Investment Migration' in Kochenov and Surak (eds), *Citizenship and Residence Sales* (Cambridge University Press 2023).

blood hierarchies that Dimitry Kochenov defines as follows: 'the central feature of the world's population management, mobilizing law, politics and international relations at the service of the blood-based aristocracy principle underpinning the distribution of resources and opportunities in the world today'.[2]

First, this chapter shows that the meritorious paradigm undergirds immigration and citizenship law and is based on skills (or, less broadly, talent) and effort, or money. Today, besides family ties (eg marriage) and fear of persecution it constitutes the main way to overcome a 'bad' passport attributed at birth (most of the time based on blood) mainly but not exclusively in former colonies (Section II). Second, it shows that behind its common understanding – skills/talent and effort or money – merit is racially and ethnically loaded, especially in immigration and citizenship law, which is morally and even legally problematic: one has to be meritorious – for example talented – per se to overcome the disadvantage of their passport embedded in racial and ethnic hierarchies (Section III). However, and third, it argues that simply suppressing these so-called meritorious programmes, including RBI and CBI programmes, does more harm than good in terms of inclusivity and equality as it does not address the deeper issue of the citizenship apartheid (Section IV). Simply put, opposing the commodification of passport for social justice reasons is illogical and contradictory. Indeed, while it only prevents a privileged few from improving their lives, it does nothing to address the bigger issue of the blood hierarchy and coloniality that lies behind the passports being purchased. Moreover, it does not tackle the system which underpins their cash value.

II. MERIT IN CITIZENSHIP AND IMMIGRATION LAW

This section defines merit, in its usual and contemporary understanding, showing that it constitutes a prevalent criterion in allocating residence permits and citizenship.

Merit as a criterion for allocating public and social goods, power, opportunities, advantages, offices and legal statuses is far from a new phenomenon. From the ancient Greek philosophers and Confucius to Emmanuel Macron and Xi Jinping,[3] merit has been used as a device in justice and politics. Merit as it is commonly used in justifying the allocation of public and social goods, power, opportunities, advantages, offices and legal statuses refers to accomplishments (or future accomplishments). Many public domains such as education, social assistance, civil service, immigration, asylum and citizenship law have (increasingly) incorporated merit (or demerit) as a key criterion for the allocation (or denial) of diplomas, social benefits, positions, residence statuses and citizenships. In this context, merit is often framed in terms of specific talents, skills, language proficiency, integration (potential), economic resources thresholds or other forms of economic added-value that an individual is deemed likely to contribute to the society.[4]

Merit is a blurred concept, though, and varies depending on the context at stake:[5] Evgeny Kissin is considered as a meritorious person when it comes to appreciating musical

[2] Kochenov, 'Citizenship Apartheid' in Kostakopoulou et al (eds), *Elgar Concise Encyclopaedia on Law and Citizenship* (Elgar 2025).

[3] Wooldridge, *The Aristocracy of Talent* (Penguin 2021).

[4] Ganty, 'The Constitutional Politics of Merit' in Tushnet and Kochenov (eds), *Research Handbook on the Politics of Constitutional Law* (Elgar 2023).

[5] Mulligan, 'Meritocracy' in Zalta and Nodelman (eds), *The Stanford Encyclopedia of Philosophy* (first published on 3 August 2023) https://plato.stanford.edu/entries/meritocracy/.

accomplishments, but his musical merits will be of little relevance for the Nobel in physics. In the usual and contemporary understanding, merit in its distributive function is identifiable through two main proxies: skills/talent and effort on the one hand, and money on the other hand. First, merit as skills/talent and effort undergirds the concept of meritocracy, attributed to Michael Young, author of the famous dystopia 'The rise of the Meritocracy'.[6] Michael Young explicitly states that 'Merit = intelligence + effort'.[7] His dystopia deals with a very narrow idea of intelligence measured on the basis of IQ and does not touch upon the broader idea of talent or skills, though.[8] Although Young writes that '[t]he lazy genius is not one', he has little more to say about effort. On the rare occasions he mentions it, it is only in relation to the assessment of wages on the basis of measured effort. In Young's dystopia, there is no competition either – all the meritorious are guaranteed a position related to their merit, that is, their IQ. It is important to understand that though today's rationale for merit is similar – an unequal system justified by talent and effort – the contours of today's merit are not those depicted by Michael Young. Indeed, the presumption that merit is based on intelligence which would be fixed, unitary and determined does not fit contemporary's dominant meritocratic logic.[9] Rather, '[i]ndividuals must now attend to their own "social mobility" [...] applying to "mastery children" who are confident in success, those who believe that they can perpetually improve'.[10] And effort plays a much more central role today, as described by Daniel Markovits in his essay 'the Meritocracy Trap', which diagnoses the harm of today's meritocracy among the US elite. Today, as opposed to Young's dystopia,[11] each individual – or her family – is responsible for identifying her own talent and intelligence and making the necessary effort to develop them – preferably from the moment of birth – to convince the elite institutions of their abilities and motivation, and to work on them to climb the ladder of the social hierarchy. Private investment in talent, skills and effort is therefore crucial in current meritocracies.[12] Skills/talent and effort grow in the intimacy of the private sphere and those who are lucky enough to be born in the right home will thrive. The notion of talent or more broadly skills that meritocratic scholars punctuate in their work is far from straightforward, however. Generally, talent refers to 'a natural skill or ability to be good at something, especially without being taught' while skills is broader as it refers to a special ability to do something well which can be natural and/or based on practice/training and therefore effort.[13] Today's understanding of talent and skills is mainly understood as technocratic expertise in government, military distinctions in the armed services, academic achievements and high-scoring test results in universities, or a person's ability to contribute to the market for immigrants or employees or entrepreneurs whose success is appreciated on the basis of the value of the goods or services they sell (ie the demand) in the economy and so on.[14] Talent and effort compensate each other in that someone less talented but hardworking is likely to be perceived as meritorious in many circumstances and vice and versa, especially when the combination of the two converge into (high)skills.

[6] Young, *The Rise of the Meritocracy, 1870–2033* (Penguin 1958); Floud et al, *Social Class and Educational Opportunity* (Heinemann 1956); Daunton, 'Michael Young and Meritocracy' (2005) 19 *Contemporary British History* 285.
[7] Young, *The Rise of the Meritocracy*, 94.
[8] Talent is indeed defined as 'a natural ability to do something well' and intelligence is far from synonymous to talent.
[9] Allen, 'Michael Young's The Rise of the Meritocracy' (2011) *Br. J. Educ. Stud.* 367.
[10] ibid 377–78.
[11] ibid.
[12] Markovits, *The Meritocracy Trap* (Penguin 2019).
[13] See 'Talent' (Cambridge Dictionary) https://dictionary.cambridge.org/dictionary/english/talent.
[14] Sandel, *The Tyranny of Merit* (Penguin 2020) 31.

Specifically, both immigration and citizenship laws are profoundly shaped by merit as it plays a determining role in allocating immigration and citizenship statuses. In Europe, the immigration process is increasingly based on skills.[15] Generally, it is well-established that many countries around the world want to attract talented, skilled and hard-working people and have put in place special facilities to achieve this, especially in some sectors such as IT.[16] In general, the perception of a migrant's integration into its host community increasingly includes an aspect related to merit or demerit based on skills and effort, assessed through the performance of those 'that live up to the ideals of today's neoliberal markets: self-sufficient, hard-working employees of the formal economy'.[17] Today's so-called civic integration policies impose demanding conditions and obligations on low-skilled migrants, usually exempting non-citizens who are 'wanted' – highly-skilled workers and their families. Furthermore, for a few years now, the concept of desert as merit[18] has played a growing role even in the field of asylum rights (where only hardship counts in principle) and scholars have increasingly showed 'how perceptions of deservingness shape access to mobility, protection and legal status, as well as reception and assistance practices for refugees or other migrants'.[19] For instance, Nathalie Welfens shows that in recent resettlement programmes refugees have to demonstrate not only that they are at risk in their countries of origin or their first country of refuge (hardship), but also that they are 'willing and able to "overcome" their vulnerability to become law-abiding, self-sufficient and culturally malleable future members of their host societies …', which has been qualified as 'promising victimhood'.[20] In other words, they have to show their potential as worthy individuals and, above all, cannot be 'demeritorious'.

In general, citizenship law also makes it easier for the meritorious (ie those who have special skills or who can offer enough economic added-value to society) to naturalise, such as in the example of acquisition of citizenship for highly skilled people or talented people who can just bypass some naturalization requirements on the basis of their skills or talents such as in Germany or in the Netherlands. Being sufficiently hard-working also pays off like in Belgium: having worked continuously for five years constitutes the 'royal road' to the acquisition of nationality as it dispenses with all the social integration conditions, including language proficiency and social integration.[21] In the same vein, Christian Joppke explains that today, social inclusion is intrinsically more closely linked to the labour market than to the nation state as a whole, motivated by an image of society as a 'machinery of performance'.[22] Economic integration is the privileged referent for social integration, but is also related to the nation state as long as it is understood as the allegiance to the *material priorities* of the state. In other words, the idea of integration also encompasses a strong dimension related to merit (making the necessary effort to acquire the necessary skills and become an economic, cultural and social fit)

[15] de Haas et al, 'Growing Restrictiveness or Changing Selection?' (2023) 52 *IMR* 324.

[16] Shachar, 'Selecting By Merit' in Fine and Ypi (eds), *Migration in Political Theory* (Oxford University Press 2016).

[17] Welfens, 'Promising Victimhood' (2023) 49 *JEMS* 1103, 1306.

[18] The concepts of merit and deservingness both relate to each other, but need to be distinguished. We understand merit as the proxy used to determine whether someone deserves a specific positive or negative treatment based on their achievements while desert or deservingness, which is broader, is the device used to determine the justness of the treatments whether legal, social, etc. In short, in line with Tošić and Streinzer, *Ethnographies of Deservingness* 1st edn (Berghahn Books 2022), we argue that merit operates as *a proxy for deservingness*, especially in the field of migration, integration and citizenship governance.

[19] Welfens, 'Promising Victimhood'.

[20] ibid.

[21] Art, 12*bis*(1), 2°, c), d) and e) of Nationality Code (BE).

[22] Joppke, 'Beyond National Models' (2007) 30 *WEP* 1, 8.

that we have called elsewhere 'meritocratic inclusion' which permits the selection and reward of the meritorious.[23]

Second, money can also be associated with merit as it is perceived as the external sign of skills/talent and effort in a capitalist society, especially in migration and citizenship law. If money is prevalent in developing talent and effort as showed by Daniel Markovits – the family enterprise – the reverse is true as well: someone who is relatively rich is likely to be regarded as more meritorious (ie more talented and hard-working) than someone who is not.[24] In other words, financial assets and economic success are proxies for evaluating merit, as diplomas are. Of course, they often overlap, but not always.

Money plays an important role in the fields of citizenship and immigration and, as with skills, is likely to be associated with merit. In fact, there is not much difference between skills or money when it comes to migration or citizenship.[25] Odile Ammann is right that 'the distinction between capital *tout court* and human capital (or talent) is not watertight in practice, and capital can very well be the fruit of a person's merit'.[26] It is certainly true that when it comes to the market and GDP: 'the common good is defined by GDP, and that the value of people's contributions consists in the market value of the goods or services they sell', as Sandel explains.[27] Certainly, not only is the moral justification of merit as market value questionable, but also the fact that someone's market value is considered as 'a good measure of his or her contribution to society'.[28] Citizens in economically unequal societies are less concerned about inequalities than those in more egalitarian societies, because the former situation is 'reflective of merit', which implies skills/talent and effort.[29] In short, that money (and more particularly market value) equals merit, constitutes a political, legal and psychological reality. Of course, this reality ignores the role of luck and the fact that the rich underestimate the importance of luck to their success, as Robert H Frank has compellingly argued.[30] More generally, several intellectuals, including Friedrich von Hayek, have also contended that it is a mistake to think that the money made on the basis of consumer preference would reflect merit. In Hayek's words, '[t]he attempt to achieve a valuable result may be highly meritorious but a complete failure, and full success may be entirely the result of accident and thus without merit'.[31] More importantly, most capital assets in the world are still transferred through the family – as are other kinds of capital.[32] Moreover, when wealth is indeed based on individual achievements (usually the two are inseparable, as money produces money), it usually concerns people who grew up in the right environment to achieve. This does not change the fact that money tends to be perceived as merit and rewarded accordingly by society, as are diplomas. In this context,

[23] Ganty, 'Integration duties in the European Union' (2021) 28 *MJ* 784.

[24] Ammann, 'Passports for Sale' (2020) 22 *EJML* 309.

[25] Erez, 'In for a Penny' (2019) 8 *MPP* 155.

[26] Ammann, 'Passports for Sale', 323. Sandel, *The Tyranny of Merit*, 113–37. Merit also echoes the concept of meritoriousness which designates the fact of being praiseworthy or 'commendable', deserving praise and approval, and comes from the Latin word *meritorious*, which literally means 'brings money'.

[27] Sandel, *The Tyranny of Merit*, 136.

[28] ibid; Anderson, 'What Is The Point of Equality?' (1999) 109 *Ethics* 287, 325.

[29] Heiserman and Simpson, 'Higher Inequality Increases the Gap in the Perceived Merit of the Rich and Poor' (2017) 80 *Social Psychology Quarterly* 243. Mijs, 'The Paradox of Inequality' (2021) 19 *Socio-Economic Review* 7. La Roex et al, 'Attitudes towards Income Inequality' (2019) 62 *Acta Sociologica* 47.

[30] Frank, *Success and Luck* (Princeton University Press 2016).

[31] von Hayek, *The Constitution of Liberty* (Chicago University Press 1978) 94–96; Scanlon, *Why Does Inequality Matter?* (Oxford University Press 2018) 125.

[32] Piketty, 2014. *Capital in the 21st Century* (Harvard University Press 2014); Bourdieu, 'The Forms of Capital' in Richardson (ed), *Handbook of Theory and Research for the Sociology of Education* (Greenwood 1986) 241–58.

antidiscrimination law – which seeks to uncover 'an apprehension of "individual merit"',[33] as discussed in the next section – indirectly justifies socioeconomic inequalities while ethically purifying the market,[34] which is allegedly accessible to all: free of any sin, capital is admired and envied, while the inequalities in the richest countries in the world continue to grow.

The residency or citizenship by investment programmes adopted by several states around the world are an example of money as merit to distribute public and social good implying opportunities and advantages attached to such residence statuses/citizenships:[35] some states consider someone worthy to become a resident or a citizen without any other condition than not being a criminal if she or he has the economic capital to 'buy' a citizenship or visa with cash or investment in the country.[36] This amount varies enormously from one state to another depending on the type of visa applied for. At the other end of the spectrum are the systems which require an individual to demonstrate the absence of demerits in order to receive a visa, for instance by proving sufficient means not to become a 'burden' for the social welfare system of the host country. In contrast to the meritocratic investment programmes, the sufficient means condition comes, of course, with additional requirements, such as having family ties in the host country.

Interestingly, the vision of EU citizenship also endorses an idea of merit based on skills and economic performance – that is, money. Per Mouritsen et al characterise EU citizenship as 'European "citizenship-lite"' and explain that 'the closure of membership is increasingly tied, not to national identity but to employment skills and economic selection within a harder outer (European Union) shell and, at the level of identity and defining values, to a simple preference for "liberal people"'.[37] In other words, EU citizenship mainly benefits a certain class of EU citizen which is even narrower than market citizens[38] – poor workers are excluded[39] – because it mainly benefits an elite, especially a Western European elite.[40]

III. MERIT AS A RACIAL DEVICE

This section explores the strong connection between the norm of merit and race/ethnic origin within the legal field, a link which is well-documented as underpinning the education system in some Western states, with parallels drawn in social welfare, immigration, and citizenship law.

Merit and anti-discrimination law have typically been viewed as ideal companions, whether when considering racial, ethnic, gender or religious discrimination. In the words of the US Supreme Court: 'One of the principal reasons race is treated as a forbidden classification is that it demeans the dignity and worth of a person to be judged by ancestry instead of by his or her own merit and essential qualities.'[41] However, the relationship between merit and equality

[33] Post, *Prejudicial Appearances, The Logic of American Antidiscrimimination Law* (Duke University Press 2001) 16.

[34] Somek, 'Antidiscrimination and Decommodification' (2005) U Iowa Legal Studies Research Paper No. 05-03; Somek, *Engineering Equality* (Oxford University Press 2011).

[35] Ammann, 'Passports for Sale'.

[36] Kochenov and Surak (eds), *Citizenship and Residence Sales* (Cambridge 2023).

[37] Mouritsen et al, 'Introduction: Theorizing the Civic Turn in European Integration Policies' (2019) 19 *Ethnicities* 595, 596.

[38] Kochenov, 'The Oxymoron of "Market Citizenship"' in Amtenbrink et al (eds), *The Internal Market and the Future of European Integration* (Cambridge University Press 2019).

[39] O'Brien, '*Civis Capitalist Sum*' (2016) 53 *CMLRev.* 937.

[40] Ganty, 'Integration Duties'.

[41] *Rice v Cayetano* [2000] 528 US 495, 517.

is much more complicated than simply combating any discrimination on grounds of a suspect criterion. Indeed, meritocracy has not achieved the promise of equality it carries; quite the opposite, I argue that it is nothing more than a reproduction of social hierarchies 'through transformation', in the words of Reva Siegel.[42]

Nowadays, that meritocracy is a failed promise in terms of equality has been widely documented in the field of education and even acknowledged by the proponents of meritocracy, arguing that this is not 'true' meritocracy:[43] merit reproduces social hierarchies, especially racial and ethnic hierarchies. In other words, race and merit are closely linked. As developed below, it is important to understand race and ethnic origin in general, including in the context of merit, as based on the social meaning giving to racial and ethnic characteristics and not limited to the mere existence of these very characteristics.

In the recent past, merit was distorted by some Ivy League schools to ensure that unwelcome talented students would not be too numerous: merit was based on holistic and dynamic assessments which justified informal quotas on Jews among others.[44] Now universities pride themselves that their need-blind admission policies through standardised merit tests select students exclusively on their talents and achievements, independently of their ability to pay, their race or their political connections. However, the picture is much less rosy and simple that it would appear. Students with political connections or money are still privileged, although soliciting or providing such preferences openly would be regarded as corruption.[45] Moreover, merit is today used to oppose programmes promoting the inclusion of racial and ethnic minorities, as done by the mainly white anti-affirmative action movement which embraces the success of Asian Americans in order to oppose affirmative action ('they were able to overcome their hardship and discrimination which proves that affirmative actions are not necessary').[46] This is also the conception embraced and recalled recently by Justice Thomas in the recent *Students for Fair Admissions v Harvard* case:

> meritocratic systems have long refuted bigoted misperceptions of what black students can accomplish … Meritocratic systems, with objective grading scales, are critical to that belief. Such scales have always been a great equalizer – offering a metric for achievement that bigotry could not alter. Racial or ethnic preferences take away this benefit, eliminating the very metric by which those who have the most to prove can clearly demonstrate their accomplishments – both to themselves and to others.[47]

However and strikingly, merit is still predominantly white (and native born citizen) in Europe and the US, as most of the racial and ethnic minorities are underrepresented in the so-called elite educational institutions, unable to match the admission criteria, including the highly selective examinations. In other words, the idea that meritocracy is 'objective' is a smokescreen and the conception of merit varies enormously, with more or less impact on certain groups.[48]

Racial and ethnic minorities do usually not perform well on the meritocratic scale, because of structural disadvantages they have faced their whole lives and for generations. Whether in France, the UK or in the US, it is striking that most of the racial and ethnic minorities are underrepresented in the best schools and universities: 'Because talent lives everywhere, but

[42] Siegel, 'Why Equal Protection No Longer Protects' (1996–97) 49 *Stan. L. Rev.* 1111; Siegel, '"The Rule of Love": Wife Beating as Prerogative and Privacy' (1996) 105 *YLJ* 2117; Ganty, 'The Constitutional Politics of Merit'.

[43] Wooldridge, *The Aristocracy of Talent*.

[44] Karabel, *The Chosen* (Houghton Mifflin 2005).

[45] ibid; Park and Liu, 'Interest Convergence or Divergence?' (2014) 85 *JHE* 36.

[46] Park and Liu, 'Interest Convergence or Divergence?'.

[47] *Students for Fair Admissions v Harvard* [2023] 600 US 181.

[48] Park and Liu, 'Interest Convergence or Divergence?'.

opportunity does not, there are undoubtedly talented students with great academic potential who have simply not had the opportunity to attain the traditional indicia of merit that provide a competitive edge in the admissions process.'[49] Interestingly, the only way for an individual at the bottom of the social ladder to climb it is to be even more meritorious than their privileged peers. In other words, the system is porous enough to let the *crème-de-la-crème* of the talented at the bottom of the society to thrive while the rest has simply no perspective of improvement, because much less opportunities. Moreover, even when some minorities perform well, such as Asian American in the US for example, they are still likely to suffer from negative action, meaning that these minorities tend to be displaced by the majority – that is, with the same test results white Americans are still more likely to be admitted.[50] In the same vein, it is not a given that white opponents of affirmative action (especially alumni funders for instance) would truly embrace standardised conceptions of merit which would imply that Asian American would suddenly dramatically increase in representation in the most-elite universities: 'they want quantifiable standards of merit when they keep out supposedly unqualified URMs but appear willing to dismiss such rigidity if it works against their self-interest'.[51] In fact

> Asian Americans complicate the affirmative action debate by providing evidence that merit is actually a highly flexible, subjective, and dynamic concept tied to the interests of various stakeholders … Asian American admissions trends demonstrate that the idea of merit is neither concrete nor transparent; rather, it is a contextually defined and determined concept.[52]

Finally, even *among* migrants or racial and ethnic minorities, merit is racially loaded. The example of the Asian American community in the US is striking since there are important disparities between Asian subgroups (Indians and Korean Americans tend to 'perform' better than Southeast Asian Americans according to today's academic standards), which even prompted some – controversially – to attribute special meritorious qualities to certain ethnic and racial groups as opposed to others.[53]

Merit (or demerit) as a means for distributing public and social goods, as well as legal statuses among others, also constitutes a racial device in contexts beyond education. Merit (or demerit) is increasingly used as an implicit or explicit heuristic device racially and ethnically biased to design social welfare requirements such as language conditions imposed in some European countries as a precondition for access to social benefits or social housing, as in Belgium, Austria and the Netherlands.[54] Language requirements serve as a means to demonstrate that applicants are potentially meritorious, or at least not demeritorious, by showcasing their self-responsibility, ability to overcome precarious circumstances, and capacity to contribute to society. Arguably, such conditions have an impact on immigrants or citizens with an immigrant background and is likely to constitute racial or ethnic discrimination. This argument has been brought before the European Court of Justice (ECJ) considering otherwise and

[49] As argued by Harvard Student and Alumni Organizations in their *Amici Curia*, ibid.

[50] Park and Liu, 'Interest Convergence or Divergence?'.

[51] ibid 46–47.

[52] ibid.

[53] Eg Chua and Rubenfeld, *The Triple Package: How Three Unlikely Traits Explain the Rise and Fall of Cultural Groups in America* (Penguin Press 2014).

[54] Art 6.20 para 1, 5° and 6°, Housing Code 2021 (for Flanders, Belgium); para 6 (9), Oberösterreichisches Wohnbauförderungsgesetz (Upper Austrian Law on Housing Construction Subsidies) (LGBl. 6/1993) (for Austria); Art 18, Wet van 2 juli 2014 tot wijziging van de Wet werk en bijstand, de Wet sociale werkvoorziening, de Wet werk en arbeidsondersteuning jonggehandicapten en enige andere wetten gericht op bevordering deelname aan de arbeidsmarkt voor mensen met arbeidsvermogen en harmonisatie van deze regelingen (Invoeringswet Participatiewet) (for the Netherlands).

adopting a very narrow definition of race and ethnic origin.[55] The narrow definition of racial or ethnic origin spelled out by the ECJ is problematic because it relies on the idea of racial and ethnic minorities as more or less static groups, whose existence can be objectively ascertained by tagging a combination of characteristics (language, religion, etc). The Court failed 'to understand the dynamics of racial discrimination which depend, ultimately, not on the existence of certain "ethnic" characteristics but on the social meaning given to them',[56] making it impossible to recognise the racial or ethnic dimension of such integration conditions imposed on migrants. The International Court of Justice (ICJ) also recently faced criticism for its approach towards race discrimination in relation to citizenship and nationality: it 'assumed that treatment based on race (which includes national origin) and nationality were mutually exclusive … [failing] to acknowledged that there might be an overlap between nationality and national or ethnic origin'.[57] Furthermore, discrimination law generally fails to grasp structural racism – understood as 'as embedded in the social, economic, cultural and political dimensions of the State itself'[58] – as argued by Shreya Atrey while racism 'exists not as a historical fact fixed in time but as a constantly evolving and mutating phenomenon whose actual modalities are forever shifting'.[59] This observation can be extended to the racism entrenched in immigration and citizenship policies since in the words of Achiume race plays the function of border: 'Race emerges as an illegality detection and production mechanism, as border infrastructure relied upon to presumptively exclude, subordinate, and immobilize through nonwhiteness, while presumptively including and facilitating the mobility through whiteness'.[60]

In fact, the use of merit operationalised through language tests mirrors a broader tendency towards the racialisation/ethnicisation of welfare support as a means of advancing welfare state cutbacks, as was done in Austria.[61] It also reflects common public views that 'the migrant "other" is often classified as *per se* undeserving' when determining 'who should get what',[62] a situation which can be overcome mainly by merit (or at least the absence of demerit) or by appealing to specific vulnerabilities,[63] when one does not have the 'right' passport.

In the context of migration and citizenship, the link between racial or ethnic origin and merit is significant. While merit increasingly influences migrant selection criteria, as previously discussed, data and reality show that citizenship and origin remain the primary determinants of who is granted entry, residence and citizenship.[64] Indeed, despite the growing importance of skills and money in migration and citizenship law, the broader citizenship system is organised today in such a way as to keep people from the former European colonies and other racialized groups out.[65] Citizenship is connected to race and ethnic origin,[66] leading Boatcă to speak of

[55] Case C-94/20 *Land Oberösterreich v KV* ECLI:EU:C:2021:477.

[56] Ganty and de Vries, 'Non-discrimination in European Social Security Law' in Vonk and Pennings (eds), *Research Handbook on European Social Security Law* (Elgar 2023).

[57] Costello and Foster, 'Race Discrimination Effaced at the International Court of Justice' (2021) 115 *AJIL Unbound* 339, 248; See in particular: *Application of the International Convention on the Elimination of All Forms of Racial Discrimination* (Qatar v UAE) [2021] ICJ Rep. 71, para 81.

[58] Atrey, 'Structural Racism and Race Discrimination' (2021) 74 *Current Legal Problems* 1.

[59] ibid 9.

[60] Achiume, 'Racial Borders' (2022) 110 *Geo. LJ* 445, 485.

[61] Schadauer, 'The Racialization of Welfare Support as Means to Further Welfare State Cutbacks' (2022) 45 *Ethn. Racial Stud.* 308.

[62] ibid; Harell et al, 'Race, Prejudice and Attitudes toward Redistribution' (2016) 55 *EJPR* 723.

[63] van Oorschot, 'Making the Difference in Social Europe' (2016) 16 *JESP* 23.

[64] Ganty et al, 'The Meritorious 'Other' and The Interconnection of Merit and Race in EU migration Law and Policy' (2025) (on file with the author).

[65] Boatcă, 'The Colonial Institution of Citizenship and Global Capitalist Dynamics' in Kochenov and Surak (eds), *Citizenship and Residence Sales*, 259.

[66] Kochenov, *Citizenship* (MIT Press 2019).

the 'coloniality of citizenship rights',[67] although the international law and the human rights system still fails to recognise it.[68] In other words, citizenship has replaced the racial hierarchies without suppressing it. Today, the citizenship(s) a person has are deemed as a justification for differentiated treatment, including when drowning in the Mediterranean or dying of cold at the EU-Belarusian border.[69] Law, in particular international and European human rights law, is in a profound denial regarding the link between citizenship and race or ethnic origin. Immigration cases brought before the European Court of Human Rights (ECtHR) are usually not perceived as racially or ethnically loaded and do not trigger the prohibition of racial or ethnic discrimination. In some instances, even the law itself explicitly refuses to draw any link or connection between immigration, citizenship and race, EU law being a paradigmatic example.[70] In this context, it is striking that merit serves as a so-called 'objective device' to select while in fact being racially and ethnically loaded. It is mainly people from the former colonies and the Global South more generally who have to show their meritoriousness to overcome the shortcomings of their passports by getting a residence status or a better citizenship.[71] In this context, merit appears to whitewash selection by origin and therefore blood.

On the one hand, when people with 'bad' passports wish to access Western countries, they are targeted through requirements such as cultural and language tests (so-called 'integration tests') which indirectly discriminate against them on grounds of race or ethnic origin. These tests measure the potential worth, making sure they are not 'demeritorious'. For instance, the Netherlands only requires migrants of certain nationalities to comply with pre-entry civic integration tests while others – the citizens of the so-called 'Western countries' – are exempted from such tests. Of course, this difference in treatment is directly based on nationality (which in principle calls for very weighty reasons).[72] But the derogation also indirectly discriminates on the basis of race and ethnic origin, because certain ethnic minorities such as migrants from the Maghreb are over-represented among the visa applicants obliged to pass those tests.[73] The indirect racial and ethnic distinction made by the pre-entry integration tests mirrors the integration requirements imposed on Dutch citizens of Caribbean origin in 2009, which was repealed 18 months after its adoption.[74] Moreover, in several European countries, Turkish

[67] Boatcă, 'The Colonial Institution', 261; the author defines coloniality of citizenship rights 'in close interconnection with modernity as a set of political, economic and sociocultural hierarchies between colonizers and colonized that emerged with the conquest of the New World in the sixteenth century. Coloniality is thus distinct from premodern forms of colonial rule in that it translates administrative hierarchies into a racial/ethnic division of labor; and it is more encompassing than modern European colonialism alone, in that it transfers both the racial/ethnic hierarchies – the "colonial difference" – and the international division of labor produced during the time of direct or indirect colonial rule into postindependence times'.

[68] Costello and Foster, 'Race Discrimination Effaced at the International Court of Justice'; Costello and Foster, '(Some) Refugees Welcome' (2022) 22 *IJDL* 244; Baumgärtel and Ganty, 'On the Basis of Migratory Vulnerability' (2024) 20 *Int'l JL Context* 92–112.

[69] Kochenov and Ganty, 'EU Lawlessness Law' (2024) 30 *CJEL* 78.

[70] Ganty and de Vries, 'Non-discrimination in European Social Security Law'.

[71] ibid; Costello and Foster, '(Some) Refugees Welcome'; Achiume, 'Racial Borders'; Achiume, 'Digital Racial Borders' (2021) 115 *AJIL Unbound* 333. de Vries and Spijkerboer, 'Race and the Regulation of International Migration' (2021) 39 *Netherlands Quarterly of Human Rights* 291; Kochenov and Ganty, 'EU Lawlessness Law'.

[72] Gerards, 'The Margin of Appreciation Doctrine, the Very Weighty Reasons Test and Grounds of Discrimination' in Balboni (ed), *The Principle of Discrimination and the European Convention of Human Rights* (Editoriale Scientifica 2017).

[73] See also FitzGerald et al, 'Can You Become One of Us?' (2018) 44 *JEMS* 27; Mügge and van der Haar, 'Who Is an Immigrant and Who Requires Integration?' in Garcés-Mascareñas and Penninx (eds), *Integration Processes and Policies in Europe* (Springer 2016).

[74] Besselink, 'Inburgeringsplichten voor Nederlanders' in Addink et al (eds), *Grensverleggend Bestuursrecht* (Kluwer 2008) 137.

families were overwhelmingly subjected to integration requirements as pre-departure conditions, exemplifying the targeting of 'non-Western' groups. On the basis of the standstill clause of the EU–Turkey association agreement, the ECJ deemed such practices in countries like Denmark[75] and Germany[76] unlawful when applied to Turks. However, the ECJ reasoning is not beyond criticism as it entirely disregards the racial and ethnic dimensions underlying such tests and conditions,[77] which are still overwhelmingly imposed on 'non-Western' migrants.

On the other hand, migrants with 'bad' passports are indirectly impacted by merit-based immigration criteria such as high skills requirements for obtaining certain types of residence permits – such as the EU blue card – which help to improve opportunities and ensure a decent standard of living. Indeed, the proportion of highly-skilled workers from non-Western countries, particularly sub-Saharan African countries, remains very low relative to their population size.[78] In this context, merit serves as a mechanism to select a limited number of individuals from the former colonies and other non-Western countries – those deemed sufficiently meritorious to contribute added-value through their skills – while enabling European countries to avoid 'a critical mass' or 'an influx' of non-Western migrants. In turn, merit becomes for them a tool to offset a 'bad' passport and overcome the implicit barriers of selection based on origin.

All in all, these migration requirements have had one common impact: excluding the demeritorious, including the meritorious and tolerating the 'neither demeritorious nor meritorious' under the condition of some potential 'promising worth' when other criteria are met (eg family ties or fear of persecution).[79] Within this dynamic, racial and ethnic criteria indirectly play a central role, creating additional tensions when it comes to the contested RBI or CBI programmes, as argued in the last section of this chapter.[80]

IV. THE CASE OF RESIDENCY OR CITIZENSHIP BY INVESTMENT PROGRAMMES

Citizenship is today's main factor in global inequality, as Milanović shows, through what he calls a 'citizenship premium' shaping the privileges awarded by the Global North citizenships and implying that being born in the Global North such as the US or Canada multiplies a person's income by almost a hundred times in comparison to a person born in the Global South, be that Congo, Cambodia or Colombia.[81] Residency or citizenship by investment allows sufficiently wealthy individuals born in the 'wrong' parts of the world to 'buy' a visa or passport to help them multiply their opportunities and improve their lives. It is important to bear in mind that people do not so much use these programmes for migratory reasons – that is, to move permanently to a specific place – but simply to upgrade their status, gain access to more rights to move freely and work around the globe and escape the burdens of their

[75] Case C-89/18 *A v Udlændinge- og Integrationsministeriet* ECLI:EU:C:2019:580; Case C-279/21 *X v Udlændingenævnet* ECLI:EU:C:2022:1019; Case C-561/14 *Caner Genc v Integrationsministeriet* ECLI:EU:C:2016:247.

[76] Case C-138/13 *Naime Dogan v Bundesrepublik Deutschland* ECLI:EU:C:2014:2066; Case C-123/17 *Nefiye Yön v Landeshauptstadt Stuttgart* ECLI:EU:C:2018:632.

[77] Ganty, 'Silence is Not (Always) Golden' (2021) 23 *EJML* 176; interestingly, the ECtHR has found that, in the case of Denmark, the integration condition of the closest link constitutes a discrimination on grounds on race/ethnic origin when only native are exempted from it as opposed to citizens holding the Danish citizenship for less than 28 years: *Biao v Denmark* [GC], no. 38590/10, 24 May 2016.

[78] Ganty et al, 'The Meritorious 'Other''.

[79] Welfens, 'Promising Victimhood'.

[80] Karabel, *The Chosen* (Houghton Mifflin 2005).

[81] Milanović, *Global Inequality* (Harvard University Press 2016).

original citizenship, among other reasons.[82] These programmes exist everywhere and grew in EU countries following the 2008 global financial crisis.[83] The EU accounts for one third of the market for the RBI, including Denmark, France, Netherlands, Portugal, Latvia, Greece and Germany. As for the CBI programmes, today only Malta has one in the EU (Cyprus did until 2020).

The limits of RBI or CBI programmes are quite blurred,[84] but whatever form they might take – entrepreneurial and business visa programmes, residence by investment programmes, discretionary economic citizenship or citizenship by investment – they all follow the neoliberal individual rationale of merit. Agreeing with Ammann, I have already explained why: there is not much difference between financial capital and human capital, that is, skills. In this section, I discuss the meritorious aspect of RBI and CBI programmes and the opposition to them, through the lens of race and ethnic origin. I argue that the objection to these programs, which amount to an anti-meritocratic stance, is also entangled with racial and ethnic biases, creating an additional quandary given the racial and ethnic dimensions that undergird such programmes.

As most immigration policies based on a merit rationale, these programmes are racially and ethnically loaded. Indeed, it is precisely the 'coloniality of citizenship rights' and therefore the racial premise that they are based on,[85] 'which makes it possible to turn the globally scarce goods of citizenship and residence of former colonial powers into commodities on investor markets'.[86] Moreover, RBI and CBI programmes from the Global North are only open to a few citizenships – second-class citizenships – and many nationalities including Iranian, Sudanese and so on, are simply excluded from these programmes. The main nationalities to benefit are Chinese, citizens from Middle Eastern countries and Russians.[87] In this context, CBI and RBI appear as another ideal target for the critiques of meritocracy. Solely based on wealth – which could in fact be family wealth and not rooted in any personal achievements – the world's second-rate citizens can simply buy what people tend to see as an uncommodified institution par excellence, which is itself a product of our colonial past. In recent years, RBI and especially CBI programmes have found very vocal and powerful opponents, including the European Commission and the European Parliament, although the idea that residency and citizenship may be obtained for a price is nothing new and can be traced back to ancient Greece.[88]

RBI and especially CBI programmes in the EU have come under strong criticism, mainly from the European Commission towards Cyprus (which has suspended its CBI programme) and Malta.[89] The main arguments against the commodification of this vaunted EU citizenship are related to security, money laundering, tax evasion and corruption,[90] as well as EU values (especially the principle of sincere cooperation) and the very concept of EU citizenship,

[82] Kochenov, 'Victims of Citizenship' in Kochenov and Surak (eds), *Citizenship and Residence Sales*.

[83] Surak, *The Golden Passport*; Surak, 'Investment Migration'; Lindeboom and Meunier, 'In the Shadow of the Euro Crisis' in Kochenov and Surak (eds), *Citizenship and Residence Sales*.

[84] Surak, *The Golden Passport*; Surak, 'Investment Migration'.

[85] Boatcă, 'The Colonial Institution of Citizenship', 261.

[86] ibid, 260.

[87] Surak, *The Golden Passport*; Surak, 'Investment Migration'.

[88] Surak, 'Investment Migration', 50; Roy, 'The "Streetlight Effect" in Commentary on Citizenship by Investment' in Kochenov and Surak (eds), *Citizenship and Residence Sales*; Prak, 'Citizenship for Sale in Pre-modern Europe' in Kochenov and Surak (eds), *Citizenship and Residence Sales*, 209–22.

[89] Interestingly, money is the main problem here while talents and skills are not.

[90] European Commission, 'Investor Citizenship and Residence Schemes in the European Union' COM(2019) 12final.

because of the alleged absence of any genuine link with a territory of the EU.[91] All these arguments have been convincingly disproved.[92] Interestingly, money (the very commodification of citizenship) appears to be the main problem here, while talents and skills are usually not: many EU countries naturalise people based on their exceptional accomplishments or talents even without residency.[93]

In fact, the genuine link argument (ie that people who invest in a country are not considered as having a genuine link when compared with people who reside or have an employment contract in the country) is an indirect opposition to economic meritocracy, implying that people are rewarded – that is, given citizenship – on the basis of their merit – that is, investment. That the genuine link principle from the infamous ICJ *Nottebohm* decision is no longer good law has been already widely commented on in the literature.[94] As put by Petra Weingerl and Matjaž Tratnik, only 'relevant links' could be considered as appropriate to justify the grant and maintenance of nationality and 'which links are relevant should be left to state autonomy, that is, it is for each individual state to decide', including the criteria of 'state interest' which can imply investment.[95] In any case, the assumption that work constitutes a real link while investment does not is quite surprising and shows the flexibility and the absolute lack of transparency of this concept, which allows those in power to use it as a device to include the wanted and exclude the unwanted. Indeed, opposing investment-based migration while welcoming skill-based migration is normatively inconsistent as Erez powerfully argued: disapproving the former should imply disapproving the latter.[96]

What is more, this genuine link is openly discriminatory on the basis of blood: having citizens in your ancestry can be sufficient per se to prove a real link while monetary investment in the country might not. As a matter of fact, blood based-transfer of citizenship has never been questioned by the EU Commission, echoing Hans Kundnani's diagnosis of *Eurowhiteness* that an ethnic/cultural version of European identity which is externally exclusive is becoming stronger and is an expression of regionalism, analogous to nationalism rather than the opposite of it.[97]

In other words, rejecting the meritorious institution of CBI programmes amounts to indirectly supporting non-disclosed nationalist and racist goals, to prevent some out-group individuals from thriving and rising according to their capacities. Indeed, opponents to citizenship by investment do not denounce it because they would like to oppose the inequalities underlying the institution of citizenship; quite the contrary – they want to keep their club limited to those who have the right blood.[98] For instance, the Council of the European Union suspended the visa exemption with Vanuatu because it considered that the CBI programmes operated by Vanuatu (mainly for Chinese citizens)[99] – 40 per cent of Vanuatu GDP – were used to circumvent the EU short-stay visa procedure and were problematic for the internal security

[91] ibid. Also, European Parliament, 'Report with proposals to the Commission on citizenship and residence by investment schemes' 2021/2026(INL) [2022] and European Commission, 'Recommendation on immediate steps in the context of the Russian invasion of Ukraine in relation to investor citizenship schemes and investor residence schemes' C (2022)2028 final.

[92] Roy, 'The "Streetlight Effect"'; Jessurun d'Oliveira in this volume.

[93] Erez, 'In for a Penny'.

[94] Spiro in this volume.

[95] Weingerl and Tratnik, 'Relevant Links' in Kochenov and Surak (eds), *Citizenship and Residence Sales*, 168.

[96] Erez, 'In for a Penny'.

[97] Kundnani, *Eurowhiteness* (Hurst 2023).

[98] Kochenov and Basheska in this volume.

[99] Surak, *The Golden Passport*; Surak, 'Investment Migration'.

of the European Union.[100] Dimitry Kochenov and Wiliam Thomas Worster argue that it constitutes the return of 'neo-colonialist practice by the former colonizing powers'.[101] Specifically, the EU Commission opposed Venuatu's CBI programme because it granted passports to individuals from 'dubious' states which are on the Schengen visas 'black list': 'the countries of origin of successful applicants include some that are typically excluded from other citizenship schemes, such as Iran and Afghanistan, and other countries whose nationals require a visa for short stays in the EU, including Nigeria, Yemen, Syria, Pakistan and Libya'.[102] It brings to light how the EU is pressuring the former colonies to keep as clear as possible the racial and ethnic divide based on citizenship which prevents many wealthy citizens from outside the Global North from enjoying better mobility and the former colonies from enjoying important incomes related to such mobility.[103] In any case, whatever reasons are advanced for rejecting such programmes, it implies an anti-meritocratic move in practice, if we agree with the definition of merit I previously provided: that merit is skills/talent, and effort and money.

Moreover, the special focus by the EU Commission against Russian citizens following the invasion in Ukraine is paradigmatic of the discriminatory rationale defended by opponents of CBI specifically targeting nationalities which overlap with racial or ethnic groups:

> It also called upon all Member States to stop operating their investor citizenship and residence schemes for all Russian applicants with immediate effects. In addition, it urged Member States to reassess all approved applications from Russian nationals over the past few years.[104]

As in the case of the visa ban against Russian citizens unlawfully imposed by the Baltic countries, Poland and Finland, and based purely on an outdated retribution against the 'enemy alien',[105] it is possible to understand such objections as targeting Russian citizens as an ethnic group, no matter how diverse that ethnic group may be. In this case, the opposition to citizenship by investment is ethnically or even racially loaded, including towards others considered as 'white' such as Russian. Certain white groups can be racialised or ethnicised and discriminated against on this basis, especially if we acknowledge that race and ethnic origin should not be restricted to some 'objective characteristics' (eg phenotypes) but rather understood in terms of their social meaning which encompasses a geopolitical-economic dimension, among other factors.[106] Of course, establishing that a difference in treatment based on nationality amounts to racial or ethnic discrimination can be challenging, particularly when interpreted in the light of the ICJ case law, as previously explained.[107] However, this case law has been widely criticised and it seems unreasonable to deny that nationality is not related to

[100] Council Decision 2022/366 on the partial suspension of the application of the Agreement between the European Union and the Republic of Vanuatu on the short-stay visa waiver [2022] OJ L69/105. In general, the concepts of 'internal security' and the so-called 'instrumentalization' have increasingly been used by the EU and its Member States to exclude undesirable non-Western citizens en masse (eg Violeta Moreno-Lax, *Crisis as (Asylum) Governance*, (2024) 9 *Eur Papers* 179; Ganty et al, 'EU Lawlessness Law at the EU-Belarusian Border: Torture and Dehumanisation Excused by "Instrumentalisation"' (2024) 16 *HJRL* 739).

[101] Kochenov and Worster, 'EU's Neocolonialism' (EU Law Live 2022).

[102] European Commission, 'Proposal for a Council Decision on the partial suspension of the application of the Agreement between the European Union and the Republic of Vanuatu on the short-stay visa waiver' COM(2022) 6 final, 2.

[103] Surak, *The Golden Passport*; Surak, 'Investment Migration'.

[104] European Commission, 'Recommendation on immediate steps in the context of the Russian invasion of Ukraine in relation to investor citizenship schemes and investor residence schemes' C (2022)2028 final, recital 11 of the preamble; para 5.

[105] Ganty et al, 'Unlawful Nationality-Based Bans from the Schengen Zone' (2023) 48 *YJIL Online*.

[106] Lewicki, 'East–West Inequalities and theAambiguous Racialisation of "Eastern Europeans"', (2023) 49 *JEMS* 1481.

[107] *Qatar v U.A.E.*, 74–105.

race and ethnic origin while most of the historical, political and sociological evidence points in that direction.[108]

In fact, applying an anti-meritocratic rationale to oppose RBI and CBI simply means indirectly supporting the reproduction and modernisation of racial and ethnic hierarchies even more than if these programmes were supported. Indeed, as in the debate for education, we should be cautious about how we use the anti-meritocratic rationale, which, like the holistic and dynamic criteria of merit itself, is geared towards the interests of white stakeholders from the Global North. The closure of CBI or even RBI programmes would restrict immigration and citizenship policies and leans towards more segregation: instead of making our society more inclusive and allowing more people to access a residence status or 'good' citizenship, we would close one of those rare doors available to people with a second-rate citizenship to improve their lives, which would simply level down the state of migration and mobility. Today, it would be unimaginable to critics of meritocracy in education that abolishing meritocracy would amount to a return to racial segregation. This is not the case when it comes to immigration and citizenship, however: rejecting meritocracy in those fields implies depriving some people from the opportunity of freeing themselves from the blood hierarchy they are trapped in, without any other alternative. Why then should CBI or even RBI programmes be closed to make the system of citizenship apartheid worse and to deprive some people of getting out of it? In this context, rejecting meritocracy amounts to support a more serious form of apartheid: the citizenship apartheid, a form of modern racial and ethnic segregation.[109]

V. CONCLUSION

Any kind of hierarchy should be treated with caution, whether it is meritocratic or anti-meritocratic. The critiques of meritocracy should be geared towards the suppression of social hierarchies rather than an ideological anti-neoliberalism which locks people in their countries, including those who are economically privileged. In other words, when a society is unable to organise itself differently, merit appears as a lesser evil, whether we are discussing the field of education, citizenship or migration and despite the major differences in legislating in those fields. It is also a symptom of a society unable to be creative when thinking and fighting against hierarchies. While the US was stuck with segregation 70 years ago, which was regarded as the lesser evil compared to slavery, today it is stuck with meritocracy as the lesser evil compared to segregation. When merit, whether talent, skills, effort or money, becomes the only way to overcome deeper disadvantages such as having the 'wrong' citizenship, it is difficult to oppose it until the moment borders and citizenship become more inclusive. It would be unthinkable today to return to a system of racial segregation in education, which this is why the critiques of meritocracy – implying, in theory, that anyone can thrive regardless of their race, gender, religion and so on – can be expressed safely. This is not the case with citizenship, where blood hierarchy is still the rule. It is therefore important to use the anti-meritocracy argument with caution in this context not to reinforce the citizenship apartheid as well as racial and ethnic divides based on passports.

[108] Costello and Foster, 'Race Discrimination Effaced at the International Court of Justice'.
[109] Kochenov, *Citizenship*.

II.

Legal Regulation: Empirical and Normative Perspectives on Investor Migration

5

Nottebohm *and 'Genuine Link'* Anatomy of a Jurisprudential Illusion

PETER J SPIRO

I. INTRODUCTION

NATIONALITY PRACTICES HAVE generally fallen outside the ambit of international law. No other major element of governance has been so untouched by international constraints. This is surprising given the place of nationality (now conceived as citizenship) in the determination of rights. But perhaps it is not so surprising. Nationality is supremely important to the state project, insofar as it is the boundary delimitation – more even than territory – that constitutes the state. Nationality is the starting point for self-determination. In that respect it allows for minimal external imposition. In the wake of the human rights revolution, international law has made some limited inroads into what was largely within the state's sole discretion.[1] But these inroads have been targeted almost exclusively at the denial or revocation of nationality. International law may be looking to put citizenship attribution to work as part of a broad agenda to expand human rights.

But there are no such international law trends with respect to the consensual attribution of citizenship. If anything, international law has come to see citizenship attribution as an unmitigated good, assuming a willing recipient. This destination is the product of the historically entrenched discretion afforded states over nationality practices now buttressed by the rights agenda. Both point to the grant of citizenship as one that should not be subject to external assessment or interference.

Among the very few derogations from this over-arching rule of non-interference looms the International Court of Justice 1955 decision in the *Nottebohm* case.[2] It looms large in part because there have been so few broad rulings relating to the attribution of nationality. It looms large because its facts, stylised as they are, could have been written for a law school examination. And, finally, the case looms large because court's opinion is broadly framed, exploring the elusive nature of the citizen-state relationship.

But none of these elements engendering *Nottebohm*'s notoriety add weight to its decisional authority. Perhaps the contrary. The case is most famous for articulating a supposed requirement that an individual have 'genuine links' to a state asserting the individual's interest on the international plane. The putative 'genuine link' requirement for the allocation of citizenship

[1] Spiro, 'A New International Law of Citizenship' (2013) 105 *AJIL* 694.
[2] *Nottebohm* (Liechtenstein v Guatemala) [1955] ICJ Rep. 4.

is loosely bandied about in some legal and policymaking circles as if it were a hard-and-fast rule of international law. In fact, the 'genuine link' test has been vigorously contested since its first articulation in *Nottebohm*. 'Genuine link' makes even less sense in the wake of globalisation than it did in the world of the mid-twentieth century. As individuals become more highly mobile and are enabled to maintain multiple citizenships, the prospect of sorting supposedly authentic citizenship from instrumental citizenship is a fool's errand. A chorus of academic commentary has declared 'genuine link' a dead letter. International law is not about to start constraining states in their allocation of citizenship among willing recipients now.

In short, 'genuine link' is not and never was a requirement for international recognition of the attribution of nationality.

II. THE HISTORICAL BACKDROP

'Genuine link' must first of all be situated against a preexisting legal backdrop in which international law imposed almost no limitation on state sovereign discretion respecting nationality practice. States could – and did – set the terms of birthright citizenship, naturalisation and expatriation as they saw fit. States could be restrictive in their grants of nationality, as was the case among some continental states like Germany, or liberal, as was true of the United States and its near-absolute rule of territorial birthright citizenship. At the other end, states could strip individuals or whole communities of nationality. Totalitarian expatriations were a moral abomination but they did not run afoul of any rule of international law.

As declared in the opening article of the 1930 Hague Convention on Certain Questions Relating to the Conflict of Nationality Laws, 'It is for each State to determine under its own law who are its nationals', providing that such determinations were 'recognized by other States in so far as it is consistent with international conventions, international custom, and the principles of law generally recognized with regard to nationality'. 'There can be no doubt that nationality questions must be regarded as problems which are exclusively subject to the internal legislation of individual States', the Polish jurist Szymon Rundstein declared in 1926. 'It is, indeed, the sphere in which the principles of sovereignty find their most definite application.'[3]

States could, of course, consent to constrain nationality practices in bilateral or multilateral agreement with other states. The Hague Convention itself supplied one such example, along with the Bancroft treaties that the United States entered into with various European states during the late nineteenth century. These comprised conventional international law limitations, undertaken by states on a volitional basis. But even these volitional constraints were thin through the middle of the twentieth century. This is notable given the serious frictions among states that resulted from conflict of nationality laws, especially where the conflicts gave rise to conflicting claims to individuals (in other words, gave rise to dual nationals). These frictions sometimes resulted in armed conflict, including the US-UK War of 1812.[4] Notwithstanding these serious consequences, states failed to harmonise nationality laws on their own or through

[3] See 'League of Nations Committee of Experts for the Progressive Codification of International Law: Questionnaire No. 1: Nationality' (Special Supp. 1926) 20 AJIL 21, 23 ('There is no rule of international law, whether customary or written, which might be regarded as constituting any restriction of, or exception to' the exclusive jurisdiction of individual states); also, eg Weis, *Nationality and Statelessness in International Law* 2nd edn (Brill 1979) 101: 'The power of a state to confer its nationality is derived from its sovereignty. It is an attribute of territorial supremacy.'

[4] For myriad examples of the sort of disputes generated by nationality-based conflicts, see volume 6 of Moore, *A Digest of International Law* (Govt Print Office 1906); Borchard, *The Diplomatic Protection of Citizens Abroad or the Law of International Claims* (Banks Law Publishing Co. 1915).

other general international law constraints. In other words, even though there was very good cause to put international law to work in the area, there was little progress towards that end.[5] Some difficulties were resolved through discretionary state policies. For example, many states came to terminate nationality upon naturalisation in another state, thus eliminating a major source of dual nationals.[6] That was permissive to states – there was no rule of international law that required the practice. Multilateral efforts such as the Hague Convention fell well short of correcting the source of the conflicts, both in terms of substance and in terms of the low number of accessions.

But for purposes of custom and generally recognised principles, states were subject to only one clear constraint: they could not naturalise an individual without his consent. This norm was established through a series of nineteenth and twentieth century cases in which Latin American states purported to naturalise nationals of the United States and European states automatically by operation of law after a certain period of residency. The laws were aimed not just at naturalising the individuals but also at depriving them of home-state nationality and the diplomatic protection that came with it. These efforts were vigorously protested by the United States, in the face of which the Latin American countries backed down. The norm precluding non-consensual naturalisation was recognised by a consensus of nationality experts, whose opinions in that era were understood to stand as authoritative sources of international law itself. As mid-century nationality scholar Paul Weis observed, 'the acquisition of a new nationality must contain an element of voluntariness on the part of the individual acquiring it, that it must not be conferred against the will of the individual'.[7]

Otherwise, it was understood that customary international law – the form of binding international law established through state practice – had no place in constraining state discretion over the allocation of nationality. Decisions of international tribunals were in concurrence, as were the commentators. Speaking of 'matters which, though they may very closely concern the interests of more than one State, are not, in principle, regulated by international law', the Permanent Court of International Justice declared in the *Nationality Decrees in Tunis and Morocco*, 'questions of nationality are, in the opinion of this Court, in principle within this reserved domain'. In this reserved domain, 'each State is sole judge'.[8]

To the extent that there were other limitations placed on the recognition of nationality, it was entirely in the context of dual nationality, the source of serious friction in state-to-state relations as each of two sovereigns laid claim to individuals representing military and economic manpower. The flashpoint was invariably the exercise of diplomatic protection, when one state would intervene on behalf of its national with another state also claiming the individual as its own. The decision to exercise diplomatic protection was itself a matter of sovereign discretion.

[5] It was not for lack of trying. Nationality law was one of only three subjects on the table at the 1930 Hague Codification Conference. In the run-up to that negotiation, John D Rockefeller, Jr, commissioned a blue-ribbon initiative to study the issue and make recommendations for rationalising nationality practice. 'The Law of Nationality' (Special Supp. 1929) 23 *AJIL* 1, 21. Nationality laws had been a major target of newly emerged networks of legal policy makers in the late nineteenth century, who repeatedly lamented the failure to reach international agreement on the subject. See, eg Scott, *Observations on Nationality* (Oxford University Press 1931) 6 (framed as a 'plea' for states to harmonise their nationality practices to avoid dual nationality).

[6] See, eg Flournoy, 'Naturalization and Expatriation' (1922) 31 *YLJ* 702.

[7] Weis, *Nationality and Statelessness*, 110. See also van Panhuys, *The Role of Nationality in International Law* (AW Sythoff 1959) 156: 'it would be hard to defend that the conferment of nationality on a person who has no connection whatsoever with the State in question may ever produce nationality within the meaning of international law'. Also, Spiro, 'Citizenship Overreach' (2017) 38 *Mich. J. Int'l. L.* 167.

[8] *Nationality Decrees Issued in Tunis and Morocco*, Advisory Opinion No. 4 (Great Britain v France) [1923] PCIJ Series B no 4, para 24.

Disputes arose where one state refused to accept the legitimacy of the other's intervention. These disputes mostly occurred outside the context of formal processes and claims resolution, as when European-born naturalised US citizens returned to visit their homeland only to find themselves facing military conscription or penalties for its evasion.[9]

But disputes relating to dual nationals also arose in the context of the many arbitration settlement processes that were established by mutual consent of states to resolve a number of nineteenth-century bilateral conflicts implicating economic loss to private individuals. In some of these processes, arbitral bodies rejected the possibility that an individual holding nationality in each of two establishing states could bring a claim against either, in the face of the dictum (rooted in sovereign equality) that international law could not hear an individual's claim against his own state of nationality. This rule was reflected in the 1930 Hague Convention, which provided that 'A State may not afford diplomatic protection to one of its nationals against a State whose nationality such person also possesses.' (Some states, notably the United Kingdom, adopted it as an operating principle in most contexts, beyond the espousal of claims.)

But other tribunals developed a doctrine of 'dominant' and/or 'effective' nationality to in effect designate a sole nationality to individuals holding nationality in each of two states constituting a claims process. In other words, individuals could bring claims against one state in which they held nationality when they held 'dominant' nationality in the other.[10] This approach looked to the relative connections of the individual to each of the two states. Although the test was in theory multi-factored, typically the state of habitual residence was deemed the dominant one. The 'dominant nationality' test supplied a mechanism for managing the conflicts rooted in the failure to eradicate dual nationality. While the approach had the effect of disregarding one of an individual's nationalities, the inquiry into an individual's ties to a state of nationality was limited to the context of dual nationality only, and then only when addressing a claim by an individual holding one nationality against another state in which he also held nationality. These cases were not about second-guessing nationality determinations generally, only about enabling claims that would otherwise be blocked by (typically) vestigial nationalities in former homelands. In other words, the dominant nationality test expanded the universe of potential claims in arbitration proceedings, allowing some individuals to bring claims who would otherwise have faced the categoric bar of the Hague Convention approach against nationals bringing claims against a state of nationality in any case.

III. THE *NOTTEBOHM* CASE

It was against this backdrop that the International Court of Justice issued its decision in *Nottebohm*. The facts will be familiar to any international lawyer. Born in Germany in 1881, Friedrich Nottebohm moved to Guatemala in 1905, where he participated in several profitable businesses, including the country's second-largest coffee producer. He did not naturalise as a Guatemalan, notwithstanding decades of residence there, maintaining his German birth nationality. With the approach of World War II, in 1939 he naturalised in Liechtenstein, where his brother lived but in which Nottebohm himself had never resided. A three-year residency requirement was waived upon the payment of a naturalisation fee and an undertaking to pay

[9] See Spiro, *At Home in Two Countries* (NYU Press 2016) ch 2.

[10] For citations to the many arbitral tribunals adopting the dominant nationality approach, see ILC, Draft Articles on Diplomatic Protection with commentaries, UN Doc. A/61/10 (2006), 34, fn 79.

an annual tax to Liechtenstein. Refusing to recognise the legitimacy of the naturalisation, Guatemala detained Nottebohm in 1943 as an enemy alien after entering into a state of war with Germany, and it also expropriated his properties in Guatemala. (Guatemala later turned Nottebohm over to the United States, where he was interned.[11]) Liechtenstein subsequently sought to exercise diplomatic protection on behalf of its national. Liechtenstein argued that the detention and expropriation were wrongful because Nottebohm was a national of Liechtenstein, a neutral state in the war, and therefore not classifiable as an enemy alien.

The majority opinion denied Liechtenstein's capacity to bring the claim. The Court found Nottebohm's naturalisation not to have international effect for purposes of espousing the claim against Guatemala. The Court explored the nature of the Liechtenstein's naturalisation decision to consider whether Nottebohm's acquisition of Liechtenstein nationality was 'real and effective'. '[N]ationality is a legal bond having as its basis a social fact of attachment', the Court observed in a much-quoted formulation, 'a genuine connection of existence, interests and sentiments, together with the existence of reciprocal rights and duties'.[12] In the Court's view, Nottebohm failed the test, 'his actual connections with Liechtenstein [being] extremely tenuous'. His naturalisation had 'the sole aim of … coming within the protection of Liechtenstein but not of becoming wedded to its traditions, its interests, [or] its way of life'. The naturalisation

> was not based on any real prior connection with Liechtenstein, nor did it in any way alter the manner of life of the person upon whom it was conferred in exceptional circumstances of speed and accommodation. In both respects, it was lacking in the genuineness requisite to an act of such importance.[13]

This 'link theory' of nationality had not been proposed to the Court by Guatemala or any other party before it. Guatemala had argued that Nottebohm had acquired naturalisation in Liechtenstein through fraud.

But the Court was careful to limit its inquiry to the international effect of Nottebohm's nationality and to preserve the state's discretion over nationality determinations for purposes of municipal law. The Court refrained from confronting the validity *vel non* of Nottebohm's naturalisation. 'It is for Liechtenstein', the Court observed, 'as it is for every sovereign State, to settle by its own legislation the rules relating to the acquisition of its nationality'. Noting that 'for most people' nationality has 'its only effects within the legal system of the State conferring it', the Court affirmed 'the wider concept that nationality is within the domestic jurisdiction of the State'.[14] The decision had nothing to say about Nottebohm's status in Liechtenstein, only that his nationality could not be deployed against another state. As J Mervyn Jones noted in an early commentary on the case, 'In the result it seems clear that [Nottebohm] did in fact become a Liechtenstein national, and the Court in its judgment did not question this fact.'[15] As J Mervyn Jones noted in an early commentary on the case, 'In the result it seems clear that [Nottebohm] did in fact become a Liechtenstein national, and the Court in its judgment

[11] On the complex parallel proceedings between the Nottebohm family and the United States (including the detention of his Guatemalan national nephews), see Buys, 'Nottebohm's Nightmare' (2011) 11 *CKJICL* 1. The US government eventually returned assets to the family that had been frozen during the War, with a concession that Nottebohm was a 'non-enemy'. See Kunz, 'The *Nottebohm* Judgment' (1960) 54 *AJIL* 536, 554.

[12] *Nottebohm*, 23–24.

[13] ibid 26.

[14] ibid 20.

[15] Jones, 'The *Nottebohm* Case' (1956) 5 *ICLQ* 230, 234; see also Kunz, 'The *Nottebohm* Judgment', 550: 'The judgment does not adjudicate upon the validity of the acquisition of Liechtenstein nationality by Nottebohm'; Sloane, 'Breaking the Genuine Link' (2009) 50 *Harv.Int'l LJ* 1, 16: *Nottebohm* 'did not establish a new rule limiting the internal competence of states to confer their nationalities'.

did not question this fact.' In other words, the majority was not denying the legitimacy of Nottebohm's nationality in Liechtenstein. Rather, it was purporting to distinguish among its nationals, recognising the country's capacity to assert claims for some nationals but not for others.

The Canadian jurist John Erskine Read issued a lengthy dissent from the decision, perhaps among the most notable dissents in ICJ history. Noting the Bancroft treaties, entered into by the United States with a range of states (not including Liechtenstein) governing the diplomatic protection of naturalised citizens who returned to their homelands, Judge Read argued that there would be no cause to devise such treaty arrangements if they were already supplied by customary law.[16] If states wanted to limit their capacity to represent nationals in the claims context, they had the means to do it, but such limitation should not be read into generally applicable international law. He distinguished decisions of arbitral tribunals as implicating dual nationality, 'an essentially different kind of relationship', in particular where states refused to recognise the naturalisation of nationals before other states, on the obvious basis that no such conflicting claims to nationality were implicated in Nottebohm's case. In any case, Read rejected the salience of Nottebohm's motivation for naturalisation. Even if Nottebohm had naturalised to avoid the possibility of detention and expropriation, in his view, it would not affect the opposability of his naturalisation by Liechtenstein.

Judge Read also refused to recognise Nottebohm's lack of residence in Liechtenstein as a decisive factor. He observed:

> Most States regard non-resident citizens as a part of the body politic. In the case of many countries such as China, France, the United Kingdom and the Netherlands, the non-resident citizens form an important part of the body politic and are numbered in their hundreds of thousands or millions. Many of these non-resident citizens have never been within the confines of the home State. I can see no reason why the pattern of the body politic of Liechtenstein should or must be different from that of other States.[17]

'Unable to disregard what really did happen',[18] Read highlighted that after the war Nottebohm established residence in Liechtenstein. Among the more curious aspects of the *Nottebohm* decision is the fact that as of the date of the Court's decision in 1955, Nottebohm had been resident in Liechtenstein for almost a decade.[19]

A. *Nottebohm*'s Errors

Nottebohm is the most famous decision of an international tribunal relating to the subject of nationality. But the ruling is famous because it was (and is) infamous, at least among the college of international lawyers studying nationality law. The decision was discontinuous with preexisting law. On the facts, the decision was riddled with contradictions. It was mostly aimed at a problem that was not before the court, that of dual nationality. It was only in that context that the ruling was thereafter applied, and then only in a sporadic fashion. The 'genuine link' concept, meanwhile, has come under increasingly withering attack from respected international law scholars.

[16] *Nottebohm*, 41.
[17] ibid 44.
[18] Read, J, dissent at 45.
[19] See Goldie, 'The Critical Date' (1963) 12 *ICLQ* 1251. The *Nottebohm* majority suggested that his residence in Liechtenstein was explained by Guatemala's refusal to allow his return to the country in 1946: *Nottebohm*, 25.

Taken on its own terms, the decision is full of contradictions. It is not clear what nationality the ICJ was ascribing to Nottebohm on application of its approach. The Court did not question the operation of German law, under which his German nationality terminated upon naturalisation in Liechtenstein.[20] In any case, Nottebohm's ties with Germany had been attenuated through his more than three decades residence in Guatemala. If 'social fact of attachment' were the appropriate metric, Nottebohm would have been a national of Guatemala. But he had not naturalised there, and there could be not question of imputing Guatemalan nationality in the absence of his consent (and, although that would have barred Nottebohm's claims in an international tribunal, it would have undercut Guatemala's basis for expropriating his property in the first place). In this sense, the ICJ denominated Nottebohm as stateless, at least for purposes of diplomatic protection. 'The judgment prevented justice from being done to Nottebohm', observed Josef Kunz, 'making him, for all practical purposes, a stateless person and depriving him of the only legal remedy he had'.[21]

The decision cannot be framed as treating Nottebohm in effect as a German national, for whom expropriation would then be just desserts. The opinion would have applied to any other claim that Liechtenstein attempted to bring on Nottebohm's behalf, even if it were completely unrelated to international law as it related to enemy aliens. Say, for example, Nottebohm had been wrongfully detained by some other state on a basis having nothing to do with his German origins. The logic of the *Nottebohm* decision would have denied Liechtenstein's capacity to intervene on behalf of its national in that case. Although Nottebohm's German origins may have driven the facts in the case before the Court, this element of the case cannot support the 'genuine link' rationale for denying the admissibility of Liechtenstein's espousal.

Nottebohm's logic seemed targeted at another problem altogether, that of dual nationality. The decision purports to isolate the 'social fact of attachment' as the fulcrum of nationality. But the opinion translates this threshold for nationality as 'the juridical expression of the fact that the individual upon whom it is conferred … is in fact more closely connected with the population of the State conferring nationality than with that of any other State'.[22] Short of the ICJ claiming the power to adduce nationality – which would be entirely inconsistent with state sovereign discretion – the test works only where an individual has more than one nationality. *Nottebohm*'s approach was ill-suited to the facts of the case, where the question was not which of multiple nationalities to validate for international purposes but whether to validate his sole nationality for those purposes. As Robert Sloane notes, 'The logic and propriety of transposing, by what amounts to *ipse dixit*, the "criteria designed for cases of double nationality to an essentially different type of relationship" is questionable.'[23] In this respect *Nottebohm* was squarely in the tradition of the dominant nationality approach to claims in which an individual brought claims against one state of nationality.

[20] Although there was nothing in the Court's opinion questioning the termination of his German nationality, the Court may have been influenced by contingencies relating to German law and policy in the months leading to the outbreak of the War. A July 1939 German Foreign Office circular urged Germans in Latin America to seek a foreign citizenship, assured of having it restored in peace. The 1913 Reich nationality law also provided for the readmission of former German nationals. These background facts may have contributed to the 'bad cases make bad law' take on the judgment. Weis, *Nationality and Statelessness*, 180.

[21] Kunz, 'The *Nottebohm* Judgment', 566; Eagleton, 'Ferment or Revolution?' (1956) 50 *AJIL* 916, 920 (decision 'could produce a new class of "stateless persons"'); Glazer, 'Affaire *Nottebohm* (*Liechtenstein v. Guatemala*)' (1956) 44 *Georget. LJ* 313, 323 (characterising *Nottebohm* as 'manifestly bad' and 'exceedingly harsh').

[22] *Nottebohm*, 23.

[23] Sloane, 'Breaking the Genuine Link', 15.

At the same time, *Nottebohm* was by its own terms limited to the context of diplomatic protection and international claims. That had been the centre of controversies implicating nationality and dual citizenship. One state seeks to espouse a claim against another state of which the individual is also a national. In that case, as described above, international tribunals (before and after *Nottebohm*) have in some cases sought to determine which nationality is 'dominant', supported by an 'effective link'. Mid-century nationality scholar Paul Weis accepts *Nottebohm*'s validity on this basis only. 'The Court did not pronounce either on the general validity of the naturalization under international law', he observed. 'It merely held that Nottebohm's nationality was not opposable by Liechtenstein against Guatemala in international judicial proceedings.'[24] Sloane agrees. '[T]he rationale for the rule limits its application to the classical context of diplomatic claims espousal.'[25]

Nottebohm was controversial from its inception. Jack H Glazer called it 'disturbing', 'a hollow triumph of form'.[26] Writing in the influential *American Journal of International Law*, Josef L Kunz noted that the 1955 judgment had 'already provoked a vast literature', much of which was 'highly critical'.[27] On the judgment's 'genuine link' dictum, Kunz noted that the Court 'was unable to quote a single judicial precedent in favor of the genuine link theory as constituting positive international law'.[28] Mervyn Jones characterised it as an 'entirely new theory of international claims', 'a novel principle'.[29]

B. *Nottebohm* in Practice

The *Nottebohm* judgment has not fared well in practice. There are no important decisions from international tribunals that have adopted its rationale. As a jurisprudential matter, it was dead on arrival.

In the 1958 *Flegenheimer* case before the Italian-United States Conciliation Commission, the first major consideration of *Nottebohm* in a claims tribunal, *Nottebohm* and 'genuine link' was brushed aside.[30] The United States sought recovery of losses incurred by Fleigenheimer, a US national, on account of the sale of capital stock made at depressed prices in the face of anti-Semitic Italian legislation. Flegenheimer, who was Jewish, had been born in Germany to a father who was a return migrant from the United States. He had inquired about the possibility that he was a US citizen *jure sanguinis* but was rebuffed by various US officials in the 1930s and 1940s, even as he was stripped of his nationality under German law in 1940. Only in 1952 was his US citizenship confirmed. Italy asserted that Flegenheimer did not qualify as a US national for purposes of the claims process at relevant dates in 1943 and 1947, and 'in view of the fact that, during half a century, the individual concerned was considered as and considered himself to be a German national by his conduct, his sentiments, his interests'. '[N]ationality is not effective when it confines itself to establishing a nominal link between a State and an individual', Italy argued, citing *Nottebohm*, 'and is not supported by a social solidity resulting from a veritable solidarity of rights and duties between the State and its national'.[31]

[24] Weis, *Nationality and Statelessness*, 179.
[25] Sloane, 'Breaking the Genuine Link', 29.
[26] Glazer, 'Affaire *Nottebohm*', 325.
[27] Kunz, 'The *Nottebohm* Judgment', 537–38, 553.
[28] ibid, 553.
[29] Jones, 'The *Nottebohm* Case', 243, 231.
[30] *Flegenheimer* (U.S. v Italy) [1958] 14 RIAA 327, 377–78.
[31] ibid 375.

The tribunal rejected *Nottebohm*'s application.

> [I]t is doubtful that the International Court of Justice intended to establish a rule of general international law in requiring, in the *Nottebohm Case*, that there must exist as effective link between the person and the State in order that the latter may exercise its right of diplomatic protection in behalf of the former.[32]

The tribunal in effect limited *Nottebohm* to its facts. The tribunal proceeded to stress that the doctrine of effective nationality was limited in application to cases in which an individual held nationality in each of two states subject to the claims resolution process. Since there was no allegation that Flegenheimer was an Italian national, the tribunal had no basis to reject recognition of Flegenheimer's US nationality, however nominal it may have been. So long as the citizenship was 'regularly acquired' (that is, acquired in conformity with the nationality law of the state in question), the tribunal would otherwise defer to the 'unquestionable principle of international law according to which every State is sovereign in establishing the legal conditions which must be fulfilled by an individual in order that he may be considered to be vested with its nationality'.[33]

Perhaps the only major litigation in which *Nottebohm* was accepted as the putative rule of decision was in the Iran-US claims tribunal A/18 case.[34] The question there was whether dual nationals could file claims before the tribunal. The claims tribunal was enabled to hear claims by nationals of the United States or Iran. The tribunal interpreted *Nottebohm* to allow an inquiry into the 'real and effective nationality based on the facts of a case, instead of an approach relying on more formalistic criteria'.[35] But the approach was deployed to soften the bar on claims by dual nationals as nationals of one state where they also held nationality in the state against which a claim was being made.[36] The tribunal was thus putting *Nottebohm* to work not in its own context (which of course did not involve dual nationality) but rather to the end of validating the 'dominant and effective' approach to claimants holding each nationality of two states constituting a claims settlement process. A/18 implicated dual nationals only, and then only in the specific context of claims processes resolving disputes between the two states of nationality. It would not have applied to a US national having no social connection to the United States if his other state of nationality were with, for instance, the United Kingdom. The ruling applied only to dual Iranian-US nationals. In that respect it was applying *Nottebohm* only orthogonally, to a conceptually distinct constellation of facts. In this respect, A/18 'repurposed' *Nottebohm* in service of the doctrine of dominant nationality, a doctrine into which (but for the fact that Nottebohm lacked dual nationality) the judgment much more comfortably fits.[37]

Closer to home, the European Court of Justice demurred from applying *Nottebohm* in the *Micheletti* case. Micheletti, a national of Italy and Argentina, sought to establish a dental practice in Spain. In the case of dual nationals, Spanish law recognised the nationality of the

[32] ibid 376.
[33] ibid 337.
[34] *Iran v United States*, Case A/18 (1984) 5 Iran-U.S.C.T.R. 251.
[35] ibid 263.
[36] As the tribunal noted, 'This trend toward modification of the Hague Convention rule of non-responsibility by search for the dominant and effective nationality is scarcely surprising as it is consistent with the contemporaneous development of international law to accord legal protections to individuals, even against the State of which they are nationals'; in other words, A/18 put *Nottebohm* to work to expand the universe of tenable claims, not restrict it. ibid 265.
[37] Thwaites, 'The Life and Times of the Genuine Link' (2018) 49 *Vic. Univ. Wellingt. LRev.* 645, 657.

last state of residence, in Micheletti's case, Argentina, and denied his right to establish the practice. Advocate General Tesauro asserted that the Spanish law violated Micheletti's rights as a national of a Member State, namely Italy. The Advocate General found it 'clear that possession of the nationality of a Member State is the only prerequisite which an individual must satisfy in order to be able to exercise the right'. The Advocate General rejected the application of 'effective nationality, whose origin lies in a "romantic period" of international relations and, in particular in the concept of diplomatic protection'; in other words, the concept was overblown and limited. The opinion in the same breath rejected invocation of *Nottebohm* itself, 'the well known (and, it is worth remembering, controversial)' judgment of the ICJ.[38] The European Court of Justice followed the Advocate General's recommendation in deeming the Spanish law inconsistent with EU commitments.

There are other contexts in which *Nottebohm* has been demoted or cast aside. Arbitration panels established under the ICSID Convention 'have disavowed the principle of the genuine link with a view to recognizing the primacy of the domestic rules on nationality'.[39] The panels have generally accepted nationality determinations by states except where they do not appear to conform with positive legal requirements. A panel rejected the claim of Italian nationality notwithstanding supporting official documentation where an individual had apparently not complied with a requirement to request the retention of Italian nationality upon naturalisation in another state. But another panel accepted the attribution of nationality by descent to reject a claim even where the individual had no other connection with the state. Assessing these and other cases, Robert Sloane concludes that ICSID tribunals 'have shown little inclination to search for robust substantive bonds of the sort stressed in *Nottebohm*. This casts further doubt on the descriptive accuracy of the genuine link theory as a general doctrine of international law.'[40]

Nottebohm has also been rejected by the International Law Commission, whose work (while not qualifying as an authoritative pronouncement of the United Nations) is afforded substantial weight as the work of a collective expert body. The Draft Articles on Diplomatic Protection adopted by the ILC in 2006 provide that 'a State of nationality means a State whose nationality that person has acquired, in accordance with the law of that State … not inconsistent with international law'.[41] The accompanying commentary explains that this provision 'does not require an effective or genuine link between itself and its national, along the lines suggested in the *Nottebohm* case'. The commentary found it appropriate 'to limit *Nottebohm* to the facts of the case in question' and concluded that the ICJ 'did not intend to expound a general rule'. As a general matter, the ILC observed that the burden of proof should be on any State challenging nationality in light of the fact that 'the State conferring nationality must be given a 'margin of appreciation' in deciding upon the conferment of nationality and that there is a presumption in favour of the validity of a State's conferment of nationality'.[42]

As for the dominant nationality approach to claims by dual nationals against one state of nationality itself, the doctrine continued to have traction through the mid-century. In the *Mergé* decision from the Italian-US Conciliation Commission, nearly contemporaneous to *Nottebohm*, the tribunal weighed the efforts of a US-born claimant who had assiduously taken

[38] Opinion of AG Tesauro, Case C-369/90 *Micheletti* ECLI:EU:C:1992:47, para 5.
[39] Sironi, 'Nationality of Individuals in Public International Law', in Forlati and Annoni (eds), *The Changing Role of Nationality in International Law* (Routledge 2013).
[40] Sloane, 'Breaking the Genuine Link', 39.
[41] Art 4 of ILC Draft Articles.
[42] Commentary to Art 4 of ILC Draft Articles.

steps to maintain her US citizenship against her habitual residence in Italy to find the latter dominant and thus preclusive of a claim against Italy.[43] As described above, the A/18 ruling is more appropriately situated in this line of decisions that in any universalised conception of 'genuine link'. Article 7 of the ILC Draft Articles on Diplomatic Protection accepts the dominant nationality approach as a default rule. More recently, there appears to be a retreat from even this limited context in which duly conferred nationality is disregarded, in recognition of the cumbersome nature of the dominant nationality determination. The UN Compensation Commission, established in the wake of Iraq's 1991 invasion of Kuwait, entertained by dual nationals holding Iraqi citizenship so long as the other citizenship was bona fide, which was interpreted to mean that the other nationality had been acquired prior to the beginning of the military conflict in August 1991.

As a general matter, international law has made some inroads into the near-complete discretion that states previously enjoyed with respect to nationality determinations. There has been some suggestion that states cannot discriminate in their nationality practices on the basis of suspect classifications, and there is some convergence in state practice toward adopting double jus soli.[44] But these norms are provisional – they have clearly not hardened into binding customary international law. With limited exceptions,[45] they implicate only the denial or withdrawal of nationality, not its conferment. Otherwise, the traditional rule that states have discretion over their nationality practices is largely intact. The first article of the1997 European Convention on Nationality, for example, provides that 'Each State shall determine under its own law who are its nationals', and that such determinations shall be accepted by other States as far as they are consistent with treaty obligations, customary international law, and 'principles of law generally recognized with regard to nationality'. This formulation is almost identical to the lead provision of the 1930 Hague Convention. There is simply no credible argument that *Nottebohm* and 'genuine link' have risen to the level of customary international law or of a general principle of law relating to nationality.[46] To the contrary, *Nottebohm*'s star, to the extent it had ever risen, has fallen rather far.

C. 'Genuine Link' in the Face of Globalisation

From a functional perspective, if *Nottebohm*'s 'genuine link' analysis made little sense in the context of the mid-twentieth century, it makes even less sense today. The *Nottebohm* period reflected perhaps the height of national loyalties and identities, that 'romantic period' of nationality, set as it was in the inter-state military conflict of the Second World War. Nottebohm's cosmopolitan identity was relatively uncommon for the time, restricted to wealthy elites who could afford the expense of frequent inter-continental travel.

[43] *Mergé* (U.S. v Italy) [1955] 14 RIAA 236.

[44] Spiro, 'A New International Law of Citizenship', 729–30. Double *jus soli* implicates the extension of nationality to the children of parents also born on state territory.

[45] In some cases, international organisations have refused to recognise the attribution of nationality where it was with the purpose of securing advantage as an employee of the organisation. See Sironi, 'Nationality of Individuals in Public International Law', 65–66. This is a minor derogation from the general rule of non-interference. Of course, the longstanding norm that states may not naturalise individuals on a non-consensual basis stands. See 'Human Rights in the Context of Automatic Naturalization in Crimea' (Open Society Justice Initiative 2018) www.opensocietyfoundations.org/sites/default/files/report-osji-crimea-20180601.pdf.

[46] See, eg Weis, *Nationality and Statelessness*, 201: *Nottebohm* approach 'can hardly … be regarded as forming part of customary international law'.

Of course, there were business persons of Nottebohm's profile who actively sustained their homeland identity at the same time that they permanently resettled in far-flung locales. It is not a coincidence that these were the stock characters in international claims cases implicating nationality disputes. More typically, migrants transferred their citizenship along with their centre of social gravity, so that their new nationality was their 'dominant' one. Or they returned to their homeland and the former nationality reverted, as was provided for under the Bancroft treaties. Dual nationality was suppressed, although in many cases the interaction of non-harmonised nationality laws left individuals with the nationality of both country of origin and resettlement. That explained why tribunals undertook to make the dominant nationality inquiry in some cases, even though the individual in many cases would have had 'genuine links' to both his country of origin and resettlement.

Today the 'genuine link' inquiry looks absurd in the face of proliferating multiple nationality and the dramatically enhanced capacity for individuals to maintain social connections to multiple countries. Multiple nationality is now a fact of globalisation. The number of states accepting the status has dramatically increased. *Nottebohm* seems perhaps no more dated in this respect than in its conception of naturalisation, which the court framed as involving the 'breaking of a bond of allegiance'.[47] Leaving aside the question of whether it remains appropriate to speak of 'allegiance' in the context of the state, it is only in a distinct minority of cases today that naturalisation in a state requires termination of one's citizenship of origin.

This has normalised the attribution of nationality on the basis of a range of social connection. In many cases, the connections and identities will be substantial, as in the case of migrants, who will typically have deep connections to both their country of origin and their country of resettlement. But in other cases, acceptance of dual citizenship enables the attribution of nationality on the basis of thin ties.

For example, many individuals are claiming the nationality of a grandparent or even more distant forbearer. Nationality based on ancestry may be meaningful in a sociological sense, or it may not be. The range will be on the one extreme those who deeply identify with the nationality of their ancestors, even if it has been centuries since the territorial link was broken. Some Sephardic Jews still closely identify with their Spanish and Portuguese roots more than half a millennium after their expulsion from the Iberian Peninsula. This will also often be the case with identification with the states from which a parent or grandparent emigrated. But it will also often be the case that the child or grandchild of an immigrant, never mind a more distant relation, identifies only weakly with the state of origin. An increasing number of countries are relaxing the jus sanguinis basis for allocating birth citizenship. Few of them subject individuals who acquire citizenship on that basis to any sort of integration test and few retain any sort of residency requirement for *jus sanguinis* citizens born abroad. They are not required to own property in their state of ancestral citizenship, maintain any other kind of vested interest, or even have visited. States thus do not sort for sociological connections – call it 'social fact of attachment' – among citizens by descent.

The same holds true in some cases for those born with *jus soli* citizenship. In states such as the United States that extend citizenship to those born on national territory on a near-absolute basis, there will be many cases in which a person does not sustain a connection to the state of birth into adulthood. That is true of the birth tourist, of course, but it is also true of the child born to the graduate student or business person on temporary assignment. As a result, a

[47] *Nottebohm*, 24.

growing number of individuals will have formal citizenship in a state with few, and often, no other ties to that state.[48]

The tenuous connection many individuals have with a state of birth citizenship brings *Nottebohm* in question in rather obvious ways. The critique is not original, to say the least. As noted by the ILC commentary on diplomatic protection, the genuine link theory by its terms

> would exclude literally millions of persons from the benefit of diplomatic protection. In today's world of economic globalization and migration, there are millions of persons who have drifted away from their State of nationality and made their lives in States whose nationality they never acquire. Moreover, there are countless others who have acquired nationality by birth, descent or operation of law of States with which they have the most tenuous connection.[49]

To the extent that a 'genuine link' test is applied only to naturalised citizens, moreover, it tends to discriminate against them. Only the nationality of the naturalised citizen is subject to scrutiny, where the birth citizen gets a pass, even if unjustified.[50]

This can be true even of those who naturalise in states imposing a residency requirement. Residency requirements typically do not implicate continuous presence. In the wake of immensely intensified communications networks and the reduced cost of travel, migrants can maintain homeland ties on a near-continuous, virtual basis. The homeland connection is compounded where there are co-ethnic migrant concentrations. One can live a fully functional professional and social existence in most world capitals in one's own language among others from one's country of origin. Of course, many states apply other requirements to test for cultural integrations. But short of minutely inspecting a person's beliefs, friends and daily interactions, these conditions are incapable of measuring a naturalisation applicant's actual connection to the existing community.

The *Nottebohm* majority spoke of Nottebohm's relationship to Liechtenstein as one of not 'becoming wedded to its traditions, its interests, [or] its way of life'. This was an almost comically nostalgic conception of nationality, if not at the time it was decided than certainly in contemporary perspective. States no longer have unitary traditions, interests or ways of life to which citizens hew. To apply a 'genuine link' test of this sort to all individuals would result in a great many losing their citizenship. Likewise with respect to the ICJ's calling Nottebohm out for not 'assuming the obligations – other than fiscal obligations – and exercising the rights pertaining to' nationality. Most of the millions of individuals who live outside their countries of citizenship assume no obligations relating to their nationality – not even fiscal ones. (The only country in the world that taxes non-resident citizens is the United States.) Even those who live within a country of nationality are unlikely to assume many citizenship-delimited obligations, most of which, like taxes, are imposed on the basis of residency, not citizenship. Nor are there many rights that are exercised on a citizenship-delimited basis. Those that are – voting in national elections representing the prime example – are abjured by many citizens. No one would suggest making the recognition of citizenship contingent on the exercise of rights today.

These observations apply today, more or less, to almost every state in a globalised world. Almost every state these days will have some number of citizens who would fail the 'genuine

[48] eg Sloane, 'Breaking the Genuine Link', 18: 'The unquestioned validity of both *jus soli* and *jus sanguinis* as bases for the ascription of nationality casts doubt on the genuine link theory, at least in the robust form expounded by the ICJ.'

[49] ILC Draft Articles, 30.

[50] Weis, *Nationality and Statelessness*, 181. See also Art 5(2) of the European Convention on Nationality (1997) ETS 166: 'Each State Party shall be guided by the principle of non-discrimination between its nationals, whether they are nationals by birth or have acquired its nationality subsequently'.

connection' as conceived by the *Nottebohm* judges. To the extent states don't police their own citizenship boundaries, they are hardly in a position to police the boundaries set by other states, for international purposes or otherwise.

Moreover, 'genuine link' seems infinitely elastic in a world in which establishing connections of various descriptions has been dramatically facilitated by the compression of space that has come with globalisation. The threshold for demonstrating links with a state, its people, and its economy are categorically lower than they have been ever been in the past. This adds additional complexity to the task of any state (or other entity) seeking to second-guess the attribution of nationality by another state. As Judge Read noted in his *Nottebohm* dissent, '[n]ationality, and the relation between a citizen and the State to which he owes allegiance, are of such a character that they demand certainty … There must be objective tests, readily established, for the existence and recognition of the status.'[51] Any move to second guess the nationality decisions of other countries would inevitably implicate a subjective element, undermining the reliance value that millions of individuals place in their nationality to facilitate their movement through the globalised world. There are other mechanisms that states have to police any perceived abuses in the attribution of nationality, for example, by modulating visa requirements for all nationals of a particular state.

D. *Nottebohm* Today: A Dead Letter

Nottebohm may be among the ICJ's most famous opinions. But it is also surely among its least respected. 'Among legal scholars who take *Nottebohm* seriously as jurisprudence', writes Audrey Macklin, 'there is strong consensus that it was wrong then, and may be even more wrong now'. She concludes that it is time to 'retire' *Nottebohm*.[52] Dimitry Kochenov concludes that the decision is an 'entirely arbitrary and potentially harmful rule of international law',[53] the genuine link model 'incoherent and logically inexplicable'.[54] Robert Sloane finds that the 'sociopolitical, romanticist vision of nationality articulated by the *Nottebohm* majority has … become increasingly anachronistic and misplaced today'.[55] Rayner Thwaites similarly characterises *Nottebohm* as a 'dead letter'. Thwaites dismisses *Nottebohm* as a '"one-off' … confined to the facts of the case'.[56] Annemarieke Vermeer-Künzli concludes that the *Nottebohm* case 'has been criticized rather strongly, and rightly so'.[57] And so on.[58]

Nottebohm remains part of the discourse in two ways, neither of which live up to its mostly underserved reputation as constraining the conferment of nationality. First is a creative

[51] Read, J, dissent at 46.

[52] Macklin, 'Is It Time to Retire *Nottebohm*?' (2018) 111 *AJIL Unbound* 492.

[53] Kochenov, 'Where is EU Citizenship Going?' in Talani (ed), *Globalisation, Migration, and the Future of Europe* (Routledge 2011), 5.

[54] Kochenov, 'Citizenship without Respect' (2010) Jean Monnet Working Paper 08/10, 46.

[55] Sloane, 'Breaking the Genuine Link', 5.

[56] Thwaites, 'The Life and Times of the Genuine Link', 661.

[57] Vermeer-Künzli, 'Nationality and Diplomatic Protection' in Annoni and Forlati (eds), *The Changing Role of Nationality in International Law* (Routledge 2013) 77.

[58] See also Dörr, '*Nottebohm* Case', in *Max Planck Encyclopedia of Public International Law* (Oxford University Press 2007): *Nottebohm* 'was not successful … in setting up the requirement of a genuine connection for the exercise of diplomatic protection in cases of nationality conferred through naturalization. Its reasoning in this respect was unconvincing, and the consequences of the genuine link rule were seen to be disadvantageous for the position of individuals in international law'; Tratnik, 'Limitations of National Autonomy' in Kraljić and Klojčnik (eds), *From an Individual to the European Integration Discussion on the Future of Europe* (University of Maribor Press 2018) 507: *Nottebohm* 'is largely overestimated' and 'belongs in the past'.

application under which some advocates are pressing states to extend citizenship to individuals having genuine links to a state, a kind of 'reverse Nottebohm'.[59] In other words, some are arguing that a state must grant citizenship to individuals with genuine links to the state. This is by way of challenging states when they deny citizenship, not grant it. There are interesting developments consistent with this argument, under which states might have a qualified obligation to extend citizenship to those with a genuine link.

But this use of *Nottebohm* is not much more than a branding exercise. The level of genuine link required to activate the norm would be obviously higher than the level of genuine link needed to satisfy the *Nottebohm* test in the context of recognising a grant of citizenship. Indeed, nothing less than habitual residence would be required to trigger an obligation to grant citizenship. In other words, it has nothing really to do with its original doctrinal meaning, nor does it validate that original doctrinal meaning in any way.

Similarly, some political theorists have latched onto the 'genuine link' formulation in an effort to shore up the state as a location for the redistribution of resources and the protection of rights. These liberal nationalists – Ayelet Shachar and Rainer Bauböck most prominently among them – have centred 'genuine links' as part of their program to limit the citizenry to those who have a common interest in collective governance and as a counterpoint to the rise of what Shachar calls 'nominal heirs', those who are allocated citizenship in countries in which they have never lived.[60]

But this turn, while powerfully argued, veers heavily to a nostalgic and romanticised view of the relationship between the individual and the state. 'Hollow citizenship' is everywhere and irreversible. 'Genuine links' as deployed by the theorists does not translate into a practical standard for the allocation of nationality. As Bauböck suggests, 'genuine links' can serve as 'a critical standard for assessing the strength of ties between and individual and a particular polity'. But he concedes that 'this strength cannot be measured in a uniform way either as a subjective sense of belonging or through objective indicators such as duration of residence or family ties in the territory'.[61] In other words it is variable in a way that cannot supply a doctrinal metric. Perhaps the most that can be said of 'genuine link' is that it supplies a heuristic for thinking about idealised conceptions of the state,[62] and perhaps there is a reason that *Nottebohm* is popular with the political theorists at the same time that it is being abandoned by legal scholars.

IV. CONCLUSION

Nottebohm is a remarkable decision in one respect only: there may be no other judgment of an international tribunal that has so much purchase on the imagination at the same time as it has so little traction on the ground. Better than any other judicial pronouncement it captures the liberal nationalist ideal of the relationship between the individual and the state. Perhaps it is something to aspire to, though prevailing trajectories point in other directions. Whether or not *Nottebohm* reflects admirable aspirations of social organisation, it does not supply a workable frame for addressing nationality and its place in relations among states.

[59] See Spiro, 'A New International Law of Citizenship', 723; Macklin, 'Is It Time to Retire *Nottebohm*?', 496.
[60] Shachar, *The Birthright Lottery* (Harvard University Press 2009) 166–71.
[61] Bauböck, 'Democratic Inclusion' in Owen (ed), *Democratic Inclusion* (Manchester University Press 2018) 3, 44.
[62] See Sloane, 'Breaking the Genuine Link', 26: 'genuine link became a kind of mantra'.

6

State Autonomy versus 'Genuine Links' Nottebohm and Beyond

MATJAŽ TRATNIK AND PETRA WEINGERL

I. INTRODUCTION

DEBATES ON A genuine link in nationality matters started in the EU around a decade ago when the Commission and EU Parliament started criticising Malta for its Citizenship by Investment (CBI) programme. Ever since, there have been discussions on the desirability and lawfulness of a genuine link requirement for the acquisition of Member States nationalities, and therewith EU citizenship, as well as for the recognition of nationality based upon CBI programmes, without a genuine link, by other Member States.

In a 2019 Report,[1] the Commission wrote:

> The Nottebohm case of the International Court of Justice establishes that, for nationality acquired through naturalisation to be recognised in the international arena, it should be granted on the basis of a genuine connection between the individual and the State in question.

In another document published in the same year,[2] the Commission went even further:

> Member States must therefore take into account all rules that form part of the EU legal order, including international law, which requires a 'genuine connection' between the State in question and the person that is granted citizenship.

In the 2019 Report, the Commission clarified that with the 'genuine connection', it has primarily in mind either 'blood connection' or effective prior residence:

> The 'bond of nationality' is traditionally based either on a genuine connection with the people of the country (by descent, origin or marriage) or on a genuine connection with the country, established either by birth in the country or by effective prior residence in the country for a meaningful duration.[3]

Based on these statements, the Commission assumes that international law requires a 'genuine connection' for every grant of nationality (*sic*!). It appears that the Commission is invoking the

[1] European Commission, 'Investor Citizenship and Residence Schemes in the European Union' COM(2019)12 final 5.

[2] 'Questions and Answers on the Report on Investor Citizenship and Residence Schemes in the European Union' (European Commission, 23 January 2019) https://ec.europa.eu/commission/presscorner/detail/ro/MEMO_19_527.

[3] European Commission, COM(2019)12final 5.

Nottebohm[4] case due to significant political pressure from the EU Parliament, which prevails over the opinion of the legal service.[5] While the Parliament has passed several non-binding resolutions calling on EU Member States to abolish such programmes,[6] the Commission went further.[7] The process with Malta's CBI programme culminated in the infringement proceedings initiated by the Commission based on Article 258 TFEU, based on this understanding of requirements of international law. The final act, an action for infringement, was brought by the Commission before the Court of Justice of the EU (CJEU) in March 2023.[8] The Commission wants the CJEU to declare that EU law precludes CBI schemes 'in exchange for pre-determined payments or investments in the absence of a requirement for a genuine link between the State and the individuals concerned'.[9] To this end, the Commission claims that Malta failed to fulfil its obligations under Article 20 TFEU (EU citizenship) and Article 4(3) Treaty on the European Union (TEU) (the principle of sincere cooperation). As Worster rightfully observes, the Commission does not argue that other Member States can disregard such grants of nationality but that Member States are violating EU law when they grant nationality by investment.[10]

This contribution will argue that neither international law nor EU law requires a 'genuine link' in the process of the acquisition and/or recognition of a foreign nationality. In fact, such a requirement can be menacing for several reasons discussed below. Section II will delve into the concept of nationality and its role, followed by Section III, which will revisit the well-known *Nottebohm* judgment, demonstrating that it is often misinterpreted in relation to the genuine link requirement in nationality matters. Section IV will shift focus to EU law, investigating the potential limitations on national autonomy in nationality matters through the principle of sincere cooperation. In that framework, the contribution provides some reflections on the inconsistencies and dangers posed by employing genuine links in nationality matters. It will conclude by asserting that the debate surrounding the genuine link is primarily driven by political, rather than legal, considerations. While the CJEU case law shows that the principle of sincere cooperation has the potential to intrude even in areas which are reserved for Member States' competence, thus also in nationality matters, such an intrusion could only be justified for the advancement of the EU objectives and should respect the sensitive division of competences in the EU. However, the Commission's employment of the genuine link requirement in this context is, in fact, itself contrary to EU objectives, most notably the internal market and the principle of free movement.

II. NATIONALITY AND ITS FUNCTION

In Article 2(a) of the European Convention on Nationality 1997 (ECN),[11] nationality is defined as 'the legal bond between a person and a State and does not indicate the person's ethnic

[4] *Nottebohm* (Liechtenstein v Guatemala) [1955] ICJ Rep. 4.

[5] See a reserved approach towards the genuine link requirement in: Fernandes et al, 'Avenues for EU Action on Citizenship and Residence by Investment Schemes' (2021) *EPRS*, www.europarl.europa.eu/RegData/etudes/STUD/2021/694217/EPRS_STU(2021)694217_EN.pdf.

[6] See eg European Parliament resolution on EU Citizenship for Sale (2013/2995(RSP)) [2014] OJ C482/117; European Parliament resolution with proposals to the Commission on citizenship and residence by investment schemes (2021/2026(INL)) [2022] OJ C347/27.

[7] For a critical analysis of these developments, see Kochenov and Basheska in this volume.

[8] Case C-181/23 *Commission v Malta* OJ C 173/27 pending.

[9] Action brought on 21 March 2023 in the Case C-181/23 *Commission v Malta* OJ C 173/27 pending.

[10] Worster, 'Reining in the *Nottebohm* Case' (2021) 41 *B.U. Int'l L.J.* 316. Also eg Van den Brink, 'Revising Citizenship within the European Union' (2022) 23 *GLJ* 79.

[11] European Convention on Nationality (1997) ETS166 (ECN).

origin'. Other definitions might also say that nationality is the status of membership in a state community,[12] or as Kochenov[13] put it, status of belonging (to a state). Nationality is a legal concept, which is necessarily connected to a public authority.[14] Nations without a state do not have nationality in this legal sense. National and international law use nationality as a connecting factor, to provide nationals of states certain rights and duties. From the perspective of states, it might be said that nationality is also used as a tool of exclusion of foreigners from certain rights. It enables them to distinguish between 'Us' and 'Them'. In addition, nationality can be (ab)used by states to discriminate between various groups of foreigners.[15] In international law, nationality is important especially in three areas: state succession, treatment of enemy aliens in case of war and diplomatic protection.[16]

When speaking of nationality in international law, Article 15 Universal Declaration of Human Rights (UDHR) guarantees the right to a nationality to everyone. There are, however, two problems with this guarantee. Regarding the first, the UDHR does not provide to which nationality this right refers. Concerning the second, the right to a nationality is not a right with a definite content. It is often described as the right to have rights in national and international law. It is not clear which rights exactly, because national legal systems may attach various rights and obligations to their nationality.[17]

Even though nationality is an important concept in international law, the issues of acquisition and loss of nationality are considered as, in principle, belonging to the *domaine réservé* of nation states. This national autonomy in matters of nationality is a longstanding principle, that has been confirmed by various decisions of international courts,[18] as well as by international legal instruments,[19] and in the doctrine.[20] The principle of national autonomy can be illustrated by Article 1 of the 1930 Hague Convention, stating that it is for each State to determine under its own law who are its nationals and that this law must be recognised by other States in so far as it is consistent with international conventions, international custom and the principles of law generally recognised with regard to nationality. Therefore, other states have

[12] See about the different meanings of the terms nationality and citizenship R De Groot and Vonk, *International Standards on Nationality Law* (Wolf 2016) 3–4. Kunz, 'The *Nottebohm* Judgment' (1960) 54 *AJIL* 536, 546. We will use the term nationality for the nationality of states and citizenship only when we will refer to the citizenship of the European Union, recognising that the distinction between nationality and citizenship may be relevant in other contexts.

[13] Kochenov, *Citizenship* (MIT Press 2019) 37.

[14] In most cases, but not necessarily a state. Some federal states have (had) subnational citizenship (eg former Yugoslavia and the Soviet Union). Also the EU has its own citizenship.

[15] Kochenov and Ganty, 'EU Lawlessness Law' (2023) 30 *CJEL* 78; See also Marilyn and Immanuel, '*The Gambia v Myanmar*' (OpinioJuris, 11 October 2022) https://opiniojuris.org/2022/10/11.

[16] Crawford, *Brownlie's Principles of Public International Law* 9th edn (Oxford University Press 2019) 495; R De Groot and Vonk, *International Standards*, 20–28 with abundant references.

[17] See extensively about the right to a nationality von Rütte, *The Human Right to Citizenship* (Brill-Nijhoff 2022); R De Groot and Vonk, *International Standards*, 41–42; R De Groot and Tratnik, *Nationaliteitsrecht* 5th edn (Kluwer 2021) 5–6. See about rights and duties states attach to nationality Kochenov and Lindeboom, 'Empirical Assessment of the Quality of Nationalities' (2017) 4 *EJCL* 314.

[18] *Nationality Decrees Issued in Tunis and Morocco*, Advisory Opinion No. 4 (Great Britain v France) [1923] PCIJ Series B no 4; *Nottebohm* [1955] ICJ Rep. 4; Case C-369/90 *Micheletti* EU:C:1992:295; see eg Jessurun d'Oliveira, 'Case C-369/90, *M.V. Micheletti and others v Delegación del Gobierno en Cantabria*, Judgment of 7 July 1992' (1993) 30 *CMLRev.* 623.

[19] See Art 1 of the Hague Convention on Certain Questions Relating to the Conflict of Nationality Law (1930) 179 LNTS 89 (The Hague Convention); Art 3(1) ECN; Art 4 of ILC, Draft Articles on Diplomatic Protection with commentaries, UN Doc. A/61/10 (2006).

[20] See extensively Brownlie, 'The Relations of Nationality in Public International Law' (1963) 39 *Br. Yearb. Int'l. L.* 284, 286–89; Crawford, *Brownlie's Principles*, 495; R De Groot and Vonk, *International Standards*, 41–44. See also Klaestad, J, dissenting in *Nottebohm*, 27.

the obligation to recognise the acquisition of another state's nationality, unless it was acquired in violation of international law.

Under modern international law, the national autonomy is not unlimited. The limitations flow from international agreements relating to nationality, as well as international human rights law.[21] We have extensively discussed the limitations of international law, and EU law, on national autonomy elsewhere.[22] In the case of the acquisition of nationality, states must draft their rules without discrimination and in such a way that statelessness does not occur. Nationality may not be removed arbitrarily, even if it does not result in statelessness. However, these limitations do not impose restraints on states as regards the possible grounds for the attribution of citizenship.[23] Here, states enjoy a large portion of discretion. There are two important limitations; states may not impose their nationality on adults without their consent[24] and they may not discriminate on grounds of race, gender and as to the birth status.[25]

As regards the recognition of nationality, other states may only refuse to recognise a nationality acquired from another state if it is acquired in violation of international law. With the exception of a few very specific cases, there is no relevant case law to demonstrate examples where the acquisition of nationality would be in violation of international law.[26]

In the EU, nationality matters remain in the competence of the Member States, too, since they have not conferred any competences on the EU in this area.[27] The Member States are, however, required to draft their nationality laws with *due regard to EU law*, as the CJEU expressly stated in *Micheletti*. To this end, the two most important principles of EU law which need to be observed in the process of the acquisition or loss of nationality are the principle of proportionality and the principle of sincere cooperation.[28] While the principle of proportionality is used by EU citizens as a shield against Member States' measures affecting their nationality, the principle of sincere cooperation could potentially be used as a shield against national measures affecting nationality by other Member States and by the EU itself.[29] De Groot recognises a problem if a Member State would (by surprise) confer its nationality to a large or disproportionate number of persons holding the nationality of a non-EU Member State, without prior consultation with the other Member States and the EU.[30] AG Maduro followed De Groot's opinion in the *Rottmann* case, in which he stated that the principle of sincere cooperation 'could be affected if a Member State were to carry out, without consulting the Commission or its partners, an unjustified mass naturalisation of

[21] R De Groot and Vonk, *International Standards*, 44–46; Donner, *The Regulation of Nationality in International Law* 2nd edn (Transnational Publishers 1994) 2; Weingerl and Tratnik, 'Relevant Links' in Kochenov and Surak (eds), *Citizenship and Residence Sales* (Cambridge 2023) 168–71.

[22] Eg R De Groot and Vonk, *International Standards*.

[23] Weingerl and Tratnik, 'Relevant Links', 180.

[24] Weis, *Nationality and Statelessness* 2nd edn (Sijthoff & Noordhoff 1979) 110; Spiro in this volume.

[25] The Convention on the Elimination of All Forms of Discrimination against Women (1979) 249 UNTS 13 (CEDAW); 1989 Convention on the Rights of the Child 1989 1577 UNTS 3; Arts 8 and 14 of Convention for the Protection of Human Rights and Fundamental Freedoms (1950) CETS 005. See *Genovese v Malta*, no. 53124/09, 11 October 2011.

[26] Weingerl and Tratnik, 'Relevant Links', 180.

[27] ibid 164; Sarmiento and Van den Brink, 'EU Competence and Investor Migration' in Kochenov and Surak (eds), *Citizenship and Residency Sales*, 183–206.

[28] Weingerl and Tratnik, 'Relevant Links', 172.

[29] ibid 176; Weis, *Nationality and Statelessness*, 110; Sironi, 'Nationality of Individuals in Public International Law: a Functional Approach' in Annoni and Forlati (eds), *The Changing Role of Nationality in International Law* (Routledge 2013) 54.

[30] R De Groot, 'The Relationship between the Nationality Legislation of the Member States of the European Union and European Citizenship', in La Torre (ed), *European Citizenship* (Kluwer Law International 1998) 115–47; R De Groot, 'Towards a European Nationality Law' (2004) 8 *Electronic Journal of Comparative Law* 1.

nationals of non-member States'.[31] Jessurun D'Oliveira is of a different opinion and considers that such a lack of notification would not violate the principle of sincere cooperation.[32] Moreover, Shaw argued that the 'mass naturalisation case' would not apply to CBIs since it concerns a limited number of persons.[33] Until now, there is no case law to evidence the influence of the principle of sincere cooperation on the nationality rules of the Member States.

The European Commission argues, however, that international law provides for more limitations of the national autonomy, which are supposedly based on the *Nottebohm*[34] decision of the International Court of Justice (ICJ) that introduced the problematic 'genuine link' that will be discussed in what follows (Section III). Contrary to what some authors and the Commission would contend, the genuine link criterion in *Nottebohm* was only applied to the recognition of Liechtenstein's nationality for the purpose of diplomatic protection, specifically against Guatemala.[35] To address the Commission's arguments in *Commission v Malta*, the analysis below discusses the genuine link criterion in EU law based on the principle of sincere cooperation both for the acquisition and for the recognition of nationality (Section IV).

III. *NOTTEBOHM* REVISITED

A. The Facts and the Decision of the ICJ

To analyse the claims of the Commission, it is necessary to take a closer look at the *Nottebohm* case. Friedrich Nottebohm was born in 1881 in Hamburg and acquired the German nationality by birth.[36] In 1905, after having spent two years in South Africa, he emigrated to Guatemala to join his elder brother's businesses there. In the 1930s, he became the head of the Nottebohm overseas companies. In autumn 1939, he visited another brother in Liechtenstein, where he acquired the Liechtenstein nationality using a privileged naturalisation procedure, available under the Liechtenstein nationality law. It also involved payment of a relatively large sum of money, therefore his naturalisation may be considered as the first famous acquisition of nationality by investment. Due to his naturalisation, he automatically lost his German nationality under Article 25 of the German Nationality Act of 1913. In early 1939, he obtained a Guatemalan visa in his Liechtenstein passport at the Consulate General of Guatemala in Zurich and returned to Guatemala. He entered the country with his Liechtenstein passport that was accepted by the immigration authorities. He was also registered as a foreigner with Liechtenstein nationality. On 11 December 1941, Guatemala declared war on Germany. It was merely a nominal declaration of war, no hostilities between the two countries took place.

On 19 October 1943, Nottebohm was arrested at the instigation of the USA and turned over to the armed forces of the United States on the same day. Three days later he was deported to the United States and interned there for two years and three months. There was no trial

[31] Opinion of AG Poiares Maduro, Case C-135/08 *Rottmann* ECLI:EU:C:2009:588, para 30.

[32] Jessurun d'Oliveira, 'Union Citizenship and Beyond' in Cambien et al (eds), *European Citizenship under Stress* (Brill-Nijhoff 2020) 28.

[33] Shaw, 'Citizenship for Sale' in Bauböck (ed), *Debating Transformations of National Citizenship* (Springer 2018) 61–64.

[34] *Nottebohm.*

[35] Van den Brink, 'Revising Citizenship within the European Union', 181.

[36] Based upon Art 3 of the Gesetz über die Erwerbung und den Verlust der Bundes- und Staatsangehörigkeit 1870 (GE), which was initially nationality law for the North German Union and became after the establishing of the Germany Empire in 1871 nationality law (Reich- und Staatsangehörigkeitsgesetz) for the whole German Empire. See R De Groot, *Staatsangehörigkeitsrecht im Wandel* (TMC Asser Instituut 1989) 54.

or inquiry in either country and he was not allowed to confront his accusers, defend himself or give evidence on his behalf.[37] Following the arrest, his property in Guatemala was seized and was subject to confiscation procedures. After his release in 1946, he wanted to return to Guatemala, but he was not admitted, so he took residence in Liechtenstein. In 1949, Guatemala adopted Decree Law No. 689,[38] which retroactively fixed the date of determination of alien status on October 7, 1938, when Nottebohm was still a German. After that the confiscation of his property in Guatemala became final. At that time, Nottebohm was already a resident of Liechtenstein for more than three years.[39] In 1951, Liechtenstein sued Guatemala before the ICJ, and in 1955, the ICJ denied Liechtenstein standing due to the lack of *genuine link* between Nottebohm and Liechtenstein.

What is this genuine link requirement? It follows from the Court's poetical definition of nationality:

> Nationality is a legal bond having as its basis a social fact of attachment, a genuine connection of existence, interests and sentiments, together with the existence of reciprocal rights and duties. It may be said to constitute the juridical expression of the fact that the individual upon whom it is conferred … is in fact more closely connected with the population of the State conferring nationality than with that of any other State.[40]

As AG Tesauro aptly remarked, the ICJ language belongs to the romantic period of international law.[41] Nonetheless, the attitude of persons regarding their nationality may be like the ICJ described it. Even though it is a legal concept, some people are very sentimental about their nationality, they are proud of it, they are irrationally attached to it, cry when their national team wins a medal, and so on. There is nothing wrong with that, though. Other people consider their nationality in a merely functional way. It guarantees them the entry to a certain, but not necessarily their favourite, state, the right to reside and work there, not to be expelled,[42] without any warm feelings about it. Nothing is wrong about that, either.

B. What Exactly did the ICJ Decide?

Not only the Commission but also several academics interpret the decision of the ICJ inaccurately.[43] It is therefore important to stress what the ICJ did decide, what it did not decide and what is the impact of the decision on the international law. The ICJ decided that because of the lack of a genuine link between Nottebohm and Liechtenstein, the latter could not exercise diplomatic protection of Nottebohm against Guatemala. The decision is limited to the issue of diplomatic protection between both countries[44] and it does not concern the

[37] Read, J, dissenting in *Nottebohm* 34.
[38] According to some sources 690 and 630.
[39] As rightfully noted by Klaestad, J, dissenting in *Nottebohm*, 31.
[40] *Nottebohm*, 23.
[41] See the Opinion of AG Tesauro in *Micheletti* ECLI:EU:C:1992:47. He rejected the application of 'effective nationality' and found it 'clear that possession of the nationality of a Member State is the only prerequisite which an individual must satisfy in order to be able to exercise the right'. Cited by Spiro in this volume; Kochenov, *Citizenship*, 115–16.
[42] Kochenov, *Citizenship*, 212.
[43] Eg R De Groot and Vonk, *International Standards*, 35; Ko Swan Sik, 'Nationaliteit en het Volkenrecht', in Ko Swan Sik, *Preadvies voor de Nederlandse vereniging voor Internationaal Recth* (Kluwer 1981) 20, referred to by R De Groot and Vonk, *International Standards*, 45.
[44] As the Court expressly noted (*Nottebohm* 17), but as Makarov commented, did not explain why Guatemala was so specific in this respect. See Makarov, 'Das Urteil des Internationalen Gerichtshofes im Fall *Nottebohm*' (1956) 16 *Zeitschrift fur Auslandisches offentliches Recht und Volkerrecht* 417.

possibility of diplomatic protection against other States (eg the USA). It also does not concern the question of recognition of Nottebohm's naturalisation in the 'international arena' as the Commission claims, in general.[45] Moreover, it does not concern the question whether genuine link is a condition for the attribution of nationality by birth or by any other mode of acquisition. In fact, the ICJ even expressly recognised that Liechtenstein had the right to naturalise Nottebohm in accordance with its internal law.[46] The ICJ also did not decide about the right of Guatemala to detain German nationals and to confiscate their property in Guatemala, even if it would be interesting whether such a right exists in cases of purely nominal declarations of war.[47]

There are commentators who contend that *Nottebohm* was not at all about genuine links, but about abuse of rights.[48] Nottebohm would supposedly abuse his right to be naturalised in Liechtenstein to change his nationality of a belligerent state to the nationality of a neutral state, and Liechtenstein would abuse its right to naturalise Nottebohm. We cannot share this opinion. First, Nottebohm most likely did not have any right to be naturalised in Liechtenstein. Naturalisation often lies in the discretion of the naturalising state.[49] Second, we also cannot agree that Liechtenstein would have abused his right to naturalise foreigners because this naturalisation helped Nottebohm to get rid of his German nationality. The right to naturalise non-nationals is a part of the national autonomy, which then and even now belongs to the *domaine réservé* of each individual state. This was even expressly confirmed by the ICJ in its decision.[50] The decision to naturalise Nottebohm also did not damage or in any way affect the rights of Guatemala, which would be the condition to apply the abuse of rights concept.[51] If Nottebohm's naturalisation affected another state, it was not Guatemala, but Germany, because he lost his German nationality and Germany lost a national, and even a very wealthy one. Moreover, we do not see that the Nottebohm's motive to change his nationality is relevant[52] or as some authors and the ICJ contend, 'ungenuine', 'insincere' or even fraudulent. At the time of Nottebohm's naturalisation, both Guatemala and Liechtenstein were neutral.[53] Guatemala declared war on Germany two years later. According to the US sources,[54] he was

[45] As also emphasised by Kunz, 'The *Nottebohm* Judgment', 551, 564.

[46] *Nottebohm*, 20.

[47] Kunz, 'The *Nottebohm* Judgment', 543; Makarov, 'Das Urteil', 425. It is not even clear whether Guatemala had the right to arrest Nottebohm and confiscate his possessions in case he would be a German national; See Potterf, 'Treatment of Alien Enemy Property in War Time and After by the United States' (1927) 2 *IND. LJ* 453. The US settled Nottebohm's claims in 1950 to the benefit of the latter; Buys, 'Nottebohm's Nightmare' (2011) 11 *Chi.-Kent J. Int'l & Comp. L.* 13–14; Kunz, 'The *Nottebohm* Judgment', 554.

[48] Sloane, 'Breaking the Genuine Link' (2009) 50 *Harv. Int'l LJ* 1.

[49] The Slovenian Nationality Act provides eight times (!) that the competent authority decides on naturalisation at its discretion. See Tratnik, *Pravo državljanstva* (Lexpera GV Založba 2018) 151.

[50] *Nottebohm* 20: 'It is for Liechtenstein, as it is for every sovereign State, to settle by its own legislation the rules relating to the acquisition of its nationality, and to confer that nationality by naturalization granted by its own organs in accordance with that legislation.'

[51] See on the issue of abuse of rights in this case also Kunz, 'The *Nottebohm* Judgment', 549 and Klæstad J, dissenting in *Nottebohm*, 31. Moreover, Read J, 37–38 wrote: 'The doctrine of abuse of right cannot be invoked by one State against another unless the State which is admittedly exercising its rights under international law causes damage to the State invoking the doctrine.'

[52] Read J, dissenting in *Nottebohm*, 42.

[53] See extensively EH Loewenfeld, 'Der Fall Nottebohm' (1956) 5 *Archiv des Völkerrechts* 387; Makarov, 'Das Urteil', 425, 426.

[54] A December 1945 Memorandum from the US Embassy in Guatemala states that 'Nottebohm's name does not appear on the Nazi party list believed to be authentic, and there is no reliable evidence to indicate that he was a member of the party or even a sympathizer of Hitler.' Memorandum on Frederico Nottebohm dated Dec. 6, 1945, Box 44, Dept. of State, Special War Problems Div., 1939-54: Name Files of Interned Enemy Aliens from Latin Am. (1942-48), Folder: "Nottebohm, Frederico," RG 59, National Archives, College Park, MD. Cited by Buys, 'Nottebohm's Nightmare', 12.

also not associated with the Nazi regime, which some accused him of. And in principle, is there anything wrong if a person being born with 'problematic' nationality uses an opportunity to change it for a more respected one?[55] Third country nationals seek naturalisation in EU Member States not necessarily because they feel attached to the Member State that grants them nationality but also or even mainly because they want to enjoy the privileges of EU citizens in the other Member States.

C. *Nottebohm* Controversies

Liechtenstein sued Guatemala before the ICJ because the latter subjected Nottebohm to treatment as an enemy German national, albeit he at the relevant time possessed exclusively the Liechtenstein nationality and Liechtenstein was a neutral state. It is true that pursuant to the Decree Law No. 689 Guatemala retroactively considered him as a German national, but this was contrary to international law, namely the 1930 Hague Convention on nationality.[56] Although Liechtenstein and Guatemala were not state parties to this Convention, both parties recognised that it represented valid international law.[57] Under Article 2, it was not Guatemala that could establish which nationality Nottebohm possessed, but Germany as to the loss of the German nationality and Liechtenstein as to the acquisition of the Liechtenstein nationality.[58] Moreover, by not recognising Nottebohm's naturalisation in Liechtenstein Guatemala infringed Article 1 of the Convention that provides that a foreign nationality law must be recognised by other states, 'in so far as it is consistent with international conventions, international custom, and the principles of law generally recognised with regard to nationality', or simply said, with international law. Guatemala argued before the ICJ that Nottebohm acquired the Liechtenstein nationality contrary to international law but was unsuccessful at this point.[59] It is interesting to mention that Guatemalan nationality law at that time provided for a similar privileged speedy naturalisation of Spaniards and 'Iberoamericans'.[60]

The ICJ did not decide that Nottebohm's naturalisation was invalid or that it would be contrary to international law. On the contrary, it even expressly recognised the right of Liechtenstein to grant its nationality to foreigners in accordance with its own internal law.[61] It only ruled that it, due to the lack of genuine link, missed full international effect, namely as regards the right of Liechtenstein to exercise diplomatic protection against Guatemala.

In accordance with Article 38(1) of its Statute, the ICJ has the obligation to apply international law; treaties, customary rules and general principles. Nonetheless, the ICJ did not apply any of that. It was not able to quote any treaties, customary international law or general principles in support of its position, that the genuine link would be a precondition to exercise diplomatic protection. The Court was also unable to quote a single judicial precedent in favour

[55] Cf Kunz, 'The *Nottebohm* Judgment': 'Even if Nottebohm had changed his nationality for the purpose of becoming the national of a neutral state there existed no rule of municipal or international law rendering his naturalisation invalid for that reason only.' See also Kochenov, *Citizenship*, 118.

[56] The Hague Convention.

[57] Loewenfeld, 'Der Fall Nottebohm', 400.

[58] See Art 2, the Hague Convention: 'Any question as to whether a person possesses the nationality of a particular State shall be determined in accordance with the law of that State.' Also Kunz, 'The *Nottebohm* Judgment', 548. Judge ad hoc Guggenheim dissenting in *Nottebohm*, 56.

[59] See Kunz, 'The *Nottebohm* Judgment', 550: 'As the case stood, it must be said that Nottebohm certainly did acquire Liechtenstein nationality, and did so validly, both under Liechtenstein and international law.'

[60] Jones, 'The *Nottebohm* Case' (1956) 5 *ICLQ* 230, 236–37.

[61] *Nottebohm* 20.

of the genuine link theory as constituting positive international law. Consequently, it based its reasoning as to Nottebohm, who all his life possessed only one nationality, on the issue of dual and multiple nationality, which as Kunz[62] rightfully noted, 'in no way fits the case'. The arbitral practice referred to by the Court[63] was dealing exclusively with cases of dual or multiple nationality. The same is true regarding Article 3(2) of the Court's Statute and Article 5 of the Hague Convention, as well as the so-called Bancroft Treaties, that were also expressly invoked by the Court.[64] All this makes the whole Court's reasoning at large irrelevant.[65] As Spiro[66] put it, the question in this case was not which of multiple nationalities to prefer for international purposes, but whether to validate his sole nationality for those purposes.[67]

Not surprisingly, the *Nottebohm* decision was harshly criticised already in the first years after it was rendered. The decision encountered criticism from a number of prominent international lawyers, such as: Makarov, Loewenfeld, Verzijl, Seidl Hohenveldern, Glazer, Merwyn Jones and Kunz, as well as the three dissenting judges Klaested, Read and ad hoc judge Guggenheim,[68] meanwhile it was appraised among others by Brownlie and Jessup.[69]

Kunz concludes as to the *Nottebohm* decision as follows:

> The judgment has hardly proved the existence of an 'absolute link' rule even in case of double nationality having nothing to do with the case at bar. Nor has the judgment proved the genuine link as a requirement of positive international law in cases where the person involved has had at all times only one nationality. The genuine link theory, as Mervyn Jones states, is a novel one, based only on the authority of the Court; the conclusion is, therefore, inescapable that the genuine link theory is not required by international law and, as applied in the Nottebohm Case, constitutes a clear-cut instance of judicial legislation.[70]

Among the most recent critics probably the most severe is Spiro. According to him *Nottebohm* may be among the ICJ's most famous opinions, but it is also surely among its least respected. As well as Thwaites,[71] he finds that the decision is a dead letter.[72] Among the contemporaneous criticists of the decision can also be found Dorr, Kochenov, Macklin, Sloane, Van den Brink, Sironi and Vermeer-Künzli.[73] Kochenov finds the decision is an 'entirely arbitrary and potentially harmful rule of international law',[74] and the genuine link model 'incoherent and

[62] Kunz, 'The *Nottebohm* Judgment', 556–60 extensively discussing the ICJ's double nationality argumentation.

[63] ibid, 22.

[64] ibid, 22–23. See Judge ad hoc Guggenheim's disssent, 59 very clearly: 'As for the Bancroft Treaties, which were invoked during the course of the proceedings, I consider it incorrect to regard these Treaties as constituting a precedent for the case of F. Nottebohm.'

[65] See also Read J, dissent in *Nottebohm*, 42; Loewenfeld, 'Der Fall Nottebohm', 400–01.

[66] Spiro in this volume; Kunz, 'The *Nottebohm* Judgment', 538.

[67] According to Brownlie, 'The Relations of Nationality in Public International Law', 354. However, the critics did not prove why the doctrine of effectiveness only applies to certain permutations of fact.

[68] All cited by Kunz, 'The *Nottebohm* Judgment', 537–38.

[69] Brownlie, 'The Relations of Nationality in Public International Law', 314: 'The doctrine of the effective link may be classified either as a rule of customary law or as a general principle of (international) law.' Jessup, in *Proceedings, Second Summer Conference on International Law* (Cornell Law School 1958) 43, 49. Jessup also wrote that the fact that the decision was not based upon the arguments of the parties is the only criticism, which can properly be directed at the Court's decision in *Nottebohm*. Separate Opinion of Jessup, J, *Case Concerning Barcelona Traction, Light, and Power Co., Ltd* (Belgium v Spain) [1970] ICJ Rep. 3, para 38.

[70] Kunz, 'The *Nottebohm* Judgment', 560.

[71] Thwaites, 'The Life and Times of the Genuine Link' (2018) 49 *VUWLR* 645, 655.

[72] Spiro in this volume.

[73] ibid. See also Sironi, 'Nationality of Individuals', 54. On the other side, Blackman, 'State Successions and Statelessness' (1998) 19 *Mich. J. Int'l. L.* 1141, 1160 wrote: 'From a common law perspective, Nottebohm can be viewed as a quite reasonable judgment about legal standing.'

[74] Kochenov, 'Two Sovereign States vs. A Human Being' in Talani (ed), *Globalisation, Migration, and the Future of Europe* (Routledge 2012).

logically inexplicable'.[75] Following Macklin, 'Nottebohm "was wrong then, and may be even more wrong now" and that it is time to "retire" Nottebohm'.[76] According to Sloane, the 'sociopolitical, romanticist vision of nationality articulated by the Nottebohm majority has become increasingly anachronistic and misplaced today'.[77] Thwaites similarly characterises *Nottebohm* as a 'dead letter' and dismisses *Nottebohm* saying that 'the "restrictive innovation" of Nottebohm has proved to be a "one-off"'.[78] Vermeer-Künzli wrote that the *Nottebohm* case has been criticised rather strongly, and rightly so.[79] Dorr, for example writes, that *Nottebohm*

> was not successful … in setting up the requirement of a genuine connection for the exercise of diplomatic protection in cases of nationality conferred through naturalization. Its reasoning in this respect was unconvincing, and the consequences of the genuine link rule were seen to be disadvantageous for the position of individuals in international law.[80]

According to Van den Brink, '[T]he facts in Nottebohm show how harmful the enforcement of a genuine link requirement can be.'[81]

D. Infringement of International Law?

It is a well-established rule of customary international law that states have the right to exercise diplomatic protection.[82] They have the right to invoke international responsibility of another state that mistreated their nationals. In the *Nottebohm* case Liechtenstein stood up for Nottebohm, because Guatemala severely violated his fundamental human rights, most notably the right to fair trial, the right to property and the right to personal freedom. Nottebohm was treated as a German, that is, an enemy national of Guatemala, while in fact he was a national of Liechtenstein at the moment he was subjected to this treatment, and Liechtenstein was a neutral state. As it was demonstrated above, the ICJ denied standing to Liechtenstein based upon arguments built upon the assumption that he was a dual national. Those arguments should be treated as irrelevant, since it was not a case of double nationality, nor a case of diplomatic protection of a double national against his other national state.[83] Yet, there was a certain resemblance to the latter. Nottebohm did not possess the Guatemalan nationality,[84] but he was a resident of Guatemala for decades. He had the centre of his interests there[85] and, undoubtedly, Guatemala was the only state with which he had a dense relationship. This last fact makes the case even more bizarre, because Guatemala mistreated a person who had a (genuine) link

[75] Kochenov, 'Citizenship Without Respect' (2010) Jean Monnet Paper No. 8/10.

[76] Macklin, 'Is it Time to Retire *Nottebohm*?' (2017) 111 *AJIL Unbound* 492. Also cited by Spiro in this volume.

[77] Sloane, 'Breaking the Genuine Link', 5.

[78] Thwaites, 'The Life and Times of the Genuine Link', 661.

[79] Vermeer-Künzli, 'Nationality and Diplomatic Protection' in Annoni and Forlati (eds), *The Changing Role of Nationality in International Law*, 77.

[80] Dörr, '*Nottebohm* Case', in Max Planck Encyclopedia of Public International Law (Oxford University Press 2007).

[81] Van den Brink, 'Revising Citizenship within the European Union', 3.

[82] *Mavrommatis Palestine Concessions* (Greece v U.K.) [1924] PCIJ Series B no. 3; *Panevezys-Saldutiskis Railway* (Estonia v Lithuania) [1938] PCIJ Series A/B no. 76; See also Crawford, *Brownlie's Principles*, 495; Makarov, 'Das Urteil', 414; Jones, 'The *Nottebohm* Case', 230; Vermeer-Künzli, 'As If: The Legal Fiction in Diplomatic Protection' (2007) 18 *EJIL* 37.

[83] See also Kunz, 'The *Nottebohm* Judgment', 561.

[84] Even if he had acquired the Guatemalan nationality, that would not protect him against the Guatemalan measures. His nephews Karl-Heinz and Kurt did have Guatemalan nationality but that did not prevent their internation as 'enemy nationals'; See Buys, 'Nottebohm's Nightmare', 8–9.

[85] As also recognised by the ICJ in *Nottebohm*, 25, 26.

to Guatemala close of that of a 'national'. Brownlie[86] even found: 'The Court decided that the effective nationality was that of Guatemala.'

By its decision, the ICJ, as Kunz rightfully observed, imposed a new restriction on the exercise of diplomatic protection, that had no basis in international law.[87] According to Mervyn Jones,[88] it was 'a novel principle', 'an entirely new theory of international claims'. The *Nottebohm* decision regarding the condition of genuine link to exercise diplomatic protection stands of course as a subsidiary source of international law, pursuant to Article 38(1)(d), but it was never confirmed in cases of single nationality.[89] The ILC Draft Articles on Diplomatic Protection 2006 even expressly rejected the decision.[90]

Said Articles[91] provide under Articles 3, 4 and 5 that every state of nationality may exercise diplomatic protection. In the case of two or more nationalities, every national state has the right to diplomatic protection, which can also be exercised jointly. There are two limitations: (i) a state cannot exercise diplomatic protection if its nationality was acquired in a manner inconsistent with international law; (ii) in case of multiple nationality, it is not allowed to exercise diplomatic protection against another national state (Article 7).[92] The second limitation allows even for an exception, namely if the nationality of the claiming state is predominant. In this last case, it may be assumed that the criterion of predominance bears a considerable resemblance with the genuine link criterion.[93] Therefore, genuine link indeed plays a role in the modern law of diplomatic protection, but a very limited one. In cases of a single nationality, the genuine link does not play any role at all. Vermeer-Künzli[94] writes: 'Even if one must criticize the dictum in the Nottebohm case for its insistence on the genuine attachment of individuals to their state of nationality in the 1950s, today such insistence is not supported by international law.' It may be concluded that the recent developments go in the direction of widening of the possibility of diplomatic protection.[95] It must however also be noted, that the issue is losing

[86] Brownlie, 'The Relations of Nationality in Public International Law', 355 citing the Court's decision at 25–26.

[87] Kunz, 'The *Nottebohm* Judgment', 562, 565; similarly, Makarov, 'Das Urteil' 414, 415. Also Judge Owada has pointed out that the genuine-link theory had never been mentioned in the textbooks before the *Nottebohm* case was decided. Cited by Andaenas, 'Jurisdiction, Procedure and the Transformation of International Law' (2011) The ICJ Cambridge University Research Paper no. 53/2011, 15.

[88] Jones, 'The *Nottebohm*', 231, 242. On the contrary, Jessup wrote in his separate opinion to the *Barcelona Traction* judgment, para 42: 'I do not agree that in that instance the Court created a new rule of law. Indeed the underlying principle was already well established in connection with diplomatic claims on behalf of corporations.'

[89] See eg *Flegenheimer* (U.S. v Italy) [1958] 14 RIAA 327, 376. *Nottebohm* was indeed applied by the Iran–US claims tribunal in *Iran v United States*, Case A/18, 5 Iran-U.S.C.T.R. 251 (1984). See the comment on both cases by Spiro in this volume.

[90] See ILC, Draft Articles (2006), Commentary to Art 4, 30: 'If the genuine link proposed by Nottebohm was strictly applied, it would exclude millions of persons from the benefit of diplomatic protection.' See also John Dugard (Special Rapporteur on Diplomatic Protection), the First Report of the Special Rapporteur on Diplomatic Protection (2000) A/CN.4/506; also cited by Macklin, 'Is It Time to Retire Nottebohm?', 492; see also Worster, 'Reining in the *Nottebohm* Case', 311; Worster in this volume.

[91] It is arguable whether the ILC Articles can be deemed to represent customary international law, but in any case, they can be considered as 'teachings of the most highly qualified publicists' under Art 38(1)(d) of Statute of the International Court of Justice (1946) 33 UNTS 993.

[92] Makarov, 'Das Urteil', 414.

[93] Commentary to Art 7 of ILC, Draft Articles (2006), 35; Vermeer-Künzli, 'Nationality and Diplomatic Protection', 82–89.

[94] Vermeer-Künzli, 'Nationality and Diplomatic Protection', 89–91 as regards Art 8 of ILC, Draft Articles (2006) providing for diplomatic protection of stateless people and refugees.

[95] See eg *Application of the Convention on the Prevention and Punishment of the Crime of Genocide* (Gambia v Myanmar), Preliminary objections [2022] ICJ Rep 477; See also Heieck, 'Judicial Intervention and the Duty to Prevent Genocide' (Opinio Juris, 25 August 2020) https://opiniojuris.org/2020/08/25/rohingya-symposium-judicial-intervention-and-the-duty-to-prevent-genocide-in-the-rohingya-genocide-case-the-role-of-obligatio-erga-omnes-and-nouvelle-protection-diplomatique/; Marilyn and Immanuel, '*The Gambia v Myanmar*'; see also Vermeer-Künzli,

its importance, due to the high level of human rights in national and international law, the existence of international human rights courts and mechanisms for the protection of investors (such as the Investor State Dispute Mechanisms – ISDS).

Looking at the case retrospectively, it might even be argued that the ICJ also infringed Notttebohm's right to a nationality.[96] Seven years before the *Nottebohm* decision, the General Assembly of the United Nations adopted the Universal Declaration of Human Rights that provides in Article 15 for the right to a nationality as a fundamental human right. Article 15(2) states that 'no one shall be arbitrarily deprived of his nationality nor denied the right to change his nationality'. By not admitting Liechtenstein to exercise diplomatic protection, the ICJ rendered *Nottebohm* as to the possibility of diplomatic protection stateless.[97] Its decision, factually on unsound grounds, deprived him of his only nationality for the purposes of diplomatic protection, which left him with no possibility of international protection. A very important implication of the right to a nationality is namely that this right implies the possibility[98] to enjoy international protection by the national state. Moreover, not recognising Liechtenstein's right to diplomatic protection had the same effect as denial of Nottebohm's right to change his nationality.[99]

To conclude our observations on Nottebohm, his only fault was probably the fact that he was born as a German and lived in a wrong time. As Andenas[100] rightfully observed:

> Kurt Lipstein would have won *Nottebohm* for Lichtenstein had it been decided today. The International Court would not have invented the requirements of 'effective nationality' and 'a meaningful connection' to the relevant state as it did under strong pressure from the victors of the Second World War. These countries had strong economic interests in not to open up other fora of review for many war–time confiscations.

It is also interesting to mention Worster's analysis of the recent decision in the *CERD Quatar v UAE*[101] case, where the author concludes that the ICJ itself seems to go back on *Nottebohm*'s genuine link theory.[102]

IV. IS THERE A GENUINE LINK CRITERION IN EU LAW?

A. The Complex Relationship between National Autonomy and EU Citizenship

As established above, there exists no genuine link requirement for the acquisition or the recognition of nationality in international law. However, the question is whether the situation may

'Nationality and Diplomatic Protection', 89–90; Andenas, 'Jurisdiction, Procedure and the Transformation of International Law'. Moreover, Art 8 of the ILC Draft Articles (2006) opened the possibility of diplomatic protection of stateless people and refugees.

[96] In this sense also Loewenfeld, 'Der Fall *Nottebohm*', 399. See also Worster, 'Reining in the *Nottebohm* Case', 316–20.

[97] Loewenfeld, 'Der Fall *Nottebohm*', 399; Macklin, 'Is It Time to Retire *Nottebohm*?', 494; Spiro in this volume; Van den Brink, 'Revising Citizenship within the European Union', 4.

[98] It is only the possibility, not a right, since individuals do not have an enforceable right to diplomatic protection against their national state.

[99] Thomas and Thomas Jr, 'Human Rights and the Organization of American States' (1972) 12 *Santa Clara LRev* 319, 362: 'many authorities believed the International Court of Justice "arbitrarily" deprived Nottebohm of his right to change his nationality'.

[100] Andaenas 'Jurisdiction, Procedure and the Transformation of International Law', 14.

[101] *Application of the International Convention on the Elimination of All Forms of Racial Discrimination* (Qatar v U.A.E.), Preliminary Objections [2021] ICJ Rep. 71, 81.

[102] See Worster, 'Reining in the *Nottebohm* Case', 301–30.

differ in EU law due to the concept of EU citizenship. Typically, the acquisition of nationality entails rights and responsibilities within the national legal framework without direct implications for other states. However, in accordance with the Treaties, particularly Article 20(1) TFEU, individuals becoming nationals of a Member State automatically obtain EU citizenship. This provision stipulates that EU citizenship 'shall be additional to and not replace national citizenship'. It is intended to be the 'fundamental status of nationals of the Member States',[103] and as such, it must be recognised and respected across all other 26 Member States.[104] Consequently, Member States have obligations under EU law concerning the treatment of nationals of other Member States as EU citizens. This dynamic highlights the intricate interplay between the regulation of a Member State's nationality, which remains within the domain of individual Member States, and the automatic attribution of EU citizenship rights to nationals of Member States, which are enforceable throughout the EU. This suggests that if a Member State adopts overly inclusive rules for the acquisition of its nationality, it could potentially pose challenges and concerns for other Member States. Could this pose a legal issue under EU law?

As aforementioned, the CJEU confirmed the national autonomy of Member States in matters of nationality already in *Micheletti*.[105] However, it also ruled that Member States must exercise their national autonomy by laying down the conditions for the acquisition and loss of nationality 'having due regard to Community law'. To date, the CJEU has addressed issues related to the loss of nationality, and to the revocation of the assurance of naturalisation that amounted in the loss of the EU citizenship. The first case dealing with the acquisition of a Member State nationality and therewith the EU citizenship is still pending.[106] In the context of the loss of nationality, the CJEU has consistently emphasised, through its rulings in preliminary reference procedures, that Member States are obliged to uphold the principle of proportionality when implementing their regulations on the loss of nationality.[107] Thus, the principle of proportionality serves as a limitation of national autonomy. It was initially applied in the *Rottmann* case and has since been further elaborated upon by the CJEU in cases referred by Dutch, Danish, Austrian and German courts (cases *Tjebbes*, *Udlændinge- og Integrationsministeriet, JY*, and *S.Ö. and others*,[108] respectively). In *Tjebbes*, the CJEU highlighted the importance of fundamental rights in the proportionality assessment, especially when deciding on the loss of nationality of children.

The principle of proportionality, together with fundamental rights, has the potential to curtail national autonomy in matters of nationality to the benefit of individuals whose nationality could be stripped away. Thus, as aforementioned, they are used by EU citizens as a shield against Member States' measures affecting their nationality.[109] However, its impact on the broader operation of nationality regulations remains somewhat limited. More consequential

[103] Case C-184/99 *Grzelczyk* EU:C:2001:458.

[104] Weingerl and Tratnik, 'Relevant Links', 182–83.

[105] *Micheletti*. See also *Tjebbes* case (Case C-221/17 *Tjebbes* ECLI:EU:C:2019:189) and its influence on the nationality laws of the Member States; R De Groot, 'Loss of nationality due to permanent residence abroad' (EU-CITZEN 2020) 21–25 https://commission.europa.eu/system/files/2022-01/eu-citzen_-_type_a_report_-_study_loss_of_nationality_due_to_permanent_residence_abroad_tjebbes.pdf; Kochenov, 'The *Tjebbes* Fail' (2019) 4 *European Papers* 319; Kochenov and D De Groot, 'Helpful, Convoluted, and Ignorant in Principle' (2022) 47 *ELRev* 699.

[106] *Commission v Malta* pending. This contribution was submitted in September 2024. In November 2024, A.G. Collins in his Opinion (ECLI:EU:C:2024:849) largely confirmed the views expressed in this contribution.

[107] Case C-135/08 *Rottmann* ECLI:EU:C:2010:104; *Tjebbes*; Case C-689/21 *X v Udlaendinge- og Integrationsministeriet* ECLI:EU:C:2023:626.

[108] Case C-118/20 *JY* ECLI:EU:C:2022:34 and Joined cases C-684/22 to C-686/22 *S.Ö. and Others* ECLI:EU:C:2024:345.

[109] Weingerl and Tratnik, 'Relevant Links', 176; See also Lenaerts and Van Nuffel, *EU Constitutional Law* (Oxford University Press 2021) 135 and references in fn 21.

for Member States' autonomy are potential restrictions imposed by other Member States and the EU through the principle of sincere or loyal cooperation requirements in the stages of acquisition or the recognition of nationality. There is so far no case law of the CJEU on this matter. However, in the pending case *Commission v Malta*, the Commission claims that Malta has supposedly infringed this principle because of its CBI programme, since it 'offers naturalisation in the absence of a genuine link of the applicants with the country, in exchange for pre-determined payments or investments'.[110] The subsequent analysis explores whether potential limitations imposed by the principle of sincere cooperation can be legally enforced under EU law or if they perhaps derive only from the political arsenal of both Member States and the EU.[111]

B. The Principle of Sincere Cooperation (Loyalty) and its Integrationist Push in the 'Federal' Order

The principle of sincere cooperation (also referred to as the principle of loyal cooperation or the duty to cooperate in good faith[112]) is enshrined in Article 4(3) TEU. Article 4 TEU is dubbed as 'a core provision to understand the "federal" nature of the European Union'.[113] It is composed of three paragraphs which try to strike a balance between the EU and the Member States. The first paragraph enshrines the so-called 'principle of presumed Member States competences', which is devoted to the vertical division of competences and strengthens the respect of the principle of conferral. The second paragraph requires the EU to respect Member States' national identities, inherent in their fundamental political and constitutional structures. The third paragraph enshrines the principle of sincere cooperation or loyalty, which should inform the cooperation among levels of government. In this respect, all the paragraphs express a sort of 'federal concern'.[114]

This 'federal' architecture of Article 4 TEU and the place of the principle of sincere cooperation in it should inform the understanding of the contours of this principle, which is a reflection of 'federal good faith'.[115] What exactly is the content and role of Article 4(3) TEU?

A closer look reveals that it contains both positive and negative obligations. Positive obligations are related to ensuring the effectiveness of EU law in the Member States and a more general duty to cooperate in the achievement of the Union's objectives. It also expresses a negative obligation on the Member States to 'refrain from any measure which could jeopardise the attainment of the Union's objectives'. The objectives referred to are found in Article 3 TEU.[116]

The principle is modelled on the international principle of good faith and the (domestic) principle of federal fidelity.[117] The principle of good faith is a general principle of international law which flows directly from the rule *pacta sunt servanda*. In this respect, a concretisation of the principle of good faith in international law manifests in the prohibition against the abuse

[110] *Commission v Malta*.

[111] See also Shaw, 'Citizenship for Sale', 61.

[112] Lenaerts and Van Nuffel, *EU Constitutional Law*, 110.

[113] Guastaferro, 'Sincere Cooperation and Respect for National Identities' in Schütze and Tridimas (eds), *Oxford Principles of European Union Law* Vol 1 (Oxford University Press 2018); on EU citizenship within the EU federal context, see contributions in Kochenov (ed), *EU Citizenship and Federalism* (Cambridge University Press 2017).

[114] Guastaferro, 'Sincere Cooperation'.

[115] Lenaerts and Van Nuffel, *EU Constitutional Law*, 110.

[116] See also Klamert, *The Principle of Loyalty in EU Law* (Oxford University Press 2014) 290.

[117] Guastaferro, 'Sincere Cooperation', 359.

of rights. This occurs when a state exercises its rights in a manner that arbitrarily infringes upon the rights of another Member State, failing to consider the legitimate expectations of the latter.[118]

The CJEU confirmed that good faith is part of the EU legal order,[119] expressly linking this general principle with the specific principle of legitimate expectations.[120] However, good faith in international law and loyal cooperation in EU law should not be seen as equivalent.[121] While both attach to the Member States similar positive duties of assistance and similar negative duties of abstention, only the EU Treaty requires Member States to 'facilitate the achievement of the Union's tasks'.[122] Thus, while good faith can have a pivotal role in the determination of obligations, it can generally not be the source of such obligations.[123] The question is: what is the extent of these obligations in EU law?

The CJEU has played a crucial role in elucidating the principle as a *legal* obligation for Member States to uphold their commitments outlined in Article 4(3) TEU in safeguarding the interests of the Union.[124] It has imposed wide-reaching obligations applying to both the judicial and the administrative authorities of the Member States.[125] In its case law, the principle of sincere cooperation has been used in connection with the implementation of EU law, either requiring Member States to put into effect some provisions of the Treaty (eg by eliminating custom duties) or preventing Member States from using provisions and practices existing within its internal legal system to justify a failure to comply with obligations laid down by EU law.[126] Moreover, it sometimes formed the legal basis for new Member State's obligations that cannot be derived from other Treaty provisions, but are necessary to attain Treaty's objectives.[127] The well-known examples of such obligations created based on the principle of sincere cooperation are, for instance, the doctrine of state liability (*Francovich*) and the creation of interim measures (*Factortame*).[128]

Thus, historically, the principle of sincere cooperation was not recognised as 'neutral'. It carried a strong integrationist force, which might favour the EU at the expense of the Member States.[129] The literature has referred to the principle as a sort of 'reverse subsidiarity'.[130] To this end, it bears the potential of intruding into Member States' autonomy (eg national procedural autonomy, also in criminal matters (*Taricco* case), also the principle of conferral).[131] Reuter called it a 'competence creep through the duty of loyalty'.[132] However, this amplifying power of the loyalty clause has its limits. As Cremona, and also Klamert, argued, the Union

[118] ibid, 359–60; Reinhold, 'Good Faith in International Law' (2013) 2 Bonn Research Papers on Public International Law No. 2/2013, 8–9.

[119] The General Court held that the principle of good faith is a rule of customary international law binding on the Union in Case T-115/94 *Opel Austria GmbH v Council* ECLI:EU:T:1997:3, para 24.

[120] Guastaferro, 'Sincere Cooperation', 360.

[121] de Baere and Roes, 'EU Loyalty and Good Faith' (2015) 64 *ICLQ* 829.

[122] Guastaferro, 'Sincere Cooperation', 361.

[123] Reinhold, 'Good Faith in International Law', 2.

[124] Lang, 'Developments, Issues and New Remedies' (2003) 27 *Fordham Int'l. LJ.* 1904; Carrera, 'The Price of EU Citizenship' (2014) 21 *MJ* 406, 420.

[125] Guastaferro, 'Sincere Cooperation', 362; Reinhold, 'Good Faith in International Law', 20.

[126] Guastaferro, 'Sincere Cooperation', 354.

[127] Herzog, 'Article 4 TEU on Relationship Between the European Union and Its Member States' in Herzog et al (eds), *Smit and Herzog on the Law of the European Union* (LexisNexis 2005).

[128] Case C-213/89 *Factortame* ECLI:EU:C:1990:257; Joined cases C-6&9/90 *Francovich* ECLI:EU:C:1991:428.

[129] Guastaferro, 'Sincere Cooperation'.

[130] ibid, 374, referring to Schütze, *European Constitutional Law* 2nd edn (Oxford University Press 2015) 218.

[131] ibid.

[132] Reuter, *Competence Creep via the Duty of Loyalty?* (Doctoral Thesis, EUI 2013).

interest in this context has been conceived 'as a restraint on but not a denial of Member State competence'.[133] It should be recalled that Article 4 TEU, in its first paragraph, itself reminds us of the principle of conferral and the sensitive division of competences in the EU. This is a more procedural limitation, related to the formal legitimacy of EU rules. Moreover, another limitation, related to the material legitimacy of EU rules, are the interests and the related objectives pursued with such a competence creep. As Klamert noted, 'loyalty does not protect the interests of one Member State against the interests of other Member States, but it is primarily about the safeguarding of Union interests'.[134]

Thus, can one legitimately claim that the principle of sincere cooperation's integrationist force can lead to the intervention into national competence in nationality matters based on the genuine link requirement? The interpretation that naturally flows from Article 4(3) TEU suggests a negative answer. As seen, the 'competence creep through the duty of loyalty' would, if at all, be justified to 'facilitate the achievement of the Union's tasks' in light of the Treaty's objectives. Which Treaty's objectives could the principle of sincere cooperation further with its intervention into nationality matters? Already here, it should be recalled that the objectives of the EU are found in Article 3 TEU, and that they do not encompass any goal in relation to discrimination on the basis of a particular type of citizenship acquisition, or any kind of ethnic nationalism based on 'purity of European blood in one's veins' as explained by Kochenov[135] and dwelled upon below. As it will be shown, the Commission's allegations that the CBI programmes pose a threat to the concept of EU citizenship and the principle of sincere cooperation, due to the lack of genuine link, suggest disrespect for the division of powers in the EU and itself contravene the EU objectives, most notably the internal market and the principle of free movement.[136]

The remaining parts of this section will discuss the lack of compelling arguments for a genuine link to be introduced as a requirement for either the acquisition or the recognition of nationality based on the principle of sincere cooperation.

C. Application of the Principle of Sincere Cooperation to Nationality Matters (Genuine Link and Other Concerns)

Nationality matters and their implications for EU citizenship are a prime example of the composite EU order reflected in the federal nature of Article 4 TEU. Since the *Micheletti* case, the Member States must consider EU law in the operation of their nationality laws. To what extent are they still free to lay down the grounds for the acquisition and loss of nationality without EU supervision and accountability? The more precise question here is whether the overinclusive attribution rules of a Member State can affect the principle of sincere cooperation. Or perhaps, the other way around, could it be limiting the EU's encroachment on the Member States' competence in the matter of nationality? To this end, it should be recalled that Article 13(2) TEU imposes the duty of sincere cooperation on the Union too.[137]

[133] Cremona, 'Defending the Community Interest' in Cremona and de Witte (eds), *EU Foreign Relations Law* (Hart 2008) 168; Klamert, *The Principle of Loyalty in EU Law*, 122.

[134] Klamert, *The Principle of Loyalty in EU Law*, 25.

[135] Kochenov, 'Policing the Genuine Purity of Blood' (2021) 25 *Studies in European Affairs* 33. See also Kochenov and Basheska in this volume.

[136] See also Kochenov and Basheska in this volume. Nevertheless, the Commission's action against Malta is provided as one of the examples of the fight for the rule of law, see 'Review 2: The Commission's Rule of Law Reporting' (European Court of Auditors 2024).

[137] It provides: 'Each institution shall act within the limits of the powers conferred on it in the Treaties, and in conformity with the procedures, conditions and objectives set out in them. The institutions shall practice mutual sincere cooperation.'

In practice, the respect of principle of sincere cooperation in matters of nationality means that Member States' actions in the nationality domain cannot negatively affect in substance the concept and freedoms of EU citizenship.[138] It is questionable whether the principle itself adds anything in this respect, since the Member States may not negatively affect the rights and freedoms of EU citizens in any case. As aforementioned, in the pending case *Commission v Malta*, the Commission claims that Malta has supposedly infringed this principle because of its CBI programme, since it 'offers naturalisation in the absence of a genuine link of the applicants with the country'.[139] How can horizontal loyalty, based on the principle of mutual trust[140] and entitling Member States to expect that other Member States fulfil their obligations under EU law, apply in such a scenario?

If the obsolete *Nottebohm* is applied to this situation, we can distinguish two scenarios. The first is the question of the acquisition of nationality through the CBI programme. The EU has no competence here, however, the EU citizenship reality brings the matter into the realm of EU law. Yet, any intervention into these matters should respect the division of powers in the EU and it should further and not obstruct EU objectives. The second situation is the question of the recognition of such nationalities, and, consequently, the additional EU citizenships in other Member States. Can the absence of a genuine link lead to rejection of such nationalities based on the principle of sincere cooperation? Can one say that Member States have the legitimate expectation not to be burdened with at least (possibly) 'problematic' newly naturalised persons? The analysis first focuses on the genuine link as a condition for the acquisition of nationality by naturalisation. and then turns to genuine the link as a condition for the recognition of nationality by other Member States.

i. Acquisition of Nationality: Genuine Link as a Limitation of National Competence?

As aforementioned, EU law, similarly to international law, does not impose the genuine link criterion as regards the acquisition of nationality. In fact, it is a national competence to decide on the acquisition and loss of national and EU citizenship. As seen from the case law of the CJEU, the principle of sincere cooperation could arguably and not entirely uncontroversially interfere with the national competence in this context, but only to 'facilitate the achievement of the Union's tasks' in light of the Treaty's objectives.

As stated above, the objectives of the EU do not encompass any goal in relation to discrimination on the basis of a particular type of citizenship acquisition or any kind of ethnic nationalism. They do, however, encompass 'the strict observance and the development of international law'. To this end, it should be recalled that international law prohibits discrimination based on a particular type of citizenship acquisition. To this end, Article 5 of ECN prohibits discrimination against naturalised citizens.[141] The two main groups of rights that

[138] Carrera, 'The Price of EU Citizenship', 406.

[139] *Commission v Malta*.

[140] Case C-359/16 *Altun* ECLI:EU:C:2018:63; Lenaerts and Van Nuffel, *EU Constitutional Law*, 113.

[141] Art 24(3) in conjunction with Art 24(1) of International Covenant on Civil and Political Rights (1966) 999 UNTS 171 prohibits discrimination regarding the acquisition of nationality between legitimate children, children born out of wedlock, children of stateless parents and based on the nationality status of one or both parents of a child. See von Rütte, *The Human Right to Citizenship*, 106. For the prohibition of discrimination on the grounds of birth (out of wedlock), see also ECtHR case *Genovese v Malta*. Another instrument prohibiting discrimination in the acquisition of citizenship is CEDAW. Art 9 CEDAW does not grant a right to nationality as such, but it prohibits discrimination on the basis of sex or gender in the acquisition and transmission of nationality, or more generally, on equality in the application of nationality laws. Thus, it has the character of an equality norm. Spiro, 'A New International Law of Citizenship' (2011) 105 *AJIL* 694, 714. Moreover, Art 1(3) of International Convention on the Elimination of All

EU citizenship grants to EU citizens concern free movement and so-called political rights. As O'Leary argued, 'one of the products of the free movement of Union citizens in an area of freedom, security and justice may be precisely a generation of Union citizens with multiple nationalities, allegiances and genuine links'.[142] Though the idea of citizenship inherently excludes and discriminates against certain people, the nationalist ethnic undertone of the argument in favour of genuine link requirement in the EU sits in stark tension with the idea of the internal market and the free movement. Discriminating against a particular type of acquisition of nationality, and thereby EU citizenship, and to this end undermining the EU's objectives of the internal market and free movement of persons in the name of sincere cooperation, which is said to have an integrationist push, seems to obstruct integration instead of advancing it.[143]

In light of the internal market objective, one can ponder whether, in fact, CBI programmes create what seems to be an ideal EU citizen in accordance with the existing EU legislation: mobile across borders, rich ('having sufficient resources') and not relying on social security and/or healthcare support in the new Member State of residence.[144] Several authors argued that, in practice, the legal framework established by Directive 2004/38 is designed for the rich, while it renders the right to free movement impossible for indigent people.[145] This is part of a broader EU's problem 'in reconciling the right to free movement and the policy objectives of fighting poverty and social exclusion'.[146] To some extent, it is echoed in the criticism that CBI programmes reflect 'the inherent lack of fairness and discrimination CBI/RBI schemes represent, relative to other pathways to residence and citizenship'.[147] However, excluding the rich most probably will not save this issue. As Van der Mei formulated: 'When taken seriously, Union citizenship ought to be developed in such a way that both the "rich and the poor" can enjoy the rights that come with it.'[148]

Thus, an introduction of a genuine link as a condition for the acquisition of nationality through the principle of sincere cooperation is not compatible either with the objectives of the EU or with the CJEU's interpretation of the contours of this principle. The European Parliament's and Commission's insistence on the genuine link as the most important dimension within the larger context of the principle of sincere cooperation can be seen as a double-edged argument raising a fundamental dilemma from the angle of EU citizenship.[149] One can legitimately claim that it will open the Pandora's box.[150] One of the issues is its vagueness. What is genuine and effective? What is precisely 'habitual', 'effective' or 'functional' residence for the purposes of EU citizenship law?[151] Putting that aside, other concerns with this requirement encompass the problems of inconsistent and arbitrary application.[152] It is a slippery slope. Genuine link cannot be applied in isolation, only to CBI programmes. Several Member States operate some sort of privileged naturalisation schemes in the 'national interest' for some

Forms of Racial Discrimination (1965) 660 UNTS 195 prohibits discrimination against any particular nationality in nationality, citizenship or naturalisation matters. von Rütte, *The Human Right to Citizenship*, 118.

[142] O'Leary, 'Nationality and Citizenship' in Lenaerts et al (eds), *An Ever-Changing Union?* (Hart 2019) 78.

[143] See extensively on this issue Kochenov and Basheska in this volume.

[144] See Directive 2004/38/EC on the right of citizens of the Union and their family members to move and reside freely within the territory of the Member States [2004] OJ L 158/77, 77–123.

[145] Verschueren, 'Free Movement of EU Citizens' (2015) 22 *MJ* 10.

[146] ibid, 10.

[147] Fernandes et al, 'Avenues for EU Action', 25–27.

[148] Van der Mei, *Free Movement of Persons within the European Community* (Hart 2003) 220.

[149] Carrera, 'The Price of EU Citizenship', 423.

[150] See also Jessurun d'Oliveira, 'Union Citizenship and beyond', 40.

[151] ibid.

[152] Weingerl and Tratnik, 'Relevant Links', 178–80; Van den Brink, 'Revising Citizenship within the European Union'.

reason, including economic.[153] Thus, can other naturalisations be in the spotlight, too, based on the (alleged) lack of it?

CBI programmes are one of the several grounds for privileged naturalisation that most Member States nationality rules provide for. Most such rules have one thing in common: naturalisation is granted, even if there is no or a very limited genuine link between the naturalising state and the persons to be naturalised. Consequently, there is a (very) limited residence requirement or even none.[154] Here must also be observed that the requirement of legal residence does not necessarily imply psychical presence.[155] In addition, also some other conditions are waived, for example, the requirement to renounce the original nationality and the language and civic test. Almost all Member States provide for a privileged naturalisation of spouses, extramarital partners and adoptive children of their nationals. The three Scandinavian Member States provide for privileged naturalisation of nationals of Nordic states.[156] Similarly, the Spanish Código civil provides for a privileged naturalisation of nationals of Latin American countries, Andorra Philippines, Portugal and Equatorial Guinea.[157] Furthermore, ethnicity (belonging to the 'state nation') is important ground for privileged forms of naturalisation in Croatia, Greece, Hungary, Italy, Latvia, Portugal, Romania and Slovenia.[158] German law provides for a wide possibility of acquisition of the German nationality on ethnic grounds for 'Germans within the meaning of Art. 116 of the Constitution' (*Deutsche im Sinne des Grundgesetzes*). Several Member States offer privileged naturalisation on grounds of 'state interest' to persons who have rendered or are expected to render outstanding achievements to the naturalising Member State. Some regulations specify the state interest by mentioning the areas of sports, science and culture, meanwhile other use some very general formulations. This ground for naturalisation is available in Austria, Croatia, Czech Republic, Estonia, France, Greece, Ireland, Latvia, Luxemburg, Netherlands, Portugal, Romania, Slovakia and Slovenia.[159] Interesting are the regulations in Spain and in Portugal that provide for a privileged naturalisation of Sephardic Jews as redress for historic injustices that happened several centuries ago.[160] Bulgaria, Cyprus, Malta and Romania provide expressly for privileged naturalisation based on investment, which does not exclude investment to be a ground for naturalisation in other Member States, where the regulation speaks vaguely of state (economic) interest.[161] Considering all the above grounds

[153] Weingerl and Tratnik, 'Relevant Links', 178, fn 97 and references therein; Van den Brink, 'Revising Citizenship within the European Union'; see the study by Kochenov and Van den Brink in this volume.

[154] Interestingly, in 2017 Slovenia even amended its Nationality Act to be able to naturalise an American basketball player who lived and worked in Spain. See Art 22(1) Código Civil 1966 and Art 6(7) of the Portuguese Nationality Act 1981 (PT).

[155] See extensively Van den Brink, 'Revising Citizenship within the European Union'.

[156] See Art 4(2) of the Danish Nationality Act 2004 (DK), Arts 21 and 30 of the Finnish Nationality Act 2003 (FIN) and Art 16 of the Swedish Nationality Act 2001 (SE).

[157] Art 22(1) Código civil 1966 (PT).

[158] See Art 11 of the Croatian Nationality Act 1991 (HR), Art 4 of the Greek Nationality Act 1984 (GR), Art 4(3) of the Hungarian Nationality Act 1993 (HU), Art 9(1)(a) of the Italian Nationality Act 1992 (IT), Art 8 of the Latvian Nationality Act 1994 (LV), Art 6(4) and 6(6) of the Portuguese Nationality Act 1981 (PT), Art 11(1) of the Romanian Nationality Act 1991 (RO) and Art 12 of the Slovenian Nationality Act 1999 (SI). See for Hungary also Bauböck (ed), 'Dual Citizenship for Transborder Minorities?' (2010) EUI Working Paper RSCAS 2010/75.

[159] See Art 10(6) of the Austrian Nationality Act, Art 12 of the Croatian Nationality Act, Art 16(1) of the Czech Nationality Act, Art 10 of the Estonian Nationality Act, Art 13 of the Greek Nationality Act, Art 12 of the Irish Nationality Act, Art 13 of the Latvian Nationality Act, Art 18(1) of the Luxembourgish Nationality Act, Art 10 Dutch Nationality Act, Art 6(6) Portuguese Nationality Act, Art 8(2)(a) of the Romanian Nationality Act, Art 7(2) of the Slovakian Nationality Act, Art 13 of the Slovenian Nationality Act and Art 21(19)(6) of the French Code Civil.

[160] See Art 22(1) Código Civil 1966 and Art 6(7) of the Portuguese Nationality Act 1981.

[161] See about Bulgaria, Cyprus and Malta, Weingerl and Tratnik, 'Relevant Links', 99–104, 162 and for Romania Art 8(2)(d), as well as Iordachi, 'Country Report: Romania' (2013) EUDO Citizenship Observatory Country Report RSCAS/EUDO-CIT-CR 2013/19, 8. See also Weingerl and Tratnik, 'Relevant Links', 162.

for privileged naturalisation without a genuine of effective link, it is arbitrary to attack only the CBI.

Can one speak of a reverse genuine link which would in some instances lead to a right to nationality?[162] All Member States provide for regular naturalisation, and most of them for various forms of privileged naturalisation. In the case of regular naturalisation, most Member States provide for rules that may be considered underinclusive. The conditions for regular naturalisation in all Member States demand even a very strong link between the Member States and the foreigners to be naturalised. They impose qualified residence requirements (five to 10 years),[163] language and civic tests, a clean criminal record, and so on.[164] Several Member States also demand that the applicant renounces (or makes everything in his/her power to lose) his/her current nationality. Considering the fact that potential naturalised persons must be, to a large extent, integrated, the genuine link criterion might even be 'reversed'. Could genuine link justify a *right* to naturalisation? According to some theorists fully integrated third country nationals would have a kind of a moral claim to be included in the national citizenry.[165]

It is believed that the debate on the genuine link is charged with political, not legal, concerns. As Kochenov and Kundnani forcefully argued, these political concerns, which contradict the objectives of the Union, find their basis also in ethnic nationalism.[166] There might be other concerns which are more apposite to be considered as a breach of the principle of sincere cooperation in cases of CBIs or other nationality rules. The EU objectives at risk must be first determined.

To this end, some argue that a more convincing case could be based on the argument that selling passports to people who want to enjoy free movement within the EU could be regarded as inconsistent with the spirit of the internal market.[167] The argument goes that Malta and other EU Member States with similar programmes act as 'free riders, charging a price for people to buy something that other EU Member States provide and pay for – residence in their country and/or Union citizenship freedoms'.[168] This argument is not convincing either. What is here approached as free-riding (free movement) is, in other situations, recognised as a proactive contribution to the achievement of the objectives of the Union. It seems to be based on the idea that free movement in cases of CBI brings costs, not benefits. However, it is argued that if CBIs pose significant security risks such as money laundering or corruption, they can be addressed under the current framework of EU law.[169] This would also be aligned with the principle of proportionality, which dictates in Article 5(4) TEU that 'the content and form of Union action shall not exceed what is necessary to achieve the objectives of the Treaties'. Thus,

[162] Spiro, 'A New International Law of Citizenship', 723.

[163] Weingerl and Tratnik, 'Relevant Links'.

[164] In Belgium for example, even a regular naturalisation is after 1 January 2013 only possible based on extraordinary achievements in the areas of science, sports or culture (Art 19(1) of the Belgian Nationality Act 1984 (BE)). See Wautelet, 'Naturalisation Procedures for Immigrants Belgium' (2013) EUDO Citizenship Observatory Naturalisation Procedures Report RSCAS/EUDO-CIT-NP 2013/16, 1–2.

[165] See Van den Brink, 'Revising Citizenship within the European Union', 2–3.

[166] Kochenov, 'Policing the Genuine Purity of Blood'; Kundnani, *Eurowhiteness* (Hurst 2023).

[167] Carrera, 'The Price of Citizenship'.

[168] ibid, 424; see also Fernandes et al, 'Avenues for EU Action', 21.

[169] Van den Brink, 'The Relationship between National and EU Citizenship' in Kostakopoulou and Thym (eds), *Research Handbook on European Union Citizenship Law and Policy* (Elgar 2022) 112. See Brillaud and Martini, 'European Getaway' (Transparency International and Global Witness 2018).

potential negative externalities that affect other states do not appear to be a valid reason for restricting the Member States' competence in this area.[170]

To sum up, based on the CJEU's case law, the principle of sincere cooperation has the potential to intrude even in areas which are reserved for Member States' competence, thus also in nationality matters. As discussed above, such an intrusion is not without limitations. To this end, an argument that a genuine link is a factor which is contrary to EU objectives and thus infringes this principle is based on shaky grounds. Moreover, it opens more dangerous doors than it allegedly closes. Therefore, it seems appropriate to ask whether the Commission is itself entering the murky waters on the edge of infringing the principle of sincere cooperation imposed on EU institutions by Article 13(2) TEU. In doing so, the Commission is apparently willing to sacrifice both the respect for vertical and horizontal division of competence in the EU, as well as the objectives of the internal market.

In adjudicating genuine link cases, the CJEU should tread carefully and recall the limits on its own jurisprudence, imposed by the principle of conferral.[171] It is an important difference between cases in the preliminary reference procedure (*Michelleti*, *Rottmann*, *Tjebbes* and others) and the infringement procedure (*Commission v Malta*). In preliminary reference procedures, it is for the national judges, in the spirit of the principle of sincere cooperation, to indicate to the CJEU in what way the dispute pending before it, even despite its purely domestic character, has a connecting factor with EU law.[172] In the infringement procedures, the limits imposed on EU institutions by EU constitutional principles are more pronounced.

ii. Genuine Link as a Condition for the Recognition of Nationality by (Privileged) Naturalisation?

As explained above, under international law, states have the obligation to recognise the acquisition of another state's nationality, insofar as it is acquired in consistence with international law.[173] In addition, non-recognition of a Member State's nationality by another Member State due to lack of genuine link would be contrary to EU law as well. One of the Treaty's goals is the internal market and free movement of persons. The most apparent legal argument against introducing a genuine link as a condition for the recognition of nationality is that allowing Member States not to recognise someone's nationality absent a genuine link would have adverse and damaging implications for free movement within the EU. The CJEU recognised this in its case law and forcefully rejected such a condition.[174]

Hitherto, there are three relevant CJEU cases to be considered, *Michelletti*, *Zhu and Chen* and *Garcia Avello*. The *Micheletti* case was about an Argentinian by birth. He lived and was educated in Argentina before he immigrated to Spain. He also acquired the Italian nationality by descent, without having any (genuine) link with Italy.[175] It therefore might be assumed that the Italian rules on acquisition of nationality were overinclusive, at least to a certain extent. Nonetheless the CJEU decided that Spain had to unconditionally[176] recognise Micheletti's

[170] Van den Brink, 'The Relationship between National and EU Citizenship', 112.
[171] See eg Vėlyvytė, Judicial Authority in EU Internal Market Law (Hart Publishing 2022).
[172] Case C-268/15 *Ullens de Schotten* ECLI:EU:C:2016:874, para 55; da Cruz Vilaça and Silveira, 'The European Federalisation Process and the Dynamics of Fundamental Rights' in Kochenov (ed), *EU Citizenship and Federalism* (Cambridge University Press 2017) 144.
[173] See Art 1 of the Hague Convention.
[174] *Micheletti*.
[175] His grandfather was Italian who as well as many Italians, emigrated to Argentina.
[176] See eg Lenaerts and Van Nuffel, *EU Constitutional Law*, 135.

Italian nationality and to grant him rights under EU law, which amounted to a rejection of the genuine link principle as regards the recognition of another Member State's nationality.[177] Also in *Garcia Avello*, the Court confirmed that

> it is not permissible for a Member State to restrict the effects of the grant of the nationality of another Member State by imposing an additional condition for recognition of that nationality with a view to the exercise of the fundamental freedoms provided for in the Treaty.[178]

In the *Zhu and Chen*[179] case, Catherine Zhu was born in Ulster and never even visited the Republic of Ireland yet she acquired the Irish nationality by birth and moved with her mother to England (from one part of the United Kingdom to another).[180] Also in this case there was no genuine or whatsoever link between Ireland and Catherine Zhu, nonetheless the UK had to respect her Irish nationality and therewith the EU citizenship and free movement and residence rights connected to it.

Both *Micheletti* and *Zhu and Chen* considered the acquisition by birth, and both Member States, Italy and Ireland, had arguably overinclusive attribution rules. However, it was not the acquisition without a genuine link which was problematic, but the non-recognition of the Italian and Irish nationality by Spain and the UK.[181] Therefore, it may be assumed that there is no genuine link requirement in EU law as regards the acquisition of nationality at birth, even in the case of overinclusive attribution rules. A newborn cannot have a (genuine) link with a state. Such a link may develop later or not at all.

Moreover, still in relation to the acquisition of nationality, the Commission's reasoning lacks in consistency since a 'blood connection' itself does not prove a special 'genuine bond' with a state.[182] It even has some 'dark' connotation. Like Micheletti, there are millions of EU citizens who never lived in or even visited their national Member State.[183] As many as 20 Member States provide namely for acquisition of their nationality *iure sanguinis* at birth, if at least one parent is their national, even in the case of birth in another state, and irrespective whether the child also acquires another nationality, mainly of the state where it was born and/or of the other parent. The other seven Member States impose additional requirements in case of birth abroad and/or in cases where the other parent is a non-national. Even those Member States however, allow for the acquisition of their nationality upon a declaration/registration by their national parent of the child.[184] Consequently, children born from EU nationals outside the EU often acquire their Member State nationality next to the foreign nationality of the other parent and/or of the state where they are born and 'give' their Member State nationality to their descendants, even for generations.[185] Only 10 Member States have limited this possibility

[177] The Court followed AG Tesauro in rejecting *Nottebohm*; Spiro in this volume.

[178] Case C-148/02 *Garcia Avello* ECLI:EU:C:2003:539, para 28.

[179] Case C-200/02 *Zhu and Chen* ECLI:EU:C:2004:639.

[180] See for the background and analysis Kochenov and Lindeboom, 'Breaking Chinese Law – Making European One', in Davies and Nicola (eds), *EU Law Stories* (Cambridge University Press 2017) 178–200.

[181] In *Zhu and Chen* at 34 the Court expressly rejected the argument of the counsel for the UK R Plender based on abuse of rights.

[182] See also Kochenov and Basheska in this volume.

[183] Judge ad hoc Guggenheim dissenting in *Nottebohm*, 56; Jones, 'The *Nottebohm*', 239–40.

[184] Art 8(1)(2)(b) of Belgian nationality law 1984 (BE), Art 5(1) of Croatian nationality law 1991 (HR), Art 8(2)) of Cypriot nationality law 1967 (CY), Art 4(4) of German Nationality Law 1914 (GE), Art 1(c) of Portuguese nationality law 1981 (PT), Art 5 of Slovenian nationality law 1999 (SI) and Art 1 of Swedish nationality law 2001 (SE). See also Vink and R De Groot, 'Citizenship Attribution in Western Europe' (2010) 36 *JEMS* 713, 716–18.

[185] See eg Kovács and Tóth, 'Country Report: Hungary' (2013) EUDO Citizenship Observatory Country Report RSCAS/EUDO-CIT-CR 2013/18, 6: 'Since 1929, millions of (lawful) emigrants and their descendants have preserved their Hungarian citizenship despite acquiring a second or third citizenship, and despite the absence of close relations

by providing for the loss of their nationality due to continuous residence abroad, provided that the targeted persons possess another nationality, as well, in order to prevent statelessness.[186]

V. CONCLUSIONS

The contribution seeks to depict the problematic employment of the Commission's genuine link rhetoric, backed with the principle of sincere cooperation, to attack CBI programmes. To this end, the contribution discusses the Commission's improper reference to the *Nottebohm* judgment, which has been misunderstood twice – first, as to the facts of the case, and second, as to its effect. The conclusion is, first, that, international law does not require that attribution of nationality must be based on a genuine link. The same applies to the issue of recognition of a foreign nationality. Member States may, however, impose such a requirement to grant nationality to individuals as part of their national autonomy, though, it is by no means required by international law to do so.

Second, EU law does not require a genuine link for the attribution and/or recognition of a Member State nationality, either. There is also no EU competence in matters of nationality, which is not likely to change. A Treaty amendment would be needed or at least an Article 352 TFEU based measure, which is practically the same.[187] The contribution shows that the Commission's employment of the genuine link concept encroaches on the vertical and horizontal division of competence in the EU, as well as contravenes the EU objectives, most notably the internal market and the principle of free movement. Moreover, the Commission does so in an inconsistent and arbitrary manner, since it does not question other privileged naturalisations in Member States. As demonstrated above, in practice, there are millions of EU citizens without (genuine) link with their 'national' Member States. To conclude, the Commission's claim against Malta is based on loose sand.[188]

(or any relation whatsoever), or cultural and ethnic affiliation to Hungary.' Kunz, 'The *Nottebohm* Judgment', 567 speaks of millions of 'overseas Chinese'; Jones, 'The *Nottebohm*', 239 of hundreds of thousands of British subjects in foreign countries who have never seen their native land and who, from generation to generation have acquired British nationality by descent. See also Spiro in this volume.

[186] See for a comparative survey R De Groot and Vink, 'Best Practices in Involuntary Loss of Nationality in the EU' (2014) CEPS No. 73/November 2014, 2–9.

[187] See extensively Sarmiento, 'EU Competence and the Attribution of Nationality in Member States' (2019) IMC-RP 2019/2; Sarmiento and Van den Brink, 'EU Competence and Investor Migration'.

[188] As already confirmed by the Opinion of A.G. Colllins, see fn 105.

7

What are the Risks of Investment Migration? Going Beyond the Status Quo

KRISTIN SURAK*

I. INTRODUCTION

IN AUGUST 2023, the Singaporean police arrested 10 people from Fujian, China in connection with a massive international money laundering and organised crime ring. The bust seized or froze over $2 billion in assets, including more than one hundred properties in some of Asia's top-end neighbourhoods, a slew of Bentley cars and Patek Philippe watches and hundreds of luxury bags and multi-coloured 'Bearbrick' figurines. It was Singapore's largest ever case of money laundering and it rocked the country for months. Hitting the headlines was not only the gang's rainbow array of costly bear dolls but also its rainbow array of passports: Cambodia, Cyprus, Dominica, Saint Kitts, Turkey and Vanuatu – all countries with citizenship by investment programmes.

In November 2023, the Organisation for Economic Co-operation and Development (OECD) and the Financial Action Task Force (FATF) released the report, 'Misuse of Citizenship and Residency by Investment Programmes' (hereafter, OECD/FATF report), an evaluative assessment of what can go wrong both with and within citizenship by investment (CBI) and residence by investment (RBI) programmes.[1] The report is measured and covers a wide range of issues around money laundering, financial crimes, corruption and tax evasion. Yet striking is what it misses when read against Singapore's massive money laundering ring. The predominant country where the illicit actors had gained citizenship through investment was Cambodia, which neither directly nor indirectly features in the OECD/FATF report. Furthermore, all the actors had obtained residence in Singapore by setting up businesses rather than through a CBI or RBI scheme of the sort spotlighted by OECD/FATF. When it comes to issues around citizenship, residence and money laundering and financial crime, what – and where – are the key risks?

* This chapter draws on research supported by ESRC Grant ES/X001342/1 and grants from LSE-RSF and STICERD. It builds on a working paper prepared for the Fifth International Research Conference on Empirical Approaches to Anti-Money Laundering and Financial Crime, hosted by the Central Bank of the Bahamas in January 2024.

[1] 'Misuse of Citizenship and Residency by Investment Programmes' (OECD/FATF 2023) www.fatf-gafi.org/en/publications/Methodsandtrends/misuse-CBI-RBI-programmes.html.

This chapter takes the OECD/FATF report as a provocation to examine the wider range of risks involving residence, citizenship and identity documents with respect to identity laundering, money laundering and tax. The OECD/FATF report assesses a number of angles involved in these programmes and offers many sound recommendations, several of which are already in practice in a number of schemes. Good practices include a clear accounting of the money coming in through the programmes and how it is channelled, close cooperation between governments and financial intelligence units to guard against illicit money flows, regular audits of programmes and public reporting of approval numbers and financial flows. The report also notes best practices that help ensure programme integrity. These include running programmes through a specialised agency within a government, which has a clear mandate, qualified workers, continued training and peer reviews; maintaining caps on applications and setting reasonable target times to ensure proper bureaucratic management; employing multi-tier vetting that includes both in-house due diligence teams and multiple international due diligence providers; ensuring clear firewalls and divisions of labour between agents, which should be licensed and regulated, and government decision-makers; and developing clear policies around and measures to prevent conflicts of interest (see Section V).

However, the report also contains errors, mistakes and inconsistencies that undermine its goals. Focusing on and developing beyond these failings can sharpen the policy tools that are available for limiting the misuses that the report targets. As such, this chapter focuses on identity laundering, money laundering and tax risks. In doing so, it does not directly handle issues raised in the Report's Section 4 on corruption[2] or in Section 5 on mitigation and good practice,[3] which are overall solid. Instead, it draws attention to the problems derived from blind spots concerning scope, including the definition of the phenomena and breadth of relevant cases, and it focuses on the implications for key financial crime risks.

First, it addresses issues in the OECD/FATF report concerning scope, including the definition of CBI and RBI and the identification of relevant cases. It draws attention to alternative modes of acquiring citizenship or residence that fit the definition of investment migration that the report employs and that carry similar vulnerabilities. These alternatives should also be taken into account when developing problem-based approaches to mitigating risks and limiting vulnerabilities that emerge in the interaction between finance and mobility or identity documents. Next, it assesses the scale of actual CBI and RBI offerings, identifying typically ignored cases that are particularly vulnerable to misuse, and it fills in absences in the depiction of the investment migration ecosystem by including powerful but overlooked actors and relationships. Finally, it discusses risks related to identity laundering, money laundering and tax. Crucial in this regard is the role of documents for building profiles that are legible and acceptable to financial institutions as indicia of a person's relationship to a jurisdiction and that can be used to establish legal 'substance' or techniques around 'ghosting residence'. The chapter discusses the extent of identity laundering risks, identifies some financial crime risks overlooked by the report, and it assesses tax risks and their relationship to investment migration programmes. Overall, it shows that the risks around identity laundering, money laundering and tax operate through profile-building around legal substance and not migration

[2] See also Surak, 'Citoyenneté à vendre: Stratégies de marchandisation de l'État' (2024) 251(1) *Actes de la recherche en sciences sociales* (ARSS) 50–73; Surak, *The Golden Passport* (Harvard University Press 2023).

[3] See also Surak, '"Citizenship and Residence by Investment Schemes: State of Play and Avenues for EU Action." European Added Value Assessment (EAVA) commissioned by the European Parliamentary Research Service (EPRS). Brussels: European Union.

or immigration per se. For this reason, a much wider range of possibilities for acquiring citizenship or residence based on financial means – going beyond merely investment migration programmes to include adjacent phenomena such as grey market options and business investor visas – needs to be taken into account if those risks are to be fully addressed. In short, a problem-based approach more accurately exposes the vulnerabilities than a programme-based approach. Though this chapter carries over the risk-framing from the OECD/FATF report, it closes by proposing that it is more effective to develop measures developed from the analysis of actual harms rather than posited risks.

A. Methods

The analysis presented here is based on 10 years of fieldwork in 20 countries that traces the global market in investment migration (Map 7.1). The focus of the fieldwork was on 'supply' countries, 'demand' areas and the network of intermediaries that build the market. The fieldwork also included ethnographic work at over 30 professional conferences and networking events on investment migration. Over the years, I conducted formal and informal interviews with over 500 individuals involved in all aspects of these programmes, including government officials, lawyers, migration agents, accountants, wealth planners, real estate developers, due diligence firms, standards boards, journalists and locals. The quantitative figures are drawn from on the InvestMig dataset that I constructed, which collates known figures related to applications, approvals and investments in CBI and RBI programmes. The dataset relies on government figures that are publicly available or gained through information requests. If these are unobtainable, it employs figures from major newspapers (often acquired through government leaks) or NGO and private sector reports. It triangulates the information from multiple sources where possible and updates the numbers as new or more accurate ones become available.

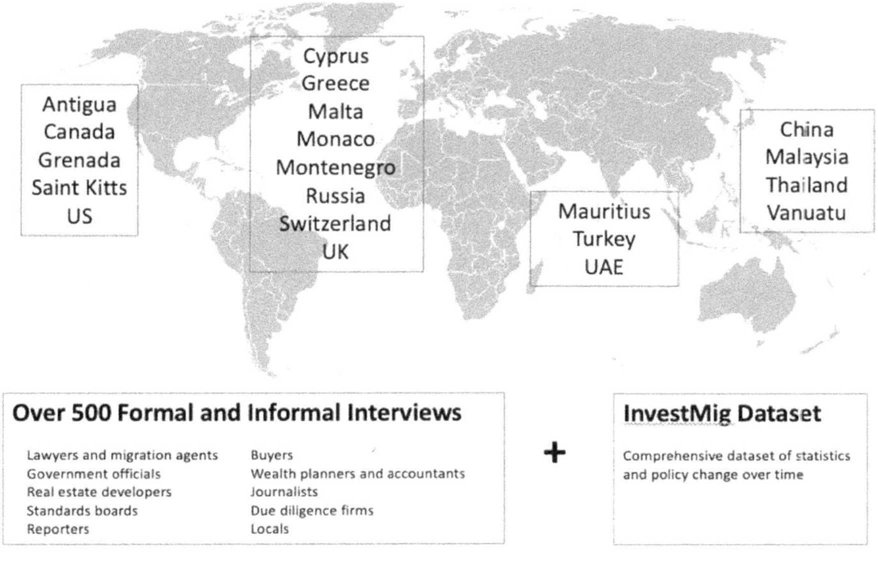

Map 7.1 Overview of Fieldwork

II. SCOPE ISSUES: WHERE ARE THE RISKS?

A key weak point of the OECD/FATF report concerns scope. It fails to adequately develop and consistently apply a precise definition of the phenomenon it aims to address – CBI and RBI – and subsequently generalises from limited cases. As a result, it fails to assess attendant risks in their full breadth and identify where they are most likely to be found. In addition, the report misses out on neighbouring phenomena – other naturalisation or residence channels – that carry similar vulnerabilities and should be taken into account when developing a problem-based approach to risk management.

The report defines investment migration as 'a type of migration where citizenship or residency in a jurisdiction can be effectively purchased through an investment in the host jurisdiction's economy'.[4] It is important to bear in mind that, particularly in the case of CBI, *migration* itself is uncommon. Instead, CBI turns on *mobility*, mainly in terms of visa-free access in the present or travel possibilities in the future, as well as related issues of risk-hedging, future-planning and business opportunities.[5] RBI programmes are more likely to see participants spending some, and sometimes substantial, time in the country where they gain residence. However, the variability of physical presence in these cases, too, is best captured by focusing on mobility rather than migration.[6] As such, rather than 'nuances related to finance and immigration and how they interact',[7] more crucial are those between finance and *mobility* and what this means for the production of documentary evidence, legal substance and profile-building.[8]

This shift in terminology may be brushed off as splitting hairs, but recognising the difference is crucial for identifying how the risks around tax, money laundering and identity laundering actually work. In these cases, it is often not the immigration of a person from Place A to Place B that is important. Instead, financial possibilities are opened based on the ways that an individual creates legal substance around movement and mobility – and how an individual cuts ties to other places. People looking to game systems manufacture a legal profile that can be used to make a case that works in their own interest. 'Ghosting residence' – or leveraging absence for advantages – for example, doesn't depend on immigration or migrating to a locale, but on building a competing profile in an alternative jurisdiction to avoid or evade taxes. In other cases, however, the accumulation of legal substance in multiple jurisdictions can work against them, leading to double or triple taxation. However, attempts at ghosting and similar forms of arbitrage only work because financial institutions rely heavily on documentary evidence indicating legal substance in order to determine whether an individual can open an account and transfer money, in addition to adjudicating where they are tax resident. The risks around identity laundering, money laundering and tax discussed below operate through such profile-building and not migration or immigration per se.

[4] OECD/FATF 2023, para 24.

[5] Surak, 'Millionaire Mobility and the Sale of Citizenship' (2020) 47 *JEMS* 166. The CBI programme in Turkey is the exception where a significant proportion of naturalisers move to the country or include it as a hub either before or after naturalisation. Cyprus saw a similar trend among the Russian naturalisers in its now defunct programme. The CBI programmes in Jordan and Egypt, by contrast, focus on mainly 'nationalising' wealthy foreigners, often who have been based in the country for decades, see Surak, *The Golden Passport*.

[6] Kochenov and van den Brink in this volume.

[7] OECD/FATF 2023, para 14.

[8] Mobility remains relevant, even if people remain immobile, because the current regime of identifying and allocating people juridically is grounded in the assumption that individuals are in 'their' state, with exceptions turning on mobility – or projected mobility – whether of people across borders or borders across people.

The misplaced emphasis on immigration and citizenship, generally built from assumptions derived from North Atlantic cases, leads to a number of unnecessary and incorrect statements in the report that distract from its overall project. For example, the report distinguishes CBI and RBI from other routes to naturalisation or residence because they allow individuals to gain rights 'by expediting or bypassing the *normal, more lengthy migration processes*'.[9] However, the pattern of immigrating to a country, accruing time there and then naturalising, is not common or even available in many parts of the world, including China and much of the Middle East, nor are immigration routes the most common way to naturalise in many European countries.[10] RBI programmes are strangely rolled together with citizenship in this statement even though they are typically managed through the same bureaucratic channels as other visas and rarely offer an unusually 'expedited' route. The same misattribution occurs in the declaration that the screening principles of investment migration 'depart from the *conventional features* of modern immigration controls'.[11] A North-Atlantic bias also lingers behind superfluous assertions such as 'investment migration … involves the creation of social contracts',[12] based on Western philosophical assumptions and debates about statecraft that have little relevance to mechanics of visa and citizenship policies globally.[13] The recommendation to '[s]trengthen the real link between recipients and the jurisdiction that designed the program', for example, builds from a standpoint that holds investment migration to a standard different to those of other visa and naturalisation channels. This bias reappears in describing the mobility of investor citizens in regional free-mobility areas as able to 'disrupt supranational agreements'.[14] The basic premise suggests that this mode of naturalisation does not entitle its beneficiaries to the same rights as natural-born citizens which are presumably not 'disruptive', or that naturalised citizens themselves are not entitled to the same rights as other citizens that are guaranteed by supranational agreements. 'While residence requirements and other traditional measures for granting residence and citizenship (language and civic knowledge, for example) are absent from many programs, these may be assessed in light of the expected engagement of the beneficiaries.'[15] Beyond the nonsensical assertion that a residence requirement is a traditional measure for granting residence in a country (most residence visas are not granted based on prior residence nor do they enforce physical presence), the meaning of the vague term 'traditional measures' is clarified through the example of 'language and civic knowledge'. However, it is extraordinarily rare to grant residence visas anywhere in the world based merely on language or civic knowledge, if such a practice exists at all. Furthermore, while language abilities or civic knowledge may be assessed as a part of some naturalisation channels, particularly in the West, these are far from being a global standard. In GCC states, for example, *wasta* or 'connections' have traditionally been crucial for naturalising. Such superfluous assertions, often logically inconsistent, are not needed to advance the OECD/FATF report's goals and instead detract from its rigour and accuracy.

[9] OECD/FATF 2023, para 1, emphasis added.
[10] Kochenov and Basheska in this volume, van den Brink and Kochenov in this volume, Ganty in this volume.
[11] OECD/FATF 2023, para 13, emphasis added.
[12] ibid, para 12.
[13] See Kochenov and Surak, 'Introduction' in Kochenov and Surak (eds), *Citizenship and Residence Sales* (Cambridge University Press 2023); Kochenov, 'The Victims of Citizenship' in Kochenov and Surak (eds), *Citizenship and Residence Sales*.
[14] OECD/FATF 2023, para 114.
[15] ibid, para 187.

The report goes on to define both CBI and RBI programmes as extending, respectively, citizenship or residence based primarily on a financial investment,[16] adding that CBI programmes do not require a significant period of prior physical residence.[17] In its introduction, the report explains that the particular method of selection – one that relies on financial investment – is risky because it selects new residents and citizens based on a 'specific transient and transferable attribute that can be gained in both legal and illegal ways: wealth' as opposed to 'non-transferrable attributes', which it identifies through the examples of family/heritage, skills including language, qualifications and abilities.[18]

The emphasis on the transient and transferable attribute of wealth that can be gained both legally and illegally is important for it is precisely these traits that bring risks related to financial flows. However, screening based on wealth is not limited to CBI or RBI, nor is it unusual.[19] It is also a defining characteristic of self-support, self-employment and business investment visas, which border on the proximate phenomena of retirement visas and digital nomad visas, in addition to discretionary grants of citizenship based on economic contributions and grey market options. These neighbouring categories are important because, as we shall see, they bring with them risks that are similar to those posed by the investment migration programmes that the OECD/FATF assessment targets, but often at lower cost and sometimes with greater speed and fewer due diligence checks. The upshot of the report's laudably terse set of definitions is that they cast a wide net encompassing far more country cases and visa and naturalisation categories than the report analyses, producing sizeable blind spots when assessing the types and areas of risk.[20]

A. Adjacent Phenomena and Alternatives

The sections below discuss the alternatives to CBI and RBI that either fit into the exact definition used by the OECD/FATF report or also bring the same risks related to the intersection of finance and mobility that emerge from selecting individuals based on wealth.[21]

[16] OECD/FATF 2023, para 25: 'CBI is the practice of granting citizenship status principally or solely in return for financial investment, without any requirement for a significant period of prior physical residency in the issuing jurisdiction'; see also para 28: 'RBI is the process by which applicants acquire a visa or residency permit that permits residency in the issuing jurisdiction in return for some type of financial investment'.

[17] The CBI definition continues in the next sentence to declare, 'A unique feature of CBI is that these programmes usually allow applicants to acquire citizenship quicker than through other, more traditional immigration channels' (ibid, para 25). This is a superfluous addendum that is factually wrong and does not contribute to identifying the phenomenon with precision. In several countries, including Italy, Romania, Bulgaria and Hungary, the majority of naturalisations by a wide margin are granted based on ancestry (with no physical presence required) rather than through putatively 'normal' or traditional immigration channels. Prospective new members must simply gather the documents to prove that an ancestor was once a subject of those governments, which can often be done in a few months and with no need to show that they have spent time in or even visited the country. The same misattribution occurs, too, in declaring that investment migration 'departs from the conventional features of modern immigration controls'. See Kochenov and van den Brink in this volume.

[18] OECD/FATF 2023, para 13.

[19] Kim, 'Migration-Facilitating Capital' (2018) 36 *Sociological Theory* 262. Surak, *The Golden Passport*; chapters by Ammann and Ganty in this volume.

[20] The definitions have weaknesses in internal consistency as well. CBI and RBI programmes are identified as employing 'transient and transferrable' qualities as the basis for naturalisation or residence, which are contrasted against the 'conventional' screening mechanisms, defined as 'non-transferrable attributes' that include 'family/heritage or skills (i.e. language), qualifications, and abilities' (para 7). The two, however, are not distinct. Heritage is clearly transferrable within families through inheritance, and skills, qualifications and abilities are transferrable between people as well. In addition, they can erode over time, whether through memory loss or simple skill obsolesce, becoming transient too.

[21] Cf OECD/FATF 2023, paras 13–14.

i. Adjacent Phenomena and Alternatives to RBI Programmes

a. Business Investment Visas

The OECD/FATF report's definition of RBI encompasses also many business investment visas (BIVs), although these do not feature in the report's analysis. BIVs can be found in nearly every country in the world and many states offer multiple programmes. In these schemes, individuals gain residence in a country in recognition of an investment made, though there is substantial variation in the qualification requirements across countries. Some business investment visas are aimed largely at entrepreneurs with business experience, others target individuals with promising ideas, while some cater to those who merely put money into a company. Within this array, there is significant variability concerning the extent of engagement required – or, put otherwise, whether the programmes require an active and passive investment. The most 'active' BIV programmes will also target skills by, for example, requiring applicants to evince a history of building businesses and assessing whether a business plan fits the individual's capabilities. They will also continue to monitor an individual's involvement in the business and its success after the initial grant of the visa. By contrast, the most 'passive' programmes will simply look for evidence that the individual has injected money into a company, which may be pre-existing or newly incorporated. In some cases, the extent of 'active' expectations is codified in law or policy; in others, it is an outcome of administrative practice. Germany, for example, moved from a passive business investment programme to one that was more active by changing its administrative procedures to more strictly assess applications and impose continued monitoring.[22] In some cases, investors prefer BIV programmes to strictly passive RBI offerings. For example, wealthy Mexicans are more likely to use the relatively swift and cheap NAFTA-based business investment options to acquire a residence permit for the US than go through the more cumbersome and expensive RBI programme, the EB-5 visa. Due diligence requirements for BIVs can also be less. For example, the Canadian entrepreneurial visa programme requires fewer checks on the source of funds than its now defunct Federal Immigrant Investor Programme (FIIP).

Notably, the 10 Chinese criminals behind Singapore's $2 billion money laundering ring established residence on the island using the BIV category 'Employment Pass' or its 'Dependent's Pass'. These permits can be applied for online and are typically processed within two to three weeks if the company is registered in Singapore and within two months if it is registered outside the country. Family office regulation in Singapore is light, rendering it straightforward to set up a family office to facilitate financial flows while simultaneously using the business to transform oneself into an employee who then qualifies for an Employment Pass residence permit. It is also possible to establish a business with no substantial operations – for example, one whose sole purpose is to facilitate property purchases – and then use that shell company to qualify for residence. This is the strategy taken by the accused money launderers, who set up shell companies that could be used to clean their ill-gotten gains and employed those shell companies to qualify for residence permits based on business investments.[23] Singapore is also home to a bubbling private market around employment visas. Individuals hoping to bank through Singapore can simply pay a local firm to employ them and grant them a residence permit. With the residence permit in hand, it is relatively easy to open a bank account.

[22] Surak, 'Who Wants to Buy a Visa?' (2020) 30 *JCES* 151.

[23] Lam, 'Purchased Passports, Shell Companies' (*Channel News Asia*, 20 October 2023) www.channelnewsasia.com/singapore/billion-dollar-money-laundering-passports-shell-companies-affidavit-3857886.

b. Self-Support and Independent Means Visas

Self-support and independent means visa programmes grant a residence permit to individuals who can prove that they have sufficient assets to support themselves. Typically, applicants must also show evidence of private health insurance and guarantee that they will not take up employment within the country. Self-support and independent means visas are less prevalent than BIVs but are particularly prominent in Latin America and parts of Europe and can be found in places including Austria, Chile, Costa Rica, France, Ireland, South Africa and Sri Lanka. Self-support visas share many similarities with self-employment visas and business investment visas that grant residence to individuals who buy, create or invest in a company in the country, and they share similarities with freelancer and digital nomad visas if they allow individuals to qualify by demonstrating sufficient income or self-employment. In these cases, an individual needs merely to incorporate a company and hire themself to qualify for a residence permit, sometimes with the additional requirement of showing some business activity. As with BIVs, they provide possibilities for acquiring the documentary indications of residence that can be used in banking and other financial activities.

c. Illegal Visa Sales

A final alternative for securing a visa for a country based on financial resources is through government corruption. The purchase of passports from corrupt embassy officials is perhaps more widely known,[24] yet it is also possible to secure a residence permit through such means. Notably, these illicit exchanges can occur on a massive scale. In the 'Visagate' scandal that broke in Poland in 2023, for example, investigative journalists found that officials facilitated a fast-track visa-approval system for kickbacks. Applicants for residence and work permits would pay several thousand dollars to brokers to ensure that their file would be swiftly approved, going through only cursory checks even if the documentation was incomplete. The Ministry of Foreign Affairs reportedly sent lists of the applicants who were to be fast-tracked to Polish embassy workers across the globe. As many as 250,000 to 350,000 visas, including temporary work visas, may have been issued in this way in consulates spanning Hong Kong, the Philippines, India, the UAE and Belarus. With the investigation still underway at the time of writing, the actual scale of the visa sale is difficult to assess. However, the number of work visas that Poland issues stands out against EU averages. In 2021 alone, it granted nearly 800,000, or more than 25 per cent of the first-time residence permits issued within the entire EU.[25] By early 2023, over 150,000 individuals with work visas were not registered as working in the country and possibly not even present in Poland.[26] The available evidence suggests that the scale of this scandal in which visas were granted without due process outstrips the number of RBI approvals in the EU by multiples. Embassies across the world are always at risk of corrupt officials granting passports,[27] but Poland's Visagate scandal points to potential problems around residence permits too.

[24] Surak, *The Golden Passport*.

[25] 'First Residence Permits Reached Pre-Pandemic Levels' (*EUROSTAT*, 9 August 2022) https://ec.europa.eu/eurostat/web/products-eurostat-news/-/ddn-20220809-2.

[26] Pawłowska, 'Afera Wizowa' (*BIQdata* 2023) https://biqdata.wyborcza.pl/biqdata/7,159116,30219125,afera-wizowa-pracuje-u-nas-mniej-osob-niz-ma-wizy-reszta.html.

[27] For a range of cases: Surak, *The Golden Passport*.

ii. Adjacent Phenomena and Alternatives to CBI Programmes

a. Discretionary Economic Citizenship

In the case of CBI, the OECD/FATF report's definition does not distinguish formal programmes from discretionary grants of citizenship as both allow a financial investment to serve as the basis of naturalisation with little to no requirement for physical presence. Any sovereign can extend citizenship in a discretionary manner, including in recognition of economic benefits. Cases are wide-ranging, but their discretionary nature renders them extraordinarily difficult to track.[28] Recently, for example, the media have exposed instances of tech billionaires securing citizenship in countries by going outside the standard rules or routes, including Paypal's Peter Thiel in New Zealand, SnapChat's Evan Spiegel in France, Apple's Steve Wozniak in Serbia and Telegram's Pavel Durov in the UAE. Austria has formalised these grants by creating a bureaucratic procedure for approving applicants who make an unspecified contribution to the country's economic success. Such cases, however, are very difficult to investigate systematically given their discretionary nature. Even if they fall under the report's CBI definition, they fall out of its purview and even discussion.

Discretion, too, can be used to approve more nefarious characters, raising questions about kickbacks to officials. For example, Montenegro naturalised former Thai leader Thaskin Shinawatra, who was carrying a criminal conviction for abuse of power, after he moved €15 million into a bank co-owned by the prime minister's brother.[29] Similarly, the president of Albania saw it fit to grant citizenship to the two Sandesaras brothers and their families, including a diplomatic post for a relative, when they promised to invest €33 million in the country even while under investigation in a $2 billion bank fraud scandal.[30] These discretionary grants can occur in countries with CBI programmes as well, operating as a parallel 'VIP track' that enables individuals to move around official bureaucratic processes.[31] For example, Ali Reza Monfared, an Iranian citizen who was both circumventing sanctions on the sale of Iranian oil and embezzling from the government in Tehran, was granted citizenship in Dominica a week after the meeting with the country's prime minister.[32] Al Jazeera exposed similar workarounds to the official CBI programme in Cyprus. Undercover journalists posing as representatives of a bogus businessperson with a criminal record revealed that high-ranking politicians were willing to circumvent the formal vetting procedures for kickbacks.[33] If a country has a CBI programme, it may provide a degree of cover and offer a post-hoc justification for citizenship acquired through corruption. This possibility is an important area for further empirical research. At the same time, such a twinned relationship is risky for a CBI programme too: the exposure of workarounds can threaten the integrity of the formal scheme, leading to the loss of visa-free access or programme closures.[34]

[28] Cf ibid.

[29] ibid.

[30] 'Above the Law' (OCCRP, 8 June 2021) www.occrp.org/en/investigations/above-the-law-how-a-wealthy-indian-family-evaded-justice.

[31] Surak, *The Golden Passport*.

[32] Hirten, 'Diplomats for Sale' (*Al Jazeera*, 2 December 2019) www.aljazeera.com/features/2019/12/2/diplomats-for-sale-how-an-ambassadorship-was-bought-and-lost. The Prime Minister denies the allegations: 'Exclusive: Caribbean officials linked to diplomatic passport sale' (*Al Jazeera*, 27 November 2019) www.aljazeera.com/news/2019/11/27/exclusive-caribbean-officials-linked-to-diplomatic-passport.

[33] 'The Cyprus Papers Undercover' (*Al Jazeera*, 12 October 2020) www.youtube.com/watch?v=Oj18cya_gvw.

[34] Surak, *The Golden Passport*.

b. Grey-Market Documents

During my fieldwork, I encountered service providers in China, the Middle East, Russia and Europe who described securing citizenship for clients in recognition of investments in places without CBI programmes, including countries in North, Central and South America; Western and Southern Africa; Western and Eastern Europe; the Balkans; and East Asia. In some cases, knowing the right officials was critical and citizenship could be gained by making a contribution to the country that would include something personally beneficial to the official as well. In others, the workarounds had become so standardised and the processing so straightforward that boutique businesses had developed to offer citizenship options off the shelf to willing buyers without individualised personal connections. Service providers working in this space described to me the grey market options as easier and cheaper than the more costly official CBI programmes that also require due diligence checks. However, grey-market documents come with more uncertainty: 'they're not fake, but it's not 100 percent legal either', as one service provider put it. The insecure future of the grey-market grants rendered them less trustworthy than CBI options.[35] As such, they are not always the most desirable option.

Though challenging to estimate, the overall scale of grey-market documents issued in countries without CBI programmes is likely to be sizeable.[36] For example, CNN in 2017 exposed the sale of nearly 150 Venezuelan passports at the country's embassy in Baghdad – about the same number of applications approved annually by smaller CBI programmes.[37] The scale, however, can be much greater. In Bulgaria, for example, prosecutors in 2020 revealed that officials were accepting bribes of around €5000 to issue fake documents attesting to Bulgarian origin, which could then be used to naturalise. More than 20 individuals were arrested in connection to the scandal. The full scale of the passport issuances in this case is unknown, but local news sources claimed that around 30 fake certificates were issued every week.[38] The extrapolated rate – around 1500 individuals gaining citizenship through this particular illicit group every year – is far greater than the number of people Malta regularly naturalises through its CBI scheme.

The Bulgarian grey market described above leveraged not a CBI programme, but a legal provision allowing naturalisation based on ancestry. Such channels are found in many countries, but the most popular ones are in southern and eastern Europe and provide access to EU citizenship. Indeed, naturalisation based on ancestry is the most common route to naturalisation in several EU countries including Hungary and Italy, with the latter having naturalised more than one million people through this route.[39] Romania, for example, is a popular choice among Russians who simply purchase false identity documents and use them to apply for ancestry-based citizenship. In 2018 alone, Bucharest naturalised 45,000 individuals due to ancestry and just over 400 based on immigration. Reporters investigating how Romanian naturalisation-through-ancestry operates in practice have uncovered hundreds of cases in which the paperwork vanished and thousands in which supplementary documents were not received yet applications labelled 'urgent' were moved directly for

[35] ibid.

[36] For an overview of historical cases operating around Hong Kong in the 1980s and 1990s, ibid.

[37] Zamost et al, 'Venezuela May Have given Passports to People with Ties to Terrorism' (*CNN* 2017) https://edition.cnn.com/2017/02/08/world/venezuela-passports-investigation/index.html.

[38] Gotev, 'Thousands Obtained EU Citizenship for €5000 in Bulgarian Scam' (*Euractiv*, 30 October 2018) www.euractiv.com/section/justice-home-affairs/news/thousands-obtained-eu-citizenship-for-e5000-in-bulgarian-scam/.

[39] Tintori, 'More than One Million Individuals Got Italian Citizenship Abroad in Twelve Years (1998–2010)' (EUDO Citizenship Observatory 2017) https://globalcit.eu/more-than-one-million-individuals-got-italian-citizenship-abroad-in-the-twelve-years-1998-2010/.

approval by high-ranking committee members.[40] Such ancestry channels are usually much cheaper than CBI options and involve only minimal due diligence, but they are not open to all since applicants must generally possess a white racial profile to present a convincing case. However, for those who fit the profile, loosely implemented provisions provide possibilities for ready access to citizenship.

A further form of fraud is found among officers who sell dated – or back-dated – entry and exit stamps for passports. Corrupt officials may be willing, for a bribe, to stamp passports to show physical presence in a country for a desired length of time either to claim citizenship or to establish tax residence. When such circuits are set up, the passports can be simply mailed to the individual in possession of the entry/exit stamp for the certification.

c. Diplomatic Passports

Individuals seeking additional protection may negotiate diplomatic posts. Diplomats are not always citizens of the countries they represent and in some countries, including the US, it is common to grant diplomatic posts to businesspeople who may aid a country in developing economic opportunities abroad. However, such posts can also be desired for the travel ease and legal protections they bring. London is a prominent example, where around 22,000 people are entitled to diplomatic immunity. The possibilities that diplomatic status carries can be particularly valuable to wealthy residents who may claim diplomatic immunity to avoid paying UK divorce settlements.[41] Not all attempts are successful: Boris Becker tried to avoid bankruptcy proceedings in the UK by asserting diplomatic immunity as a representative of the Central African Republic only to discover that the documents issued were fake.[42] However, the demand for such documents is substantial. Countries with CBI programmes have also issued diplomatic credentials for questionable reasons, as seen in the Monafred case introduced above. It remains unclear whether such issuances are more or less frequent than in similar countries without CBI programmes.

d. Black Market Documents

For those who are not connected, passports can be readily acquired on the dark web. For a profile from an EU country, fake documents cost around $1500 and a real passport around $14,000.[43] It is also possible to purchase images of individuals holding their passports beside their faces, which can be used for online identification purposes, as will be discussed later. As with the grey market, these black-market documents are significantly cheaper and more readily had than acquiring a passport via CBI, but there is more uncertainty over whether they will be successfully recognised when used or continue to work over time.

[40] Pocotilă, 'Romania Has Allegedly Allowed Russians and Ukrainians to Buy EU Passports' (*Vice*, 12 March 2020) www.vice.com/en/article/akwe34/romania-has-allegedly-allowed-russians-and-ukrainians-to-buy-eu-passports#.

[41] See for example, 'Saudi Billionaire Denied Diplomatic Immunity in UK Maintenance Battle' (*The Guardian*, 8 February 2016) www.theguardian.com/world/2016/feb/08/saudi-billionaire-sheikh-walid-juffali-denied-diplomatic-immunity; see also 'Hammond Criticises Judge for Stripping Diplomatic Immunity from Saudi Billionaire' (*The Guardian*, 22 March 2016) www.theguardian.com/law/2016/mar/22/hammond-criticises-judge-for-stripping-diplomatic-immunity-from-saudi-billionaire.

[42] Henley, 'Boris Becker's Diplomatic Passport Is a Fake, Says CAR' (*The Guardian*, 19 June 2018) www.theguardian.com/world/2018/jun/19/boris-beckers-diplomatic-passport-is-a-fake-says-car.

[43] 'Different Countries Passports are Selling on Dark Web' (*GBHackers*, 9 October 2018) https://gbhackers.com/passports-dark-web/.

III. IDENTIFYING CBI AND RBI AND THE INVESTMENT MIGRATION ECOSYSTEM

To decrease the conceptual muddiness, this paper advances an alternative definition of CBI and RBI to the one employed by the OECD/FATF report that distinguishes the phenomena from neighbouring cases. Citizenship by investment programmes can be defined as formal, bureaucratic schemes that enable individuals to naturalise based on a defined donation to a government or passive investment in a country. They establish minimum investment amounts and types, have a clearly defined and bureaucratic application procedure, and can be readily applied for by anyone who can tick the correct boxes. Formalisation is an important element of this definition as it distinguishes CBI from merely the grant of citizenship based on individualised negotiations with a government or set of officials, a practice that can be found globally.[44] Formalisation is important as well because it facilitates predictability, catering to a mass market, profitability, programme growth and the elaboration of an investment migration ecosystem. As such, formalisation is a key precondition of the particular risk profiles that may subsequently emerge.

Residence by investment programmes enable countries to extend temporary or permanent residence to individuals based on a defined donation to or passive investment in a country. As with CBI programmes, they too establish set investment amounts and types, have a clearly defined and bureaucratic application procedure, and can be readily applied for by anyone who ticks the correct boxes. Traditionally, it has been the passive nature of investments that has provoked debates about the rich 'paying to play', which are rarely raised in the context of business investor visas and sub-genres like entrepreneurial visas. BIVs can encompass both active and passive investments, depending on the de jure programme structure and its de facto implementation in practice, and thus may partly overlap with RBI programmes. Due to this fuzziness, this chapter employs a strict definition of RBI programmes, defined as having at least one qualifying investment option that is passive by nature, such as investing in real estate, bonds, stocks or funds.[45]

By these definitions, at least 22 countries have had legal provisions facilitating CBI within the past 10 years (Map 7.2),[46] and at least 60 countries and six dependencies have legal provisions enabling RBI (Map 7.3).

Map 7.2 Countries with Legal Provisions Enabling CBI During the Period 2014–23

[44] Surak, *The Golden Passport*.

[45] For a discussion of scope, see Surak and Tsuzuki, 'Are Golden Visas a Golden Opportunity?' (2021) 47 *JEMS* 3367.

[46] The 10-year limit is chosen because most passports are issued for 10 years and this chapter focuses on the risks associated with identity documents. The limit is imperfect because passports can be renewed or revoked. However, the definition captures the main cases of interest.

Map 7.3 Countries with Legal Provisions Enabling RBI (2023)

However, a provision on paper does not equal an active programme that is not only accepting applications but also approving significant numbers of individuals. Samoa, for example, passed a law in 2016 that enabled CBI. However, it has seen only one application which was revoked before it was fully assessed, producing no investor citizens to date.[47] CBI programmes currently approving at least 100 applications per year include Turkey, Saint Kitts, Dominica, Vanuatu, Grenada, Antigua, Malta and Saint Lucia (see Figure 7.1). Cyprus also approved at least 100 applications annually in the years before it closed its programme in 2020. In some years, Jordan and Montenegro have approved more than 100 applications, but the approval rates are inconsistent across time and are often under 100. It is important to note that, on average, each application includes 1.7 family members in addition to the main applicant.[48] As such around 2.7 individuals typically gain citizenship for each application approved.

Figure 7.1 Annual Approval Numbers for CBI Applications

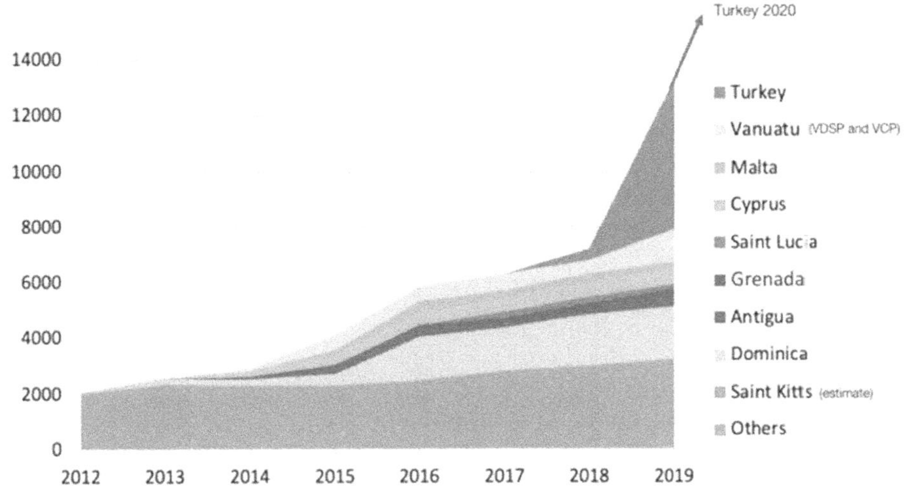

[47] Surak, *The Golden Passport*.
[48] Surak, 'Do Passports Pay off?' (2024) *JEMS*.

The figures for global annual approvals run only through 2019, before the emergence of Covid-19. The pandemic significantly interrupted application submission, along with normal bureaucratic functioning, in many countries. Only now are statistics becoming available that can be used to construct a global image of approval rates, but they remain incomplete for some key cases. If, however, the graph was extended, it would show that the approvals in Turkey have skyrocketed. In 2021, the Minister of the Interior reported that the government was approving around 1000 applications per month, which would constitute around half of all global approvals. In 2022, Turkey raised the minimum investment amount from $250,000 to $400,000, but it remains a popular choice in a region of great insecurity. It also continues to accept applications from Russian citizens, currently a major source of demand for citizenship options.[49]

Within this field, annual application approval figures for two countries – Comoros and Cambodia – are not known and therefore are not included on the graph. Complete figures for all of Vanuatu's channels are also unknown. There have been substantial irregularities in programme operation in these countries that can justify categorising them, or individual programmes within them, as operating in a grey legal area and outside fully formalised programmes. However, this chapter includes them within its scope as they raise a number of concerns with respect to financial crimes. The Comoros channel, for example, distributed passports in bulk and operated in violation of international law.[50] The country has subsequently not recognised many if not most of the citizenships granted and has refused to renew passports on that basis.[51] Cambodia's channel is accessed not through a completely de-individualised bureaucratic procedure, but through government connections. Vanuatu has hosted seven different CBI channels over the past decade, some with conflicting government information, and figures are known for only two of the channels.[52] Notably, citizenship in Cambodia was the prime choice of the money launderers in Singapore, with six of the 10 carrying its passport, followed by Vanuatu, which naturalised five of the ringleaders. Furthermore, the scale of issuances in these cases can be substantial. Vanuatu naturalised at least 2200 individuals through some of its CBI options in 2020 alone. In the case of Cambodia, only total naturalisation figures are available, but CBI likely accounts for a substantial proportion of the cases. Since 2017, it has been naturalising at least one hundred individuals each year, rising to as high as 725 in 2019. The largest by far, however, has been the Comoros, which issued at least 50,000 passports through its channel between 2008 and 2018.[53]

Global figures on the far more numerous RBI programmes have not yet been systematically collected. Such an exercise presents challenges as many countries do not regularly release details about the number of residence permit issuances in any visa category, including RBI programmes. Furthermore, RBI programmes are also found in authoritarian regimes that rarely offer information about visa approvals or respond to information requests. Figure 7.3 offers a partial view of this field, tracing application approvals through the eve of Covid-19 when the pandemic disrupted application processing and government reporting, from which is only beginning to recover. The figure reveals the decline of Canada's FIIP and QIIP, the relatively steady popularity of the US's EB-5 programme which is subject to a maximum cap,

[49] Surak, 'Turkish Citizenship is a Hot Commodity' (*The Wall Street Journal*, 8 September 2023) www.wsj.com/world/europe/turkish-citizenship-is-a-hot-commodity-50668d4b#.

[50] Spiro, 'Investment Citizenship and the Long Leash of International Law' in Kochenov and Surak (eds), *Citizenship and Residence Sales*, 137–60.

[51] Surak, *The Golden Passport*.

[52] ibid.

[53] ibid.

and the miniscule numbers in Australia and New Zealand. Programmes were offered in 13 EU countries during these years and have continued to be popular.

Figure 7.2 Annual Approval Numbers for RBI Applications

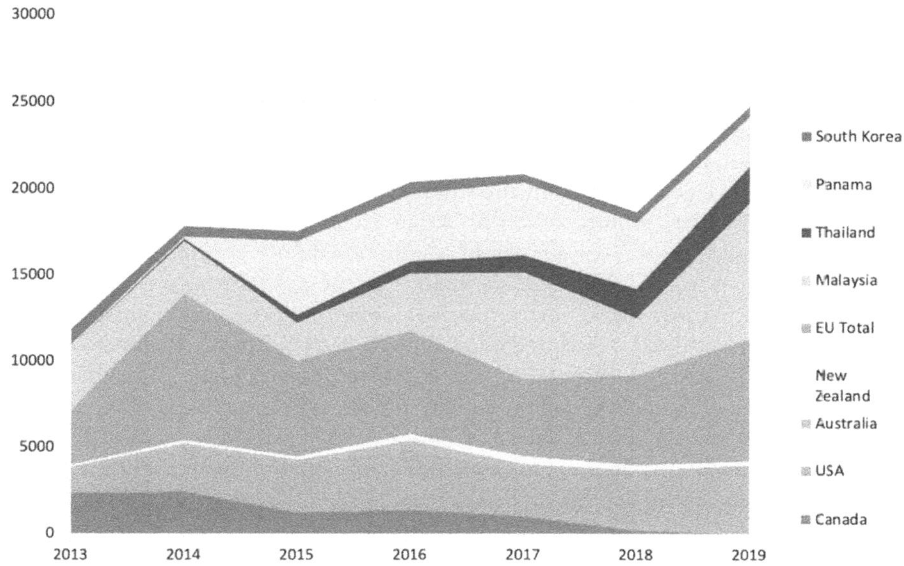

However, the available data show that the biggest RBI programmes are in the Global South. By 2019, the largest single programme was Malaysia's My Second Home scheme, which in some years was approving more individuals than all EU programmes combined. Thailand and South Korea were more popular than Australia and New Zealand, and Panama was also approving more individuals than the US in some years.[54] Even though data are available for only a subset of Global South cases, their pooled approvals outstrip those of Europe, the US, Canada, Australia and New Zealand combined. This important development, typically overlooked in discussions of investment migration,[55] suggests that RBI programmes are not merely an open door for South-North migration, as is often presumed, but an important form of South-South connectivity and even North-South connectivity.

Within this field, the UAE is the giant that dwarfs the rest. In 2019, it began its golden visa programme, which offers residence permits valid for five or ten years in recognition of an investment or property purchase of around \$550,000. Based on information from lawyers and statements by officials in the UAE, the government had granted 150,000 visas by the end of 2022, rising to a total of 250,000 by the end of 2023. As such, it is the largest RBI programme in the world by multiples and possibly accounts for more than 80 per cent of all approvals globally. The reality, however, is a mixed bag since the visa also includes widely used options for skilled workers.[56] Still, this massive scale requires that the UAE be included as an influential

[54] Notably, the US's EB-5 programme has an annual cap of 10,000 individuals. The actual number of approvals fluctuates around this limit, but the upshot is that in most years only around 3500 applications are approved.

[55] For an exception, see Surak, 'Investment Migration' in Kochenov and Surak (eds), *Citizenship and Residence Sales*, 25–69.

[56] It is important to recognise, however, that the UAE's golden visa programme is large because it also serves as a privileged visa for highly skilled workers. Historically, workers in the UAE have received only two-year visas.

part of the equation when calibrating working assumptions about investment migrations programmes. It is also a particularly important case to focus on when evaluating risks around financial crime.

The absence or only faint presence of significant cases[57] – especially the UAE, Comoros, Vanuatu and Cambodia – is a critical blind spot in the OECD/FATF report. As a result, the report produces a far too limited characterisation of the field and how it operates, which inhibits its effectiveness in addressing issues around financial crime. For example, due diligence is thin at best, if carried out at all, and does not involve private sector actors in the cases of Comoros, Vanuatu and Cambodia, alongside Turkey's massive scheme and the much smaller programmes in Jordan, Egypt and elsewhere.[58] Neither Vanuatu nor Cambodia requires applicants to submit a police certificate from their home country verifying that an individual has no criminal record. Turkey requires one only from an individual's place of residence over the proceeding twelve months. None of these countries have a separate bureaucratic unit to handle application assessment.[59] Indeed, the reality of the programme structure – from the application submission process through to the assessment processes – in countries outside the Caribbean and those in the EU or EU neighbourhood is vastly different than what is captured by the OECD/FATF report's general model. These differences in actors, assessment stages and administrative processes, as well as public-private interface in programme operation, have a significant impact on the types of risks raised and how they can be addressed. For example, the report's extended sections on due diligence are largely non-applicable and the discussions of various government layers are spurious in precisely the cases that pose a greater risk for financial crimes.

Ignoring Global South cases and connections also results in a limited characterisation of the role of the private sector, or 'investment migration industry', within the wider investment migration ecosystem. The report asserts that only a 'small number of firms' operate in this space[60] when the actual numbers are substantial, particularly in key 'sending' areas, whether global hubs or countries of origin. A sense of the scale can be gained from China where until 2018 all immigration firms had to be licensed by the government. An analysis of their licensing certificates shows that by a conservative estimate around 5000 firms operated in this space and that as many as 27,000 were offering immigration services.[61] Notably, too, the dominant Chinese firms are massive, counting more than 500 and sometimes over 1000 employees. The vast majority offer services beyond merely investment migration programmes, but nonetheless remain a definitive part of the Chinese investment migration scene. The great scale and operation of the migration industries in the 'sending' areas – places like Dubai and Hong Kong are also bubbling hubs – need to be taken into account, alongside the complex web of 'business-to-business' (B2B) relationships, which the report reduces to only 'concierge

The golden visa, however, can be granted for as long as 10 years, thereby offering greater future security. The result is that many elite workers, such as CEOs, high-level managers and university professors, have moved to golden visas as a part of a deluxe migration package. A golden visa can be acquired by purchasing real estate, investing in equities, investing in property, advancing a business project, or exhibiting outstanding specialised talent. It is the final category that offers the flexibility to use the programme as a channel for highly skilled workers.

[57] Vanuatu is mentioned once in a footnote.

[58] cf OECD/FATF 2023, para 18.

[59] cf ibid, paras 51 and 16–17.

[60] ibid, para 104.

[61] Surak, *The Golden Passport*; L Xiao, '猜猜看，全国有多少家移民中介公司？调查报告来了' [Guess how many immigration agencies there are in the country? The survey report is here!] (Lao Xiao Talks about Immigration, 4 September 2019) https://mp.weixin.qq.com/s/VYcAVBQ3Wtgv4VocSfjFAQ.

services', to offer an accurate assessment of risks and mitigation techniques around documentation, scams, fraud and money laundering.[62]

As the OECD/FATF report describes, a large and transnational investment migration industry interacts with governments to form an ecosystem of public and private actors that facilitates investment migration.[63] However, the report focuses only on a limited range of

[62] Surak, *The Golden Passport*. Some comparative work has assessed the economic outcomes of both CBI programmes (Surak, 'Investment Migration'; Surak, 'Do Passports Pay off?') and RBI programmes (Surak and Tsuzuki, 'Are Golden Visas a Golden Opportunity?'). Though these implications are, in the main, only tangentially related to the goals of the OECD/FATF report, the report still contains several errors worth noting as they can lead to distorted assessments. It is not the case that '[m]any countries have … raised thresholds or phased out real estate investment' in response to 'concerns about distortion of the real estate market and negative impact on accessibility for residence to [*sic*] rental [*sic*] and purchased [*sic*] property' (OECD/FATF 2023, para 112). Portugal fits this characterisation, but the other cases of change (a small proportion of RBI programmes overall), such as the US, Turkey and Malaysia did not make such a shift in response to concerns about property market distortions. Instead, change was driven other factors, including fluctuations in overall approval numbers, inflation rates and internal political debates. The empirical work on the impact of CBI and RBI programmes on real estate prices is nascent but shows that in most cases there is no impact at the national level (see Surak and Tsuzuki, 'Are Golden Visas a Golden Opportunity?'; Surak, 'Citizenship and Residence by Investment Schemes'; Surak, *The Golden Passport*; Surak, 'Do Passports Pay off?'). Where it does occur, the risk is concentrated within specific cities or districts (see Viesturs et al, 'Limiting the Program of Temporary Residence Permits for Foreigners Based on Real Property Investment in Latvia' (2017) 5 *BJREECM* 248; Surak and Tsuzuki 2021; Surak, 'Do Passports Pay off?. Cf OECD/FATF 2023, para 185).

In addition, there is no evidence to date that Covid-19 'led several tourism-dependent countries to seek alternative source of revenues through CBI/RBI programs', which the report specifies as 'more recent' schemes (OECD/FATF 2023, para 112). At the time of writing, no new CBI programmes have appeared since Russia's in 2020, which was already in the works before Covid, and most of the new RBI programmes have been countries that are not dependent on tourism, with the Bahamas and Sri Lanka as possible exceptions. The report also speculates about the fiscal cost of CBI naturalisers who become resident in a country and subsequently may draw on social security provisions and the education system (ibid, para 112). However, research shows that most naturalisers do not move the CBI country, that their qualifying economic contributions are typically greater than what an average taxpayer contributes to government coffers, and that when they do relocate, they have a preference for relying on private education and private care which is usually superior to public provisions in these countries (Surak, 'How COVID-19 will transform the market in investment migration' (Globalcit, 3 June 2020) https://globalcit.eu/how-covid-19-will-transform-the-market-in-investment-migration/; Surak, *The Golden Passport*). The main exception, which should be empirically investigated, is the possibility that RBI participants in programmes offered by wealthy countries where migrants are likely to settle, such as Australia or Canada, subsequently benefit more from public services that what their qualifying investment contributes to the government.

[63] Surak, 'Investment Migration'; Surak, 'Citizenship for Sale'; Surak, *The Golden Passport*. Dating the inception of the 'modern investment migration ecosystem' to 1984, the year that Saint Kitts and Nevis established a CBI provision the OECD/FATF report (para 15), misses out on the historically contingent co-constitution of the ecosystem itself and the formalisation and expansion of CBI programmes (Surak, 'Marketizing Sovereign Prerogatives' (2021) 52 *EJS* 171; Surak, *The Golden Passport*). It is precisely the formalisation of the programmes through the variable and contingent interactions between governments and the private sector that allowed this ecosystem – as well as the CBI programmes in particular – to grow. The flattened account also fails to capture the much older history of contemporary RBI programmes. This is an under-researched field, but it goes back further than Canada's FIIP (cf OECD/FATF 2023, para 15). Spain and Portugal, for example, offered residence to individuals making a passive investment in real estate from at least the early 1980s, and Malta has been doing so since it gained independence in 1964, with successive programmes folding into each through to its present RBI schemes (Surak, *The Golden Passport*). To date, no comprehensive study has examined the history of these older RBI channels or the migration industries surrounding them. Yet dissecting the vagaries of both CBI and RBI histories and the varying relationships between governments, applicants, and private sector interests is essential for isolating risks and mitigation techniques around corruption, kickbacks, workarounds and loopholes that may compromise the integrity of programmes. The report does a commendable job of listing a wide range of issues that may emerge, but a more rigorous attention to contingent historical developments can add needed specificity to the precise patterns of potential misuses, which can vary greatly from jurisdiction to jurisdiction. For example, a closer analysis of the migration industries around these older RBI programmes could spotlight the changing roles of private due diligence firms within the wider ecosystem or the transformations in regulation and de-regulation in countries where demand originates. Analysis of transformations in such public-private partnerships over time can also be used to identify how risk profiles can change both positively and negatively, as well as isolate the success rates of mitigation techniques in particular circumstances (see Surak, 'Citizenship for Sale'; Surak, *The Golden Passport*).

actors and roles without tracing the length of the supply chains and elaborating on the possible configurations they can take, such as in Figure 7.3. Notably, the supply chains cross jurisdictional boundaries, which facilitates arbitraging regulations and creates challenges to enforcing country-based rules that must be adequately addressed when fleshing out vulnerabilities and adequate courses of action.[64]

Figure 7.3 Supply Chain (basic form)

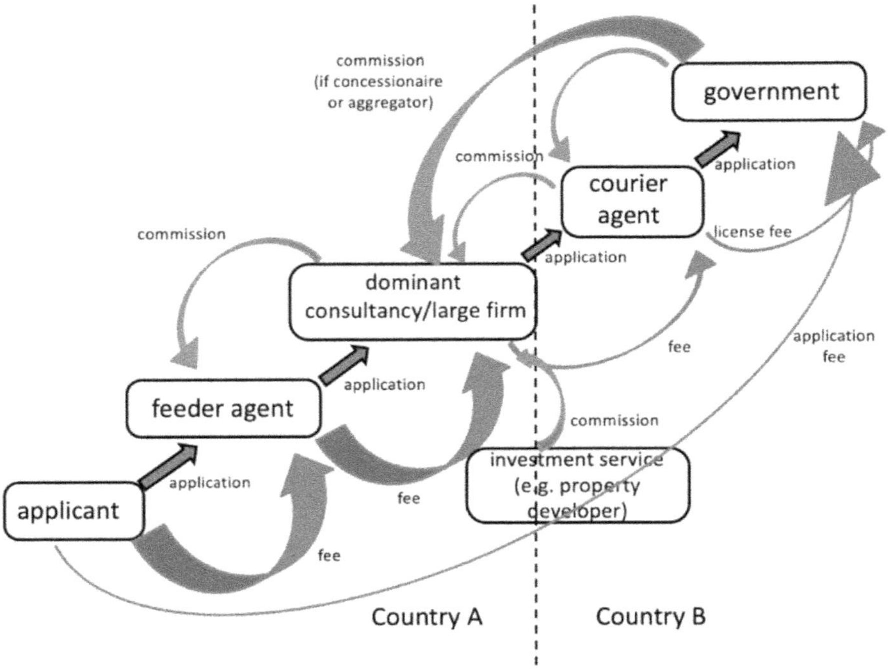

A major gap in the OECD/FATF report's ecology of public and private actors is the role of global superpowers and supranational organisations, which wield substantial influence over several CBI programmes outside their own jurisdiction. Microstates in the US's and EU's sphere of influence have, over time, acquiesced to several demands from these larger powers by changing their programme formats, administrative procedures, and due diligence regimes. They have also followed US State Department guidance on banning particular nationalities from applying for their programmes and have sought its endorsement of pre-approval lists of individuals.[65] Since 2023, the US has made its influence more public. In February of that year, the US Department of Treasury met with the five Caribbean countries with CBI programmes and issued a list of 'Six Principles' that the countries agreed to implement. Within months, the countries began to apply these changes, which include interviews with applicants, measures to prevent 'forum shopping' by rejected applicants, enhanced due diligence checks, periodic audits, retrieval of revoked passports, and the suspension of applications from Russians and Belarusians. Crucially, the Department of Treasury has been holding follow-up meetings to

[64] Surak, *The Golden Passport*.
[65] ibid.

ensure implementation, which actors in the region confirm is needed to safeguard compliance. This form of intervention appears, thus far, to be an effective way to encourage governments in a competitive environment to agree to common standards and limit programme vulnerabilities. Indeed, in cases where actors like the US supply a backstop to programmes as discussed above, it can also become possible for global powers to track and identify illicit actors who have received citizenship and passports through these channels.

The European Commission and European Parliament, by contrast, have wielded influence largely by pressuring countries in the accession process to close programmes or halt planned options before they open, and by threatening to revoke visa-free access for others. EU interests concerning cross-border movement have also guided how CBI countries that are in its sphere of influence select applicants. Caribbean CBI countries, for example, have agreed to reject applicants who have been denied a visa for the EU's free mobility region (the Schengen Zone) and for the UK, and such denials are checked during the application process.[66] Additionally, Malta requires its CBI applicants to obtain a Schengen visa before approval to ensure that other Schengen-area countries will accept the individual crossing their borders visa-free. Malta is the only CBI country with visa-free access to the US, but as with all foreign nationals, including those with visa-free access, its citizens must first apply for approval through the Electronic System for Travel Authorization (ESTA) to enter, giving Washington the final decision on who can enter visa-free. Since 2018, the EU has been intending to implement a similar system known as the European Travel Information and Authorization System (ETIAS), but the rollout has faced continuous delays stretching on for years, with a mid-2025 launch now projected. Once it is in place, it will also give the EU the final decision on who can access its travel area visa-free.

IV. VULNERABILITIES AROUND IDENTITY LAUNDERING, MONEY LAUNDERING AND TAX

The OECD/FATF report identifies investment migration as posing financial risks in three areas: identity laundering, money laundering and tax. In the context of financial crime, CBI and RBI programmes do not directly supply mechanisms for moving, hiding or transforming wealth itself, but rather make legal identities, residence possibilities and profile-building opportunities available to individuals – as do citizenship and residence acquired through any means. The following section assesses these risks vis-à-vis identity laundering, money laundering and tax.

A. Identity Laundering Risks

The OECD/FATF report spotlights identity laundering as a 'benefit' of CBI.[67] However, the connection is not straightforward in the limited set of country cases that the report assesses, and how it works in practice is more complicated than readily gaining the '[o]pportunity to acquire a travel and identification document under a different nationality or name, which can be used to represent who the holder is in a novel way, or otherwise obfuscate the person's original identity'.[68] Notably, none of the recent reports by OECD/FATF on the techniques used by criminal actors to finance illicit activities hinges on identity laundering, including the

[66] Rigour in enforcing this agreement may vary across countries and across time.
[67] OECD/FATF 2023, para 26.
[68] ibid.

areas of crowdfunding for terrorism financing, ransomware financing, the art and antiquities market, environmental crime, trade-based money laundering and others. However, a false or new identity can, as the OECD/FATF report on investment migration notes, facilitate layering that renders illicit financial flows more difficult to trace.

All countries with active CBI programmes list place of birth in the passport (Table 7.1). Thus, any disjuncture between a person's birthplace and country of citizenship is readily visible to border guards when assessing an individual, even absent the two-track passport system that the OECD/FATF report proposes.[69] In addition, biometric passports and retina scans make it difficult for individuals to simply drop prior identities by naturalising and acquiring a new travel document. For example, border guards in the UAE use biometrics to immediately identify whether an individual is entering under a different nationality than one used previously. Biometric systems are not yet universal and not all passports issued by CBI countries currently in circulation include biometric data, but as countries move to this standard, it will be more difficult for individuals to avoid identity-matching.

Table 7.1 Passport Information

Country	Includes Place of Birth	Biometric Passport (introduction date)
Antigua	Yes	Yes (2017)
Cambodia	Yes	Yes (2014)
Comoros	Yes	No information
Cyprus	Yes	Yes (2010)
Dominica	Yes	Yes (2021)
Egypt	Yes	Yes (2006)
Jordan	Yes	No
Malta	Yes	Yes (2008)
Moldova	Yes	Yes (2011)
Montenegro	Yes	Yes (2010)
North Macedonia	Yes	Yes (2007)
Saint Lucia	Yes	Yes (2022)
Saint Kitts	Yes	Yes (2015)
Vanuatu	Yes	Yes (2010)

Note: Only countries with known CBI approvals between 2014 and 2023 are included.

The OECD/FATF report identifies name changes as a perfectly legal option that criminals might exploit for nefarious ends. Within this vulnerability, it is important to bear in mind that most name changes are mundane. A typical example is altering a name upon marriage or divorce, but the most common cases are due to cultural complexities. Moving from one writing system to another regularly produces challenges around standardisation that can produce such requests, as well as irregularities across documents. Russia, for example, has changed the standard format for Romanising names from Cyrillic several times in recent decades. As a result, it is not unusual for a single individual to find their name written differently across

[69] ibid, paras 164–65.

official documents when recorded in Roman letters. Cultural complexities in naming practices, such as including parents' and grandparents' names as a part of a given name in some documents and not others, are found in countries across Latin America and the Middle East. In a recent fieldwork example, a successful applicant to a CBI programme in the Caribbean was seeking a name change because the common practice in his country of origin was to list the father's and grandfather's names as a part of the baby's name on its birth certificate. However, the individual's other official documents, including his home-country passport and bank accounts, employed a Westernised standard that listed only two names: his given name and surname. The country where he became an investor citizen printed the six-part name from his birth certificate onto his passport and he was seeking to have this shortened to the two that he uses to conform with Anglophone standards so that it would align with his other identification documents. Due diligence service providers note that such cultural complexities are common and usually not an indication of nefarious activities. However, they do present one of the key challenges of their work.

There is substantial variation across countries and across time in the ease of changing names. Caribbean countries with CBI programmes no longer allow names to be changed in the application process and have moved to systems designed to limit the possibility of identity laundering:[70] individuals wishing to alter a name must submit documentation that it has been legally changed within their home country before the official name in the CBI country, including the name on the passport, can be altered. Interviews with service providers suggest that name changes are challenging to implement in Turkey and Malta. However, previously in places including Dominica and Saint Kitts, changing a name was a relatively straightforward process that could be carried out after acquiring citizenship and before applying for a passport. Notably, changing name is relatively easy in Cambodia and as many as a third of all naturalisers do so. Beyond the possibility of altering names officially, identity laundering is a significant vulnerability in cases where the bureaucratic vetting procedures within governments are extremely weak. The countries of greatest risk for such cases are Comoros, Vanuatu and Cambodia.

Previous research has identified cases of 'serial investor migrants' among approved applications whereby individuals acquire citizenship through investment and subsequently use it to acquire an additional citizenship or residence through investment.[71] In the case of the UK's now defunct RBI programme, the Tier 1 (investor) visa, such serial investor migrants represented 1.0 per cent of main applicants and 1.2 per cent of family dependants – a small proportion of cases for a programme known for having particularly lax due diligence checks.[72] Serial investor migration is, in itself, not a crime and may even result by default when, for example, an individual renounces their original citizenship, takes on an investor citizenship and subsequently applies for an RBI programme. However, it poses a risk if an individual lies about possessing multiple citizenships and presents only one, thereby cutting biographic ties.[73]

[70] Madatali and Blanckaert, 'Visa Suspension Mechanism' (2023) *EPRS*.

[71] Surak, 'Who Wants to Buy a Visa?' (2020) 30 *JCES* 151; Surak, 'Citizenship and Residence by Investment Schemes'; Surak, *The Golden Passport*.

[72] Sumption in this volume; Until 2016, the Home Office assumed that the banks were carrying out due diligence on the individuals applying for investor residence when they opened an account, and the banks assumed that approval for Tier 1 was a signal that an individual had been cleared by the Home Office. The circularity resulted in few effective background checks carried out during the application process, as was widely known among service providers dealing with the programme.

[73] Surak, 'Millionaire Mobility and the Sale of Citizenship'; Surak, 'Citizenship and Residence by Investment Schemes'; Surak, *The Golden Passport*.

B. Money Laundering and Financial Crime Risks

International actors have raised concerns over the use of CBI and RBI programmes for money laundering and illicit financial activities.[74] Investigative journalists have exposed some major cases of criminals in possession of citizenship gained through CBI programmes who have carried out billions of dollars in financial crimes. What remains unknown is the actual incidence rate of money laundering or financial crimes carried out via these programmes which now naturalise around 50,000 people each year in the case of CBI[75] or extend residence to hundreds of thousands of individuals annually in the case of RBI.[76] To date, no empirical study has assessed or established a reasonable estimate of the number or proportion of people with criminal backgrounds who have been approved by CBI or RBI programmes, or – a greater challenge to intercept – people with criminal intents who apply for the programmes, alongside the actual use of investor citizenship or residence to carry out criminal activities.

The OECD/FATF report identifies a set of risks and vulnerabilities that investment migration programmes present regarding money laundering. According to the report, CBI facilitates this kind of financial crime by (1) altering identities, (2) enhancing freedom of movement, (3) facilitating the establishment of legal persons in other jurisdictions.[77] RBI does the same by allowing actors to (1) move to new places, (2) justify large cross-border capital flows, (3) purchase high-value goods and services, (4) set up businesses and (5) ultimately obtain a new citizenship.[78]

The list, however, lacks the precision needed to adequately address the risks. It is unclear why the 'benefits' of RBI programmes are not also listed among those for CBI schemes, though they are acquired as well. More importantly, some of the 'benefits' are only secondary to the financial flows involved in money laundering. Attributing them to investment migration muddies the water when attempting to address the source and extent of the risks with precision. For example, 'sending children to private schools and using real property'[79] and 'gain[ing] enhanced freedom of movement'[80] are hardly needed for illicit actors to carry out financial crimes or money laundering, and it is only in unusual cases that a visa or citizenship is needed to 'purchase high value goods and services'.[81] The report's limited case analysis also leads to inaccurate claims such as 'RBI programmes normally lead to settled status and can lead to citizenship through naturalization over time … bringing with [this] many of the same risks as a CBI programme, albeit on a slower basis'.[82] Notably, settled status is not available to the vast majority – likely upward of 85 per cent – of RBI participants, nor is 'ultimately obtaining[ing] a new citizenship'[83] even a possibility in these cases, particularly within the very popular programmes in the Global South. For reasons described in the first part of this chapter, the risks around altering identities may be much greater in the grey market that operates

[74] European Parliamentary Research Service 2020; FATF 2023, OECD 2023.

[75] Surak, *The Golden Passport*.

[76] RBI programmes supply residence permits that can be permanent (sometimes subject to conditions for retention) or temporary and subject to renewal. Residence visas are offered for different lengths of time and can be lost as well, rendering it extraordinarily difficult to assess how many people currently possess such permits globally. Given, however, that the UAE alone has extended around 250,000 'golden visas' that remain active, the global total runs in the hundreds of thousands.

[77] OECD/FATF 2023, para 25.

[78] ibid, para 36.

[79] ibid.

[80] ibid, para 35.

[81] ibid, para 36.

[82] ibid.

[83] ibid.

outside the official programmes. Furthermore, possibilities to establish legal persons, move to new places and set up businesses are available through any sort of visa, not only those gained through RBI. If focusing on the opportunities opened by wealth, then the business investor visas, self-support visas and similar categories discussed above present similar risks on a wide basis.

Financial institutions play a critical role in the operation of CBI and RBI programmes as they serve as the gateway for qualifying funds to enter a country. The OECD/FATF report assesses a number of risks involved in the movement of funds during the application process. To this list, it is important to add those around escrow accounts. Such accounts are employed in the qualification process for citizenship in several CBI programmes, and the vulnerabilities they present may also extend to RBI programmes if they are used. Escrow accounts that do not have independent oversight are vulnerable to mismanagement or misappropriation, particularly if actors 'play' with the funds and seek to turn a profit for themselves before the funds are disbursed. In extreme cases, as with the CIIP in Vanuatu and the offering in Comoros, the qualifying funds have been transferred not to the government, but to an overseas escrow account maintained by a service provider.[84]

However, a much larger risk concerns financial crimes that occur after the application process. In these cases, the operation of financial institutions is crucial. The success of laundering an identity with the goal of accessing a financial system, for example, depends on a bank's procedures for verifying an identity. Some banks require only two forms of identification, such as a passport and a utility bill, and will even accept expired documents as sufficient evidence. Online banks may rely solely on the online verification of identity documents, rendering these financial institutions vulnerable to exploitation by actors who simply purchase identity images from the dark web.[85] In many cases, however, identity laundering is not necessary. Jho Low, the alleged mastermind of the 1MDB scandal, used Deutsche Bank to clear €6 million that he moved Cyprus when applying for citizenship by investment, which occurred after the emergence of allegations of massive embezzlement.[86]

The OECD/FATF report discusses the positive role that professional due diligence firms can play in screening applicants and their source of funds and wealth. Though due diligence firms have become integrated into the CBI screening processes of several countries, including those in the Caribbean and Europe or its periphery, such as Malta and Montenegro,[87] they do not feature in the cases beyond, including Turkey, Egypt, Jordan, Comoros, Vanuatu and Cambodia.[88] Nor do they play a role in vetting applicants for RBI programmes beyond any screening they might supply for banks or financial institutions. Within the due diligence field, however, the type of firm matters. Missed in the report is that governments may appoint small, boutique due diligence firms whose main source of income is the contract to screen for an investment migration programme, which can render the firm vulnerable to bribery or collusion. Large, multinational due diligence firms with a diversified clientele and an interest in maintaining professional integrity to preserve their much wider business interests present much less of a risk.

[84] Surak, *The Golden Passport*.

[85] One way to limit such vulnerabilities – and one more realistic than the recommended retrieval of passports, which is challenging even for powerful countries (cf OECD/FATF 2023, para 86) – would be to require banks to check passports against a revoked passport list similar to ones used by airlines.

[86] Peel and Olaf, 'Deutsche Bank Cleared Cyprus Funds for Businessman Jho Low' (*Financial Times* 2020) www.ft.com/content/5b329f78-6220-11ea-b3f3-fe4680ea68b5.

[87] On the history of this integration, see Surak, 'Marketizing Sovereign Prerogatives'; Surak, *The Golden Passport*.

[88] cf OECD/FATF 2023, para 56.

C. Tax Evasion and Avoidance Risks

International institutions have raised concerns about tax evasion risks presented by investment migration programmes[89] and some analysts have targeted CBI programmes for allowing individuals to avoid reporting under CRS.[90] The OECD/FATF report is inconsistent on the implications: it cites the work of the OECD to assert that only 22 out of 100 investment migration programmes are high risk,[91] but elsewhere claims that 'All CBI/RBI programmes present a high risk of being used to circumvent international tax information exchanges under the CRS'.[92] In addition, what 'high risk' might mean in practice is not straightforward since the CRS's automatic exchange of information (AEOI) is based solely on an individual's *tax residence* and not their citizenship or residence permits, nor even their domicile or purely physical residence. As a result, merely participating in a CBI or RBI programme is insufficient to avoid AEOI under CRS.

Whether or not a risk is present depends primarily on how financial institutions identify the tax residence of their clients. This is typically through self-declaration under threat of perjury: most banks allow clients to self-certify their tax residency, placing the burden on the client to honestly declare their situation. There is great variability in the extent to which financial institutions attempt to ensure that clients are making true statements and variability in the type and extent of documentation they require. Some oblige clients to supply a variety of supporting evidence and carry out tests to potentially 'trip up' individuals making false claims, while others do not. They also vary in what triggers red flags and how they handle them. A citizen or resident might apply for a tax identification number from a country, for example, but it is up to the bank – and the decisions of its compliance department – to decide whether this is taken as definitive of tax residence and whether they should investigate for tax residencies elsewhere. My interviews show that the introduction of CRS has led to some cases of individuals becoming serial investor migrants in attempts to avoid automatic reporting to their place of tax residence. However, follow-up fieldwork suggests that such manoeuvring is not always effective in practice.[93] Success depends on whether a bank accepts proof of citizenship and potentially also a tax identification number as sufficient verification of a person's tax residence and accepts that as definitive of a person's sole tax residence.

Because financial institutions rely on self-certification and profile-building to determine tax residence, obtaining *any* kind of residence visa in the *same* country as the banking relationship represents the greatest opportunity for avoiding AEOI under CRS. Usually, banks regard

[89] European Parliamentary Research Service 2020; OECD/FATF 2023; OECD 2023.

[90] Langenmayr and Zyska, 'Escaping the Exchange of Information' (2023) 221 *Journal of Public Economics*. Their investigation is a study in what can be done methodologically with extraordinarily limited data. Unfortunately, however, these limits means that the authors can generate only indirect evidence that automatic information exchanges may be avoided, and they do not allow them to suggest how common such cases may be: Is the effect due to one individual moving large sums or many individual moving smaller sums? The authors also mischaracterise the risk when they make claims such as, 'CBI programmes enable tax evaders to escape tax information exchange'. Rather, the risk is that programmes might serve as a basis for an individual to gain documents that they can use to falsely present themselves to banks. Unfortunately, they are unable to account for any bias in their sample, which consists of only six, sometimes four, countries (out of a wider field of over twenty) and ignores all large countries operating in the space. Finally, in two out of the four cases, they operationalize the year of "program introduction" based on an ad hoc decision of when a particular reform – out of a string of reforms – was significant. Due to such fundamental issues with the inputs, it is not possible to accept the outputs as meaningful.

[91] OECD/FATF 2023, para 117.

[92] ibid, para 118. Perhaps the most straightforward way to avoid reporting under CRS is the 'US solution': simply open a bank account in the United States, which hasn't signed the agreement and is unlikely to become a signatory.

[93] Surak, 'Citizenship and Residence by Investment Schemes'; Surak, *The Golden Passport*.

individuals who have residence in the same country where they are opening an account as a 'non-reporting person' and do not collect information for CRS. If a person with a Turkish passport attempts to open a bank account in London and claim Maltese tax residence, it will likely raise a red flag. However, if the person has a basic work permit or any kind of residence visa for the UK, along with basic supporting evidence such as a utility bill or rental agreement, they will likely be seen by the London bank as a 'non-reporting person' and categorised as a UK tax resident. Often, too, financial institutions do not press on to identify any additional tax residencies once they have identified one. As such, it is not that CBI and RBI programmes themselves 'present a high risk of being used to circumvent … CRS',[94] but that residence documents *of any sort* present challenges to banks as they try to determine an individual's tax residence. For this reason, the business investor visas, self-support visas and other forms of independent-means visas discussed earlier in this working paper are essential to take into account if the actual vulnerabilities around 'ghosting residence' to avoid AEOI for tax reasons are to be addressed.

Among the countries that offer RBI, the UAE programme presents perhaps the greatest risk in this regard given the scale of its approvals and the ease of claiming tax residence in the country known for having very low tax rates. To qualify for a tax residence certificate, a person simply needs to be in the UAE for one day every six months. Taiwan is another important case to note as it has not signed onto CRS. It is also highly unlikely to report to the People's Republic of China, which makes Taiwan's RBI programme highly desirable for Chinese nationals. Finally, any country that has opted for 'voluntary secrecy' by being listed under Annex A of the MCAA agreement will submit – but not receive – information under CRS. The OECD does not publish a list of countries that have opted for voluntary secrecy. However, it is possible to estimate which jurisdictions have selected this option based on OECD data on active exchange relationships.[95] Countries and dependencies that receive information from no jurisdictions are likely to have chosen voluntary secrecy and include Anguilla, Bahamas, Bahrain, Belize, Bermuda, British Virgin Islands, Brunei, Cayman Islands, Dominica, Kuwait, Lebanon, Marshall Islands, Montserrat, Nauru, New Caledonia, Niue, Oman, Qatar, Saint Vincent, Samoa, Sint Maarten, Trinidad, Turks and Caicos, UAE and Vanuatu. In addition, Macau is receiving information only from a single jurisdiction, Costa Rica. If an individual is able to persuade a financial institution that they are a tax resident in one of these jurisdictions, they will also be considered 'non-reportable' and their information will not be collected.

At the same time, the shift in international tax enforcement towards requiring 'substance' works in favour of some CBI and RBI programmes. The trend has been towards taxing profits in the place where the profit-generating economic activities occur. This creates an incentive for producing more physical, economic and statutory 'substance' in low-tax jurisdictions, or effectively a form of 'mid-shoring'.[96] Particularly with CBI, in which physical presence has traditionally remained rare among naturalisers outside the case of Turkey, calls by international institutions for investor citizens to spend more time in the CBI country and generate 'real links'[97] or 'genuine links' also encourage the production of 'substance' for wealth-structuring purposes.[98] Notably, the traditional 'core market' of CBI programmes has been in low-tax

[94] OECD/FATF 2023, para 118.

[95] 'Corruption Risks Associated with Citizen- and Resident-by-Investment Schemes' (OECD 2023) www.oecd.org/tax/automatic-exchange/crs-implementation-and-assistance/residence-citizenship-by-investment/.

[96] Surak, *The Golden Passport*.

[97] eg OECD/FATF 2023, para 187.

[98] On this unintended consequence, ibid.

jurisdictions that offer beneficial tax rates to individuals who are resident but not domiciled in the country. 'Real link' requirements can contribute to the substance needed to claim these wealth structuring possibilities that might otherwise be ignored since physical presence requirements have traditionally been a detriment to the popularity of individual CBI programmes. Individuals may end up spending 60 days – sometimes less – in a country,[99] alongside joining some clubs, donating to some charities, and moving some business and wealth structures into a country, to produce not only 'real links' but also facilitate the profile-building that results in a convincing 'whole picture' of the person's mode of existence from a taxation perspective. Similar possibilities can be found in the 'resident non-domiciled' ('res non-dom') options, such as Portugal's Non-Habitual Residency Program and Spain's 'Beckham Law', maintained in some countries with RBI programmes. Notably, these tax structures are not built into the RBI programmes themselves but operate – and in most cases are created -- independently of them.[100] Indeed, it is not an RBI visa, but rather any sort of residence permit for the country that is a prerequisite for accessing such tax statuses.

V. CONCLUSION

As with any policy, investment migration options present various risks and the costs must be weighed against the benefits. Furthermore, any comprehensive assessment must take into account the reality of how programmes operate on the ground. For countries going forward with investment migration, there are a number of ways in which programmes can be designed and implemented to diminish various risks. For international agencies concerned with identifying and mitigating risks, it is crucial that the empirical phenomena of concern are precisely identified and accurately assessed, and that models are built from indicative samples. It is also crucial to assess the scale of the risks and whether they are more prevalent in neighbouring cases that may be off the radar. Adequately addressing these issues around design and scope is crucial for developing suitable and accurate policy tools.

This chapter has identified limits and inaccuracies in the OECD/FATF report concerning what investment migration is, how it operates and the risks it brings, and it has identified adjacent phenomena that produce similar outcomes, sometimes on a much larger scale. It has addressed various gaps in the depiction of investment migration and its accompanying ecosystem, and identified some vulnerabilities overlooked in the report. It has also assessed risks around identity laundering, money laundering and tax, and spotlighted a key mechanism facilitating risks involved around tax and accessing financial systems: namely the role of documents in building profiles and legal substance. If those risks are to be addressed, further work should move beyond a programme-driven approach, such as one that starts from only CBI and RBI schemes, and adopt a problem-driven approach, such as one that starts from the full range of possibilities for accruing documents that enable individuals to build profiles that can be used for illicit ends.

Although this chapter carried over the risk-and-vulnerabilities approach used in the OECD/FATF report, future research should consider shifting to an analytic framework that

[99] In Cyprus, for example, it is possible to apply for and gain a tax residence certificate verifying one's intention to make it one's tax residence after only a few weeks.

[100] Portugal's non-habitual residence scheme and Spain's 'Beckham Law', for example, predate each country's current RBI offerings. Malta, with its long history of combining RBI visa categories and tax benefits, is the main exception (Surak, *The Golden Passport*).

emphasises real harms rather than potential risks when identifying programme vulnerabilities. In any domain, potential risks are myriad, while those actually exploited and causing real harm are more limited. Identifying where the real harms have occurred, as well as their frequency and scale, would facilitate more targeted policy responses with stronger efficacy against actual damage. Further work should fully identify the scale and scope of actual harms to produce a better understanding of risk profile patterns that can feed into greater precision around regulation and workable best practices.

8

Legal Residence and Physical Presence

The Law and Practice of Naturalisation in EU Jurisdictions

DIMITRY V KOCHENOV AND MARTIJN VAN DEN BRINK*

I. INTRODUCTION

LEGAL RESIDENCE AND physical presence – two of the most common legal concepts in European migration and nationality laws. The relationship between both concepts may seem simple, but anyone who has followed the disputes over national and European residency requirements before the Court of Justice of the European Union (CJEU) knows otherwise. It was recently examined whether third-country nationals lose their right to reside as long-term residents if their presence on EU territory is limited to a few days per year. Ruling against Austria, the Court found that such a short presence is sufficient to prevent the loss of long-term residence.[1] Moreover, and politically more interesting, the European Commission has initiated infringement proceedings against Malta for awarding national and EU citizenship to wealthy investors 'absent any genuine link to the country or its citizens'.[2] The Maltese scheme places an obligation of one year of legal residence on those who want to obtain Maltese nationality by means of investment, but it does not demand any physical presence on the territory of Malta. The European Commission claims that Member States should not award their citizenship to persons without a genuine connection to their society,[3] by which it explicitly thinks of 'residence-based naturalization'.[4]

While scholars have debated whether naturalisation must be conditional on the existence of such a connection, as well as whether it can be required under EU law that such a connection exists,[5] less attention has been paid to the empirical side of the Commission's claim. How

* We are grateful to Emma Schulte for research assistance.

[1] Case C-432/20 *ZK* ECLI:EU:C:2022:39.

[2] 'Investor citizenship schemes: European Commission opens infringements against Cyprus and Malta for "selling" EU citizenship' (*European Commission*, 20 October 2020) https://ec.europa.eu/commission/presscorner/detail/hu/ip_20_1925.

[3] European Commission, 'Investor Citizenship and Residence Schemes in the European Union' COM(2019)12 final.

[4] Annex III to the European Commission Report COM(2019) 12 final.

[5] van den Brink, 'Revising Citizenship within the European Union' (2022) 23 *GLJ* 79; cf Jessurun d'Oliveira, in this volume; Sarmiento and van den Brink, 'EU Competence and Investor Migration' in Kochenov and Surak (eds), *Citizenship and Residence Sales* (Cambridge University Press 2023); Weingerl and Tratnik, 'Relevant Links' in Kochenov and Surak (eds), *Citizenship and Residence Sales*; Kochenov, 'Genuine Purity of Blood' (2020) LEQS Paper No. 164/2020.

rare is it that states allow naturalisation without a requirement of legal residence or physical presence? And how connected are both concepts in the law and practice of naturalisation in Europe? These questions have been little discussed despite their relation to and relevance for the normative and conceptual debate about the conditions for the acquisition and loss of both citizenship and the right to reside, either temporary or permanent. What does it mean that someone needs to 'reside' somewhere for several years to have a right to naturalise? How much overlap can one observe between residence and presence? Our aim is to expose the complexity of the relationship between two of the most basic terms used in naturalisation laws on the European continent, which we do by disentangling the meaning of 'legal residence' and 'physical presence' in these laws and the practice of their application in the EU Member States. We will do the same for similar rules at the supranational level. To this end, we studied the relevant legal material together with documents, statements and explanations given by the competent institutions on this material's application.

Our study reveals that the disconnect separating legal residence from physical presence is not nearly as exceptional as one could think. First, and unsurprisingly, the requirements of legal residence and physical presence hardly ever overlap fully: short periods away from the territory do not normally interrupt the continuity of legal residence. Second, and more interestingly, the disconnect between legal residence and physical presence in both national and EU law is often quite substantial – as is observable in the law itself, through the practice of the law's application by the competent authorities, or both. The relevant legal requirements vary widely across the EU, in terms of both the duration of legal residence required to be able to naturalise and the period of physical presence to be met to fulfil the conditions of legal residence. However, when examining whether the required period of legal residence is met, the competent authorities are concerned mainly with the *continuity* of legal residence – that is, the uninterrupted enjoyment of the right to be physically present – and less so with physical presence in the territory, that is, the actual exercise of the legal right. In other words, most Member States ask for proof of legal residence, such as an address in the country, registration in the municipality of legal residence or an employment contract with a local undertaking; they do not measure physical presence per se.

Furthermore, long absences from the national territory are often expressly permitted under national legislation. In some Member States, most citizenship acquisitions even proceed through procedures that impose either minimal to no requirements of legal residence or physical presence for those who want to naturalise. On top comes the reality of open internal borders within the EU, which creates a very specific context that needs to be taken into account. It is doubtful whether or to what extent physical presence is measurable in this context. Our study of national practices suggests that most Member States that have physical presence conditions on the books hardly assess whether such conditions are met in practice. Of course, the cases discussed in this chapter – the naturalisation of foreigners – are in themselves a minority: the vast majority of individuals with a European nationality acquired this status at birth. Yet the acquisition of nationality at birth is not the subject of our study.

Our analysis of the requirements of legal residence and physical presence in EU law leads to very similar conclusions. Following established approaches in national law and practice, EU legislation on the position of third-country nationals and the free movement of EU citizens also distinguishes between legal residence and physical presence. Even if EU law provides a uniform legal framework, its implementation in practice allows for significant national variation. This is, first, because EU legislation offers Member States flexibility regarding the implementation of the provisions on physical presence, but also because the enforcement of these provisions happens in accordance with national standards, policies and practices.

Regarding the scope of our study, two clarifications are in order. First, to obtain citizenship or permanent residence, foreigners must usually meet multiple requirements, ranging from proof of a clean criminal record, of financial self-sufficiency or of language proficiency. These criteria vary from one Member State to another but will not be discussed in this work. Second, we will not address the normative question of whether physical presence should play a (greater) role in the context of naturalisation and acquisition of permanent residence. Instead, our aim is to provide a clearer picture of the current state of the law on legal residence in the EU. We will not discuss all national legislation in equal detail, however, as some Member States provide more guidance on the implementation of their laws than others and, hence, offer more useful insights in respect of the interaction between legal residence and physical presence. Existing legal rules and practices will be discussed to the extent necessary to offer a good illustration of the legal diversity and practical complexity when it comes to rules requiring legal residence and physical presence, as well as their enforcement.

This contribution is structured as follows: Section II discusses our findings regarding the requirements of legal residence and physical presence in the nationality laws of the Member States. Section III examines the implementation of these laws by the responsible national authorities. Section IV examines the provisions on legal residence and physical presence and their interpretation in EU legislation on the right of long-term residence of third-country nationals and of the right of permanent residence of EU citizens. In the conclusion, we summarise our findings and consider their broader relevance.

II. LEGAL RESIDENCE AND PHYSICAL PRESENCE IN EU MEMBER STATE NATIONALITY LAWS

This section examines the requirements of legal residence and physical presence in the national citizenship codes of EU Member States. Naturalisation is defined as 'all modes of acquisition after birth other than those for which birth in the territory or to citizen parents is a condition'.[6] As is well known, Member States regulate naturalisation in very different ways, and there is variation not only between, but also within, them: national laws on the acquisition of citizenship distinguish between different categories of persons and the requirements for naturalisation are tailored to these categories. Thus, the same Member State may impose different naturalisation requirements for different categories of individuals, including different requirements of legal residence and physical presence.

In what follows, we offer a comparative overview of these requirements. We first discuss ordinary naturalisation procedures, which is followed by an analysis of the preferential regimes Member States have established. The ordinary naturalisation procedure is the default procedure for foreigners who do not qualify for any of the more preferential regimes. It is important to note, however, that the ordinary procedure is not necessarily the procedure that most individuals use to naturalise. On the contrary, most citizenship acquisitions may take place under preferential procedures. Thus, while we will, in accordance with common terminology, use the term ordinary procedure for the national default procedures, we are aware that these procedures may provide a far less popular path to citizenship than preferential procedures.

[6] 'Glossary on Citizenship and Electoral Rights' (EUI Globalcit 2020) https://cadmus.eui.eu/bitstream/handle/1814/67362/RSCAS_GLOBALCIT_Glossary_2020.pdf?sequence=1&isAllowed=y.

A. Ordinary Naturalisation

Ordinary naturalisation procedures usually require applicants to have resided legally in the country for a certain period before they are eligible to apply for nationality. The periods of legal residence required by the Member States vary considerably, but in most cases are between five[7] and 10 years.[8] Legal residence implies a continued possession of a right to be present in the territory in accordance with the terms of validity of a residence permit. In many countries, the period of validity of temporary residence permits also counts toward the residence requirements for naturalisation, but some Member States expect foreigners to hold a permanent residence permit, and sometimes to have held it for a number of years, before they can apply for naturalisation.[9] The practical implication of such a requirement to have permanent residence status before one can apply for naturalisation is that the periods of residence required for naturalisation can be (much) longer than a cursory reading of the different nationality laws would suggest. For example, a person who is not a Bulgarian citizen can obtain Bulgarian citizenship if he or she has held a permanent residence permit for five years on the date of application.[10] But since a foreigner must have been in legal residence for a period of (at least) five years before he can obtain a permanent residence permit,[11] he must have been legally resident for at least ten years before an application can be successfully made to become a Bulgarian citizen.

In most Member States, the period of legal residence must be continuous. An important exception to this rule is Germany, which allows previous periods of residence to be taken into consideration.[12] However, continuous legal residence does not imply continuous physical presence. In some respect, this is both unexpected and entirely logical: otherwise, very few foreigners would ever be eligible for citizenship, since periods of presence are often interrupted by periods abroad for reasons related to work, health, study, family or vacation. Moreover, in a world of increasing mobility, some people cross borders with high frequency, sometimes de facto and/or de iure residing in two or more different countries at the same time. Not surprisingly, many Member States make an explicit distinction between the requirements of legal residence and physical presence in order to allow for such travel, including those without such an explicit distinction in their legislation. For example, while the Spanish nationality law requires residence to be 'legal, continuous and immediately before the application',[13] without specifying whether absences are allowed, the Spanish Supreme Court has ruled that short trips abroad do not interrupt the continuity of residence.[14]

Between those Member States that do specify how much absence is allowed, there are significant differences. At one end of the spectrum, we find countries like Poland, Denmark, and Hungary, which allow very limited absences from their territory. The Law on Polish Citizenship requires uninterrupted legal residence for a relatively long period of 10 years before a claim

[7] Art 13(2)(a) of the Nationality Law 2003 (FI); Art 21-17 of the French Civil Code 1804 (FR); Art 12(1)(1) of the Nationality Law 1994 (LV); Art 8(1) of the Nationality Law 1984 (NL); Sect 11(4)(c) of the Nationality Act 2001 (SE); Art 12bis of the Nationality Act 2013 (BE).

[8] Art 10 of the Nationality Act 1985 (AT); Art 9(1)(f) of the Nationality Act 1992 (IT); Art 18(1) of the Nationality Law 2002 (LT); Art 22(1) of the Civil Code 1889 (ES).

[9] Art 12(1)(1) of the Nationality Act 1994 (LV); Art 12(2) of the Nationality Law 1999 (BG); Art 8 of the Nationality Law 1991 (HR); Art 6(1)(2) of the Nationality Act 1995 (EE); Art 18(1) of the Nationality Act 2002 (LT).

[10] Art 12(2) of the Nationality Law 1999 (BG).

[11] Art 25 of the Foreigners in the Republic of Bulgaria Law 1998 (BG).

[12] Art 12(b) of the Nationality Law 1913 (DE).

[13] Art 22(3) of the Civil Code 1889 (ES).

[14] R Rubio-Marín et al, 'Country Report on Citizenship Law: Spain' (EUDO Citizenship 2015) 25.

to acquire Polish citizenship can be made.[15] Residence is considered uninterrupted, according to Article 30(3) of the same law only if, during this 10-year period, none of the periods spent abroad exceeded six months and all these periods did not exceed 10 months in total. Denmark requires nine years of residence before naturalisation is an option, during which the foreigner must not have been absent from the territory for a total of more than one year.[16] Applicants for citizenship of Hungary must not have left the country for more than six months during the required eight years of continuous residence.[17]

However, these countries appear to be the exception rather than the rule. Most Member States allow foreigners to be absent from their territory for more extended periods. For instance, Estonia and Lithuania require legal and continuous residence for relatively long periods – eight and 10 years respectively[18] – but allow absences of around six months per year.[19] The German Nationality Act offers even greater flexibility. Like Estonia and Lithuania, Germany considers ordinary residence to be uninterrupted by stays abroad not exceeding six months.[20] However, for foreigners who exceed this period, Article 12(b)(2) of the German Nationality Act specifies that previous periods of residence may be counted toward the period of residence required for naturalisation, up to a period of five years.

Another example of a Member State that expects foreigners to spend a certain amount of time in the territory before qualifying for permanent residence or nationality, but allows them to leave the country regularly, is Finland. Finnish law allows short periods of absence to be counted towards the continuous period of residence and defines with precision what counts as a short period. According to Section 16(2) of the Finnish Nationality Act, this includes:

1) periods of absence not exceeding a month;
2) a maximum of six periods of absence exceeding one but not exceeding two months;
3) a maximum of two periods of absence exceeding two but not exceeding six months.

The same section also provides that temporary absences of more than six months, but less than one year, shall not be counted in the continuous period of residence nor interrupt it. Since, according to Section 13(1)(2) of the Nationality Act, one of the conditions for obtaining Finnish citizenship is that foreigners have resided and domiciled in Finland for five years without interruption, it seems that they may remain outside Finnish territory for considerable periods without being disqualified for Finnish nationality.

Some countries specify in their immigration laws, rather than in their nationality laws, how long applicants may have been abroad. For example, Portugal, which is known for its inclusive citizenship regime,[21] requires six years of legal residence before an application for Portuguese citizenship can be made.[22] Legal residence requires the regularisation of stay in accordance with Portuguese immigration law. This law sets out the conditions under which temporary and permanent residence permits can be obtained or lost. In the case of Portugal, temporary

[15] Art 30(1)(6) of the Nationality Law 1962 (PL).
[16] Art 9 of the Circular Letter No. 61 on Naturalisation 2008 (DK).
[17] 'Access to Citizenship and its Impact on Immigrant Integration: ACIT Handbook for Hungary' (EUI Migration Policy Group 2013) http://cadmus.eui.eu/bitstream/handle/1814/29771/ACIT_Handbook_Hungary_ENGLISH.pdf?sequence=1.
[18] Art 6(2) of the Nationality Law 1995 (EE); Art 18(1) of the Nationality Law 2002 (LT).
[19] Art 11 of the Nationality Law 1995 (EE); Art 2(18) of the Nationality Law 2002 (LT).
[20] Art 12(b)(1) of the of the Nationality Act 1913 (DE).
[21] 'Access to Citizenship and its Impact on Immigrant Integration: ACIT Handbook for Portugal' (EUI Migration Policy Group 2013) http://cadmus.eui.eu/bitstream/handle/1814/29770/ACIT_Handbook_Portugal_ENGLISH.pdf?sequence=1.
[22] Art 6 of the Nationality Law 1981 (PT).

residence is lost when the foreigner is absent for 'six consecutive months or eight interpolated months, within the overall validity of the authorisation'.[23] Permanent residence is lost after an absence of '24 consecutive months or, in a period of three years, 30 interpolated months'.[24] Hence, once obtained, foreigners have the right to leave the country for long periods of time without having their residence permits revoked. This implies that such absences also are also in accordance with the residence requirements for obtaining Portuguese nationality.

In addition to these standard rules for authorised absences, some Member States allow longer periods of absence in the event of special circumstances. Germany allows longer absences if the foreigner has to perform military service in the country of origin.[25] Under Danish law, periods spent abroad can be twice as long as under the default rules in case of education or training, military service in the applicant's country of nationality or visits to close family due to serious illness in the family.[26] Likewise, the Netherlands does not consider that the foreigner has changed his residence when he stays abroad for military service, work or education.[27]

Yet another group of Member States provides that persons applying for citizenship must have been both legally resident and domiciled there for a certain period.[28] Domicile is the place where a person has his or her main or habitual residence, that is, the place where the person and his or her family usually reside. Legal residence and domicile are, of course, not separate issues. Under Belgian law, for example, a person is habitually resident if she has established part of her life there.[29] This requires, among other things, that she is legally resident.[30] Likewise, the immigration authorities of the Netherlands stipulate that legal residence is lost if a person moves her main residence to another country.[31] That said, it is possible to be legally resident but not be habitually resident. This is certainly the case for EU citizens, who can have a right of residence under EU law without having a residence permit.[32] Thus, absences from the territory that entail the loss of habitual residence need not automatically entail the end of legal residence.

More important for our purpose is the relationship between domicile and physical presence. These, too, are not entirely separate. For example, the German nationality law provides that the '*gewöhnliche Aufenthalt*' is not interrupted by stays abroad not exceeding six months.[33] Longer periods abroad may affect one's domicile. Likewise, according to the Dutch immigration authorities, longer periods abroad affect a person's main residence. When a person holds a temporary or permanent residence permit, she may stay outside the Netherlands for up to

[23] Art 85(2)(a) of Act 23/2007 (PT), amended by Act 29/2012 (PT), on the conditions and procedures on the entry, stay, exit and removal of foreign citizens from Portuguese territory, as well as the long-term resident status.

[24] Art 85(2)(b) of Act 23/2007 (PT), amended by Act 29/2012 (PT), on the conditions and procedures on the entry, stay, exit and removal of foreign citizens from Portuguese territory, as well as the long-term resident status.

[25] Art 12(b)(1) of the Nationality Act 1913 (DE).

[26] Art 9(ii) of the Circular Letter No. 61 on Naturalisation 2008 (DK).

[27] Decision of the State Secretary for Security and Justice No. WBV 2014/23 (NL) amending the Aliens Circular 2000.

[28] In addition to the Member States discussed here, see also: Art 11 of the Nationality Law 2001 (SE); Art 8 of the Nationality Law 1991 (RO).

[29] Art 3 of Law on population registers, identity cards, foreigners' cards and residence documents 1991 (FR) amending the law of 1983 on organising a national register of natural persons.

[30] Art 7bis of the Nationality Law 2013 (BE).

[31] The Dutch authorities explain the consequences of moving one's main residence for legal residence here: 'Main residency' (Immigratie-en Naturalisatiedienst, 25 April 2024) https://ind.nl/en/living-in-the-netherlands-with-a-residence-permit/main-residency.

[32] According to CJEU, residence permits only have a declaratory character. Case C-325/09 *Dias* ECLI:EU:C:2011:498, para 54.

[33] Art 12(b) of the Nationality Law 1913 (DE).

six consecutive months. Students, highly skilled migrants and investors may stay abroad for longer periods.[34] At the same time, domicile is often about more than just physical presence, and a person's principal residence need not be affected by regular stays abroad. For example, the Dutch authorities hold that someone's main residence is not interrupted if, on the basis of the correct legal residence permits, she moves abroad for work.[35] Moreover, domicile is often determined by much more than physical presence alone. Other considerations include having paid taxes, registration with local authorities, and having a bank account or real estate in the country.[36] Domicile and physical presence should therefore not be confused. Even in countries where domicile is required, continuous legal residence does not require continuous presence.

B. Preferential Naturalisation

All Member States have important exceptions to the default naturalisation rules described above. Their preferential naturalisation procedures allow foreigners to obtain citizenship with much shorter and sometimes no legal residence or physical presence requirements. We focus on three important exceptions that allow accelerated naturalisation for specific categories of foreigners with expedited naturalisation: the exceptions for family members, individuals with special historical ties to the state awarding citizenship and those that can make a contribution deemed valuable by the state in question. Such procedures are proving very popular in some countries, which may mean that many of the new citizens have hardly resided in the territory legally or physically. The Italian and Hungarian examples that we will explore demonstrate this quite clearly: hundreds of thousands of newly naturalised Europeans have in fact never lived in the EU; many of these EU citizens have never been to Europe.

i. Family Ties

It is common for countries to facilitate the naturalisation of relatives of those who already possess or apply for nationality. This applies to the children and the partner/spouse of the citizen, who can obtain citizenship under preferential conditions and after a simplified process in most of the Member States. In the past, citizenship was often transferred from the husband to his spouse, but those rules have disappeared.[37] Instead, partners of both sexes can obtain citizenship under preferential conditions in most Member States.

Most Member States have shorter residence requirements for the partner of someone who already is a national. Austria requires six years of continuous legal residence instead of 10,[38] and the partner of a Croatian national must have a permanent residence permit but need not meet the requirement of eight years of continuous residence in Croatia.[39] Similarly, Finland requires four years of continuous legal residence instead of five,[40] and Hungary allows the partner of a national to apply for citizenship after three years of continuous legal residence instead of eight, if the partner has lived in the household of a Hungarian citizen for at least

[34] 'Main residency' (Immigratie-en Naturalisatiedienst, 25 April 2024).
[35] Art 6.2.1. of the Aliens Circular 2000 (NL).
[36] See for some criteria: 'Main residency' (Immigratie-en Naturalisatiedienst, 25 April 2024).
[37] Bauböck and Goodman, 'Naturalisation' (2010) EUI EUDO Citizenship Policy Brief No 2. https://cadmus.eui.eu/bitstream/handle/1814/51625/RSCAS_EUDO_CIT__PB_2011_02.pdf?sequence=1&isAllowed=y.
[38] Art 11a of the Nationality Act 1985 (AT).
[39] Art 10 of the Nationality Law 1991 (HR).
[40] Art 22(2)(a) of the Nationality Law 2003 (FI).

three years in a lawful marriage.[41] Under the previous version of the relevant Italian legislation, spouses could apply for nationality already after six months of residence, in contrast to the 10 years required under the ordinary naturalisation procedures. Consequently, spousal naturalisation became the main procedure used, and it remains popular even if the required legal period of residence for family members has been extended to two years, which is still five times shorter than the period required under the ordinary procedure.[42]

Some Member States do not impose any requirement of legal residence at all for certain family members. Article 3(1)(a) of the Nationality Law of Portugal provides that a foreigner married to a Portuguese citizen for more than three years may acquire Portuguese citizenship by declaration.[43] Italy allows the foreign partner of an Italian citizen to obtain citizenship if he or she has legally resided in Italy for two years after the marriage, but also after three years from the day of the marriage when the foreigner has resided abroad.[44] Likewise, France allows the spouse of a French citizen to acquire French citizenship from two years after the day of the marriage if the spouse has sufficient command of the French language. The duration is three years if the foreigner cannot prove that he or she has continuously resided in France for at least one year since the day of marriage.[45] The Netherlands equally does not require the family to reside in the country before the non-citizen family member applies for naturalisation.[46] Finally, the Slovenian Nationality Act provides that a foreigner married to a Slovenian citizen may be granted nationality after three years of marriage and one year of continuous residence in Slovenia prior to submitting the application. The law adds, however, that the criterion of continuous residence may be fulfilled even when the person is not physically present, which is to the discretion of the Slovenian government.[47]

ii. Historical Ties

Many countries offer preferential access to citizenship to persons with special, often historical (and barely existing), ties to the country, in some cases dating back to times predating both their birth and the country's creation. Such preferential regimes have been set up by Member States with former colonies, with a significant expatriate community, and by those wishing to redress a historic injustice. For example, Bulgaria, Croatia, Greece, Hungary, Ireland, Lithuania and Portugal all allow individuals that can prove that they are descendants to obtain nationality even if they are not domiciled or resident in the country.[48] Other countries do impose a residency requirement, but usually one that is considerably shorter than the requirement under their ordinary naturalisation procedure. Under Italian law, direct ancestors in the second degree can become Italian citizens after two years of legal residence in Italy and a declaration of intent to become an Italian citizen.[49] Slovenian expatriates and their descendants up to the fourth generation have a right to obtain Slovenian citizenship if they have lived

[41] Art 4(2)(a) of the Nationality Law 1993 (HU).
[42] Art 5(1) of the Nationality Law 1992 (IT).
[43] Art 3(1) of the Nationality Law 1981 (PT).
[44] Art 5(1) of the Nationality Law 1992 (IT).
[45] Art 21-2 of the French Civil Code 1804 (FR).
[46] Art 8(2) of the Nationality Law 1984 (NL).
[47] Art 12 of the Nationality Law 1999 (SI).
[48] Art 15(1) of the Nationality Law 1999 (BG); Art 16 of the Nationality Law 1991 (HR); Art 10 of the Greek Nationality Act 1984 (GR); Art 4(3) of the Nationality Law 1993 (HU); Art 16 of the Nationality Law 1956 (IE); Art 10 of the Nationality Law 2002 (LT); Art 6(4) of the Nationality Law 1981 (PT).
Art 5(1) of the Nationality Law 1992 (IT).
[49] Art 4 of the Nationality Law 1992 (IT).

for at least one year in Slovenia before applying for citizenship.[50] Finally, Spain is known for the preferential conditions it has for nationals of Latin American countries, the Philippines and Equatorial Guinea, who can apply for Spanish citizenship after two years of legal residence, instead of the 10 years that the ordinary procedure imposes.[51]

The preferential naturalisation procedure in Spain also covers Sephardic Jews, if they have resided in Spain for at least two years.[52] Spain provides the Sephardic community preferential access to its nationality in order to correct a historical injustice, namely the Inquisition against this community. For this reason, the Spanish authorities have also used the discretionary powers they have under the Spanish Civil Code to grant nationality to Sephardic Jews who did not meet the residency requirements.[53] Portugal follows the Spanish example. It allows Sephardic Jews who can demonstrate that they belong to a community of Portuguese origin to be naturalised without having to reside in Portugal.[54] Descendants of people who were exiled long ago are thus entitled to both Spanish and Portuguese citizenship without residence there.[55]

Preferential citizenship regimes for those with historical ties have proven extremely popular in some Member States. Statistics show that the vast majority of Spanish citizenship acquisitions are by persons from Latin America.[56] Likewise, the number of foreigners of Greek origin in Greek naturalisation statistics is much higher than the number of foreigners without Greek origin,[57] which suggests that most persons who obtain Greek nationality do so under a procedure that does not require them to have resided in Greece. Finally, the Irish rule, which allows the Minister to grant an application for a certificate of naturalisation 'where the applicant is of Irish descent or Irish associations'[58] has become highly popular after the Brexit referendum, as many British citizens have sought to obtain Irish and EU citizenship through this procedure.[59]

iii. Special Achievements and Investments

Third, EU Member States have established preferential naturalisation regimes for those who have made or are likely to make a contribution deemed of sufficient value to distinguish such applicants from the general group of applicants for naturalisation. Preferential routes to

[50] Art 12 of the Nationality Law 1999 (SI).

[51] Art 22(1) of the Civil Code 1889 (ES).

[52] ibid.

[53] The discretionary procedure is laid down in Art 21(1) of the Civil Code 1889 (ES). For further information about the discretionary conferral of citizenship to Sephardic Jews, read: Rubio-Marín et al, 'Country Report' 22.

[54] For an analysis of the Portuguese as well as Spanish law, read Jessurun d'Oliveira, 'Iberian Nationality Legislation and Sephardic Jews' (2015) 11 *EUConst* 13.

[55] Lesperance, 'Even for the Super-Rich, Citizenship by Descent Is Extremely Useful' (IMI Daily, 5 January 2022) www.imidaily.com/reasonable-doubt/even-for-the-super-rich-citizenship-by-descent-is-extremely-useful-lessons-from-abramovich/; the simple fact that blood lineages are as irrational a mode of status and rights distribution as one gets revealed anti-Semitic inclinations even among those, who initially supported the remedying of the wrongs vis-à-vis the Sephardic community: when a Portuguese MEP, Ms Gomes, learnt that a Russian-Israeli oligarch, Mr Abramovich, acquired Portuguese citizenship due to Sephardic connections, she apparently concluded that he was the 'wrong Jew' for the Portuguese law, not the kind of Jew she had in mind. She twitted 'Why is Russian kleptocrat #Abramovich not included in #EU sanctions list? Well, now he is … Portuguese!' (1 March 2022).

[56] Rubio-Marín et al, 'Country Report' 34.

[57] Christopoulos, 'Country Report on Citizenship Law: Greece' (EUDO Citizenship Observatory 2013) 14.

[58] Art 16 of the Nationality Law of Ireland also specifies that one is of Irish association if 'related by blood, affinity or adoption to a person who is an Irish citizen or entitled to be an Irish citizen', or 'related by blood, affinity or adoption to a person who is deceased and who, at the time of his or her death, was an Irish citizen or entitled to be an Irish citizen'.

[59] 'Huge Rise in Britons Applying for Irish Citizenship after Brexit Vote' (*The Guardian*, 13 October 2016) http://www.theguardian.com/world/2016/oct/13/huge-rise-in-britons-applying-for-irish-citizenship-after-brexit-vote.

citizenship have been created for athletes, stellar scientists and investors. Procedures of this kind have been described as creating a form of 'Olympic citizenship'[60] or investment citizenship.[61]

Member States usually allow discretionary naturalisation for people who have made an outstanding contribution to the country.[62] Croatian law permits the discretionary naturalisation of foreigners if this is in the interest of Croatia,[63] and Latvia and Lithuania may grant citizenship to foreigners for achievements of special merit to their society.[64] Other Member States allow for the naturalisation of those who can make a special scientific, cultural or athletic contribution.[65] Discretionary naturalisation is often also possible for persons without legal residence, but there are exceptions. Romania allows 'internationally famous personalities' to obtain Romanian citizenship if they have been domiciled for half as long as that required under the ordinary naturalisation procedure (four instead of eight years),[66] and Lithuanian law provides that the beneficiary must have integrated into the Lithuanian society.[67]

Some Member States have preferential naturalisation schemes for persons willing to make a substantial financial investment or donation. Until recently Cyprus allowed investors to directly acquire nationality following the investment required by the Cypriot Civil Registry Laws and the acquisition of real estate in the amount of €500,000, plus VAT.[68] Cyprus suspended its scheme following pressure from the European Commission,[69] despite the absence of EU competence in this field.[70] In contrast to Cyprus, where investments were preferred, Malta offers citizenship to those making the required non-refundable donation, acquiring or renting a property of a certain value, and residing legally in the country for 12 months.[71] The requirement of legal residence is not a requirement of physical presence, as investors only have to visit the island once. This requirement is nonetheless more extensive than what, for example, Cyprus, Austria, Croatia and Latvia require under their Olympic/investment citizenship acquisition schemes, as well as many other preferential naturalisation regimes.

In most Member States, foreigners can obtain a residence permit in exchange for an investment.[72] For instance, it is possible to acquire permanent residence in Latvia for five years in exchange for an investment in the equity capital of a company, in state securities, or by making a bank deposit.[73] Investors are not required to be physically present in Latvia for

[60] Shachar, 'Picking Winners' (2017) 120 *YLJ* 2088.

[61] Surak, *The Golden Passport* (Harvard University Press 2023); Kochenov and Surak (eds), *Citizenship and Residence Sales* (Cambridge University Press 2023); Kälin, Ius Doni *in International Law and EU Law* (Brill-Nijhoff 2019).

[62] See also Kochenov and Basheska in this volume.

[63] Art 12 of the Nationality Law 1991 (HR).

[64] Art 20(1) of the Nationality Law 2002 (LT); Art 13(1) of the Nationality Law 1994 (LV).

[65] Art 16 of the Nationality Law 1999 (BG); Art 16(1) of the Nationality Law 1993 (CZ); Art 10 of the Nationality Act 1995 (EE); Art 7(2)(b) of the Nationality Law 1993 (SK).

[66] Art 8(2) of the Nationality Law 1991 (RO).

[67] Art 15 of the Nationality Law 2002 (LT).

[68] Art 111A of the Civil Registry Law 2002 (CY). On the potential breaches of EU free movement of capital law in this context, which obliged a category of naturalised EU citizens to keep investments in a particular country, see Kudryashova, 'The "Sale" of Conditional Citizenship', in Cambien et al (eds), *European Citizenship under Stress* (Brill-Nijhoff) 413.

[69] Jessurun D'Oliveira, 'Golden Passports'; Kochenov and Basheska in this volume. Since the less transparent investor citizenship schemes of Austria and Croatia were not challenged, this seems to show that the more economically beneficial the scheme are, the less politically acceptable they are. Sumption, 'Can Investor Residence and Citizenship Programmes Be a Policy Success?' in Kochenov and Surak (eds), *Citizenship and Residence Sales*, 377. See also, Surak, 'Investment Migration' in Kochenov and Surak (eds), *Citizenship and Residence Sales*, 25.

[70] Sarmiento and van den Brink, 'EU Competence and Investor Migration'; Kochenov and Basheska, as well as Weilerr in this volume.

[71] Individual Investor Programme of the Republic of Malta Regulations 2013 (MT).

[72] Commission Report COM(2019) 12 final.

[73] Sect 23(28) of the Immigration Law 2003 (LV).

the duration of their permit: legal residence is offered as a right and does not require physical presence. Greece offers visas in exchange for investments in real estate and, like Latvia, does not require physical presence.[74] Spain requires that the investor travels 'to Spain at least once during his or her authorised residence period'.[75] Slightly more demanding is Portugal, where investors must be present for seven days, continuous or not, during the first year, and for 14 days, continuous or not, during the subsequent two years.[76] However, unlike Greece and Latvia, Portugal allows individuals with an investment residence permit to apply for permanent residence or citizenship later, meaning that those who obtain a residence permit through investment can at some point obtain permanent residence or citizenship without having been physically present in Portugal for a substantial period of time.[77] The Spanish regime also offers more favourable access to citizenship. Holding a Spanish investment visa for 10 continuous years is sufficient to obtain the Spanish nationality.[78]

III. PHYSICAL PRESENCE IN PRACTICE

However diverse Member States' rules on the acquisition of nationality are, some important conclusions can be drawn from the discussion in the previous section. First, legal residence is not always an indispensable element in the acquisition of citizenship by naturalisation. In the case of ordinary naturalisation, legal residence for a certain period is a requirement in all Member States, but in the case of preferential naturalisation, this requirement is usually either shortened or abolished altogether. It is not surprising, in this context, that 'ordinary naturalisation' is frequently not the most popular way to naturalise in practice – pointing to a possible misnomer. Second, legal residence only partially coincides with physical residence, and many preferential naturalisation schemes allow naturalisation without a requirement of physical residence. This, however, is only the law on the books. If, in addition, the practical enforcement of the legal requirements of legal residence and physical presence are considered, an additional layer of complexity comes to light. It then becomes apparent that some of the existing legislation seems mostly aspirational in nature.

Because intra-EU border controls have largely disappeared, individuals can cross borders without national immigration authorities being able to verify where they are staying or moving to. And not only have internal border controls disappeared, but external border controls have become less stringent for some persons. Passports of persons with the nationality of an EU/EEA country or Switzerland are not stamped, just like the travel documents of foreigners who enjoy a right of residence as relatives of an EU citizen and who can prove this by presenting a 'residence card of a family member of a Union citizen'.[79] Stamping passports makes a difference, as the Schengen Border Code clarifies: 'Stamping makes it possible

[74] Law 4146/2013 (GR).

[75] Carrera, 'How Much Does EU Citizenship Cost? The Maltese Citizenship-for-Sale Affair: A Breakthrough for Sincere Cooperation in Citizenship of the Union?' (2014) CEPS Paper No. 64, 16. For more nuanced takes on the nature of EU citizenship and sincere cooperation, see Jessurun D'Oliveira, 'Golden Passports'; Margiotta, 'Ricchi e poveri alla prova della cittadinanza europea' (2020) *Ragion Pratica* 513; Kochenov and Basheska in this volume.

[76] Art 5 of Order No. 11820-A/2012 (PT), amended by Order No. 1661-A/2013.

[77] Art 5(3) of Order No. 11820-A/2012 (PT), amended by Order n. 1661-A/2013.

[78] Carrera, 'How Much Does EU Citizenship Cost?', 16.

[79] See Art 10(2) of Regulation No 562/2006/EC establishing a Community Code on the rules governing the movement of persons across borders (Schengen Borders Code) [2006] OJ L105/1, in combination with Art 10(1) of Directive 2004/38/EC on the right of citizens of the Union and their family members to move and reside freely within the territory of the Member States.

to establish, with certainty, the date on which, and where, the border was crossed'.[80] That certainty disappears when stamping disappears. As a result, Member States can more easily check whether the requirements of legal residence have been met than whether applicants for naturalisation have been physically present for the required period. As we show, the procedures of many national immigration and naturalisation services do not seem designed to establish whether physical presence criteria are met. Also in practice, legal residence is not physical presence.

A study of the supporting documents that applicants must submit with their naturalisation file suggests that only two EU Member States request information on arrival in and departure from the territory. These are Ireland and Cyprus, which, not surprisingly, are both non-Schengen countries, and thus in a position to verify to some extent, on the basis of the documents submitted, that legal requirements of physical presence have been met.[81] This is not to say that both countries can fully verify that applicants of their nationality have met the legal presence requirements, if only because they also have borders porous by law. Ireland has a common travel area with the UK and the Channel Islands that allows travel with minimal immigration controls. Someone with a residence permit for one country can in principle travel to the other.[82] Similarly, the Green Line between the north and south of Cyprus, is normally crossed without a passport stamp to indicate that such a trip has been made. Finally, the restrictions imposed by EU law on stamping travel documents also undermine the ability to verify physical presence based on applicants' travel documents.

Perhaps for this reason, these countries may require EU/EEA and Swiss nationals to present different evidence as part of their nationality application than other foreigners. Ireland illustrates this well. Eligibility for Irish citizenship under the ordinary naturalisation procedure requires applicants to have resided legally in Ireland for five years during the nine years preceding the date of application. Of these five years, the last year must be continuous.[83] In addition, Irish law requires applicants to have accumulated sufficient 'reckonable residence'. Reckonable residence is the period during which applicants have resided in Ireland with the required immigration permits. What evidence must be presented to prove reckonable residence is different for EU/EEA and Swiss nationals than for other foreign nationals. Those who are not EU/EEA or Swiss nationals must show that they have 1825 or 1826 days of reckonable residence over nine years based on their accumulated permission stamps, including one year of continuous residence immediately prior to the date of application.[84] EU/EEA and Swiss nationals must submit different proof of their residence in Ireland. While the legal residence of other foreign nationals is controlled by passport stamps, those holding the nationality of an EU/EEA country or Switzerland are 'required to reach a score of 150 points in each of the years proof of residency is required. They do this by submitting proofs with a predetermined value.'[85] This may include

[80] Recital 9 of Regulation No 562/2006/EC.

[81] The information on the supporting documents to be provided in an application for Cypriot citizenship is published here: 'Due to Years of Residence' (Civil Registry and Migration Department) www.moi.gov.cy/moi/crmd/crmd.nsf/duetoyears_en/duetoyears_en?OpenDocument; Ireland is less clear about this matter but makes a distinction between nationals from EU/EEA countries and other foreigners: www.irishimmigration.ie/wp-content/uploads/2023/04/FORM-8-CTZ3-Version-7.0-Apr-23.pdf.

[82] Some exceptions are laid down in The Immigration (Control of Entry Through Republic of Ireland) Order 1972 (IE).

[83] Art 15 of the Nationality Law 1956 (IE).

[84] 'Naturalisation Residency Calculator' (Immigration Service Delivery) www.irishimmigration.ie/naturalisation-residency-calculator/.

[85] 'Proofs of Residence' (Immigration Service Delivery) www.irishimmigration.ie/how-to-become-a-citizen/become-an-irish-citizen-by-naturalisation/proofs-of-residence/.

mortgage or rent agreements, employment or medical details or proof of tax payments. Such documents do not provide proof of physical presence in the same way as passport stamps.

As for the other EU Member States, we can see considerable variation. Some still attach great importance to physical presence, not only in law but also in practice, while others no longer control this at all. An example of a country that still emphasises the importance of legal residence and actual presence is Austria. Under the old Nationality Act, applications for Austrian citizenship had to meet a condition of continued residence, which meant being registered with the police for the required period. Time abroad was deemed unimportant.[86] However, since the Nationality Act was amended in 2005, applicants must, in accordance with Article 10(1), have lawfully resided in the federal territory for an uninterrupted period of at least 10 years, including at least five years as a settled resident. Furthermore, Article 15(1)(3) of the Nationality Act stipulates that applicants must not have resided outside the federal territory for more than 20 per cent of that period.

Both requirements make things more difficult for many persons interested in obtaining Austrian citizenship. Uninterrupted residence requires uninterrupted residence permits, meaning it is interrupted if the applicant is without a residence permit, even for a short period.[87] In addition, the 20 per cent rule may make it more difficult to obtain Austrian citizenship for individuals who need to spend an extended period of time abroad for (say) work or study.[88] However, it remains uncertain to what extent the competent authorities can verify whether a person has spent the required time in Austria. Applicants for naturalisation must submit extensive documentation as part of their application, including documents authorising their stay in the country. Such documents allow the authorities to determine whether the condition of continuous legal residence is met,[89] but not whether the requirement of physical presence is complied with.

A development opposite to that in Austria is that which has occurred in Finland, which has moved away from the use of residence as an important criterion for access to citizenship. Finnish legislation is very specific regarding periods of absence from Finnish territory that do not interrupt continuous residence,[90] but the latest amendments to the Finnish Nationality Act were introduced partly because residence was not considered essential for integration.[91] Rather, priority was given to language requirements, as an adequate understanding of the Finnish language was considered more important for integration into Finnish society. Applicants for Finnish nationality no longer need to submit proof of continuous legal residence. They only need to submit a valid identity card, a certificate demonstrating language proficiency and information of their current and previous income.[92]

That countries are not actually interested in the question of how long the applicant has been present in the national territory during the required periods of legal residence is also evident from the way in which the Netherlands applies its legislation in practice. To be eligible for Dutch nationality, the applicant must have been admitted to and have his main residence in the Netherlands.[93] To prove admission, the Dutch authorities require that applications be

[86] Stern and Valchars, 'Country Report: Austria' (EUDO Citizenship Observatory 2013) 21.

[87] ibid.

[88] Migration Policy Group, 'Access to Citizenship and Its Impact on Immigrant Immigration: Handbook for Austria' (EUDO Citizenship Observatory 2013) 13.

[89] ibid 16.

[90] Sect 16 of the Nationality Law 2003 (FI).

[91] Brander, 'The 2011 Amendment of the Finnish Nationality Act' (EUDO Citizenship Observatory 2011).

[92] Information about an application for Finnish citizenship at 'Citizenship for Adults' (Finnish Immigration Service) https://migri.fi/en/citizenship-for-adults.

[93] Art 8(c) of the Nationality Law 1984 (NL).

supported by proof of valid residence. Normally, this is a valid residence permit, but those with the nationality of an EU/EEA country or Switzerland do not need to provide proof of residence; local authorities check how long the applicant has lived in the Netherlands in the municipal personal records database.[94] Using this database, it is assessed whether the applicant has his main residence in the Netherlands.[95] EU/EEA citizens and Swiss nationals therefore meet the conditions for naturalisation – legal residence and main residence – if they are registered in the municipal personal records database. Other foreigners must also submit proof of legal residence. But none of the other supporting documents – a copy of a passport, a birth certificate and proof of civic integration[96] – attests to physical presence. Hence, although one may lose one's main residence in the Netherlands due to prolonged absences, this does not seem to be a legal requirement that the national authorities are concerned with during the naturalisation process.

The situation in Sweden seems similar. Sweden has a slightly different regime for EU/EEA citizens compared to foreigners from other countries. EU/EEA citizens do not have to hold a residence permit while residing in Sweden, but before they can apply for nationality, they must present evidence that they have the right of residence or that they have fulfilled the requirements needed for the right of residence.[97] In addition to legal residence, applicants must also be habitually resident in Sweden. According to the responsible authorities, habitual residents are those with long-term residence and the intention to remain in Sweden. The main rule is that residence based on permits leading to permanent residence counts as habitual residence.[98] But to prove both their legal and their habitual residence, EU/EEA citizens must submit documents showing that they have worked, been self-employed, had their own financial assets, or have studied in Sweden. (Self)-employment can be demonstrated by submitting contracts or tax statements, periods of studies based on transcripts and financial self-sufficiency by submitting bank statements and other relevant documents.[99] In other words, none of the requested documents show how long applicants for nationality have been physically present in the country. They may have spent significant periods abroad.

So, while physical presence is an important legal requirement under many naturalisation schemes, compliance with this requirement is often not examined in practice – and is in many situations not easily examinable. What we see, therefore, is that national authorities have become more interested in the kind of activities applicants for citizenship have undertaken in their country, for which they are asked to present documents such as rental contracts, certificates of ownership or information about their living arrangements.[100] To what extent applicants have physically lived in the country often seems less relevant, even if the law suggests otherwise.

[94] 'Becoming a Dutch National through Naturalisation' (Immigratie-en Naturalisatiedienst, 5 April 2024) https://ind.nl/en/dutch-citizenship/becoming-a-dutch-national-through-naturalisation.

[95] Besluit van de Staatssecretaris van Veiligheid en Justitie van 12 december 2013, nummer WBN 2013/6, houdende wijziging van de Handleiding voor de toepassing van de Rijkswet op het Nederlanderschap 2003 (NL).

[96] 'Becoming a Dutch National through Naturalisation' (Immigratie-en Naturalisatiedienst, 5 April 2024).

[97] 'Citizenship for Adults' (Migrationsverket, 6 May 2024) www.migrationsverket.se/English/Private-individuals/Becoming-a-Swedish-citizen/Apply-for-citizenship/Citizenship-for-adults.html.

[98] 'Apply for citizenship – for adults' (Migrationsverket, 6 May 2024) www.migrationsverket.se/English/Private-individuals/Becoming-a-Swedish-citizen/Apply-for-citizenship/Citizenship-for-adults.html#MoredocumentsforEUEEAcitizens.

[99] ibid.

[100] Another example is the naturalisation process in Romania, Barbalescu, 'Naturalisation Procedures for Immigrants: Romania' (EUDO Citizenship Observatory 2013) 11–12.

A. Physical Presence in EU Law and Practice

This section discusses the extent to which EU law distinguishes between legal residence and physical presence, by studying the relevant legislative provisions and the case law of the CJEU. It should be clarified from the outset that the provisions discussed do not concern the acquisition of national citizenship. The EU is not competent to define who can be a citizen of the Member States and of the Union.[101] Article 20(1) TFEU states clearly that 'every person holding the nationality of a Member State shall be a citizen of the Union' and that EU citizenship 'shall be additional to and not replace national citizenship'. The CJEU has also affirmed on different occasions that it is in principle 'for each Member State … to lay down the conditions for the acquisition and loss of nationality'.[102] The EU enjoys competence, however, to determine the conditions under which EU citizens can exercise the right of free movement and residence across the Member States and to develop a common immigration policy that determines the conditions under which third-country nationals can reside legally in the EU.[103]

In accordance with this competence, the EU has adopted detailed legislation on the right of residence of third-country nationals in the EU and the right of free movement and residence of EU citizens across the Member States. It is these legislative acts that are the subject of our inquiry. As we will see, EU legislation conditions the enjoyment of specific rights on legal residence, but like national legislation, distinguishes between legal residence and physical presence. Moreover, as we explain, this distinction is a consequence not only of the written law but also of the fact that its application is left to the Member States, which may use their own methods to determine whether the legal requirements have been met.

Let us first analyse Directive 2003/109/EC concerning the status of third-country nationals who are long-term residents (Long-Term Residents Directive).[104] Article 4(1) of that Directive provides that 'Member States shall grant long-term resident status to third-country nationals who have resided legally and continuously within its territory for five years immediately prior to the submission of the relevant application'. So, like most Member States, the EU requires residence to be both 'legal' and 'continuous'. However, the legislature also decided that third-country nationals do not need to be continuously present during these five years. According to Article 4(3),

> periods of absence from the territory of the Member State concerned shall not interrupt the period … and shall be taken into account for its calculation where they are shorter than six consecutive months and do not exceed in total 10 months within the period referred to in paragraph 1.

Member States have considerable latitude under the Long-Term Residents Directive in determining whether a foreigner is legally resident. As the CJEU held, the Directive 'does not lay down the conditions which the residence of those nationals must satisfy for them to be

[101] Sarmiento and van den Brink, 'EU Competence and Investor Migration'; D Kochenov, '*Ius Tractum* of Many Faces' (2009) 15 *CJEL* 169; van den Brink, 'The Relationship between National and EU Citizenship' in Kostakopoulou and Thym (eds), *Research Handbook on European Union Citizenship Law and Policy* (Elgar 2022). The de facto impact of EU law on the nationalities of the Member States has been growing, however: in many EU jurisdictions EU citizens naturalise easier than third country nationals: EU citizens naturalise in other Member States much easier than third country nationals and the discrepancies between the rules applicable to Europeans and non-Europeans in this context has only been growing: Kochenov, 'Member State Nationalities and the Internal Market', in Nic Shuibhne and Gormley (eds), *From Single Market to Economic Union* (Oxford University Press 2012) 241.

[102] Case C-135/08 *Rottmann* ECLI:EU:C:2010:104, para 39; Case C-221/17 *Tjebbes* ECLI:EU:C:2019:189, para 30.

[103] Arts 21(2) and 79 TFEU. Sarmiento and van den Brink, 'EU Competence and Investor Migration'.

[104] Council Directive 2003/109/EC concerning the status of third-country nationals who are long-term residents.

regarded as legally resident in the territory of a Member State'.[105] Therefore, 'Member States are to grant long-term resident status to those nationals who, *in accordance with their national law*, have resided legally and continuously within their territory for five years immediately prior to the submission of the relevant application'.[106] This does not mean that Member States may issue permanent residence permits under the Directive to persons who have not legally resided in their territory for five years,[107] but it does mean that Member States have considerable discretion in deciding when persons enjoy legal residence under EU law. Moreover, Member States are of course allowed to grant permanent residence to anyone under national law, which is not limited by the conditions for legal residence in the Directive.

Member States also have considerable discretion in determining when absences from their territory interrupt the five-year period of residence. We just saw that absences that are shorter than six consecutive months and do not exceed 10 months in total during this five-year period do not interrupt this period. Article 4(3) adds, however, that '[i]n cases of specific or exceptional reasons of a temporary nature and in accordance with their national law, Member States may accept that a longer period of absence … shall not interrupt the [five-year] period'. This provision also provides that Member States are allowed to let 'periods of absence relating to secondment for employment purposes, including the provision of cross-border services' count towards the calculation of the five-year period. A study by the Commission has shown that many Member States have used the freedom provided to allow longer periods of absence.[108] What we see, then, is not only that legal and continuous residence does not require continuous physical presence, but also that Member States have different views on how much physical presence should be expected.

Finally, additional diversity is provided by the fact that Article 7(1) requires the applicant for a long-term residence permit must submit 'documentary evidence *to be determined by national law* that he/she meets the conditions set out in [the Directive] as well as, if required, by a valid travel document or its certified copy' (emphasis added). It is thus up to the Member States to determine how to assess whether the conditions of the Directive are met. Looking at the national conditions, it appears that they do not always attach much importance to establishing whether applicants have been present within their national borders. For example, Sweden requires that applications for long-term residence status are accompanied by a passport and documentary evidence that the applicant has been able to support himself and his family for the past five years.[109] The Netherlands requires applicants to demonstrate that they are in the possession of sufficient financial resources and have successfully passed their civic integration exam.[110] Both countries thus seem more concerned with whether applicants can contribute to their country and whether there are risks of the applicant becoming a social burden than with actual physical presence.

The Long-Term Residents Directive also defines the conditions under which long-term resident status may be lost or withdrawn. According to Article 9(1), third-country nationals are

[105] Case C-40/11 *Iida* ECLI:EU:C:2012:691, para 36.

[106] ibid, para 37 (emphasis added).

[107] This would arguably be against the Directive's purpose to promote the 'mutual confidence between Member States', see recital 17, Directive 2003/109/EC.

[108] European Commission, 'Report from the Commission to the European Parliament and the Council on the application of Directive 2003/109/EC concerning the status of third country nationals who are long-term residents' COM(2011)585 final.

[109] See the information provided by the Swedish authorities at: www.migrationsverket.se/English/Private-individuals/EU-citizens-and-long-term-residents/Long-term-residents/Long-term-resident-in-Sweden.html.

[110] See the information provided by the responsible Dutch authorities at 'Aanvraag verblijfsvergunning EU langdurig ingezetene of een verblijfsvergunning regulier voor onbepaalde tijd' (Immigratie-en Naturalisatiedienst 2023) https://ind.nl/en/Forms/6009.pdf.

no longer entitled to this status when it has been obtained fraudulently, when an expulsion measure has been issued against them,[111] and, most importantly, in case of 'absence from the territory of the Community for a period of 12 consecutive months'. According to Article 9(4), third-country nationals are not entitled to maintain their status 'after six years of absence from the territory of the Member State that granted long-term resident status'. However, these provisions allow Member States to derogate from these rules and determine that an absence exceeding these periods shall not entail the loss of that status in specific or exceptional circumstances. More importantly, individuals with long-term resident status hardly need to be physically present during these periods to maintain this status. In *ZK*, the CJEU interpreted Article 9(1) literally and held that any physical presence in the territory of the European Union during a period of 12 consecutive months, even if limited to a few days, is sufficient to prevent the loss of long-term resident status.[112] There is no reason to think that the CJEU would rule differently with respect to the conditions in Article 9(4), which would mean that long-term residents can maintain their status if they visit the European Union once a year and the Member State that granted long-term residence status once every six years.[113]

We see a very similar picture when analysing Directive 2004/38/EC on the right of EU citizens and their family members to move and reside freely within the territory of the Member States (the Citizenship Directive).[114] According to Article 16(1) of the Citizenship Directive, 'Union citizens who have resided legally for a continuous period of five years in the host Member State shall have the right of permanent residence there'. However, EU citizens do not need to be continuously present during that period. Article 16(3) provides that 'continuity of residence shall not be affected by temporary absences not exceeding a total of six months a year'. It is worth noting that EU citizens may be absent for longer periods than third-country nationals. EU citizens must have resided legally and continuously in the host Member State for five years to qualify for permanent residence, but they may be away for approximately half of that period as long as their absences do not exceed six months per year. Finally, in the absence of border controls and reporting requirements, it cannot be ruled out that EU citizens may qualify for permanent residence if their absences exceed that period.

It also follows from several CJEU judgments that legal residence under the Citizenship Directive means residence in accordance with the conditions set out therein.[115] In *O and B*, it addressed the question of whether legal and continuous residence under the Directive requires continuous presence. Advocate General Sharpston argued that she did not think that 'residence requires constant physical presence in the territory of a single Member State'.[116] Otherwise, 'one could be found to be resident in a Member State only if one had not exercised the right to freedom of movement'.[117] She also explained that EU citizens may reside in two or more Member States:

> In many cases, the exercise of the right to reside freely in the European Union will involve moving residence from one Member State to another, without keeping any meaningful connection with the former place of residence. In other cases, however, it will be expedient for various reasons to maintain significant ties.[118]

[111] Case C-488/19 *WT* ECLI:EU:C:2020:467.
[112] Case C-432/20 *ZK* ECLI:EU:C:2022:39.
[113] See also, Peers, 'EU Law Analysis: Residents of Everywhere?' (EU Law Analysis, 26 January 2022) http://eulawanalysis.blogspot.com/2022/01/residents-of-everywhere-cjeu-rules-on.html.
[114] Directive 2004/38/EC of the European Parliament and of the Council.
[115] Joined cases C-424&425/10 *Ziołkowski and Szeja* ECLI:EU:C:2011:866, para 46. See also Case C-162/09 *Lassal* ECLI:EU:C:2010:592, paras 52–56.
[116] Opinion of AG Sharpston, Case C-456/12 *O and B* ECLI:EU:C:2013:837, para 102.
[117] ibid.
[118] ibid, para 103.

The CJEU agreed, ruling that to determine whether someone is resident in the host Member State, his presence must not be continuous, but 'genuine'[119] – a rather vague term, it must be said. The CJEU clarified that 'short periods of residence such as weekends or holidays' do not satisfy the conditions for a right of residence,[120] but it is clearly not a requirement to be continuously present in the host state.

Moreover, like the Long-Term Residents Directive, the Citizenship Directive leaves it to the Member States to determine how to assess legal and continuous residence. According to Article 21, 'continuity of residence may be attested by *any means of proof in use in the host Member State*' (emphasis added). Thus, although the Directive provides precise guidance on the permitted periods of absence from the host state, the application of these criteria will vary from one country to another, depending on how continuity of residence is demonstrated at the national level. Not only that, given the general difficulty of investigating actual presence, it will often be difficult to prove that EU citizens have not met the requirements. This difficulty is reflected in the way Member States apply the permanent residence provisions. As we have seen, the Swedish authorities require EU and EEA nationals to prove that they have met the conditions for permanent residence by showing that they have been employed or self-employed, have sufficient financial resources, or have been students for the past five years.[121] The Netherlands checks primarily whether EU citizens have an address in the Netherlands.[122] If these conditions are met, the permanent residence permit is granted; presence does not seem to be checked.

Finally, Article 16(4) specifies the conditions under which the right of permanent residence is lost: 'only through absence from the host Member State for a period exceeding two consecutive years'. Contrary to the plain meaning of the provision, the CJEU once held that 'the undermining of the link of integration between the person concerned and the host Member State justifies the loss of the right of permanent residence *even outside* the circumstances mentioned in Article 16(4)',[123] but it said this in passing and it is unlikely that this is a binding interpretation of the provision.[124] On the contrary, the CJEU has generally emphasised that this provision 'refers to loss of the right of permanent residence on account of absences of more than two consecutive years from the host Member State'.[125] The question on which the CJEU has not yet ruled is how much absence is allowed, but it is likely that the interpretation of Article 9(1) of the Long-Term Resident Directive in the *ZK* judgment applies by analogy to Article 16(4) of the Citizenship Directive. In *ZK*, the CJEU suggested that the provisions of both Directives may need to 'be interpreted in a similar way'.[126] If so, EU citizens could maintain their permanent residence status if they visit the Member State once every two years.

IV. CONCLUSION

We studied the requirements of legal residence and physical presence in Member State nationality laws and EU legislation governing the right to move and reside freely of third-country

[119] Case C-456/12 *O and B* ECLI:EU:C:2014:135, paras 53–57.

[120] ibid, para 59.

[121] www.migrationsverket.se/English/Private-individuals/Becoming-a-Swedish-citizen/Citizenship-for-adults/How-to-apply/Further-documents-for-EU-citizens.html.

[122] 'Becoming a Dutch National through Naturalisation' (Immigratie-en Naturalisatiedienst, 5 April 2024).

[123] Case C-378/12 *Onuekwere* ECLI:EU:C:2014:13, para 25 (emphasis added).

[124] For criticism, Bełavusaŭ and Kochenov, '*Kirchberg* Dispensing the Punishment' (2016) 40 *ELRev* 557; Nic Shuibhne, 'Limits Rising, Duties Ascending' (2015) 52 *CMLRev.* 889, 920.

[125] *Lassal*, para 55; Case C-325/09 *Dias* ECLI:EU:C:2011:498, para 59.

[126] Case C-432/20 *ZK* ECLI:EU:C:2022:39, para 43. See also, Peers, 'EU Law Analysis'.

nationals and EU citizens. Three conclusions can be drawn from our analysis. First, while legal residence is a requirement to be met for persons who seek to obtain citizenship through ordinary naturalisation procedures, it is not for many who can obtain citizenship through preferential naturalisation – often the most popular method of naturalising in the EU. Second, legal residence does not coincide with physical presence, either in EU law or in national law. The required duration of physical presence is always shorter than that of legal residence, often considerably shorter, or, not infrequently, absent altogether. Third, national authorities often do not examine whether applicants for naturalisation meet the physical presence requirements, and indeed cannot easily examine this in a Union where internal borders have largely disappeared.

These findings are relevant for ongoing debates about the rules and practices regarding the acquisition of nationality in Europe, more specifically regarding the European Commission's argument that nationality should not be awarded absent a genuine connection of the applicant with the state. Our analysis does not allow direct conclusions on the validity of the Commission's claim as a matter of legal fact or normative principle. It does shed doubt, however, on its claim, or at least the underpinning presumption, that naturalisation is normally possible only once a genuine link with the state granting nationality has been established. The Commission claims that immigrants ordinarily have 'the possibility to naturalise as citizens, provided they fulfil certain integration conditions and/or show a genuine connection to the country'.[127] It means 'residence-based naturalisation',[128] possibly combined with additional requirements that would demonstrate a genuine connection, such as language or civic integration tests.[129] The Commission is right, of course, that ordinary naturalisation procedures typically require the applicant to have been legally resident for an extended period of time, and also that states typically require applicants to pass such tests as part of their application for citizenship.[130] Yet while ordinary naturalisation schemes are residence-based, not all of them require extensive physical presence on the national territory. More importantly, there are numerous preferential naturalisation practices that allow citizenship to be acquired by persons that have only briefly or never resided, let alone been physically present, in the state awarding citizenship. It may well be that the only link these people have with the state that provided them citizenship is the legal link of citizenship itself.

This means one of two things for the Commission's arguments. On the one hand, if the claim it makes in the context of its challenge to citizenship by investment, that citizenship should not be granted without a 'genuine link' is legally credible, then it logically follows that other national citizenship laws and practices also violate EU law.[131] However, as it is a national competence to lay down the rules on the acquisition and loss of citizenship, there does not seem to be any basis under EU law for its claim and, more generally, for challenging the citizenship pluralism as it currently exists in the EU.[132] On the other hand, it could mean, following Petra Weingerl and Matjaž Tratnik, that a broader account of 'relevant links' is required.[133]

[127] Commission Report COM(2019) 12 final, 2.

[128] ibid, Annex III.

[129] ibid.

[130] Ganty, 'Integration Duties in the European Union' (2021) 28 *MJ* 784; Orgad, 'Naturalization' in A Shachar et al (eds), *The Oxford Handbook of Citizenship* (Oxford University Press 2017). cf Kochenov, *Citizenship* (MIT Press 2019) 73ff.

[131] See also, van den Brink, 'EU Competence and Investor Migration'.

[132] Kochenov and Lindeboom, 'Pluralism through Its Denial', in Davies and Avbelj (eds), *Research Handbook on Legal Pluralism and EU Law* (Elgar 2018) 179.

[133] Weingerl and Tratnik, 'Relevant Links'.

But if the Commission considers applicants' distant ancestral ties, their sports achievements, marriage certificates, or contribution to the arts and sciences, as 'genuine links', it is unclear why the depth of their pockets, that is, their financial contribution to a state, would not. In any event, as this study has demonstrated, physical presence and/or legal residence is not at all indispensable, as the EU and national law and practice stands today, for the establishment of such links and successful naturalisation.

9

Investor Citizenship Cartels, Residence by Investment Cartels and EU Competition Law

GARETH DAVIES

I. INTRODUCTION

MANY STATES IN the world effectively sell their citizenship and/or the right to live in their territory.[1] The purchasers are not usually interested in the cultural particularities of the state in question, even less in settling there. Where citizenship is concerned, their major interest is typically in possessing a passport which allows them freer, and more visa-free, international travel than that of their home state.[2] If going for a residence scheme, they may want access to a safe and stable jurisdiction for funds, family and schooling for their children.[3] They may also be interested in the fact that an investor residence permit is, in some states, a first step to citizenship.[4] Where it is an EU Member State offering the residence permit, the purchaser may be attracted by the access offered to other Member States within the EU's borderless Schengen area.

Each scheme offers its own unique combination of the above advantages, for its own unique price.[5] However, at least to some extent, the selling states are in competition with each other for

[1] Kochenov and Surak, 'Introduction' in Kochenov and Surak (eds), *Citizenship and Residence Sales* (Cambridge University Press 2023); Parker, 'Commercializing Citizenship in Crisis EU' (2017) 55 *JCMS* 332; European Commission, 'Investor Citizenship and Residence Schemes in the European Union' COM(2019) 12final; Džankić, 'Investment-Based Citizenship and Residence Programmes in the EU' (2015) EUI Working Papers RSCAS 2015/08; Džankić, *The Global Market for Investor Citizenship* (Palgrave Macmillan 2019); Sumption and Hooper, 'Selling Visas and Citizenship' (Migration Policy Institute 2014). See also henleyglobal.com for an overview of schemes worldwide.

[2] Harpaz, 'Citizenship and Residence Rights as Vehicles of Global Inequality' in Kochenov and Surak (eds), *Citizenship and Residence Sales*; Surak, 'Millionaire Mobility and the Sale of Citizenship' (2021) 47 *JEMS* 166.

[3] van den Brink, 'Investment Residence and the Concept of Residence in EU Law' (2017) Investment Migration Working Papers IMC-RP 2017/1; Bongardt and Neves, 'The Chinese Business Community at a Crossroads Between Crisis Response and China's Assertive Global Strategy' (2014) EUI Migration Policy Centre Research Report 2014/02, 29.

[4] Džankić, 'The Pros and Cons of *Ius Pecuniae*' (2012) EUI Working Papers EUDO/RSCAS 2012/14; Boatcă, 'Commodification of Citizenship' in Wallerstein et al (eds), *Overcoming Global Inequalities* (Paradigm 2014) 12.

[5] Surak, 'Citizenship and Residence by Investment Schemes' (European Parliament Research Service, 2021); Džankić, 'The Pros and Cons'; Kochenov and Lindeboom (eds), *Quality of Nationality Index* (Hart 2020); Carrera, 'How Much Does EU Citizenship Cost?' (2014) CEPS Paper No. 64/2014; Gamlen et al, 'Re-thinking Immigrant Investment Funds' (2016) Investment Migration Working Papers IMC-RP 2016/2.

the same pool of wealthy potential buyers.[6] It is therefore perfectly likely that at some point, if not already, those selling states will take into account each other's pricing and communicate with each other in order to prevent the market value of a passport or residence permit being driven too low.

This would, if these were normal products and states were normal undertakings, be a simple example of a cartel. However, can the selling of citizenship or residence rights be seen as an economic activity falling within the scope of EU competition law?[7] This chapter argues that substantively it is, and that where it is EU states involved in this business, it is not impossible that they might find themselves in legal trouble, although it is not certain either: there are enough legal ambiguities to allow a court, or EU commission, wary of politics to shy away.

The issue may matter, because while these schemes are controversial, and many would like to see them done away with,[8] they offer concrete economic benefits to the selling states which might easily outweigh the somewhat amorphous and theoretical harms to identity and community that they are claimed to cause too.[9] They may therefore be durable, so that at some point discussion will move from whether they should be allowed at all to how they should be regulated. That is the question to which this chapter contributes.

The focus is on EU competition law, because EU law provides us with the unique situation of a number of states that market their passports and residence documents, and whose documents are in direct competition with each other, and which states are within the framework of a hard and enforceable competition law regime that is not scared off by concepts such as sovereignty. The ingredients for legal action are present here if anywhere.

The conclusion is that while the law could go either way, a consideration of the core factors on which legality turns tells us in any case something about what is at stake. The major conceptual obstacle is not really whether selling passports is economic: it is, because Member States have made it so. Rather, the major obstacle to legal action is that the victims are outside the EU. Most cartels which competition law engages with consist of undertakings exploiting European consumers or businesses. There is a supposed welfare decrease for Europeans as a result. By contrast, an investment passport cartel would consist of Europeans exploiting non-Europeans, increasing EU welfare at the expense of citizens of other states. Enforcement would be apparently welfare decreasing for the EU. That is an uncomfortable position for competition law to be in. Does it, should it, apply to situations where the European consumer, via their state, is the profiteer rather than the victim?

The chapter first explains how the selling of citizenship or residence permits might amount to a cartel in normal, economic terms, with all the expected effects on welfare. It then considers the conditions for the application of competition law to activities that are traditionally a privilege of the state. Finally, it considers the jurisdictional problem of European cartels exploiting victims abroad.

[6] Shachar and Hirschl, 'On Citizenship, States and Markets' (2014) 22 *JOPP* 231; Parker, 'Commercializing Citizenship'; van den Brink, 'Investment Residence and the Concept of Residence in EU Law'.

[7] Case C-364/92 *SAT Fluggesellschaft mbH v. Eurocontrol* ECLI:EU:C:1994:7, para 30. See also the Advocate General's Opinion in C-181/23 *Commission v Malta* ECLI:EU:C:2024:849.

[8] Shachar and Hirschl, 'On Citizenship, States, and Markets'.

[9] Surak and Tsuzuki, 'Are Golden Visas a Golden Opportunity?' (2021) 47 *JEMS* 3367.

II. DE FACTO INVESTOR CITIZENSHIP CARTELS AND RESIDENCE BY INVESTMENT CARTELS

A. The Mechanisms of Payment

Investor citizenship and residence schemes typically provide a passport or residence permit to foreign individuals who are prepared to comply with some combination of three requirements: they maintain legal – not necessarily physical[10] – residence in the providing state for a certain period; they invest in the local economy via real estate or business investments, the type and location of investment sometimes being specified; they donate money to a government fund or programme, or purchase government bonds, thereby effectively lending money to the state.[11]

Donations to government funds or programmes can be seen as simple payments for the relevant document. An institution of the state receives money from the individual, and another arm of the state provides them with valuable documents. This is a sale, pure and simple.

Where investment is concerned it could be argued that this is also of value to the state. Although the investor retains ownership, and entitlement to profits, their investment is clearly of benefit to local people and businesses – that is the premise of the scheme.[12] Since these are actors to whom the state also has a responsibility it could be argued that assistance to them is of value to the state. Politically this is manifestly the case. Thus, although any transfer of value is to a third party here, reasonably it could still be said that there is a contractual type of relationship between the state and the individual: you do something that is of value to us (help our economy) and we will transfer documents of value to you.

An actual residence requirement would not fit the contractual paradigm so easily. It would be more of a residual moral condition. However, investor schemes work almost exclusively with legal residence requirements, so that the investor is recorded as residing, but does not have to have be actually present for any particular period of time.[13] To some extent, such conditions can be seen as an attempt to give purely financial transactions a more substantive and participatory veneer, as if the investor is becoming a part of the national community. More realistically, legal residence may bring with it certain tax obligations. It can then be best understood as just another mechanism for arranging financial transfer to the state.

Given that the very idea of investment schemes is that individuals are granted some form of membership rights in a society because of their direct financial contribution to it, it is therefore reasonable to conceptualise these as a form of contract, and so as a form of sale – you give money, we give rights. The fact that there may be peripheral conditions associated with this sale, varying from the residence requirements mentioned above, to a maximum limit on the number of sales per year, or completion of satisfactory background checks does not alter the underlying economic nature of the transaction.

[10] Kochenov and van den Brink in this volume.

[11] Sumption and Hooper, 'Selling Visas and Citizenship'.

[12] Lindeboom and Meunier, 'In the Shadow of the Euro Crisis' in Kochenov and Surak (eds), *Citizenship and Residence Sales*.

[13] Kochenov and van den Brink, 'Legal Residence but Physical Presence'.

B. The Residence-Citizenship Link

The two kinds of scheme are not only linked by their similar mechanisms and consequences. One can also be a path to the other: sometimes a period of investment-based legal residence can be used as a foundation to acquire citizenship.[14] Thus residence by investment can be seen as a slow-burn and indirect form of investor citizenship. This varies from state to state, depending on the precise criteria for acquiring citizenship.

Alternatively, a five-year residence permit such as is often issued to investors, may enable the investor to obtain the status of 'long term resident' which, as a matter of EU law, gives them rights very similar, if slightly less robust and more conditional, to Union Citizenship.[15] Technically, long term resident status is only acquired after five years of actual, physical, residence in a Member State, which will not be the ambition of many investors.[16] However, it may be for some, or for some of their family members. Moreover, it may well be the case that this physical residence is not actually checked, so that after a period of five years of possession of an investor's residence permit it can in fact, whether or not this is strictly legally correct, be changed into an EU long term resident's card.[17] This might be attractive for those who do wish to have residence in the EU, but whose home state excludes dual nationality, as is the case with China.[18] Either via this route, or via citizenship, a residence by investment scheme will typically offer a pathway to permanent residence rights throughout the EU.

C. Competition between Programmes

What makes these sales legally interesting within the EU is that the documents issued by different Member States are directly in competition with each other.[19] That is to some extent the case globally, in that any candidate for an investment scheme will canvas the various possibilities available. However, the nature of the products within the EU stands out for the degree of their interchangeability. This is most strikingly the case with citizenship, thanks to the fact that any citizen of an EU Member State is also a citizen of the Union, and entitled to live, work, study and enjoy equal treatment in any other Member State.[20] All EU passports therefore grant full access to the entire EU. Unless an investor is particularly concerned with their right to vote, which is unlikely to be a primary consideration, all EU passports have essentially the same value within the EU. The choice of which to purchase will be partly influenced by the access they offer to third countries – not all EU passports offer visa-free access to the US, for example – and further by the price, conditions and availability. The nature of the issuing Member States itself will be of marginal importance. Hence the success of the Maltese and Cypriot (now suspended) schemes.[21]

[14] Džankić, 'The Pros and Cons'; European Commission Report COM(2019)12 final.

[15] Council Directive 2003/109/EC concerning the status of third-country nationals who are long-term residents [2004] OJ L 16/44; Sarmiento and van den Brink, 'EU Competence and Investor Migration' in Kochenov and Surak (eds), *Citizenship and Residence Sales*.

[16] Art 4 of Directive 2003/109/EC; Carrera, 'How Much Does EU Citizenship Cost?'.

[17] See discussion of the claims to this effect in van den Brink, 'Investment Residence', 14.

[18] ibid.

[19] Parker, 'Commercializing Citizenship'.

[20] Arts 20 and 21 TFEU; Directive 2004/38/EC of the European Parliament and of the Council on the right of citizens of the Union and their family members to move and reside freely within the territory of the Member States.

[21] Brillaud and Martini, 'European Getaway' (Transparency International and Global Witness 2018).

Long-stay residence permits of up to five years are not quite so interchangeable. They are issued by a single Member State, under national law, and so only grant residence rights in that state. There is thus a meaningful difference between their values. On the other hand, if that Member State is a Member of the Schengen area, as most EU Member States are, including all of the wealthier ones plus Norway and Switzerland, then the residence permit automatically grants the right to stay up to 90 days in any given 180 days in any of the other Schengen states.[22] Moreover, in practice, travel within Schengen is formality free and uncontrolled. De facto, the possessor of a long-stay residence permit can spend their time almost wherever they like within the Schengen area without unpleasant controls or visa applications. Officially at least half their time should be either in the state which issued their residence permit – if that state requires this, which many do not for investors – or outside the EU, but in practice this will not be checked or enforced. For the investor who is prepared to have a more or less nominal base in one of the countries of the EU, a residence permit offers them the day-to-day freedom of Europe – as well as a route to long-term residence status with its genuine right to live and work wherever they like. The residence permits of different Member States do thus compete to a significant extent.

D. Market Definition

Competition law uses the Small but Significant Non-Transitory Increase in Price (SSNIP) test to determine whether products are in competition, and so to determine market definition.[23] This test asks whether a small but significant non-transitory increase in price would cause customers to switch products. This is ultimately a matter for empirical research. Its application to the products discussed here would in some ways be complex – price variations of the order of the 5–10 per cent typically discussed in a SSNIP test may have relatively little effect, for example. However, the SSNIP test is not definitional, but a tool to be used to discover whether customers consider two products to be viable alternatives. If so, the question is what causes them to choose one over the other, whether it be price or other factors, and any agreement on those factors is prima facie a restriction of competition.

Those who have researched the way that investors make their choices to date, have not done so specifically from the perspective of competition law. However, there is a widespread agreement among them that investors shop around, and that de facto the products form a (or more than one) competitive market.[24] The precise scope of the relevant market in any particular case is something that would require further investigation, but it is not obviously an obstacle to the absence of competition law: the markets exist.

E. Cartelisation

There is no suggestion that the Member States of the EU have made agreements regarding the prices of their citizenship and residence packages. Nevertheless, given that these programmes

[22] Regulation No. 265/2010 of the European Parliament and of the Council amending the Convention Implementing the Schengen Agreement and Regulation (EC) No. 562/2006 as regards Movement of Persons with a Long-Stay Visa [2010] OJ L85/1.

[23] Commission Notice on the definition of relevant market for the purposes of Community competition law [1997] OJ C372/03.

[24] Surak, 'Citizenship and Residence by Investment Schemes'; Džankić, 'The Pros and Cons'; Parker, 'Commercializing Citizenship'; Surak, 'Millionaire Mobility'.

are created to boost state finances and economies, one could expect states to be concerned if others significantly undercut them, so that, for example, the residence by investment scheme of Spain suddenly sees all its customers defect to Portugal (actually the two schemes offer very similar terms). In periods when such schemes are popular, which is largely driven by factors outside the EU, such as political instability in countries like China and Russia, then a clear motivation would exist for small Member States, for whom these schemes potentially represent a proportionally more important source of income, to lower their price and soften their terms to the point where they attract the largest share of applicants.[25] It is no coincidence that most discussion on this topic has concerned Malta and Cyprus.[26]

An equally clear motivation would exist for other Member States to take action against this. On the one hand, they may object to another state essentially selling access to their own territory – Malta offering documents to people who will choose to spend their time in Paris.[27] On the other hand, they may wish to protect their own schemes.

One approach that they can take is to try EU legal action against states whose price has dropped to the point that they are selling significant numbers of permits. They will not be able to object to the price as such – that would be too transparently cynical – but they may be able to argue that a state is violating the EU Treaty duty of loyalty in exploiting its open borders with other states in this way, and either themselves, or via the Commission, try to use the law to set limits.[28] A distinction could be drawn between a 'genuine' scheme, which rewards individuals who participate importantly in the life of a state with the right to live or become a citizen, and an 'abusive' scheme, which is merely the sale of access to Schengen.[29] That distinction is somewhat artificial, since the terms of both 'types' would be substantively the same.[30] It would also face the problem that there is no clear dividing line between citizenships or residence permits awarded on the basis of birth, family, work or money, but rather a huge variety of schemes combining these in different ways and forming a continuum on any given axis – with a trend towards instrumentalisation and commercialisation in recent decades.[31] Nevertheless, some kind of distinction is just about arguable, and discussions have indeed taken place on whether investor citizenship programmes in several Member States violated EU law. The Commission has begun infringement actions.[32] Although success is not certain, this is in some ways an attractive issue for it to pursue: it entails a chance to expand the scope of EU law, and the offending states are small ones, while the ones offended are large.

Nevertheless, the legal path is a longish and uncertain one, which for Member States runs the risks of unpleasant side effects: that perhaps these kinds of schemes might end up getting banned altogether, or limited to an extent that even complaining states did not want. Even

[25] Džankić, 'Investment-Based Citizenship and Residence Programmes in the EU' 20; Parker, 'Commercializing Citizenship'.

[26] Parker, 'Commercializing Citizenship'; Bauböck, *Debating Transformations of National Citizenship* (Springer 2018).

[27] Davies and Rostek, 'The Impact of Union Citizenship on National Citizenship Policies' (2007) 22 *Tulane European & Civil* LF 89.

[28] Opinion of AG Poiares Maduro, Case C-135/08 *Rottmann* ECLI:EU:C:2009:588; van den Brink, 'Revising Citizenship within the European Union' (2022) 23 *GLJ* 79. C.f. Advocate General, *Commission v Malta*.

[29] Džankić, 'Investment-Based Citizenship'; European Commission Report COM(2019)12 final.

[30] See also Kochenov, 'Citizenship for Real: Its Hypocrisy, Its Randomness, Its Price' in Bauböck (ed), *Debating Transformations of National Citizenship* (Springer 2018) 51; Davies and Rostek, 'The Impact of Union Citizenship'.

[31] Parker, 'Commercializing Citizenship'; Joppke, 'Citizenship by Investment as Instrumental Citizenship' in Kochenov and Surak (eds), *Citizenship and Residence Sales*; Džankić, 'Investment-Based Citizenship'; see also Davies and Rostek, 'The Impact of Union Citizenship'. See also Advocate General, *Commission v Malta*.

[32] Advocate General, *Commission v Malta*.

more importantly, legal action, if successful, might establish a degree of EU competence over nationality law that could have implications beyond the immediate context.[33]

There would thus be a motivation for Member States to try and solve the problem more informally – by negotiation with the undercutting states. An obvious path would be to agree to certain minimal requirements for residence documents and passports, and perhaps also to agree on maximum numbers that each state would issue. That way, the number of individuals acquiring documents in one Member State in order to spend their time in others would be limited, as would the impact of one national scheme on others. Both total output, and the division of market shares, would be managed. No Member State corners the market, and each Member State can reserve a slice of the pie for itself.

More realistically, there might not be a perfect and comprehensive agreement, but Member States might at least communicate enough to ensure that none dropped their prices or increased their volume beyond the point that others could tolerate. Political or legal conflict could be avoided by a degree of awareness of, and sensitivity to, each other's concerns.

This is what we call a cartel, or in the words of EU competition law, an agreement to restrict competition.[34] The fact that it may have social purposes – restriction of indirect immigration of wealthy individuals – as well as economic ones does not change this. Many agreements between public undertakings in restraint of competition have multiple purposes, for example an agreement between hospitals to allocate patients or an agreement between universities to limit the number of foreign students they admit or to offer a common price for degrees. These factors enter the law, if at all, at the stage of justification.[35] It would be an interesting and controversial question, outside the scope of this chapter, whether an inter-state citizenship or residence agreement might be able to benefit from one of the exemptions or justifications which competition law is notoriously so reluctant to concede. The question here, by contrast, is whether competition law applies. Prima facie, there are reasons to think that it should, because whatever public policy arguments might later be made, it remains the fact that the object or effect of any agreement on investor citizenship or residence by investment would be to restrict competition, and to maintain prices above a competitive level, with a consequent loss of welfare for the actual and potential consumers of the product. That is precisely the kind of situation that competition law exists to prevent.

III. THE APPLICATION OF COMPETITION LAW

A. Can Inter-State Agreements be Subject to Competition Law?

The conceptual and factual basis for the application of competition law is in place. However, there are complications because the undertakings are states, and the product is citizenship or residence permits. Were these to be ordinary states it would be a challenge to consider who would have jurisdiction, and whether sovereign states could be called to account in any actual court for this kind of price fixing. The situation would have echoes of the discussion around OPEC, which is widely agreed to be a cartel in substance, but which has not been successfully

[33] Maas, 'European Governance of Citizenship and Nationality' (2016) 12 *JCER* 532; Sarmiento and van den Brink, 'EU Competence and Investor Migration'.

[34] Art 101 TFEU.

[35] Dunne, 'Public Interest and EU Competition Law' (2020) 65 *The Antitrust Bulletin* 256; Case C-309/99 *Wouters* ECLI:EU:C:2002:98.

challenged in court anywhere, because its nature as an agreement between sovereign states gives it either legal or political exemption – or a combination of both – from enforcement.[36]

However, Member States of the EU cannot rely on their sovereignty to escape EU law. They are subject to its rules, and there is no prevailing presumption that action against Member States is politically problematic. Indeed, precisely the opposite is one of the foundation stones on which the EU and its legal system is built. The idea that Member States should be compelled to respect the Treaties is a guiding principle for both the Court of Justice and the Commission and is reflected in the many enforcement actions against Member States, as well as the legal mechanisms which have been developed to allow individuals to prevent unlawful national action.[37] Admittedly, the Commission still exercises a certain political judgment in deciding which issues to push and which to overlook, but broadly speaking, if national behaviour is contrary to EU law then there is a good chance that a motivated and funded actor would be able to establish this in court.

B. The Distinction between Public Power and Economic Activity

There is no doubt that competition law can apply to public bodies, but it only does so if they are engaging in economic activity.[38] There is a distinction in the law between an organ or arm of the state acting as a public authority, and one acting as an undertaking. An undertaking is defined as 'any entity engaged in an economic activity, that is an activity consisting in offering goods or services on a given market, regardless of its legal status and the way in which it is financed'.[39] The question here is whether a state selling passports or residence permits, for financial motives, on a competitive market for these products, is acting as an undertaking.

An important point in the definition above is that legal form does not matter: even a ministry of the central government could be subject to competition law if it was, in fact, offering goods or services on a given market. It is established that bodies owned by the state are so subject, and it would undermine the effectiveness of the law if states could escape its application simply by having transactions done directly by the state itself, rather than via an entity it owned. The phrase 'regardless of its legal status' should be taken seriously given the Court's historical preparedness to hold Member States to account.

Given all that, it looks as if (i) there is a competitive market for investor citizenship and residence documents, and that (ii) services are most definitely offered to investors, and that (iii) the fact that it is the state offering services is irrelevant. It would therefore seem, following the definition of an undertaking, that the case is closed: competition law applies.

However, there is a complication. The Court does, in several cases, try to make a distinction between economic activities and governmental ones in a way that is sufficiently ill-defined to create legal uncertainty. It does this with the phrase, repeated in several cases, that 'activities which fall within the exercise of public powers are not of an economic nature justifying the application of the Treaty rules of competition'.[40] The implication here is that activities fall

[36] Lento, 'Shifting Sands' (2014) 2 *JERL* 281.

[37] Jakab and Kochenov (eds), *The Enforcement of EU Law and Values* (Oxford 2017).

[38] Case C-41/90 *Hoefner and Elser* ECLI:EU:C:1991:161.

[39] Commission Notice on the concept of undertakings concerned under Council Regulation (EEC) No. 4064/89 on the control of concentrations between undertakings [1998] OJ C 66/03; *Hoefner and Elser*; Case C-205/03 *FENIN* ECLI:EU:C:2006:453.

[40] Case C-113/07 *SELEX* ECLI:EU:C:2009:191, para 70; *SAT Fluggesellschaft mbH v Eurocontrol*, para 30; Case C-343/95 *Cali* ECLI:EU:C:1997:160.

into one of these two groups, either public power or economic. That however, becomes troublesome in a situation such as the one here, where the state essentially puts the exercise of its public power up for sale.[41] It is then exploiting its public power for economic purposes, and the activity in question would seem to fall within both groups. How to fit that situation into the law?

It is perhaps tempting to think that a certain activity – the cases concerned air traffic control and pollution regulation, for example – falls inherently within one, and only one, of the two categories.[42] The market, perhaps, provides clothes and food, and the sale of these is thus inherently 'economic', and could never be public power. The state, however, is responsible for security and citizenship, and the provision of these is inherently part of public power, and could never be economic. However, this perception would be wrong, both as a matter of logic and of law.

First, states are capable of reserving almost any kind of activity to themselves and providing the service in question in a non-profit and public interest way – state monopoly transport, education, energy production, healthcare and security services are not unknown. Second, markets are also capable of providing almost any kind of service. Not only can they provide the services just mentioned, but in theory they can also provide law or citizenship. For example, commercial standard setting bodies may be allowed to draw up standards, and other undertakings in the relevant field may be required to sign up, for payment, with one of these bodies in order to carry out their business.[43] A market for law is essentially created, with the substance of the law provided by undertakings. Certainly, those standard setting bodies act within a legal framework determined by the state, but so do restaurants, clothes shops and accountants. This cannot be a criterion that prevents an activity being 'economic'. Considering the issue of this chapter, it is imaginable that a state might allow private and commercial undertakings to issue residence permits or citizenship, against payment, within a certain legal framework:[44] it is really just a certification process, and we know these can be privatized. De facto that private authority may not even be so far from the reality regarding some residence permits, since it may sometimes be the input of an employer that is decisive. That is not to say that this is how investor residence or citizenship schemes are constructed, but rather to make the point that there are in fact no government services that are inherently uneconomic, impossible to imagine in a market context.[45] Rather, whether an activity is economic or not is a question of how it is organised.[46] Citizenship, law, security, healthcare, education and sandwiches can all be offered for sale on a market, and could all be provided by commercial undertakings.

This focus on organisation is what the case law shows too. *SAT* and *Selex* concerned Eurocontrol, a body providing air traffic control services, while *Diego Cali* concerned pollution surveillance in harbours.[47] The bodies providing the services were actually private in these

[41] See Cholbi, 'Public Cartels, Private Conscience' (2018) 17 *Politics, Philosophy & Economics* 356; Joelson and Griffin, 'The Legal Status of Nation-State Cartels under United States Antitrust and Public International Law' (1975) 9 *Int'l. Lawyer* 617.

[42] Kloosterhuis, 'Defining Non-Economic Activities in Competition Law' (2017) 13 *Eur. Compet. J.* 117.

[43] eg Case C-171/11 *Fra.Bo* ECLI:EU:C:2012:453.

[44] See, similarly, Johnson, 'A Citizenship Market' (2018) *Univ. Ill. LRev.* 969.

[45] eg ibid.

[46] Commission Notice on the notion of State aid as referred to in Article 107(1) of the Treaty on the Functioning of the European Union [2016] OJ C 262/1, paras 12–17; Nistor, *Public Services and the European Union* (TMC Asser Press 2011) 144; Davies, 'Welfare as a Service' (2002) 29 *LIEI* 27.

[47] *SELEX*, para 70; *SAT Fluggesellschaft mbH v Eurocontrol*, para 30; *Cali*.

cases, but the Court nevertheless found that they were not undertakings in this respect, and not subject to competition law, because their activities should be seen as the exercise of 'public power'. Speaking of the activity undertaken by the body in *Diego Cali* the Court said that it was 'connected by its nature, its aim and the rules to which it is subject with the exercise of powers … which are typically those of a public authority'.[48] It used functionally identical phrases in the other cases.

The unfortunate phrasing implies that things that states 'typically' do are outside competition law. However, the substantive reasoning in the cases did not follow this approach. The Court was interested in the actual details of the bodies in question and their functioning. It found that these bodies were entrusted with a public interest task – managing air space safely and preventing and watching out for pollution – and that while users of air space and harbours were required to pay fees to fund this task, these should be understood as proportionate contributions to the cost of that public interest task, not as payments for a commercial service. Rather than conceptualising the situation as airlines and shipping companies buying services from a business, on a market for those services, it was more analogous to taxation on, for example, car owners, who are required to contribute to the state because of the burden that they also place on it.

That distinction is rather slippery, certainly at the margins, but it is clear that the Court was interested in a global assessment of the core question: were Eurocontrol and Cali doing business, or doing government? Were they acting commercially, on an actual or potential market, or in the public interest, carrying out a state responsibility? The line may be blurred, but a centre of gravity may exist, and here it was on the side of public power.

By contrast, it is evident, even uncontroversial, that the answer could have been different if matters had been organised differently. Precisely the same services might well have been subject to competition law if the states in question had made different choices. For example, let us assume that instead of coming together to create monopoly bodies responsible for air traffic control or pollution surveillance, the Member States in question had chosen to licence multiple and competing commercial operators to undertake these activities, requiring users of air space or harbours to contract with one of these operators. It is structurally quite plausible: the same space can be surveilled or supervised by multiple eyes, albeit that they may need to communicate, but then so do telecoms companies. There is no doubt that in such a situation price agreements or market sharing between the various licenced operators would be of interest to competition law. That would be equally true if all the undertakings in question were in fact state-owned, because the states in question had decided to award the limited licences to their own undertakings. As the Court says, ownership is irrelevant.[49] A transnational cartel of public undertakings, on a market from which private undertakings are excluded by national laws, would fall within Article 101 TFEU. The application of this to citizenship markets is clear.

One can continue this thought experiment to other fields. If a number of regional educational authorities, providing free education at state institutions, decide to co-ordinate certain activities in the public interest, competition law will not consider this to fall within Article 101. If, on the other hand, a Member State fulfils its universal education obligation by providing parents with vouchers carrying value, and then allows its schools or universities to charge fees, and to keep profits, and those schools or universities co-ordinate their activities or prices in the

[48] *Cali*, para 23.
[49] *Hoefner and Elser*.

interests of dividing and managing the market, competition law will certainly be engaged.[50] Mutatis mutandis health care.[51]

In short, it is not possible to distinguish between governmental and economic activities by looking purely at the nature of the activity itself – education, air traffic control, pollution surveillance. Rather, it is the way in which an activity is provided to users which determines the camp in which it falls, and whether or not the provider is acting as an undertaking.[52] The nature of the activity may play some evidential role – some things are easier to see as public interest or essentially commercial – but it is not decisive. The assessment is global, or, as the Court puts it, a product of the activity's 'nature, its aim and the rules to which it is subject'.[53] When an activity is typically a core state activity, and it is carried out in the public interest, in a way that excludes commercial development, competition or profit making, with funding by the state or by compulsory contributions, it is likely to be public power. When an activity is typically provided on a market, on a voluntary and contractual basis, and is carried out in order to make money, in a competitive and commercial spirit, it is likely to be economic.

C. The Economic Nature of Selling Passports

The normal provision of citizenship or residence permits falls within the category of public power. These are granted because an individual has some kind of bond with a society and is seen as therefore deserving of a corresponding legal status. There may be a fee to be paid but this is akin to the air traffic control fees in *SAT*, and does not make the grant of a first passport or residence permit into an economic activity. When the state awards a person citizenship because of their family ties or length of residence, they are not doing business.

However, the same activity can, in principle, be carried out for different reasons and in different contexts, both economically and non-economically. The issuing of passports of residence documents in the context investment schemes is different from the issuing of passports and residence documents on more traditional grounds in several important ways, which justify treating it differently, and as an economic activity.

First, most obviously, the primary motivation for these schemes is economic: that is why states run them.[54] Their economic interest may arise because investors make direct payments to public bodies, or it may arise indirectly through tax incomes from the required investments. In both cases, investment schemes are ways for the state to raise funds.

Admittedly, in some investment-only schemes the state may not get directly richer. It may be the economy and local businesses which are the primary winners.[55] On the one hand, the state will still benefit. Aside from the political gains, there will be indirect financial benefits, such as

[50] Nistor, *Public Services and the European Union*, 144; Amato and Farbmann, 'Applying EU Competition Law in the Education Sector' (2010) 6 *IJELP* 7; Gideon, 'Higher Education Institutions and EU Competition Law' (2012) 8 *Competition LRev* 169–84.

[51] Joined cases C-159&160/91 *Poucet and Pistre* ECLI:EU:C:1993:63; *FENIN*; D Gallo, 'Functional Approach and Economic Activity in EU Competition Law' (2020) 26 *EPL* 569; Nikolić, 'Applicability of European Union Competition Law to Health Care Providers' (2021) 46 *J. Health Pol. Pol'y & L.* 49; van de Gronden and Guy, 'The Role of EU Competition Law in Health Care and the "Undertaking" Concept' (2021) 16 *HELP* 76.

[52] Noted, but regretted, in Kloosterhuis, 'Defining Non-Economic Activities in Competition Law'; Commission Notice on the notion of State Aid as Referred to in Article 107(1) of the Treaty on the Functioning of the European Union [2016] OJ C262/1, paras 12–17; Nistor, *Public Services and the European Union*, 144; *Poucet and Pistre*; *FENIN*; Gallo, 'Functional Approach and Economic Activity in EU Competition Law'.

[53] *SAT Fluggesellschaft mbH v Eurocontrol*; Case C-82/01 *Aeroports de Paris* ECLI:EU:C:2002:617.

[54] Sumption and Hooper, 'Selling Visas and Citizenship'.

[55] Surak and Tsuzuki, 'Are Golden Visas a Golden Opportunity?'.

the tax revenue mentioned above or the reduction in unemployment and its associated burdens. On the other hand, investment schemes with no direct payments to the state might be given a more altruistic and less commercial spin.

Perhaps it is the case that each scheme needs individual assessment. In some cases a residence by investment programme may look more akin to giving a residence permit to someone getting a job: a recognition of their desire to participate in the country, and their potential value to it, but not so much an earning opportunity for the state. However, as a general rule, the states' only interest in an investor is in their money, and in seeing a sum of that money paid into a destination designated more or less precisely by the state. That is the condition for beginning the process. It is, on the whole, an effort *not* to see this as payment.

Second, the schemes are structured as transactions: if you do X, which is of value to us, then we will do Y, which is of value to you. They are far more contractually presented than a normal process of gaining citizenship or residence rights. Instead of rights being recognised because of a person's substantive characteristics – their family, language or place of residence or work – they are recognised on condition that certain payments are made. The contractual nature is clear, and it becomes quite natural to regard this as the 'sale' of the rights in question.[56] The fact that the payments may be made to a third party, as in property or company investments, does not change this: that the state wants these payments to be made is sufficient to establish that they are, in contractual terms, valid consideration. I can ask you to pay my fees to my friend, and the contract is still binding on us both.[57]

Third, these products take place in a competitive context. A person normally applying for citizenship or a residence permit does not think 'which states shall I choose?' They have a family, job or other relationship with a particular state which gives them rights that they may decide to use. By contrast, the investor will certainly consider their options and decide which of the offers that states are making is most attractive to them. The situation is similar to the ones posited above, where a number of bodies compete to provide pan-European air traffic control or accreditation services. An activity over which the state enjoys ultimate responsibility has been marketised.

In conclusion, all things considered, the 'nature, aim and relevant rules' of investment schemes look a lot more economic than public authority-like. They are not about recognition of moral, cultural or familial bonds with the state. They involve valuable rights, granted to those prepared to pay, out of economic motives, in a competitive context.

D. Inter-State Markets

Nevertheless, many will struggle to accept competition law's application because this involves such core activities of the state. Certainly, in theory, one can conceive of private undertakings granting passports, but realistically this is not about to happen, and courts are too conservative to base their decision-making on its likelihood. From the perspective of EU law, we must accept that only states will run commercial citizenship or residence permit schemes.

This seems problematic because one way that the Court decides whether a body is an undertaking is by asking whether it is doing something that could be done by private bodies on

[56] See discussion in Prats, 'Are Citizenship-by-Investment Programs Legitimate?' in de Lange et al (eds), *Money Matters in Migration* (Cambridge University Press 2021) 263; Tanasoca, 'Citizenship for Sale' (2016) 57 *EJS* 169.

[57] See eg 'Privity of Contract: Contracts for the Benefit of Third Parties, Presented to Parliament by the Lord High Chancellor by Command of Her Majesty' (Great Britain, Law Com No. 242 Cm 3329, HMSO 1996).

a market.[58] That was part of its reasoning in *Hoefner*.[59] It wants to know whether the state is doing something essentially un-marketable, or whether it is replacing what businesses would otherwise do, and it is the finding of the latter that ultimately justifies applying market law. *Hoefner* involved employment services, and there were no doubt businesses who would have liked to enter this market, if only it had been allowed. There are no businesses ready with their concept passports if only the states will allow them to compete (yet).

However, the situation of investment schemes involves something unique and novel in competition law: a market between states. Usually when public undertakings are subjected to competition law scrutiny it is because of their actual or potential competition with private bodies. Here, by contrast, public undertakings are competing with each other, in a market that is as close to being inherently public as is realistically possible, but which is in other respects no less a market. What should the law do about that? Are markets only markets if they can be populated by private businesses?[60]

The logic of excluding public power from competition law is twofold. Partly, it is the fact that within this sphere of imperium it is non-economic interests which prevail, and if there are economic or efficiency concerns they are necessarily subordinated to something else – the protection of the environment, or air safety, or the maintenance of a just community of identity. Additionally, it is that public power is often understood as that which cannot be marketised (at least realistically).[61] It is about the delivering of goods which markets are simply incapable of providing, for various reasons, at least to the extent required. Universal education, clean harbours, and the equality of all citizens are not expected to be the result if the state was to walk away from these questions and let the market prevail. Hence applying competition law to the state's *imperium* seems nonsensical, because it would push for optimal economic outcomes in a context where economic effects are but a secondary concern, and for competition, in situations where competition is expected to deliver bad results. Market law is for markets, not for governance.

However, in the case of citizenship and residence by investment schemes, the logic above takes us in a different direction. For here there is a market, and those putting their services for sale in that market are doing so for traditional market reasons. Documents are not being awarded in the pursuit of non-economic public interest goals, but out of soundly economic motives that every business could relate to. The market structure is odd in that the undertakings are public, but otherwise there is no reason to think that the dynamics of competition is different from other markets – cartels and abuse will be inefficient, dynamic competition will increase overall welfare. As *Hoefner* reminds us, the public/economic distinction is not to do with the public or private character of the market actors, but with the nature of what they do. An inter-state market for a service should therefore be treated no differently from a market where that service is provided by private undertakings. *A fortiori* because states are using their powers to create exclusive goods, in a way analogous to the exploitation of intellectual property. Oligopolies, even public oligopolies, deserve particularly strict scrutiny. If states want to turn themselves into undertakings, they should expect to be treated as such.

[58] *SAT Fluggesellschaft mbH v Eurocontrol*, para 9; See also, implying a more nuanced position, *Aeroports de Paris*, para 82.

[59] *Hoefner and Elser*.

[60] cf *Aeroports de Paris*, para 82.

[61] Kloosterhuis, 'Defining Non-Economic Activities in Competition Law'.

E. Jurisdiction

A bigger problem for the application of competition law is that the victims of a cartel would be, by definition, based outside the EU. Typically, EU competition law is concerned with anti-competitive behaviour which affects consumers or businesses within the EU. It is EU welfare which is being protected. This is sometimes used to claim jurisdiction over mergers or behaviour outside the EU, on the basis that it has effects within.[62] It is the location of the effects which is crucial, not the location of the anti-competitive actors or agreements.[63]

By contrast, here the situation is turned around. An essentially European cartel would be exploiting actors outside the EU, reducing 'their' welfare in order to increase 'ours'.[64] The European, via their state, could be argued to benefit from artificially high citizenship and residence rates, since these are charged to those outside the EU.

There is no precedent for using competition law to prevent Europe profiting from non-Europeans. At the same time, it is not explicitly excluded. Article 101 requires that an agreement affect competition in the internal market and be of a scale sufficient to affect trade between Member States, as conditions for its application.[65] While generally these effects arise because the victims of anti-competitive behaviour are located in within the internal market, other mechanisms are possible. Competition and trade could also be affected because the competitors are located in the EU.

In this case, a cartel would affect the competition between states – thus within the internal market – by affecting how many passports and permits they sold, and at what price. It would also, in doing this, affect inflows of investment funds and the location of establishment of foreign individuals. Given the scale of the citizenship and residence markets, this would seem to be enough to affect trade between Member States, and to affect the structure of various markets.[66] Thus even while the primary victims of a cartel would be outside the EU, the effects of that cartel on competing states, and on investment and establishment within the EU, ought to be sufficient to engage the law.

Nevertheless, this does raise questions about what competition law is for. Is it really an abstract normative framework for economic activity, aimed at promoting efficiency wherever it can? Or is it more narrowly a mechanism for promoting specifically European welfare, and inapplicable wherever that welfare might benefit from the exploitation of others? Perhaps that question is made more complicated by the fact that the customers of investor citizenship and residence schemes do not always have a good press, and sometimes for good reasons. A moral argument for the protection of fleeing oligarchs is not the easiest one to make. However, the righteousness of the customers of investment schemes is a factor which belongs in another stage of the law, and is not relevant to the legitimacy of any Member State cartel. To rob a thief is still theft.

[62] Behrens, 'The Extraterritorial Reach of EU Competition Law Revisited' (2016) Europa-Kolleg Hamburg, Institute for European Integration Discussion Paper No. 3/16, 3; Zelger, 'EU Competition Law and Extraterritorial Jurisdiction' (2020) 16 *Eur. Compet. J.* 613.

[63] ibid.

[64] It would not be necessary to prove the welfare loss in the case of an agreement whose object was to restrict competition, ie an explicit cartel: Art 101 TFEU; Dunne, 'Characterizing Hard Core Cartels Under Article 101 TFEU' (2020) 65 *The Antitrust Bulletin* 376.

[65] Art 101(1) TFEU.

[66] Joined cases C-501, 513, 515 & 519/06 P *Glaxo SmithKline* ECLI:EU:C:2009:610.

IV. CONCLUSION

Normative questions around investor citizenship and residence by investment have tended to concern whether or not citizenship and residence rights should be sold at all.[67] Are they not something special, above the market? Does sale not damage their nature?

This chapter suggests that as long as such sales are permitted, and occur, there is another layer of normativity which requires investigation: should those sales be regulated, or are Member States in this respect above the law? Are they free to – acting out of purely economic motives – offer products for sale for which the markets are inherent oligopolies (Union Citizenship and Schengen residence), collude on those markets, take the profits and then claim either that they were not economically active, or that it doesn't matter if they were because the victims are foreign and rich? A proposition like that would bring competition law into disrepute.

Rather, it should be accepted that when states have special rights and responsibilities, they can exercise these in economic or non-economic ways. The choice is always controversial, as we have seen in the public and academic discussions about market mechanisms within health-care and education. However, once governments have chosen, there are legal consequences. Citizenship need not be sold, and perhaps it should not be sold, but if it is put on the market, then this ought to be done fairly and according to the laws of the marketplace.

[67] Johnson, 'A Citizenship Market'; Kochenov, 'Citizenship for Real'; Shachar and Hirschl, 'On Citizenship, States, and Markets', 231.

10

Nothing to Hide? Transparency Requirements, Accountability and Privacy in Investment Migration

JACQUELYN D VERALDI* AND OSKAR J GSTREIN**

I. INTRODUCTION

IN RECENT YEARS, intense scrutiny from various angles has been placed on citizenship by investment (CBI) and residence by investment (RBI) schemes,[1] sometimes referred to as producing 'golden passports' or 'golden visas'.[2] One of the core concerns is that some of those who are 'being let in' present a greater risk than acceptable. In that regard, it is generally recognised that the investment migration industry is particularly prone to risks related to security, money laundering, organised crime, corruption and tax evasion, amongst others.[3] Many applicants may acquire CBI/RBI for reasons considered 'legitimate' by a given jurisdiction (eg with the main motivators being identified as 'mobility, education and lifestyle, business opportunities and the preservation of wealth').[4] However, it is also a reality that '[b]y their very nature, golden visa schemes are attractive to the criminal and the corrupt'.[5] These are risks inherent to the trading of large amounts of money for mobility rights.

* CEU Democracy Institute.
** University of Groningen.

[1] In the academic literature, see eg Shachar, 'Citizenship for Sale?' in Shachar et al (eds), *The Oxford Handbook of Citizenship* (Oxford University Press 2017); Mavelli, 'Citizenship for Sale and the Neoliberal Political Economy of Belonging' (2018) 62 *ISQ* 482. In civil society, see Brillaud and Martini, 'European Getaway' (Transparency International and Global Witness 2018); Global Witness, 'Europe's Golden Doors' (2020) www.globalwitness.org/en/campaigns/corruption-and-money-laundering/europes-golden-doors/.

[2] 'MEPs Demand a Ban on "Golden Passports" and Specific Rules for "Golden Visas"' (*European Parliament*, 9 March 2022) www.europarl.europa.eu/news/en/press-room/20220304IPR24787/meps-demand-a-ban-on-golden-passports-and-specific-rules-for-golden-visas; '"Golden Passport" Schemes: Commission Proceeds with Infringement Case against Malta' (*European Commission*, 6 April 2022) https://ec.europa.eu/commission/presscorner/detail/en/IP_22_2068.

[3] eg European Commission, 'Investor Citizenship and Residence Schemes in the European Union' COM(2019)12 final; Surak, 'Citizenship and Residence by Investment Schemes' (2021) *EPRS* 31.

[4] Fernandes et al, 'Avenues for EU Action on Citizenship and Residence by Investment Schemes' (2021) European Parliamentary Research Service PE 694.217, 17, see for a detailed explanation 21–23.

[5] Brillaud and Martini, 'European Getaway', 19.

The mechanisms in place to process such applications are hence being placed under a microscope by European institutions and civil society,[6] and it is time for scholars (and states) to critically examine and reflect on CBI and RBI programmes. It is in the direct interests of states with such programmes to minimise the risks presented thereby. As noted by Surak, the value of citizenship or residence itself can be eroded by a failure to do so, as other countries may regard a sale of citizenship or residence 'as dubious, illegitimate, or a security threat, and can react, for example, by removing visa-free access'.[7] This may not only be the case where the process is blatantly insufficient to preclude the entry of high-risk individuals, but also where opacity exists to such an extent that may give rise to concerns as to the sufficiency of the process.

In the European Union (EU), it has been found that there is a severe transparency deficit in respect to the operation of Member State CBI and RBI programmes. The desirability of transparency in this context seems to stem from the issue of accountability: Numerous scandals have been exposed by civil society groups and the media in recent years, whereby individuals with questionable backgrounds, associations, and sources of wealth have been approved by CBI or RBI administrators in countries such as Cyprus and Malta.[8] Yet, often few details exist as to how these approvals came to be: Was there a lack of or insufficient due diligence, a lack of appropriate and detailed governance frameworks, or corruption? These are questions that matter for the purposes of accountability, but which cannot be answered without greater transparency. At the same time, this gives rise to the question of just how far transparency should go to facilitate accountability. Potentially, an inappropriate amount of transparency could result in severe harms for vulnerable individuals and groups.

The extent of the transparency advocated for has varied. It has included measures as extensive as the publication of the names of those who naturalise or obtain residence status via CBI or RBI schemes. This has been called for by Transparency International and Global Witness, for instance.[9] The European Commission has similarly criticised the lack of 'comprehensive information available about the identity of people who successfully obtain citizenship on the basis of investment and their countries of origin'.[10] In Malta also (where the names of those who naturalise more generally are published) the parliamentary opposition called for the publication of a separate list containing the names of those who naturalise specifically via the CBI programme. This was rejected by the government.[11]

While such a rejection might seem opportunistic with obvious motives for some observers, publishing the names of the respective individuals along with relevant details such as their

[6] eg Fernandes et al, 'Avenues for EU Action'; Council of Europe Parliamentary Assembly Resolution, 'Investment Migration' [2020] Res. 2355 https://storage.polit-x.de/media/EU_COE_EN/pdf/2020-12/47e9a384977bbc0961728c3d7973aebb.pdf; European Commission Report COM(2019)12 final; 'Corruption Risks Associated with Citizen- and Resident-by-Investment Schemes' (OECD 2019) www.oecd.org/corruption/integrity-forum/oecd-corruption-risks-of-citizen-and-resident-by-investment-schemes-scoping-note-2019.pdf.

[7] Surak, 'Marketizing Sovereign Prerogatives' (2021) 62 *EJS* 275, 287.

[8] Harding and Pegg, 'How "Golden Passports" Firm Lays on VIP Service to Colourful List of Clients' (*The Guardian*, 22 April 2021) www.theguardian.com/world/2021/apr/22/how-golden-passports-firm-lays-on-vip-service-to-colourful-list-of-clients; 'The Cyprus Papers' (*Al Jazeera*, 2020) https://interactive.aljazeera.com/aje/2020/cyprus-papers/index.html; Peel and Hope, 'Cyprus Clings to "Golden Passports"' (*Financial Times*, 24 November 2019) www.ft.com/content/9e2a67f6-06cd-11ea-a984-fbbacad9e7dd; O'Murchu, 'Malta Grants EU Citizenship to Legatum Backer' (*Financial Times*, 29 January 2018) www.ft.com/content/110f57ee-02a3-11e8-9650-9c0ad2d7c5b5; Khan, 'EU Prepares Crackdown on "Citizenships for Sale"' (*Financial Times*, 8 December 2018) www.ft.com/content/9a6eb914-9e23-11e8-85da-eeb7a9ce36e4.

[9] Brillaud and Martini, 'European Getaway', 38, 51; Fernando et al, 'Citizenship for Sale' (2021) *International Monetary Fund Finance & Development* 50, 52.

[10] European Commission Report COM(2019)12 final 19.

[11] Cube, 'Malta Will Not Publish the Names of Investors on Separate Lists' (Immigrantinvest, 21 July 2020) https://immigrantinvest.com/insider/publication-names-applicants-in-malta-en/.

birth date must not be taken lightly. Highlighting the privacy implications, the data provided can turn out to be highly sensitive – and even dangerous – information. In an increasingly 'datafied' society,[12] it seems very likely that a combination of inference points such as family name, place of origin, date of naturalisation, birth date (etc) might make it possible to identify individuals, their families and stories when combining this information with other data sources. These include records of other governments that are increasingly easy to retrieve, information available on various social media outlets, news articles, blog posts and the internet in general. It should also be borne in mind that an increasing number of professionals, such as self-employed persons, advisers in different fields, academics and many other professional groups are increasingly dependent on an active and well-maintained online presence. This dynamic results in the question as to what extent such increased transparency through datafication in a wider sense should be considered when publishing CBI and RBI information openly to all members of society. The potential harms stemming from re-identification, profiling, tracking, defaming, stalking and blackmailing out of various – potentially dubious or outright illegitimate – motives seem easier to manifest compared to decades ago. There might be individuals that abuse CBI and RBI schemes, but that does not justify the assumption that everyone who uses them should remain on display via the public record for the rest of time.

In the interest of striking the appropriate balance between the relevant privacy and transparency interests at stake, it must be asked which objectives such measures pursue and whether they are fit for purpose. It is argued that while certain transparency-related measures may enable and facilitate accountability without affecting the privacy of individuals, the singling out and publishing of names of those who apply for or acquire CBI/RBI status might be a 'bad compromise', as it only addresses a symptom rather than the root of the problem.

At the same time, the publishing of names of individuals may fuel existing prejudices against particular nationalities. Already, the European Commission, Parliament, civil society and the media consistently highlight that individuals with Russian and Chinese citizenship are the dominant applicants for the programmes.[13] However, knowing someone's name or country of origin does not sufficiently speak to the degree of risk they – as individuals – present to the Member States or the EU as such. What is most important for the purposes of minimising these risks is using equally stringent criteria designed to catch all risks, no matter the country of origin of an applicant or beneficiary. All CBI and RBI applications carry an inherent degree of risk as mechanisms involving the trading of money for legal status, and so all individuals should be treated with the same amount of suspicion the situation calls for.

Furthermore, from a human rights perspective it is problematic that increasingly a 'nothing to hide' dynamic emerges in this domain, through which all individuals potentially concerned must prove a certain status. Rather, it is the governments themselves who need to develop clear,

[12] Gstrein and Beaulieu, 'How to Protect Privacy in a Datafied Society?' (2022) 35 *Philosophy & Technology* 3.

[13] eg Petrequin, 'EU Wants to End Golden Passport Schemes, Targets Russians' (*AP News*, 28 March 2022) https://apnews.com/article/russia-ukraine-immigration-business-european-commission-malta-b79cf4711e93d970c3d64a1c59af1dd4; Fernandes et al, 'Avenues for EU Action', 15–17 and 20; Brillaud and Martini, 'European Getaway', 12. Bedingfield, 'How the Golden Visa Scheme Let Russian Money Pour into the UK' (*WIRED UK*, 23 July 2020) www.wired.co.uk/article/russia-report-golden-visas; Schmidt et al., 'Portugal Golden Visas' (*Bloomberg*, 4 August 2022) www.bloomberg.com/news/articles/2022-08-02/portugal-golden-visas-rich-chinese-lose-their-favorite-escape-route-to-europe; May, 'UK Has Granted "golden Visas" to Foreign Investors since 2008' (*Daily Mail*, 23 July 2020) www.dailymail.co.uk/news/article-8553639/Tens-thousands-golden-visas-granted-wealthy-foreign-investors.html; Similarly invoking a sense of prejudice, the Commission has encouraged Member States to withdraw Russian and Belarusian citizenship or residence granted on the basis of investment: European Commission, 'Recommendation on immediate steps in the context of the Russian invasion of Ukraine in relation to investor citizenship schemes and investor residence schemes' C(2022)2028 final.

transparent and sufficiently detailed governance frameworks that manifest the rule of law. At the same time, states must develop reliable oversight and enforcement structures capable of enforcing the provisions. 'Nothing to hide' dynamics regularly emerge when governments/authorities are afraid of losing control over a particular issue, especially in cases of perceived emergencies relating to security. A recent example to illustrate this includes the rushed mass-adoption of digital certificates to demonstrate vaccination against SARS-CoV-2 (eg EU Digital COVID Certificate). While it seems sensible from the outset to require more monitoring and control of this public health emergency, the hasty adoption and rushed development of accompanying legal frameworks failed to acknowledge considerable governance challenges and privacy risks relating to sensitive health data.[14] At the same time, the question of efficacy of this measure remains unknown. The possibility of indirect discrimination based on nationality also exists.[15] This is because the measure affects those of particular nationalities more than others. It is also disproportionate, since the publishing of personal data is not necessary to achieve the relevant objectives of ensuring transparency and proper oversight of the relevant CBI and RBI programmes.

We begin this chapter by outlining the general legal landscape and re-visiting our findings related to Member State practice concerning the publication of naturalisation details.[16] We find that while it appears to still be considered lawful in many Member States, there has nevertheless been a clear trend towards increased privacy since the entry into force of the 2016 European Union General Data Protection Regulation (GDPR).[17] Building on this analysis, we provide recommendations for measures to be put in place that allow the public to recognise trends and developments in CBI and RBI schemes, while limiting the exposure of individuals to cases where this is clearly in the legitimate and overarching interest of the general public. Additionally, we propose that instead of transparency in respect to the identities of those who naturalise, greater emphasis should be placed on increasing the transparency and sufficiency of due diligence procedures and oversight mechanisms. This is the best way to achieve the ultimate objectives of greater transparency in respect to CBI and RBI programmes, namely, to increase accountability and thereby the quality of these programmes.

II. APPROACHING THE 'NOTHING TO HIDE' DEBATE

From the outset, the question arises as to who stands to benefit from the publication of facts relating to the identities of the applicants. States and the public might simply be interested in who is joining the citizenship or residence community. Besides, members of the public might have an expectation that only those individuals should join their established groups if they have 'nothing to hide'.[18] However, from the perspective of human rights this cannot be considered as a legitimate interest, certainly not in European countries. Both the European Convention of Human Rights of 1951 (ECHR) of the Council of Europe with 46 member states, as well as

[14] Gstrein et al, 'A Terrible Great Idea?' (2021) COMPAS Working Paper No. 153; Gstrein, 'The EU Digital COVID Certificate' (2021) 12 *EJRR* 370.

[15] Kochenov and Veraldi, 'The Commission against the Internal Market and European Union Citizens' Rights' (2021) 12 *EJRR* 404.

[16] This builds on our work as published in the HJIL: Kochenov et al, 'The Naturalization-Privacy Interface' (2019–20) 42 *Houst. J. Int'l. L.* 237.

[17] Regulation no. 2016/679 on the protection of natural persons with regard to the processing of personal data and on the free movement of such data [2016] OJ L119/1; Hoofnagle et al, 'The European Union General Data Protection Regulation' (2019) 28 *Information & Communications Technology Law* 65.

[18] On the nothing to hide issue, see eg Solove, *Nothing to Hide* (Yale 2011).

the Charter of Fundamental Rights of the EU from 2009 (CFR) enshrine considerable privacy protections.

The ECHR can still be considered as the leading human rights treaty in Europe.[19] Here the right to privacy – including the protection of family life, home, correspondence and personal honour – is stipulated in Article 8 ECHR. As such, the right to privacy is a non-absolute right. In other words, it may be limited through state intervention on the basis of a specific law that serves a legitimate public interest (eg national security, public safety or the economic well-being of the country). Additionally, each interference of the right to privacy is subject to a case-based proportionality test. Although there is an ongoing academic discussion when it comes to what such a test entails, the general objective is to identify whether a law-based infringement is

1. Able to realise the aim/legitimate public interest;
2. Taking place using the least invasive instrument in the specific case and finally;
3. Whether the infringement is proportionate when considering what must be sacrificed to achieve the aim/legitimate interest ('proportionality stricto sensu').

Since the ECHR is considered a 'living instrument',[20] the concrete definitions of the substantive dimension of the right to privacy, the legitimate interests, as well as the understanding of proportionality are subject to constant change.[21] This changing interpretation is rendered through the case law of the European Court of Human Rights in Strasbourg (ECtHR) and summarised in 'factsheets' highlighting the most prominent developments.[22]

With the rapid datafication of society,[23] non-absolute rights such as privacy are changing their nature and dimension, as well as their meaning. This can even be seen when comparing the ECHR – drafted right after World War II – with the EU CFR – drafted in the early 2000s,[24] with increasing Internet access and emerging Big Data infrastructures. Not only does Article 7 CFR guarantee a right to privacy that has many parallels to the ECHR, but additionally Article 8 CFR enshrines the protection of personal data. This raises the question to which degree the rights differ from each other in their essence and implementation. From a historic perspective, it is fair to state that the regulation of the automated processing of personal data has increasingly moved from an administrative issue to a fundamental rights concern, particularly in Europe with the turn towards the twenty-first century.[25] However, the jurisprudence of the CJEU remains ambiguous whether and which differences exist between Article 7 and 8 CFR.[26] If anything, it seems that Article 8 – specifically in paragraphs 2 and 3 – makes clear that automated information processing is within the scope of the CFR, and that the individual

[19] Wouters and Ovádek, *The European Union and Human Rights* (Oxford University Press 2021) 212; Dalla Corte, 'On Proportionality in the Data Protection Jurisprudence of the CJEU' (2022) 12 *Int. Data Priv. L* 259.

[20] This is a settled interpretation of the convention by the court, settled in case law such as *Mamatkulov and Askarov v Turkey* [GC], nos. 46827/99 and 46951/99, ECHR 2005-I; *Tyrer v UK*, 25 April 1978, Series A no. 26; *Marckx v Belgium*, 13 June 1979, Series A no. 31; *Chassagnou and Others v France* [GC], nos. 25088/94 and 2 others, ECHR 1999-III; *Dudgeon v the United Kingdom* (Article 50), 24 February 1983, Series A no. 59.

[21] Theil, 'Is the "Living Instrument" Approach of the European Court of Human Rights Compatible with the ECHR and International Law?' (2017) 23 EPL 587, 600–02.

[22] 'Factsheet: Personal Data Protection' (ECtHR Press Unit, June 2022) www.echr.coe.int/Documents/FS_Data_ENG.pdf; 'Factsheet: Protection of Reputation' (ECtHR Press Unit, June 2022) www.echr.coe.int/Documents/FS_Reputation_ENG.pdf.

[23] Gstrein and A Beaulieu, 'How to Protect Privacy in a Datafied Society?'.

[24] Rosas, 'The Charter and Universal Human Rights Instruments' in Peers et al. (eds), *The EU Charter of Fundamental Rights* (Hart 2014) 57.43–57.48.

[25] González Fuster, *The Right to the Protection of Personal Data and EU Law* (Springer 2014) 213–52; van der Sloot, 'Do Data Protection Rules Protect the Individual and Should They?' (2014) 4 *Int. Data Priv. L* 307.

[26] Kranenborg, 'Article 8' in Peers et al (eds), *The EU Charter of Fundamental Rights* (Hart 2014) 08.27–08.46.

concerned is entitled to increased individual control (eg through consenting to the processing of personal data), accuracy and purpose limitation of the processing, as well as the duty of states to establish competent and independent data protection authorities for oversight. These general rules are more concretely manifested in the 2016 GDPR, which is also based on Article 8 CFR.[27]

The GDPR itself can be understood as a regulation that manifests the more abstract human rights provisions as outlined above. In its essence, it is a technology neutral and principle-based framework (an 'omnibus approach') that covers the automated processing of personal data, with a focus on principles and corresponding individual rights. This puts it in contrast to regulation in other countries such as the United States or the People's Republic of China, where sectoral regulation with a focus on a certain data use or the business sector is the dominant paradigm.[28] The relevant GDPR principles can be found in Article 5 GDPR, and include lawful, fair and transparent processing of personal data, use of personal data for a specific purpose, data minimisation, accuracy, storage limitation, integrity and confidentiality, as well as accountability. While it is sometimes claimed that the GDPR is a revolutionary regulation, its substantive approach is fully in line with the incremental establishment of these principles through related European data protection law frameworks since the 1970s.[29] What probably helped GDPR to gain its prominence is the fact that the automated use of personal data has become increasingly important with the turn to the new millennium, the establishment of a broad set of individual rights (e.g. the erasure of data or access to data collected by companies) that correspond to the GDPR principles in Article 5, as well as a considerably redefined and strengthened sanctioning regime. Furthermore, the principle-based nature makes the regulation relatively flexible in addressing emerging technologies. Today it can be stated that the GDPR has become the global benchmark for regulation in its area, with 157 countries having national data protection laws in 2022, usually following the GDPR approach, or revising existing laws to adopt its principles.[30]

Before we go on to exploring the impact of the emergence of GDPR when it comes to publication of names of CBI/RBI applicants in the next section, we can summarise what has been stated so far as follows: if EU Member States wish to publish the names of those who naturalise or receive residence status this can be lawful. However, there needs to be a specific legal framework for publication that responds to a legitimate public aim in a democratic society. Here the question arises what such a specific legitimate aim could be. Examples include the preservation of public order, responding to concerns relating to security or crime, as well as the protection of the economic interests of the state (eg in tax matters). When referring to one or more of these legitimate public interests, states also need to provide concrete evidence that supports and motivates their choices. Beyond this, a specific law should also include the

[27] For the sake of accuracy, it must be added that GDPR is additionally based on Art 16 TFEU, which is a provision dedicated to personal data protection. Art 16 has also been included in the TFEU with the Treaty of Lisbon, to respond to evolving CJEU case law covering data protection matters with a broad legal basis directly enshrined in primary law. To a certain extent, this creates another parallel legal basis when it comes to data protection. The first legal bases covering data protection in European Law in general – although with much more limited scope – were introduced with the Amsterdam Treaty in 1999, namely Art 286 TEC and Art 30(1)(b) TEU. For more background information on the development of data protection provisions in EU primary law see Docksey and Zanfir-Fortuna, 'Article 16 [Protection of Personal Data]' in Blanke and Mangiameli (eds), *Treaty on the Functioning of the European Union* (Springer 2021).

[28] Hoofnagle et al, 'The European Union General Data Protection Regulation', 67.

[29] Ukrow, 'Data Protection without Frontiers' (2018) 4 *EDPL* 239.

[30] Greenleaf, 'Now 157 Countries' (2022) 176 *Privacy Laws & Business International Report* 1, 3–8. Gstrein and Zwitter, 'Extraterritorial Application of the GDPR' (2021) 10 *Internet Policy Review* 1, 2–7.

procedure and means of publication (eg web-based publication via an archive with dedicated user account management, or a web page that is generally available to the public and contains names and addresses), as well as consideration of whether less privacy-invasive measures such as publication can serve the legitimate aim.

All of these measures need to consider the risks and potential harms of publication of citizenship or residence by investment. As has already been stated in the introduction, the published data can be easily combined with other openly available databases and sources on the internet such as social media profiles, news articles, blog posts, public announcements on government websites, and so on. Hence, there will be ways to profile and track the respective individuals using their names and other information as a point of departure, as well as their families, especially if a more comprehensive set of data is revealed. This might lead to stigmatisation, discrimination based on ethnicity or nationality, defamation through publications that connect the available data with hardly known or claimed circumstances, blackmailing, and many other potentially very (psychologically/physically) harmful consequences. Any publication of data should be done in a way that understands and responds to these potential risks, also taking the situation in the states into account where those people come from (eg citizens of the Russian Federation, Belarus or Hong Kong trying to leave a country whose authorities they fear and where retaliation when living abroad might be possible). Finally, in each individual case a proportionality assessment needs to be carried out. This can avoid that a legally justified infringement of the right to privacy results in disproportionate harm (eg discrimination or physical harm) for particularly sensitive individual cases. Finally, although the right to privacy is an individual right, it also seems sensible to extend such a case-by-case proportionality assessment to particularly vulnerable families and societal groups.

III. EU MEMBER STATE PRACTICE

Research into EU Member State practice on the issue of publishing the fact of naturalisation – whatever its legal basis – demonstrated great variance, albeit with a clear trend towards greater protection of the privacy of the applicants. Whereas publication was once the default option, the increased prominence of privacy concerns has necessitated scrutinising the status quo. As already mentioned, the entry into force of GDPR in 2016 might play a role here. Another driving factor might result from the fact that publication used to be a paper-bound process (eg through an official government journal), but has increasingly moved to online outlets and platforms that are instantly available to a much wider public. Internet users might retrieve sensitive information almost incidentally via the search of someone's name through a search engine.

The majority of EU Member States (16) do not appear to publish information related to the naturalisation of individuals. This includes Austria, Croatia, Cyprus, the Czech Republic, Estonia, Germany, Hungary, Ireland, Italy, Latvia, Luxembourg, Slovakia, Slovenia,[31] Sweden,[32] Denmark and Poland.[33] By contrast, it was found that 11 Member States still disclose varying

[31] In Slovenia, the authorities exceptionally publish the information of successfully naturalised citizens if the individual's address is unknown: '*Ad-Hoc* Query on Naturalisation' (European Migration Network, 9 November 2015) www.udi.no/globalassets/global/european-migration-network_i/ad-hoc-queries/compilation-ie_ad_hoc_query_on_naturalisation_open.pdf.

[32] ibid.

[33] On Poland, see 'Confirmation of Polish citizenship or its loss' (Ministry of the Interior and Administration of the Republic of Poland) www.gov.pl/web/mswia-en/confirmation-of-possession-or-loss-of-polish-citizenship. On Denmark, see the Annex in 'Bekendtgørelse om forskellige forhold vedrørende Statstidende' (Retsinformation 2014) www.retsinformation.dk/eli/lta/2014/349#B1.

amounts of personal information pertaining to naturalisation. In France, for instance, decrees are published in the *Journal Officiel* in line with Articles 50 and 51 of Decree no. 93-1362 of 1993.[34] They contain the name of the newly naturalised individual, date and place of birth, and the same information of their eligible children.[35] For its part, Lithuania publishes the name, date of birth, country of birth and current residence of newly naturalised citizens in the online Register of Legal Acts,[36] in accordance with its law on citizenship.[37] Likewise, the following details of naturalised Greeks are also published online in the Greek *Gazette*: full names, country of birth, city of residence and Special Identity Card numbers.[38] Belgium also publishes the full name, date and place of birth of new citizens in their *Official Monitor*,[39] which are available upon a simple search for 'naturalisations'.[40] In Portugal, since 2007 the *Diário da República* publishes the name, birth date and city of birth of naturalised individuals concerned,[41] as provided for by Article 19 of their 1992 Nationality Regulation.[42] Finally, Spain and Malta also publish the names of such individuals in their official journals.[43]

In some of the Member States that have abandoned the practice, however, far more extensive personal details were published in government Gazettes. In Ireland, for instance, the home addresses of those who naturalised were also published in the *Iris Oifigiúil*, along with the name, date of naturalisation and whether they were an adult or a minor.[44] These details were indexed by search engines.[45] In 2015, attention was drawn to this in the media through a newly-naturalised citizen and,[46] upon review by the relevant Data Protection Commissioner, the practice was originally claimed to have a legal basis and be in the public interest.[47] After investigation by the Justice minister, however, including a request for an ad-hoc query through the European Migration Network of the EU, the practice was ultimately suspended in April 2016.[48] It does not seem to have been reinstated, though the relevant legislation and information concerning publication online remain.[49]

[34] Arts 50 and 51 of Décret n° 93-1362 relatif aux déclarations de nationalité, aux décisions de naturalisation, de réintégration, de perte, de déchéance et de retrait de la nationalité française 1993 (FR).

[35] ibid, Art 50.

[36] 'Register of Legal Acts' (Office of the Seimas of the Republic of Lithuania 2014) www.e-tar.lt/portal/en/index.

[37] Art 36 Law on Citizenship No. VIII-391 1991 (LITH) as amended in 2010.

[38] Above note 13, see also Greek Gazette No. 3184 of 12 September 2017 (GR).

[39] eg 'Loi accordant des naturalisations' No. 2018013138 of 11 July 2018 (BE).

[40] 'Moniteur Belge: Nouvelle recherche' www.ejustice.just.fgov.be/doc/rech_f.htm.

[41] It appears the authorities have not been particularly expeditious in publishing such information, however, as they are still retroactively publishing naturalisations from 2007, see eg Aviso n.° 14404 of 30 November 2017 (PT).

[42] Decree no. 332/82 Portuguese Nationality Regulation 1981 (PT).

[43] For Spain: When the term 'nacionalidad' is searched within Section III documents of the Spanish OJ, it populates decisions granting naturalisation from 1960 to present: 'Buscar' (Boletin Oficial del Estado) www.boe.es/buscar/. For Malta, see Ch. 188, Sect 25 Malteze Citizenship Act 1965 (MT). The latter almost stopped doing so in 2020 but quickly reversed that decision: Investment Migration Insider, 'Malta Reverses Decision to End Publishing of CIP Applicant Names' (*Investment Migration Insider*, 30 December 2020) www.imidaily.com/program-updates/update-malta-reverses-decision-to-end-publishing-of-cip-applicant-names/.

[44] Form 13 of the Irish Nationality and Citizenship Regulations SI No. 569 of 2011 (IE).

[45] Edwards, 'Online publication of new citizens' personal details is unwise' (*The Irish Times*, 21 August 2015) www.irishtimes.com/news/ireland/irish-news/online-publication-of-new-citizens-personal-details-is-unwise-1.2323443.

[46] O'Halloran and Edwards, 'Government publishes personal details of new citizens online' (*The Irish Times*, 21 August 2015) www.irishtimes.com/news/ireland/irish-news/government-publishes-personal-details-of-new-citizens-online-1.2323501.

[47] Edwards, 'Online publication of new citizens' personal details is unwise'. See also E Edwards, 'Migrant Rights Group "Astounded" Citizen Data Published Online' (*The Irish Times*, 21 August 2015) www.irishtimes.com/news/ireland/irish-news/migrant-rights-group-astounded-citizen-data-published-online-1.2324498.

[48] Edwards, 'Online publication of new citizens' personal details is unwise'.

[49] eg 'Citizenship Law, Policy and Guidance' (Department of Justice, Immigration Service Delivery) www.irishimmigration.ie/how-to-become-a-citizen/citizenship-law-policy-and-guidance/; Form 13 of the Irish Nationality and Citizenship Regulations SI No. 569 of 2011 (IE).

More restrictive approaches to publication have been observed in Bulgaria and the Netherlands. In the former, decree certifications can be obtained in person by appointment,[50] whereas in the latter after 100 years the information of those who naturalise is published.[51] Otherwise, in Romania[52] and Finland[53] – and until more recently Italy – the names of those who *apply* to naturalise are published.[54]

Whereas a not insignificant number of Member States still publish the names and usually other information of newly naturalised citizens, the majority still choose to comprehensively protect privacy. There appears moreover to be a trend towards increasing privacy protection. For instance, Ireland, Latvia and Luxembourg previously had a practice of publication, but changed it in recent years. Whereas the first two have rendered past entries related thereto private (as recently as 2016[55] and 2017[56]), Luxembourg has maintained their availability in their *Journal Officiel*.[57] Moreover, changes towards less transparency have been done directly in light of legal privacy frameworks. For instance, in Italy, Ireland, Latvia and France this has been the case. The first three completely ceased the publication of individual names upon naturalisation, whereas in France the system was changed so that the names can now no longer be indexed by search engines.[58]

Overall, it is evident that there is substantial variance in Member State practice concerning the publication of individual naturalisation details. However, it is also clear that the status quo of publication is increasingly questioned and overruled on the basis of emerging awareness and legislation relating to privacy and data protection.

IV. DISCLOSURE OF IDENTITIES OF INVESTOR MIGRANTS: A BAD COMPROMISE?

If a Member State wishes to disclose the identities of those who naturalise, this might be lawful so long as the right conditions are in place. Any such disclosure would have to be based on a dedicated and clear legislative framework, pursue a legitimate objective, be as non-invasive as possible, and be proportionate in light of the harm that could be caused by disclosing information. Ultimately, these hurdles might prove rather difficult to meet, as suggested by the abolition or modification of such measures by Member States that have in fact taken the time to formally review the publication of naturalisation details. These hurdles would be even more significant if an attempt is made to single out investor migrants, as the objective differences between the different classes of migrants might not be sufficient to justify such discrimination.

[50] 'Obtaining certificates in execution of a decree' (Ministry of Justice) bit.ly/2DqHvls.

[51] Besluit Nr. 68091 van de Minister van Justitie en Veiligheid tot beperking van de openbaarheid van het naar het Nationaal Archief over te brengen digitale archief 'Vreemdelingendossiers en Naturalisatie- en Nationaliteitsaangelegenheden van de Immigratie- en Naturalisatiedienst, 2006–2010' of 23 November 2017 (NL).

[52] 'Citizenships' (Monitorul Oficial) bit.ly/2PYUufp.

[53] 'Ad-Hoc Query on Naturalisation' (European Migration Network, 9 November 2015) 4–7.

[54] 'Lista delle richieste di appuntamento per il riconoscimento della cittadinanza italiana' (Consolato Generale d'Italia San Paolo, 4 September 2007) www.conssanpaolo.esteri.it/consolato_sanpaolo/it/la_comunicazione/dal_consolato/lista-requerimentos.html.

[55] Edwards, 'Publication of New Irish Citizens' Data Put on Hold' (*The Irish Times*, 11 April 2016) www.irishtimes.com/news/ireland/irish-news/publication-of-new-irish-citizens-data-put-on-hold-1.2605504.

[56] 'Datu valsts inspekcija Nr. 2–4.3/820-N' (Latvijas Vestnesis, 4 August 2017) www.vestnesis.lv/wwwraksti/PAZINOJUMU_PIELIKUMI/LEMUMS_PAR_PERSONAS_DATU_DZESANU.PDF.

[57] See eg London Gazette Issue 4684 of 24 July 1959 www.thegazette.co.uk/London/issue/41773/page/4684/data.pdf; 'Lois du 7 november 2008 conférant la naturalisation' (LegiLux, 24 November 2008) https://legilux.public.lu/eli/etat/leg/loi/2008/11/07/n2/jo; It appears the Edinburgh and Belfast gazettes have not historically published information related to naturalisation.

[58] Arts L221-14 (translated), which was amended by Art 1 of Loi n° 2015-1713 (FR).

This is aggravated by the fact that the disclosure of identities in this way may not contribute to the objective it seeks to achieve in any significant way. The purpose of such disclosure would be to facilitate transparency, defined in the sense of 'the availability of information about an actor allowing other actors to monitor the workings or performance of this actor.'[59]

The desire for greater transparency in respect to state decision-making is generally to facilitate accountability – through 'the power of shame',[60] in the case of publishing the names of CBI and RBI beneficiaries. But this is only possible under the right conditions, which have been forwarded as including 'when it actually presents a significant increase in the available information, when there are actors capable of processing the information, and when exposure has a direct or indirect impact on the government or public agency'.[61] Yet, the publication of names would not present a significant increase in available information – nothing would be known about the basis for the decision behind the fact and it would not get the general public any closer to figuring out the underlying motives and reasons. This would also hamper the capacity of any actor to process that information or influence government policy. The publication of the identities of investor migrants thus does very little, if anything, to facilitate accountability and yet raises considerable privacy concerns for the individual concerned. At the same time – as alluded to earlier above – the right to privacy as an individual does not fully capture the harms that could occur to groups that might be identified based on the rough estimation of family names, connecting the disclosed information with other online sources, or using other available information that enables the drawing of more or less accurate inferences. The academic discussion around group privacy exists, but it is still in its early stages.[62] In conclusion, the publication may therefore be considered a bad compromise. Thus, we explore other measures that could make a greater contribution to accountability as the overarching objective: stronger and more transparent due diligence mechanisms, as well as increased oversight.

V. DUE DILIGENCE, A DIFFERENT KIND OF TRANSPARENCY AND OVERSIGHT

Due diligence mechanisms assist in directly filtering out risks, whereas oversight measures ensure those due diligence mechanisms are being properly implemented. In both areas, however, existing EU Member State CBI and RBI programmes appear fundamentally deficient across the board.[63] In respect to both, there is a notable lack of any public information on the existence of such measures in the majority of Member States. Where they are available, they can hardly be described as fit for purpose. At the same time, aggregated information and data sets could be used to report to the public a general picture of the status of CBI and RBI programmes, which might allow the opening of a debate on principles – where necessary – without sacrificing the right to privacy of individuals.

While there are good reasons for rejecting the nothing to hide argument when it comes to the individuals concerned, the same is not true of public institutions. Indeed, transparency is

[59] Meijer, 'Transparency' in Bovens et al (eds), *The Oxford Handbook of Public Accountability* (Oxford University Press 2014) 511.

[60] Fox, 'The Uncertain Relationship between Transparency and Accountability' (2007) 17 *Development in Practice* 663, 665.

[61] Meijer, 'Transparency', 512.

[62] Taylor et al, 'Conclusion' in Taylor et al (eds), *Group Privacy* (Springer 2017).

[63] As noted in Corrado and Marsh, 'Compliance in the Immigrant Investor Industry' in Kochenov and Surak (eds), *Citizenship and Residence Sales* (Cambridge University Press 2023) 488. In general 'there is neither a common standard of due diligence nor an oversight body … for CBI and RBI programs'.

essential for democracy, allowing the public to scrutinise the actions and decisions of those governing on their behalf. Transparency of the public business is also critical to support the rule of law; politicians and public actors must be capable of proving that they are abiding by the law and common values. Thus, in the sections below we argue that due diligence and oversight mechanisms are fundamental to mitigating risks associated with CBI and RBI programmes.

A. Due Diligence Mechanisms

In respect to due diligence, this is a 'term used to describe a series of investigative processes that identify, corroborate and verify information about an individual or a business entity, and assess their eligibility and risk profile in order to protect against security, criminal, reputational and political risks'.[64] Although several preliminary studies have now been conducted on due diligence in the contemporary investment migration industry, they themselves are limited by the opacity of these mechanisms. While the studies have involved the use of information requests from governments and media reports, information on the application processes is still limited to such a general level that the studies can tell us nothing about the degree of risk acceptable to a given Member State. A study commissioned by the industry body the Investment Migration Council has itself noted 'the questionable transparency of due diligence processes as they apply to investment migration'.[65] This opacity is problematic, since the 'availability of relevant information is one of the prerequisites for the information phase of any accountability process'. Nevertheless, these studies can still provide a degree of insight into the current state of due diligence mechanisms in investment migration practices.

First, in some Member States such mechanisms are insufficient simply due to their non-existence. For instance, it is reported that in Portugal '[t]he current legal framework does not explicitly mandate that Immigration and Borders Service conduct due diligence on applicants or determine whether applicants are politically exposed persons (PEPs)'.[66] Thus, 'There also seem to be no checks on applicants' source of wealth and funds used for investment.'[67] However, Portugal is one of the top performers of EU countries in the investment migration industry, having the largest RBI scheme.[68] In recent years, there has also been an ongoing scandal related to corruption and a host of individuals with questionable backgrounds having RBI applications approved.[69] However, strong due diligence criteria are vital for the survival of these programmes: 'As demonstrated by the abolition of the Cyprus Investment Programme, failure to implement comprehensive due diligence processes in time can come with grave consequences, including permanent damage to a programme's reputation.'[70]

Second, while a total lack of due diligence procedures seems to be the exception, a core problem with the governance of the industry appears to be that there is hardly any information available on the due diligence processes that do exist. Nevertheless, we know based

[64] 'Due Diligence in Investment Migration: Current Applications and Trends' (Oxford Analytica, January 2020) 2 https://investmentmigration.org/wp-content/uploads/2020/07/DD-in-IM-Current-Applications-and-Trends-January-2020-1.pdf.

[65] ibid, v.

[66] Brillaud and Martini, 'European Getaway', 37.

[67] Ibid.

[68] Fernandes et al., 'Avenues for EU Action', 12.

[69] Above note 3.

[70] 'The 2021 CBI Index' (2021) 7 https://cbiindex.com/reports/; This follows in particular from 'The Cyprus Papers' (*Al Jazeera*, 2020).

on contemporary research that 'some of these programmes' checks and verifications remain inadequate when assessing the risk profile of applicants'.[71] Perhaps most concerning is the fact that we do not know that the programmes result in the exclusion of what might reasonably be considered high-risk individuals.

In other words, being identified as a potential high-risk individual does not necessarily prohibit success of a CBI or RBI application. This relates not to just to the fact that some Member States authorities maintain discretion to accept applicants 'even when the applicants do not meet certain security requirements'.[72] It also relates to the due diligence thresholds themselves. For instance, Malta has long been said to have the most stringent CBI due diligence process,[73] but the information available in this respect is of such a general level that it seems impossible to determine whether the programme is sufficiently stringent. Thirty per cent of the applications were refused from July 2019 to December 2020.[74] Moreover, numerous instances of apparently high-risk individuals nevertheless obtaining Maltese – and hence EU citizenship/ residence – have been identified by the media and civil society.[75] Thus, while the risk matrix used by the government's Community Malta Agency to assess applications does document how wealth has been accumulated, or whether an applicant is politically exposed, no information is available as to how the ultimate decision has been reached. It is also not expressly indicated that the application of someone whose wealth is of questionable origin or who is politically will be rejected by the Agency. Thus, if Malta's programme is this opaque and it is yet 'known to be the most thorough scheme worldwide in terms of due diligence', what this seems to really imply is that we do not know much at all about due diligence processes in the investment migration industry.

Without transparency with regards to the rules outlining how these due diligence mechanisms operate and how the ultimate decisions are being reached in principle, there can be no scrutiny. There can also be no accountability, since it is entirely unclear what the standards for accountability are.

B. A Different Kind of Transparency

In terms of the special oversight mechanisms that do exist, these generally consist of reporting obligations, the degree of transparency of which varies. In Spain, the responsible Ministry must prepare a report every year on the implementation of their RBI scheme, to be submitted to the government (the Council of Ministers).[76] By contrast, in Portugal the RBI scheme is audited annually by the General Inspection department of the Ministry of Internal Affairs, the conclusions of which are to be published on the Government's website. However, this has apparently only in fact been done once.[77] In Malta, an independent regulator was established,[78] which also

[71] 'Due Diligence in Investment Migration' (Oxford Analytica, January 2020) 13.

[72] Commission Report COM(2019)12 final, 12.

[73] Eg Malta earns a joint top score on the due diligence indicator of 'The 2021 CBI Index' (2021) 10, 23. See also Balakrishnan, 'How Malta Does Vetting on Candidates?' (Best Citizenships 2020) https://best-citizenships.com/2020/12/20/how-malta-does-vetting-on-candidates/.

[74] 'Seventh Annual Report on the Individual Investor Programme of the Government of Malta' (Office of the Regulator: Granting of Citizenship for Exceptional Services, April 2021) 12 https://orgces.gov.mt/en/Documents/Reports/Annual%20Report%202020%2025_01_2022.pdf.

[75] Above note 8.

[76] Commission Report COM(2019)12 final, note 110.

[77] ibid.

[78] Brillaud and Martini, 'European Getaway', 31.

monitors and reports on various aspects of the CBI and RBI schemes.[79] Published statistical information relates to the applications submitted (number, gender, origin, number of different citizenships, dependants); outcomes thereof (approved and rejected), naturalisations (number, origin, employment status, education, age), properties (purchased versus leased, locations), investments in government stocks, contributions and fees paid, donations made and agents.

While such statistics are potentially helpful to provide an overall picture of the situation and give general information to the public without sacrificing the privacy of individuals concerned, these statistics do very little to tell us anything about the degree of risk acceptable to the government and agents involved in processing CBI or RBI applications. They provide a useful window into the operation of these programmes, but for proper oversight to be achieved the relevant overseer needs more than simple aggregated statistics. Only then can critical reflection develop as to whether the correct balance is being struck. Thus, reports should also include a detailed impact assessment in terms of, for example, benefits to the economy, impact on local housing markets, instances of crime or other security issues, and so on. This would enable comprehensive scrutiny by citizens, their representatives in Parliament and civil society, as well as enable genuine reflection on behalf of Member State governments as to the future direction of CBI or RBI programmes.

C. Oversight

Proper oversight by an independent body of CBI and RBI programmes could also mitigate risks associated with less transparency. Greater oversight would assist with facilitating accountability by enabling the oversight agency to ensure that the relevant rules and procedures of the programme are being followed. (Again, however, this only works if the problems with due diligence mechanisms in the first place are addressed.) This reduces the need for transparency while at the same time protecting the privacy rights of applicants: it pursues the same legitimate objective of mitigating the identified risks, while at the same time not giving rise to privacy concerns in the first place.

In contrast, the reality in the EU Member States is that the above-described lack of transparency into the functioning of existing due diligence mechanisms is aggravated by the fact that 'Specific monitoring mechanisms and reporting obligations exist in a very limited number of Member States'.[80] According to the Commission, this means that 'in most cases, the oversight of the scheme is left to general monitoring mechanisms when they exist, such as parliamentary scrutiny, administrative liability, general reporting of activities to the government, or access to documents requests'.[81] However, the contemporary risks and scandals associated with CBI and RBI schemes arguably demonstrate that more than these general mechanisms are necessary.

What might oversight designed to facilitate accountability look like? Oversight of the operation of CBI or RBI programmes should be done by bodies that are independent from any parties involved in the application, in particular public or private parties involved in submitting or processing applications. These bodies should have access to all the information necessary to understand the basis for the decisions, to render conclusions as to the risks taken on by the relevant state during the reporting period. Without needing to put at risk the privacy of

[79] eg 'Seventh Annual Report on the Individual Investor Programme of the Government of Malta' (Office of the Regulator: Granting of Citizenship for Exceptional Services, April 2021) 10.

[80] Commission Report COM(2019)12 final, 20.

[81] ibid.

the relevant applicants, oversight reports should also be published so that the public is kept informed 'of the risks and rewards that come with selling citizenship and residency'.[82]

VI. CONCLUSION

On 29 September 2022, the Commission referred Malta to the ECJ for its citizenship by investment programme scheme.[83] Hence, it is clear that governments, regional institutions and civil society will continue to debate the desirability of CBI and RBI programmes. However, to date this debate has only been necessarily minimally informed owing to the opacity of schemes; not only in terms of the basis on which decisions are made, but also with regards to the riskiness of the programmes themselves. The opacity of the sector has not done itself any favours. The lack of knowledge on the nature of the due diligence checks necessarily leads to speculation about the degree of risk entailed by the programmes. The truth is that we just do not know. Empirical evidence that would enable meaningful conclusions is lacking in respect to a majority of the benefits or risks typically associated with CBI or RBI programmes.[84] Thus, to label these programmes 'dangerous'[85] may be an exaggeration – but it also might not. Indeed, it would also be naïve to assume these programmes are bullet proof when a wide range of preliminary evidence suggests some of these risks – in particular corruption and acceptance of high-risk individuals – have actually materialised, in some cases leading to the annulment of the citizenship or residence,[86] the prosecution of public officials[87] or the closure of schemes altogether.[88] Indeed, Member States that are unwilling or unable to adopt mechanisms sufficient to mitigate these risks should not have such programmes.

The preliminary research by regional institutions and civil society into the lay of the land of the risk entailed by CBI and RBI programmes is therefore a welcome step towards greater transparency. However, research is also necessary that enables comprehensive critical reflection on the desirability of CBI and RBI schemes – we know too little at present to be fervent supporters or critics, based on their risks discussed in this piece. However, this research is not possible until governments produce more information on the nature of these programmes, and so it is with them that the next step towards greater transparency and reflection lies.

As we observed and discussed above, greater transparency seems necessary to facilitate accountability and thereby mitigate risks associated with these programmes. However, publication of the identities of those who naturalise may ultimately be a 'bad compromise', unfit to achieve the overarching purpose. In essence, it is not individuals who have to demonstrate that they have 'nothing to hide', but public actors. The publication of names of new citizens/

[82] Brillaud and Martini, 'European Getaway', 51.

[83] 'Investor Citizenship: Commission Refers Malta to the Court of Justice' (*European Commission*, 29 September 2022) https://ec.europa.eu/commission/presscorner/detail/en/IP_22_5422.

[84] eg on money laundering Annex II by Surak, 'Citizenship and Residence by Investment Schemes', 31.

[85] PACE 'Investment Migration', 2.

[86] eg Nesheim, 'Cyprus to Revoke Another 45 Citizenships Obtained by Investment' (*Investment Migration Insider*, 16 October 2021) www.imidaily.com/europe/cyprus-to-revoke-another-45-citizenships-obtained-by-investment-further-revocations-expected/; Desku, 'Four More Russian Billionaires Lose Cypriot Citizenship, Following EU Sanctions' (*Schengen News*, 8 August 2022) www.schengenvisainfo.com/news/four-more-russian-billionaires-lose-cypriot-citizenship-following-eu-sanctions/.

[87] 'Four Charged over Cyprus "Cash-for-Passports" Scheme' (*Al Jazeera*, 16 July 2022) www.aljazeera.com/news/2022/7/16/four-charged-over-cyprus-cash-for-passports-scheme.

[88] Eg 'Tier 1 Investor Visa Route Closes over Security Concerns' (United Kingdom Home Office, 17 February 2022) www.gov.uk/government/news/tier-1-investor-visa-route-closes-over-security-concerns; on Hungary, Brillaud and Martini, 'European Getaway', 20, 40–41.

residents cannot constitute an appropriate substitute for the implementation of effective due diligence and oversight mechanisms, which are essential to safeguarding democracy and the rule of law.

However, we found that those responsible for the operation of CBI and RBI programmes in the EU Member States have been opaque as to how they function: this begs the question as to what is being concealed by those who *should* have nothing to hide (ie the state), and why? It could be that governments are concerned further details will attract further negative attention, but this is exactly the sort of debate that needs to happen if these schemes should be considered legitimate. The severe opacity has seriously hampered the ability of investigations by regional institutions and civil society groups into the existence or functioning of the due diligence and oversight mechanisms to provide further insight on these programmes. What has emerged clearly from this research, however, is that a concerning amount of Member States appear to totally lack due diligence or oversight measures. Therefore, if the objective is to mitigate the risks associated with CBI and RBI programmes – such as those related to security, money laundering, organised crime, corruption and tax evasion – greater pressure should be placed on Member States to implement strong due diligence and oversight mechanisms. This is a crucial steppingstone towards realising accountability and therefore legitimacy in the EU investor migration sector, without sacrificing the privacy of individuals.

11

Can Investor Visas be Made to Work? Lessons from the United Kingdom and United States

MADELEINE SUMPTION

I. INTRODUCTION

INVESTOR VISA PROGRAMMES, also known as residence by investment, offer residence permits in return for a passive financial investment or transaction. They have become widespread over the past two decades. A 2019 review identified 60 different immigrant investor programmes (IIPs) (including citizenship by investment) in 57 countries, of which half had been established since the year 2000.[1] In the European Union, half of Member States had an investor programme by 2019, up from only four in 2010.[2]

Investor programmes are often portrayed as a ruthlessly utilitarian strategy to extract economic benefits from the mobility of the wealthy. However, evaluations have sometimes found that the programmes fell short of expectations. For example, official evaluations in Australia, Canada and the UK concluded that IIPs had brought only modest economic benefits.[3] Other studies found that the investment migrants themselves fared surprisingly badly in the labour market after migration, including in Canada, Australia and New Zealand.[4] While a few programmes have received at least some praise from evaluators, such as the United States' EB-5 programme,[5] they have also faced criticisms of insufficient transparency or fraud.[6]

Despite policymakers' apparent enthusiasm for investor programmes in the 2010s – particularly in Europe – there are also signs of sellers' remorse in some quarters. Canada closed its main investor programme in 2014,[7] and the United Kingdom followed suit in 2022. Australia

[1] Gamle et al, 'Citizenship as Sovereign Wealth' (2019) 10 *Global Policy* 527.

[2] Surak, 'Who Wants to Buy a Visa?' (2022) *JCES: 151-169.*

[3] 'Evaluation of the Federal Business Immigration Programme' (Citizenship and Immigration Canada 2014) www.canada.ca/en/immigration-refugees-citizenship/corporate/reports-statistics/evaluations/federal-business-immigration-program.html; 'Migrant intake into Australia' (Australian Government Productivity Commission 2016); 'Tier 1 entrepreneurs: Review of the Tier 1 Entrepreneur and Graduate Entrepreneur routes' (MAC 2014).

[4] Chiang, 'The Dynamics of Self-Employment and Ethnic Business Ownership Among Taiwanese in Australia' (2004) 42 *International Migration* 153; Ley, *Millionaire Migrants* (John Wiley & Sons 2011).

[5] Henry et al, 'Estimating the Investment and Job Creation Impact of the EB-5 Program. US Department of Commerce' (U.S. Department of Commerce 2017) www.commerce.gov/data-and-reports/reports/2017/01/estimating-investment-and-job-creation-impact-eb-5-program.

[6] 'Immigrant Investor Program' (GAO 2015) www.gao.gov/products/gao-15-696.

[7] Cohen in this volume.

indicated in 2023 that it would replace its investor programme because it was 'delivering poor economic outcomes'.[8] And in 2024, Spain announced its intention to close its investor visa. These moves do not necessarily amount to a systematic turn away from investor visas across the board, but they do signal that getting the programmes to deliver what policymakers want might be harder than expected.

Lacklustre evaluations and apparent doubts among some policymakers about the programmes' value raise an important question for the future of the programmes worldwide: why has it been so difficult to design successful investor visa programmes?

To start to answer this question, I draw on a study of investor visa programmes in two high-income countries: the United States (1990 to the present) and the United Kingdom (1994 to 2022).[9] The UK and US contexts don't represent all countries that have or are considering investor programmes. But the findings from the study nonetheless help to illustrate some general challenges that any residence by investment programme must address, such as how to ensure that investment funds are put to good use and what policymakers can realistically expect in the way of economic contributions from the investment migrants themselves.

A. Residence by Investment: The Basics

In this study, I define investor visa programmes (or residence by investment) as policies in which the government awards residence permits in return for a financial transaction or passive investment, with relatively limited requirements to be actively involved in the day-to-day operations of a business.

The main eligibility criterion for investor visa programmes is the financial transaction the programmes require. The qualifying investments range widely, from investments in private sector businesses or residential real estate, to transactions that are not really investments – such as transferring bank deposits to the country or making charitable donations.[10] Most programmes also have at least some other criteria. For example, investor programmes will generally require applicants to provide evidence of the source of their wealth and the funds they are investing, to address concerns that the programmes might attract illicit wealth.[11]

Some programmes require applicants to have a business background, demonstrate a given net wealth or assets (beyond what they are investing) or meet language proficiency requirements.[12] Some have residency requirements ranging from trivial (a few days) to substantial (half of the year or more).[13] In some cases, the initial residence permit comes with relatively few criteria, but applicants who want to move on to permanent status or citizenship must meet

[8] Review of the Migration System: Final Report 2023 (Australian Government, Department of Home Affairs 2023) www.homeaffairs.gov.au/reports-and-pubs/files/review-migration-system-final-report.pdf.

[9] Sumption, 'An analysis of success and failure in the immigrant investor programmes of the United States and the United Kingdom' (Doctoral Thesis, Maastricht University 2023).

[10] For example, as of 2024 Portugal rewarded private sector business investments and donations to arts or research; Greece allowed real estate investments, business investments, or bank deposits; and Italy rewarded share purchases, investments in government bonds, or charitable donations, see 'Investment Migration Programs 2024' (Henley & Partners 2024).

[11] Veraldi and Gstrein in this volume.

[12] For example, as of 2024 New Zealand required applicants to have basic English language skills and to meet health requirements and background checks; Quebec required applicants to demonstrate a net worth of CAD 2 million, though the actual investment capital required was 1.2 million, see 'Investment Migration Programs 2024'.

[13] For example, as of 2024 Latvia had no residence requirement, New Zealand required an average of just over 29 days per year, while Singapore required visa holders to be present for at least half of the time, see 'Investment Migration Programs 2024'.

more requirements. For example, the United Kingdom programme that closed in 2022 had no language requirement at entry, but applicants for permanent status needed to pass the same language and civic integration tests as migrants coming through other routes.

i. The US and UK Investor Programmes

The US and UK investor programmes underwent significant changes over the past decade, and indeed the UK programme closed entirely in early 2022.

The fieldwork for this study predated new legislation that reformed the US investor programme in 2022, following years of wrangling between constituencies with different visions of how it should work. It also predated the closure of the UK programme. This study does not examine the post-reform policies, but instead uses the analysis from the previous programmes to derive some general lessons about the challenges designing successful residence by investment programmes. While not all of the challenges will apply in quite the same way in other countries, many of them will.

At the time the study took place, the US and UK qualifying investments both required investment in private-sector companies. However, the US EB-5 programme required investments based on more complex criteria that attempted to target specific types of job-creating activity, with a requirement to show the investment would create at least 10 jobs. By contrast, the Tier 1 Investor programme allowed applicants to choose from a broader list of options, including simply buying shares in listed companies. Details of the two programmes appear in Table 11.1.

Table 11.1 US and UK investor programme details at the time the study was conducted

Characteristic	United States (before 2022)	United Kingdom
Type of investment	Investment 'at risk' in private sector project.	Wide choice of investments, including low-risk listed companies.
Investment amount	Before 2019: \$500,000 (TEA) or \$1,000,000 (non-TEA). From November 2019–June 2021: \$900,000 (TEA) or \$1,800,000 (non-TEA).	Before 2014: £1,000,000. From November 2014: £2,000,000.
Conditions on success of investment	Must be expected to create at least ten jobs.	No job creation requirement but investment must still exist when extending visa or applying for settlement.
Duration of investment	Variable depending on green-card waiting times.	Five years (or two to three years for higher investment amounts).
Waiting times	Median application processing time 32.5 months in year ending September 2021. Additional waits for green card availability, varying by country of nationality.	Less than one month.

(continued)

Table 11.1 *(Continued)*

Characteristic	United States (before 2022)	United Kingdom
Residence expected	No fixed physical presence requirement but to maintain green card, US must be main place of residence; absences of more than two years not permitted. Green-card status of children does not depend on parents' residence.	During two to five year temporary visa phase: children *and both* parents need at least 185 days of physical presence per year. After receiving permanent status: no absences of more than two years.
Conditions and rights attached to status	No requirements to be doing any specific activities (eg work, study).	No requirements to be doing any specific activities (eg work, study).

The governance of the US programme was more chaotic than the UK one. Processing times for applications had ballooned to around three years and many applicants faced additional long waits to receive a green card, because the number of green cards that could be issued each year was capped and oversubscribed. In the UK, meanwhile, applications were usually processed within a few weeks, giving applicants a smoother, less stressful and more predictable experience.

The US EB-5 programme has had a more complex history than the UK's Tier 1 Investor visa. While the UK investor programme was largely ignored for much of its existence with only a few tweaks to the criteria, the US one has undergone numerous policy changes. Administrative reorganisations, legislation, regulations and policy guidance have repeatedly sought to reshape how money flowed through the programme.

One result has been that the US programme became more complex over time. While the UK imposed few restrictions on where applicants could invest, the US rules are highly prescriptive. This complexity may well have improved the economic impacts of the programme to a certain extent, but not always in the ways policymakers hoped and not without unwanted consequences, as I explain below.

B. Methodology

The study employed a qualitative methodology, drawing on semi-structured interviews with 63 people involved in the design and implementation of the US and UK investor programmes and a review of official documents and transcripts of legislative debates. Interviews with policymakers and political insiders were used to understand the objectives of the programmes, the factors that contribute to their perceived successes and legitimacy within government, design and implementation challenges and the factors that affected policy decisions and policy change. Interviews with investor-programme professionals – including immigration lawyers, wealth managers and businesses receiving investments from investor applicants – were used to understand the programmes' day-to-day operation and the impacts of policy choices on applicants and on demand for IIPs. A full description of the methodology, recruitment and analysis processes can be found in Sumption.[14]

[14] Sumption, 'An Analysis of Success'.

II. OBJECTIVES

Policy debates tend to proceed on the assumption that we all know what the programme is supposed to achieve. However, a study that surveyed programme designs across the world argued that 'remarkably few' investor programmes had well-specified objectives and that this lack of clarity contributed to the inefficient use of financial capital.[15] This was also a running theme in interviews with policymakers, particularly but not exclusively in the UK. Nonetheless, some clear themes emerged.

US policymakers interviewed for the study said that, for them, the money was the most important benefit. While they might also like to attract entrepreneurial business people, that wasn't the main goal.

In the UK, the opposite was true. Policymakers said they were most interested in attracting 'go-getters' – motivated business people who could replicated their overseas success in the UK. The investment itself was an added benefit.

But before we assume these programmes are all about economics, it's important to note a third objective: politics. In fact, the objective mentioned most often in the United Kingdom was not the economic impact of the investments or the investors but rather the programme's ability to send a message that the UK was 'open for business'. This was particularly the case in the early 2010s, when the government was introducing more restrictive policies in other parts of the migration system. As one UK policymaker put it:

> Essentially, the economic benefit was important and something that we thought about, but it's fair to say that an important driver was that we needed a response to [other departments'] allegations or attacks that our policies would damage the economy. Investor visas provided a good line to say 'look at this good thing that we're doing'. (UK1)

Previous research suggests the UK is not alone in appreciating the potential political value of investment migration policies. A study from Canada, for example, finds that the Business Immigration Programme there had not simply been a tool to bring about specific economic objectives; policymakers had also used it to project a particular image of Canada's ability to attract entrepreneurial migrants. Indeed, he found that policymakers turned a blind eye to the programme's poor economic performance because they were too attached to the 'convenient fictions' it offered.[16]

The next sections examine the quest to meet each three of the objectives laid out here, and the challenges policymakers have faced along the way.

III. MONEY

The economic impact of investments coming through investor programmes depends in large part whether it actually stimulates new economic activity that would not otherwise have happened. When assessing the potential impact of investments, we need to understand whether the investment was genuinely additional to investment that would otherwise have taken place. In particular, we must ask:

Would the investments have taken place anyway, even if the programme did not exist?
Did the investments displace other funding?

[15] Gamlen et al, 'Citizenship as Sovereign Wealth', at 532.
[16] Ley, *Millionaire Migrants*, 428.

If the answer to both of these questions is 'no', we have the conditions for an investment programme that stimulates new economic activity. That's not to say the money will always be put to good use or that it will go towards the types of activity policymakers or the public approve of.

In both the UK and the US, interviews with investment advisors and immigration lawyers indicated that most applicants would not have made the same set of investments without the incentive of getting an investor visa. This was particularly true of the United States, where EB-5 investments offer a bad deal by commercial standards. No person of sound mind would choose them for purely financial reasons, since EB-5 packages offer a substantially below-market return. Even in the UK, where applicants could buy into normal commercially competitive funds, they would not necessarily have chosen to invest the specified amount in UK-based companies.

The more demanding question is whether the investments simply displaced other investment. To see why this matters, it's useful to examine the UK programme before its closure in 2022. Applicants could invest in almost any UK-registered private company,[17] buying shares on the secondary market. Almost none injected new capital into the businesses.

If an average of 500 investors invested £1 billion in FTSE 100 listed companies in 2021, this would have made up around 0.1 per cent of these companies' combined market capitalisation (£1.9 trillion in August 2021).[18] Investor capital was broadly irrelevant in the grand scheme of the UK stock market.[19] In other words, the UK model made effectively no effort to ensure that qualifying investments stimulated new economic activity or to push them towards high-risk investments that might not otherwise have had access to funds.

In the United States, there is a stronger case that the EB-5 investments stimulated new economic activity. This is because they reduced the cost of capital businesses faced, primarily in the real estate sector. For example, a business receiving a $500,000 EB-5 loan would at the time have paid around 5 per cent per year, after including intermediaries' cut (the investors themselves received much less). If the alternative was paying 10 per cent, this means they might save around $87,000 over a three-year period. A lower cost of capital stimulates additional economic activity.[20]

What the EB-5 programme did less successfully was push funding towards businesses that would not otherwise have been able to secure any capital at all. Some policymakers saw this as the programme's main objective, and they were disappointed. This happened for two main reasons.

First, even though the EB-5 market is a strange one, it is a market nonetheless. Applicants wanted to reduce their risk, ensure they received their capital and make sure they would get a green card at the end of the process. They were not looking to receive high returns, as they were not normal investors: they were in it for the immigration benefits. As a result, they gravitated towards safe bets. This made big property developers in New York City more attractive

[17] Subject to minor restrictions such as a requirement that the company have employees based in the UK and not be principally engaged in property investment.

[18] 'FTSE 100' (London Stock Exchange 2021) www.londonstockexchange.com/indices/ftse-100/constituents/table.

[19] Even if investments affected share prices at the margins, the impact on the company's market capitalisation should not last very long. In an efficient market where shares were correctly priced before immigrant investors bought in, increases in the share price should be counterbalanced by other investors selling to benefit from the (marginally) elevated stock values.

[20] Chatelain and Teurlai, 'The Impact of the Cost of Capital and on the Decision to Invest or to Divest on Investment Behavior' (MMF Research Group Conference 2003).

than care homes in Ohio. Without totally rethinking the structure of the EB-5 programme (in which applicants choose what to invest in and any business can sign up to participate in the programme), pushing funding towards businesses that really wouldn't have received funding otherwise is an uphill struggle. As one industry professional put it: 'How do you write a rule that says that this money can only go to projects that are so crappy that nobody else would fund it?' (US30)

Second, the US programme criteria arguably pushed funding further towards the larger, more professionalised businesses that policymakers did *not* typically envisage receiving the funding, because these businesses were better able to meet conditions such as compliance reporting, pay fees and guarantee job creation. They were also better able to handle the US programme's rather chaotic governance, with long processing times and unpredictable timelines for investors to receive their funds back.

Finally, US policymakers were clear that they wanted the programme to bring investment, rather than simple payments. Policy interviewees rejected the idea of cash for green cards as undignified or unethical. However, they presided over a model in which businesses and applicants collaborated to transform something that superficially looks like an investment into something that is really more like a payment in disguise. Ironically, this payment-like arrangement was part of the reason the programme is likely to have been economically beneficial, even if they money did not flow to the types of businesses many policymakers had envisaged should benefit.

A. Side Effects of the US Model

The US model, despite some economic benefits, came with costs. In particular, a long history of fraud and abuse has dogged the EB-5 programme, and government agencies have struggled to prevent it. It is difficult to quantify the prevalence of fraud in the EB-5 industry, either today or in the past. Presumably, the vast majority of projects are professionally run and comply with the rules. However, interviewees in both government and EB-5 industry agreed that the programme had been poorly regulated in the early days, as monitoring failed to keep up with the growth in the EB-5 industry. One industry professional described the period from 2008 to 2012 as a 'wild, wild west' where people with histories of fraud or bankruptcy could raise money from China with almost no oversight (US27).

While professionals and policymakers agreed that things had improved, some features of the EB-5 model have nonetheless made it more susceptible to fraud than models that allow applicants to choose commercially viable investments, like the UK's Tier 1 Investor visa. There were three main reasons. First, the EB-5 programme pushed applicants into financial transactions they would otherwise have preferred not to conduct and were not always equipped to scrutinise (most did not have backgrounds in finance or the US markets they were investing in, and some lacked the English skills to conduct their own due diligence). Some were thus vulnerable to unscrupulous business or agents.

Second, the decentralised investor visa market allowed almost anyone to set up a regional centre to receive EB-5 funds, and some turned out to be unscrupulous or incompetent.

And third, the complexity of the financial transactions and the decentralised market put heavy demands on the immigration agency, USCIS. Applications required extraordinary volumes of information including a detailed financial paper trail showing the applicant's wealth, business plans and statistical modelling demonstrating job creation plans, and financial information about the commercial enterprise handling the funds. One US policymaker described the resulting complexity:

> It's gotten to the point now where the types of deals and investments that are being proffered for [the agency's] approval, are just so complicated that it's impossible for a regular adjudicator to understand. The nature of the submissions that are given to us, all the evidence and supporting documentation is unbelievably voluminous, and it's terabytes of data that come in, and it's unbelievable. (US7)

It took an iterative process over many years for USCIS to develop rules and expertise to monitor the programme.

For all the economic drawbacks of the UK programme, its qualifying investment created fewer monitoring and compliance challenges. Indeed, both policymakers and industry professionals who worked with applicants were sceptical about the benefits of pushing applicants towards risky investments. As one UK immigration lawyer put it when describing direct investments (as opposed to share purchases), 'we are very wary of these structures and try to keep our clients away from them' (UK4).

Dealing with complex financial instruments is not necessarily a strong suit for immigration agencies. The US and UK cases both show how a lack of expertise with financial instruments can put pressure on casework operations. In the United States, it took many years for the immigration agency to build up a cadre of expert staff, and it continued to face problems recruiting enough qualified people to run the programme efficiently. The complexity of the programme contributed to outlandishly long processing times. Even in the much simpler UK programme, some policymakers said that the complexity of financial transactions made the programme difficult to monitor.

In both countries, policy development over time reveals a learning process as unanticipated problems emerged. For example, the United Kingdom improved its due diligence procedures after identifying flaws in the pre-2015 policies, although only after admitting substantial numbers of investors with limited scrutiny. The United States built up more financial expertise in the immigration agency and started to collaborate more closely with the financial regulator – although the agency was still stymied by a lack of legal authority to regulate the programme properly until 2022. With the benefit of hindsight, the initial policy design in both cases was naïve in failing to anticipate the operational and integrity risks that investor programmes might present.

Given that other immigration categories typically do not involve complicated financial transactions (with the possible exception of entrepreneur programmes), these oversight challenges are also likely to face immigration bureaucracies implementing investor programmes in other countries.

B. Is there a Better Way?

On the face of it, neither the UK nor the US model look particularly attractive to countries considering adopting a residence by investment scheme. The UK qualifying investment brought no economic benefits, while the US one was difficult to regulate. Are there models that would make more sense?

To answer this question it is worth stepping back a bit. Given that one of the primary practical functions of IIPs is to induce investment, we must ask whether there is actually an investment problem that needs to be fixed and if so, what it is. Relatively few policymakers interviewed for this study identified investment-related problems that they thought the investor programme should address. One US policymaker did mention the high cost of capital in the real estate sector as a problem the EB-5 programme should address. But for the most part, the mentality was 'here is some money, what should be direct it towards' rather than 'here is an investment problem, how can we fix it'.

Indeed, it is possible that in some countries, there is not a significant problem with investment. When the Australia Productivity Commission (2016) examined Australia's investor visa, for example, it argued that while immigration policymakers had developed a strand of the investor programme to push funding towards high-risk venture capital, there was no need for government intervention to expand venture capital and the route was not bringing many benefits.[21]

If policymakers believe there *is* a problem to be fixed, they will need to be realistic about the prospects that an immigrant investor programme can fix it. Applicants are not venture capitalists. The vast majority will invest not because they want to but because the immigration system requires them to. As a result, applicants will gravitate to low-risk options that already have relatively good access to capital elsewhere, unless they are forced to do something different.

If policymakers are serious about channelling funding towards businesses or causes that do not have good access to capital, using a decentralised web of private-sector intermediaries to do this will be an uphill struggle. Governments may need to take a stronger role in deciding what gets funded – for example, through a centralised fund. Some countries already have small business loan programmes or similar support for entrepreneurs, unrelated to the immigration system. It may be more efficient to add investor programme funding to existing programmes such as these rather than creating a new structure with its own demands on administrative resources and oversight.

If we follow this argument to its logical conclusion, we arrive at a system of non-refundable payments to government funds that stimulate new economic activity. From an economic perspective, a donation is much more useful than a genuine investment that is highly likely simply to displace other sources of investment. Payments are controversial, however. Policymakers who baulk at this idea may prefer a structure that looks less like a payment, such as zero-interest loans to a government fund. But the reality is much the same.

Alternatively, policymakers may prefer to abandon the idea that the investment will bring substantial benefits. This could mean dropping the investment requirement entirely, and using other criteria to assess whom to admit (this is discussed in the next section). Or it could mean giving the investment a largely symbolic role. Under this rationale, the purpose of the investment is not to stimulate economic activity but to create the impression that applicants are 'contributing'. A reasonable observer might conclude that this is pointless and that perhaps we should be more honest about what is really going on. But if symbolism is nonetheless the goal, the investment should arguably be simple as possible. Policymakers should avoid complex criteria that immigration caseworkers will have to monitor and that might push migrants with limited financial expertise into potentially fraudulent transactions. In this scenario allowing investments in listed companies – as the UK did until 2022 – is not such a bad idea. After all, investments in listed companies can be conducted via regulated wealth managers in markets where mainstream financial regulations protect the investors.

[21] 'Migrant intake into Australia' (Australian Government Productivity Commission 2016).

IV. PEOPLE

Rhetoric about residence by investment often portrays the programmes as a way to admit entrepreneurial people. The United Kingdom illustrates a case where this was a central objective of the programme. UK policymakers' vision of the desirable applicant was both vague and demanding. They said they wanted to attract 'go-getting' applicants or 'captains of industry', including successful overseas business people, who would make further investments after arriving in the UK and perhaps move parts of their overseas businesses to the UK.

US policymakers were less concerned about the applicants, and more interested in the money – indeed, given that their investment model actually brought some economic benefits, they had the luxury of not needing to worry too much about whether the people also did so.

UK policymakers were disappointed that the applicants they received were not the ones they had originally envisaged. In both countries, interviews with intermediaries suggested that applicants fell into three main groups:

- Leisure and education migrants: people looking for a better quality of life or educational opportunities for their children, with no particular plans to work or run businesses.
- Professionals who were eligible for other visas but wanted an immigration status with fewer restrictions, eg the right to run a business on the side (in the UK) or to get a faster path to a green card (in the US).
- People with entrepreneurial plans. UK respondents characterised this group as a tiny minority, although US professionals were more likely to say they had encountered people planning to conduct business after migrating.

Why did the programmes appear to attract relatively few entrepreneurs, particularly in the UK? First, successful overseas businesspeople whom policymakers often envisage admitting do not necessarily want to relocate their businesses or start new businesses in a completely different business environment. Even wealthy migrants can face the same barriers identified in the literature on migrant entrepreneurship, such as a lack of social capital and local business knowledge.[22] As a result, the target group of the investor applicants UK policymakers considered most desirable – successful business people willing to move to the UK – is likely to be relatively small.

This is consistent with previous research on investment migration, which has generally found that when investment migrants move at all, they typically do not set up flourishing businesses at destination. Many move as leisure migrants and don't plan to work, while those who wanted to set up businesses often struggled to adapt to a new business environment and had poor outcomes in the labour market.[23]

Second, defining reliable criteria to identify economically active people through investor programmes is difficult. Requiring an investment screens people based on their wealth, and

[22] Jones et al, 'Transnationalism as a Force for Ethnic Minority Enterprise?' (2010) 34 *IJURR* 565; Jones et al, 'Migrant Entrepreneurship' in Hytti et al (eds), *The Dynamics of Entrepreneurial Contexts* (Elgar 2018); Kloosterman et al, 'Mixed Embeddedness' (1999) 23 *IJURR* 252; Naudé et al, 'Migration, Entrepreneurship and Development' (2017) 6 *IZA Journal of Migration*.

[23] 'Evaluation of the Federal Business Immigration Programme' (Citizenship and Immigration Canada 2014); Chiang, 'The Dynamics of Self-Employment and Ethnic Business Ownership Among Taiwanese in Australia' (2004) 42 *International Migration* 153; Coates et al, 'Rethinking Permanent Skilled Migration after the Pandemic' (Grattan Institute 2021) https://grattan.edu.au/report/rethinking-permanent-skilled-migration-after-the-pandemic/; Ho and Bedford, 'The Asian Crisis and Migrant Entrepreneurs in New Zealand' (1998) 24 *New Zealand Population Review* 71; Ley, *Millionaire Migrants*; Liu-Farrer, 'Migration as Class-Based Consumption' (2016) 226 *The China Quarterly* 499.

wealth alone is not a good way of identifying people who plan to be active in business. More broadly, the characteristics policymakers were interested in were either too nebulous to be written into transparent selection criteria (eg being 'dynamic') or were forward-looking (eg the intention to be actively involved in investment activities), so policymakers could not rely on a measurable track record.

Third, UK policymakers faced tensions between the different things they were trying to achieve. On one hand they wanted a programme that would be attractive to successful business people. On the other, they wanted applicants to establish themselves in the UK. To achieve this second goal, they introduced a hefty residence requirement: anyone who wanted to secure permanent status had to be physically present for at least half the year. However, this residence requirement put off prospective applicants with successful businesses overseas, because they did not really want to establish themselves full time in the UK. A lower residence requirement would have made the programme much more attractive, but would presumably have done less well at attracting people willing to spend a lot of time in the UK. In effect, the two desired characteristics of overseas business success and commitment to the UK conflicted.

Even for applicants who were willing to establish themselves in the UK, policymakers faced a tension trade-off between offering more rights and flexibility to make the programme attractive, and screening the applicants more effectively. In principle, the government could have required temporary visa holders be economically active, conducting specified types of activity. However, this would likely have reduced demand among the target applicants. The greater flexibility for applicants meant less control for policymakers, who could not specify what people should do after they arrived.

A. Who should Policymakers Try to Attract?

Policymakers operating investor visa programmes may thus need to decide whether they are happy to accept substantial numbers of applicants who do not fit the vision of the ideal entrepreneurial migrant, to make sure the programme continues to be attractive to those who do.

One of the main groups of people interested in using investor visas is best described as lifestyle migrants, including people who do not intend to work and are accompanying children for education or want a pied-a-terre in another country. The economic benefits of admitting them are expected to be smaller than the benefits of admitting the elusive go-getting entrepreneurs this study has discussed at length. But some modest benefits may nonetheless result from their discretionary spending, and their wealth reduces the likelihood that they will impose substantial economic costs. One option for policymakers is thus to embrace the role of investor programmes as a leisure visa, and hope that a handful of the entrepreneurial migrants they most wanted to attract will also materialise.

If policymakers are not keen to admit leisure migrants on investor visas – for example, because they are keen to lower overall migration levels – this puts them in a difficult position. Specifying reliable selection criteria to screen them out – and *only* admit successful overseas businesspeople who plan to be economically active at destination – is difficult. Policymakers in this camp might reasonably conclude that having an investor visa is not worth the trouble.

On the other hand, if policymakers *want* to admit leisure migrants or at least do not mind doing so, their task is much easier. It does still leave them with the question of whether they need to require an investment, or whether they would be better off with a less complex programme design that simply requires people to have the means to support themselves.

B. Screening Out 'Bad Actors'

One of the charges frequently levelled at investor programmes is that they admit people who earned their money through illicit means. This was a particular concern among policymakers in the UK, who frequently voiced concern that the programme attracted people who were 'not exactly wholesome' (UK9). Concerns about applicants' backgrounds have also been shared by think tanks and NGOs,[24] although there is very little information in the public domain to assess the scale of the problem.

Perhaps surprisingly, some private-sector intermediaries interviewed for this research shared these concerns about the backgrounds of applicants, some of whom were their clients. One wealth manager who had been involved in conducting due diligence checks, for example, said that 'You could go back over a bunch of these people who've got ILR *[indefinite leave to remain]* and I would probably say that at least 20 per cent are full-on crooks by anyone's standards' (UK13).

Some policymakers felt that admitting people with illicit wealth was an unavoidable consequence of having an immigration route for wealthy people. Due diligence processes are not perfect, after all. Some people's wealth is inherently more difficult to investigate than others, particularly if they made their money in business environments with poor record-keeping, and in some cases the required documents can be bought and sold.

However, it's also clear that some due diligence procedures are stricter than others. Little is known about the practical effectiveness of screening checks in residence by investment programmes, and indeed governments tend not to publish much detail about what applicants have to demonstrate and how checks are conducted.[25] In this study, however, the comparison between the US and UK was interesting. While some US policymakers mentioned the risk of admitting people with illicit wealth, this risk was much less salient than in the UK. One potential explanation is that US due diligence processes were more effective. It is difficult to compare the US and UK due diligence processes directly, because US checks were conducted 'in house' by specialised immigration officers while UK checks were outsourced to private financial institutions via a requirement for applicants to open a bank account. However, it is notable that while several US intermediaries said that the paperwork required for due diligence was a common factor preventing people from applying, while UK intermediaries did not. Indeed, some UK intermediaries indicated that applicants rejected from one financial provider could often just shop around until they found a bank willing to accept them. This does seem to indicate that the US checks were more effective at screening out people with illicit wealth – and probably also some with legitimate wealth too.

V. POLITICS

Success isn't just a question of social or economic benefits: politics matters as well. Programmes that lack political support may not survive. Indeed, the UK investor programme became so unpopular in its later years that it was closed in 2022 with cross-party support.

[24] Hawley et al., 'Red Carpet for Dirty Money' (Spotlight on Corruption 2021) www.spotlightcorruption.org/report/new-briefing-red-carpet-for-dirty-money-the-uks-golden-visa-regime/; Heathershaw et al, *The UK's Kleptocracy Problem* (Chatham House 2021).

[25] Veraldi and Gstrein in this volume.

The US and UK case studies both show that the political success of investor visa programmes is far from guaranteed. This is interesting since at least in the UK, policymakers portrayed political benefits as one of the main benefits of the programme in the early 2010s.

First, negative narratives about the programmes compete with the positive ones. The political arguments in favour of the programmes rely on the economic benefits, either of the investment or the investors themselves. Negative arguments included the risks of admitting people with illicit wealth or facilitating fraudulent business transactions.

While the abstract argument about economic benefits played well in the UK in the early 2010s, by the middle of the decade the costs were more salient. Politicians could not point to specific businesses or amenities that had resulted from the investor programme, but newspapers could point to money launderers suspected of holding the visas. As one policymaker put it, framing the investor visa in a positive light was a challenge because there was 'this constant thing nagging at the back of everyone's brain: it's going to be the cronies, it's going to be the Russian mafioso' (UK7).

In the United States, the economic benefits were more tangible because applicants had to invest in specific projects. The benefits were concentrated locally, which meant that some politicians had an interest in enabling their constituents to access EB-5 funding. On the other hand, high-profile fraud cases undermined the US investor programme's reputation by casting doubt on the integrity of the businesses using the funds.[26] Indeed, US Senator Patrick Leahy turned from being one of the EB-5 programme's boosters to one of its most vociferous critics, after a high-profile fraud scandal in his state, Vermont. Nonetheless, the politics of the EB-5 programme in the United States were more favourable to the programme's survival: narratives about tangible benefits competed with narratives about tangible costs.

Second, the politics of qualifying investments constrain policymakers' options. In theory, the simplest way to ensure economic benefit and reduce the operational chaos seen in the US investment model would be to accept a non-refundable donation and get the government to direct it to causes it considers worthwhile. The causes might be business related (eg grants to small businesses that struggle to raise finance) or they might not. Policymakers in a system along these lines would still face the challenge of deciding how to target the funds. Presumably, this process would be more legitimate and transparent in some states than others. But assuming the funds were managed competently, a system based on non-refundable payments would cut out much of the complexity and risks of abuse that result from the attempts to regulate private transactions between investors and private-sector businesses.

Interviews with intermediaries in both the UK and the US suggested that many investors would actually prefer to make a non-refundable donation if it reduced the hassle and risks of managing a qualifying investment. Applicants would not have to worry about whether they could trust the private-sector operator they selected.

The barrier to cash-based investor programmes was not that the applicants were unwilling to part with their money but that policymakers did not want to take it. Taking a non-refundable donation from investors was considered a political non-starter in both countries. US policymakers said there had been no serious discussion of implementing a model along these lines.

Indeed, the idea of auctioning investor visas had been widely discussed in the United Kingdom because the Migration Advisory Committee (MAC) formally recommended doing so in 2014. At the time, MAC recommendations were usually always accepted. On this occasion,

[26] McCullum and D'Ambrosio, 'A ski resort, a dream and greed' (Burlington Free Press, 15 December 2020) https://eu.burlingtonfreepress.com/in-depth/news/local/vermont/2020/12/14/how-jay-peak-vermont-fraud-became-example-greed-flawed-oversight/6177757002/.

however, there was never any serious suggestion that the recommendation might be adopted. It was politically 'unsellable' (UK29). The MAC recommendation may have been economically efficient but it was arguably the worst possible design from a political perspective, as it involved *literally* selling to the highest bidder.

Politically perceptions also played a role in the design of the US programme. The job creation requirement in the US EB-5 programme was, for example, helped create a positive narrative about the programme's benefits. Whatever its substantive merits, it enabled proponents of the route to point to tangible, quantifiable benefits. As one US policymaker put it, 'Whatever you were doing … you still had to create a certain number of jobs. You can't get around that. Because that's the one fig leaf they have that makes it not be citizenship for sale' (US7).

In both countries, framing the financial transaction as an investment rather than a payment made the politics of the investor programme more favourable. In reality, the line between payments and investments in investor programmes is fuzzy. Industry professionals typically said that applicants saw the investment as a cost they had to pay to secure status. In the US EB-5 programme, applicants already effective paid a direct subsidy to the businesses that used their funds, as described above. Even if the line is fuzzy in practice, it may appear clearer in the political debate.

As a result, policymakers face a trade-off between investment models that are (a) economically beneficial and operationally tractable and (b) politically palatable.

VI. CONCLUSION

Why have investor visas been difficult to design, and can the problems be overcome? The UK and US case studies suggest there is no perfect option: policymakers face trade-offs that can't be avoided entirely. In particular, challenges can arise for three main reasons.

First, investor programmes' different objectives may conflict. For example, politicians may be interested in 'genuine investments' but it is likely that allowing investors to choose commercially viable investments will greatly reduce the economic benefits of the programme by enabling applicants to displace other funding. The easiest way to ensure an economic benefit is to accept a non-refundable donation, but this may not be politically palatable. Politics may thus push policymakers towards models that are less economically beneficial or more difficult to operate.

Second, the vision of the entrepreneurial applicant is both vague and demanding, and it is often not obvious that policymakers have thought through who they want the programmes to admit and whether those people really want to move. Policymakers who are happy to accept applicants who either (a) don't have to live in the country full time, or (b) have no entrepreneurial or further investment plans, will face an easier ride admitting non-trivial numbers of applicants, though these applicants will not necessarily bring large economic benefits.

Third, investor programmes can have unintended consequences, including accidentally admitting people with illicit wealth or facilitating fraudulent transactions. The harms resulting from these problems are difficult to assess.[27] At the same time, immigration agencies lack expertise in financial matters. This makes it harder for them to vet applicants' financial history and scrutinise investments. Policymakers may initially underestimate the requirements

[27] Surak, 'The misuse of citizenship and residence by investment' (2024) LSE Department of Social Policy Working Paper www.lse.ac.uk/social-policy/Assets/Documents/PDF/working-paper-series/WPS-02-24-Kristin-Surak.pdf.

for specialist expertise, either in-house within the immigration agency or through cross-government collaboration.

The scale of investor programmes varies, but in many high-income immigration destinations (the focus of this particular study), they make up a small share of immigration. They will often also make up a small share of the economy (with some exceptions).[28] The smallness of the programmes in the grand scheme of many high-income countries raises the question whether it's worth all the fuss. In theory, perhaps policymakers could introduce investment models that have some benefits. Is it worth it? Perhaps it could be. But equally, the money may not be big enough to make much difference.

Investor programmes interact in interesting ways with the rest of the immigration system, creating a kind of residual category for people who don't fit other immigration routes or don't find them attractive. Demand depends at least partly on what is missing from other parts of the immigration system. As a result, the value of using an investor programme to admit individuals may vary depending on how significant those gaps are. For example, the EB-5 programme filled large gaps in the creaking and dysfunctional US immigration system, but was arguably less necessary in the UK, where other routes already existed for many of the people UK policymakers considered desirable.

Policymakers contemplating immigrant investor programmes in order to bring economic benefits would thus be well served to put careful thought into the question of what they really expect the programme to achieve and whether they need one at all. As one UK policymaker put it: 'There needs to be clearer vision of who these people are, why we should bother, and how you would design the scheme to attract those people. And I think that's where it's all been pretty vague' (UK20).

[28] Surak and Tsuzuki, 'Are Golden Visas a Golden Opportunity?' (2021) JEMS: 3367–3389.

III.

Investment Migration Regulation in Europe and the World

12

Wealth Influx, Wealth Exodus
Investment Migration from China to Portugal

LUUK VAN DER BAAREN* AND HANWEI LI

I. INTRODUCTION

PORTUGAL HAS BEEN hailed as one of the most popular European destinations for wealthy emigrants, in particular for those of Chinese origin. This development was offset by the introduction of the ARI[1] in 2012, commonly known by its marketing name, the 'golden visa'. The introduction of the ARI enables third country nationals to obtain a Portuguese residence permit in exchange for certain predefined investments. After the introduction of the Portuguese investment programme in 2012, Chinese investors quickly became the programme's primary beneficiaries. Chinese investors comprised the majority of approved applicants until 2016, but subsequently investors from other countries gradually surpassed them in prominence and Chinese demand did not return to the pre-2016 level in the post-Covid era either.[2] Despite its popularity, the programme and its wider context have been little studied. This chapter describes how the investment programme has developed during a peak period of Chinese interest (approximately 2012–18) and whether it has lived up to its ambitions at the time. How did the Portuguese investment programme work and can it be regarded as a success? And what drove the Chinese demand for the Portuguese investment programme? These are the questions that this chapter aims to address. Acknowledging that the one country's wealth influx can be the other country's wealth exodus, the chapter examines the investment programme both from a Portuguese as well as a Chinese perspective. In the first section, the nature of the Portuguese investment programme is discussed, as well as the political context in which it came about. In the second section, key factors that drove wealthy Chinese to make use of investment programmes at the time – and the Portuguese programme in particular – are discussed. Next to that, it discusses the ways in which wealth emigration affects China and the countermeasures that the Chinese government has taken during that period. Taken together, the chapter aims to provide a more complete picture of investment migration and a better understanding of the dynamics that have contributed to its emergence.

* Centre for Global Mobility Law, Copenhagen University (funded by DNRF Grant No DNRF169).

[1] 'Autorização de Residência para atividade de Investimento': 'Residence permit for Investment Activities'.

[2] Nesheim, 'Chinese Investors' Share of Portugal Golden Visa in Q1 at Highest Level Since 2016' (*IMI Daily*, 8 April 2021) www.imidaily.com/europe/chinese-investors-share-of-portugal-golden-visa-in-q1-at-highest-level-since-2016/.

II. THE PORTUGUESE WEALTH INFLUX

A. The Development of the Investment Programme: Rise and Decline between 2012 and 2018

Portugal was among the hardest hit European states in the 2007 financial crisis and the subsequent 2011 budgetary crisis. In addition to austerity measures, the Portuguese government has introduced a wide array of measures aimed at economic reform. In 2012, a legislative proposal with such measures was presented, which included a proposal for a Portuguese residence-by-investment programme. Its explanatory memorandum referred briefly to this investment programme. It stated that the goal of the investment programme was to 'boost economic diplomacy'.[3] The Portuguese government interprets this term as the utilisation of State activities and public institutions abroad for – in short – stimulating international trade and investment.[4] In the light of this strategy, an institutional reform had taken place which increased the collaboration between the Ministry of Foreign Affairs and the Ministry of Economic Affairs. Logically, Portuguese embassies and consulates also played a key role in this strategy.[5] The term became even more of a buzzword under the XIX Portuguese Government (2011–15). In practice, it combined traditional international trade policies, like the conclusion of trade agreements, with a more innovative 'commercialisation' of State institutions. The embassies and consulates were tasked with stimulating collaboration with foreign companies and attracting activities and investments of non-residents, but also to 'relaunch the brand Portugal' and improve the country's reputation.[6] The ultimate goal was to create economic growth by making the Portuguese economy more internationally oriented.[7] The introduction of a residence permit for investors can be seen as a part of this strategy. 'If you help us, we will treat you well', as the Portuguese vice-president summarised it.[8] In conclusion, the ultimate goal of the investment programme was to internationalise the Portuguese economy by attracting foreign investors.

In 2012, only two applications were approved. Since then, the figures rapidly increased. By 2014, the number had risen to already 1,526 investors and 2,395 family members.[9] Therefore, the Portuguese investment programme gained more and more attention from the international media.[10]

In November 2014, the rise of the golden visa plunged. An investigation by the Portuguese Central Department of Investigation and Penal Action (DCIAP), codenamed Operation Labyrinth, had brought to light numerous suspicions of high-level fraud related to the investment programme. Suspects include the head of the Portuguese Institute for Registries and Notaries (IRN), the Minister of Internal Affairs and the Secretary-General of the Portuguese

[3] Legislative Proposal 50/XII 2012 (PT).

[4] Resolution of the Council of Ministers 152/2006 (PT).

[5] ibid.

[6] Presidência do Conselho de Ministros, Programa do XIX Governo Constitutional 2011-2015 (PT), 104.

[7] ibid 106.

[8] 'Paulo Portas diz que Portugal tem de "tratar bem" quem invista em dívida soberana' (*Jornal de Negocios*, 20 December 2012) www.jornaldenegocios.pt/economia/ajuda-externa/detalhe/paulo_portas_diz_que_portugal_tem_de_tratar_bem_quem_invista_em_divida_soberana.

[9] 'Relatório de Imigração, Fronteiras e Asilo' (SEF 2014), 13.

[10] 'Golden chance to soak up sun' (*South China Morning Post*, 20 March 2013) www.scmp.com/property/international/article/1194671/golden-chance-soak-sun; 'EU States dangle visas for foreigners' (*New York Times*, 11 October 2013) www.nytimes.com/2013/10/11/greathomesanddestinations/eu-states-dangle-visas-for-foreigners.html; 'Immobilier: le Portugal, nouvel eldorado européen?' (*Le Figaro*, 15 September 2014) www.latribune.fr/vos-finances/immobilier/20140915tribd4addf9ff/immobilier-le-portugal-nouvel-eldorado-europeen.html.

Ministry of Justice. The suspects were charged with crimes of corruption, influence peddling, embezzlement and money laundering.[11] The corruption trial damaged the reputation[12] as well as the implementation of the investment programme. The handling of the applications was slowed down and eventually even came to a standstill. The primary reason was the chaotic situation at the SEF caused by the investigations and raids. In response, SEF employees stated they were no longer willing to process applications until the regulation was made clearer. Multiple investors who had expected an easy and quick procedure now instead became stuck in a legal limbo.[13] Although the SEF has admitted that applications were delayed for several months, some investor migrants stated that they have been waiting for a response to their applications for more than a year.[14] The delays have caused severe problems for the investors, as their Schengen visas inevitably expired after 90 days. These problems could have been avoided if the investors had obtained an ordinary residence visa – the visa that is usually granted to those wishing to apply for a residence permit. Although a residence visa is more difficult to obtain, it can be extended in case the procedure for obtaining the residence permit takes longer than expected.

In response to the corruption trial, the Minister chose not to repeal the investment programme, but to amend it instead.[15] Four new investment options were added.[16] The explanatory memorandum stipulates that the added options should stimulate investment in a more diverse set of sectors and also outside Portugal's major cities. This cannot be seen separately from the reputational damage that the programme suffered and the subsequent need for a 'charm offensive'. Nevertheless, there was clearly also a genuine need to diversify the investment programme, as the abundant majority of investors had opted for real estate investment in similar areas (see Section II.A).

Several procedural amendments were also introduced, including an extension of regulatory guidance regarding the documentation that investor had to submit.[17] The decree also introduced a yearly audit to be executed by IGAI, the conclusions and recommendations of which are to be presented to a parliamentary commission.[18] Third, it required that a procedural manual be produced for the use of SEF staff.

In May 2017, a bill was presented to amend the investment programme once more.[19] It was proposed to further reduce the minimum requirement for an investment fund. Next to

[11] 'Vistos Gold: 11 detidos por suspeitas de corrupção' (*Observador*, 13 November 2014) http://observador.pt/2014/11/13/diretor-nacional-sef-detido-por-suspeitas-de-corrupcao-na-atribuicao-dos-vistos-gold/; 'Como funcionava, afinal, a rede ilegal dos vistos Gold' (*Observador*, 15 November 2014) http://observador.pt/2014/11/15/como-funcionava-afinal-rede-ilegal-dos-vistos-gold/; 'Portuguese police detain 11 in "golden visa" corruption raids' (*Financial Times*, 14 November 2014) https://next.ft.com/content/fa7412b8-6be7-11e4-b939-00144feabdc0.

[12] The Chinese state press agency Xinhua reported extensively on the Portuguese corruption scandal. See: 'Portuguese prominent figures to stand trial over golden visa scandal' (*China.org.cn*, 13 May 2014) www.china.org.cn/world/Off_the_Wire/2016-05/13/content_38441980.htm.

[13] 'Chinese Stuck in Portugal's Visa Limbo' (*Bloomberg*, 20 January 2016) www.bloomberg.com/news/articles/2016-01-20/chinese-property-buyers-stuck-in-portugal-s-golden-visa-limbo.

[14] 'Chineses dos vistos gold sentem-se enganados por Portugal' (*TSF*, 10 October 2016) www.tsf.pt/economia/interior/chineses-dos-vistos-gold-sentem-se-enganados-por-portugal-5433247.html.

[15] Act 63/2015 (PT).

[16] These options were the purchase of real estate at least 30 years old or located in urban recovery areas (350,000 euros), investment in scientific research (350,000 euros), investment in arts and culture (250,000 euros) and investment in an investment fund aimed at small or medium-sized businesses (500,000 euros). On all the new options as well as the existing option in job creation, the investor obtains a 20 per cent reduction if the investment is made in an area with a low population density or a GDP per capita rate lower than 75 per cent of the national average. The options are discussed in greater detail in Section II.B.

[17] Art 65-A to 65-E of Decree 15-A/2015 (PT).

[18] Art 65-I of Decree 15-A/2015 (PT).

[19] Legislative Proposal 86/XIII 2017 (PT).

that, a new investment option was proposed, namely an investment in a small or medium-sized Portuguese business. In a parliamentary debate, the Secretary of State and Foreign Trade Paulo Ferreira presented the amendments as a part of a set of measures which should support Portuguese companies in need of recovery and restructuring.[20] In July 2017, the bill was adopted and entered into force in November 2017.[21]

During the course of 2016 and 2017, the programme had got back up to speed and reached the same levels of approvals as the period preceding the corruption trial. Nevertheless, the SEF remained to struggle with backlogs at the time.[22] During the period 2016–18, the share of Chinese applicants continued to decline; in 2017 Chinese investors no longer formed the majority of approved applicants for the first time in the history of the Portuguese investment programme.[23]

B. The Development of the Investment Programme

Under the terms of Act 29/2012, it was made possible to issue a temporary residence permit to third country nationals making an investment within Portugal. A brief overview of the investment programme can be found in Table 12.1. The law introduced four investment options, namely purchases of real estate, deposits in a Portuguese bank account, investments in companies or job creation.[24] Such investments had to be sustained for at least five years.[25] The investor did not have to apply for a so-called residence visa entailing a multitude of administrative requirements.[26] Instead, the investor could travel to Portugal on an ordinary Schengen ('tourist') visa with a (non-extendable) validity of 90 days.[27] Besides this visa exception, the investor needed to fulfil the regular conditions for obtaining a temporary residence permit, the most relevant of which relate to an absence of criminal convictions and alerts in the Schengen information System.[28]

In the first year, the investor was obliged to be present in Portugal for at least seven days per year. In the subsequent years, this requirement was raised to 14 days per period of two years.[29] The validity of the residence permit was one year. After that, it could be extended for periods of two years.[30] Extension of the residence permit did not necessarily require proof of this presence, as it is merely stated that the applicant *may be asked* to provide evidence of presence in Portugal. Thus, providing such proof was in principle not necessary.[31] As Portugal is an EU Member State and part of the Schengen area, the holder of the permit was permitted to stay in other Schengen States for up to 90 days in a 180-day period.[32] After fulfilling the regular

[20] Diário da Assembleia da República, Serie I, No. 101, 2017 (PT), 4.

[21] Diário da República, Serie I, No. 165, 2017 (PT).

[22] 'Atrasos na atribuição de vistos Gold afasta investidores' (*SIC Notícias*, 5 January 2018) https://sicnoticias.pt/economia/2018-01-04-Atrasos-na-atribuicao-de-vistos-Gold-afasta-investidores.

[23] 'Chinese Investors' Share of Portugal Golden Visa in Q1 at Highest Level Since 2016' (*IMI Daily*, 8 April 2021).

[24] Art 3, sub. d of Act 23/2007 (PT), amended by Act 29/2012.

[25] Art 4 of Order 11820-A/2012 (PT).

[26] Art 58 ff. of Act 23/2007 (PT), amended by Act 29/2012.

[27] Art 90-A, para 1, sub a and d of Act 23/2007 (PT), amended by Act 29/2012.

[28] Art 77 of Act 23/2007 (PT), amended by Act 29/2012.

[29] Art 5 of Order 11820-A/2012 (PT), amended by Order 1661-A/2013.

[30] Art 90-A, para 3 of Act 23/2007 (PT), amended by Act 29/2012.

[31] Form can be found here: www.sef.pt/documentos/56/iii_Purchaseovalueequalorabove500_ren.pdf.

[32] Art 5 of Regulation No 610/2013 of the European Parliament and of the Council amending Regulation (EC) No 562/2006 of the European Parliament and of the Council establishing a Community Code on the rules governing the movement of persons across borders (Schengen Borders Code), the Convention implementing the Schengen Agreement, Council Regulations (EC) No 1683/95 and (EC) No 539/2001 and Regulations (EC) No 767/2008 and (EC) No 810/2009 of the European Parliament and of the Council [2013] OJ L 182/1.

requirements, an investor migrant could obtain permanent residence or apply for naturalisation in Portugal.

C. The Non-Habitual Residence Tax Regime

An often overlooked advantage of taking up residence in Portugal is the existence of the Non-Habitual Residence Tax Regime. This taxation scheme was introduced in 2009, with the aim of (re)attracting talent and high net worth individuals.[33] Anyone who has not been a tax resident in Portugal during the preceding five years and takes up residence in Portugal is eligible to participate in this scheme.[34] For 10 years, the migrant can profit from advantageous tax rates.[35] The migrants' Portuguese sourced income will be taxed at a flat rate of 20 per cent if the income is derived from 'high value activities', while many forms of foreign source income (including foreign source pensions) are exempted from taxation. Moreover, Portugal does not impose wealth taxes. Becoming a Portuguese tax resident requires residing in Portugal for at least 183 days in a 12-month period.[36] A person who does not fulfil this requirement can still be considered a tax resident in Portugal if he has a home in Portugal which is intended to be his permanent residence.[37] It must be noted that Portugal is not the only EU Member State that has introduced a beneficial taxation scheme for third-country nationals. The Netherlands, for example, has introduced the so-called '30 per cent facility', which entails that highly skilled workers from a third country are exempted from taxation on 30 per cent of their remuneration.[38]

Table 12.1 Portuguese Residence permit for Investment Activities as at 1 January 2018

Investment	A. Capital transfer of at least 1,000,000 euro
	B. Creation of at least 10 jobs
	C. Purchase of real estate to the value of at least 500,000 euros
	D. Purchase of real estate for at least 350,000 euros. Construction is older than 30 years or in an urban recovery area
	E. Capital transfer of research activities at an institution integrated into the national scientific/technological system of at least 350,000 euros
	F. Capital transfer in arts, national heritage reconstruction, through the local and central authorities, public institutions or private institutions for public interest of at least 350,000 euros
	H. Capital transfer for shares in investment funds or in venture capital for small or medium-sized companies of at least 350,000 euros
	I. Capital transfer for (the creation of) a company of at least 350,000 euro and the creation/retention of at least five permanent jobs for at least three years *Art 3 par d Act 23/2007, amended by Act 29/2012, Act 63/2015 and Act 165/2017*

33 Preamble Decree 249/2009 (PT).
34 Art 16, para 6 of Decree 249/2009 (PT).
35 ibid, Art 16, para 7.
36 Art 16, para 1, sub a of Código do Imposto sobre o Rendimento das Pessoas Singulares 2014 (PT).
37 ibid, Art 16 para 1 sub b.
38 Art 10ea of Uitvoeringsbesluit loonbelasting 1965 (NL).

D. The Nature of Investments in Portugal (2012–18)

The total amount invested from October 2012 to May 2018 was 3,768,808,068 euros.[39] In this period, 6,159 residence permits were granted to main applicants and 10,396 to family members, of whom more than 60 per cent were Chinese. The investors mostly opted for real estate investment. In fact, almost 95 per cent of the resident permits were granted in exchange for real estate investments. The investments were predominantly done in the Lisbon region. In 2014 more than 90 per cent of the total investments was invested in real estate within the Greater Lisbon Region, Setúbal and the Algarve.[40] In 2013, 80 to 90 per cent of the investments were done within the Lisbon region.[41]

The predominance of real estate acquisitions can partially be explained by the existence of a 'real estate migration industry' consisting of Portuguese governmental institutions, Portuguese real estate agencies and Chinese migration agencies. First of all, two governmental organs (AICEP and EPE) are responsible for the promotion of the investment programme.[42] They have promoted the investment programme at real estate fairs in multiple sending states, together with the real estate sector association APEMIP. The promotion is also executed through diplomatic and consular networks.[43] A number of Portuguese real estate agencies work independently to attract Chinese investors, attending real estate fairs in China to promote their activities themselves. However, most agencies collaborate with China-based migration consultancy firms. The consultancy firms are able to recruit potential investors and are thereby the first link in the chain. The real estate agencies then set up a portfolio of real estate likely to be of interest for the particular investor. The investor will then make a short trip to Portugal (about three days) in order to visit the selected locations. On the last day, the acquisition decision is made, after which a Portuguese bank account is opened and the administrative procedure initiated. After that, the investor can return to his place of residence.[44]

Due to problems with language and a lack of knowledge of the Chinese market, Portuguese firms are often dependent on Chinese consultancy firms. Therefore, the bargaining position of the Chinese consultancy firms enables them to charge high fees.[45] Cases have been reported in which such fees were added to the value of the real estate price without the investor being informed, after which the investor is left with an overpriced purchase.[46]

It is often assumed that investors obtain their residence permits in exchange for 'buying a house'. In reality, the issue is more complex. First of all, it is sometimes necessary to buy several houses or apartments to reach the minimum investment level, as the level of real estate prices in Portugal is relatively low. In other cases the acquisition consists of a pre-formed 'package deal' of real estate to be rented out with a promised ROI-rate of around 5 per cent.[47] The investment programme is moreover in principle applicable to *all* forms of real estate.

[39] 'Golden Residence Permit Program (ARI) data from 8th of October 2012 to 30th of April 2018' (SEF 2018).

[40] 'Relatório de Imigraçao, Fronteiras e Asilo' (SEF 2014), 13.

[41] 'Os vistos gold vieram dar novo folego ao mercado de luxo' (*Público*, 16 January 2014).

[42] Art 65.º-F of Regulatory Decree 15-A/2015 (PT).

[43] Art 65.º-G of Regulatory Decree 15-A/2015 (PT).

[44] Quintela, 'A Imigração De Negócios E O Desenvolvimento Local Num Contexto De Crise' (Doctoral Thesis, University of Lisbon 2014), 78 ff.

[45] cf ibid 84.

[46] 'Chineses com vistos "gold" queixam-se de burla imobiliária' (*Diário de Notícias*, 19 June 2014) www.dn.pt/portugal/interior/chineses-com-vistos-gold-queixamse-de-burla-imobiliaria-3979283.html; 'Chineses com vistos gold "roubados" por mediadoras' (*Notícias ao Minuto*, 15 February 2014) www.noticiasaominuto.com/economia/174842/chineses-com-vistos-gold-roubados-por-mediadoras.

[47] eg www.goldenvisas.com/portugal-guaranteed-rental-5-percent-5-years/.

As could be expected, the investment programme has been enthusiastically received by the real estate sector. The investment programme was introduced at a time when the real estate sector was stuck in a deep recession. Therefore, foreign investment in real estate was most welcome. According to estimates of the real estate association APEMIP, 23 per cent of house acquisitions in 2014 were by non-Portuguese, 23,000 in total. Of this, 18 per cent (or 4,140 properties) are said to have been bought by Chinese nationals. Other major groups are British nationals (23 per cent) and French nationals (16 per cent), reportedly attracted by the Non-Habitual Residency Tax programme.[48]

The level of investment attracted from October 2012 to May 2018, more than three billion euros, is substantial given the size of the Portuguese economy.[49] Foreign investment in real estate can have multiple positive effects. First of all, foreign real estate investment tends to be non-mortgaged, which was greatly beneficial in the Portuguese case, as the country's real estate market was badly affected by the financial crisis and credit availability was constrained. This way, the golden visa programme could contribute to the stability of the real estate market. Second, in the Portuguese case, investors often acquire renovated or newly constructed buildings. In general, such investment has wider positive effects ('trickle-down effects') than acquisition of existing properties as such.[50] Third, foreign investment has increased the value of properties in certain areas, most notably the historical centre of Lisbon. Within certain areas, sales prices per square meter have reportedly increased as much as 30 per cent within one year.[51]

Nevertheless, the long-term effects of the investment programme remain uncertain. The regulation requires the investment to be sustained for five years, after which permanent residence or EU-residence can be obtained. This entails that, in practice, the properties acquired can come back on the market from 2018. In a policy paper, the International Monetary Fund warns that citizenship and residence-by-investment schemes are indeed prone to such 'sudden-stop' risks.[52] Next to that, the rising prices of properties within the city centre of Lisbon also come with disadvantages, as these properties are becoming unaffordable for the original inhabitants.[53] Lastly, even though the programme has delivered significant economic contributions, it is unlikely that it has fundamentally altered the Portuguese economic landscape by attracting more international business activity, as was intended by the legislator.[54]

[48] 'Franceses aproximam-se dos chineses na compra de imóveis em Portugal' (*Publico*, 10 February 2015) www.publico.pt/economia/noticia/francesas-aproximamse-dos-chineses-na-compra-de-imoveis-em-portugal-1685577. The figures are estimates and were distributed by the sector association APEMIP. There are no official figures of the above-mentioned real estate acquisitions by non-Portuguese available.

[49] For purposes of comparison, Portuguese foreign direct investment inflows in 2016 alone were estimated at 8.41 billion euros in total, see: 'Foreign direct investment, net inflows (BoP, current US$)' (World Bank Open Data) https://data.worldbank.org/indicator/BX.KLT.DINV.CD.WD.

[50] See Rosen et al, 'Breaking Ground' (Asia Society Special Report 2017). However, others doubt whether the multiplier effect of real estate investment through the Portuguese investment programme is substantial, see eg Ferras, 'Corrupção em Portugal' (*Correio do Minho*, 29 November 2014) https://correiodominho.pt/cronicas/corrupcao-em-portugal-o-caso-dos-vistos-gold/6338.

[51] Guimarães, 'Num semestre Lisboa vender 909 imóveis a compradores internacionais' (2017) 3 *Revista Confidencial Imobilário*.

[52] Xin et al, 'Too Much of a Good Thing?' (2015) IMF Working Paper No. 15-93, 30.

[53] Lestegás, 'The Global Rent Gap of Lisbon's Historic Centre' (2018) 13 *IJSDP* 683, 690.

[54] Gamlen et al argue that investment programmes often suffer from a lack of engagement of investor migrants, see Gamlen et al, 'Re-thinking Immigrant Investment Funds' Investment Migration Council Working Paper 1/2016, 8ff.

III. WEALTH EXODUS FROM CHINA

A. Causes of Investment Migration from China

Portugal's investment programme has for several reasons been successful in attracting investor migrants from China during the period studied in this chapter. This can partially be attributed to the lenient requirements of the Portuguese scheme at the time, but there are other underlying causes that are also applicable to a wider context beyond the Portuguese case, explaining why wealthy Chinese are keen to move themselves, their assets and their family abroad.

The low presence requirement of the Portuguese scheme is especially important to Chinese investment migrants. It enables investors to legitimately hold a Portuguese residence permit while spending most of their time in the country of origin. Presence requirements is sometimes referred to among Chinese emigrants as a 'migration prison'. According to interviews among Portuguese real estate agents, the vast majority of Chinese investment migrants choose to stay in China.[55] In the meantime, their properties can be rented out. The low requirement meets the Chinese investors' demands, since they would often prefer to continue to reside in China after obtaining a residence permit for Portugal.[56] The rationale behind this phenomenon is firstly that the Chinese investors' businesses and (political) careers are rooted in China and therefore they cannot afford to live abroad for significant periods of time.[57] Second, the Chinese investors often lack the language skills, cultural knowledge or the social networks to set up an equally successful business in another country.[58] Next to that, a residence permit can be obtained to ease international travel. Holders of a Portuguese residence permit can reside in other Schengen Area Member States for 90 days in each 180-day period and are therefore exempted from cumbersome visa application procedures.[59]

To conclude, some of the Chinese investor migrants only migrate on paper, not necessarily in practice. This leads to a new form of 'quasi-migration' in which the purpose of migration is not necessarily to move to another country, but rather to be prepared to do so at any time, or to ease their mobility by avoiding visa restrictions. The investment migration scheme can therefore serve as an insurance against potential political and economic risks, or as a strategic choice. All in all, these Chinese investment migrants can be called 'voluntary immobile migrants' who are 'standing on two boats at the same time'. While the Portuguese government would expect and hope that the investment migrants would bring international business opportunities to boost the Portuguese economy, the concept of 'voluntary immobility' seems to contradict such expectations.

Another important factor that contributes to the success of the Portugal investment migration scheme is that it allows investor migrants to invest in real estate. As mentioned above, investment in real estate is by far the most popular option of the Portuguese scheme. The acquisition of real estate is regarded by wealthy Chinese as a safe and stable investment.[60] It is suggested that in the majority of cases, the property acquired through investment programmes

[55] cf Quintela, 'A Imigração De Negócios E O Desenvolvimento Local Num Contexto De Crise', 78.

[56] Liu-Farrer, 'Migration as Class-based Consumption' (2016) 226 *China Quarterly* 499, 508.

[57] Miao and Wang, *International Migration of China* (Springer 2017) 22.

[58] See, for example, David Ley's ethnographic study to the difficulties investor migrants encountered in Canada: Ley, *Millionaire Migrants* (Wiley-Blackwell 2010).

[59] Art 5 of Regulation No 610/2013 Schengen Borders Code [2013] OJ L 182/1.

[60] Szto, 'Representing Chinese Real Estate Investors in the United States' (2014) 23 *Minn. J. Int'l L.* 173, 177; cf Miao and Wang, *International Migration of China*, 23.

will not be used as a primary residence and can therefore serve as a holiday home and eventually be rented out.[61]

Some wealthy Chinese investors are emigrating in search of political stability. After the current Chinese President Xi Jinping started a systematic and forceful anti-corruption campaign in China, many higher and lower level officials ('tigers' and 'flies', in Jinping's metaphor) in the government were under investigation.[62] This anti-corruption campaign not only affects the political figures, but also businesspersons, as business in China is often closely related with politics.[63] Despite their wealth, many businesspeople have to rely heavily on connections with authorities, as they are in need of the support of the administration. The line between cooperation and corruption is often thin, as a certain form of 'gift-giving' is seen as a natural way to maintain *guanxi* (social networks and relationships of influence).[64] Therefore, these connections with the authorities make them vulnerable to corruption charges. Portugal is a politically stable country, where such they can preserve their wealth in case of a sudden policy change or social conflict endangering their wealth in China. The fact that they hold a Portuguese residence permit make sure that they are ready to leave at any time.

A quest for economic safety is also driving demand for investment programmes. While the Chinese real estate market offers abundant opportunities on the one hand, it is also volatile on the other. This is illustrated by the fact that house prices in major Chinese cities have soared, leading to the risk of an overheated property market and the formation of a real estate bubble.[65] The potential bursting of this real estate bubble is estimated to have a limited effect on Chinese economic development as a whole, but investment in Chinese real estate is nevertheless deemed to entail high risks.[66] In order to cool down property markets, several Chinese cities have taken measures to curb the purchase of properties for individuals who already own housing.[67] As wealthy Chinese are aware of these risks, they tend to distribute their wealth partially abroad.[68]

Investment migration is also an important family livelihood planning strategy in which the wealthy Chinese seek to invest in their children's quality of life. One of the main reasons for the surge of Chinese demand for investor residence permits is that it provides a way to secure their children's (primary and secondary) education abroad.[69] Next to education, less tangible issues as concerns about environmental pollution also play a role.[70] The Portuguese investment programme includes relatively extensive provisions for family reunification, including dependent parents and dependent (underage or adult) children. Chinese parents often prefer

[61] Chen and Lazarus, 'Rising Outbound Flows' (CBRE Research 2015) 6 https://f.tlcollect.com/fr2/715/78861/CBRE_-_Outbound_PPT_(Webinar)_(EN).pdf; 'Casas com vistos gold cada vez mais arrendadas' (*Expresso*, 13 May 2018) https://expresso.pt/economia/2018-05-13-Casas-com-vistos-gold-cada-vez-mais-arrendadas.

[62] Yuen, 'Disciplining the Party' (2014) 3 *China Perspectives* 41.

[63] See for example Cheng Li's report, describing the power-capital nexus within the Chinese tobacco industry through corporate and industrial interest groups: Li, 'The Political Mapping of China's Tobacco Industry and Anti-Smoking Campaign' (Brookings 2012) www.brookings.edu/articles/the-political-mapping-of-chinas-tobacco-industry-and-anti-smoking-campaign-2/.

[64] Szto, 'Chinese Gift-Giving, Anti-Corruption Law, and the Rule of Law and Virtue' (2015) 39 *Fordham Int. LJ* 591, 609; Luo, 'The Changing Chinese Culture and Business Behavior' (2008) 17 *IBR* 188.

[65] Glaeser et al, 'A Real Estate Boom with Chinese Characteristics' (2017) 31 *JEP* 93.

[66] Wu et al, 'Evaluating the Risk of Chinese Housing Markets' (2016) 39 *China Econ. Rev.* 91; Fang et al, 'Demystifying the Chinese Housing Boom' (2015) NBER Working Paper 21112, 105; Guo and Huang, 'Does "Hot Money" Drive China's Real Estate and Stock Markets?' (2010) 19 *IREF* 452.

[67] '2017 Pacific Real Estate Market Outlook – Greater China' (CBRE Research 2017).

[68] Cf Chen and Lazarus, 'Rising Outbound Flows', 6.

[69] Simons et al, 'Chinese Investment in US Real Estate Markets Using The EB-5 Programme' (2016) 30 *Econ. Dev. Q.* 75. For tertiary education, obtaining a residence permit through investment is not necessary, as students can obtain a residence permit for study purposes.

[70] Miao and Wang, *International Migration of China*, 4.

their children to have a Western education because of the heavy burden of Chinese compulsory education and fierce competition in the *Gaokao* (the university entrance examination). Second, a western education is widely perceived as more prestigious and has become a status symbol.[71] Since the local Portuguese high schools teach in Portuguese, Chinese parents would often choose to send their children to international schools.[72]

Demand for the Portuguese investment programme is also stimulated by the highly developed Chinese 'migration industry'.[73] As the investment migration procedures tend to be complex, Chinese investor migrants are prepared to hire agencies that help them handle the investment migration procedures. In 2011, there were 730 migration agencies operating under licence from the Chinese Ministry of Security.[74] The most important task of the migration industry is to deal with the administrative burden of the emigration process and connect the Chinese investors to suitable investment options, next to consulting for the right migration destination. Furthermore, the Chinese migration industry is connected with agents working in destination countries, whereby potential investors can overcome language barriers.

B. The Consequences of the Wealth Exodus from China

This section mainly addresses the consequences of investment migration from China to western countries. Investment migration from China to Portugal is a prism through which to scrutinise the volume and dynamics of the wealth exodus from China in general. We mainly discuss the consequences of the wealthy migrating from China, the impact of their migration on China, and the countermeasures employed by the Chinese government.

i. Emigration Restrictions

In the Chinese perception, investment migration is often framed as a channel for corrupt officials and businessmen to escape from prosecution in China as well as a mechanism for money laundering.[75] For example, the Chinese government has requested Australia to help to hunt down fugitives who allegedly have fled China through the Australian investment programme.[76] The Chinese media have reported extensively on cases of corrupt officials who have escaped the arm of the law by using investment migration channels.[77] Cases are known of exiles involving top Chinese government officials with highly classified political documents, as was seen in

[71] ibid, 3; Liu-Farrer, 'Migration as Class-based Consumption', 513.

[72] Revez, 'Depois dos russos, os chineses chegam ao Algarve à procura de ar puro e golfe' (*Publico*, 6 April 2014) www.publico.pt/2014/04/06/economia/noticia/russos-ja-estao-no-algarve-os-chineses-vem-ai-1631039.

[73] This is complemented by a rapidly developing migration industry that operates on a global level. See for an account of the development of the citizenship-by-investment industry: Surak, 'Global Citizenship 2.0' (2016) Investment Migration Working Papers IMC-RP2016/3, 25 ff.

[74] Xiang, 'Changing Patterns of Out-Migration and Identity Implications' in Iredale and Guo (eds), *Handbook of Chinese Migration* (Elgar 2015) 285.

[75] Fangmen, 'Millionaire Emigration' (MPI 2017).

[76] The Economic and Commercial Section of the Consulate General of the PRC in China, *China Requests Australia's Cooperation in Chasing Fugitives* http://sydney2.mofcom.gov.cn/article/bilateralcooperation/inbrief/201410/20141000760011.shtml; 'China requests Australia's cooperation in chasing fugitives' (*Global Times*, 14 October 2014) www.globaltimes.cn/content/886259.shtml.

[77] 'Insecurities of rich drive US visa rush' (*Global Times*, 1 April 2014) www.globaltimes.cn/content/852110.shtml; 'Hunt for corrupt officials fleeing overseas meets legal barriers' (*Global Times*, 9 April 2014) www.globaltimes.cn/content/853506.shtml.

the case of Chinese businessman Ling Wancheng fleeing to the USA after his once powerful brother Ling Jihua was taken into custody.[78] Besides the obvious capital drain, this can also have an adverse effect on society at large, as it creates the impression that elite officials place themselves above the law, which could lead to more societal grievances over the inequality between different social classes, leading to potential social and political instability.

For the abovementioned reasons, the Chinese government has imposed stringent regulations on the travel of Chinese government officials abroad. In general, limitations of the right to leave are based on Article 8 paragraph 5 of the Law on the Control of Exit and Entry of Citizens 1985. This clause states that exit approval shall not be granted to persons whose exit will 'be harmful to State security' or 'cause a major loss to national interests'. This clause is further specified in the secondary legislation, which also addresses limitations for government officials. There is also a multitude of restrictions in place for the acquisition of a Chinese passport. Depending on the passport category one has to apply for, there can be cumbersome administrative requirements as well as diverse grounds for outright refusal.[79]

According to our interviewees,[80] two main measures are taken to fight against corrupt officials leaving China to prevent the exit from China of corrupt officials. First, all government officials are subjected to yearly scrutiny procedures of their backgrounds, in which they have to submit a form that includes detailed information about their own nationalities, as well as their children and spouse' nationalities, current place of residence, and their ownership of (overseas) property. In case of falsification of information, the official may face severe retribution. Such scrutiny is carried out by the Central Commission for Discipline Inspection. The Central Commission for Discipline Inspection (CCDI) is the highest internal control institution of the Communist Party of China (CPC), tasked with enforcing internal rules and regulations and combating corruption in the Communist Party.[81] If it is found that both the children and the spouse of a senior government official have moved abroad, he or she will be required to resign from the current post and be demoted to a lower position in the government or to move their children or spouse back to China. Second, when Chinese officials reach *ke ji* (section) level their passports will be confiscated. Travel abroad would have to be reported to the higher officials and getting official approval for this is needed.

The right to leave one's own country is protected under international law through multiple international treaties as well as international customary law. In the academic literature, the right to leave is predominantly studied from the perspective of the International Covenant of Civil and Political Rights (ICCPR).[82] However, the ICCPR has not been ratified by China.

Moreover, the right to leave one's own country is widely considered to be part of international customary law.[83] In one of the rare studies on the right to leave in Chinese law, it is argued

[78] 'Top China defector passes secrets to US' (*Financial Times*, 4 February 2016) www.ft.com/cms/s/0/4e900936-cb20-11e5-a8ef-ea66e967dd44.html.

[79] Liu, *The Right to Leave and Return and Chinese Migration Law* (Brill–Nijhoff 2007) 246.

[80] The following information on regulations of Chinese officials going abroad is based on an interview with Chinese officials working for the Commission for Discipline Inspection.

[81] Gong, 'The Party Discipline Inspection in China: Its Evolving Trajectory and Embedded Dilemmas' (2008) 49 *Crime, Law and Social Change* 139.

[82] Kochenov, 'The Right to Leave Any Country including Your Own in International Law' (2012) 28 *Conn. J.Int'l L.* 44; Hannum, *The Right to Leave and Return in International Law and Practice* (Brill–Nijhoff 1987).

[83] Chetail, 'The Transnational Movement of Persons Under International Law' in Chetail and Bauloz (eds), *Research Handbook on International Law and Migration* (Elgar 2014) 20; Storey, *Foundations of International Migration Law* (Oxford University Press 2013) 78.

that the Chinese restrictions are in general inconsistent with international customary law.[84] We would add that the case may be different regarding the emigration restrictions in place for senior government officials as these restrictions can be defended as a necessity to protect public order due to such persons' access to sensitive information. Nevertheless, the principles of proportionality and necessity have to be taken into account in each individual case.

ii. Capital Outflow

The most direct impact of investment programmes on China is that they cause an outflow of capital. More and more middle- and upper-class Chinese families are relocating their assets abroad, often in contravention of capital control measures. The Chinese government has sought to entice capital flow back and to prevent more capital from fleeing. There is a limit in place of (the equivalent of) 50,000 US dollars annually per capita for foreign currency purchases.[85] There are also restrictions in place for international transfers with UnionPay credit and debit cards, including limitations on the purchase of overseas insurance and investment products. As UnionPay has a near monopoly position on the Chinese market, these limitations have a powerful impact.[86] Since 2016, control over whether individuals adhere to these restrictions has been intensified. Hence Chinese banks are obliged to report transactions above a limit of (the equivalent of) 10,000 US Dollars to the State authorities.[87]

However, there are numerous other methods which investor migrants can use to transfer money abroad, including underground banks, transfers through Hong Kong money changers, pooling the quotas of family and friends, bogus purchases of overseas services and commodities, for example intentionally unsuccessful bidding at foreign art auctions), getting an overseas mortgage based on savings in China or simply carrying cash across the border.[88]

iii. Long-Term Effects of China's Wealth Exodus: Reproduction of Social Inequality?

Investment migration can cause social inequality to be reproduced locally and transnationally. Investment migration is unattainable for low- and middle-income Chinese households, while wealthy Chinese households have access to migration information as well as the funds to pay for migration agencies and can therefore obtain visas, residence permits or even acquire nationalities that allow them to become a citizen of the world. This substantiates the argument that in the era of globalisation, the rich become the global and the poor remain the local. Social inequality can also be reproduced transnationally through investment migration. The offspring of such families can obtain an international upbringing and education, enabling them to better compete in a global market. This 'head start' of the *fu'erdai* (or the second generation of wealthy Chinese) has the potential to exacerbate Chinese social inequality at a global level.

[84] Liu, *The Right to Leave*, 94.

[85] Art 2 of Detailed Measures for the Implementation of the Measures for the Administration of Individual Foreign Exchange.

[86] Wang, 'Inner Workings of the Chinese Economy' (2016) University at Buffalo Working Paper https://papers.ssrn.com/sol3/papers.cfm?abstract_id=2752030.

[87] Art 5 of Order No. 2 of the People's Bank of China on Measures for the Administration of Financial Institutions' Reporting of High-Value Transactions and Suspicious Transactions 2006 (CN).

[88] Cf Wang, 'Inner Workings'; 'China's money exodus' (*Bloomberg*, 3 November 2015) www.bloomberg.com/news/features/2015-11-02/china-s-money-exodus.

IV. CONCLUSION

This chapter started from the premise that an inflow in a receiving country, be it in people or in capital, must logically be preceded by an outflow from a sending country. Therefore, the aim was to study the Portuguese investment programme by combining a 'Portuguese perspective' with a 'Chinese perspective'.

The Portuguese investment programme was announced as a boost to Portugal's 'economic diplomacy', aiming to internationalise the Portuguese economy and improve its international reputation. Therefore, the investment programme exemplifies an intriguing merger of the public and the private, in which embassies and ministries are teaming up with real estate agents to maximise their gains. It is clear that the number of (notably Chinese) investors and the size of their investments has been substantial and have made a significant contribution to the Portuguese economy. The investor has also contributed greatly to the urban regeneration of certain areas of Lisbon. However, it is doubtful whether the investments attracted during the period 2012–18 internationalised Portugal's economy, as the investments mainly ended up in the domestic real estate sector.

On the Chinese side, the causes of migration from China to Portugal show that conditions such as low residence requirements, access to the Schengen Area and an option to invest in real estate are likely to attract Chinese investors to the Portuguese investment programme. Other factors of importance are the wish of wealthy Chinese to partially distribute their wealth abroad and the preparation of a potential 'escape route'. Meanwhile, it is important to acknowledge that investment migration is often a household-level strategy, for example to enable children to have a western education at a young age.

The consequences of the wealth exodus from China are viewed mainly as negative from the point of view of the Chinese State. To name a few, capital outflow is perceived to lead to a capital drain and impede the robust growth of the Chinese economy, while investment migration is also perceived by the Chinese political left as an escape route for corrupt officials and businessmen facing prosecution. Investment migration used as a preservation of wealth, and investment in the future for their children's education can also directly or indirectly contribute to the reproduction of inequality. The Chinese government has implemented measures to curb capital outflow, prevent the exit of officials, and to halt the wealth exodus. However, economic instability and a multitude of factors impeding quality of life in China maintain the demand for emigration among wealthy Chinese, while the Chinese 'migration industry' is more than willing to assist them. Investor migration programmes offer them unprecedented freedom of mobility and can strategically assist their families to become part of a global elite, while being served by exceptionally lenient migration policies and tax incentives rates along the way. All in all, it seems that the migrants themselves will turn out to be real 'winners' of the golden visa saga.

13

Investment Residence in Greece

Analysing the Attractiveness and Challenges of the Golden Visa Programme

NIOVI VAVOULA AND VASILIKI APATZIDOU*

I. INTRODUCTION

THE GREEK GOLDEN visa programme was designed in 2013 and has grown significantly since 2017. The programme has undergone several legislative reforms with the most recent one from April 2023, when its regulation was incorporated in the new Greek Immigration Code.[1] The programme has attracted a large number of investors (mainly investing in real estate) due to its advantages among which the threshold of €250,000 to purchase a property or multiple properties to complete the minimum required amount, no requirement of physical presence in Greece, and the long duration of the programme which is five years with the possibility of unlimited renewals. However, the chapter will demonstrate that the societal impact of the golden visa programme is considerable, mainly regarding the consequences on the real estate market because of the increase that is witnessed in the prices that local residents have to afford to rent or buy a property. Furthermore, as it will be explained below, the limited scrutiny conducted before and after the issuance of the residence permit may raise security concerns, as well as possible risks of money laundering.[2] The new Immigration Code brings some amendments among which on the investment thresholds, which are increased, in many cases, to €500,000. It remains to be seen how this increase will affect the 'success' of the programme in Greece and if this measure will be enough to alleviate the adverse impacts of the scheme.

Against this backdrop, this chapter aims to critically evaluate the advantages and flaws of the legal framework of the Greek golden visa programme. According to Surak and Tsuzuki, until 2019, Portugal, Spain, Greece and Latvia were responsible for 70 per cent of the approved golden visa applications in the EU.[3] Particularly in Greece, the golden visa programme has

* Both authors are grateful to the officers at the Greek Ministry of Migration and Asylum for valuable information regarding the practical application of the 'golden visa' programme.

[1] Immigration Code of Greece 2023 (GR).

[2] Pavlidis, 'A Case of Insufficient Safeguards or State-Enabled Money Laundering?' (2021) 22 *J. Invest. Compliance* 170; European Commission, 'Investor Citizenship and Residence Schemes in the European Union' COM(2019)12 final.

[3] Surak and Tsuzuki, 'Are Golden Visas a Golden Opportunity?' (2021) 47 *JEMS* 3367.

increased tremendously over the last years to the extent that it has been heralded as one of the most advantageous and attractive schemes in the EU[4] and has generated more than €2.5 billion in proceeds since its launch.[5] Nevertheless, it has only received scant attention in the literature that deals with investment residence.[6] In our research, we have primarily relied on a black letter analysis of legal and policy-related documents, including publicly available statistical data on the issuance of residence permits. To gain insights into the implementation of the programme in practice, the policy analysis is complemented by informal discussions that we conducted with the competent unit of the Greek Ministry of Migration and Asylum. The chapter is organised as follows: the next section provides an outline of the legal framework on investment residence programmes in Greece, followed by an analysis of its practical application. Then, we examine the programme in terms of its advantages, which have raised its attractiveness and its flaws. With regard to the flaws, we emphasise three aspects: the impact on the residential market; the pre- and post-issuance checks and the potential impact on the fight against money laundering. The chapter concludes with a summary of the main findings of the research.

II. AN OUTLINE OF THE GREEK GOLDEN VISA PROGRAMME

The Greek golden visa programme launched in 2013 via Law 4146/2013, in the hope of boosting market confidence and enhancing state's savings.[7] Soon that legislation was replaced by Law 4251/2014 – the Immigration and Social Integration Code[8] – which introduced important reforms on granting residence permits to third-country nationals, including by investment. Law 4251/2014 has been amended multiple times through Laws 4332/2015,[9] 4399/2016,[10] 4540/2018,[11] 4546/2018,[12] 4587/2018,[13] 4589/2019,[14] 4605/2019,[15] 4634/2019,[16] 4764/2020[17] and 5007/2022[18] to primarily fill in legislative gaps. As the Immigration and Social Integration

[4] Enterprise Greece – the competent national authority for attracting foreign investment has noted that since 2013 the number of residence permits granted have been: 20 in 2013, 364 in 2014, 773 in 2015, 1258 in 2016, 2216 in 2017, 4107 in 2018, 7535 in 2019 and 7905 in 2020.

[5] 'Τι σημαίνει το φρένο από Κομισιόν στη «Χρυσή Βίζα» (λίστες)' (*Newmoney*, 10 April 2022) www.newmoney.gr/roh/palmos-oikonomias/tourismos/ti-simeni-to-freno-apo-komision-sti-chrisi-viza-listes/.

[6] For the most comprehensive analysis of Greek golden visas see Archontaki, *Golden Visa* (Nomiki Vivliothiki 2021). There is some reference to Greece's golden visa programme in Surak, 'Who Wants to Buy a Visa?' (2022) 30 *JCES* 151. Also see Surak and Tsuzuki, 'Are Golden Visas a Golden Opportunity?'; Džankić, 'Immigrant Investor Programmes in the EU' (2018) 26 *JCES* 64.

[7] Law on Creation of a Development Friendly Environment for Strategic and Private Investments 2013 (GR); See Carassava, 'Bond Buyers to Land Greece's Golden Visa' (*The Times*, 22 October 2018) www.thetimes.co.uk/article/bond-buyers-to-land-greece-s-golden-visa-wplx6qp62.

[8] Immigration and Social Integration Code of Greece 2014 (GR).

[9] Law 4332/2015 (GR).

[10] Law 4399/2016 (GR).

[11] Law 4540/2018 (GR).

[12] Law 4546/2018 (GR).

[13] Law 4587/2018 (GR).

[14] Law 4589/2019 (GR).

[15] Law 4605/2019 (GR).

[16] Law 4634/2019 (GR).

[17] Law 4764/2019 (GR).

[18] Law 5007/2022 (GR).

Code was followed by many legislative amendments and additional Ministerial Decisions that regulated not only investment residence permits, but also other kinds of residence permits, the Ministry of Migration and Asylum proposed in March 2023 the codification of all relevant provisions that concern 'legal' migration in an 'Immigration Code'.[19] The investment visa is regulated in Articles 94 to100 of the Immigration Code, but there are no substantive differences from the previous legal framework.[20]

At the time of writing, the applicable legislation was Law 4251/2014, and the analysis in this chapter is primarily based on its provisions. However, with the new Code of Law coming into force on 1 January 2024, this chapter also highlights relevant amendments and substantive changes introduced by the updated legal framework.[21] Law 4251/2014 envisages two types of golden visas: (a) in accordance with its Article 16; these concern individuals whose investment will have a positive impact on national growth and economy (Article 16A); strategic investments (Article 16B); or investments in products, such as the acquisition of bonds (Article 16Γ); and (b) in accordance with Article 20B, concerning permanent residence permits granted to individuals who purchase property in Greece or enter a long-term lease agreement concerning a touristic property. The following subsections will examine each in turn and then look into the application process and rights derived from the issuance of an investment residence permit.

A. Investment Residence Permits under Article 16 of Law 4251/2014

Article 16 of Law 4251/2014 foresees the issuance of residence permits in respect of investment activities under the following requirements: (a) the applicant must be a third-country national (non-EU/EEA and non-Swiss);[22] (b) who has lawfully entered Greece holding a national or Schengen visa or is lawful resident in Greece, irrespective of the type of residence permit or visa, which may even be issued by another EU Member State. This means that even a short-stay (type C) visa or a long-stay (type D) visa which may be issued by another Schengen country gives the applicant the ability to enter Greece and settle issues regarding the purchase of the property as well as to apply for the golden visa; (c) the applicant must conduct investment activities in Greece. Depending on the type of the investment, Article 16 distinguishes among three types of investment residence permits.

The first one is regulated by Article 16A and concerns a five-year investment residence permit to be issued for an investment that will have a positive impact on national growth and the economy. What this vague legal term means is determined by the Ministry of Development and Investments, which is responsible for assessing the investment.

[19] Law 5038/2023 (GR).

[20] The new provisions are codified as such: Art 94: 'Requirements for the applicants', Art 95: 'Duration of residence permits for investment reasons', Art 96: 'Strategic investments' (Type B1), Art 97: 'Residence permits for the establishment of business' (Type B2), Art 98: 'Executives of companies established in Greece, affiliated companies located in Greece that carry out commercial or other activity' (Type B3), Art 99: 'Investments in assets' (Type B4), Art 100: 'Investments in property' (Type B5).

[21] The new Immigration Code only codifies the previous provisions that regulated investment visa, and thus, the applicable rules and framework remain almost the same. That said, the requirements, the procedure, the duration of valid residence permits, the notion of 'family members' and most of the golden visa thresholds remain the same. In some cases, such as investments in assets, the threshold is increased.

[22] Citizens of the United Kingdom can apply for the golden visa programme as of January 2021.

The Ministry enjoys discretion, but factors that are taken into account for assessing the impact on national development are job creation, promotion of domestic resources and vertical integration of domestic production, export orientation, innovation and adoption of new technology, without though providing any quantitative indicators (eg precise number of jobs) that will be taken into account to assess the positive impact on national development and economy.[23] The legislation also does not provide much clarification as regards the type of investment and the financial threshold that is required. There are no restrictions regarding the sector of activity or the location of the investment project, the only requirement being that the investment is to have a positive impact on national growth and the economy. The legislation also does not set specific limits regarding the total cost of the investment project, however, pursuant to Joint Ministerial Decision 53969/2014,[24] each investor applying under this programme should contribute to the investment with an amount of at least €250,000 available through their own funds (therefore not through a loan obtained in his country of origin).[25] This amount has been increased to €500,000 as of 1 September 2024.[26] The investment activity may be pursued by either a natural person or a legal entity, which can be either foreign or constituted under domestic law, in which case depending on the amount of the investment the beneficiaries of the residence permits may be up to three third-country nationals who are shareholders or executives of the legal entity.[27]

The second type of investment residence permit is regulated in Article 16B and concerns a 10-year permit[28] to be issued for strategic investments. The term strategic investment is chosen to denote their strategic importance for the national or regional economy in that they can bring about considerable results quantitatively and qualitatively to the increase in employment, what is termed as 'productive restructure' – a concept understood as mechanisms to re-integrate unemployed persons in production – and the promotion of the country's environment, including the cultural one.[29] Law 4864/2021 sets the specific requirements that are needed to consider an investment as 'strategic investment'.[30]

The strategic investments are categorised depending on the budget and new employment posts in five groups, as indicated by Table 13.1 below. Depending on the category, there may be other incentives, for example in relation to taxation.[31]

[23] 'Residence Permits: For Investment activity in Greece' (Enterprise Greece 2017) 8 www.enterprisegreece.gov.gr/images/public/pdf-files/resident-permits-AUG16_EN_WEB.pdf.

[24] Joint Ministerial Decision No 53969/2014 (GR).

[25] 'Residence Permits: For Investment activity in Greece' (Enterprise Greece 2017) 8. The funds must come from the investor themselves, which means that a loan is not sufficient.

[26] Art 92 of Law 5079/2023 (GR).

[27] Under the residence by investment which will have a positive impact on national growth and the economy and the residence by strategic investment schemes, entry and residence are allowed to a maximum of nine other third-country nationals (investors, experts and executives) to implement the investment.

[28] The duration of the residence permit issued for strategic investments will be reduced to five years according to Art 95 of the Immigration Code 2023 (GR), which specifies that all residence permits for investment purposes will be of five-year duration.

[29] Archontaki, *Golden Visa*, 36.

[30] Art 2 (2) of the Law 4864/2021 (GR).

[31] The details that concern strategic investments were initially regulated in Law 4608/2019 (GR) which was then replaced by the Law 4864/2021 (GR). The many incentives that concern strategic investments are regulated in this legal framework and concern spatial (location) incentives, tax incentives, 'fast track' licensing, and aid for operating expenditure (Arts 7, 8, 9 and 10 of the Law 4864/2021). For further information, see Archontaki, *Golden Visa*, 36–48.

Table 13.1 Strategic Investment Categories

	Budget and employment thresholds	Spatial (location) incentives	Tax incentives	"Fast track" licensing	Aid for operating expenditure
Strategic Investments 1	> EUR 75 million	X	X*	X	
	> EUR 40 million and ≥ 75 FTEs	X	X	X	X**
Strategic Investments 2	≥ EUR 20 million (in various fields)		X	X	X**
	> EUR 30 million and ≥ 50 FTEs		X	X	X**
	> EUR 20 million and ≥ 40 FTEs (organized recipients/industrial areas)		X	X	X**
Flagship investments of exceptional importance	Distinguished legal entities that promote the green economy, innovation, technology, as well as a low energy and environmental footprint economy	X	X	X	X**
Fast-track strategic investments	> EUR 20 million and ≥ 30 FTEs			X	X**
	> EUR 10 million and ≥ 30 FTEs (already existing strategic investments)			X	X**
	> EUR 15 million and ≥ 100 FTEs (existing investments in restructuring)			X	
Automatic strategic investments	> EUR 20 million for investments under Law 3389/2005 and investments for European Energy Projects of Common Interest (IPCEI)		X*	X	
	Strategic investments of spatial organization of enterprises for the development of business parks under Law 3982/2011 (area of 500 acres and budget> EUR 10 million)	X	X	X	

Source: Deloitte (Deloitte | tax@hand (taxathand.com)).

* Only stabilization of income tax rate.

** Conditions apply.

Regarding the procedure for the characterisation of an investment as 'strategic investment', the Law foresees that the applicant should lodge the application and the necessary documents[32] to Enterprise Greece SA and pay the fee equal to 0.01 per cent of the total investment cost.[33]

[32] The proposed investment's business plan, a financial analysis of the total investment budget and the financing structure, documentation that proves the ownership status of the investment, an investment impact assessment, proof of payment of the fee, supporting documentation such as a detailed description of the aid requested and the costs incurred.

[33] Art 12 of the Law 4864/2021 (GR).

The Enterprise Greece SA will conduct the assessment and provide an opinion regarding the characterization of the investment as 'strategic'.[34] This assessment and the file will then be forwarded to the General Secretariat for Private Investments of the Ministry of Development and Investments which will decide whether to classify the investment as strategic and decide for the granted incentives.[35] The General Secretariat will also be responsible for the monitoring of the implementation process of each investment.

Third, as for investments under Article 16Γ, these concern the following eight categories of acquiring intangible instruments (securities):

(a) Contribution of funds amounting at least to €400,000 (this amount will be increased to €500,000 according to Article 98 of the Immigration Code) to a company with registered seat or an establishment in Greece for the acquisition of stocks through a capital stock increase or acquisition of bonds in the case of issuance of a bond;

(b) Contribution of funds amounting at least to €400,000, to a Real Estate Investment Company (ΑΕ Επενδύσεων σε Ακίνητη Περιουσία (ΑΕΕΑΠ)) the purpose of which is investing solely in Greece[36] for the acquisition of stocks through a capital stock. The fact that the company is investing in property in Greece does not prevent the investor in making investments in other Member States and therefore freedom of movement of capital is violated.

(c) Contribution of funds amounting at least to €400,000, to an Alternative Investments Scheme (Οργανισμός Εναλλακτικών Επενδύσεων ΟΕΕ) and in particular in a Venture Capital Company (Εταιρεία Κεφαλαίου Επιχειρηματικών Συμμετοχών (ΕΚΕΣ)), regulated in Article 5 of Law 2367/1995,[37] to acquire stocks, or to a venture fund (Αμοιβαίο Κεφάλαιο Επιχειρηματικών Συμμετοχών (ΑΚΕΣ), regulated in Article 7 of Law 2992/2002.[38] A condition is that the specific Alternative Investments Schemes (OEE) are willing to exclusively invest in enterprises with registered seat or an establishment in Greece.

(d) Purchase of Greek Government bonds with an acquisition value of at least €400,000 and remaining term of at least three years. The purchase must be realised via credit institution established in Greece;

(e) Fixed term deposit of and amount of at least €400,000 in a Greek bank with at least a term of one (1) year, with a fixed renewal;

(f) Purchase of stocks, corporate bonds or Greek Government bonds with an acquisition value of at least €800,000 which are traded in regulated markets or via multilateral trading facilities in Greece;

(g) Purchase of shares with an acquisition value of at least €400,000 in a mutual fund incorporated in Greece whose object is exclusively to invest in stock, corporate bonds and./or Greek Government Bonds in regulated markets or via multilateral trading facilities in Greece;

(h) Purchase of shares or stocks of at least €400,000 in an Alternative Investment Scheme (OEE) incorporated with the purpose of investing in real estate in Greece only.

[34] The characteristics that are assessed to characterise an investment as 'strategic' include among others financial sustainability, extroversion, innovation, competitiveness, universal planning, environmental, economic and social impact in local and national level, saving of natural resources, perspective of cyclical economy, high added value especially in the sectors of financial activities regarding international traded goods and services.

[35] Arts 13 and 15 of the Law 4864/2021 (GR).

[36] For the restrictions on the capital movement and possible justifications, see Kudryashova, 'The Sale of Conditional EU Citizenship' (2018) 3 *European Papers* 1265. For an overview, see Horsley, 'Death, Taxes and (Targeted) Judicial Dynamism' in Arnull and Chalmers (eds), *The Oxford Handbook of European Union Law* (Oxford University Press 2015).

[37] Law 2367/1995 (GR) as amended.

[38] Law 2992/2002 (GR).

In such cases, a five-year residence permit can be issued following a decision by the Minister of Migration and Asylum, and the permit can be renewed with the same duration each time, as long as it is certified that the investor still holds the investment.

B. Investment Residence Permits under Article 20B of Law 4251/2014

With regard to investments under Article 20B, which regulates investments in property, it foresees that the application must be lodged either to the competent Decentralised Administration unit (Συντονιστής της Αποκεντρωμένης Διοίκησης),[39] or since 2020, to the competent department for investment residence permits of the Greek Ministry of Migration and Asylum (Υπουργείο Μετανάστευσης και Ασύλου). Thus, there is a co-responsibility of the aforementioned authorities; in fact, since 2020 most of the applications are centrally lodged in the Ministry of Migration and Asylum. However. according to a new Ministerial Decision no. 674588/2022,[40] all applications for a golden visa should be lodged exclusively online as of 14 November 2022.[41]

The residence permit is issued for five years, provided that the eligibility criteria are met.[42] These are the following: (a) the applicant must be a national of a non-EU/EEA state and must have entered Greece lawfully with any type of visa (either Schengen[43] or national visa) or be lawfully residing in the country, even if the residence permit does not allow change of purpose for residence;[44] (b) with a clear criminal record;[45] and (c) medical insurance both for themselves and for any accompanying family members. In terms of the investment-related criteria, the applicant must own real estate property in Greece – through purchase, inheritance or donation – either personally or through a legal entity of which they own the total of the company shares, provided the minimum value of the property is €250,000.[46] The investment

[39] The Decentralised Administrations are regional administration units that operate under the Ministry of Interior, but are not part of the local government; For more details, see 'Decentralized Administration' (Αποκεντρωμένη Διοίκηση Πελοποννήσου-Δυτικής Ελλάδας-Ιονίου) www.apd-depin.gov.gr/index.php/2018-11-18-00-35-23/organization-chart-english.

[40] Ministerial Decision 674588/2022 (GR).

[41] The competent processing authorities remain the same: the Decentralised Administrations and the Ministry of Migration and Asylum.

[42] In the case of golden visas issued on account of strategic investments, the duration of the residence permit is 10 years.

[43] Even if that Schengen visa was issued by another Member State.

[44] If these requirements are not met, then it is necessary that the individual obtains a national visa for the issuance of a residence permit by residence. The issuance of the permit can be done either after the conclusion of the contract or before it even starts or during the process.

[45] The criminal record is verified as follows: the applicant must provide a copy of their criminal record by the foreign authorities. In case where a judgment irrespective of the sentence has been issued, and in order to detect whether the criminal offence is connected to reasons creating a risk for public order or public security, specific justification is required by balancing different factors such as the seriousness of the offence, whether the offender is a repeat one and in general the criminal behaviour of the third-country national. See 'Χορήγηση άδειας διαμονής στην Ελλάδα λόγω αγοράς ακινήτων ή στρατηγικής επένδυσης' (Ministry of Foreign Affairs, July 2013) www.mfa.gr/missionsabroad/images/stories/missions/uae/docs/adeies_ependytes_el.pdf.

[46] This includes acquisition of land on which construction takes place. What matters is the actual price paid, therefore even if the objective value of the property is less than €250,000, this is not an obstacle for the application so long as the contract refers to an amount equal or above the minimum requirement. In case of inheritance, the objective value of the property is important at the time of the inheritance. Therefore, for example, if a minor inherits property below the required amount, even if that property increases in value until the minor reaches the age of 18, they still cannot apply for a residence permit. Moreover, cases of acquisition of property even before 2014 is possible provided the requirements are fulfilled. Co-ownership signifies that each of the owners must have invested at least €250,000. Finally, it does not matter whether the investment is one property or more with total value of more than €250,000.

amount has been increased to €500,000, according to Article 100 of the new Immigration Code, in some areas such as in the greater area of Athens (centre, northern and southern suburbs), the Municipality of Thessaloniki, Mykonos and Santorini.[47] For the other regions of Greece, the amount will remain at €250,000; or they make a leasing agreement with a minimum term of 10 years for the lease of hotel accommodation or furnished tourist residences in tourist accommodation complexes which are worth minimum €250,000; or they make a time sharing agreement (lease) for at least 10 years in respect of property which is worth a minimum of €250,000; such an agreement is the commitment of the lessor to grant, each year, to the lessee, for the duration of the timeshare, the use of the tourist accommodation and to provide to them the relevant services for the determined period of time according to the contract, and the lessee must pay the agreed rent.

Since 2019, there is also the possibility for a capital contribution with a minimum level of €400,000 to a company with its registered office in Greece for the acquisition of shares of real estate property, companies or bonds. In addition, there is the option to acquire a permit if the applicant makes a deposit of €400,000 to a Greek bank or an investment of €800,000 in corporate or government bonds. Finally, according to the Greek Legal Council of the State,[48] cases of naked selling, whereby the applicant has given the full or part of the amount of money for the purchase before the contract, at a time where the seller had not been owner of the later sold property are not precluded from the application process.[49]

There are limitations as regards the property; Article 25 of Law 1892/1990 prohibits third-country nationals (and to foreign legal entities) to purchase land or acquire other interests in land in remote areas (such as certain islands, or regions close to the Northern and Eastern borders) without prior issuance of relevant permit by the Greek Ministry of Defence.[50] Third-country nationals may apply for purchasing properties in those regions stating among others the purpose for which the property will be used. A dedicated committee decides on lifting the ban in each concrete case.[51] Therefore, in cases where land is situated in those areas, prospective buyers have to undergo the same process. Furthermore, in December 2022 Law 5007/2022 was adopted increasing the threshold in connection with specific regions in Athens (city centre, northern and southern suburbs), Thessaloniki, Mykonos and Santorini.[52] Furthermore, in such cases the possibility that the investment may involve several properties is abolished The revised legal framework entered into force at the end of 2023, and a transitional period was foreseen during which applicants could still benefit from the lower threshold to apply for a residence permit. In particular, applicants had until the 31st of July 2023 to sign draft agreements for the purchase of real estate property (accompanied by a 10 percent deposit), with the finalisation of contracts required by the end of 2023. If, for any reason, there was no longer an agreement, prospective applicants could sign a draft agreement for another property even after 31st July 2023, provided the purchase was completed by the end of 2023.[53] In practice, the transition

[47] Art 100 of the Law 5038/2023 (GR). This amendment came into force on 1 September 2024.

[48] The Greek Legal Council of State is the body providing legal assistance to the Greek Government, for example, by representing the Government before national, EU and international courts and providing legal opinions on matters requested by the administration.

[49] Opinion 184/2021, Legal Council of the State (GR).

[50] Law 1892/1990 (GR).

[51] Art 26 of Law 1892/1990 (GR).

[52] The same is foreseen in the forthcoming Immigration Code of Greece (Art 100). Thus, there will be two different thresholds depending on the area that the property is located.

[53] Nesheim, 'Greece extends Golden Visa Transition Period by another 3 Months to July 31st' (*Imidaily*, 1 April 2023).

period was extended even further following the entry into force of the new Immigration Code, with the new thresholds becoming applicable as of September 2024.

The extent to which the residence permit may be issued to minors has been subject to debate. The Greek Legal Council of State in its Opinion 22/2020 clarified that there is no requirement under Article 20B that the residence permit applicant must be an adult except in cases where the individual comes by the property through inheritance or parental donation, thus without financial inflow in the country.[54] Indeed, a teleological interpretation of the legislation points in the direction that the national legislator linked the issuance of the permit with the lawful financial investment in Greece and the guarantee that the individual's presence will not jeopardise public order or public security. Requirements of subjective nature concerning the age of the individual are not requirement. As a result, even minors through their parents and/or guardians have the right to apply and acquire a residence permit in Greece if the conditions mentioned above are met.[55]

C. Application Process, Beneficiaries and Rights

The application process for the residence permit comprises of four steps, including as a first step the lodging of an application for a visa or residence permit, in case the applicant does not hold one. The application for an investment residence permit constitutes the second step, whereby the applicant must gather the relevant documents, laid down in Ministerial Decision 30825/2014,[56] which are the following: the application form, a certified copy of a valid passport or other travel document recognised by Greece with the valid national visa, four photographs, a certificate of payment of the €2,000 application fee,[57] service fee (€16), comprehensive sickness insurance, certificate on whether the property has been used for the issuance of investment residence permit, signature sample and documents concerning the investment property. This concerns documents, such as the contract and registration of the contract with the Greek Land Register, a certificate issued by the notary who composed the purchase contract, invoices issued by the contractors and other necessary certificates and evidence that concern the investment.[58] In relation to applications for residence permits under Article 16, these are subject to additional requirements regarding documentation, which differ depending on the types of investments (under Articles 16A, 16B or 16Γ).[59]

[54] Opinion 22/2020, Legal Council of the State (GR). See Art 3(2) of Law 4587/2018 (GR).

[55] There is a minority opinion according to which residence permits applicants must be adults.

[56] Joint Ministerial Decision 30825/2014 (GR) specifying the documents for the issuance of national entry permits and the grant and renewal of residence permit in accordance with the provisions of Law 4251-2014 (GR).

[57] For family members the fee is 150 and there is no fee for children below 18. However, it has been observed that in practice with regard to children above the age of 13 an application fee is also requested considered that at the end of the five-year residence permit they will be 18. This interpretation is not supported by the law or by any ministerial guidance. See Archontaki, *Golden Visa*, 72–73.

[58] The specifying documents can be found on the website of the Ministry of Migration and Asylum, 'Golden Visa' (Ministry of Migration & Asylum, 21 May 2020) https://migration.gov.gr/en/golden-visa/; in principle the value of the property is estimated based on what is mentioned in the contract and must have been paid in full until lodging the application for a residence permit.

[59] For example, with regard to investments under Art 16A it is necessary to provide documentation presenting the investment plan, presenting the investor (eg a biographical note) and documentation regarding the feasibility of the investor to cover the investment through own funds. Under Art 16B a document necessary is one by the Ministerial Group on Strategic Investments that the investment is considered as strategic. Finally, for Art 16Γ documentation regarding the type of investment is also necessary verifying the investment. For the detailed list of those necessary documents see Joint Ministerial Decision 46440/2019 (GR).

Under the third step, the relevant documents must be lodged for consideration. Article 155 of Law 4764/2020 foresees the possibility of applying for an investment residence permit via a lawyer, who has been specifically authorised to do so on behalf of the investor.[60] This means that the applicant is not required to be physically present in Greece to submit the application and accompanying documentation, provided that the residence permit concerns cases under Article 20B. The applicant is then required within 12 months to enter Greece to provide their biometric data, namely two fingerprints. This rule was expanded to cases of Article 16A and 16Γ following the adoption of Law 5007/2022.

Provided that the application fulfils all the requirements, under the fourth step the residence permit will be issued. The processing period is two months, but there may be delays due to incomplete application files or other impediments. According to the Ministry of Migration and Asylum, the golden visa application is usually decided within six months but it may take even longer if the submitted file is not complete.[61] Investment residence permits under Article 16B though are granted within five days.

Furthermore, with regard to the beneficiaries of residence permits, there are two main issues to be clarified; first that under the Article 16 rules it is possible for more than one person to be granted a residence permit depending on the value of the investment. Second, in relation to family members of the residence permit holder they can apply for a residence permit in Greece, which will be valid for the same duration with the initial investor's residence permit.[62] This concerns the spouse or the partner of the investor, the parents of both the investor and their spouse or partner, and their unmarried mutual children below the age of 21, including the partner's children if they are also recognised by the applicant.[63] Spouses are considered those that are married, or in civil marriage, while partners in registered partnership have also the right to apply for an equal duration residence permit. The law does not specify further whether it concerns same-sex or different-sex couples, but the important factor is to be married or in registered partnership. Also, the law refers to only one spouse or partner, thus solely one partner can benefit from this scheme, in case for example it concerns application from a polygamous applicant. Also, the law specifies that the application concerns both the biological and adopted children, as well as the legally recognised children of the investor that are below the age of 21.

The validity of the residence permits under Article 20B is initially for five years and can be renewed every two years throughout the period that the investor remains the owner of the property. Therefore, if in the meantime, the individual sells the property and buys another one still fulfilling the required amount of money, the permit will not be renewed, because the permit is attached to the specific property. The validity of the residence permits under Article 16 varies depending on the investment (five or ten years, as mentioned above).

[60] See Art 155, Law 4764/2020 (GR).

[61] Applications for cancellation of a decision on the rejection, withdrawal or renewal of a residence permit (appeals) must be filed with the competent administrative court within a reasonable period of time and not more than six months from delivery of the contested decision in accordance with the provisions of Art 15 of Law 3068/2002 (GC) (Law on Compliance of the Administration with judicial decisions, promotion of judges of regular administrative courts to the level of State Counsellor and other provisions of 14 November 2002 (Νόμος Υπ' Αριθμό 3068 Συμμόρφωση της Διοίκησης προς τις δικαστικές αποφάσεις, προαγωγή των δικαστών των τακτικών διοικητικών δικαστηρίων στο βαθμό του συμβούλου Επικρατείας και άλλες διατάξεις), Law 3036/2002 (GC).

[62] See Art 20B (4) of Law 4251/2014 (GR); all family members will have to pay the application fee and lodge a separate application.

[63] In the case of children above the age of 21, they are able to renew the residence permit for three years with the sole requirement to submit the previous residence permit for family reunification reasons. After the age of 24, further renewal is possible in accordance with domestic provisions.

Furthermore, the investment residence permit under Article 16 can be renewed for the same duration, as long as the investor still maintains the investment. Revocation of the residence permit is possible when the requirements for its issuance are no longer fulfilled, in particular when the property is sold[64] or there are changes to the realisation of the investment under Article 16. It has been rightly argued that if the third-country national commits a criminal offence abroad or in Greece this is also a reason for revoking the permit.[65]

The investment residence permit affords recipients a diverse range of rights, extending beyond those already mentioned above and includes the right to stay in Greece, even though this is not strictly required; as such, the Greek Legal Council of State has opined that the programme envisages a right to stay.[66] The residence permit holders also benefit from free movement in the Schengen area, pursuant to the Schengen Borders Code.[67] It also allows access for short stays to Bulgaria, Cyprus and Romania based on the unilateral recognition of residence permits by these Member States. Moreover, there may be an impact on the acquisition of the EU Long-Term Residence status, which is conferred on third-country nationals who have resided legally and continuously in an EU Member State for five years.[68] Importantly, the five years for which the residence permit is valid are counted towards the total of seven years that are required for the acquisition of Greek citizenship,[69] as long as the other conditions for such acquisition such as language criteria, pass of the Greek citizenship test and other due diligence requirements are also met.[70] Physical presence of at 183 days per year for the entire period is also necessary for acquisition of citizenship. With regard to the right to employment, there exist divergent rules depending on the type of investment residence permit, In particular, investment residence permits under Article 16 of Law 4251/2014 allows holders to exercise the particular entrepreneurial activity for which the permit has been granted; it is precisely due to their status as shareholders or CEOs of the legal entity that will exercise the activity or their participation in the strategic investment that are granted the permit. However, Article 20B(6) grants the right to employment to individuals only when it involves the exercise of economic activity in the capacity of a shareholder or Chief Executive Officer of companies established before the application for a residence permit under this scheme. This is by contrast to other similar programmes running in EU Member States, such as in Spain, where a golden visa allows the investor to live and work in the country.[71] Family members who are issued a residence permit do not have similar access to the labour market, but they do have access to public education.

[64] Art 20B(5)(γ) of Law 4251/14 (GR).

[65] Archontaki, *Golden Visa*, 96. How the commission of a criminal offence abroad would become known to the authorities is however unclear.

[66] Opinion 22/2020, Legal Council of the State (GR) 21–22.

[67] Regulation No 2016/399 Union Code on the rules governing the movement of persons across borders (Schengen Borders Code) [2016] OJ L77/1.

[68] Council Directive 2003/109/EC concerning the status of third-country nationals who are long-term residents [2004] OJ L 16/44. See further in Sarmiento and van den Brink, 'EU Competence and Investor Migration' in Kochenov and Surak (eds), *Citizenship and Residence Sales* (Cambridge University Press 2023).

[69] According to Art 4, Income Tax Code 2013 (GR), an individual is a tax resident of Greece, provided that they: (a) have their permanent or principal place of residence or habitual residence or the center of their vital interests, namely their personal or economic or social ties in Greece; and (b) have a physical presence in Greece for a period of more than 183 days in any 12-month period, uninterruptedly or with breaks.

[70] Arts 89–90, Law 4251/2014 (GR). For the acquisition of citizenship see Art 5 of Law 3284/2004 (GR) as amended by Ministerial Decision 130181/6353/7.3.2018 (GR); see also Mavrommatis, 'Greek Citizenship Tradition in Flux?' (2018) 46 *Nationalities Papers* 484; see also Kokkinidou et al, 'Naturalisation and the Acquisition of Citizenship' in Mattheoudakis et al (eds), *Migration and Language Education in Southern Europe* (Cambridge Scholars Publishing 2021).

[71] Holleran, 'Buying up the Semi-Periphery' (2021) 86 *Journal of Anthropology* 730.

III. PRACTICAL IMPLEMENTATION

Regrettably, there is no statistical information available regarding the issuance of investment residence permits under Article 16, but there are data on those granted in accordance with Article 20B, albeit provided in a fragmentary manner. As Figure 13.1 shows, in the first years of the residence by investment scheme – 2014–17 – almost 6,000 golden visas were issued.[72] Under the right-hand bars, residence permits of both initial investors and their family members are indicated and the left-hand bars correspond to the residence permits issued only for the investors.

Figure 13.1 Breaking Down the Investment Residence Permits Issued per Year (2014–17)

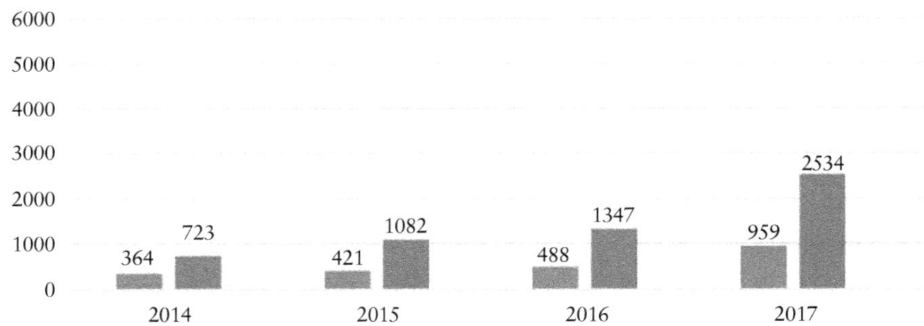

Source: Tyrovolas, 2020.

As shown by Figures 13.2 and 13.3, between 2018–22, 16,411 investment residence applications were lodged, leading to 11,763 issued permits, 4,483 pending permits, 112 rejections and 63 withdrawals. The decrease in the number of applications since 2020 is attributed to the COVID-19 pandemic mainly due to travel restrictions hindering applicants from coming to Greece (ie to give fingerprints).

Figure 13.2 Total number of golden visa applications in the period 2018–22

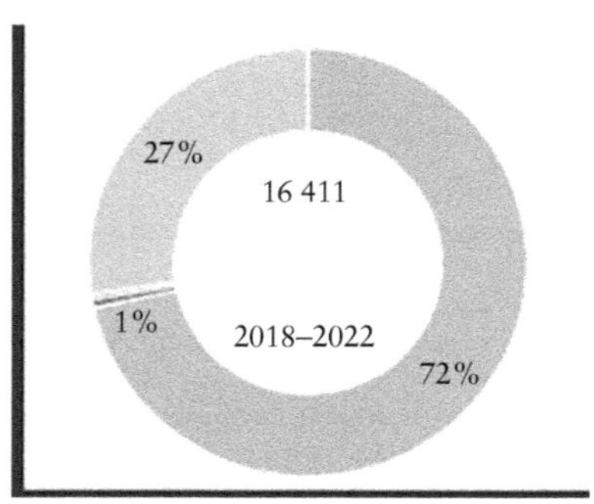

Source: Greek Ministry of Migration and Asylum (December 2022).

[72] In the years 2014–17, the Ministry of Migration and Asylum was not the competent authority for the issuance of residence permits based on the Greek golden visa programme and thus there are no official data published for that period. For this reason, we refer to the data that concern the issued residence permits (2014–17) as they were provided by the Ministry of Citizen Protection.

Figure 13.3 Breaking Down the Applications per Year (2018–22)

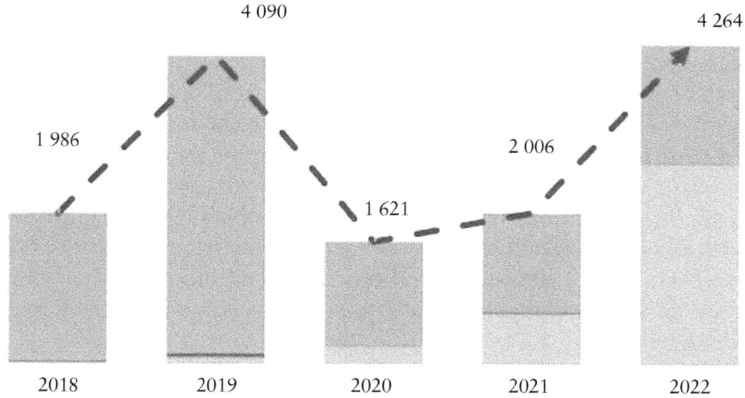

Source: Greek Ministry of Migration and Asylum (December 2022).

Overall, 72 per cent of the applications were successful, 27 per cent are pending cases, while only a striking 1 per cent of submitted applications were rejected. According to informal discussions with the officers of the relevant department of the Greek Ministry of Migration and Asylum, the rejections mainly concern the lack of submission of certain essential documents. The role of the lawyer is important in the process as she or he informs the applicant about the documents that are needed as well as the application process. Also, as they have expertise in the applicable legal framework, they can provide sound legal advice on the applicants' investment and ways to avoid a possible rejection. It is however possible to apply without a lawyer. The competent authority conducts a procedural check of the submitted documents, and in cases where all the necessary documents are submitted along with the application form, the residence permit is issued. Therefore, it is possible that lawyers representing their clients minimise the risk of rejection, given their expertise in the process. While the approval rate for golden visa applications is relatively high, these programs are typically vetted for financial eligibility, as they involve substantial investments, rather than the traditional criteria applied to Schengen visas which are issued for short-term travel purposes and also have a high approval rate (12.5 per cent rejection rate).[73] That said, a more holistic check must have been conducted when the applicant applies for a visa, in accordance with the Visa Code, or residence permit, under national law, as a prerequisite for applying for an investment residence permit, in which case the applicant must further submit a criminal record and a health certificate. In most cases, a common reason for turning down an application has been the failure of the applicant to comply with the specific procedure that must be followed regarding the payment for the property; either because the means of payment used was not in line with the requirements of the law – this was particularly the case prior to the adoption of Law 4635/2019 which allowed Point of Sale (POS) transactions as an acceptable means of payment[74] – or because the full

[73] See '2022 Schengen Visa Statistics for Schengen Countries' (SchengenVisaInfo) https://statistics.schengenvisainfo.com/.

[74] One such example is the case of Papaevangelou who had set up a company selling property to Chinese nationals using POS, though not foreseen under the Greek law, as a means to bypass capital controls in China. A series of transactions were made prior to the adoption of the law, but the Law 4635/2019 (GR) applies in retrospect since 1 January 2017, thus lifting the unlawful character of these transactions.

amount was not paid before the completion of the contract.[75] Nevertheless, there is no statistical information on the visa or residence permits applicants who intended to apply for an investment residence permit and were rejected.

With regard to the total number of currently valid residence permits, Figure 13.4 demonstrates that this corresponds to more than 30,000 active residence permits as of December 2022. The majority of the valid residence permits concern the family members of the initial investor (56 per cent), whereas only 31 per cent of the valid residence permits corresponds to the initial investor's permit.[76] The remaining 13 per cent concerns renewals of residence permits, either of the initial investor or their family members. During informal discussions with the Ministry it was clarified that most residence permits by investment concern the investor's family members, as the law fosters a rather wide definition of who can be considered as a 'family member' of the initial investor, which goes a bit beyond the immediate family, which typically includes partner and children.

Figure 13.4 Total number of valid investment residence permits as of December 2022

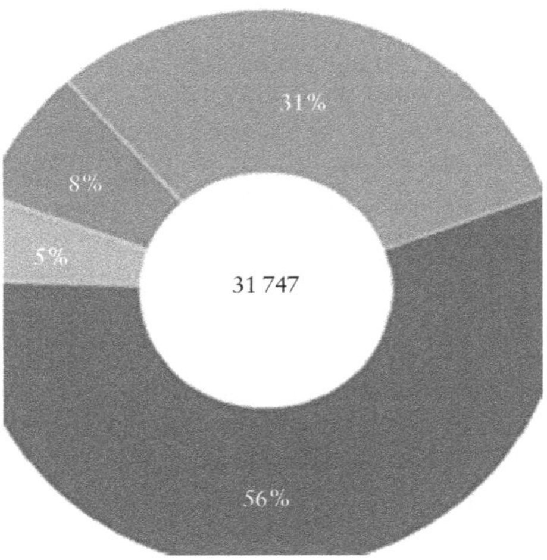

Source: Greek Ministry of Migration and Asylum.

Finally, in terms of the nationalities that usually benefit from the Greek 'golden visa' programme, the first years it attracted Chinese nationals and third-country nationals from Egypt, Lebanon and Russia. Following the failed *coup d'etat* in Turkey in 2016, Turkish nationals also sought to benefit from the investment visa programme in Greece in order to acquire a residence permit and use it a 'safe pathway' to the West.[77] Overall, from the establishment of the scheme until the end of 2022, 62.8 per cent of all investment residence permits have been granted to Chinese investors; followed by Turkish (6.4 per cent) and Russian (4.1 per cent) nationals. 4 per cent of residence permits holders come from Lebanon, 2.8 per cent from Iran and another 2.8 per cent from Egypt.[78] That said, since March 2022, the Ministry of Migration and Asylum

[75] For example, see Decision 488/2020, Athens Administrative Court.

[76] The most recent data report was issued in December 2022. Important data and statistics can be found at 'Information Note' (Ministry of Migration and Asylum 2022) Αύγουστος-2022_ΥΜΑ-GR-Ενημερωτικό-Αύγουστος-Β-Νόμιμη-Μετανάστευση_ΝΕΑ-ΕΚΔΟΣΗ.pdf (migration.gov.gr).

[77] Carassava, 'Turks mop up property in Greece' (*Deutsche Welle*, 14 May 2017).

[78] See all the reports, 'Statistics' (Ministry of Migration and Asylum) Στατιστικά | Υπουργείο Μετανάστευσης και Ασύλου (migration.gov.gr).

has suspended the examination of applications for investment residence permits by Russian nationals and this concerns both pending applications and new applications.[79] The suspension of the examination of the applications from Russian nationals has happened in the shadow of the general EU policy to respond to the 'Russian aggression against Ukraine' where both the Parliament and the Commission referred to the need for a strict regulation of the residence by investment programmes, calling for the immediate termination of existing programmes to Russian and Belarusian nationals without though assessing the possible implications of this action to the success of the programme.[80] However, this recommendation was made in breach of EU law, which prohibits such nationality discrimination.[81] This is one of the reasons that Russian investors, as of the end of 2022, represented the 4.1 per cent of the total investors, while in the end of 2021, Russian nationals were representing 6.2 per cent of top 10 investors' nationalities (which was very close to Turkish, which is the second most common nationality since 2016, after Chinese). A lower percentage of residence permit holders corresponds to applicants from the United States of America (USA) (1.8 per cent) and the United Kingdom (2.0 per cent). Finally, 1 per cent concerns Israeli and 0.9 per cent Iraqi nationals.

IV. AN ANATOMY OF THE INVESTMENT RESIDENCE PERMITS IN GREECE: ARE THEY ATTRACTIVE AND, IF SO, WHY?

The interest of Greece in enhancing its economy through foreign investment in the post-crisis era, has turned the Greek 'golden visa' rules, particularly under Article 20B, into one of the most advantageous, affordable and thus overall attractive programmes in the EU, which represents a high number of the total approved permits in the EU alongside Portugal, Latvia and Spain.[82] Third-country nationals have the possibility to invest in properties in countries such as Greece or Portugal, which entitles them and their families to travel to the Schengen area for 90 days in any 180-day period and a pathway to citizenship.[83] However, the Greek golden visa scheme does not give the right to investors to work in Greece, while investors cannot also stay for a long period of time or work in other EU Member States, as the rule of a maximum stay of 90 days in any 180 days in the Schengen countries without a visa applies.[84] To acquire long-term residence status and be able to reside in another Member State for more than three months, the investor should fulfil the requirements envisaged in the Long-Term Resident Directive, such as legal and continuous residence within the territory of a Member State for five years.[85]

In the case of Greece, its attractiveness compared to other EU Member States may be attributed to three additional factors: first, for years the Greek legislation required one of the lowest investment thresholds which amounts to only €250,000 for real estate. There are some other

[79] 'Greece Freezes Golden Visa Program for Russian Citizens' (*Greek Travel Pages*, 28 February 2022) https://news.gtp.gr/2022/02/28/greece-freezes-golden-visa-program-for-russian-citizens/.

[80] See Kochenov and Basheska in this volume; Also see also European Parliament resolution on the Russian aggression against Ukraine (2022/2564(RSP)) [2022] IO C 125/2 and European Commission, 'Recommendation on immediate steps in the context of the Russian invasion of Ukraine in relation to investor citizenship schemes and investor residence schemes' C (2022)2028 final.

[81] For an overview, see Ganty et al, 'Unlawful Nationality-Based Bans from the Schengen Zone' (2022) 48 *YJIL* online 1.

[82] Surak and Tsuzuki, 'Are Golden Visas a Golden Opportunity?'.

[83] Berger, 'The ultra-wealthy are abandoning the American Dream for second residences in Portugal and Greece' (Portuguese Chamber of Commerce in the UK, 21 June 2022).

[84] Scherrer and Thirion, 'Citizenship by Investment (CBI) and Residence by Investment (RBI) schemes in the EU' (2018) EPRS.

[85] Chapter II of the Council Directive 2003/109/EC [2004] OJ L16/44; See also van den Brink, 'Revising Citizenship within the European Union' (2022) 23 *GLJ* 79.

EU countries that have a lower threshold such as Malta, or equal, such as Portugal and Latvia, while in countries such as Italy, Spain or Bulgaria the threshold for investments is €500,000 or above.[86] Also, the main applicant can purchase several properties to reach the investment amount of €250,000 in any part of Greece.[87] Thus, this amount may correspond to one or more properties. Article 20(B)(2) of Law 4251/14 allows the Minister of Finance, Development and Investment and the Minster of Migration and Asylum to amend the threshold though Joint Ministerial Decisions, as well to compile list of areas in the country for which a differentiated regime will be applicable with regard to the necessary threshold. Factors to be taken into account in this respect are the developmental objectives, touristic development, geographical position, and the prices of the real estate property in those areas. It appears that this clause has not been used yet; instead, in September 2022, the Greek Prime Minister announced the Government's intention to increase the investment threshold from €250,000 to €500,000 in some parts of Greece.[88] Indeed, as it was mentioned also earlier, the new Immigration Code increased the threshold in connection with specific regions in Athens (city centre, northern and southern suburbs), Thessaloniki, Mykonos and Santorini, to €500,000. Even with this amendment the Greek threshold will still be one of the lowest investment thresholds in the EU, matching that of Spain, as mentioned above. Whether the attractiveness of the Greek programme will remain is unclear, but one should also take into account that one of the competitive schemes, namely from Portugal will be scrapped in its entirety.[89]

Second, the residence permit issued is valid for five years, while in other countries such as Portugal and Spain, the first residence permit by investment is valid for two years only, with a possibility of renewal.[90] Moreover, the residence permit can be extended to the applicant's family members with the same validity period. The definition of family, as applied in this context, is quite liberal, enabling even the parents from both sides (the investor and their spouse /partner to benefit from a residence permit. In addition, with regard to citizenship rights, it is true that the legal framework does not grant holders of residence permits the automatic right to obtain citizenship. Therefore, the beneficiaries of these schemes must go through the ordinary naturalisation procedure to obtain citizenship,[91] which requires possession of a (permanent or long-term) residence permit and lawful residence in Greece for seven years;[92] sufficient knowledge of the Greek language, history and culture; a clear criminal record; sufficient subsistence means; and oath of allegiance within the year after the person has been naturalised. That said, for an investor who wishes to continue residing in Greece after five years of residence, the residence permit can be renewed for two years, and after seven years it is possible to apply for the Greek citizenship.

[86] The minimum investment amount for Malta Permanent Residence Programme is €150,000. In Latvia, the investment threshold is €250,000. In Portugal, the threshold is lower (€250,000) when it concerns investments in arts, reconstruction or refurbishment of works of national heritage. In Spain and Italy, the threshold is €500,000 and in Bulgaria €512,000. See Archontaki, *Golden Visa*, 11–20; 'European Golden Visas' (SchengenVisaInfo) www.schengenvisainfo.com/eu-golden-visas/.

[87] Botsiou, 'Greece welcomes investors golden visa and other residency programmes' (*Khaleej Times*, 28 October 2021).

[88] Considering the inflation rate in Greece in 2022 has been 9.3 per cent and in 2023 has been until August 2023 around 4 per cent this amounts to a significant increase.

[89] Nesheim, 'Portugal to Close Golden Visa Program in Its Entirety' (*Imidaily*, 16 February 2023 www.imidaily.com/program-updates/portugal-closes-golden-visa-program-in-its-entirety/.

[90] Gaspar and de Haro, 'Buying Citizenship?' (2020) 58 *International Migration* 58.

[91] Art 5, Law 3284/2004 (GR).

[92] As mentioned earlier, this entails the physical presence requirement is 183 days per year so that the permit holder can be considered a tax resident.

Third, there is no requirement for the investment residence holder to be physically present in Greece, not even to come to Greece to lodge the application. The applicant is only required for a one-off visit in Greece for the collection of biometric identifiers (facial image and fingerprints), which is required for the issuance of all residence permits, plus every time (s)he applies for a renewal of the permit. Such provision may only be found in two other countries, Malta and Bulgaria, therefore it contributes to the distinctive appeal of the Greek programme.[93] The fact that there is no requirement of physical presence in Greece signifies that the invested property may be rented without losing the residence permit and the benefits derived from it. This means that investors are not compelled to maintain a permanent residence or address in Greece to retain their rights. This flexibility allows investors to derive income from their property by benefitting from long-term rentals or other short-term renting platforms such as Airbnb, while still enjoying the advantages of their Greek residence permit by solely maintaining the ownership of the property. It offers a significant advantage, particularly for those who may not plan to reside permanently in Greece but seek to make strategic real estate investments while benefiting from the perks of the residency program. In addition to this, Greece has facilitated the tax regime for investors, who are considered as non-habitual residents.[94] By contrast, the Portuguese law requires a minimum stay of 35 days during a five-year period to retain the residence status.[95] In Cyprus, the residence permit holders must visit the country once every two years.

At the same time, the procedural difficulties of the Greek scheme must be viewed in the broader context of the increased bureaucracy stemming from the need to provide at least 10 different certificates that must be provided as accompanying documents to the application, the whole process may last up to six months and despite the low threshold there still exists increased taxation on property years after the end of the financial crisis. Besides, a significant amount of properties are still subject to bank mortgages and other burdens, thus affecting the appeal of the scheme. The additional costs surrounding these programs for paying the professionals such as lawyers and real estate agents are often high. Lawyers often assist with legal aspects of the application, ensuring compliance with regulations. Real estate agents aid in property selection and transactions, helping investors navigate the real estate market. Their fees vary, but usually, the estate agent's fee for example, including VAT (24 per cent), amounts to 2 per cent of the property value. Finally, on the negative aspects, it must be recalled that the investors may wish to have access to the labour market, which the Greek permits do not allow.

V. FLAWS OF THE GREEK INVESTMENT RESIDENCE SCHEME

In addition to the considerations mentioned above, there is a series of gaps in the legal framework that can be identified. This section will highlight three such flaws: (a) the pressure on the internal residential market; (b) challenges posed by the lack of an in-depth pre-vetting of the applicants and ex-post checks that the requirements are fulfilled; (c) risks of money laundering.

[93] European Commission, Report COM(2019) 12 final, 9.

[94] Džankić, 'Immigrant Investor Programmes'; Greece differentiates between 'residence' and 'tax residence', whereby only those present on the country's soil for over 183 days are subject to the regular tax regime. The Greek Golden Visa programme does not require investors to be physically present on its soil for extended periods of time and in this way, it can facilitate tax obligations In Greece, non-habitual residents are taxed only for their Greece-based income and are not considered 'tax residents' if they do not stay for long periods of time (more than half a year) in Greece.

[95] Arcibal, 'Golden visa fuels demand for Greek homes' (*South China Morning Post*, 9 May 2022).

A. Pressure on the Residential Market

Although concerns have been raised across the EU that the residence by investment programmes may distort real estate market, the repercussions are often sidelined.[96] The case of Greece is paradigmatic in this context.[97] A study from 2018 demonstrated that almost half of the amount of money placed in the local property market concerned property purchased by foreign investors.[98] Thus, this capital raised by foreign investors constitutes a substantial proportion of the total property market. The impact is already apparent on the internal residential market as the property market in Greece shows signs of destabilisation and locals have been largely affected by this housing 'crisis'.[99] Available information on the areas where residence permit-seekers are looking for purchasing real estate demonstrates that there is a huge demand in Athens, as well as in islands such as Santorini, Mykonos and Corfu.[100] As confirmed by the Ministry, the vast majority of the investment is concentrated in property located in Athens and thus the scheme has never had its country-wide appeal that was originally expected. However, the prolonged financial crisis in Greece has put local property holders under significant pressure to sell their properties at a higher price to third-country nationals that wish to benefit from the 'golden visa' programme. It has been highlighted that there are cases where the parties deliberately increase the price in the contract to meet the threshold for the investment residence permit and then bilateral arrangements the surplus is returned following and distributed among middlemen.[101] Although this may have had a positive impact for property owners that have managed to sell their property at a beneficiary rate, usually at the threshold that is required to acquire an investment visa or sometimes even higher,[102] there has been a domino effect to the local population. First, local residents experience difficulties to buy a house at a reasonable price as the 'golden visa' programme has contributed, among other factors, in pushing the costs upwards.[103] Second, the impact of the increase in investment residence is also profound in the rental market. The local population, especially in Athens cannot afford renting a house, especially in the city centre,[104] where investors tend to buy houses in order to rent them or benefit from the Airbnb scheme. This is not merely a speculation; it is precisely this increase in Airbnb that has driven the Greek Government to change the minimum threshold especially in some regions where the impact is significant.[105] Indeed, there is a rise of properties registered in Airbnb is currently witnessed in big cities,[106] especially Athens, as well as in the islands.

[96] Scherrer and Thirion, 'Citizenship by Investment (CBI) and Residence by Investment (RBI) schemes in the EU'.

[97] Surak and Tsuzuki, 'Are Golden Visas a Golden Opportunity?'.

[98] Roussanoglou, 'Foreign Investors are Spending More on Greek Real Estate' (*GreeceIs*, 24 June 2019).

[99] Bourro, 'How has the Golden Visa impacted the Greek Real Estate Market' (*Imberal*, 2 November 2023).

[100] Alderman, 'In Greece, an Economic Revival Fueled by "Golden Visas" and Tourism' (*The New York Times*, 20 March 2019) www.nytimes.com/2019/03/20/business/greece-economy-golden-visas-tourism.html.

[101] Archontaki, *Golden Visa*, 133–34.

[102] Many medium sized apartments in Athens, Thessaloniki and islands are priced at exactly €250,000, which is the minimum threshold for acquiring a golden visa. This shows the tension of the homeowners to attract foreign investors.

[103] The central bank data shows, in the second quarter of 2019 apartment prices are estimated to have increased year-on-year by 11.1 per cent in Athens, 7.0 per cent in Thessaloniki, 4.1 per cent in other cities and 4.9 per cent in other areas of Greece. The prices fell in the period 2020–21 mainly because of the Covid-19 pandemic, but have shown again a rise of almost 12 per cent in Athens in 2022; see in 'Residential and Commercial Property Price Indices and Other Short-Term Indices' (Bank of Greece) www.bankofgreece.gr/en/statistics/real-estate-market/residential-and-commercial-property-price-indices-and-other-short-term-indices.

[104] '"All my wage goes to the house": A rental crisis brews in Greece' (*Al Jazeera*, 25 July 2022) www.aljazeera.com/features/2022/7/25/housing-crisis-in-greece-with-increased-rent.

[105] 'Golden Visa: Προωθούνται αλλαγές με στόχο τη μείωση των ενοικίων' (*Oikonomikos Taxydromos*, 22 December 2022).

[106] Balampanidis and Papatzani, 'Airbnb and the future of housing in Greece' (*Eteron*, 9 April 2023).

The increase of short-lease apartments has driven up rent prices.[107] This has made people move either to the suburbs of Athens, or even leave Athens to seek accommodation at an affordable price in smaller cities. Such repercussions may have been prevented had the golden visa programme been accompanied by any coordinated state housing policy.[108] However, since the emphasis has been on the inflow of money in the Greek market, such considerations were set aside.

It is because of the housing crisis that the threshold for investing in real estate in Greece has increased to €500,000, so that the market for Greek middle-class families can become more accessible. The increase in the threshold will have a significant impact on the regions in which the investments will take place. The legislative reform seems to strike a better balance between the competing driving forces of rejuvenating specific regions, whilst taking into account the residential market crisis. Therefore, it is expected or at least hoped that investments will be more controlled, in certain more affluent areas in the southern suburbs of Athens and the Greek islands, and the differentiated thresholds will increase the affordability of real estate for locals and stabilise the market, potentially reigniting interest in real estate investment, touristic development and potentially new job opportunities in rural areas that have immediate needs.[109] A similar approach was followed by the Portuguese regime that disincentivised investors who wish to purchase property in Lisbon, Porto and Algarve in order to delimit profiteering practices and retain affordable prices in the largest cities of the country and encourage investment in regions with less dense population to increase their economic development. The increase in the threshold may also be seen as a legislative trick to motivate investors to benefit from the currently applicable advantageous regime as soon as possible, considering that the first half of 2022 showed a decline not only in the form of less applications for new residence permits, but also through the withdrawal from the programme by reselling the invested property, which is coupled by an overall decline in the number of applications due to the COVID-19 pandemic and the fact that the Ministry of Migration and Asylum decided the suspension of the 'Golden Visa' programme for Russian nationals who were amongst the most common nationalities applying for investment residence permits in Greece.[110] Indeed, even before the adoption of the legislation, the announcement of a forthcoming revision boosted the golden visa programme in Greece even more, and it is estimated that the demand has been increased to 290 per cent in comparison with the same months (September, October and November) of 2021.[111] The potential investors are all too ready to apply for the golden visa before the entry into force of the amendment. In any case, considering the cases of increasing the price solely to meet the threshold, it is also necessary to accompany differentiated rules with provisions establishing a mechanism for the correct evaluation of the value of the property as a requirement prior to granting an investment residence permit.[112]

[107] Barker, 'The Airbnb Effect on Housing and Rent' (*Forbes*, 21 February 2020).

[108] Edelman and Geradin, 'Efficiencies and Regulatory Shortcuts' (2015–16) 19 *STLR* 293.

[109] 'Golden Visa' (*Ethnos*, 13 October 2022) www.ethnos.gr/opinions/article/228203/goldenvisatafoplakahependytikotexnasmahayxhshtoyorioyependyshssta500000eyro; according to the statistics provided by the Ministry of Migration and Asylum, in 2021, a total of 599 permits were granted to Russian investors which represented 6.2 per cent of the top 10 nationalities with investment residence permit in Greece, while in the end of 2022, the Russian investors represented only the 4 per cent of the top 10 nationalities.

[110] ibid.

[111] 'Μεγάλη αύξηση ζήτησης ακινήτων για Golden Visa' ['The demand for investment residence in Greece is highly increased'] (*SofokleousIn*, 24 October 2022).

[112] Archontaki, *Golden Visa*, 134; For an overview on the need to re-assess the value of properties backing investment residence on an annual basis, see in Park, *Citizens without Nations* (Cambridge 2018) and Park, 'Citizenship for Sale in Pre-modern Europe' in Kochenov and Surak (eds), *Citizenship and Residence Sales*.

B. Checks Before and After the Issuance of a Residence Permit

The procedure for granting an investment residence permit seems to be rather formalised in the sense that the legislation does not require the competent authorities to subject applicants to extensive pre-vetting and the investors are primarily screened based on their financial contributions.[113] Arguably, the applicant will have already undergone through extensive background checks in the first step of the application process which requires a visa or a residence permit. Therefore, for the purposes of applying for the investment residence, it could be held that it is not necessary for the applicant to go through extensive pre-vetting. There are a series of reasons why this simplified approach may raise concerns: first, there may be some time passed between the issuance of the visa or residence or permit and the submission of the investment residence permit applications; second, the permit will be issued for a significant period of time and, as it will be discussed below, there are inadequate mechanisms for ensuring that the requirements for issuing residence permits remain fulfilled, which also raises non-discrimination concerns against applicants for residence permits applicants using other grounds; third, if there is no meaningful check the individual risks having their application rejected and that rejection may be accompanied by a return decision; and fourth, the lack of a requirement on behalf of the investor to demonstrate the lawfulness of the money that has been used for purchasing the property may create risks for money laundering. That said, in our discussion with the Ministry it was stated that during the assessment of the application for an investment residence permit there is formal communication between the competent authorities and the Police and the latter conducts the background check on the applicants. Presumably the checks involve at least checking the Schengen Information System (SIS), as it is also a requirement under Regulation (EU) 2018/1861 to conduct a check with the system prior to the issue of all residence permits.[114] However, in view of numerous pathogenic features of the SIS these checks may not be sufficient and additional checks against other national, EU, such as the Visa Information System (VIS) or the forthcoming European Criminal Record Information System for Third-country Nationals (ECRIS-TCN) and international databases, such as certain Interpol databases (SLTD and TDAWN) could be foreseen.

Furthermore, considering the emphasis on the investment to issue a residence permit instead of a more holistic check on the applicant's profile, it is problematic that there is no mechanism reviewing on a periodical basis whether the conditions of issuing these permits continue to be met throughout their period for which the residence permits are valid. Indeed, re-checks of the conditions take place only when the validity of the residence permit expires, as all other categories of residence permits. This is related to the requirement to revoke a residence permit in cases where the property is sold in accordance with Article 20B(5), which only refers to situations where the new owner is also a third-country national, in which case they are entitled to exercise their right to apply for an investment residence permit. Because of this, there has been a case of carousel fraud, whereby five third-country nationals each contributed €50,000 to purchase a property by one of them. Within three months, the property was sold and the price was given to another member of the team that purchased the first property, who in turn bought another property. As a result, all five original purchasers obtained investment residence permits whereby instead of investing €1,250,000, they only invested €250,000. The fact that the properties were sold to Greek nationals was central for not being detected during the application

[113] Surak and Tsuzuki, 'Are Golden Visas a Golden Opportunity?'.

[114] Regulation No 2018/1861 on the establishment, operation and use of the Schengen Information System (SIS) in the field of border checks [2018] OJ L 132/14.

process. As stressed by Archontaki, these gaps could be filled in different ways; reducing the validity period of the residence permit, which will also bring the Greek scheme closer to the standards applicable in other Member States, but may reduce its attractiveness; conduct of at least once checking before the renewal of the residence permit or the expiry of its validity; or the creation of a dedicated database in land registry offices or notaries with all the properties based on which applications have been lodged to monitor their subsequent ownership.[115] The requirement that the applicant provides a certificate on whether the property has been used for the application of an investment residence permit is also important in this context, provided that the competent authority follows up closely on the fate of the property in cases the certificate mentions that such an application has been made.

C. Combating Money Laundering

According to the fifth Anti-Money Laundering (AML) Directive, third-country nationals who apply for residence rights or citizenship in the Member State in exchange of capital transfers, purchase of property or government bonds or investment in corporate entities in that Member State are designated as high risk thus requiring enhanced customer due diligence.[116] However, the Directive lays down these obligations only in relation to economic operators and does not cover governmental organisations and agencies, which are thus not included in the list of obliged entities. This means that the authorities responsible for assessing residence permit applications are not covered. At the same time, Article 18(3) of the fourth AML Directive requires both Member States and obliged entities when assessing the risks of money laundering to take into account a series of factors listed in Annex III of that legislation, which includes customers who are third country nationals who apply for residence rights or citizenship in the Member State in exchange of capital transfers, purchase of property or government bonds or investment in corporate entities in that Member State. This does not mean national authorities are entrusted with customer due diligence tasks. The provision merely requires Member States to take certain factors into account when deciding whether to require obliged entities, as laid down in Article 2(1), to perform enhanced customer due diligence. In a report on Investor Citizenship and Residence Schemes in the European Union, the Commission stressed the need for measures checking the origin of the amounts of money invested,[117] which could be conducted by national authorities, as in the case of Bulgaria or Spain or by private entities and freelancers.[118] The degree of background checks differs among Member States; for example, in Croatia, Portugal and Hungary such checks are not laid down in law.[119] In the case of Greece, the lack of a requirement of the national authorities to conduct a background check as regards the origins of the investment capital is problematic. The way in which this has been addressed is through Law 4251/2014, which requires that the payment for purchasing (or in the case of a hotel its rental) takes place via the involvement of banks or payment service providers operational in Greece (either a crossed cheque to a bank account registered in Greece, or a bank transfer, POS established by a provider of payment services which operates

[115] Archontaki, *Golden Visa*, 132–33.
[116] Art 2(1), Directive 2018/843 on the prevention of the use of the financial system for the purposes of money laundering or terrorist financing [2018] OJ L 156/43.
[117] European Commission Report COM(2019)12 final.
[118] Archontaki, *Golden Visa*, 136.
[119] ibid 137.

in Greece, or by credit or debit card of the investor to an account registered by a payment service provider which operates in Greece). The involvement of the Greek banking system is due to the obligations of the banking system, notaries and lawyers to report any suspicious transactions and carry due diligence checks in accordance with the EU anti-money laundering legislation.[120] POS transactions were only made possible via Law 4635/2019, but the previous legislative choice was also found to be lawful by the Greek Council of State claiming that from a holistic interpretation of the law, these means of payment safeguard the objectives of the legislation including the full check of the relevant financial transaction and the exclusion of false transactions or money laundering.[121] As a result, the burden on background checks is solely on obliged entities detecting and reporting potentially suspicious financial transactions and not on national authorities.

VI. CONCLUSION

This chapter mapped the Greek law and practice underpinning Greek investment residence permits oriented at plugging economic gaps caused by the financial crisis and to critically evaluate its advantages, that have made it one of the popular ones in the EU, as well as its flaws stemming both from the contextual framework within which the 'golden visa' programme operates and the legislation. It has been shown that the programme has attracted particular attention since its launch due to its flexibility, the low threshold on the value of the invested property, the rather liberal understanding of who constitutes a family member and the long validity period of the permits. At the same time, the attractive low threshold has put significant pressure on the real estate market, significantly contributing to the housing crisis. Furthermore, the application though inherently bureaucratic, it does not necessarily allow for meaningful checks either prior or after the issuance of the permits and the risk for money laundering may not be sufficiently addressed. The consecutive legislative reforms have rectified a number of problematic features, but challenges remain, some of which pertain to the design of the programme, such as the need to ensure better follow-up checks after the issuance of a permit, whereas others relate to structural, extra-migration matters and thus may be much more difficult to change. In any case, a holistic evaluation of the programme is due to determine its effectiveness and if, it is not proven then withdrawing the programme or drastically changing its requirements may have to be considered. With the new threshold now in effect, it remains to be seen the extent to which the Greek investment residence permits will be still so appealing or not.

[120] In accordance with the fifth AML Directive, notaries and other independent legal professionals, where they participate, whether by acting on behalf of and for their client in any financial or real estate transaction, or by assisting in the planning or carrying out of transactions for their client concerning among others the buying and selling of real property or business entities.

[121] Judgment 2036/2019, Legal Council of State (GR); Commented by Archontaki, 'Σχολιασμός ΣτΕ 2036/2019' ΕΜΕΔ, N 1/2018, 50.

14

The Rise and Fall of Investment Immigration in Canada

MIRIAM COHEN*

I. INTRODUCTION

CANADA HAS LED the way in providing permanent residency, which may eventually lead to obtaining Canadian citizenship, to foreign individuals seeking to immigrate to Canada in exchange of an investment.[1] While investor immigration programmes in Canada have gone through some changes over the years since it was first established in 1986, foreign investors have always had to meet specific economic criteria; the common denominator has been a large sum of investment in exchange for the right to reside in Canada, and eventually the ability to become a Canadian citizen. This Chapter aims to engage in a historical overview of Canadian investment immigration policies, their genesis and their current status. An underlying question in such an analysis is whether investor-type immigration is justifiable in the Canadian context.

Immigration forms part of the fabric of Canadian society and is a crucial topic in Canadian politics. Having been a pioneer in investment migration globally (where foreign investors immigrate through financial contribution),[2] the Canadian Federal Government implemented a pilot programme for immigration through investment, the 'Immigrant Investor Venture Capital (IIVC) Pilot Program' (the 'Program' or the 'IIVC Program').[3] The IIVC Program had made significant changes to previous investment immigration rules, including the total amount of investment required and the timeframe that the investment is locked in for. Through the IIVC Program, investors with a net worth of CAD 10 million or more, and who were willing to make 'an at-risk investment which is not guaranteed of CAD 2 million in the Immigrant

* The author thanks the Foundation for Legal Research for a research grant without which this project would not have been possible. The author also thanks Ryan Lemay, Allister McGillivray, Sarah-Michèle Vincent Wright and Rodrigue Oloudé for invaluable research assistance. Last, thanks to the anonymous peer reviewers for all comments and suggestions. An earlier draft of this chapter appeared in Investment Migration Working Papers 2017.

[1] Distinct from other countries, Canada's investment immigration is not a citizenship by investment programme; investor immigrants can become permanent residents and may later apply for citizenship following the same process as other permanent residents.

[2] Ley and Kobayashi, 'Back to Hong Kong' (2005) 5 *Global Networks* 111.

[3] Sect 12 of Immigration and Refugee Protection Act 2001 (CA); Ministerial Instructions 18 (MI18): Instructions respecting the Immigrant Investor Venture Capital Class 2015 (CA). At the time of writing, in 2022, the IIVC Program is no longer in operation. The various economic immigration programmes in Canada, such as the 'Start-up Visa Program', launched in 2013, are outside the scope of this Chapter, see: IRCC, 'Evaluation of the Start-Up Visa (SUV) pilot' (November 2016) 2; https://www.canada.ca/en/immigration-refugees-citizenship/corporate/reports-statistics/evaluations/start-visa-pilot.html.

Investor Venture Capital (IIVC) Fund', could apply to become permanent residents.[4] Thus, under certain circumstances, foreign investors were effectively allowed to immigrate to Canada in exchange for an investment. Developments in immigration policies underscore important questions, including how immigration laws and policies may ultimately shape the future of Canada's economy and society. While investment immigration has existed in Canada for some time (and is a global phenomenon), the topic remains under-theorised and under-studied. With the successive changes to the federal investment immigration programme, this book is a crucial avenue for further analysis of (defunct) investment immigration programmes and their drawbacks to inform future developments in the field, both in Canada and beyond.

In light of these questions, while not focusing on all categories of economic immigration, this chapter has the object of tracing the evolution of investment immigration in Canada. The backdrop of this chapter is an inquiry into whether Canadian citizenship should be a commodity traded for an investment. Through an examination of the historical evolution of investment immigration in Canada and interdisciplinary scholarship in the theme, this chapter maps the evolution of investor migration in Canada.

Section II of this chapter provides a broad overview of the Canadian immigration legal framework, which will serve as the background for the following analysis. Section III reviews the evolution of Canadian investment immigration laws. Section IV looks at the global investment migration phenomenon and juxtaposes the old Canadian Federal IIVC Program with its counterparts in other countries. Section V looks at some of the issues raised by the Program in the context of a broader discussion of immigration policies.

II. AN OVERVIEW OF THE CANADIAN IMMIGRATION LEGAL FRAMEWORK

Immigration is a cornerstone of Canadian society: not only does it populate a country with vast landmass and resources, but it also brings diversity and prosperity into Canada.[5] Immigration has always been part of Canadian history and immigrants contribute to the multicultural society that Canada is today. Given Canada's stated goal to honour its humanitarian traditions as well as its aspiration to foster a stronger economy, immigration will undoubtedly play a fundamental role in shaping the Canadian ethos in years to come.[6]

The Canadian immigration legal system is far from straightforward, however. Its intricacies stem from the Canadian Constitution Act of 1867,[7] section 95 of which provides that jurisdiction over immigration should be shared among the federal, provincial and territorial governments.[8] That said, authority over immigration is not distributed equally: a provincial or territorial law related to immigration deemed to be 'repugnant to any Act of the Parliament of

[4] Having permanent resident status is not equivalent to being a Canadian citizen. Permanent residents do not have the right to run for political office, nor do they have the right to vote in elections. Furthermore, permanent residents have 'the right to enter and remain in Canada, subject to the provisions of the [IRPA]'. Canada's constitution does not contain a definition of citizenship and it does not provide for the means by which citizenship may be acquired or lost. Although it is necessary that an immigrant become a permanent resident prior to applying for Canadian citizenship, there are a number of additional requirements that must be met. These include, and are not limited to, passing the citizenship test, taking the citizenship oath, demonstrating adequate knowledge of English or French and meeting the residency requirements.

[5] Atkey, 'Canadian Immigration Law and Policy' (1990) 16 *CAN.-U.S. L. J.* 59, 60–65. See the '2024 Annual Report to Parliament on Immigration' (Government of Canada 2024) 4: 'immigration brings in new workers, attracts new investments, and supports Canada's economic growth'.

[6] Alexander, 'From Supply to Demand-driven in Immigration' (Canadian Politics and Public Policy 2014) 34, 35 http://policymagazine.ca/pdf/10/PolicyMagazineNovember-DecemberAlexander-14.pdf.

[7] The Constitution Act 1867 (CA).

[8] Liew and Galloway, *Immigration Law* 2nd edn (Irwin Law 2015) 32.

Canada' has no force or effect.[9] Additionally, section 91(25) of the Constitution Act extends legislative power over 'naturalization and aliens' to the Federal Government. Although the Canadian judiciary is still filling out the exact contours of this phrase, the federal government has jurisdiction, inter alia, over the process of citizenship.[10] In this respect, the Federal Government has responsibility for immigration matters, though the provinces undoubtedly have an appreciable influence.

Perhaps the clearest manifestation of this coexistent jurisdiction over immigration is the dual system that exists between the province of Quebec and the Federal Government. The Federal Government and the Province of Quebec signed in 1991 the Canada–Québec Accord relating to Immigration and Temporary Admission of Aliens,[11] which gives Quebec the exclusive responsibility for selecting immigrants to the province.[12]

Canada's immigration legal framework is dictated primarily by the Immigration and Refugee Protection Act (IRPA).[13] In 2002, this statute replaced the former Immigration Act, altering various aspects of Canada's immigration system such as the composition of the Immigration and Refugee Board and the configuration of the points-based screening system.[14] Although the general structure of Canada's immigration scheme has remained unchanged since the implementation of the IRPA, many of the programmes which serve as a gateway to Canada have been subject to extensive revisions.[15] This is exemplified in part by the numerous changes that Canada's Federal Immigrant Investor Program has undergone since its inception, as will be detailed in Section III.

The overall purpose of the IRPA – operating in conjunction with the Immigration and Refugee Protection Regulations (Regulations) – is to regulate who can come to Canada and under what immigration status. This entails the delineation of the administrative process for decision-making pertaining to immigration and deportation.[16] It includes an explanation of the rights and obligations bestowed upon immigrants.[17] Additionally, section 12 of the IRPA establishes three overarching categories by which a candidate may be chosen to immigrate to Canada as a permanent resident.[18]

The first category is commonly referred to as the family reunification class. This programme allows Canadian citizens and permanent residents to sponsor family members to come to Canada. In order to immigrate under the family class, there is an application process that must be successfully completed by both the sponsor and the foreign national. For the sponsor, proof of financial stability is required.[19] Other restrictions are also imposed on sponsors; for example, residency requirements and an absence of certain prior criminal convictions.[20] For the foreign national applicant, the legal definition of 'a member of the family class' as contained in the IRPA Regulations must be met.[21] In 2023, Canada welcomed 471,808 immigrants: there were

[9] ibid.
[10] ibid 33–34.
[11] Canada–Québec Accord relating to Immigration and Temporary Admission of Aliens 1991 (CA).
[12] This unique relationship will be explored further in the following sections of this chapter.
[13] Immigration and Refugee Protection Act 2001 (CA).
[14] Dauvergne, 'Evaluating Canada's New Immigration and Refugee Protection Act in its Global Context' (2003) 41 *Alta LRev.* 725, 726.
[15] Alboim and Cohl, 'Shaping the future' (Maytree 2012) 2 https://maytree.com/wp-content/uploads/shaping-the-future.pdf.
[16] ibid 38–40.
[17] Fournier-Ruggles, *Canadian Immigration and Refugee Law for Legal Professionals* 2nd edn (Emond Montgomery 2013) 23.
[18] Waldman, *Canadian Immigration & Refugee Law Practice* (LexisNexis Canada 2012) 64.
[19] Fournier-Ruggles, *Canadian Immigration and Refugee Law*, 164.
[20] ibid 164–65.
[21] ibid 171.

109,730 immigrants in the family category, 272,744 economic immigrants, 51,081 refugees and Protected Persons, and other immigrants.[22]

The second category is the refugee/humanitarian route. Essentially, Convention refugees or those in similar circumstances may be permitted to immigrate to Canada under this category.[23] A number of requirements for successful immigration are detailed by section 139 of the IRPA Regulations.[24] For example, there must be no reasonable prospect 'of a durable solution in a country other than Canada'.[25]

The third category is the economic stream, under which there are a number of immigration programmes, including the investment immigration programmes. The IRPA explains that this class is designed for those who have the 'ability to become economically established in Canada'.[26] There are several subcategories within the economic class, including the Start-Up Visa programme.

Citizenship and Immigration Canada ('CIC') releases statistics capturing the number of permanent residents who immigrated to Canada annually. Since 2005, Canada has admitted between 236,753 and 280,687 immigrants each year. As of 31 March 2024, a total of 471,808 permanent residents were permitted to enter Canada.[27] As can be gleaned from these numbers, most immigrants who settle in Canada do so under one of the economic immigration programmes.

III. THE EVOLVING FACES OF INVESTMENT IMMIGRATION IN CANADA

Canadian immigration policy has historically been economically driven.[28] This has not changed much – for example, the *2024 Annual Report to Parliament on Immigration* states that 'the economic immigration class is the largest source of permanent resident admissions, at approximately 58% of all admissions in 2023'.[29]

In 1976, the Immigration Act set Canada's Business Immigration Program in motion.[30] The purpose of this enactment was to generate an influx of business immigrants in the hope of accelerating economic growth across Canada.[31] Initially, the Business Immigration Program included only two categories of immigrants: entrepreneurs and the self-employed.[32]

The investment migration in Canada can be largely grouped into three phases. First, in 1986, the investor category was created, seeking to draw significant investment capital to Canada.[33] Furthermore, some attempt was made to overcome the flaws in government monitoring practices related to the programme.[34] For example, penalties for fund managers who did not comply with the Immigration Act were prescribed.[35]

[22] '2024 Annual Report to Parliament on Immigration' (Government of Canada 2024) 5, 16, 17; www.canada.ca/en/immigration-refugees-citizenship/corporate/publications-manuals/annual-report-parliament-immigration-2024.html.

[23] Fournier-Ruggles, *Canadian Immigration and Refugee Law*, 76.

[24] ibid.

[25] ibid 77.

[26] Sect 12 of Immigration and Refugee Protection Act 2001 (CA).

[27] '2024 Annual Report to Parliament on Immigration' (Government of Canada 2024) 38.

[28] *Green and Green, 'The Economic Goals of Canada's Immigration Policy' (1999) 25 Canadian Public Policy* 425.

[29] '2020 Annual Report to Parliament on Immigration' (Government of Canada 2020) 17.

[30] Ch 52 of Immigration Act 1976 (CA); See DeRosa, 'The Immigrant Investor Program' (1995) 27 *Case W. Res. J. Int'l L.* 359.

[31] Grant and Oertel, 'Diminishing Returns to Immigration?' (1998) 30 *Can. Ethn. Stud.* 56, 67–68.

[32] Wong, 'Canada Business Migration to Australia, Canada and the United States' (2003) 12 *Asian Pac. Migr. J.* 301, 311.

[33] Fournier-Ruggles, *Canadian Immigration and Refugee Law*, 351.

[34] ibid.

[35] ibid 15.

In its early years, the Federal Investor Immigrant Program required applicants to have a net worth of at least CAD 500,000, obtained by the immigrant investor's own endeavours.[36] A minimum investment of CAD 250,000 for three years (five years after 1990) was also mandatory. However, it should be noted that a three-tiered investment structure was in effect at this time.[37] As such, the precise amount required to be invested was contingent upon which province the money was being invested into. Applicants were also required to have successfully operated, controlled or directed a business or commercial venture.

In a second phase, from 1 April 1999, fairly significant changes to Canada's Federal Immigrant Investor Program came into effect.[38] The purpose of these changes was, inter alia, to augment the economic gain for Canada while simultaneously reducing fraud and the operating expenses associated with carrying out the programme.[39] The specific changes to the programme included an increase in the minimum amount required to be invested (ie CAD 400,000 for all investors, regardless of province or territory of investment).[40] Additionally, the minimum net worth for investors increased to CAD 800,000.[41]

Finally, in 2014, the Federal Immigrant Investor Program was terminated and replaced by the IIVC Program (which is also no longer existent).[42] As a result, an amendment to the IRPA on 19 June 2014 (section 87(5)(1) IRPA) 'terminate[d] all visa applications by foreign nationals under the investor … class which had not met certain requirements by February 11, 2014'. This led to some cases before the Federal Courts challenging the constitutionality of this amendment.[43]

Under the IIVC Program, an applicant had to allocate CAD 2 million to the Immigrant Investor Venture Capital Fund for approximately 15 years.[44] From there, the money was invested in 'innovative Canadian start-ups with high growth potential for the benefit of Canada'.[45] BDC Capital (the investment arm of the Business Development Bank of Canada) was responsible for managing the fund. Significantly, the investment that applicants had to make was 'at-risk' and 'non-guaranteed'.[46] This means that because the proceeds received from the fund were contingent upon its performance, an applicant could lose some or all of their investment.

In addition, the Program required applicants to have a net worth of at least CAD 10 million. Importantly, the applicant's wealth must have been 'acquired through lawful business or investment activities'.[47] If an applicant proceeded in the review process, they would be required to obtain a due diligence report from an acceptable service provider (to confirm the legitimacy of their net worth). Furthermore, candidates applying to this investor programme must have reached a specified level of proficiency in English or French. The Canadian Language Benchmarks (CLB) is the 'Canadian standard used to describe, measure and recognize … [the] language ability of … immigrants'.[48] Investor immigrants were required to attain at least

[36] ibid 14.
[37] ibid 370.
[38] Berger, 'Canadian Immigrant Investor Program' (2000) 25 *International Legal Practitioner* 27.
[39] ibid.
[40] ibid.
[41] Fournier-Ruggles, *Canadian Immigration and Refugee Law*, 351.
[42] Costigan et al, 'Beyond Economics' (2016) 48 *Can. Ethn. Stud.* 19, 21.
[43] See eg *Dhaliwal v Canada (Minister of Citizenship and Immigration)* [2015] 483 F.T.R. 88; *Jia v Canada (Minister of Citizenship and Immigration)* [2014] 457 F.T.R. 73; cf *Tabingo v Canada (Minister of Citizenship and Immigration)* [2013] 431 F.T.R. 118.
[44] Ministerial Instructions 18 (MI18): Instructions respecting the Immigrant Investor Venture Capital Class 2015 (CA).
[45] ibid.
[46] ibid.
[47] ibid.
[48] ibid. See also 'Immigration and Citizenship Help Center Glossary' (Government of Canada 2021) www.canada.ca/en/services/immigration-citizenship/helpcentre/glossary.html.

Canadian Language Benchmark 5 in English or *Niveau de compétence linguistique canadien* 5 in French.[49] Finally, applicants to the Program needed to have a 'Canadian post-secondary degree, diploma or certificate of at least one year, or the foreign equivalent as validated by an Educational Credential Assessment (ECA)'.[50] Importantly, those who could demonstrate a net worth of at least CAD 50 million could be exempted from this requirement. The one-year IIVC programme was intended to be open until a maximum of 500 applications; a total of seven applications were received.[51] On 30 December 2015, applications stopped being received and the programme closed.[52]

It is apparent from all the different versions described above that Canada's federal investment immigration programme has been reinvented many times since its inception in 1986. However, a recent face of federal investment immigration had multilevel requirements that were not part of previous versions. Simply from this brief description, it is apparent that there were many hoops to jump through before an applicant could qualify as an investor immigrant. This version of the federal programme was not in line with other investment immigration programmes around the world or within Canada (in Quebec), as it set out a complex scheme that made it less competitive in the market. The following section overviews investment migration globally to compare and contrast with the IIVC Program and the context in which it existed and operated.

IV. THE DEMISE OF THE CANADIAN FEDERAL PROGRAM

While Canada led the way in investment migration globally in 1978, there are currently numerous investment immigration programmes worldwide. However, applications to the IIVC Program stopped being accepted on 30 December 2015, and the programme was officially announced to be closed and removed from the permanent resident programmes list on 29 January 2021.[53] It is apparent from the number of applications described above that it has not been attractive to potential investors.[54]

In this light, to assess investment immigration in Canada and the IIVC Program more specifically, it is relevant first to discuss some of the main characteristics of other selected investment immigration programmes.

A. Competition from Within: The Evolution of the Quebec Investment Immigration Program

As explained above, under the IIVC Capital Pilot Program, an applicant had to devote CAD 2 million to the Immigrant Investor Venture Capital Fund for approximately 15 years.

[49] ibid. See also, www.cic.gc.ca/english/immigrate/business/iivc/eligibility/language-testing.asp.

[50] ibid. See also, www.cic.gc.ca/english/immigrate/business/iivc/assessment.asp.

[51] Mas, 'Millionaire immigrant investor program lures only 7 instead of 60' (*CBC*, 22 January 2016) www.cbc.ca/news/politics/immigration-investor-pilot-program-1.3331204.

[52] 'Program Delivery Update' (Refugees and Citizenship Canada Immigration, 29 January 2021) www.canada.ca/en/immigration-refugees-citizenship/corporate/publications-manuals/operational-bulletins-manuals/updates/2021-ivcc.html.

[53] ibid.

[54] Singer, 'Canada Losing Wealthy Immigrant Investors' (Keynote Speech, Immigration Summit, Ottawa, 5 April 2016).

From there, the money was invested in 'innovative Canadian start-ups with high growth potential for the benefit of Canada'. Significantly, official sources clearly state that the investment was 'at-risk' and 'non-guaranteed', and thus investors could lose their entire investment capital. On the flip side, it was also unpredictable how well the Capital Fund would perform, and applicants could lose some or all of their investment because the proceeds received from the fund were contingent upon its performance.

When the Federal government terminated Canada's Immigrant Investor Program in 2014, Quebec's Investor Program was not affected.

Someone wishing to immigrate to Quebec must be selected *and* admitted. Responsibility for selection means that Quebec gets to establish the criteria for choosing applicants. Responsibility for admission means that the Federal Government has the final say on whether someone can come to Canada (ie by carrying out security/health checks, etc).

To apply under the Quebec Investor Program,[55] an applicant must have 'net assets of at least $ 2,000,000'. These assets may belong solely to the principal applicant or be held with an 'accompanying spouse [...] no later than 120 days following the date on which the Ministère requests this'. The wealth must not have been acquired illegally. Furthermore, any donations received less than six months before the date on which the application was filed are excluded from the count. The applicant must also 'enter into an investment agreement with a financial intermediary that has signed a participation agreement with the Ministère and with Investissement Québec Immigrants Investisseurs Inc'. On 1 January 2024, the Financial intermediary that has signed the participation agreement are: Arton Investments, AURAY Capital Canada inc., Sherbrooke Street Capital (SSC) Inc., Dubeau Capital, iA Private Wealth inc., Société de fiducie Blue Bridge inc., Trust Eterna inc., and Valeurs mobilières Peak inc.[56] Unlike Canada's IIVC Program, the investment (CAD 1,000,000) that applicants must make (for a five-year term) 'is guaranteed by the Government of Quebec'. The income generated by the investment 'is paid to the Business Assistance – Immigrant Investor Program (BAIIP) and the Fonds de développement du marché du travail (FDMT)'. Once the five-year term is completed, the investor is reimbursed the amount they invested, without interest, within 30 days.

Applicants to Quebec's Investor Program must also have 'management experience for at least two years in the five years preceding the application for selection'. Other factors taken into consideration during the assessment of each application (for a certificate of selection) include the nature and duration of their professional training and language skills: applicants must 'have a knowledge of spoken French' (Québec scale of French proficiency levels, level 7). In addition, as of 1 January 2020, if requested by the Ministry as soon as their file is opened and within a maximum of 60 days, candidates must demonstrate through an attestation that they have knowledge of the democratic values and Quebec values expressed in the Charter of Human Rights and Freedoms. This attestation is required for the applicant, his or her spouse and children aged 18 and over. Last but not least, applicants must also plan to reside in Quebec for at least 12 months in the two years following the delivery of his/her work permit.

[55] Conditions for immigrating to Québec as an investor; www.quebec.ca/en/immigration/permanent/immigrate-business/investors/conditions.

[56] ibid.

V. ASSESSING INVESTMENT IMMIGRATION IN CANADA

Having overviewed the immigration framework in Canada, both at the federal and provincial levels, this chapter now focuses on a scholarly assessment of Canada's investment immigration policy, which raises the question at the heart of this chapter: should permanent residency (which can lead to Canadian citizenship) be traded in for some investment?

A. A Critical Outlook on Canada's Investment Immigration Policy

The comparative analysis above indicates that the reinvented IIVC federal Program was lacking competitiveness in the market. It is reported that rather than attracting 500 applications (the maximum number of applications which would be accepted) in the limited period it was open for applications (initially only for two weeks, but later extended), it attracted seven applicants.[57] This data alone should raise some questions about the basic usefulness of the IIVC Program to foreign investors and give the Federal Government pause.

I argue however that the problem goes beyond purely market competition; it is more fundamental. When we look at the many overlapping investment immigration programmes that have existed throughout the years, it appears arguable that Canada should not be in the business of investment immigration as it was historically conceived.

Immigration forms the building blocks of a country's society, identity, culture and economy. Allowing an investor to become a resident of Canada simply due to his or her net worth poses a number of challenges.

Research has demonstrated that the investment made by potential immigrants is not always beneficial to the economy in the long term.[58] The Government of Canada stated that

> [r]esearch shows that immigrant investors pay less in taxes than other economic immigrants, are less likely to stay in Canada over the medium to long term, and often lack human capital qualities – including official language proficiency – to integrate as well as other immigrants from the same countries.[59]

Investment immigration should be taken as integral to Canada's broader immigration policy and priorities. The vision of the investment immigration programme in Canada was not delivering on the stated objective of boosting the Canadian economy. In fact, drawing from scholarly analysis, Professor Kristin Surak states that:

> [while] the Canadian Federal Immigrant Investor Program and its Entrepreneur Program, which ran from 1986 to 2014, were by far the largest of their kind, with over 190,000 principal applicants and family members acquiring permanent residence visas between 1994 and 2013 alone … [t]he direct contribution to the Canadian economy, however, was far less. … A World Bank auditor described the program in 1999 as a 'massive sham', and by 2014 it was suspended due to little evidence of significant economic return'.[60]

[57] Mas, 'Millionaire immigrant investor program'. 'Why Canada's Immigrant Investor Program Will Fail' (*Mondaq*, 13 February 2015) www.mondaq.com/canada/general-immigration/374660/why-canadas-immigrant-investor-program-will-fail.

[58] '2020 Annual Report to Parliament on Immigration' (Government of Canada 2020) 4.

[59] ibid.

[60] Surak, 'Global Citizenship 2.0' (2016)' Investment Migration Working Papers IMC-RP2016/3, 18–19 citing Ley, 'Seeking Homo Economicus' (2003) 93 *Ann. Am. Assoc. Geogr.* 426; Ley, *Millionaire Migrants* (Wiley-Blackwell 2010).

As discussed above, the rationale for terminating the former investment immigration programme in 2014 was that '[t]he government [would] replace these programs with more focused and effective pilot programs that [would] ensure that immigrants who come to Canada deliver meaningful benefits to [the Canadian] economy'.[61]

Looking back further than the IIVC Program, in 2014, the Federal Government Budget critically concluded that on the basis of research, investor immigrants make minimal contributions to Canadian society and economy:

> For decades, [investment immigration] has significantly undervalued Canadian permanent residence, providing a pathway to Canadian citizenship in exchange for a guaranteed loan that is significantly less than our peer countries require. There is also little evidence that immigrant investors as a class are maintaining ties to Canada or making a positive economic contribution to the country. Overall, immigrant investors report employment and investment income below Canadian averages and pay significantly lower taxes over a lifetime than other categories of economic immigrants.[62]

The reality of investment immigration in Canada was far less beneficial to Canada as a whole than may be perceived. The issues described in these various reports have given rise to a review of federal investment immigration policies and led to the creation of the IIVC Program, with the hope of attracting a smaller pool of ultra-high net worth investors.

Nevertheless, the revamped IIVC Program also had stringent conditions. The Program imposed mandatory language testing. This is a significant (additional) hurdle for potential investors and it is possible to have reduced demand for the programme. Further fuelling criticism of the IIVC Program, such language and education requirements, if met, would mean that the potential investors could also potentially be eligible in other categories of immigration that do not require an investment for an extended period, as is required of the investor category.

Beyond the lack of economic benefits to the country, another trait of Canada's investor immigration policy was – until the IIVC Program was launched in 2014 – the long waiting periods for applications to be processed. The entire process was heavily backlogged, and applicants were often forced to wait four to five years. To make matters worse, when the previous investment immigration programme was terminated in 2014, pending applications were also terminated, as discussed above.

Beyond the specific challenges to the revamped Canadian investment immigration programme, legal and interdisciplinary scholarship has focused on some challenges and criticisms of investment immigration more generally. While at the time of writing this chapter (2022), there is not much in the literature critically analysing investment immigration in Canada, a review of some studies in the field is useful to highlight some of the scholarly critique of investment immigration in Canada.[63]

B. Scholarly Critique of Investment Immigration in Canada

While the driving force for establishing immigration by investment is to boost the economy and to bring economic benefits to the country as a whole, there are some crucial (if not existential) questions for this form of immigration. Some of these criticisms shed light on the challenges of investment migration, specifically as applied to the Canadian context.

[61] 'Building a Fast and Flexible Immigration System' (Government of Canada, 11 February 2014) www.canada.ca/en/news/archive/2014/02/building-fast-flexible-immigration-system.html.

[62] Federal Government Budget 2014 (CA) 81.

[63] The review refers to investment immigration generally rather than focusing on the IIVC Program more specifically.

One important critique concerns the potential of greater disparity between developed countries and countries under development. It is submitted in this regard that 'unless in clear surplus, [migration of the] elite may consequently create an enormous vacuum draining the sending country of its driving force for development and well-being'.[64]

Thus, if an investor who would have otherwise helped establish infrastructure and employment in his/her home country is enticed to migrate to a developed nation, the development of the investor's home country is likely to be impeded. This criticism is augmented by a discussion of the likelihood of elite migrants returning to their home countries and the developmental effect of remittances to the sending country.[65]

It has also been observed that many people feel the immigrant investor programme simply provides wealthy people with a means of buying 'their way into Canada without providing a corresponding benefit to Canada as a whole'.[66] The commodification of immigrant visas is problematic because it runs counter to 'the democratic and egalitarian notions on which [Canada] is based'.[67] In a similar vein, 'to the degree that citizenship becomes a commodity, its intrinsic value may be diminished'.[68] This is problematic because it could eventually play out to the point where the entire notion of citizenship is called into question, ultimately 'lessening the legitimacy of the state'.[69] Investment immigration creates a situation where citizenship may be construed on a dollar amount.

Importantly, there are also a number of concerns about the economic impact of Canada's policies on investment immigration. Apparently, Canada's investment immigration programme has yielded far fewer jobs than was initially expected. This is due to the fact (at least in part) that in the early years of the programme (before certain types of investments were restricted), many investors became involved in projects which were non-labour intensive (eg real estate ventures).[70] Similarly, one scholar noted that as of 1998, there had been no 'compelling evidence that business immigrants have made a significant contribution to capital formation or employment creation'.[71] In sum, the original goal of Canada's investment immigration (ie attracting 'capital, innovation, and jobs through high-technology firms and businesses') has not been substantially realised.[72]

Additionally, one major issue raised was how many investor immigrants actually stayed in Canada once they obtained Canadian citizenship, which can certainly lead to questioning the long-term benefits of granting citizenship to investor immigrants. It has been observed that many immigrant investors will choose not to conduct their business in Canada despite having obtained permanent resident status 'because they are less governed by geographical boundaries in a globalized economy'.[73] If their business is not carried out in Canada, then the country is missing out on the associated economic benefits.

[64] Tanner, 'Brain Drain and Beyond: Returns and Remittances of Highly Skilled Migrants' (2005) 24 *Global Migration Perspectives* 3.

[65] ibid 5–7.

[66] Taniguchi, 'Buying or Bringing in Talent' (1994) 19 *LawNow* 13.

[67] ibid 15.

[68] Harrison, 'Class, Citizenship, and Global Migration' (1996) 22 *Canadian Public Policy* 7, 19.

[69] ibid 7, 19.

[70] See Wong, 'Canada Business Migration'.

[71] Grant and Oertel, 'Diminishing Returns to Immigration?', 71.

[72] Jones, 'Canada and the Globalized Immigrant' (2004) 47 *Am. Behav. Sci.* 1263, 1270.

[73] ibid 1270.

Additionally, Canadian investment immigration is based on the assumption that one geographic location's success is probably transferable to another location. This is problematic because entrepreneurial success is not automatic in all places across the globe, where there may be different social and economic circumstances impacting entrepreneurial success.[74]

VI. INVESTMENT IMMIGRATION IN CANADA: SOME LESSONS

The review of the programmes above indicate that investment immigration in Canada has not yielded the positive results aimed for. The reinvention of investment immigration with the introduction of the bold IIVC Program has proven problematic. It has not attracted nearly as many interested investors as initially anticipated.

Importantly, it is also not evident whether, even if the IIVC Program did succeed in attracting the number of applications hoped for, it would actually have benefited the Canadian economy. Research from previous investment immigration programmes does not support the conclusion that, in the long term, investor immigrants are always beneficial to Canada as a whole.

Canadian immigration policy has been described as an 'individually-oriented class system' which is 'increasingly focused primarily on economic considerations'; an excessive emphasis on economic benefit leads to an implicit disregard for the 'important contributions that immigrants make to Canada's multicultural society'.[75] These may be in the form of sports, arts or culture, which form the multifaceted mosaic that is Canadian society. In fact,

> since Canada's inception in 1867, the Canadian identity has been formed by the diverse cultures, religions, histories and languages of English, French and the Indigenous Peoples. Immigration has also played a key role in advancing Canada's tradition of bringing diverse peoples together to live within the same national community. Immigrants to Canada come from many source countries and possess a wide variety of cultural and religious backgrounds, and are able to integrate effectively in communities across the country.[76]

As a corollary, it is suggested that perhaps a nation's prosperity should not be judged solely (or even primarily) in terms of its economic success, especially when the extent to which investors bring lasting economic prosperity to Canada is debatable.[77]

This discussion begs the question whether rather than using resources to craft an investment immigration policy that will indeed benefit Canada as a whole, one should focus on other categories of immigration. The latter may, instead of bringing fast money, bring in lasting skills and the likely desire to set roots in Canada, and thus to contribute in the long-term to the economic prosperity of the country. Immigrants will likely become Canadian citizens – thus, while not directly trading in citizenship for an investment, this is the ultimate outcome of an investment immigration policy. Investing in human capital might bring more benefits, such as building the Canadian identity as a country of innovators and business people who will

[74] See Hiebert, 'The Spatial Limits to Entrepreneurship' (2002) 93 *Tijdschrift voor Economische en Sociale Geografie* 173.

[75] Costigan et al, 'Beyond Economics', 36.

[76] '2020 Annual Report to Parliament on Immigration' (Government of Canada 2020) 8.

[77] Costigan et al, 'Beyond Economics', 36.

succeed within Canada.[78] In reality, 'immigration will continue to be a key driver in advancing Canada's economy, especially in the context of low birth rates and its vital role in growing the working-age population, and it will remain so into the future'.[79]

The growth of Canada's population in the early 2030s will likely be based on immigration alone.[80] Many source countries of Canada's immigration system have similar demographic challenges due to aging populations and declining birth rates.[81] Therefore, it is important to be internationally competitive, especially since the significant impact of COVID-19 on Canada's prosperity and economy.[82]

It is no longer 1986 and Canada is as multicultural as ever. Immigration policies affect not only the Canadian economy but also Canadian society, and weave together the fabric of Canadian identity. Immigration, in all its categories, should go beyond pure economics, and mirror the values upon which the Canadian society is built.

[78] Wong, 'Canada Business Migration', 328, which claims that there should perhaps 'be a greater emphasis on recruiting businesspersons who have the potential to achieve success, rather than on those who have already had success'.

[79] '2020 Annual Report to Parliament on Immigration' (Government of Canada 2020) 5; 'Canada's Population Estimates: Age and Sex, July 1, 2019' (Statistics Canada, 30 September 2019) www150.statcan.gc.ca/n1/daily-quotidien/190930/dq190930a-eng.htm.

[80] ibid, citing El-Assal and Fields, 'Canada 2040' (Conference Board of Canada, 2018) www.conferenceboard.ca/e-Library/document.aspx?did=9678.

[81] ibid citing Yssaad and Fields, 'The Canadian Immigrant Labour Market' (Statistics Canada, 24 December 2018) www150.statcan.gc.ca/n1/pub/71-606-x/71-606-x2018001-eng.htm.

[82] '2020 Annual Report to Parliament on Immigration' (Government of Canada 2020) 5, 14.

15

'Internal' Investment Migration

The Case of Investment Migration from Mainland China to Hong Kong

QISHI FU

I. INTRODUCTION

FUELLED BY THE demand for foreign residence rights and citizenship in emerging economies, an increasing number of states now offer investment-based migration schemes for prospective investors. As a major source country, Chinese migrants have long dominated programmes in the United States, Canada and Australia.[1] In a 2013 survey jointly conducted by Bain & Company and China Merchants Bank, 44 per cent of Chinese high-net-worth individuals were reported to have already emigrated through investment migration schemes or were considering to do so.[2] The ongoing outmigration of the ultra-rich has led the Chinese media to speak of an 'investment migration wave', often associated with corruption and illicit financial outflows.[3] In a similar vein, some Chinese scholars situate the phenomenon in the grander 'third wave of Chinese outmigration' featured by the increasing share of the talented and the rich in the composition of emigrants.[4]

Apart from the traditional immigration countries in North America and Australasia, Hong Kong is another major destination for Chinese immigrant investors. Despite having a population of 7.2 million, Hong Kong's Capital Investment Entrant Scheme (hereinafter, CIES) had 9,227 successful applicants in 2013 alone, compared with the 7,139 visas

[1] Sumption and Hooper, 'Selling Visas and Citizenship' (MPI 2014).

[2] '2015 China Private Wealth Report" (China Merchants Bank and Bain & Company 2013) https://media.bain.com/Images/2013_China_Wealth_Report.pdf.

[3] eg Yan, '移民潮加速中国资本外逃' [Migration Wave Hastening Chinese Financial Outflows] (HKCD, 24 July 2010) http://203.85.54.57/content/2010-07/24/content_2562499.htm; Yang, '中国大陆富人现疯狂投资移民潮' [Mad Investment Migration Wave by the Ultra Rich in Mainland China] (*Radio Free Asia*, 8 February 2015) https://www.rfa.org/mandarin/yataibaodao/shehui/yf1-02082015094310.html; H Chen, '近二十年中国大陆海外移民潮之原因与影响' [The Causes and Effects of Investment Outmigration From Mainland China in the Past Two Decades] (OCAH) http://ocah.org.tw/.

[4] eg Xiang, 'The Upward Concentration of Chinese Emigration and the Rise of China' (COMPAS, 23 September 2014) http://compasoxfordblog.co.uk/2014/09/the-upward-concentration-of-chinese-emigration-and-the-rise-of-china/; Xiang, 'Emigration Trends and Policies in China' (MPI 2016); Wang, *Yi Min Chao* [The Migration Wave] (China Critic Press 2013).

issued under the EB-5 programme in the same year.[5] Among all the individuals securing CIES visas from 2003 to 2012, 90.2 per cent were from mainland China.[6] In addition to this large intake, another important feature of the CIES relates to the constitutional status of Hong Kong. Hong Kong is a special administrative region of China, and thus the legal status conferred through CIES is not of Hong Kong citizenship but of Hong Kong permanent resident status.[7] However, mainland immigrants could apply for a Hong Kong Special Administration Region passport, as distinct from a People's Republic of China passport, on obtaining permanent residence.

By examining investment migration in the context of – strictly speaking – internal migration, CIES reminds us of the diverse backdrops against which investment migration can occur. This chapter examines the mainland China–Hong Kong investment migration, focusing on the CIES-related legal issues and the practice of purchasing third-country permanent residence rights for CIES application.

First, I will briefly introduce the Hong Kong Capital Investment Entrant Scheme. Second, I will discuss the nationality issues of Hong Kong Special Administrative Region (HKSAR) permanent residents, the eligibility for and entitlements of HKSAR permanent resident status, as well as the HKSAR passport. Third, I will describe the practice of purchasing third-country permanent residence rights for CIES application.

II. OVERVIEW OF HONG KONG CAPITAL INVESTMENT ENTRANT SCHEME (CIES)

The Capital Investment Entrant Scheme was launched in 2003, when the Hong Kong economy was battered by the Severe Acute Respiratory Syndrome (SARS) crisis.[8] It offers temporary residence rights (renewable for up to seven years) for individuals who invest no less than HKD 10 million (approximately EUR 1.1 million) into 'permissible investment asset classes', including equities, certificates of deposits, subordinate debts and others. The programme was suspended in January 2015.[9] As part of a policy package to stimulate the Hong Kong economy, the CIES was relaunched in March 2024 with an increased investment threshold of HKD 30 million. Notably, the restriction towards Mainland Chinese remains as only those who are also permanent resident of another country are allowed to apply for the 'New CIES'.

The CIES has a nationality requirement which precludes Chinese nationals (excluding those from Macau and Taiwan) and citizens of Afghanistan, Cuba and North Korea from applying. Along with this general rule is an exception providing that mainland Chinese citizens who have obtained permanent resident status in a foreign country are eligible to apply.[10] Of the mainland Chinese who have secured CIES visas, 6639 (57.3 per cent) hold Gambian permanent residence rights, 2057 (17.8 per cent) are permanent residents of Guinea-Bissau, 1020 (8.8 per cent) of Canada, 490 (4.2 per cent) of the Philippines,

[5] '景鸿料投资移民减三成' [Jing Hong's Prediction of a 30% Decrease of Investment Migration] (*Apple Daily*, 10 September 2014) http://hk.apple.nextmedia.com/financeestate/art/20140910/18860986; 'Report of the Visa Office 2013' (U.S. Department of State – Bureau of Consular Affairs) http://travel.state.gov/content/dam/visas/Statistics/AnnualReports/FY2013AnnualReport/FY13AnnualReport- TableII.pdf.

[6] 'Statistics on the Capital Investment Entrant Scheme' (Hong Kong Immigration Department) www.immd.gov.hk/eng/facts/visa-control.html.

[7] Provided that the seven-year residence requirement has been met.

[8] 'Immigration Control' (Hong Kong 2004) www.yearbook.gov.hk/2004/en/20_03.htm.

[9] However, the suspension of the CIES does not affect applications received by the Immigration Department before the suspension date; 'Capital Investment Entrant Scheme' (GovHK, 1 March 2024) www.immd.gov.hk/eng/services/visas/capital_investment_entrant_scheme.html.

[10] ibid.

295 (2.5 per cent) of New Zealand, 291 (2.5 per cent) of Niger, 232 (2.0 per cent) of Australia, 168 (1.5 per cent) of the United States, 165 (1.4 per cent) of Singapore, 84 (0.7 per cent) of Nauru and 144 (1.2 per cent) from all other countries.[11] The two small West African states – Gambia and Guinea-Bissau – account for 75 per cent of the total. As I will demonstrate later, the convenient permanent residence programmes offered by some West African and Pacific Island states form the backdrop for these statistical outcomes. Nevertheless, it is important first to lay out the constitutional arrangements which enabled the mainland China–Hong Kong investment migration in the first place.

III. LEGAL ASPECTS OF CIES

A. Constitutional Status of Hong Kong

After the defeat of China in the First Opium War in 1842, Hong Kong was colonised by the British with the cession of Hong Kong Island, followed by the Kowloon Peninsula and the New Territories. Negotiations between the UK and China began in the 1980s and led to the adoption of the 1984 Sino-British Joint Declaration, which proclaimed the resumption of Chinese sovereignty over Hong Kong in 1997. On 30 June 1997, the former British colony became a special administrative region of the People's Republic of China (PRC).[12]

The HKSAR is a local administrative region of the PRC and comes directly under the Central People's Government.[13] However, according to the Basic Law (the constitutional document of the HKSAR), Hong Kong enjoys a 'high degree of autonomy' and 'executive, legislative and independent judicial power, including that of final adjudication'.[14] HKSAR maintains its immigration policy independently of mainland China.[15]

B. Hong Kong as a Separate Immigration Territory

Hong Kong's autonomy in immigration control is a complex issue. On the one hand, the Basic Law recognises Hong Kong's autonomy in administering its 'external' borders. 'The Government of the HKSAR may apply immigration controls on entry into, stay in and departure from the Region by persons from foreign states and regions.'[16] On the other hand, there is no similar legal basis authorising the HKSAR to apply immigration control over people entering the HKSAR from the mainland. Instead, Article 22(4) of the Basic Law provides that, 'for entry into the Hong Kong Special Administrative Region, people from other parts of China must apply for approval'.[17]

The provision was later elaborated in the Interpretation of the 'Standing Committee of the National People's Congress Regarding Paragraph 4 in Article 22 and Category (3) of

[11] The figures are based on data as of 29 February 2012, provided in 'Chinese African in HK' (Webb-site Reports, 15 April 2012) https://webb-site.com/articles/CIES.asp.

[12] Crawford, *The Creation of States in International Law* 2nd edn (Oxford University Press 2007) 245–50.

[13] Art 12, Basic Law 1990 (HK).

[14] ibid.

[15] 'Immigration Clearance' (Hong Kong Immigration Department) www.immd.gov.hk/eng/services/immigration_clearance.html.

[16] Art 154, Basic Law 1990 (HK).

[17] Art 22(4), Basic Law 1990 (HK).

Paragraph 2 in Article 24 of the Basic Law of the Hong Kong Special Administrative Region of the PRC in 1999' (1999 Interpretation). It provides that,

> people from all provinces, autonomous regions, or municipalities directly under the Central Government … who wish to enter the HKSAR for whatever reason, must apply to the relevant authorities of their residential districts for approval … and must hold valid documents issued by the relevant authorities before they enter the HKSAR.[18]

Implemented in practice, the 'PRC Permit for Proceeding to Hong Kong and Macau' and the 'Exit Endorsement' with which mainland Chinese are granted leave to enter the HKSAR (for short stays) are both issued by the mainland Chinese Ministry of Public Security instead of the HKSAR Immigration Department.[19]

Nonetheless, for long stays such as employment and study, an 'Entry Permit' issued by the HKSAR Immigration Department is also required.[20] Instead of full autonomy, shared authority between the central government and the HKSAR is a better description of the arrangement in place for Hong Kong in the area of immigration.[21]

C. Jurisdictional Grey Area and the Nationality and Residence Requirement of CIES

This jurisdictional grey area is also reflected in the layout of the entry categories set by the HKSAR government. There is a divide between categories applicable to mainland Chinese and to foreigners, even for the same entry purposes.[22] For example, to take up highly skilled employment in Hong Kong, foreign nationals need to obtain a visa under the 'General Employment Policy' category; for the same purpose, mainland Chinese are required to enter through the 'Admission Scheme for Mainland Talents and Professionals'.[23] Similar arrangements can also be found in other visa types.[24]

In addition, exceptions are made for entry schemes which are in principle not applicable to mainland Chinese. As noted earlier, the CIES is applicable to mainland Chinese who have obtained permanent resident status in a foreign country. The 'Investment as Entrepreneurs' entry scheme is not only open to mainland Chinese with permanent resident status in a foreign country but also to those who 'have been residing overseas for at least one year immediately before the submission of application and that the application is submitted from overseas'.[25]

The existence of this jurisdictional grey area, I think, is the primary reason for the inclusion of the third-country permanent residence requirement in the CIES. Emphasising mainland applicants' foreign resident status is an attempt on the part of the HKSAR government to avoid crossing the jurisdictional boundary drawn by Article 22(4) of the Basic Law and the 1999

[18] Interpretation by the Standing Committee of the National People's Congress Regarding para 4 in Art 22 and Category (3) of para 2 in Art 24, Basic Law (HK) www.npc.gov.cn/englishnpc/Law/2007-12/12/content_1383897.htm.

[19] 'Entry Arrangement for Mainland, Macao, Taiwan, & Overseas Chinese Residents' (Hong Kong Immigration Department) www.immd.gov.hk/eng/services/visas/overseas-chinese-entry-arrangement.html.

[20] ibid.

[21] In some cases, entry into HK is unilaterally authorised by the mainland authorities, whereas in some other cases authorisations from both sides are required in order for a mainland Chinese national to legally reside in the HKSAR.

[22] 'Visas/Entry Permits' (Hong Kong Immigration Department) www.immd.gov.hk/eng/services/index.html.

[23] ibid.

[24] For example, 'Students' (Hong Kong Immigration Department) www.immd.gov.hk/eng/services/visas/study.html.

[25] 'Capital Investment Entrant Scheme' (Hong Kong Immigration Department) www.immd.gov.hk/eng/services/visas/capital_investment_entrant_scheme.html; 'Investment as Entrepreneurs' (Kong Immigration Department) www.immd.gov.hk/eng/services/visas/investment.html.

Interpretation. This makes the CIES fall within the scope of Article 154 Basic Law where the HKSAR enjoys full control over its 'external' borders.[26] From a pragmatic perspective, letting the CIES fall within the jurisdiction of central government is to empower the mainland Ministry of Public Security to require exit permission from those who want to transfer 10 million Hong Kong dollars out of its own jurisdiction through the CIES. This is a particular concern, as this migratory flow was often portrayed by the media as associated with corruption and illicit financial outflows.

IV. LEGAL STATUS OF THE HONG KONG PERMANENT RESIDENT

A. Nationality of HKSAR Permanent Residents

The current rules on the acquisition of Chinese nationality are in the Chinese Nationality Law 1980.[27] The principle mode of acquisition of Chinese nationality at birth is *jus sanguinis*, provided in Articles 4 and 5. Article 4 stipulates that 'any person born in China whose parents are both Chinese nationals or one of whose parents is a Chinese national shall have Chinese nationality'.[28] Article 5 reads that

> any person born abroad whose parents are both Chinese nationals or one of whose parents is a Chinese national shall have Chinese nationality. But a person whose parents are both Chinese nationals and have both settled abroad, or one of whose parents is a Chinese national and has settled abroad, and who has acquired foreign nationality at birth shall not have Chinese nationality.[29]

The requirement of having at least one Chinese national parent to acquire Chinese nationality sits uncomfortably with the fact that a large proportion of Hong Kong residents held British National (Overseas) status prior to the handover.[30] One year before the transfer of sovereignty, in May 1996, the Standing Committee of the National People's Congress in Beijing stipulated in the 'Explanations of Some Questions by the Standing Committee of the National People's Congress Concerning the Implementation of the Nationality Law of the People's Republic of China in the Hong Kong Special Administrative Region' (1996 Explanations) that 'where a Hong Kong resident is of Chinese descent and was born in the Chinese territories (including Hong Kong), or where a person satisfies the criteria laid down in the Nationality Law of the People's Republic of China for having Chinese nationality, he is a Chinese national'.[31] It follows that according to Chinese nationality law, the distinction between the mainland and Hong Kong legal statuses is not one of 'nationality'. For mainland immigrants, CIES and the eventual obtainment of HKSAR-PR status do not trigger a change in nationality.

[26] Art 154, Basic Law 1990 (HK).

[27] National laws are in principle not applicable in the HKSAR according to Art 18, Basic Law. However, the same article also provides that national laws listed in Annex III to the Basic Law should be applied in the HKSAR. Chinese Nationality Law 1980 was listed in Annex III in the original Basic Law and thus has been in force in Hong Kong since 1997, see Nationality Law 1980 (CN) Annex III, Basic Law 1990 (HK).

[28] Art 4, Nationality Law 1980 (CN).

[29] In addition, Art 6 provides a supplementary mode, 'any person born in China whose parents are stateless or of uncertain nationality and have settled in China shall have Chinese nationality'; see also Arts 5 and 6.

[30] British Nationality (Hong Kong) Act 1990 (HK).

[31] Explanations of Some Questions by the Standing Committee of the National People's Congress Concerning the Implementation of the Nationality Law of the People's Republic of China in the Hong Kong Special Administrative Region (The National People's Congress of the People's Republic of China) www.npc.gov.cn/englishnpc/Law/2007-12/12/content_1383896.htm.

B. Eligibility for the Hong Kong Permanent Resident Status

As pointed out by Ghai, 'the Basic Law goes further than any scheme in providing for a local identity, which not only separates regional residents from other nationals, but also facilitates the participation and integration of non-nationals'.[32] According to Article 24 of the Basic Law, six categories of people are HKSAR permanent residents. The first three apply to Chinese citizens:

1. Chinese citizens born in Hong Kong before or after the establishment of the Hong Kong Special Administrative Region;
2. Chinese citizens who have ordinarily resided in Hong Kong for a continuous period of not less than seven years before or after the establishment of the Hong Kong Special Administrative Region;
3. Persons of Chinese nationality born outside Hong Kong of those residents listed in categories (1) and (2).[33]

There are also three categories of non-Chinese citizens:

1. Persons not of Chinese nationality who have entered Hong Kong with valid travel documents, have ordinarily resided in Hong Kong for a continuous period of not less than seven years and have taken Hong Kong as their place of permanent residence before or after the establishment of the Hong Kong Special Administrative Region;
2. Persons under 21 years of age born in Hong Kong of those residents listed in category (4) before or after the establishment of the Hong Kong Special Administrative Region; and
3. Persons other than those residents listed in categories (1) to (5), who, before the establishment of the Hong Kong Special Administrative Region, had the right of abode in Hong Kong only.[34]

To obtain HKSAR permanent residency, mainland immigrants admitted through the CIES would need to satisfy the residence requirements set out in section 2 of the above article: that is, 'ordinarily resided in Hong Kong for a continuous period of not less than seven years'. However, neither the Basic Law nor HKSAR immigration law specify what exactly constitutes 'ordinary residence'. The only related official statement is the Immigration Department's 'Explanations of Key Terms'. It provides that 'a person has ordinary residence in Hong Kong if he/she remains in Hong Kong legally, voluntarily and for a settled purpose (such as education, employment or residence), whether of short or long duration'. In addition, a number of determinants are mentioned, such as the 'reason, duration and frequency of absence' and the 'whereabouts of family members'.[35] Nevertheless, the fact remains that a 'minimum duration of residence' required for establishing ordinary residence is absent in the HKSAR immigration law.

C. Rights of Hong Kong Permanent Residents

Permanent residents of the HKSAR enjoy a right of abode which confers the right 'to land in HKSAR, to be free from any condition of stay (including a limit of stay) in HKSAR, not to be

[32] Ghai, 'Citizenship and Politics in the HKSAR' (2001) 5 *Citizenship Studies* 143, 150.
[33] Art 24, Basic Law 1990 (HK).
[34] ibid.
[35] 'Meanings of Right of Abode and Other Terms' (Honk Kong Immigration Department) www.immd.gov.hk/eng/services/roa/term.html.

deported from HKSAR, and not to be removed from HKSAR'.[36] Besides the more conventional rights associated with permanent residence, such as the right to work and the right to social benefits, HKSAR permanent residents also enjoy electoral rights. Permanent residents aged 18 or over can register to vote regardless their nationality.[37] However, for mainland immigrants, the benefits of HKSAR-PR status are not confined to the rights and entitlements they can claim within Hong Kong.

V. THE HONG KONG SAR PASSPORT

Mainland immigrants can, upon obtaining permanent residence, apply for a Hong Kong Special Administration Region passport as distinct from the People's Republic of China passport. A person is eligible to apply for a HKSAR passport if he or she is 'a Chinese citizen, a permanent resident of the HKSAR and a holder of a valid Hong Kong permanent identity card'.[38] As Hong Kong is authorised to conclude visa waiver agreements with foreign states, 154 countries or territories have granted visa-free access or visa-on-arrival to HKSAR passport holders.[39] This contrasts with the 50 countries granting visa-free travel or visa-on-arrival to PRC passport holders.[40]

A. Dual and Multiple Passports

In addition to visa-free travel, another 'external' benefit of HKSAR-PR status (for Chinese nationals) is the de facto exemption from the principle of non-recognition of dual nationality in Chinese nationality law. The Nationality Law 1980 explicitly states that China does not recognise dual nationality for any Chinese national.[41] Yet there are currently 3.4 million British National (Overseas) passport holders in Hong Kong.[42] An exception has been made for dual and multiple passports for Hong Kong in the 1996 Explanations. It provides that:

> All Hong Kong Chinese compatriots are Chinese nationals, whether or not they are holders of the British Dependent Territories Citizens passport or British National (Overseas) passport. With effect from 1 July 1997, Chinese nationals mentioned above may, for the purpose of travelling to other countries and territories, continue to use the valid travel documents issued by the Government of the United Kingdom but they shall not be entitled to British consular protection in the HKSAR and other parts of the PRC on account of their holding the above mentioned British travel documents. Likewise, Chinese nationals of the HKSAR with right of abode in foreign countries may, for the purpose of travelling to other countries and territories, use the relevant documents issued by the foreign governments and again they will not be entitled to consular protection in the HKSAR and other parts of the PRC on account of their holding the above mentioned documents.[43]

[36] ibid.

[37] 'Voter Registration' (Hong Kong Government) www.voterregistration.gov.hk/eng/register-gc.html.

[38] 'Application for HKSAR Passport' (Hong Kong Immigration Department) www.immd.gov.hk/eng/service/travel_document/apply_for_hksar_passport.html.

[39] Art 155, Basic Law 1990 (HK); 'Visa-free access or visa-on-arrival for HKSAR Passport' (Hong Kong Immigration Department) www.immd.gov.hk/eng/service/travel_document/visa_free_access.html.

[40] 'The Henley & Partners Visa Restrictions Index 2016' (Henley & Partners) www.henleyglobal.com/files/download/HP/hvri/HP%20Visa%20Restrictions%20Index%20160223.pdf.

[41] Art 3 of Nationality Law 1980 (CN).

[42] 'The UK and Hong Kong as Partners' (UK Parliament) www.publications.parliament.uk/pa/cm201415/cmselect/cmfaff/649/64907.htm#note27.

[43] Explanations of Some Questions by the Standing Committee of the National People's Congress Concerning the Implementation of the Nationality Law of the People's Republic of China in the Hong Kong Special Administrative

Similar arrangement has also been made for Macau. In 1998, one year before the return of Macau to China, the Standing Committee promulgated the 'Explanations of Some Questions by the Standing Committee of the National People's Congress Concerning the Implementation of the Nationality Law of the People's Republic of China in the Macau Special Administrative Region' (hereinafter, 1998 Explanations).[44] Just as the 1996 Explanations serve as the legal basis of the exception made for Hong Kong, the 1998 Explanations has the same effect for Chinese nationals that are Macau permanent residents. In both cases, the Chinese government allows the holding of dual or multiple passports by its nationals (not limited to those issued by the two previous metropoles, namely, the UK and Portugal). Therefore, the primary difference between the effects of these two arrangements lies not in the stances of the Chinese government but in the different types of legal statuses granted to their previous subjects or citizens by the UK and Portugal, after the transfers of sovereignty.

The UK grants the British National (overseas) status to a large portion of Hong Kongers but this status does not confer its holders a right of abode in the UK.[45] Portugal, however, did not create different categories of Portuguese nationality and a significant portion of Macau residents are thus entitled to the 'actual' and full Portuguese citizenship.[46] At the EU level, the 'Macau Chinese Portuguese' are also EU citizens enjoying all the rights conferred through EU citizenship unlike the British National (overseas) passport holders in Hong Kong.

Although these preferential treatments were rarely criticised in their own right, it was used by Chinese scholars as an argument for the recognition of dual nationality for all Chinese nationals. For them, recognising dual nationality for only one class of Chinese citizens damages the integrity of Chinese nationality law and hinders the transnational mobility of overseas Chinese of mainland origin.[47]

B. Purchasing Convenient Permanent Residency

Despite the CIES's third-country permanent residency requirement for mainland applicants, the vast majority of successful applicants are mainland Chinese.[48] The practice of first acquiring convenient permanent residency in a small state and then applying for CIES with the acquired status is termed 'double investment migration' by a senior Hong Kong investment migration consultant.[49]

Gambia is one of the main suppliers of such programmes. The documents required to obtain Gambian PR status include a copy of the passport, a passport photo, a police certificate

Region (The National People's Congress of the People's Republic of China) www.npc.gov.cn/englishnpc/Law/2007-12/12/content_1383896.htm.

[44] '全国人民代表大会常务委员会关于《中华人民共和国国籍法》在澳门特别行政区实施的几个问题的解释' [Explanations of Some Questions by the Standing Committee of the National People's Congress Concerning the Implementation of the Nationality Law of the People's Republic of China in the Macau Special Administrative Region] (The National People's Congress of the People's Republic of China) www.npc.gov.cn/npc/gadbzl/amdbdj_12/2012-06/06/content_1724386.htm.

[45] 'Types of British Nationality' (UK Government) www.gov.uk/types-of-british-nationality/british-national-overseas.

[46] Mendes, *Portugal, China and the Macau Negotiations, 1986–1999* (Hong Kong University Press 2013) 56.

[47] eg Xiao and Guo, '全球化视野下的双重国籍' [Dual Nationality From the Perspective of Globalization] (2006) 5 *Wuhan University Journal* 581; Guofu and Jiaquan, '境外国籍法的新发展与中国国籍法的渐进改革' [The Recent Development of Foreign Nationality Law and the Incremental Reform of Chinese Nationality Law] (2009) 1 *Journal of Huaqiao University* 51.

[48] 'Chinese African in HK' (Webb-site Reports, 15 April 2012).

[49] '投资移民非洲之路' [The African Route of Investment Migration] (Apple Daily, 16 April 2012) http://hk.apple.nextmedia.com/news/art/20120416/16251393.

and a medical certificate, as well as a birth certificate, marriage certificate or certificate of kinship for dependants. The application fee is approximately EUR 11,000 for each applicant and a EUR 2700 (approximate) charge for each dependant. The application process takes around 15 working days.[50]

The Vanuatu PR programme is also widely used by mainland immigrant investors. Unlike the Gambian programme which was used for CIES applications for more than a decade, the Vanuatu scheme only entered the market in 2011. As a consequence, it is not featured in the aforementioned figures on the 'residency' composition of successful mainland applicants.

The documents required to obtain Vanuatu permanent residence include those needed for the Gambian programme in addition to a proof of income, a certified letter of undertakings and certificate of registration. Certificate of registration refers to a certificate of incorporation of a Vanuatu registered company.[51]

Registering a corporation in Vanuatu is required but incurs no additional cost (the application fee is similar to that of the Gambian programme).[52] This requirement can be regarded as an attempt to promote the Vanuatu Offshore Financial Services, another programme which Vanuatu has been forcefully marketing in China. Despite the additional documents and company registration procedure required, the application process takes only one to two working days.

In addition, the legal basis of the PR programme is provided in Vanuatu Immigration Visa Regulation Order No 180 of 2011 (of the Immigration Act No 17 of 2010).[53] Virakwahe, a Vanuatu immigration officer, is delegated the powers to implement the regulation. A trade commission has also been created in Hong Kong to promote both the PR programme and Vanuatu's offshore financial services. Furthermore, PRG Consulting Limited, a Hong Kong based company, was appointed the sole distributor of the PR programme.[54] All applications are referred to PRG Consulting Limited before being considered by the Vanuatu authorities.

In addition to competition between intermediaries, the existence of competing convenient permanent residency programmes and the different alliances formed between the supplying states and the intermediaries can create conflicts of interest. In 2012 Virakwahe, the immigration officer in charge of the Vanuatu PR programme, filed a lawsuit in the Hong Kong High Court against Kwan, a director of a large Hong Kong migration intermediary, over his comments on Vanuatu's permanent residence programme which were quoted in a Hong Kong magazine.

According to the magazine article, Kwan considered Vanuatu as 'politically unstable' and there was 'no certainty and security in any co-operation with the Vanuatu government' and that 'he had also turned down the offer to be a consultant for Vanuatu'. Virakwahe alleged that the publication of the article has seriously affected the Vanuatu permanent residency

[50] In addition to secondary sources, I drew on interviews I conducted with three Chinese investment migration consultants specialized in mainland China–Hong Kong migration for details of the Gambian and Vanuatu PR programmes.

[51] '永久居留权' [Permanent Residence Rights] (PRG Consulting Limited) www.hkprg.com/PublishWebSite/hkprg/gallery/getCMSPage.asp?url=/PublishWebSite/hkprg/big5/contentPag e41404.htm.

[52] 'Vanuatu Immigration Visa Regulation Order No 180 of 2011' (Government of Vanuatu) https://governmentofvanuatu.gov.vu/images/Regulations/Immigration/order%20no.%20180%20of%202011.pdf.

[53] The regulation notes that the programme applies only in Greater China (mainland China, Hong Kong, Macau and Taiwan), ibid.

[54] 'Statement by Embassy' (PRG Consulting Limited) www.hkprg.com/PublishWebSite/hkprg/gallery/7818a2a2-b9c3-4613-a8c4-73ac0c2a389f.pdf.

programme's reputation and applications have declined substantially as a consequence. He also mentioned that

> the defendant is in the business of immigration services and is an agent for the marketing of the permanent residence status of Gambia which is in competition with [Vanuatu] and must have made and published the defamatory words with an intent to defeat the PR Visa Program.[55]

VI. CONCLUSION

As a special administrative region of China, Hong Kong is a separate immigration territory from the mainland. The rights and opportunities associated with Hong Kong permanent resident status along with the usefulness of the HKSAR passport are strong 'pull' factors for mainland immigrant investors to participate in CIES. Although this scheme is in principle designed for foreign nationals, the vast majority of its successful applicants are from the mainland. Interestingly, the tactical requirement of third-country permanent residency for mainland applicants has fuelled a demand for convenient permanent residency programmes which are met by supply from small West African and Pacific Island states.

[55] 'Statement by the Honorable Moana Carcasses (MP), Prime Minister of the Republic of Vanuatu' (PRG Consulting Limited) www.hkprg.com/PublishWebSite/hkprg/gallery/67f4a68e-deb8-430f-878e-11cb2efd54f0.pdf; Chiu, 'Vanuatu Sues Immigration Agent For Libel Over Visa Scheme' (South China Morning Post, 21 December 2013) www.scmp.com/news/hong-kong/article/1387061/vanuatu-sues-immigration-agent-libel-over-visa-scheme.

16

Will Virtual Become Real? Ten Years of the e-Residency Programme in Estonia

VADIM POLESHCHUK*

I. INTRODUCTION

ESTONIA BECAME THE first country to offer non-residents a transnational digital identity. Relevant amendments to the Identity Documents Act[1] entered into force in December 2014.[2] E-residents receive smart ID cards ('Digi-IDs') which provide them with: digital identification and authentication to secure services; digital signing of documents; digital verification of document authenticity; and document encryption.[3]

According to the Ministry of Economic Affairs and Communications, e-Residency was 'a step towards fulfilling Estonia's aspirations of pioneering the first borderless e-society, and is the first government-backed digital identity in the world'.[4] Policymakers decided to avoid exclusive terminology such as 'a non-resident', preferring the inclusive 'e-resident'. The Explanatory Note attached to the bill described an e-resident as a 'person residing in the e-state', a 'permanent virtual inhabitant of the e-state'.[5] Rein Lang MP, who was responsible for the Bill in Parliament, argued before the final vote these changes 'are epoch-making and they may potentially draw international attention and move the Estonian agenda forward'.[6] Such grand statements require proper contextualisation.

According to the Digital Agenda for Estonia 2020, the fundamental pillars of the development of the Estonian information society were the public sector's active role in the uptake and procurement of innovative solutions and the shaping of the overall conditions for development; investments in new technologies by the banking and telecommunications sectors; and the readiness of the population to use new ICT solutions.[7] Internet is accessible nearly everywhere in

* This chapter does not reflect the official opinion of the EU or the European Parliament. Responsibility for the information and views expressed in the piece lies entirely with the author.

[1] Identity Documents Act (*Isikut tõendavate dokumentide seadus*) 1999 (EE), 25, 365.

[2] Identity Documents Act and State Fee Act Amendment Act (*Isikut tõendavate dokumentide seaduse ja riigilõivuseaduse muutmise seadus*) 2014 (EE), 1.

[3] Poleshchuk, 'Making Estonia Bigger' (2016) Investment Migration Policy Briefs IMC-PB 2016/1.

[4] Press release of 13 May 2015 (Estonia, Ministry of Economic Affairs and Communications) http://www.mkm.ee.

[5] Explanatory Note to the Draft of the Identity Documents Act and State Fee Act Amendment Act (EE), 12.

[6] Parliament, Minutes of the Plenary Session of 21 October 2014 (EE).

[7] 'Digital Agenda 2020 for Estonia' (Ministry of Economic Affairs and Communications 2020).

Estonia. In 2016, when the programme had just started, fixed or wireless broadband access was enjoyed by 77.2 per cent of all households; mobile access by 67.2 per cent.[8] Estonia is pioneering in the uptake of electronic identity and the use of e-voting.[9]

Estonia's technical successes in the e-government sphere were rightly viewed as part of the neoliberal reforms which broke with the country's Soviet past, its IT backwardness and its clumsy bureaucracy.[10] Budnitsky rightly concluded that e-Estonia became 'political dogma, the questioning of which is seen as tantamount to undermining Estonia's Euro-Atlantic credentials and benefiting Russia'.[11] Against such a background, it is not surprising that '... the branding of the country through e-Residency appeals to the global competitiveness of the country. Through e-Residency, 'e-Estonia', previously a symbol of a digitally advanced *national* society, is being transformed into the image of a globally open *transnational* society. The imagery constructed around the notions of the 'virtual state' and 'virtual Residency' presents a commodified version of the national space described by global reach and accessibility, transnational character and technological attractiveness'. [12] From the start, the project has an important PR-component.

One of the objectives of the Estonian authorities is to boost economic development: e-Residency permits the holder to establish a company online within a day and administer it via internet from anywhere in the world. According to official estimates, 30,000 e-residents bring about EUR 60 million to Estonian economy annually.[13] In 2015 the authorities expected about 40,000 e-residents to register in a three-year period, or even up to 60,000 provided that additional investments were secured.[14] In May 2024, there were more than 114,400 e-residents of Estonia, who had established more than 30,600 companies.[15] By August 2023, the economic impact generated by the programme for Estonia was estimated to amount to a total of EUR 183 million.[16]

Given the size of the population and the economy (1.3 million people or 0.3 per cent of the total EU population[17] and with an economy equal to 0.2 per cent of the entire EU economy),[18] it is not uncommon for Estonians to worry about the future. In some cases, PR campaign participants openly spoke about the expectation that e-residents would help the survival of Estonian culture, language, nature and social development.[19] One of the first detailed academic analyses of the e-Residency programme ends with the conclusion that '[o]ne of the main implications of the e-Residency project has been that Estonia has gained popularity and recognition internationally ... Such attention is hoped to bolster the state's chances of survival in the long run'.[20]

[8] 'Table IT21: H Households Having Internet Connection at Home' (Statistics Estonia).

[9] 'Internet voting in Estonia' (Valimised) www.valimised.ee/en/internet-voting-estonia.

[10] Norberg and Norberg, 'Estonia's "Return to Europe"' (2024) 108 *Political Geography* 103009.

[11] Budnitsky, 'A Relational Approach to Digital Sovereignty' (2022) 16 *Int. J. Commun.* 1918, 1931.

[12] Tammpuu and Masso, 'Welcome to the Virtual State' (2018) 21 *Eur. J. Cult. Stud.* 543, 556.

[13] Press release of 23 July 2015 (Estonia, Ministry of Economic Affairs and Communications).

[14] ibid.

[15] 'E-Residency in Numbers' (E-Residency) www.e-resident.gov.ee/dashboard.

[16] Ristoja, 'E-Residency Reports Close to 40 Million Euros in State Revenue' (E-Residency, 31 August 2023) www.e-resident.gov.ee/blog/posts/eResidency-reports-40million-state-revenue.

[17] Population Change (Eurostat 2024) https://ec.europa.eu/eurostat/databrowser/view/DEMO_GIND__custom_7127262/default/table.

[18] GDP and Main Components (Output, Expenditure and Income) (Eurostat 2024) https://ec.europa.eu/eurostat/databrowser/view/NAMA_10_GDP__custom_8987645/default/table?lang=en.

[19] Adee, 'Forget Trump and Brexit' (*New Scientist*, 9 November 2016) www.newscientist.com/article/mg23230992-500-rise-of-digital-citzenship-how-to-emigrate-from-your-sofa/.

[20] Peets, 'The Implications of the Estonian E-Residency Project on Statehood and Territoriality' (MA Thesis, Charles University 2017) 73.

Not all national experts greeted the introduction of the e-Residency programme with uncritical enthusiasm. For instance, some expressed concerns related to potential identity crime and fraud.[21] Questions were also asked about possible tensions between the Estonian project and EU law and policy. Importantly, the implementation of the eIDAS Regulation[22] as a whole did not encounter any major issues.[23] Kerikmäe and Särav insisted that 'more lucrative objectives should be prioritised … by contributing to provide a techno-legal model for other Member States to fully exploit the e-services at the EU Digital Single Market'. At least partially, this remains the case today. The Estonian e-Residency programme aroused considerable interest among experts due to its thoughtful elaboration and the demonstrated will of the political leadership to develop further the project.[24]

II. WHO ARE E-RESIDENTS ACCORDING TO LAW?

Article 20-5 (2) of the amended Identity Documents Act (IDA) provides that '[t]he objective of the issue of an e-resident's digital identity card is to promote the development of the Estonian economy, science, education or culture by providing access to e-services with the Estonian digital document'.

In May 2015 Estonia launched its e-Residency application portal: e-resident.gov.ee. The online application is quite simple. After paying a modest fee and completing a background check, e-residents can collect their Digi-IDs at an Estonian embassy or a consulate, or at a Police and Border Guard Board service point in Estonia. The entire application process was expected to take an average of just one month.[25] In practice, initially it took longer than expected due to the high number of applications.

Rhetorically, e-Residency in Estonia is defined as membership in the virtual polity which does not limit itself but exceeds the polity of Estonian nationals and resident aliens. Researchers and policymakers use various fancy terms such as virtual diaspora,[26] virtual state,[27] and so on. Quite predictably, however, there is no direct connection between the e-resident's status with the status of any ordinary resident. e-Residency as such does not grant the right to visit or to reside in Estonia (which normally requires a visa, a residence permit or a right of residence).

From the legal perspective, e-Residency is endorsed by the release of a digital document enabling digital identification and digital signing. Digi-IDs are issued in accordance with the IDA and relevant secondary laws. Similar digital documents which prove digital identity have previously been and are still issued to Estonian nationals and resident aliens (Article 20-1, IDA). However, there are significant differences in procedure for these categories of applicants. The Explanatory Note states that access to e-Residency is an advantage (*hüve*), not an individual right.[28]

[21] Sullivan and Burger, 'E-Residency and Blockchain' (2017) 33 *Computer Law and Security Report* 470, 481.

[22] Regulation (EU) No 910/2014 on electronic identification and trust services for electronic transactions in the internal market [2014] OJ L 257/73.

[23] Aavik and Krimmer, 'Integrating Digital Migrants' (2016) LNCS-9820 *Lecture Notes in Computer Science* 151.

[24] Estonia's Digital Agenda 2030 (Ministry of Economic Affairs and Communications 2021) www.mkm.ee/sites/default/files/documents/2022-04/Digi%C3%BChiskonna%20arengukava_ENG.pdf.

[25] Estonia, Ministry of Economic Affairs and Communications, Press release of 13 May 2015.

[26] Rodima-Taylor and Grimes, 'Virtualizing Diaspora' (2019) 19 *Global Networks* 349.

[27] Tammpuu and Masso, 'Welcome to the Virtual State'.

[28] Explanatory Note to the Draft of the Identity Documents Act and State Fee Act Amendment Act (EE), 3.

Estonia has deliberately decided to apply the same principles to the processing of e-Residency requests as to visa proceedings.[29] The burden of proof rests with the applicant (Article 20-7 (1), IDA). The applicant's right of access to the relevant documents or files in the course of the proceedings may be restricted, also in the interests of security and the protection of public order (Article 20-7 (3), IDA). Upon resolving a challenge filed against a decision to refuse to issue, suspend the validity of or revoke an e-resident's digital identity card, the circumstances or evidence on which the challenged administrative act is based will not be stated in the decision on appeal (Article 20-7 (5), IDA). All in all, the issuance procedure for an e-resident's digital identity card is different from the rules which normally apply in Estonian administrative proceedings.[30]

Article 20-8 IDA authorises the Police and Border Guard Board, the Estonian Security Police (special service) and the Estonian Tax and Customs Board to exercise state supervision over the use of an e-resident's digital identity card.[31] Any other administrative body or service provider is required to forward to the Police and Border Guard Board service, any information which may result in the revocation or suspension of validity of the e-resident's digital identity card. The identification of the person and the verification of the identity of the e-resident (Article 20-9, IDA) is regulated by the relevant provisions of the Aliens Act,[32] including Article 270 (2) which permits the processing of a foreigner's personal data, including private and sensitive personal data, without his or her consent and without separately notifying him or her.

As a positive sign, the criteria for e-Residency were worded in general and inclusive terms. Initially, a Digi-ID could be issued to a person who 'has a relationship with the Estonian state or legitimate interest in the use of e-services of the Estonian state' (Article 20-6 (1), IDA). However, from July 2016 these criteria have been repealed, meaning that there are no longer any explicit individual criteria. An absolute prohibition for the issuance of Digi-IDs only applies to persons who are deemed to pose a threat to public order or national security; if the ID is applied for a prohibited economic activity; if the applicant cannot be clearly identified or if there is a reason to doubt the true identity thereof (Article 20-6 (2), IDA). The release of an e-resident's digital identity card can be refused, in the sense that the authorities may use their right of discretion, in cases where there is a basis for refusal to issue a visa or temporary residence permit, or to refuse entry to the country on arrival. Also, the document can be denied if it does not comply with the objectives of the issuance of the e-resident's digital identity card (Article 20-6 (3), IDA). Logically, an e-resident's digital identity card may be revoked under the same conditions (Article 20-6 (4), IDA).

In a policy brief written in 2016, I suggested that the Estonian judiciary might decide to limit the discretion of the authorities:[33] e-residents are private persons or businessmen who enter into 'effective' social relations in the Estonian territory. They establish relations with the

[29] ibid, 4.

[30] For instance, in ordinary administrative proceedings everyone has the right to examine relevant documents and files, if such exist; and the negative decision on a challenge shall be reasoned. Art 37(1), 86 (2), Administrative Procedure Act (*Haldusmenetluse seadus*) 2001 (EE), 58, 354.

[31] A digital identity card is 'an important identity document' for the purposes of the Division 2 of Ch 19, Art 350 of the Penal Code 2001 (EE). That means that crimes related to digi-IDs are punishable according to Art 347 (falsification of important ID), Art 348 (obtaining, use or grant of permission to use falsified important identity document) and Art 349 (fraudulent use of important ID) of the Penal Code. In practice there might be some problems as regards territorial scope of the penal law of Estonia insofar as it applies to acts committed within the territory of Estonia (Art 6 (1) of the Penal Code) and exceptions to these rules (Art 6 (2) and 7) are hardly relevant in the context of digi-IDs. Nevertheless, physical infrastructure that enables use of these documents as well as 'territorial points' of provision of e-services are mostly anchored to Estonia and therefore to territorial scope of the Estonian penal law.

[32] Aliens Act (*Välismaalaste seadus*) 2010 (EE), 3, 4.

[33] Poleshchuk, 'Making Estonia Bigger', 5–6.

Estonian state which provides them with Estonian personal codes and special IDs. The digital ID is also impossible without certain infrastructure, which is 'physically' located in Estonia. In the medium-term 'effective' social relations will render e-residents somewhat similar to ordinary residents who enjoy protection under Article 26 of the Estonian Constitution, which provides for the inviolability of the private and family life. In other words, under some circumstances, e-Residency might gradually become a 'right' rather than an 'advantage' and it may even come to be relied on in support of claims to be permitted to enter and remain in Estonia.[34]

However, this has never happened in practice.[35] The Estonian courts have continued to interpret the situation of e-residents quite rigidly, recognising the broad discretion of the migration authorities. This became very obvious after the outbreak of Russia's war in Ukraine, which led to the freezing of many ties between Europe, including Estonia, and Russia, as well as causing a process of regional fragmentation in international politics and economics. Currently, the issuance of first-time e-Residence cards to Russians and Belarusians is suspended by the police authorities, and renewal may be refused.[36] Accordingly, the initial claims about a certain universalism of the e-Residency programme have collided with harsh geopolitical realities.

III. COULD E-RESIDENCY BECOME SOMETHING MORE? REALITY VERSUS 'VIRTUALITY'

Soon after the start of the e-Residency programme, Roots suggested that the idea could be used for the common e-citizenship of the European Union.[37] Dumbrava went on to argue that the design and the discursive framing of the scheme could bring e-Residence closer to citizenship: in practical terms, e-Residence status amounts to a form of participation, which is an important dimension of democratic citizenship; e-residents form some links with the country, which moves it towards the formula of 'genuine connection' commonly used to designate 'classical' citizenship; the scheme also includes an element of contribution to the common good, which is important for modern understandings of citizenship.[38]

Indeed, a study of Estonian e-residents showed that although they normally perceive their relationship with the Estonian state as a client-service provider relationship, nevertheless, some of them already have a certain sense of community and belonging.[39] The emergence of such positive emotions is partly explained by what Kochenov praised as a compensation mechanism for the 'deficiencies of the statuses of citizenship, which the vast majority of the world's population got by birth'.[40] However, it is worth mentioning that five out of the top 10 most common citizenships held by e-residents are citizenships of EU Member States.[41]

[34] Provided certain conditions are met, an e-resident (as any other foreigner) may apply for a temporary residence permit for enterprise, see Subsect 5, Ch 3, Aliens Act 2009 (EE). However, several applicable rules are quite rigid (especially those related to capital).

[35] Author's analysis of court judgements published online, see 'All legal proceedings' (Riigi Teataja) www.riigiteataja.ee/kohtulahendid/koik_menetlused.html.

[36] 'Restrictions on Russia and Belarus' (e-Residency, Republic of Estonia, 24 March 2024) https://learn.e-resident.gov.ee/hc/en-us/articles/4575271559441-Restrictions-on-Russia-and-Belarus.

[37] Roots, 'E-citizenship as a Tool to Increase the European Identity' in Matiuta (ed), *Democratic Governance and Active Citizenship in the European Union* (Lambert 2015).

[38] Dumbrava, 'Welcome to E-stonia!' (EUI Globalcit, 9 September 2015) https://globalcit.eu/welcome-to-e-stonia-e-residence-and-citizenship-in-an-electronic-republic-2/.

[39] Tammpuu et al, 'Estonian e-Residency and Conceptions of Platform-Based State-Individual Relationship' (2022) 26 *Trames* 3, 16.

[40] Kochenov, 'Escapist Technology in the Service of Neo-Feudalism' in Bauböck (ed), *Debating Transformations of National Citizenship* (Springer 2018) 326.

[41] See Table 16.1.

As explained above, the rules for e-Residency are worded in quite inclusive terms, but Estonian authorities enjoy a wide margin of appreciation when deciding whether to issue, suspend or revoke their e-residents' Digi-IDs. The liberal access to e-Residency seems to benefit most non-resident aliens who have no plans to live in Estonia. In turn, e-Residency is supposed to promote Estonia's economy, science, education or culture 'at a distance'. Just as e-citizenship is not citizenship when subjected to strict legal scrutiny, so is e-Residency not residence or migration, since strict boundaries between the real and virtual worlds are maintained, and the latter is always dependent on the former.

These distinctions become especially clear if we recall the Estonian situation 'on the ground'. The country is still home to a huge number of Russian citizens and stateless persons (persons with 'unspecified citizenship').[42] They were part of the permanent population who were not recognised as Estonian citizens after the restoration of independence in 1991.[43] Both groups are active users of e-government services (just like Estonian nationals), which has no impact on their status or their legal rights and obligations (or lack thereof). Even if we consider e-Residency as a sort of protective measure (especially in the case of third-country nationals such as Russians), 'an e-resident does not acquire political rights, only the permission to use the Estonian digital infrastructure'.[44] Furthermore, according to Estonian scholars, the existing divisions in Estonian society have not eased amid the implementation of the e-Residency project:

> E-Residency provides progressive and positive meanings as an alternative to the past-oriented connotations related to the post-Soviet transformation of the country. But it also contributes to the reproduction of the exclusionary understanding of the nation, which creates tensions in the processes of the internationalisation of the society, considering the relatively negative attitudes towards immigrants in the European context, as well as drawing clear linguistic-cultural borders between national groups in Estonia since the Soviet time as indicated in previous studies.[45]

IV. LESSONS LEARNED

A. Digital is Good …

The proven interest in Estonian e-Residency shows that its authors were able to offer a truly desirable product, and earlier than others. It is clear that the first-mover advantage of originality and exclusivity will fade over time, as increasingly many similar programmes appear on the international market, sometimes also with the right of temporary residence (nomad visas).[46]

The statistics about programme participants also show that for many of Estonia's neighbours (including former neighbours in the 'Soviet dormitory') e-Residency has become a convenient opportunity to gain access to the EU market (see Table 16.1). However, the

[42] Altogether more than 10 per cent of the total population. 'Table RV068: Population By Citizenship and Place of Residence, 1 January' (Statistics Estonia) https://andmed.stat.ee/en/stat/rahvastik__rahvastikunaitajad-ja-koosseis__rahvaarv-ja-rahvastiku-koosseis/RV068.

[43] Poleshchuk, 'The JOKK Predicament: Access to Citizenship and Limits to EU Member States' Power' (Doctoral Thesis, University of Groningen, 2021).

[44] Hoffmannand and Solarte, 'The Estonian e-Residency Programme and its Role beyond the Country's Digital Public Sector Ecosystem' (2022) 13 *CES Derecho* 184, 198.

[45] Tammpuu and Masso, 'Welcome to the Virtual State', 557.

[46] Sánchez-Vergara et al, 'Home Office is the Here and Now' (2023) 65 *World Leisure Journal* 236. However, the Estonian e-Residency programme is not a classical nomad visa scheme while it does not encompass the right of physical presence in the country.

popularity of the programme among EU citizens also indicates that technology development in many Member States remains at an unsatisfactory level and Estonia can still offer unique opportunities at this juncture.

The risk factors for the programme, as events of recent years have shown, lie not only in the classic problems associated with cybercrime and cyber-fraud, identity theft, and so on. On the contrary, problems of a geopolitical nature, including risks associated with illegal circumvention of the sanctions regime, and so forth, will probably take first place.

B. … But the Digital is Subordinate to the Real

The emergence of e-Residency gave rise to high expectations of its potential to change the nature of migration and citizenship legislation, which generally did not materialise. Despite the high-flying rhetoric used by the Estonian authorities and programme executives as part of the PR campaigns for the programme, e-Residency remained the same as it was before, that is, an access point to digital public and private services, although the geography of the possible uses for e-identity has considerably expanded. e-Residency was not planned to be a tool for expanding the rights of foreign nationals or residents in Estonia, and this remains the case. The passion for everything 'digital' should not hide the fact that a 'digital service' is still a service, and digital is only the means by which it is provided. However, the form per se cannot change the actual essence of a service.

e-Residency has allowed Estonia to attract significant capital from outside without changing the fundamentals of citizenship and migration policy. Access to the programme did not require national cultural or other loyalty and linguistic competencies, and participation in the programme does not make you a full-fledged participant in Estonian life. This process had a dual nature: while solving some of the problems of holders of 'weak' passports or of passports from countries lagging behind in the field of IT, the programme did not in any way affect the internal structure of Estonian society, with its striking ethnocultural dividing lines. Virtual reality is not a suitable means by which to achieve such considerable changes.

Table 16.1 e-Residency numbers, top 10 countries by citizenship, 14 May 2024

Citizenship	No of e-residents	No of companies
Ukraine	7139	2434
Germany	6805	2368
Spain	6269	2603
Finland	6221	999
Russia	5748	1806
China	5192	502
France	4781	1638
UK	4657	1142
Turkey	4590	1788
Italy	4421	1376

Source: Republic of Estonia, e-Residency, www.e-resident.gov.ee/dashboard/.

17

Foreign Nationality Acquisition in Late Imperial China

Change of Personal Status as Pathway to Opportunities and Personal Security

SAU KONG LEE

I. INTRODUCTION

NATIONALITY DENOTES A person's status as a 'belonger' to a state. International law treats nationality as a uniform concept. The international community assumes that nationality epitomises human dignity and declares aspiringly that everyone has the right to a nationality.[1] Yet the quality of nationality (and subcategories of nationality) varies greatly across states depending on the bundle of rights, opportunities, obligations and restrictions that come with that status. Despite the supposed equality of mankind, the assignment of nationality at birth is a random birthright lottery[2] casually doling out rights, opportunities, personal liberties and security underpinned by the rule of law, or the 'penal status of privation and exclusion from dignity'.[3]

Globalisation liberates information flow and lines up different nationalities for comparison in a beauty parade. This task is facilitated by ranking indices such as the Quality of Nationality Index developed by Christian Kälin and Dimitry Kochenov which measures the quality of nationality based on internal factors (economic strength, human development, peace and stability) and external ones (travel freedom, settlement freedom);[4] the Henley Passport Index that measures the travel freedom of nationalities based on visa-free access with passports;[5] and the Citizenship Quality Index proposed by Yossi Harpaz that measures the value of citizenship (based on security, economic opportunity and civil and political rights) and mobility freedom (based on visa-free access of passport).[6] For persons born of an 'inferior' nationality,

[1] Art 15 of Universal Declaration of Human Rights 1948.

[2] Shachar, *The Birthright Lottery* (Harvard University Press 2009).

[3] Kochenov, 'Victims of Citizenship' in Kochenov and Surak (eds), *Citizenship and Residence Sales* (Cambridge University Press 2023) 71; Kochenov, *Citizenship* (MIT Press 2019).

[4] Kochenov and Lindeboom (eds), *Quality of Nationality Index* (Hart 2020).

[5] 'Passport Index' (Henley & Partners) www.henleyglobal.com/passport-index.

[6] Harpaz, *Citizenship 2.0* (Princeton University Press 2019) 20–22. Harpaz, 'Compensatory Citizenship' (2019) 45 *JEMS* 897.

the acquisition of foreign nationality or residence provides them with an alternative pathway to access rights and freedoms they do not otherwise enjoy or to ensure security of the person.[7] This is aided by the trend towards toleration of dual nationality especially since 1990s, and at the height of globalisation, a forceful argument has been advanced that dual nationality should now be recognised as a human right.[8] At the same time, the proliferation of 'citizenship-by-investment' and 'residence-by-investment' schemes has raised controversies over the morality and political implications of 'citizenship sales'. Schemes that award 'golden passports' without requiring residence in the country have attracted the strongest criticisms, not in the least because of concerns about the abuse of citizenship by corrupt individuals to perpetrate crimes and escape justice.[9]

As home to the world's second largest population,[10] China has been producing some of the world's wealthiest persons. In 2022, China came second only to the United States in the number of high net-worth individuals as well as ultra-high net-worth individuals.[11] Chinese nationals are also among the largest groups of clients of CBI and RBI schemes in the world, accounting for approximately 80 per cent of the world's applicants of residence programmes.[12] Inevitably, some of them also become embroiled in allegations of 'citizenship abuses'.[13]

Just as 'citizenship sale' has historical roots in the practices of urban centres in pre-modern Europe,[14] Chinese practice of acquiring or changing nationality is not a recent phenomenon either, but dates back to the imperial period. This chapter seeks to provide historical context by examining the acquisition and use of foreign nationality by Chinese during China's last imperial, Qing dynasty (1644–1912). It hopes to contribute to the existing scholarship on two fronts. It seeks to contribute to the literature on citizenship studies by exploring nationality's 'compensatory', 'opportunity-enhancing' function[15] from the individual's standpoint and show that the acquisition of foreign nationality is not necessarily an 'abusive' practice. It also seeks to supplement an additional perspective on the discourse on the 'unequal treaty system' in late imperial China.

[7] Harpaz, *Citizenship 2.0*, 20–22. Harpaz, 'Compensatory Citizenship', 897. Surak, *The Golden Passport* (Harvard University Press 2023) 211–15.

[8] According to the Global Dual Citizenship Database, by 2020, 76 per cent of the countries in the world had come to allow their nationals to acquire another nationality without requiring compulsory expatriation, a remarkable jump from 1960 when 62 per cent of countries in the world did not allow dual nationality: Vink et al, 'MACIMIDE Global Expatriate Dual Citizenship Dataset' (Harvard Dataverse 2015) https://dataverse.harvard.edu/citation?persistentId=doi:10.7910/DVN/TTMZ08. As to the proposition that dual nationality should be regarded as a human right, see Spiro, *Beyond Citizenship* (Oxford University Press 2008); Spiro, *At Home in Two Countries* (NYU Press 2016) 111–30; Spiro, 'Dual Citizenship as Human Right' (2010) 8 *I•CON* 111.

[9] See eg contributions from Shachar, Armstrong, Bauböck, Ochoa Espejo in Bauböck (ed), *Debating Transformations of National Citizenship* (Springer 2018); 'Misuse of Citizenship and Residency by Investment Programmes' (FATF and OECD 2023) www.fatf-gafi.org/content/fatf-gafi/en/publications/Methodsandtrends/misuse-CBI-RBI-programmes.html.

[10] 'Population, total' (World Bank 2022) https://data.worldbank.org/indicator/SP.POP.TOTL.

[11] Individuals with liquid assets of at least US$1 million and those with a net worth of at least US$30 million respectively: 'Global Wealth Report 2023' (Credit-Suisse 2023) 27–28, 31.

[12] 'Investment Migration Yearbook 2021/2022' (4th edn, IMC 2022) 6; Surak, *The Golden Passport* 17; Brillaud and Martini, 'European Getaway' (TI and Global Witness 2018) 15, 63.

[13] eg Baruch et al, 'Citizenship for Sale' (*Le Monde*, 11 October 2023) www.lemonde.fr/en/les-decodeurs/article/2023/10/11/citizenship-for-sale-dominica-s-golden-passports-go-haywire_6163322_8.html.

[14] Prak, *Citizens without Nations* (Cambridge University Press 2018) 251–73. Prak's work also examined the practice of citizenship in imperial China through civic institutions in urban centres. This chapter on the other hand examines how Chinese subjects make use of the *legal* institution of nationality (subject status) to overcome discrimination and become 'equal' citizens.

[15] eg Shachar, *The Birthright Lottery*; Harpaz, *Citizenship 2.0*; Harpaz, 'Compensatory Citizenship'; Harpaz, 'Ancestry into Opportunity' (2015) 41 *JEMS* 2081.

The Qing dynasty is a crucial period of study because China's understanding of 'nationality' went through a fundamental shift during this period. From the 1840s onwards, China progressively opened its door to foreign trade and activities pursuant to treaties concluded with foreign states, primarily those in Europe and the Americas. This new wave of 'internationalism' led to a change in the conception and practice of 'nationality' in China: moving beyond an inward-looking focus on Chinese 'subjecthood' and interactions between the different categories of Chinese subjects, to focusing on the external aspect of 'nationality' which distinguished between Chinese subjects and foreign nationals. This resulted in Chinese subjects acquiring foreign nationality for use in China. Some foreign consulates even connived in the process by selling 'naturalisation certificates' to these persons.

This change in nationality practice took place at a time when China's state power suffered a sharp decline. As the Qing government struggled to cope with internal turmoil and external military threats, it conceded territory and signed off valuable rights in the process. By the late 1890s, Qing officials and scholars had become concerned that China was treated as an 'inferior' state by the foreign powers and that the treaty terms were highly unfavourable to China.[16] Against this background, Chinese who acquired foreign nationality were often seen by their contemporaries as self-seekers who would betray their own people and 'pretend' to be foreigners in order to enjoy treaty benefits.

By the 1920s, a coherent narrative of China's 'unequal treaties' emerged, emphasising that the Sino-foreign treaties were unfair and unequal to China by pointing out the harshness of the treaty terms, the lack of reciprocity as well as the circumstances in which they were concluded (i.e. under duress), so that Chinese sovereignty was jeopardised.[17] This narrative focuses on inequality as between the treaty states and attributes the unequal treatment between foreigners and Chinese to the treaties. However, the treaties conferred rights and privileges on foreigners in China but did not dictate how Chinese subjects should be treated. Further, the treaties were not only international agreements operating at the international level but had to be operationalised within the domestic context. This gives rise to a further dimension which was not addressed by the 'unequal treaties' narrative, namely, the Qing government's latitude as policymakers to adjust the Qing domestic regimes which applied to Chinese subjects in order to mitigate the unequal treatment between foreigners and Chinese. It was the gap between treaty treatment and treatment under Qing domestic law that drove Chinese subjects to acquire foreign nationality and obtain more favourable treatment.

This chapter thus examines how Qing Chinese made use of the legal institution of nationality to respond to inequalities. It focuses on the acquisition and use of foreign nationality by Chinese subjects *within* China rather than in the country of naturalisation or other countries.[18]

[16] Wang, *China's Unequal Treaties* (Lexington Books 2005) 24–27; Chiu, 'Comparison of the Nationalist and Communist Chinese Views of Unequal Treaties' in Cohen (ed), *China's Practice of International Law* (Vol 2, Harvard University Press 1972) 243–44.

[17] eg the Nationalist Party's two declarations of 23, 28 June 1925 calling for the repeal of the unequal treaties (1925) 14 *Generalissimo Government Gazette* 197–200. See also Wang, *China's Unequal Treaties*, 64–66. Chiu, 'Comparison of the Nationalist and Communist Chinese Views', 245–48. For a discussion of how the treaty terms undermined different aspects of Chinese sovereignty, see Tung, *China and the Foreign Powers* (Ocean 1970) 107–27.

[18] There is a rich body of literature on how overseas Chinese merchants made use of multiple nationalities to secure more favourable business treatment in different jurisdictions, hedge against business risks and expand their local and international business empires. eg Lin, 'Overseas Chinese Merchants and Multiple Nationality' (2001) 35 *Modern Asian Studies* 985; Zhu, *Changqi huashang: Taichanghao, Taiyihao maoyi shi (1862–1940)* [The Chinese Merchants of Nagasaki: A Business History of Taichanghao and Taiyihao (1862–1940)] (Xiamen University Press 2016); Chung, 'Samuel Samuel & Co Ltd and Industrial Development in Early Japanese Colonial Taiwan' (2018) 25 *Taiwan Historical Research* 97.

It makes two assertions. First, foreign nationality was not only acquired by Chinese for corrupt or abusive purposes. It was an important means for ordinary subjects to access opportunities and ensure personal security when faced with inequalities in Qing society. Second, while the Sino-foreign treaty system was a major source of inequality in late Qing China, this chapter moves away from the traditional narrative which focuses on the unfairness of the Sino-foreign treaties on China and examines the Qing government's role in exacerbating the inequality between Chinese subjects and foreigners during treaty implementation. Specifically, the government rigidly insisted on treating the two differently and failed to adapt the domestic regimes for Chinese subjects or address their inadequacies. This turned Chinese nationality into part of the unequal institutions which treated Chinese subjects less unfavourably than foreigners in their own country. Overall, this chapter argues that due to Qing government failures, Chinese subjects acquired and made use of foreign nationality as a self-help measure to level the playing field. This debased Chinese nationality and eroded the foundation of Qing rule.

This chapter is divided into two parts. The first part examines nationality within the national setting. It focuses on Chinese subjecthood in Qing traditional society and examines Chinese subjects' practice of changing subject statuses to access opportunities. Chinese subject statuses were akin to 'quasi-nationalities' within a national setting, while Chinese subjects were engaging in acts that mirrored naturalisation, expatriation and nationality fraud in an international setting. The second part of the chapter focuses on the treaty port era from the 1840s. During this period, Chinese subjects adapted their practice and progressively made use of foreign nationality to enjoy the benefits of the treaty regime and to protect themselves from arbitrary treatment by Qing officials.

II. 'NATIONALITY' IN CHINA BEFORE THE TREATY SYSTEM

A. Overview: 'Nationality' in Qing China as an Inward-looking Concept

Before the onset of the treaty system in the 1840s, 'nationality' was largely an inward-looking concept in Qing China. The 'external' aspect of nationality: that is, interactions between Chinese subjects and non-subjects (foreigners), was under-developed. The Qing rulers, like their immediate predecessors, had sought to secure their empire from external threats and influence by generally prohibiting Chinese subjects from leaving the country.[19] Foreign admission into China was also tightly controlled. Trade was the main activity between Chinese subjects and foreigners and took place in the specific context of 'tribute missions' or at specific locations in the empire's frontier regions.[20] The western population in China consisted mainly of maritime traders and was small.[21] Since 1757, they could only trade at Guangzhou (Canton) and must leave China or retire to Macao after each trading season.[22] As foreigners lived in their own communities separate from local inhabitants, the general Chinese population had limited interactions with them. China did not see the need to have a law on 'nationality' to address the status of Chinese subjects in a transnational context.

[19] Art 225 of GQ Code.

[20] DQHDZL (QL), Scroll 94.

[21] As of January 1837, there were 307 foreign residents in Guangzhou and Macao, excluding Portuguese and excluding family members stationed in Macao, see CR, vol 5, 427–29, 432.

[22] van Dyke, *The Canton Trade* (HKU Press 2005) 16. By 1837, foreigners were allowed to stay in Guangzhou beyond the trading season, see CR, vol 5, 426.

In contrast to the external aspect of nationality, within the domestic context, the concept of Chinese subjecthood was highly developed. The imperial rulers of China had a long history of identifying subjects and formalising their status through registration. As early as the Shang dynasty (circa 1570–1045 BCE), when recorded history in China began, rulers were registering subjects for the purpose of raising a conscript army.[23] By the Qing dynasty, elaborate systems had evolved to classify subjects into different subject categories, entailing different treatment in law.

B. Chinese Subjecthood in Qing China: Pluralistic and Complex

Qing China was a multiethnic empire of conquest and the rulers governed their vast empire by applying different administrative-legal regimes to different territories and 'peoples'. This pluralistic style of governance permeated into the classification and registration of subjects, adding complexity to the range of subject categories within China.

First, after the ethnic Manchu rulers from the State of Qing[24] invaded Ming China (1368–1644) and moved their political seat to the Ming capital of Beijing, 'China' now covers the entire Qing territory,[25] while the territory of former Ming China became the 'regular provinces' of the expanding Qing empire. Here, the Qing rulers largely adopted the Ming systems of subject classification and registration. Since the regular provinces were the most populous regions in Qing China, the standard systems prevailing there also became the mainstream systems of Qing China. Second, to reinforce the distinct identity of a core group of subjects who were the regime's most reliable supporters, the Qing rulers continued to organise original Qing subjects and their descendants into military-administrative units (banners). These 'Banner people' were registered under Banner registers separate from other subjects.[26] Third, in the frontier regions of the empire such as Mongolia and Xinjiang, the local inhabitants were organised according to their tribes (banners) and were governed and registered by their local chiefs.[27]

Apart from establishing different subject registration systems for different territories or 'peoples', multiple categories of subjects also existed *within* a system. Within the Banner system, Banner divisions and units were distinguished according to ethnicity and affinity to the Emperor, with implications on prestige and access to resources and promotion opportunities. Bondservants were hereditary servants (de facto 'slaves') attached to their masters' households. They were not entitled to separate registration as independent subjects.[28] In the regular provinces, subjects were classified under various socio-occupational categories ('households'). Most of them were 'civilians' (*min*) who, together with 'military personnel' and 'salt-workers',[29] were ordinary subjects. Within these broad categories were various

[23] Song, *Zhongguo huji zhidu shi* [The History of Household Registration in China] (Sanqin Chubanshe 2016) 23.

[24] Roughly corresponding to present-day Liaoning, Jilin, parts of Heilongjiang and east Mongolia.

[25] Manchu text of the Sino-Russian Treaty of Nerchinsk 1689, referred to in Zhao, 'Reinventing China' (2006) 32 *Modern China* 3, 8.

[26] DQHD (QL), Scroll 9; DQHDZL (QL), Scroll 32; Rhoads, *Manchus & Han* (University of Washington Press 2000) 19.

[27] Meng, *Yuan Qing Huzheng Kao* [A Study of Household Administration in the Period of Yuan and Qing] (China Social Sciences Press 2014) 121–22. See also the registration and resettlement of Russian Kazakhs under various tribes in Xinjiang in 1907–08, see DAAS, item 02-10-012-01-014.

[28] Elliott, *The Manchu Way* (Stanford University Press 2001) 79; Rhoads, *Manchus & Han*, 19, 24.

[29] DQHD (GX), Scroll 17. The household category of 'builders and smiths' was abolished in 1645, see QWT, Scroll 21.

sub-categories, such as ethnic *miao* and *hui* Muslims who were sub-categories of civilians.[30] In contrast to ordinary subjects, who were regarded as persons of 'good standing', persons in certain socio-occupational households were socially ostracised and were known as *jianmin* ('despicable subjects'). These not only included bondservants but also included other social outcasts such as prostitutes and fishermen in Guangdong and Zhejiang.[31]

C. Chinese Subjecthood: Misogynistic, Hierarchical, Restrictive and Rigid

Subject status was underpinned by registration[32] and passed down through patrilineal descent. A primary distinction was drawn between male and female subjects. In the misogynistic Qing society, male subjects, or the head of 'households', were the primary subjects of registration. Female subjects were generally treated as dependants, subsumed under the registration of male subjects. Political and social opportunities in Qing society were likewise overwhelmingly reserved for male subjects.[33]

Second, registered subject status not only conferred a public identity on the holder but it determined their treatment in law. In the hierarchical Qing society, extensive rights and privileges were enjoyed by an elitist minority. For example, Banner subjects enjoyed many privileges despite their small population (constituting slightly over 1 per cent of the Chinese population in the mid-nineteenth century).[34] They were disproportionately represented in senior positions in central government and in the provinces.[35] They enjoyed a higher rate of passing the imperial examinations and, until the early nineteenth century, had the option of sitting a different (and easier) examination.[36] They also enjoyed privileges and exemptions in the Qing justice system, including exemption from kneeling before the magistrate, and being given a lighter sentence if convicted.[37]

Ordinary subjects in the regular provinces were commoners who bore the brunt of tax obligations and enjoyed few special rights. However, male ordinary subjects had access to one important facility that gave them opportunity for social advancement. Tax-paying ordinary subjects were allowed to sit the imperial examinations. Candidates who passed the primary level examination were formally admitted to the elite gentry class, opening the door to legal privileges and social status. Depending on the level of examination achievements, they could become government officials, the ultimate career aspiration. As one worked his way up the examination or career ladder, he would increasingly access exclusive rights and privileges such as reduced crop tax rates, privileges and exemptions in the justice system, free access to the magistrate and miscellaneous privileges relating to dress code and ceremonial matters and so on.[38]

[30] DQHD (GX), Scroll 17.

[31] DQHD (GX), Scroll 17; Art 76 of GQ Code.

[32] Art 76 of GQ Code.

[33] The nationality practices discussed in this chapter largely relate to male subjects. The nationality practices of female subjects is an unexplored topic. It is beyond the scope of this chapter to consider this topic in detail, which may form the focus of a separate study in future.

[34] Rhoads, *Manchus & Han*, 34, 45.

[35] ibid 45–46, 48.

[36] Exam Regs, Scroll 19; Rhoads, *Manchus & Han*, 43–44; imperial clansmen enjoyed further privileges: Ho, *The Ladder of Success in Imperial China* (Columbia University Press 1967) 23.

[37] Art 9 of GQ Code; Rhoads, *Manchus & Han*, 42.

[38] Ho, *The Ladder of Success in Imperial China*, 18; Chü, *Local Government in China and the Ch'ing* (Harvard University Press 1962) 173–75, 185–87.

In contrast to gentry and ordinary subjects, *jianmin* were at the bottom of the social hierarchy, taking up jobs regarded as too demeaning for ordinary subjects.[39] This small population[40] of *jianmin* suffered not only social prejudices but systemic discrimination under Qing law. They were denied civilian registration and precluded from the imperial examinations. They were banned from marrying ordinary subjects.[41] If a *jianmin* assaulted an ordinary person they would receive an aggravated sentence. Conversely, an ordinary subject who assaulted a *jianmin* would receive a mitigated sentence.[42] Like other Chinese subjects, *jianmin* had to abide by dress code which marked them out as visible targets for discrimination.[43] Since *jianmin* was not exhaustively defined in the laws, the status also came to be arbitrarily ascribed to other vulnerable members of society such as those undertaking jobs of low social status, or persons who somehow fell out of the subject registration system and became undocumented persons.[44]

Subject status came not only with rights and privileges but could also impose restrictions on the holder. For example, Banner subjects were subject to severe occupational constraints to keep them as the state's military reserves. They could only join the army or the civil administration or engage in farming, and were expressly prohibited from entering into business.[45] They lived in quarters separate from the local inhabitants and could not leave their garrison area without the approval of their commanders.[46] Given the scarcity of military posts, these restrictions pushed many lower Bannermen into poverty, a problem continuing to the last days of the dynasty.[47] Subject status could be restrictive even for the majority of the population who were civilians in the regular provinces and not subject to specific occupation constraints. For them, restriction took the form of geographical constraint of their subject registration. Civilians were organised into decimal household formations of *jia* and *li* and registered under local *lijia* tax registers.[48] The locality of *lijia* registration became the civilian's official 'hometown', akin to legal domicile, forming part of the person's hereditary subject status.

Subject status was particularly restrictive because subject category and locality of subject registration were difficult to change.[49] For example, after moving to another locality, the civilian family would have to acquire land and pay taxes continuously for 20 years, and establish ancestral graves in the locality, before they could apply for admission to the local *lijia* register and be treated as a native inhabitant.[50] This stringent threshold for change affected social

[39] Jing, *Qing dai shehui de jianmin dengji* [The Status of Despicable Subjects in Qing Society] (China Renmin University Press 2009) 32–33.

[40] Ho estimates that *jianmin* constituted 'a small fraction of 1%' of the total population of China: Ho, *The Ladder of Success in Imperial China*, 19.

[41] Arts 76(16), 115 of GQ Code.

[42] Arts 313, 373 of GQ Code.

[43] Jing, *Qing dai shehui de jianmin dengji*, 35.

[44] Kisimoto, 'Mao juan maokao susong yu Qing dai difang shehui [Litigation concerning the Use of False Registration in Title Purchases and Examination Candidature in Qing Local Society]' (Conference on the Power and Culture in the Practice of Ming-Qing Law, Taipei, 2005) 11–13.

[45] Rhoads, *Manchus & Han*, 38.

[46] ibid 36–38, 40.

[47] 'Qi ji (Banner registration)' in Zheng Guanying (ed), *Shengshi weiyan zengding xinbian* [Revised Edition of the Words of Warning in a Prosperous Age], Scroll 13; Zhao Erxun, *Qing shi gao* [Draft History of Qing], Scroll 120, 'Shi huo 1'.

[48] DQHDZL (QL), Scroll 33.

[49] Ho considers that since the regulations on subject statuses were not effectively enforced, there was considerable mobility across different subject statuses in practice, see Ho, *The Ladder of Success in Imperial China*, 54. However, the numerous examples of circumvention show all the more that the institutions were overly rigid and that there were few lawful means to change status.

[50] Exam Regs, Scroll 35.

advancement: as discussed below, the location of *lijia* registration affected a candidate's chances of succeeding in the imperial examinations. More immediately, the stringent threshold reinforced localism and xenophobia, pitching native inhabitants against migrants and hindering the latter's assimilation into local society.[51]

Of all subjects, *jianmin* had the worst deal by far. The strict prohibitions imposed on them meant they had few prospects for upward mobility under the law unless they were released from the *jianmin* status. One notable class of *jianmin* were the bondservants, the de facto 'slaves' in Qing society. These persons or their ancestors might have been ordinary subjects who became war captives of the Qing invaders and were forced into hereditary servitude, or they might have been sold into servitude by destitute families or sentenced to this status by the State as punishment. Some were even orphans sold into gentry families out of 'charity' for their 'protection'.[52] Locked into a hereditary low status, *jianmin* could only hope to be emancipated from their grim fate by their masters (in the case of bondservants) or by an act of imperial grace. For example, the Emperor Yongzheng (1723–35) was known for taking strides in abolishing many *jianmin* categories.[53] Despite this, ex-*jianmin* continued to suffer discrimination after becoming civilians. For example, their descendants had to meet more stringent conditions before being allowed to sit the imperial examinations. Social prejudices against ex-*jianmin* lasted up to the late Qing period.[54]

D. Overcoming the Handicap of Birth Status: Change of Subject Status

The multiplicity of Chinese subjecthood served the interests of imperial rulers: to reward the regime's elites and loyalists and ensure their staunch support; maintain a stable workforce supply in critical sectors; keep everyone in their rightful place according to Confucian ideals of a hierarchical and harmonious society; and protect the general populace from 'contamination' by perceived bad elements of society. However, institutional rigidity resulted in hardship and injustices in individual cases which were often overlooked by bureaucrats taking a top-down approach in administering a vast empire. As a result, subject status became an arbitrary legal institution. It could facilitate the holder to participate meaningfully in public life, resulting in a successful and enriching life experience. It could also be obstructive and lead to disappointment and even humiliation and suffering.

In face of inhibitions, resourceful subjects sought to overcome the constraints of birth status by acquiring another subject status, such as through adoption.[55] As it was difficult to change subject registration under the law, subjects even resorted to means that were legally dubious, if not plainly illegal. For example, in 1708, the Lans of Wangchun, Fujian province obtained the coveted civilian subject status by 'purchasing' a registered 'household' on the local *lijia* register.[56] Lower Bannermen were known to adopt fake Han names to pass off as civilians in order to take up jobs in other parts of China.[57]

[51] For an example of the clashes between migrant descendants and native inhabitants over imperial examinations, see Zheng, *Yimin, huji yu zongzu* [Migrants, Household Registration and Clans] (SDX Joint Publishing Company 2009) 64–84.

[52] Jing, *Qing dai shehui de jianmin dengji*, 55–71, 115–18.

[53] ibid 131–33, 136, 174, 176, 184–85; compare Ho, *The Ladder of Success in Imperial China*, 19.

[54] *QWT*, Scroll 19; Jing, *Qing dai shehui de jianmin dengji*, 184–85, 190–91.

[55] eg Exam Regs, Scroll 35; Lai, 'Cong falü kan Qing chao de qi-ji zhengce [Exploring the Banner People Register Policy from the Law of Qing Dynasty]' [2011] *Qing History Journal* 39.

[56] Szonyi, *Practicing Kinship* (Stanford University Press 2002) 76–78.

[57] Zheng Guanying, 'Qi ji'.

The imperial examination system provides unique insights into the practice of acquiring subject status because of its political and social importance. It was (male) ordinary subjects' main avenue for upward mobility, giving them an opportunity to join the government and move up the social and political ladder. A candidate's subject status could greatly affect his chances of passing the examinations. Candidates were divided into examination constituencies according to their place of *lijia* registration or their special household category (where applicable). Each constituency was allocated a pass quota capping the maximum number of passes (eg 45) in that constituency. Some constituencies were allocated a pass *ratio* (eg 5 per cent) in addition or instead.[58] Candidates competed against other candidates in the same constituency to pass the examination within these parameters. The combined effect is that the examination was easier to pass in some constituencies while excessively competitive in others. For example, in the early eighteenth century, the success rate of provincial examination was less than 1 per cent in the provinces of Zhejiang, Anhui and Jiangsu, but about 5 per cent in the metropolitan area.[59] In 1850, the *per capita* pass quota for provincial examination in Zhili (ie Hebei) province was almost four times that of populous Anhui.[60] Pass quota and ratio aside, since candidates must take all examinations except the final levels in their home county or province, migrant descendants suffered the additional hurdle of having to travel to their distant 'hometown' to sit the examinations, which could be prohibitive for indigent candidates.

Uneven distribution of opportunities across constituencies incentivised candidates to acquire subject registration in localities or subject categories with a higher examination success rate. Some candidates went to stay with relatives, clan members or family friends, and some were even formally adopted by them or by unrelated persons for money. Others simply claimed to be descendants or household members of registrants in the desired locality/subject category. Some candidates even went as far as to assume the identity of another person.[61]

The metropolitan area traditionally enjoyed a high success rate and by the beginning of the eighteenth century, the two metropolitan counties of Wanping and Daxing had become popular localities for 'subject registration fraud'.[62] Other popular constituencies included Sichuan, Yunnan, Guangxi and Hunan and Taiwan. Some of them enjoyed a more generous pass quota aimed to benefit local ethnic minority communities while others were less competitive due to their sparse population.[63] Some candidates paid to be adopted by Banner subjects so they could sit the examination as one.[64] Salt-merchant registration was another sought-after commodity. Special registers were created in major salt trade centres so that salt-merchants and descendants could take the examinations in their place of trade.[65] Candidates in this constituency enjoyed a more generous pass ratio (2 per cent) compared

[58] Exam Regs, Scrolls 19, 20, 21.

[59] Xia, 'Lun Qing dai fen sheng qu shi zhi [Selecting Officials by Provinces in the Qing Dynasty]' (2002) 3 *Historical Review* 47, 50.

[60] Based on a comparison of the provincial pass quotas in the Examination Regulations against the official provincial population recorded by Ping-ti Ho: 106 passes for a population of 23.4 million in Zhili; 45 for 37.6 million population in Anhui, see Exam Regs, Scroll 19; Ho, *The Ladder of Success in Imperial China*, 223.

[61] Exam Regs, Scroll 35.

[62] ibid.

[63] Memorial dated 6 March 1736 from Xie Jishi, Jiangnan Circuit Intendant; memorial dated 8 June 1760 from Qu Kai, Guangxi Commissioner of Education; memorial dated 11 June 1761 from Chen Quan, Sichuan Commissioner of Education; memorial dated 2 October 1771 from Li Shiyao, Governor General of Liangguang; memorial dated 20 March 1810 from Zhu Shaozeng, Treasurer of Hunan, see QJ, 13–14, 17–19, 22, 27.

[64] Exam Regs, Scroll 35.

[65] Eg Zhili (Hebei), Shandong, Guangdong, see Exam Regs, Scroll 20.

to candidates in other constituencies.[66] In 1760, the Zhejiang Commissioner of Education concluded following investigation that some 70 per cent of over 1,000 candidates on the Hangzhou salt-merchant register were not entitled to be so registered.[67]

The Qing government undertook a range of measures to combat 'subject registration fraud'. This ranged from leniency (such as permitting candidates who had confessed to their wrongdoing to re-sit the examination in future) to punishing the offenders severely (such as disqualifying them from the next examination sitting or for life; removal from office and even sentencing those involved to caning and penal servitude).[68] These measures did not stop the practice. In fact, procedural requirements introduced by the Qing government to combat fraud were themselves used to facilitate fraud. For example, a candidate's subject registration was required to be authenticated by designated personnel. Corrupt officials and salt-merchants turned this into a business opportunity and offered to certify 'fake' subject registration for candidates.[69] In 1774, 14 years after the Zhejiang Commissioner of Education's purge of the Hangzhou salt-merchant register, 'some seven or eight out of every ten candidates' on the salt-merchant register were still said to be native inhabitants rather than genuine salt-merchants.[70]

The rampancy of contravention went beyond isolated instances of violation of laws and points to the existence of more fundamental problems: that opportunities for upward mobility in Qing society fell excessively short of meeting the aspirations of a growing population of intelligent subjects. Although the pass quota system sought to ensure that government career opportunities could be shared across the country, this system became unfair and arbitrary when pass quotas failed to be updated to reflect population growth and economic and cultural development in different provinces.[71] Inequality was further exacerbated by the designs of the examination system which clear favoured the social and political elites. Competition became so fierce that ordinary subjects exploited affirmative policies aimed at benefitting underprivileged communities. The draconian residence requirements, coupled with abuses at the local level, meant that migrant families often struggled to obtain local registration decades and generations after resettlement. This motivated subjects to twitch their subject status to gain entry to the examination system.[72] Ultimately, over-reliance on using subject status to allocate social opportunities, together with a high threshold for changing subject status, left subjects few legitimate ways to redress their grievances. Once subject status was illegally changed, the status passed through patrilineal descent, magnifying the number of persons with 'wrongful' registration over time.

Qing officials would have understood the root causes of the problems as they had gone through the examination system themselves, and some would have acquired or inherited wrongful subject registration.[73] Nonetheless, the government, taking a regulator's perspective, had focused on law-enforcement options to combat abuses instead of introducing fundamental

[66] Lü, 'Qing Qianlong shang-ji gaige dui keju gongpingnxing de zhuiqiu ji qi xiandu [Merchant Registration Reforms in the Qing Dynasty during the Reign of Qianlong: Furthering Fairness in the Imperial Examination and their Limitations]' (2013) 6 *Journal of Ancient Books Collation and Studies* 70, 71.

[67] Memorial dated 2 August 1760 from Li Pei'en, Zhejiang Commissioner of Education, see QJ, 18.

[68] QJ, 17, 19–20, 22; Exam Regs, Scroll 35.

[69] Memorial dated 13 July 1761 from Zheng Huwen, Guangdong Commissioner of Education, see QJ, 19; Exam Regs, Scroll 35.

[70] Lü, 'Qing Qianlong shang-ji gaige dui keju gongpingnxing de zhuiqiu ji qi xiandu' 71.

[71] Ho, *The Ladder of Success in Imperial China*, 233–37.

[72] Exam Regs, Scroll 35; memorial dated 4 January 1744 from Yin Jishan, Acting Governor General of Liangjiang, see QJ, 14.

[73] eg many candidates registered in the metropolitan counties of Daxing and Wanping as at 1777 were said to be from families of officials all over the country, see Exam Regs, Scroll 35.

institutional reforms to tackle systemic problems such as extreme competition, inequalities and arbitrary administration. As a result, 'subject registration fraud' continued. As of 1850, some 80–90 per cent of candidates registered in the metropolitan counties of Daxing and Wanping were found to be non-natives who should have been registered elsewhere.[74]

E. Summary: Chinese Subject Statuses as 'Quasi-nationalities' Providing Access to Opportunities

Subject status in Qing China was critically important in determining a person's prospects in life. Enterprising individuals sought to transcend the constraints of an unequal society by acquiring a different subject status, turning Chinese subject status into a 'tradable commodity' in the process.[75] Although the general public had limited experience with foreign 'nationality' in a transnational context, within the domestic context, the different types of Chinese subject statuses functioned like 'quasi-nationalities'. When Chinese subjects changed subject status, they engaged in acts mirroring naturalisation, expatriation or nationality fraud in an international setting. This experience prepared Chinese subjects for the treaty port era when they adapted their practice and made use of foreign nationality to access facilities.

III. FOREIGN NATIONALITY IN THE TREATY PORT ERA

A. The Treaty System as an Entrenched Administrative-legal System in China

The 1840s marked a watershed in Sino-foreign relations. After China signed the Treaty of Nanjing and related agreements with Britain in 1842–43, other countries soon approached the Qing government to establish treaty relations. Within a decade, China had concluded treaties of 'peace, friendship and commerce' with the United States, France and the United Kingdoms of Sweden and Norway, confirmed bilateral trade with Belgium and expanded its trade arrangement with Russia.[76] These treaties opened four ports to foreign trade in addition to Guangzhou.[77] They fixed the import and export tariffs on a schedule of goods and capped the transit duty on foreign goods and the purchases of foreign traders.[78] Foreigners could now reside at the treaty ports with their families indefinitely, while the jurisdiction of consuls was enlarged to cover all disputes where the defendant was a national, including homicide and grave crimes involving Chinese victims.[79] International treaties between governments had replaced Qing government prerogative as the primary source of law for regulating foreign trade and activities in China.

[74] ibid.

[75] Compare the view that citizenship-by-investment schemes turn citizenship into a tradable or global commodity: Surak, *The Golden Passport*, 21, 24–25; Bauböck, 'What is Wrong with Selling Citizenship?' in Bauböck (ed), *Debating Transformations of National Citizenship* (Springer 2018).

[76] Treaty of Wangxia (Wang-Hea) July 1844 (US); Treaty of Huangpu (Whampoa) October 1844 (France); Treaty of Guangzhou (Canton) March 1847 (Sweden-Norway); imperial letter issued to Belgium in July 1845; Treaty of Kuldja July 1851 (Russia).

[77] Fuzhou (Foochow) and Xiamen (Amoy) in Fujian; Ningbo in Zhejiang; Shanghai in Jiangsu.

[78] eg Art X of Treaty of Nanjing 1842; Declaration Respecting Transit Duties 1843 (UK). The cap on inland transit duty was only agreed in 1858: Art XXVIII of Treaty of Tianjin (Tientsin) 1858 (UK).

[79] eg Art II oF Treaty of Nanjing 1842; Art XIII of General Regulations of Trade and Tariff.

The treaties with Britain were a necessary evil to end the war.[80] The treaties granted certain 'concessions' to nationals of the treaty states ('treaty foreigners') but the Qing government had no intention to extend treaty treatment to Chinese subjects. Nationality thus stood at the centre of the treaty system as the key criterion for determining the treatment to be accorded to a person in China: treaty foreigners would enjoy rights and benefits to the extent conceded by the treaties. By default, Chinese subjects would receive treatment under Qing laws according to their subject status. The external dimension of nationality – the distinction between Chinese subjects and non-subjects, now assumed legal prominence in China.

The Qing government had reasons to view the treaties as creating small exceptions for an exclusive population. After all, the scope of the treaties was specific, mainly relating to foreign trade. The foreign population in China was also small.[81] The government expected the existing regimes to continue to apply to Chinese subjects and did not see the need to adjust their treatment in view of rights granted to treaty foreigners. Rather, it confined foreign activities to the treaty ports and designated remote locations for foreign settlement to contain foreign presence and segregate the Chinese and foreign communities as far as possible.

Over the next few decades, the Qing government's bifurcated approach became increasingly at odds with changes ongoing in China. Sino-foreign economic interactions grew after the 1840s treaties. With the abolition of the Co-hong monopoly over foreign trade,[82] foreign merchants could now trade directly with a wider group of Chinese merchants. This led to the rise of compradors as a new class of Chinese merchants expert at mediating between Chinese and foreign businesses.[83] The opening of the treaty ports also brought a steady flow of Anglo-Chinese (ethnic Chinese born in British territory) into China, especially from the Straits Settlements.[84] Their assertion of British nationality in China challenged the Qing government's definition of Chinese subjects by perpetual patrilineal descent.[85] Physical segregation of foreign and Chinese settlements had been breached since the 1850s when Chinese subjects fleeing rebels of the Small Swords Society and then the Taiping Army took refuge in the international settlement in Shanghai.[86]

The biggest challenge to the logic of the dual-track approach came from the progressive expansion of the treaty regime over the next few decades, so that it could no longer be regarded as a regime of minor importance. In the 1840s, there were only five treaty states. By 1907 there were 20.[87] The number of treaty ports also increased from five originally to a total of 86 ports throughout China open or committed to be open to foreign trade in 1907.[88] Initially the

[80] Wang, *China's Unequal Treaties*, 11–12.

[81] As at January 1844, there were only around 550 foreign residents at the five treaty ports, Macao and Hong Kong (excluding military and government personnel but including those temporarily absent). Only 39 of them had brought their family with them, see 13 CR, vol XIII, 3–7.

[82] Art V of Treaty of Nanjing.

[83] For a study on the rise of Chinese compradors, see Hao, *The Comprador in Nineteenth Century China* (Harvard University Press 1970).

[84] For a study on the activities of Anglo-Chinese in the nineteenth century China: Murakami, 'Qing mo Xiamen Ying-ji huaren wenti [Anglo-Chinese in Xiamen During the Late Qing Period]' in Mori (ed), *Ershi shiji de Zhongguo shehui* [Chinese Society in the Twentieth Century] (Vol 1, Social Sciences Academic Press 2011).

[85] Qing officials found the use of birthplace as the basis for conferring British nationality extremely lax and arbitrary compared to the stringent standards for changing subject registration under Qing laws. Hence, they had difficulty accepting Anglo-Chinese's assertion of British nationality in China, see *DAAS*, item 01-02-001-02-023.

[86] Pott, *A Short History of Shanghai* (Kelly&Walsh 1928) 37, 39, 50–51.

[87] 'Guanyu chuanjiao tiaoyue zhi yanjiu [A Study on Treaties concerning Missionary activities]' (1908) 5(2) *Eastern Miscellany* 1. Norway and Sweden are counted separately after dissolution of their union in 1905. Japan and Korea (Choson) are counted separately (the latter was annexed by Japan in 1910).

[88] 'Zhongguo shangbu jilue [A Concise Account of the Trading Ports of China]' (1907) 186 *Diplomatic Review* 167. Only four provinces in China had no such port: Shanxi, Shaanxi, Henan and Guizhou. Another list prepared by the

treaties mainly concerned foreign trade, including fixing or capping taxes and duties at favourable rates.[89] From the 'second treaty settlement' of 1858–60 onwards, the treaties progressively struck at China's core economic interests, eventually giving foreign states the right to navigate and trade along main inland waterways,[90] the right to set up manufacturing industries at the trading ports[91] and valuable mining and railway rights.[92] Importantly, 'most-favoured-nation' ('MFN') provisions weaved bilaterally negotiated terms into a *network* of binding commitments enjoyed by all MFN states, albeit to varying extent depending on the breadth of the clause.[93] Once locked into the MFN system, the commitments became difficult for China to negotiate down or away. Instead of being a minor regime for a fringe community in China, the trade treaties had evolved into a major administrative-legal system of its own.

As the treaty system expanded, treaty foreigners progressively accessed rights originally enjoyed only by Chinese subjects. Conversely, Chinese subjects were not given access to the more favourable treatment under the treaties. Since the Qing government's long-term goal was to scale back on the special rights for foreigners through negotiations,[94] *extending* those rights to Chinese subjects was beyond their contemplation. However, the practical effect of the government's dual-track regulatory approach was that Chinese subjects were treated less favourably in some cases. The gap in treatment also widened over time. Of course, Chinese subjects still enjoyed some important, exclusive rights such as the right to reside, set up businesses and acquire property in inland China, not to mention the opportunity to enter officialdom through the imperial examination route.[95] However, juxtaposition of the treaty regime alongside the domestic regimes made the differences in treatment plainly visible to Chinese subjects. Where the advantage gap was significant, Chinese subjects tried to find ways to access treaty treatment. The old practice of 'upgrading' their subject status became useful, only that foreign nationality now offered an alternative pathway to success.

B. Assertion of Foreign Nationality: From Indirect Use to Direct Acquisition

Soon after the opening of the treaty ports, the Qing authorities became aware of instances of ethnic Chinese seeking to enjoy treaty treatment. Murakami has illustrated how Anglo-Chinese in Xiamen asserted British nationality to enjoy treaty treatment and obtain consular assistance in disputes, much to the annoyance of Qing officials who considered them to be Chinese subjects.[96] Apart from these individuals who were born with dual nationality, local Chinese merchants also started to access treaty treatment by making use of foreign businesses. Initially,

British legation in Beijing counts 25 ports of call plus 68 ports open to foreign trade as at April 1911: Wellington Koo, *The Status of Aliens in China* (Longmans 1912) 265.

[89] Above note 78.

[90] eg Art X Treaty of Tianjin 1858 (UK), which allows British vessels to trade along the Changjiang, expanding to all inland waterways under Art IX of Mackay Treaty 1902 (UK).

[91] Art VI(4) of Treaty of Shimonoseki 1895 (JPN); Art IV of Treaty of Commerce and Navigation 1896 (JPN).

[92] eg mining rights in Shanxi granted to the (British) Pekin Syndicate in 1898; railway rights granted to Germany, France, Belgium, Britain, Russia under various agreements in 1898–1900.

[93] For a survey of the MFN clauses in China's treaties, see Liang Qichao, 'Zhong-Ri gai yue wenti yu zuihuiguo tiaokuan [Treaty Re-negotiation between China and Japan, and the Most-favoured-nation Clause]' (1907) 4(2) *Eastern Miscellany* 1.

[94] Wright, *The Last Stand of Chinese Conservatism* (Stanford University Press 1957) 232, 251.

[95] Although foreigners could not sit the imperial examinations, they could be recruited directly into government service.

[96] Murakami, 'Qing mo Xiamen Ying-ji huaren wenti'.

Chinese merchants resorted to simple smuggling – mixing their goods and purchases among those of a foreign firm in order to take benefit of the favourable tax treatment enjoyed by foreign goods and purchases. Chinese compradors, as purchasing agents of foreign firms, were conveniently placed to resort to such arrangement.[97] Some foreign firms then turned this into a *business* of lending their firm's name to Chinese merchants for customs clearance.[98] Some of these 'foreign' firms were in fact beneficially owned by Chinese subjects.[99]

The smuggling of goods continued to the last days of the Qing dynasty.[100] However, as treaty port activities grew after the second treaty settlement of 1858–60, new forms of Sino-foreign business collaborations emerged. When American firm Russell & Co started a steam navigation business in China in 1861–62, the bulk of the capital was raised locally from Chinese and British merchants. Amongst the investors were some 'old Chinese friends', including the firm's Chinese compradors and a leading silk merchant in Shanghai.[101] Apart from investing in foreign enterprises and projects, Chinese merchants also sought to form partnerships with treaty foreigners or set up foreign companies or firms with their own capital.[102] These merchants saw commercial opportunities in foreign commerce and made use of business models that were commonplace in the West and which did not categorically reject investments in commercial enterprises based on the nationality of the investors. However, the Qing government was not concerned with business facilitation but with treaty administration. To the government bureaucrats, Sino-foreign business models were inherently suspect and should be banned in order to preserve the bright line between treaty and domestic regimes and preclude 'free-riders' of either regime.[103] Their regulator's mindset also reflected traditional Confucian economic values which exalted agriculture and deprecated commerce, and it was Confucian philosophy which guided the 'self-strengthening' reforms of 1861–95.[104] The government's restrictive policy did not stop Sino-foreign joint ventures completely. For example, Faure estimates that some 70 per cent of all 'Western' shipping operating in China was funded by Chinese capital.[105] However, it prevented Chinese businesses from making the most of the commercial opportunities under the treaties. Thus, the Qing government lost an opportunity to share the benefits of foreign trade with local businesses at large thereby 'neutralising' the unequal effects of the treaty system at a time when it still had policy space to do so.[106] From the 1890s onwards, successive new treaties extracted hefty indemnity and expansive economic rights from the Qing government, notably the Treaty of Shimonoseki 1895 and the Boxer

[97] Hao, *The Comprador in Nineteenth Century China*, 98–99.

[98] eg, in Xinjiang, Russians were selling 'road permits' to Chinese traders to facilitate the passage of their goods through customs barriers: DAAS, item 01-17-042-09-001.

[99] eg, the case of Xie Xiaoyuan, arrested in 1880, see DAAS, items 01-31-007-02-001 to 004.

[100] See for example the telegram dated 25 June 1907 from the Governor of Jiangxi to the Foreign Ministry, see GC Telegrams, vol 33, item 446.

[101] Liu, 'Financing a Steam-Navigation Company in China, 1861-62' (1954) 28 *Business History Review* 154, 162, 169–70.

[102] eg, American firm Holmes & Co in Shanghai was set up in 1868 by Chinese merchants Gao Jiushan and Li Jinyu and American Matthew Holmes. Gao was said to have contributed the bulk of the capital, see *DAAS*, item 01-20-009-07-002; *Zhong-Mei Waijia shiliao: Tongzhi II* [Academia Sinica, Historical Materials on Sino-American Relation: Tongzhi, Part II], item 914.

[103] Correspondence in July to November 1875 between Li Hongzhang, Superintendent for Northern Trade and the Chinese foreign office (*zongli yamen*), see DAAS, items 01-20-009-07-001 to 003; See also Fairbank (ed), *Cambridge History of China* [Late Ch'ing Part I] (Vol 10, Cambridge University Press 1978) 513.

[104] Wright, *The Last Stand of Chinese Conservatism*, 148–50.

[105] Faure, *China and Capitalism* (HKU Press 2006) 51.

[106] The legality of Sino-foreign cross-investments was finally recognised by the Qing government in 1902: Art IV. of Mackay Treaty 1902 (UK).

Protocol 1901. This severely strained Qing treasury and constrained the government's ability to fund reforms to close the competition gap between local and foreign businesses.

Up to the early 1890s, apart from Anglo-Chinese, most Chinese sought to access treaty treatment by *indirectly* relying on foreign nationality: through foreign business vehicles or business arrangements with foreign entities. The major turning point came in the late 1890s. From then onwards, Qing government records frequently feature cases of ethnic Chinese directly asserting foreign nationality in China.[107] A major cause was China's cession of Taiwan to Japan following the Sino-Japanese War 1894–95. Taiwan residents were given a period of two years to relocate to China and retain their Chinese nationality. Unsurprisingly, only a handful of residents (5,460 persons, constituting about 0.21 per cent of the population) chose to migrate by the deadline while the vast majority, some 2.6 million residents, became Japanese subjects on 8 May 1897.[108] At the time, around 80–90 per cent of Taiwan businesses had branches or agencies in the Chinese mainland.[109] These now counted as foreign businesses in China. Taiwan residents aside, this period also saw the return of overseas Chinese into China, whether to seek out business opportunities, to retire in their hometowns, or because they were chased out of their host countries by hostile legislation.[110] Many overseas Chinese had also acquired the nationality of their host countries through naturalisation,[111] adding to the pool of 'foreign nationals' when they returned to China.

These individuals had acquired foreign nationality by operation of law (treaty), by birth or by naturalisation after an extended period of residence overseas. However, foreign nationality was also popular among local Chinese. China's defeat in the Sino-Japanese War had ushered in the Scramble for Concessions whereby the Qing government was forced to make major economic concessions to foreign states, including the right to set up industries at treaty ports and important mining and railway rights.[112] Just as the rise of steam navigation business in the 1860s attracted Chinese investments into the sector,[113] these treaty concessions translated into lucrative commercial opportunities which Chinese merchants also wanted to utilise. Meanwhile, after the Qing government's disastrous handling of the Boxer Rebellion 1900–01, foreign states became more aggressively resolute in protecting the interests of their nationals. Some Chinese subjects acquired foreign nationality so that they could invoke consular assistance in legal disputes and even avoid Qing law and jurisdiction altogether.

By 1898, agencies in Shanghai were already offering to help Chinese subjects acquire foreign nationality.[114] The demand for foreign nationality continued to grow in the next decade. Even consulates in China were involved in nationality sales. By 1906, the Spanish Consulate in Shanghai had become infamous for granting naturalisation certificates to Chinese subjects in China and providing consular assistance to these nationals in legal disputes.[115] This practice was finally stopped in August 1908 when Fernandez Arias, the incoming Spanish Consul

[107] Based on a survey of archival materials in DAAS and GC Telegrams.

[108] Art V of Treaty of Shimonoseki 1895. Within three years, about 360 persons also returned and re-registered themselves in Taiwan, see TWHM, 38, 48–68.

[109] Report dated 8 August 1896 by Sawamura Shigetarō of the Civil Department, dispatched to Xiamen, see TWHM, 159.

[110] eg the Chinese Exclusion Act 1882 (US) amended in 1884 and renewed by the Geary Acts of 1892 and 1902 until made permanent in 1904.

[111] Correspondence from Deshou, Acting Governor General of Liangguang to the Foreign Ministry, received on 7 July 1903, see DAAS, item 02-13-020-02-006.

[112] Above notes 91 and 92.

[113] Liu, 'Financing a Steam-Navigation Company in China, 1861–62'.

[114] 'Q&A: Question no. 178 and Answer' (1898) 14 *Scientific Review (China)* 14.

[115] Chinese Mail (Hong Kong, 15 June 1906) 4; Shun Pao (Shanghai, 18 May 1906) 4.

in Shanghai, revoked the naturalisation certificates of some 100 ethnic Chinese, much to the Qing authorities' approval.[116] Taiwan registration status was another popular choice due to its accessibility. Given the strong family and business ties between the residents in Taiwan and Fujian, it was not difficult for Fujianese to find someone in their extended family or clan willing to certify (fake) their Taiwan connections in support of their application. As at 1905, Taiwan residents were helping Chinese subjects to acquire registration certificates for around $200–300 to $500–600 silver dollars.[117] By 1907, ethnic Chinese holding Japanese nationality (Taiwan registration status) could be found 'everywhere' throughout Fujian.[118] Alarmed that local staffers at Japanese consulates in China had colluded with Chinese subjects in perpetrating nationality fraud, the Taiwanese government ordered rigorous background checks to be conducted on all applicants for Taiwanese registration.[119] Spain and colonial Taiwan aside, Portugal, Italy and Russia were also known for granting 'naturalisation certificates' to Chinese subjects liberally.[120]

Unlike 'long-distance citizens' who make use of foreign nationality to access facilities *outside* their country of original nationality, the 'naturalisation certificates' obtained by local Chinese were primarily used by them *within* China. In the absence of a law on 'nationality' it was unclear how nationality could be changed. This gave rise to procedural irregularities. Many Chinese subjects acquired foreign nationality without informing the Qing government and hence were not officially 'expatriated'. Yet these 'dual nationals' then purported to assert their foreign nationality in or against China, their state of nationality.

C. Chinese-Foreigners: Unprincipled Villains or Victims of Inequality?

Qing officials were scandalised by ethnic Chinese attempting to assert foreign nationality in China. They considered two types of conduct especially abusive. One was 'double-dipping' – the selective assertion of Chinese and foreign nationalities at different times to enjoy domestic as well as treaty treatment. Second, the acquisition of foreign nationality by an individual *after* becoming involved in a dispute, for the sole purpose of obtaining consular assistance, and even avoiding Qing law and jurisdiction altogether.[121]

While there were clearly cases of abuses, a closer examination of the foreign nationality cases gives a more nuanced picture. In the context of trade, not only were Chinese businesses required to pay taxes on goods at the full rates, but they were vulnerable to arbitrary taxation by local officials. The *likin*, an additional transit duty introduced from the late 1850s, was particularly problematic. The tax rates varied widely across provinces and goods types and were liable to random determinations by officials and negotiation with tax collectors.[122]

[116] *Qing dai Waiwubu Zhong-wai guanxi dang'an shiliao congbian, Zhong-Xi guanxi juan* [Archival Materials on Sino-foreign Relations in the Qing Period: Sino-Spanish Relations], vol 3, items 347, 361.

[117] Chinese Mail (Hong Kong, 9 November 1905) 4.

[118] Correspondence dated 22 November 1907 from Governor General of Minzhe to the Chinese Foreign Ministry, see DAAS, item 02-21-015-02-010.

[119] Internal circular issued by the Civil Department of Taiwan on 24 May 1906, TWHM, 121–22.

[120] See for example correspondence from Duanfang, Governor General of Liangjiang received by the Chinese Foreign Ministry on 30 September 1908, see DAAS, item 02-10-012-02-009; 'Zicha ru E-ji Mengmin [Investigation into Mongolian Subjects who had Acquired Russian Nationality]' (1909) 248 *Diplomatic Review* 17.

[121] Correspondence within the Qing government in 1903, see DAAS, items 02-13-020-02-006, 02-13-020-02-012; memorial from Liu Shixun, Chinese Minister to France, Spain and Portugal in 1908, see DAAS, item 02-21-015-03-001; see also the Case of Wang Zhou Lizhen (1908-9), concubine of the Late Wang Yifu, widely reported in the newspapers in Shanghai, including Shun Pao and the North China Herald.

[122] Williams, 'Taxation in China' (1912) 26 *Quarterly Journal of Economics* 482, 499.

In day-to-day operations, Chinese businesses were also vulnerable to harassment and extortion by petty officers and local thugs. An investigation report by the Civil Department of Taiwan in 1896 found that Chinese businesses in Xiamen used to 'borrow' foreign business registration from Anglo-Chinese firms to forestall harassment and avoid incessant demands of 'miscellaneous fees'.[123] In Shanghai, some Chinese merchants moved to the international settlements so that they could conduct business without government interference.[124] In other words, Chinese traders sought foreign nationality for equal treatment, business certainty and protection from administrative arbitrariness.

Whereas there is considerable scholarship on the inadequacies and abuses of treaty states' extraterritorial justice in China,[125] the case of Taiwanese merchant Lin Mouchang in 1905–06 provides a glimpse into the use of foreign nationality in legal disputes as between ethnic Chinese before the Chinese court.[126] Lin Mouchang's father, Lin Dunyan, owned a successful tea business in Xiamen. In 1905, a dispute arose between the firm and its business partner Wanbaoyuan over the settlement of accounts. Each firm claimed that the other owed money to it. Wanbaoyuan had powerful backing: two of its three partners were prominent merchants holding Qing office titles. One of them, Guangzhou Prefect Chen Binghuang, worked behind the scene to ensure Wanbaoyuan's success in the litigation. Chen used his brother, a French national, as Wanbaoyuan's 'representative' in the litigation even though the brother otherwise had no connection with the business. The Chens then secured French Consul AJM Fanque's support in raising the matter with the Assistant Prefect of Xiamen. The judge cowered under pressure from the French Consul intervening on behalf of a business backed by two officials of more senior rank. He ordered his men to suspend Lin's business operations and restrain his goods.

Lin Duanyan petitioned the Ministry of Commerce in Beijing but passed away before the matter was fully resolved. Thereafter, his son Mouchang took over the business and lawsuit. Lin Mouchang obtained Taiwan registration status in September 1903.[127] However, since his father was a Chinese subject, he continued with the proceedings without invoking his Japanese nationality. As it turns out, Wanbaoyuan's claim had been grossly exaggerated. In February 1906, the Xiamen Chamber of Commerce determined that after set-off Wanbaoyuan still owed sums to Lin's business.[128] Contrary to customary practice, the court did not defer to the Chamber's determination. Rather, the litigation dragged on in court.

The matter took a drastic turn on 1 July 1906 when Lin Mouchang was suddenly arrested by the Xiamen Circuit Intendant,[129] probably out of vengeance to punish the Lins for petitioning the ministries in Beijing directly. The Japanese Consulate in Xiamen asked the local authorities to hand over Lin for investigation and trial pursuant to the treaty arrangement[130] but the authorities refused, claiming that the arrested person was not Japanese but a Chinese

[123] Report dated 8 August 1896 by Sawamura Shigetarō of the Civil Department, dispatched to Xiamen, see TWHM, 159–60.

[124] Pott, *A Short History of Shanghai*, 67.

[125] eg Scully, *Bargaining with the State from Afar* (Columbia University Press 2001); Ruskola, *Legal Orientalism* (Harvard University Press 2013); Cassel, *Grounds of Judgment* (Oxford University Press 2012).

[126] Except where stated, the description of this case is based on the petition of Lin Mouchang received by the Chinese Foreign Ministry on 12 February 1906, see DAAS, item 02-09-006-06-001, supplemented by Hsieh, 'Nationality Choices and Commercial Disputes between Taiwanese and Fujianese Merchants in Early 20th Century: The Case of Lin Mou-chang' (2017) 24 *Taiwan Historical Research* 83.

[127] Report no. 12985 dated 27 October 1906 of the Taipei Police, see TWHM, 384.

[128] Internal notes of the Taiwanese authorities dated November 1906, see TWHM, 366.

[129] Report dated 21 November 1906 by Taketomi Kunikane, Commander of the South China Fleet of Japan, see JACAR, item C06091840800.

[130] Arts XXII, XXIV of Treaty of Commerce and Navigation 1896.

subject called 'Lin Jiangshu'.[131] In the next five months, the Qing and Japanese authorities were at loggerheads over the transfer of Lin. They argued over the true identity and nationality of the arrested person, including whether 'Lin Jiangshu' and 'Lin Mouchang' were two different persons or two names of the same person, whether Chinese subject 'Lin Jiangshu' was fraudulently using the identity of Taiwan registrant 'Lin Mouchang', and whether there were in fact two different persons named 'Lin Mouchang'.[132] The Qing authorities shifted their reasons for arresting Lin and their version of facts, and were self-conflicting at times.[133] Following months of impasse, in November 1906, Japanese Minister to China Hayashi Gonsuke delayed the departure of Japanese warship *Takachiho* from Xiamen and instructed the commander to help secure Lin Mouchang's transfer. Lin was finally handed over to the Japanese authorities on 20 November 1906. Due to his 'tired state' he was allowed to remain at home under caution pending investigation.[134]

This case illustrates how, under the treaty system, foreign nationality could be used by parties to a dispute to increase their chances of success in litigation, thereby turning a dispute between ethnic Chinese into a Sino-foreign dispute and even one between foreign nationals. Further, foreign nationality could function as a 'sword' or a 'shield', causing, amplifying or reducing inequality of arms between the parties. For the Lins, the litigation was an unequal contest to start with. They were up against a business backed by powerful merchant-officials, adjudicated by a judge who was keen to show deference to his 'peers'. Despite the Qing government's distain for ethnic Chinese asserting foreign nationality in litigation, Chen Binghuang, a merchant-official, had bent the rules to invoke foreign nationality in order to crush his litigation opponent. It did not help that the French Consul had dived into the dispute to side with Wanbaoyuan, believed to be a French firm, without investigating the merits of its claim of French nationality or its monetary claim. By contrast, Japan, a colonial power new to the game, had proceeded more cautiously. Initially, the Japanese authorities stepped back from Lin Mouchang's litigation in China.[135] After receiving a complaint of Lin's alleged nationality fraud, the Taiwanese authorities conducted a detailed investigation into his Taiwan registration application.[136] At the same time, after Lin Mouchang's arrest, they actively intervened to procure his transfer, holding their grounds based on the treaty terms and mindful of the need to meet 'the expectations of the 1,000 or so Japanese residents in Xiamen'.[137] Unhappily for China, Qing government maladministration caused the Japanese Minister to China, Hayashi Gonsuke to resort to a veiled military threat to procure Lin's early release. The apparent 'effectiveness' of this strategy set an ominous precedent for Sino-Japanese relations, emboldening Japan to resort to military threats when the two countries clashed again shortly afterwards over the *Tatsumaru* incident.[138]

As to Lin Mouchang, just like the Chinese merchants who 'borrowed' foreign business registration from Anglo-Chinese to avoid harassment by local officials, Lin could not simply

[131] Report dated 18 July 1906 from Ueno Senichi, Japanese Consul in Xiamen to Hayashi Gonsuke, Japanese Minister to China, see JACAR, item C06091840800.

[132] TWHM, 367–69.

[133] Above note 129.

[134] Confidential report no. 40 dated 28 November 1906 from consular officer Yoshida in Xiamen to Hayashi Gonsuke, Japanese Minister to China, see TWHM, 324.

[135] Above note 128.

[136] TWHM, 318–71.

[137] Confidential report no. 23 dated November 1906 from Yoshida in Xiamen to Hayashi, see TWHM, 323.

[138] Telegram dated 11 March 1908 from the Foreign Ministry to the Governor General of Guangdong, see GC Telegrams, vol 24, item 55; Hsu, '1908 nian Zhong-Ri Erchenwan an jiaoshe shimo [Negotiations of the Tatsu Maru Event between China and Japan 1908]' (2009) 22 *Soochow Journal of History* 131, 152.

be dismissed as an unprincipled 'double-dipper' who switched between Chinese and foreign nationalities for self-serving ends. Lin obtained Taiwan registration because his business was based in Taiwan. However, Lin had been trading in China and also identified himself as Chinese. Initially, the Lin father and son had tried to resolve the business dispute with Wanbaoyuan under the Qing justice system but they faced an uphill battle. Lin Mouchang's life was even placed in peril. It was not that Lin Mouchang particularly preferred Japanese to Chinese nationality but that the Qing justice system had failed him and his father. Ironically, it was his colonial nationality that helped secure his release.

IV. CONCLUSION

After the opening of the treaty ports in the mid-nineteenth century, Chinese subjects adapted their practice of changing subject statuses and started to acquire and assert foreign nationality, first indirectly, then directly. This practice was controversial. From the Qing government's perspective, these individuals were self-seekers who made use of foreign nationality for personal gain, relying on foreign help to oppress compatriots and evade Qing law and jurisdiction.[139] Historical records reveal a more complex position. Foreign nationality was not only manipulated by scoundrels for corrupt and abusive ends. It also protected ordinary subjects from administrative abuses and arbitrary rule. Chinese businesses that used foreign nationality to access treaty treatment might be profit-chasers, but in so doing, they also became more competitive.

If inequalities and injustices faced by Chinese subjects stemmed from the treaty system, Qing government policies exacerbated the problem. From the outset, the Qing government had set its mind on subjecting foreigners and Chinese to different regulatory regimes. This inflexible mindset made the government oblivious to the need to enhance the treatment of Chinese subjects to a comparable level. Abuses by Qing officials added to the woes of Chinese subjects. Chinese nationality thus became part of the unequal legal institutions whereby Chinese subjects were treated less favourably than treaty foreigners in their own country. Foreign nationality became a tool for equalising rights and opportunities and ensuring personal security *within* China. However, the acquisition and use of foreign nationality in China inevitably undermined Qing law and institutions, debased Chinese nationality and eroded the foundation of Qing rule.

In March 1909, the throne finally approved China's first piece of nationality enactment.[140] The primary aim of this law was to 'preserve' Chinese subjecthood, by encouraging overseas Chinese to retain Chinese nationality[141] and by regulating expatriation from Chinese nationality. Importantly, Qing government approval was required for voluntary expatriation while ex-nationals were expressly prohibited from enjoying the rights of Chinese subjects.[142]

[139] Above note 121.

[140] *Da Qing guoji tiaoli* (Great Qing Nationality Regulation), the related Implementation Rules as sanctioned by the throne on 28 March 1909. The texts of the instruments are set out in the Official Gazette version of the memorial from the Constitutional Investigation Board (*Xianzheng Biancha Guan*) dated 28 March 1909, as endorsed by the throne, see XZSL, 403; For an English translation of these instruments and contemporaneous commentary, see 'Law on the Acquisition and Loss of Chinese Nationality' (1910) 4 *AJIL* 160 and Tsai, 'The Chinese Nationality Law 1909' (1910) 4 *AJIL* 404.

[141] Especially Chinese in the Dutch East Indies: see petition of the Nanyang Surabaya General Chamber of Commerce received by the Foreign Ministry on 25 February 1909, see DAAS, item 02-14-008-03-003; see also Chen, 'The Evolution of Modern Chinese Nationality Law: A Historical Perspective' (2023) 23 *China Review* 123, 128.

[142] Arts 11, 12, 16 of Great Qing Nationality Regulation; Art 8 of Detailed Implementation Rules.

In other words, nationality law was the instrument whereby the Qing rulers reasserted their authority over Chinese subjects and reined in their behaviour. At the same time, the government had also come to realise the need to improve the 'citizenship package' for its people. It had embarked on a series of 'new policy reforms' and had also mapped out a constitutional and law reform roadmap that would enhance the rights of Chinese subjects, including giving them important constitutional rights.[143] Nonetheless, these reforms came too late and too slowly. In October 1911, the Xinhai Revolution broke out. With the abdication of the throne in February 1912, China became Asia's first modern republic.

[143] Memorial dated 27 August 1908 from the Constitutional Investigation Board and the National Assembly: *Qing mo choubei lixian dang'an shiliao* [Archival Materials relating to the Preparation of the Adoption of a Constitution in the Late Qing Period] (Vol 1, Wenhai Publishing Co Ltd 1987) 54–67.

IV.

Investment Migration Conundrums in the European Union

18

Golden Passports

European Commission and European Parliament Reports Built on Quicksand

HANS ULRICH JESSURUN D'OLIVEIRA

'European values are not for sale.'[1]

I. INTRODUCTION

THIS CHAPTER ANALYSES two reports and one recommendation by the European Commission (EC) and the European Parliament (EP), all concerned with citizenship by investment (CBI), *vulgo* golden passports, leaving golden visas out of the picture. These documents purport to ban CBI's in order to safeguard the integrity of Union citizenship, the corollary of possession of the nationality of a Member State (MS). Which are the legal bases for these interventions proffered by the EU institutions? Two strongholds have been put forward and will be commented upon: the theory of the genuine link (*Nottebohm*), and the obligation for genuine cooperation by the Member States. Both foundations are built on quicksand, as the analysis below demonstrates.

II. THE COMMISSION'S REPORT OF 23 JANUARY 2019

In her first State of the Union speech as president of the EC on 16 September 2020 Ursula von der Leyen vowed to defend 'the rule of law and the integrity of our European institutions'[2] and she explained that one of the targets would be the sale of golden passports: 'European values are not for sale.'[3] A compelling and stirring slogan.[4] A month later infringement procedures were launched against Cyprus and Malta. It remains to be seen, however, to what extent these European values are at stake. Von der Leyen's position was undoubtedly based on the

[1] von der Leyen, 'Building the world we want to live in' (State of the Union Address, Brussels, 16 September 2020) https://ec.europa.eu/commission/presscorner/detail/ov/SPEECH_20_1655.

[2] ibid.

[3] ibid.

[4] The rule of law is such a value. The Commission is lenient towards the Member States such as Poland, thereby undercutting the case law of the ECJ and weakening its position: von der Leyen, Rule of law and the potential approval

Commission Report on Investor Citizenship and Residence Schemes in the European Union, published one and a half years earlier.[5] The EP had urged the Commission to take action and the Member States involved were requested to phase out their schemes.

Already in the first sentence of the introduction to this Report one feels which way the wind's blowing in the Commission: 'concerns about certain inherent risks, in particular as regards security, money laundering, tax evasion and corruption'. This is the thrust of the measures taken by the Commission against Member States as Malta, Cyprus and Bulgaria, and against a candidate such as Montenegro,[6] and even third countries. Vanuatu is a case in point, where visa-free travel to the Schengen area is suspended for Vanuatu citizens holding passports issued after 25 May 2015.[7]

In its Report, the Commission draws a distinction between 'ordinary naturalisation procedures' and 'discretionary naturalisation procedures'; the latter based on 'the national interest' and 'highly individualized'. These are excluded from the report, although it observes that a number of MS define the national interest in terms of economic or commercial advantages. It is therefore unclear why this distinction is made and why these schemes are left out in the report. Indeed naturalisations are by definition taking place 'by a discretionary decision of the competent authorities', be it Parliament, King, President, Minister or other authority. The distinction between 'ordinary' naturalisations and other naturalisations does not lie in the discretionary character of the second category, but in their special conditions. And most legislators provide for special procedures for special people. These form part and parcel of the municipal codes of nationality. In most systems even 'normal' naturalisations are discretionary. Denmark and Belgium, for example, naturalise persons by (discretionary) Act of Parliament.[8] In the Netherlands the official manual to the Code of Nationality lists 'economic and cultural interests' as interests of the State allowing naturalisation dispensating persons from a number of general requirements for ordinary naturalisation.[9] In this way guidelines are laid down for personnel of companies that are important for the Dutch economy.[10] By the way, 'ordinary' naturalisation procedures are all but uniform, share discretionary elements, and even take the form of conditional option and allow exemption of certain conditions. Although these special discretionary naturalisations are granted on an individual basis, the scheme lays down general rules for specific groups such as talented sportspersons.[11] The state has reduced its discretion in this way, as it is bound by rules of application it has developed.

To label the investment naturalisations as a novel and anomalous form, 'as they systematically grant citizenship of the MS concerned, provided the required investment is made and

of the Polish national recovery plan, Strasbourg, 7 June 2022, https://ec.europa.eu/commission/presscorner/detail/en/SPEECH_22_3528; cf Mayer, 'Die Kapitulation' (VerfBlog, 2 June 2022) https://verfassungsblog.de/die-kapitulation/; Bárd and Kochenov, 'War as a Pretext to Wave the Rule of Law Goodbye?' (2022) 27 *Elj* 39.

[5] European Commission, 'Investor Citizenship and Residence Schemes in the European Union' COM(2019)12 final.

[6] Montenegro, an EU candidate country, has extended its investor citizenship programme for the year 2022, although it announced earlier, urged by the Commission, that it would discontinue the scheme by the end of 2021 as 'contrary to EU's principles'. Until June 2021 the programme involved some 700 persons, including 300 Russian citizens, 150 from China, 50 US citizens and 40 Lebanese citizens.

[7] Kochenov and Worster, 'EU's Neocolonialism' (EU Law Live, 8 March 2022) https://eulawlive.com/op-ed-eus-neocolonialism-safeguarding-the-purity-of-ni-vanuatu-blood-through-blackmailby-dimitry-v-kochenov-william-thomas-worster/.

[8] de Groot and Vonk, *International Standards on Nationality Law* (Wolf 2015) 60.

[9] Manual to Art 10, Sub.2(1) of the Code of Nationality 1984 (NL).

[10] Future wives and husbands of the (future) Kings and Queens have been fast-tracked in this way, the idea being that their offspring should be fully Dutch.

[11] It is well-known that states pay sometimes large sums to the sport federation concerned of the country of origin to enable sportspersons to take part immediately in international competitions for their new country: reverse golden passports. cf Siekmann, *Introduction to International and European Sports Law* (TMC Asser Press 2012) 241–68.

certain criteria fulfilled' is inadequate to distinguish them from the diversified 'ordinary naturalisations'. It seems that the report is intended to frame the Golden Passport and Residence schemes as *novel and exceptional* in the world of nationality law and therefore to be suppressed. As a matter of fact, these special procedures belong to the normal repertory of the codes of nationality all over the world; excluding them is to highlight the genuine link principle and to discard beforehand national interest as a legitimate grounds for granting citizenship. The dice are loaded. Worth noticing is that the European Convention on Nationality (ECN) (1998) states in its Preamble that 'account should be taken both of the legitimate interests of States and those of individuals', and that it refrains from providing a thick, substantive, definition of 'nationality', but simply indicates that it is 'a legal bond between a person and a State'.[12] Sure, the Explanatory Report to the ECN hinted that the concept of nationality was 'explored' by the International Court of Justice in the *Nottebohm* case, without, however, endorsing any results of this exploration.

Another most important, indeed central, body of nationality law is excluded from the report is the acquisition of nationality at birth, be it by *ius soli* or by *ius generationis* and the mixed forms in between. Are these supposed to always contain the holy grail of the genuine link?

III. THE EUROPEAN PARLIAMENT REPORT OF 7–10 MARCH 2022

In the plenary session of 7–10 March 2022 of the EP a Report by the Committee on Civil Liberties, Justice and Home Affairs with proposals to the Commission on citizenship and residence by investment schemes[13] was adopted with 595 votes for, 12 against and 74 abstentions. Again, I will not deal with the Golden Visas, but focus on the parts that are concerned with the CBI schemes. This report refers to the Commission Report of 23 January 2019, and the State of the Union Address of 16 September 2020 by the President of the Commission, mentioned earlier.

The Parliamentary Report states:

> Since 2014, Parliament has been calling for a ban of CBI/RBI schemes, but so far the Commission has not put forward any proposals. Although the Commission claims it has no legal basis for legislative action, it did launch infringement proceedings against Cyprus and Malta in October 2020.[14]

And the last paragraph of the document reads:

> Thus far, the Member States have been reluctant to address the matter, to the point of refusing to engage in talks.[15] But the fact that granting citizenship as such is an exclusive national competence is no pretext for inaction when Union law and values are damaged. Union citizenship and residence are not a commodity. We all have a duty to protect it.[16]

[12] Art 2(a), European Convention on Nationality (ECN) (1997) ETS 166.

[13] European Parliament 'Report with proposals to the Commission on citizenship and residence by investment schemes 2021/2026(INL) [2022].

[14] ibid 18.

[15] Indeed, a Group of Experts from the Member States appointed by the Commission convened four times in 2019 without arriving at any result. Even about the nature and legal basis of their conclusions disagreement reigned supreme: they would suggest, advise, and certainly not recommend. A stakeholders group met concurrently and showed strong resistance against measures to be taken. The EP in its Report 'regrets that the group of Experts … has not agreed on a common set of security checks as it was mandated to do by the end of 2019; finds that the failure to agree on a common set of security checks shows the limits of adopting an intergovernmental approach … and underlines the need for Union action', ibid 20.

[16] ibid 18.

Here we see the predicament spelled out: The EP urges the EC into action, but the EC denies having the competence to do so where citizenship of the MS is at stake. Given the reluctance of the MS to see their laws on nationality, considered to belong to their reserved domain, as acknowledged by the EP, subjected to Union law and principles, legislative initiatives, if at all launched by the Commission, will in all probability not be embraced by the Council. Although the pressure is intensified by the war in Ukraine, and the need to target Russian oligarchs is obvious and fully understandable, MS will be wary and may think *hodie tibi, cras mihi*.

Nudging the Commission into action concerning the CBI schemes, the EP suggests as part of a comprehensive legislative package the introduction of measures disallowing MS to introduce new CBI programmes, and obliging MS with existing CBI schemes to phase these out 'reaching zero in 2025'. It invokes again Article 4(3) TEU as the legal basis for this legislative action. As a matter of fact it repeatedly implores the Commission in this document to support the right of initiative of Parliament in following-up Parliament's own-initiative legislative reports with legislative acts. It shows well-founded doubts about the willingness of the Commission to act on the proposal. Even less certain is the reception by the Council of any proposal to curtail the autonomy of the MS in the area of citizenship.

Commissioner for Justice and Consumer Affairs Didier Reynders disagreed with the need for new rules on sale of citizenship; he pointed out that the Commission was already pushing legal proceedings to shut down existing Golden Passport schemes in Malta, Cyprus and Bulgaria. He would, however, assess the need for new laws to tighten golden *visa* schemes. Furthermore, a non- binding recommendation would be issued on EU MS issuance of golden passports and residence permits to Russians.[17]

IV. THE EUROPEAN COMMISSION'S RECOMMENDATION OF 28 MARCH 2022

This Recommendation stated that CBI schemes are not compatible with the principle of sincere cooperation and with the concept of Union citizenship, and recommended: 'Any Member State operating such an investor citizenship scheme needs to ensure compliance with its obligations pursuant to these Treaty provisions by repealing it immediately.'[18] And it adds, for good measure:

> any MS that has naturalised Russian or Belarusian nationals based on an investor citizenship scheme should immediately assess, in accordance with the principles resulting from the case law of the CJEU, including the principle of proportionality and the protection of fundamental rights, whether these individuals' naturalisations should be withdrawn.[19]

The reason for the withdrawal would be the fact that the person involved is or becomes subject to the EU restrictive measures, or because he supports significantly by any means the war in Ukraine. Outcome of the assessments should be reported to the Commission by the end of May 2022.

There is no trace in this Recommendation of Article 21(2) of the Charter: 'Within the scope of application of the Treaties and without prejudice to any of their specific provisions

[17] The Recommendation materialized later in the month, European Commission, 'Recommendation on immediate steps in the context of the Russian invasion of Ukraine in relation to investor citizenship schemes and investor residence schemes' C (2022)2028 final.

[18] ibid 5.

[19] ibid 3.

discrimination on the grounds of nationality is prohibited.' The Commission points out that the assessment has to take place with the protection of fundamental rights in mind. This would include the right not to be discriminated on the grounds of possession of a specific other nationality than that of a MS. And: why are naturalised Syrians not included? The assessment has to take place within two months. And decisions to withdraw the naturalisation may need intervention by the lawmakers of the MS concerned.

It is abundantly clear that the Commission is reluctant to engage in proposing new, harmonising rules on citizenship of the MS. And the practical effects of new banning measures for golden passports are minimal, given that Cyprus and Bulgaria have already decided to phase out their Golden Passport programmes. At the time of writing only Malta shows some resistance.

V. THE GENUINE CONNECTION REVISITED

As both institutions rely on the 'genuine link' it is necessary to explore the genuine connection element in the many definitions of nationality and more specifically in the *Nottebohm* case.[20] As the Permanent Court of International Justice explained in its Advisory Opinion a century ago 'the question whether a certain matter is or is not solely within the jurisdiction of a State is an essentially relative question'.[21] The relativity of the reserved domain is not only a matter of time, but also one of the subject matter involved.

In *Nottebohm* diplomatic protection on the basis of nationality was at stake. Was Liechtenstein allowed under international law to exercise diplomatic protection concerning its citizen, a former German national, against Guatemala, the country where he had lived and worked the larger part of his life? As a satellite state of the US Guatemala had deprived him during WW II of his assets and had him deported to the US as an 'enemy alien'. The ICJ did not dispute that Nottebohm had acquired the Liechtenstein nationality in 1939 through naturalisation (that involved at least some 40,000 Swiss francs being paid to the State and the Commune of Mauren – a golden passport.) It held, however, that in order to exercise diplomatic protection against Guatemala successfully – the situation as to other states was not discussed – the link between Liechtenstein and its national should be 'genuine', that is, representing the centre of one's life and work. His ties with Guatemala had been much stronger in 1939 than with Liechtenstein. Nottebohm was even castigated by the Court for his motives to become a citizen of Liechtenstein: 'it was to enable him to substitute for his status as a national of a belligerent State that of a national of a neutral State, with the sole aim of thus coming within the protection of Liechtenstein'.[22] It seems to me that the ICJ in 1955 still was in the thrall of World War II, seeking revenge on 'enemy aliens', and not heeding the precept of the preamble to the ECN, that 'account should be taken both of the legitimate interests of States and those of individuals'.[23] Is it not legitimate to try to save your skin and your assets in an oncoming war in which you do not want to be involved? What about the many Jews who had as 'sole aim' to avoid being murdered in acquiring a life-saving nationality or at least a

[20] *Nottebohm* (Liechtenstein v Guatemala) [1955] ICJ Rep. 4. I am in full agreement with Spiro in this volume, and with Weingerl and Tratnik, 'Relevant Links' in Kochenov and Surak (eds), *Citizenship and Residence Sales* (Cambridge University Press 2023).

[21] *Nationality Decrees Issued in Tunis and Morocco*, Advisory Opinion No. 4 (Great Britain v France) [1923] PCIJ Series B no 4, para 20.

[22] *Nottebohm*.

[23] ibid.

(forged) passport of a country with which they had no connection whatsoever?[24] Are motives relevant in nationality law?[25] Is diplomatic protection to be withheld from persons who seek refuge by acquiring the nationality of another state with which they have no further ties than their rope to life and security? Is this what the ICJ meant?

For many reasons *Nottebohm* should be discarded. Nottebohm was left with no diplomatic protection at all, as the only nationality he possessed was that of Liechtenstein. Although he was considered by the Allies to be an enemy alien, he had lost his German nationality and could not be protected by the successor State to the Third Reich. Germany recognised Nottebohm's Liechtensteiner nationality, by attaching the loss of German nationality to his naturalisation, as confirmed by the Federal Republic in front of the ICJ. Thus the naturalisation according to Liechtenstein's municipal law had clearly its effect on the international level. This is a reason to restrict the precedent of *Nottebohm* to the topic of diplomatic protection; other effects, especially recognition by other states, including the state of former nationality, are not envisaged. Nottebohm had but one nationality and was allowed under international law, to return to Liechtenstein., with or without genuine link.

That is why the reasoning of the Court, derived from principles concerning dual nationality, was unconvincing: if a court has to choose between two nationalities, for example in matters of private international law, and prefers one above the other on grounds that that citizenship is stronger and more effective, real, than the other, the person involved in still in possession of that other citizenship. It seems that the ICJ considered Guatemala as the state with which Nottebohm had the stronger 'nationality'. He was a virtual binational but was left without any protection.[26] The Court has made the impression of scrutinising the bond of naturalised persons with their state more intensely than that same bond of nationals by birth.[27] I will return to this issue.

Nottebohm is unworkable as well: if in all cases in which diplomatic protection is exercised on behalf of a citizen the genuineness of her link has to become a preliminary issue, a bar eventually to be decided by courts or tribunals, the effectiveness of the tool of diplomatic protection is jeopardised.

If a precedent at all, it should be construed as narrowly as possible. It is even questionable whether it should still play a role in the international law and principles concerning the law of nationality. It has been superseded by more recent developments in international law. In the *Flegenheimer* Claim, decided by the United States-Italian Conciliation Commission in 1958 it

[24] Cf Kisch, 'De Winter sous l'occupation' (1972) 19 *NILR 102*, 102–06, also in Jessurun d'Oliveira (ed), *Uitgelezen opstellen* (Tjeenk Willink 1981) 408–12. Here the story is told of my predecessor Prof. De Winter who had laid his hands on a number of passports issued by a Swiss former consul of Paraguay that proved life-saving for Jews who had no connection whatsoever with Paraguay. See also Brokken, *De Rechtvaardigen* (Atlas Contact 2018). The Dutch honorary consul in Riga issued thousands of visas for Dutch colonies to mostly Jews from Eastern Europe, who could, with help of the Japanese consul in Riga, travel on that basis to Japan and China, through USSR, and survived. Not to forget Raoul Wallenberg, the Swedish diplomat who saved between 30.000 and 100,000 Hungarian Jews by handing out Swedish passports, and disappeared in the Soviet Union, most likely murdered.

[25] The argument is dismissed in Case C-369/90 *Micheletti* ECLI:EU:C:1992:295; Case C-192/99 *Kaur* ECLI:EU:C:2001:106; Case C-148/02 *Garcia Avello* ECLI:EU:C:2003:539 and, especially, Case C-200/02 *Zhu and Chen* ECLI:EU:C:2004:639, paras 35–40: 'although it is true that Ms Chen's purpose in giving birth in Ireland was to secure for her child and herself a long-term right to reside in the United Kingdom, nevertheless it is for each Member State, having due regard to Community law, to lay down the conditions for acquisition of its nationality; other Member States are not allowed to restrict the effects of the grant of nationality by imposing additional conditions.'

[26] Boll, *Multiple Nationality and International Law* (Brill-Nijhoff 2007) 113.

[27] Weis, *Nationality and Statelessness in International Law* (Brill-Nijhoff 1979) 181. Weis considered the context of Nottebohm's naturalisation as 'quite exceptional' and the principle developed by the ICJ not lending itself to generalisation.

was held that the genuine connection test should not be applied to persons holding a single nationality.[28] It stated:

> But when a person is vested with only one nationality, ... the theory of effective nationality cannot be applied without the risk of causing confusion. ... There does not in fact exist any criterion of proven effectiveness for disclosing the effectiveness of a bond with a political collectivity, and the persons by the thousands who, because of the facility of travel in the modern world, possess the positive legal nationality of a State and made their lives in foreign States where they are domiciled and where their family and business centre is located, would be exposed to non-recognition at the international level, of the nationality with which they are undeniably vested by virtue of the laws of their national State, if this doctrine were to be generalized.[29]

The International Law Commission (ILC) in its Commentary to Article 3 of the Draft Rules on diplomatic protection (2006)[30] took its distance from *Nottebohm* as well, even in the area of diplomatic protection:

> Paragraph two[31] does not require a State to prove an effective or genuine link between itself and its national, along the lines suggested in the Nottebohm case as an additional factor for the exercise of diplomatic protection. ... Moreover, the Commission was mindful of the fact that if the genuine link requirement proposed by Nottebohm was strictly applied it would exclude millions of persons from the benefit of diplomatic protection as in today's world of economic globalization and migration there are millions of persons who have drifted away from their state of nationality and made their lives in states whose nationality they never acquire ... or have (nationality) acquired by birth or descent from states with which they have a tenuous connection.[32]

According to the ILC a tenuous connection as ascribed to *Nottebohm* is not enough to block diplomatic protection; it furthermore explained that the ICJ judgment should not be used as a general principle.

I submit that *Nottebohm* is not only wrongly decided and a relic from the past, but it is being misused as well. This is especially the case in the EC's Report where it reads: 'The *Nottebohm* case of the ICJ establishes that, for nationality granted through naturalisation to be recognised in the international arena, it should be granted on the basis of a genuine connection between the individual and the State in question.'[33] This misinterpretation is far too wide and at the same time too narrow. It overlooks the limited issue before the ICJ: is Liechtenstein allowed under international law to protect its citizen against Guatemala? The Commission generalises the particular issue of diplomatic protection to the whole body of international law. It suggests furthermore that the genuine link plays a role, according to the ICJ, with regard to nationality acquired by naturalisation only (and not generally).

What is to be learned from *Nottebohm* as a parallel or precedent is this: the bought citizenship of Liechtenstein is recognised internationally by the ICJ and by Germany, but not all effects in the internationals arena are attached to it: diplomatic protection may not be exercised

[28] *Flegenheimer* (US v Italy) [1958] 14 RIAA 327; one of the members of the Conciliation Commission was Professor Sauser-Hall, Counsel for Liechtenstein in the *Nottebohm* case.

[29] ibid.

[30] This draft is to be considered as reflecting modern international customary law on the subject.

[31] Art 3(2) of ILC, Draft Articles on Diplomatic Protection with commentaries, UN Doc. A/61/10 (2006) reads as follows: 'For the purpose of diplomatic protection of natural persons, a State of nationality means a State whose nationality the person sought to be protected has acquired by birth, descent, succession of States, naturalization or in any other manner not inconsistent with international law.'

[32] ILC Draft Articles (2006), 33. cf Jessurun d'Oliveira, 'Nationaliteit en diplomatieke bescherming' de Boer et al (eds), *Strikwerda's conclusies* (Kluwer 2011) 247–63.

[33] European Commission Report COM(2019)12final, 5.

against Guatemala (against the USA would be another matter). In the same reasoning Golden Passports are legally valid under international law, but not all effects of Union citizenship are necessarily attached to it. This leads inexorably to a weakening of the link between national citizenship and Union citizenship and one can understand why the Commission and the EP do not want to engage into that road. It would imply amending article 20 TFEU. This is however the impractical but unescapable effect of the *Nottebohm* decision as read by the EC and as applied to the EU legal order.

The Commission Report continues to explain that citizenship of the Union is an automatic consequence of holding nationality of a Member State, and that all other Members States have thus to recognise this Union citizenship, without additional requirements as to the roundness or effectiveness of the nationality. This obligation is indeed the gist of *Micheletti*,[34] who had a most tenuous connection with Italy and was first and foremost an Argentinean citizen, and who was allowed to settle and practice as a dentist in Spain, where he was considered to be Argentinean. Nominal nationality did the trick. A genuine link check was not involved. I may be allowed to quote from the Opinion of AG Tesauro in this case:[35]

> I do not believe that the case before the Court constitutes an appropriate setting in which to raise the problems relating to effective nationality, whose origin lies in a 'romantic period' of international relations and, in particular, in the concept of diplomatic protection; still less, in my view, is the well-known (and, it is worth remembering controversial) Nottebohm judgment of the International Court of Justice of any relevance.

The learned AG considered as the only limits a Member State could rely on, denying the benefits of the rights of Article 52 EEC Treaty, those concerning public policy and public security. The European Court refrained from mentioning *Nottebohm* in its *Micheletti* judgment, while legiferating in the notorious and ominous obiter dictum that 'under international law it is for each Member State, having due regard to Community law, to lay down the conditions for the acquisition and loss of nationality'. The Court refrained from checking whether Italy had laid down these conditions with due regard to Community law concerning this son of Italo-Argentineans who had emigrated to South America. Is *ius sanguinis* as such enough, even if a person has never lived in the state of his European nationality? Mr Micheletti's nominal Italian nationality turned out to be sufficient basis for the exercise of the freedom of settlement and services in Spain (and elsewhere). Thus, the Court denied the impact of *Nottebohm* for Community purposes.

The referral to the municipal law of the Member States was confirmed in *Kaur*.[36] The case was decided on the basis of a Unilateral Declaration by the UK to the European Community (1972) at the occasion of its accession. Persons in the situation of Kaur were excluded from the declaration by the British Government concerning their nationality for Community purposes. Although this exclusion could be considered as a fine example of race discrimination,[37] the Court held that Kaur never had possessed the quality of British citizen and thus was rightly excluded from the freedom of movement under the Treaty. Unilateral declarations as to who can count as national of the Member State for Community purposes are taken at face value and have never been assessed in terms of their compatibility with Community law.

[34] *Micheletti*.

[35] Opinion of AG Tesauro, *Micheletti* ECLI:EU:C:1992:47, para 20.

[36] *Kaur*.

[37] It was indeed to be held to constitute racial discrimination by the European Commission of Human rights in *East African Asians v The United Kingdom*, no. 4403/70, 14 December 1973.

In *Garcia Avello v Belgium*, the Court, referring to *Micheletti*, repeated that

> it is not permissible for a Member State to restrict the effects of the grant of a nationality of another Member State by imposing an additional condition for the recognition of that nationality with a view to the exercise of the fundamental freedom provided for in the Treaty.[38]

A year later the European Court of Justice (ECJ) in *Zhu and Chen*[39] again denied the Member States the right to impose additional conditions for recognition of the nationality of other Member States of the Union. Catherine Zhu had acquired the nationality of the Irish Republic on the basis of article 6 (1) of the Irish Code on nationality, stating that every person born on the island, would *ex lege* acquire the nationality of the Irish Republic. Her mother had travelled to Belfast in Northern Ireland with the aim of this conferral to her daughter, that would enable her daughter (and herself) to settle afterwards in the UK. Even the fact that the Irish Republic conferred its nationality to a person born *outside* the Irish Republic but on the island in the UK did not bring the ECJ from its path: to withhold to the baby the fundamental freedom of movement was not allowed, 'merely because the nationality of a Member State was in fact solely acquired in order to secure a right of residence under Community law for a national of a non-member country' (ie the mother).[40] Suspect motives, so relevant in *Nottebohm*, do not count for the ECJ.[41] The Irish Republic, however, intended to remedy what it considered to be an abuse: the conferral of citizenship on persons with no tangible link to the nation or the state. Where this right was only recently laid down in 1999 in the 19th Amendment to the Constitution, the Constitution was amended already five years later, in 2004, by the 24th Amendment, restricting the *iure soli* acquisition by birth to those 'who are born on the island of Ireland to at least one parent who is … an Irish citizen'. The upshot of this development, partly inspired by the prospect of the upcoming decision by the ECJ, is that the Irish Republic discards *ius soli* as representing a genuine link. The place where the umbilical cord is buried does not count there as such link.

It was only in *Rottman*,[42] *Tjebbes*[43] and *JY* that the European Court unsheathed the sword of Union law by demanding that MS nationality laws comply with Union law, more specifically the principle of proportionality. In the meantime, Union citizenship had been upgraded by the ECJ in settled case law as 'destined to be the fundamental status of nationals of the Member States'. With a slight, but important legerdemain it was recently even promoted by the Grand Chamber to 'constitute the fundamental status of nationals of the Member States'.[44] So, the Union citizens seem to have arrived at their final destination, that of the fundamental status, as opposed to the fading status of being a national of a Member State.

Because of the axiomatic automatic conferral of this fundamental status to Member State nationals, the thundering conclusion of the EC is that 'each Member State needs to ensure that

[38] *Garcia Avello*, para 28.

[39] *Zhu and Chen*.

[40] ibid, para 40.

[41] On the backgrounds of the case, involving evasion of the one-child policy of China, see Kocherov and Lindeboom, 'Breaking Chinese Law, Making European One' in Nicola and Davies (eds), *EU Law Stories* (Cambridge University Press 2016).

[42] Case C-135/08 *Rottman* ECLI:EU:C:2010:104.

[43] Case C-221/17 *Tjebbes* ECLI:EU:C:2019:189. Interestingly the Commission quotes (Report, p. 5, fn. 27) *Tjebbes* as endorsing the 'due regard' clause but adds that the case is still pending. Did the Commission have a sneak preview?

[44] Case C-118/20 *JY* ECLI:EU:C:2022:34, para 58. This paragraph refers to paras 38 and 46 that both speak of 'destined'. The referral is thus misleading. Or are we confronted with a *lapsus linguae*? To refuse naturalisation because of a number of minor traffic offences is not compatible with the Union principle of proportionality. And: a former Union citizen who became stateless is still covered by Union law.

nationality is not awarded absent any genuine link to the country or its citizens'.[45] This is a sweeping statement indeed, needing inspection. In a footnote, it hides another argument: the principle of sincere cooperation with other Member States and the Union, Article 4(3) TEU, that would entail introducing a genuine link criterion in the Member States laws on nationality over the board.

VI. SINCERE COOPERATION

The Commission and Parliament thus add another major argument: the principle of sincere cooperation with other Member States and the Union. In the various infringement procedures launched by the Commission the principle of sincere cooperation as enshrined in article 4 (3) of the TEU is put forward as the main obstacle against golden passport schemes.[46]

This general obligation of sincere cooperation would imply that all MS are obliged, in shaping their laws on nationality, to have due regard to the whole bulk of Union laws and principles; quite an expansion from the duty to comply with the principle of proportionality as up till now laid down by the ECJ. Given its undefined and undefinable content, this cure-all is unworkable and an arbitrary tool in the hands of the Commission and other institutions of the Union.[47] That obligation, moreover, concerns 'the obligations arising out of the Treaties'. It is highly questionable whether such an obligation of the MS to adjust their codes on nationality and introduce a genuine link criterion arises indeed from the Treaty. I see no traces.

The conundrum of what is to count as a genuine link is central to doctrine and practice of the law on nationality, both municipal and international. It is significant that the ECN does not list the genuine link condition as one of its principles on which the acquisition of the nationality of each State party shall be based. It defines nationality in a neutral and minimalistic way by stating that it is a legal bond between a person and a State. The 'bedrock' of this legal bond, is, according to the ECJ, 'the special relationship of solidarity and good faith … and also the reciprocity of rights and duties'.[48] This 'essence' of citizenship is introduced by the Court as a *result* of its existence *not* as a condition for its acquisition. This phrase cannot be used to underpin the genuine link requirement at the moment of acquisition, certainly not at birth.

If the Commission demands from the MS that their laws on nationality contain the threshold of the genuine link, not only in the area of naturalisation, but generally, and thus also as concerns acquisition at birth, as a necessary consequence of the fundamental status of Union citizenship attached to it, that would necessitate a complete overhaul of the existing laws on nationality of the MS. Another consequence: loss of Union citizenship whenever the genuine link with a MS falls away, according to the perspective of the EU and its institutions.

Does birth on a certain territory, for example, represent such a genuine link? Certainly not in the *Nottebohm* definition, or in that of the ECJ: where is the relationship of solidarity and good faith of the newborn baby? And does birth from parents of a certain nationality

[45] European Commission Report COM(2019)12 final.

[46] eg against Malta and Cyprus, 'Investor citizenship schemes: European Commission opens infringements against Cyprus and Malta for "selling" EU citizenship' (*European Commission*, 20 October 2020) https://ec.europa.eu/commission/presscorner/detail/en/ip_20_1925.

[47] Upholding the rule of law would be one of the central obligations of Member States under the heading of sincere cooperation. In the case of Poland, the Commission turned out, in a fit of *Realpolitik*, to take its distance from rulings of the ECJ on the independence of the Polish Judiciary, and to reward the Polish Republic for its stand in the Ukraine-Russian war at the cost of the central tenet of the rule of law, selling its birthright for a mess of pottage. Passports may not be for sale, but the rule of law is.

[48] eg in *JY*, para 52, but already in *Rottman* and *Tjebbes* as well.

(or different nationalities), constitute such a genuine link? If the Commission want to rely on *Nottebohm*, it should bear in mind what the ICJ had to tell about the subject:

> The reason for (the fact that international law leaves it to each State to lay down rules governing the grant of its own nationality) is that the diversity of demographic conditions has thus far made it impossible for any general agreement to be reached on the rules relating to nationality.[49]

In other words: it is simply not true, as the Commission pretends,[50] that there exists 'a common understanding of the bond of nationality' as a necessary condition for accepting Union Citizenship.

Another consequence of introducing a genuine link condition: would indeed Union Citizenship fall away whenever the genuine link of nationality with a MS ceases to exist according to the views of the EU institutions?

I take a few examples, derived from the Dutch code on nationality. The Dutch nationality may be revoked by the Minister of Justice of persons condemned for having perpetrated certain terrorist crimes.[51] This is consonant with Article 7 (1) of the ECN that allows States to provide for the loss of its nationality in case of 'conduct seriously prejudicial to the vital interests of the State Party', a phrase derived from the 1961 Convention on the Reduction of Statelessness and repeated in Article 7 ECN. But the case law in the Netherlands on the provision goes a step further. Derived from the parliamentary documents, and in order to determine whether this withdrawal of nationality is to be considered as punishment or as an administrative measure, the Dutch Council of State has emphasised that 'with the withdrawal it is expressed that when a person has seriously prejudiced the essential interests of the Netherlands in this way the link with the Netherlands cannot exist any longer'.[52] To stress the impossibility of maintaining the ties with the Netherlands is, according to the court, even the purpose of the provision. In this way, a collision with the ne bis in idem principle in criminal law is parried. But this ideological turn is exposed to other criticisms. If indeed the purpose of the provision is not to increase the state's safety, but to express the view that the legal bond of nationality cannot exist anymore, it is difficult to see how this can be coupled with the fact that the minister has to effectuate a comprehensive proportionality test before the revocation of the Dutch nationality. 'Il faut qu'une porte soit ouverte ou fermée' as Alfred de Musset stated. The conviction for terrorist acts, sufficient for the loss of nationality according to the ECN, is in itself not sufficient for withdrawal of the Dutch nationality: a proportionality test has to decide whether the bond of nationality can still exist, and this test has nothing to do with the conviction. Strangely enough, monopatride Dutch persons, convicted of the same crimes, retain their nationality, although according to the prevailing ideology their bond cannot exist anymore either. It is only because of the prohibition to cause statelessness that their nationality subsists. The position is riddled with contradictions. This is a case of Christian Morgensterns' 'Weil, so schliesst er messerscharf: nicht sein kann was nicht sein darf.' This ideological frame, consistent with the 'bedrock' formula of the ECJ, encounters the paradox that only binationals are considered to have shown behaviour such as to break the genuine link, whereas mononationals retain this 'relationship of solidarity and good faith'. This goes to show that a pumped-up notion of nationality encounters serious intellectual problems. The fact that the ECN *allows,* not: *obliges to* withdraw the nationality in the case of conduct seriously prejudicial to the vital

[49] *Nottebohm*.
[50] European Commission Report COM(2019)12 final, 5.
[51] Art 14(2), Nationality Act 1984 (NL).
[52] Case no. 19/3504 ECLI:NL:RVS:2020:3045, paras 4.2, 4.3, 6.3, 7.2.

interests of the State is already an indication that a genuine link element is not involved or is superfluous.

And what about the situation that the binational holds the nationality of another member state? Will she be considered as having broken the bond of nationality with that other state as well? If not, why not?

In the aftermath of *Tjebbes*[53] the Netherlands were obliged to introduce a proportionality check to the legislation that withdraws automatically Dutch nationality from Dutch nationals, in possession of another nationality, habitually residing abroad, if they have not manifested the desire to retain their nationality by receiving a renewed passport or other identity document within a 10-year period.[54] These nationals were deemed to have lost touch with the Netherlands and to have severed the genuine link. A recent amendment to the Dutch code introduced a new right to 'opt'[55] retroactively for the Dutch nationality for those who lose their citizenship according to the still existing old law; the option is also available for new cases. In the course of handling such requests the Union principle of proportionality would duly be applied. (Automatic reinstatement in the Dutch nationality for all those who had lost it was of course out of the question: involuntary (re)acquisition *ex lege* of a lost nationality would be an unpleasant surprise for those who had acquiesced to the deprivation.)

Interestingly, in the amendment the period within which the Dutch diaspora has to receive (on request) a new document is extended to 13 years. This extension is not introduced in view of altered ideas about the moment of severance of the genuine link, but for the bureaucratic reason that the period for the validity of passports had been prolonged to ten years. Here bureaucratic reason blurs the frame of loss of real links.

Interesting as well is the situation of Dutch citizens settled in the territory of the other MS of the Union: they do not lose their nationality in the first place because that would violate their right as Union citizens, especially their freedom of movement. In other words: there still exists a genuine link with the Netherlands *because* they are Union citizens and have availed themselves of the freedom of movement. This is the world turned upside down: Union citizenship provides the genuine link with the MS of which one possesses the nationality.[56] Or: notwithstanding the loss of a genuine link, Union Citizenship will still result from an empty nationality. A person living in a third country loses *ex lege* her nationality after thirteen years if not receiving a new passport in time, whereas a third or fourth generation emigrant to another MS is still deemed to be connected genuinely to the country of her ancestors.

To be stressed is the fact that *Tjebbes* and other cases concern dual nationality. If the second nationality is one of the other Member States, no loss of Union citizenship is involved by losing the nationality of a MS. But if the other nationality is one of a third country, loss of the MS nationality becomes problematic: Union citizenship is jeopardised. In *Tjebbes* the ECJ engages in a repechage, in that it gives an opening towards maintaining Union citizenship notwithstanding the lack of a genuine link according to the municipal law of the MS.[57]

What is important here is that the Dutch provision on automatic loss stays in place and was not censored by the ECJ in *Tjebbes*, although the only way in which the Dutch citizen abroad

[53] *Tjebbes*.

[54] This provision of Art 15(1)(c) of Nationality Act 1984 (NL) is in line with Art 7 (1)(e) of the ECN (1997) ETS166: lack of a genuine link between the State Party and a national habitually residing abroad. This provision, concerning dual nationals, residing for generations abroad, is the only place in the ECN where (lack of) a genuine link is mentioned.

[55] Option in the Dutch system is a misleading term: it is not a unilateral act, but a naturalisation with less conditions.

[56] Jessurun d'Oliveira, 'Nationaliteitsrechtelijke oogst van het Programakkoord' (2022) 290 *NJB* 339.

[57] cf somewhat differently, Kochenov, 'The *Tjebbes* Fail' (2019) 4 *European Papers* 319.

is allowed to demonstrate her genuine link with the Netherlands consists of the request for and granting of(renewal of) a passport. Nothing else is required. Is this what is meant by genuine link, or the values of the EU, or the essence of Union citizenship? Here again: a passport is a manifestation or attestation of holding a certain nationality, but in this scheme it is the other way round: granting the passport (or other identity paper) in time by the authorities confers the genuine link and the (prolongation of) nationality.

In combination with the conferral of the Dutch nationality at birth by being born from at least one Dutch parent this state of affairs may go on for an indefinite number of generations of citizens settled abroad. Public international law allows this, but it allows states at the same time to break the chain of intergenerational bestowal of citizenship at one place or another. In France the loss may be established by the court for French citizens who have never lived in France, and whose parents have lived abroad for at least half a century.[58] Italy draws no time limits on the possession of its nationality; it just allows persons who settle abroad to renounce their Italian *cittadinanza*, if not becoming stateless.[59] In Poland involuntary loss of citizenship because of absence of a genuine link is not allowed; Poles may lose their nationality only on request and with the consent of the President, who has constitutional prerogative powers to deny or grant the renouncement. Polish history explains this lenient provision.[60]

It is as legitimate in terms of the genuine link criterion for states to exclude their citizens because of severance of this link by staying too long abroad – be it 10 years or 50 years – as it is to bind their diasporas as long as possible to the state until the umpteenth generation. It is as legitimate to propose that birth on a territory creates a genuine link to that state as it is to deny that this fleeting moment can convey nationality to the new-born baby. By the way: in most cases ius soli coincides or combines with ius sanguinis: the hard core of what is silently considered by most people as the real stuff.

An example where, after some five centuries, 'prodigal sons' were allowed to become again members of the household is provided by Spain and Portugal that introduced legislation concerning Sephardic Jews. They had been persecuted and banned from the Iberian peninsula in 1492 and following years. Officially this legislation was put into place to right a historical wrong. Does the wish to repair wrongs perpetrated half a millennium earlier constitute a genuine link? Unofficially the desire to attract new investors may have played a role in Spain and Portugal. What is relevant here is the fact that the Portuguese enactment does not require these Sephardim to reside in Portugal; in Spain the period of residence was reduced to two years. They furthermore are allowed to keep their nationality of origin. Mostly Sephardim from third countries have applied for the scheme.[61] UK citizens of Sephardic descent, seeking to maintain their freedom of movement after Brexit, now covet an Iberian nationality.

If indeed 'due regard to EU law', including the obligation to cooperate loyally and the principle of proportionality, would oblige states to introduce a genuine link criterion into their laws on nationality, and that is clearly the position of the Commission as shown in the infringement procedures, this would not only require an enormous overhaul of the codes on nationality of the Member States, but also a spectacular inroad into the identity of the Member States, as guaranteed in article 4(2) of the TEU. Where will the duty of sincere cooperation collide

[58] Art 23(6), Code Civil 1804(FR).

[59] Art 11, Act No. 91 of 5 February 1992(IT).

[60] Art 13, Citizenship Act 2009(PL).

[61] Jessurun d'Oliveira, 'Iberian Nationality Legislation and Sephardic Jews' in Nunez and de Groot (eds), *European Citizenship at the Crossroads* (Wolf 2015) 251–65; van der Baaren, 'On Emigrant Nationality' (Doctoral Thesis, University of Liège 2020) Ch 5.

with the respect for identity of the MS in such a sensitive area as that of defining the personal substratum of the member states? Aren't citizens a constituent part of the definition of any state? Have the MS transferred the paramount power to define who are their citizens to the EU in so many words in any Treaty document? Did they open up their *reserved domain* tacitly? In the context of EU law, especially article 4(1) of the TEU, the term 'reserved domain' is even somewhat misleading: the MS did not transfer this central element of their sovereignty.[62]

In this regard it is important to notice that the MS of the EU as members of the Council of Europe have refused to add the right to a nationality as a Protocol to the ECHR, because that would imply jurisdiction by the European Court of Human Rights (ECtHR). 'It proved politically unfeasible to require States to forgo their sovereignty in the realm of nationality law.'[63] That is why a separate ECN was drafted in 1997, again without jurisdiction of the Strasbourg Court. A clear indication that MS resist any interference by an international court with their laws on nationality.[64] The same unwillingness is shown by quite a number of EU MS that did not even ratify the Convention.[65]

There are of course many more indications. The Charter of Fundamental Rights does not mention nationality, except for the prohibition of discrimination on the grounds of nationality.[66] Nationality is however mentioned in the specific General Declaration of the (Maastricht) Conference on the nationality of a Member State, attached to the Maastricht Treaty, stating:

> The Conference declares that, wherever in the Treaty establishing the European Community, reference is made to nationality of the Member States, the question whether an individual possesses the nationality of a Member State shall be settled solely by reference to the national law of the Member State concerned. Member States may declare, for information, who are to be considered their nationals for Community purposes by way of a declaration lodged with the presidency and may amend such declarations when necessary.[67]

I highlight two elements of this declaration: in the first place no mention is made of any 'due regard to community law', as expounded by the ECJ. This declaration, then, is a clear token of the resistance by the Council against any inroads into the exclusive jurisdiction of the MS in this area. Second: nationality for Union purposes is a *functional* nationality, not necessarily identical with nationality according to the national codes on nationality. In declarations by Germany, the UK and Denmark the categories of nationals to be considered as nationals for Union purposes are indicated, and these declarations bind the EU and the MS.[68] Thus, MS may declare that persons availing themselves of the CBI schemes will not be nationals for Union purposes. But what they are not allowed to do is to exclude (former) nationals of a third state,

[62] see also Declaration 18 annexed to the Final Act of the Intergovernmental Conference which adopted the Treaty of Lisbon [2007] OJ C 306/1.

[63] de Groot and Vonk, *International Standards on Nationality Law* (Wolf 2015) 41; Jessurun d'Oliveira, 'Het Europees Verdrag Inzake Nationaliteit' in Jessurun d'Oliveira (ed), *Trends in het nationaliteitsrecht* (Sdu 1998) 8.

[64] It is significant that in a recent case before the ECtHR, *Adam Johanssen v Denmark*, no. 27801/19, 1 February 2022, concerning deprivation of nationality and expulsion, the ECtHR quoted the ECN (1997) ETS 166 extensively in the paragraphs concerning the facts, but concentrated its assessment on Art 8 ECHR, without so much as mentioning the ECN: a no-go area.

[65] As per 30 March 2022 of the 46 member states of the Council of Europe 21 have ratified the Convention. Salient absentees for various reasons: Belgium, France, Greece, Ireland, Italy, Poland, Spain, the UK, the Baltic States.

[66] Art 21(2) of the Charter of Fundamental Rights of the European Union (CFR).

[67] TEU, Declaration on nationality of a Member State [1992] OJ C191/98.

[68] Jessurun d'Oliveira, 'Nationality and the European Union After Amsterdam' in Twomey and O'Keeffe (eds), *Legal Issues of the Amsterdam Treaty* (Hart 1999) 395–412; Kojanec, 'Citizenship of the European Union' in van der Velden and Zilverentant (eds), *Aan de grenzen van het Nederlanderschap* (Ministerie van Justitie 1998) 135.

for example, Russians from this functional nationality, because the EU Charter does not allow discrimination on the grounds of nationality.

And if the principle of sincere cooperation demands from MS to accommodate a genuine link into their codes of nationality, why is it then that settled case law set by the ECJ in *Micheletti*, *Kaur* and *Zhu and Chen* prohibits other MS to test the genuineness of the link or the motives of persons, who are their nationals in acquiring a nationality? The ECJ has stated repeatedly that MS are obliged to refrain from imposing additional conditions for recognition of the nationality of other MS, in several cases where the (non-)existence of a genuine link was at stake. Why is it then, that they are not requested by the EC to cooperate in implementing this test? And why does the Commission allow itself to impose additional conditions on the acquisition of MS nationality? *Quod licet Iovi non licet bovi*? It is no accident that the Commission does not mention this well-established jurisprudence of the ECJ in its Report at all. Why would only the EU Commission be legitimised to impose the genuine link element on the MS codes of nationality? The principle of sincere cooperation is far too vague to be of any use in defining what actions are required from which MS: according to the Court they are to abstain, according to the Commission and Parliament they are obliged to take action. To my mind there is a clear clash between the position of the ECJ and that of the Commission and Parliament. Will MS have to cooperate sincerely with the ECJ or with the Commission and Parliament? Or rally with the position of the Council or the Conference? And what will the Council say, in the event that the Commission, beseeched by the EP, notwithstanding their acknowledgement of the fact that the Commission denies having any competence in this area, should come up with a legislative proposal concerning the (non) acceptability of the MS provisions on nationality, in view of the entailing Union Citizenship?

And what about diplomatic and consular protection to be exercised by MS on behalf of nationals of other MS that are not represented in a third State?[69] Are they to apply a genuine link test before taking up this task? Or are they to refrain from this check and take the nationality of such other MS for granted? The Decision concerned[70] states that the show of a passport or other identity document will suffice for demonstrating the nationality. According to the ILC a genuine link test is not required by international law, but the question arises whether EU law obliges the MS involved to ascertain whether the national on whose behalf diplomatic protection shall be exercised is a genuine citizen of the non-represented MS. And how about the cooperation and coordination by the EU? Should this involvement include ascertaining the genuineness of the link? I do not think so: it is for the incriminated state to allege the absence of an effective link.

Arriving at an interim conclusion I submit that *Nottebohm* was wrongly decided, and wrongly applied by the EC, and that a round definition of nationality of the MS for Union purposes by including a genuine link ingredient is not feasible. Not only because this would imply a drastic overhaul of the national codes of nationality of the MS, but also because of the impossibility, both intellectually and politically, to arrive at common ideas about genuineness. The principle of sincere cooperation moreover leads to paradoxical and conflicting conclusions, because there are conflicting views between the institutions of the Union concerning this issue, and even concerning EU competence in this area.

[69] Art 23 TFEU; Art 43 CFR; Council Directive 2015/637 on the coordination and cooperation measures to facilitate consular protection for unrepresented citizens of the Union in third countries [2015] OJ L 106/1.

[70] Decision of the Representatives of the Governments of the Member States meeting within the Council of 19 December 1995 regarding protection for citizens of the European Union by diplomatic and consular representations [1995] OJ L 314/73.

VII. CITIZENSHIP IN EARLY MODERN TIMES IN EUROPE

In its Report, the Commission considers the naturalisation procedures concerning golden passports as 'new',[71] or even novel. Is this indeed the case?

On my desk lies a doctoral dissertation at the University of Utrecht, defended in the year 1853. Its title reads: *Specimen historico-juridicum inaugurale de peregrinis receptis et civitate donatis in patria nostra usque ad annum MDCCXCV (1795)*.[72] The author, SJ van Geuns, describes in this work in detail the situation of foreigners and immigrants and the ways in which they could become citizens, 'burgers' or 'poorters' in the cities of the Netherlands until the year 1795, when the unitary Batavian Republic – a vassal state of France- was established. The acquisition of 'burgerschap' in the Republic of the seven United Provinces since 1588 rested in the hands of the local authorities that issued by-laws and took individual decisions.

There existed basically three ways to become a 'poorter' or 'burger' (citizen). First by marriage to a 'poorters' daughter or widow. (Acquisition by women of the status of 'burger' by marriage to a 'poorter' was a matter of course.) In some cities one had to pay a fee, and had to take a poorters' oath, swearing to behave as a good and loyal poorter and to fulfil all the duties incumbent on him.[73]

Second, by complimentary bestowal on groups or individuals: in Amsterdam tradesmen and shopkeepers in textiles, professors and ministers, protestant refugees from France and the like were welcomed.[74]

And third and most important in terms of quantity, foreigners, male immigrants and unmarried women, could buy burgerschap. The sum to be paid changed according to time and place. In Amsterdam 'in 1624 14 guilders and 6 pennies; in 1630 30, in 1634 40 and in 1650 50 guilders'.[75] Poorterschap was coveted because one of the important legal, political, social and economic rights attached to it was admissibility to one of the many guilds. On average in the seventeenth century every year some 400 foreigners bought their burgerschap in Amsterdam, mostly to enable them to become a member of a guild, but others, such as mariners, soldiers, labourers, were primarily interested in the existing welfare institutions such as the municipal orphanage (now the Amsterdam Museum), open only to children of burgers. As there was a steep increase of orphaned children in the orphanage between 1587 and 1633, from about 200 to nearly a thousand, the trustees urged the mayors of the city of Amsterdam to raise the fees for bought burgerschap and to tighten the rules for admission to the orphanage.[76] A direct relationship between the steady increase of the purchase price and the burdens on the budget of the city seems probable.[77]

[71] European Commission Report COM(2019)12 final, 3.

[72] The title page is, however, in Dutch: *Proeve eener geschiedenis van de toelating en vestiging van vreemdelingen in Nederland tot het jaar 1795*. The author was granted the right by the university authorities to write his thesis in Dutch and not in Latin as was customary at the time.

[73] One of the duties mentioned was to take part in cutting holes in the ice to hinder enemies to enter the city.

[74] One of them was the first Earl of Shaftesbury (1621–1683), who had fled, accused of treason, to Amsterdam in 1682. Shaftesbury was a former Lord Chancellor of England and had fiercely opposed the Dutch Republic in the successive Anglo-Dutch wars. As a Cato redivivus he even invariably had exclaimed in parliament 'delenda est Carthago'. The Amsterdam municipality explained benevolently:'Carthago non adhuc deleta Comitem de Shaftesbury in gremio suo recipere vult.' See van Geuns, 'Specimen historico-juridicum inaugurale de peregrinis receptis et civitate donatis in patria nostra usque ad annum MDCCXCV (1795)' (Doctoral Thesis, University of Utrecht 1853), 273.

[75] van Geuns, 'Specimen historico-juridicum', 275. Fifty guilders in 1650 represent around 500 euro nowadays. An example: immigrant carpenter Jacob Wesselsz Wiltingh buys his poorterschap of Amsterdam on 20 January 1650 for 50 guilders: Ponte and Schmitz, 'Rembrandt paints master carpenter Jacob Wesselsz Wltingh', *Kroniek van het Rembrandthuis* 2021, 18–29.

[76] Frijhoff and Prak (eds), *Geschiedenis van Amsterdam 1578–1650* (SUN 2004) 200–01.

[77] Maas, 'Immigrant Integration' (2013) 1 *Politics, Groups, and Identities* 390, 396.

All three ways to citizenship, existing in early modern cities in the sixteenth to the nineteenth century all over Europe, are still common in modern codes of nationality. Local citizenship developed into national citizenship in the newly formed nation-states after the French revolution. Marriage to a national still allows easier naturalisation or option, and was for women for a long period even the automatic effect of marriage. Award of citizenship in the national interest by discretionary naturalisation procedures, for example, for outstanding achievements in sports, culture or science still finds it place in national codes on nationality; and likewise acquisition by investment in the economy of the political entity (purchase) is still with us. These categories are not watertight, however. As mentioned before, quite a number of states define the 'national interest' as encompassing economic or commercial interests.[78]

Leo and Jan Lucassen, writing on immigration in the Low Lands in the seventeenth and eighteenth century state:

> 'Common to the cities in the coastal areas, compared with those in the inlands and especially Germany, were the low costs involved in acquisition of official citizenship. Were they in the maritime Dutch areas equal to one or a few months' wages, in the East they amounted to twice or thrice as much and in Germany the tariffs equalled some years' wages – inaccessible therefore for the average immigrant.[79]

As a leading specialist in the field, Maarten Prak, writes on the modes of access to formal legal citizenship in pre-revolutionary Europe: 'On a European scale there were two main routes into citizenship: birth ("patrimony") and purchase. It is relatively easy to establish the scale of the second route because records were kept.'[80] And Julius Kirshner reminds us that already Bartolo de Sassoferrato (1313–57), the most prominent postglossator, is mentioning the common division of the *cives in civitate* into two categories – original and non-original citizens – of which the last group could acquire citizenship by paying taxes or by buying a house in the city: CBI.[81]

As to naturalisation in the Provinces of the Dutch Republic: the States could confer the status of 'inboorling' (native) to persons or groups of persons from abroad. According to a Resolution of the Province of Holland in 1748 one had to pay a fee of 500 guilders; the names of the new citizens were registered.[82]

Acquisition of citizenship by foreigners through marriage, by bestowal and primarily by purchase thus belong to the perennial common heritage of Europe. Acquisition *iure pecuniae* of a nationality is not 'a new form of naturalisation' as the Commission suggests,[83] but a long-standing practice all over Europe to incorporate newcomers, a way of dealing with foreigners originating in its cities. It had existed 'for the best part of a millennium', as Maarten Prak writes.[84] Certainly this is a somewhat oversimplifying statement, but it can be maintained

[78] European Commission Report COM(2019)12 final, 3. eg Art 21 (21), Code Civil 1804 (FR).

[79] Lucassen and Lucassen, *Vijf eeuwen migratie* (Atlas Contact 2018) 37; Lucassen and Penninx, *Newcomers: Immigrants and Their Descendants in the Netherlands 1550–1995* (Aksant Academic Pub 1998) 91. They explain: 'There were four ways of becoming a freeman: by being born to a freeman, by marriage to the daughter or a widow of one, by grant, or by purchase. The recommended method for newcomers was generally purchase, and occasionally grant or marriage.'

[80] Prak, *Citizens without Nations* (Cambridge University Press 2018) 34.

[81] Kirshner, 'Civitas Sibi Faciat Civem: Bartolus of Sassoferrato's Doctrine on the Making of a Citizen' (1973) 48 *Speculum* 694, 702. See Riethdorf, 'A New Citizenship? National and European Identities from a Historical Perspective' (Project for Democratic Union 2014) on the split between cities' citizenship and citizenship of the Roman empire (the case of Dante and his banishment from Florence): one could lose citizenship in the city, but still be connected to the Empire.

[82] Van Geuns, 'Specimen historico-juridicum', 281.

[83] European Commission Report COM(2019)12 final, 4.

[84] Prak, 'Citizenship for Sale in pre-Modern Europe' in Kochenov and Surak (eds), *Citizenship and Residence Sales* (Cambridge University Press 2023).

that the mode of acquisition of the central status in the cities by purchase has been a tradition in early modern Europe, and has found its way into the codes of nationality since the early nineteenth century. What is new, however, is the systematical minimising of the residence requirements in the conditions of sale in some countries. Old customs may be outdated, but they are not 'novel'.

VIII. CONCLUSIONS AND SOLUTIONS

I have tried to show a number of weaknesses and misrepresentations in the Reports of the EC and the EP:

a. Leaving out discretionary naturalisation procedures in the MS, although these are the vehicle for acquisition by investment, in order to enhance 'normal' naturalisation procedures. Discretionary naturalisation is normal and common.
b. Emphasis on the 1955 *Nottebohm* decision of the ICJ, whereas this has been relegated to legal history through later developments such as the Draft Rules on Diplomatic Protection by the ILC. Misinterpretation of *Nottebohm* by maintaining that the genuine link criterion is not only barring diplomatic protection in specific circumstances, but counts as a positive obligation of states to include it in their nationality arrangements over the board.
c. If anything is learned from *Nottebohm* as a parallel or precedent it is this: A purchased citizenship is recognised as legally valid internationally both by the ICJ and by Germany; it is only in the realm of effects an inroad had been made as to the diplomatic protection against Guatemala (against the USA would have been another matter). Transposed into terms of Union law: Golden passports are to be recognized, by the other MS and the Union, but not all effects of Union citizenship need to be be attached.
d. Neglecting and leaving out the rulings of the ECJ that MS have to recognise the nominal nationality of other MS for Union purposes, without additional conditions, in order to create a level playfield. This prohibition to impose additional conditions is 'with due regard of Community law', as the Court repeatedly stated. Thus the case law of the ECJ conflicts with the views of the Commission and Parliament.
e. To invoke the principle of sincere cooperation opens the door to arbitrary inroads into the laws on nationality of the MS by Union institutions. It represents a power grab by these institutions. Furthermore, the ECJ, the Commission and Parliament and the Council show opposed views; with which institution to cooperate sincerely? The last word is with the ECJ.
f. Purchase of the status of citizen is not at all novel: before the French Revolution it was widespread in Europe and it found its way into various national Codes of nationality.
g. The genuine link criterion may be useful in situations of plural nationality (eg in private international law), albeit refused by the ECJ, but should not be introduced generally as a principle underlying the nationality codes of the MS. There does not exist a sufficient *communis opinio* about what constitutes such a genuine or effective link; A genuine link test is not without reason absent among the principles of the ECN.

This brings me to my own position in this heated debate. Point of departure is my opinion that the EU should be very reluctant in interfering with the reserved domain of the MS to define their citizens, even in the light of the Siamese bond with Union citizenship. To instruct MS to accommodate their nationality codes to the genuine link criterion makes an unnecessary and undefinable inroad into a sensitive area of law, directly linked to the sheer existence and identity of the MS with their individual histories. The high coefficient of sensitivity is demonstrated by the existence of the ECN. Nationality is neither listed in the ECHR nor in later Protocols as an independent fundamental right precisely because the MS of the Council of Europe and the EU refused to see their codes of nationality being subjected to scrutiny and definitional power by an international court such as the ECtHR or other supranational institutions. It is no accident that the ECN lacks such supervision, and that the ECHR takes its distance.

The grounds adduced for trying to impose this rearrangement are weak and wobbly. Invoking *Nottebohm* means not taking into account the development of international law in the last 50 years that witnesses a withdrawal from that notion. Into the bargain *Nottebohm* is misread: if anything the judgment introduces a negative test to be applied in the international arena, and only in the area of diplomatic protection. It did not challenge the legitimacy of the purchased nationality of Liechtenstein involved.

If indeed the existence of Union citizenship with the rights (and duties) attached to it as the fundamental status of MS citizens demands the introduction of a genuine link test in the nationality law of the MS, both in the provisions on acquisition and in those of loss, then this requirement should hit all MS, and not selectively be applied on a few MS while targeting only one type of acquisition. A thorough investigation of the national rules on loss of citizenship, not only in terms of proportionality, should include parameters to measure the provisions on unvoluntary loss in terms of their representing the severance of a genuine link with the individual MS. Which generation, living in non-EU countries, can be considered to have lost an effective link?[85] Are rules to prevent multiple nationality acceptable if a MS nationality is lost by an individual in the process of voluntary acquisition of a third state nationality, while staying in the EU? Many more questions can be asked if a genuine link is to be imposed by EU law on the MS nationality codes.[86]

Nationality law is targeted by the Commission as a tool to combat money laundering, corruption, tax evasion and the like. These are without doubt 'areas for concern'. But the instrumentalisation of nationality law for these purposes follows a dangerous indirect path and is undesirable. To fight against money laundering, corruption, tax evasion and to abate concerns about security, specific tools should be and are as a matter of fact already abundantly put into place.

Directive 2015/849 on the prevention of the use of the financial institutions for the purpose of money laundering or terrorist financing offers a number of mechanisms to deal with this plague. Article 1(2): 'Member States shall ensure that money laundering and terrorist financing is prohibited.' Should the specific instructions contained in this directive prove to be insufficient, the right way of action is implementation and eventually amendment of the directive.[87]

Directive 2014/42 on freezing and confiscation of instrumentalities and proceeds of crime in the EU tells us in article 5(2) that 'criminal offence' 'shall include at least the following: (a) active and passive corruption … in the private sector as well as active and passive corruption involving officials of the institutions of the Union and of the Member States'. Should the specific instructions contained in this directive prove to be insufficient, the right way of action is implementation or eventually amendment of the directive.[88]

[85] As shown, the Member States have widely different views on the moment in which the genuine link has evaporated.

[86] See Jessurun d'Oliveira, '"Latent" Citizens. What Do They Tell Us About the Concept of Citizenship?' in Pfeiffer et al (eds), *Liber Micorum Monika Pauknerová* (Wolters Kluwer 2021) 297–307.

[87] Directive 2015/849 on the prevention of the use of the financial system for the purposes of money laundering or terrorist financing [2015] OJ L141/73.

[88] Directive 2014/42/EU on the freezing and confiscation of instrumentalities and proceeds of crime in the European Union [2014] OJ L 127/39; Art 3 mentions host of international and EU instruments in this area.

The Reports mention a plethora of additional measures, all directly addressing the concerns about money laundering, financing of terrorism, tax evasion. May I add to this cornucopia as a powerful tool Regulation 2020/2092 on a general regime of conditionality for the protection of the EU budget?[89] On the 16 February 2022 actions by Poland and Hungary against this this Regulation have been dismissed in their entirety by the full ECJ.[90] In its article 4 the Regulation defines quite a number of situations that are exactly the concerns of the Commission about the Golden Passports: money laundering, tax evasion, terrorist financing and so on. The Council, on proposal of the Commission, can step in with monetary measures to nudge the MS involved into compliance. Let the European Anti-Fraud Office (OLAF) and European Public Prosecution Office (EPPO) do their jobs!

Given this variety of mechanisms, the fundamental principles of subsidiarity and proportionality[91] should have discouraged the Commission and the EP to choose to interfere with the nationality of the MS.[92] And if the EU really wishes to maintain or rather introduce the genuine link to a MS as a precondition for Union citizenship, it could sacrifice the holy cow of the immutable connection between the two, by breaking the automatism: if in individual cases the genuine link is absent, Union citizenship will not be entailed by MS citizenship.[93]

This is of course a highly impractical implication; one reason more to abandon the road towards imposing conditions on the nationality codes of the MS, even if this implies the existence of a number of free riders and paying guests tot Union citizenship. And we should not forget about the people with strong connections in the EU: long term residents from third countries. They are denied Union citizenship although they may have much more intense ties and richer attachments with a MS or the Union as a whole, than many formal MS nationals.[94]

To be sure, acquisition of citizenship by investment is not primarily about residence but about mobility. EU MS nationality is coveted for its access to mobility in the first place by individuals holding the nationality of third states that allows them considerably less mobility in the world and other drawbacks. We have to acknowledge the fact that nationalities differ widely in what they are able to promise in terms of rights, both in the municipal environment and internationally, as Kochenov and Kälin have convincingly demonstrated.[95] It is therefore understandable that individuals want to improve their situation by acquiring in one way or the other a richer nationality that allows them to travel around the world. Isn't that a legitimate interest? Marriage, convenient or not, is one of the gateways to the coveted nationality, available for the average person.[96] The same goes for recognition, adoption or legitimation. Purchase is for the happy cleptocracy and that is the exasperating aspect of the phenomenon. Why should privileged people be still more privileged? But this is a moral or political point

[89] Regulation 2020/2092 on a general regime of conditionality for the protection of the Union budget [2020] OJ 2020 L 4331/1.

[90] Case C-156/21 *Hungary v Parliament and Council* ECLI:EU:C:2022:97; Case C-157/21 *Poland v Parliament and Council* ECLI:EU:C:2022:98.

[91] Art 5(3) and Protocol no 2 TEU.

[92] In the same vein Sarmiento and van den Brink in Kochenov and Surak (eds), *Citizenship and Residence Sales.*

[93] Cf the fate of Dante Alighieri: banned from the city of Florence and thus losing his citizenship of Firenze he still remained a citizen of the Roman Empire.

[94] Their 'genuine link' may be compared with those of Nottebohm with Guatemala.

[95] Kochenov and Lindeboom (eds), *Quality of Nationality Index* (Hart 2020).

[96] Jessurun d'Oliveira, 'The Artefact of "Sham Marriages"' (1999) 1 *Yearbook of Private International Law* 49. 'Sham' marriage is an arbitrary frame by a state to avoid effects that are considered unwelcome, be it a nationality, a nobility title, housing, access to the labour or services market or other advantages. According to most private law systems, motives for entering into marriage are irrelevant and not to be scrutinized by the state. The secular state is concerned with form and procedure, not with the substance of marriage.

of view. And their coming out ahead is a sociological fact, whether it concerns air crashes, Titanics, diseases, floodings, earthquakes and other disasters.[97]

Possessing the nationality of a MS gives access to a large bundle of rights and duties in a political community. But it can also be qualified as a commodity most people in the EU have been granted for free, by birth or marriage. They are the free riders. For outsiders costs are involved in terms of integrational efforts and spending money.

Purchase can be discouraged through the implementation, application and monitoring of all the EU instruments that are already abundantly available. There is no need to open the box of Pandora in scrutinising nationality laws on overall bowing to an elusive genuine link principle. This amounts to putting the cat of the genuine link among the pigeons or swaying the ambiguous flag of sincere cooperation. European values and principles as subsidiarity and proportionality and upholding the identity of the MS mark the boundaries of interfering with the nationality laws of the MS. Purchasing citizen status represents moreover a millennium-old European legal practice.

[97] Cf the seminal and inspiring essay by Galanter, 'Why the Haves Come out Ahead' (1974) 9 *Law and Society Review* 95. The *Zhu and Chen* case is a fine example: a wealthy family gets what it wants by hiring expertise: an extra child, a new nationality and a residence right.

19

Investor Citizenship under EU Law
Recent Trends and Constitutional Implications

DANIEL SARMIENTO AND GUILLERMO ÍÑIGUEZ

I. INTRODUCTION

ALTHOUGH INVESTOR CITIZENSHIP schemes are by no means a new phenomenon, they have become increasingly contested under European Union law. This chapter explores recent legislative trends and assesses their constitutional implications from the point of view of Union law. It argues that the Union lacks the competence to regulate Member States' decisions to award citizenship by investment (CBI), and that recent attempts to do so may breach the division of competences at the heart of the EU treaties. In order to do so, it begins by understanding the legal framework on EU citizenship by reference to both the Treaties (Section II) and the case law of the Court of Justice (Section III). This paves the way for a discussion on the legal nature of citizenship by investment (Section IV) and on the recent moves by the EU legislator, which has become increasingly belligerent in its attempts to tackle Member States' CBI schemes (Section V). Section VI builds on the above to ask when – if at all – the Union can legislate in matters of CBI, and what implications this has for the federal allocation of power set out in the Treaties. Section VII discusses a related question regarding the scope of the Court of Justice review over national decisions on the award of nationality. Section VIII concludes.

II. NATIONAL CITIZENSHIP AND EU LAW: WHAT DO THE TREATIES SAY?

In European Union law, the principle of conferral establishes that the Union can only legislate where it is expressly authorised to do so by the EU treaties. Accordingly, 'competences not conferred upon the Union in the Treaties remain with the Member States'.[1]

EU citizenship is governed by Part II of the Treaty on the Function of the European Union (TFEU), which sets out both its content and the process by which it may be acquired. According to the TFEU, the award of nationality is an exclusive competence of the Member States which is not conferred upon the Union. This follows from Article 20(1) TFEU, which holds that '[e]very person holding the nationality of a Member State shall be a citizen of the Union'. This

[1] Art 5(2) TFEU.

provision also specifies that Union citizenship 'shall be additional to and not replace national citizenship', a wording replicated in Article 9 Treaty on the European Union (TEU). That the Member States did not intend to confer upon the Union the competence to govern questions of nationality is further emphasised by Declaration No 2 on nationality of the Member States (Declaration No 2),[2] which was annexed to the Treaty on European Union prior to the latter's ratification. According to this Declaration, which was subsequently reiterated in the 'Edinburgh Decision' of 11 and 12 December 1992,[3] 'the question whether an individual possesses the nationality of a Member State shall be settled *solely* by reference to the national law of the Member State concerned'.[4]

Therefore, although Union citizenship confers autonomous rights upon EU nationals, it cannot be dissociated from national citizenship.[5] Instead, it is the Member States who are the 'gatekeepers' of Union citizenship, with their respective citizenship rules providing the mechanisms by which an individual can acquire the latter.[6] In the words of Advocate General Collins, this

> explicit choice by the Member States not only renders the European Union powerless to create Union citizenship independently from nationality as conferred by the Member States, but also raises a *constitutional barrier* to such a power being implied under Union law.[7]

As the following sections will make clear, this unequivocal division of competences is crucial in the ongoing legal debate concerning the status of investor citizenship under Union law.

III. THE COURT'S CASE LAW

Following the ratification of the Maastricht Treaty, EU citizenship soon made its way to the Court of Justice. In *Grzelczyk*, the Court declared that Union citizenship was 'destined to be *the fundamental status of nationals of the Member States*, enabling those who find themselves in the same situation to enjoy the same treatment in law irrespective of their nationality'.[8] As the number of citizenship-related cases grew, this dictum became central to the analyses advanced by the Court of Justice, which relied on it for two purposes. First, to imbue EU citizenship with meaning, developing the implications of Articles 20 and 21 TFEU in contexts such as the exercise of the free movement provisions,[9] the enjoyment of social assistance[10] or the rights derived by the family members of EU nationals.[11] Second, to grant itself a broader scope to review Member States' nationality-related decisions.

In order to understand the Court's case law and its implications for investor citizenship schemes, it is worth drawing a distinction between three different scenarios in which EU citizenship may clash with a Member State's nationality rules: on the one hand, those involving

[2] TEU – Declaration on nationality of a Member State [1992] OJ C191/98.

[3] Decision of the Heads of State and Government, meeting within the European Council at Edinburgh on 11 and 12 December 1992, concerning certain problems raised by Denmark on the Treaty of European Union [1992] OJ C348/1.

[4] Declaration on nationality of a Member State (emphasis added).

[5] Case C-673/20 *Préfet du Gers* ECLI:EU:C:2022:449, paras 46–48.

[6] As illustrated by Case C-192/99 *Kaur* ECLI:EU:C:2001:106, paras 19–27.

[7] Opinion of AG Collins, Case C-673/20 *EP v Préfet du Gers* ECLI:EU:C:2022:129, para 22 (emphasis added).

[8] Case C-184/99 *Grzelczyk* ECLI:EU:C:2001:458, para 31 (emphasis added).

[9] Case C-413/99 *Baumbast* ECLI:EU:C: 2002:493, paras 82–84.

[10] Case C-456/02 *Trojani* ECLI:EU:C:2004:488, para 31.

[11] Case C-34/09 *Ruiz Zambrano* ECLI:EU:C:2011:124.

the revocation (Section III.A) and the recognition of Member State nationality (Section III.B); on the other, those concerning the acquisition of Member State nationality (Section III.C).

A. Revocation

The bulk of the Court's citizenship case law has centred on situations of revocation: in other words, those in which an individual has had their national citizenship withdrawn and thus faces the prospect of losing their Union citizenship.[12] In such cases, the Court of Justice has adopted a broad, teleological interpretation of the Treaties, granting itself the prerogative to review Member States' decisions in the name of upholding the rights conferred by EU citizenship. This, the Court of Justice has argued, is necessitated by the *consequences* of a Member State's revocation decision. Given that EU citizenship derives from national citizenship, an individual who is deprived of the latter will also lose their status as an EU citizen, and hence the rights derived therefrom.[13] In light of the above, Member States will have to have 'due regard to Union law' when adopting such decisions.[14]

Even in such cases, however, the Court has often shown itself deferential, imposing procedural obligations on Member States. *Rottmann*[15] provides a good example of how this can play out. The applicant was an Austrian national who applied for German nationality. In his application, however, he omitted that he was being investigated for serious fraud in Austria. He obtained a German naturalisation certificate in 1999, which entailed the automatic loss of his Austrian citizenship. Several months later, the German authorities became aware of this investigation and sought to have his award of German nationality withdrawn on the grounds of deception. Dr Rottmann appealed this decision, arguing, among others, that loss of German citizenship when he had already lost his Austrian nationality would render him stateless. The dispute eventually made its way to the Court of Justice, which declared that Germany's decision to revoke the applicant's nationality award was not contrary to Union law 'on condition that the decision to withdraw observes the principle of proportionality'.[16] This proportionality requirement, which has been replicated in subsequent judgments,[17] allows the Court of Justice to strike a balance between upholding the fundamental rights of EU citizens and respecting – rather than second-guessing – Member States' decisions.

B. Recognition

A second scenario which the Court's case law has addressed is that of *recognition* of Member States' decisions to award nationality. In *Micheletti*,[18] the applicant, who held dual Italian and Argentinian citizenship, applied for permanent residence as an EU national to set up a dental practice in Spain. However, the Spanish authorities refused to recognise his Italian nationality,

[12] See, inter alia, Case C-135/08 *Rottmann* ECLI:EU:C:2010:104; Case C-221/17 *Tjebbes* ECLI:EU:C:2019:189; *Préfet du Gers*; Case C-118/20 *JY* ECLI:EU:C:2022:34; Case C-689/21 *Udlændinge- og Integrationsministeriet* ECLI:EU:C:2023:626; Case C-684/22 *Stadt Duisburg* ECLI:EU:C:2024:345.

[13] *Rottmann*, para 42; *Tjebbes*, para 32.

[14] *Stadt Duisburg*, para 36.

[15] *Rottmann*.

[16] ibid, para 59.

[17] Most recently, see: *Udlændinge- og Integrationsministeriet*, para 30; *JY*, para 51; *Stadt Duisburg*, para 36.

[18] Case C-369/90 *Micheletti* ECLI:EU:C:1992:295.

concluding that, given his habitual residence prior to the application, it was his Argentinian nationality that took precedence. The Court deemed this practice incompatible with Union law, holding that Member States could not second-guess each other's decisions to award nationality 'by imposing an additional condition for recognition of that nationality with a view to the exercise of the fundamental freedoms provided for in the Treaty'.[19] In essence, *Micheletti* constitutes a straightforward application of the joint principles of mutual recognition and mutual trust: it is for Member States to decide who their nationals are, and such decisions must be recognised by all other Member States, who must presume that they are made in good faith – and in compliance with Union law – and may not second-guess each other's nationality awards. The Court's ruling stands stark contrast with *Nottebohm*,[20] the famous decision by the International Court of Justice in which Guatemala was allowed to refuse the recognition of Mr Nottebohm's nationality given the latter's absence of a 'genuine link' with Liechtenstein.[21]

Therefore, in situations involving the revocation or recognition of an individual's nationality, Article 20 TFEU allows the Court of Justice to step in, exercising a standard of review which upholds the effective enjoyment of Union citizenship. In the first scenario, this protects EU citizens' enjoyment of their fundamental rights, ensuring that their EU citizenship can only be revoked in certain well-justified cases. In the latter instance, it upholds the principles of mutual recognition and mutual trust, ensuring the smooth operation of the Union's legal order, including its internal market. None of this, however, questions the fundamental premiss set out in the TFEU: namely, that it is ultimately for Member States to decide who enjoys the benefits of their national citizenship, and that under Union law, both the other Member States and the EU itself must recognise such decisions.[22]

C. Acquisition

The third possible scenario where EU citizenship may clash with national competence involves those rules governing the *acquisition* of the nationality of a Member State. In accordance with Article 20 TFEU, where an individual acquires the nationality of a Member State, he or she will also benefit from the rights emanating from Union citizenship, including the enjoyment of the free movement provisions and of the rights enshrined in the CFR. Indeed, it is on this basis that the Commission has tried to bring these situations within the scope of Union law: given that nationals of the Member States automatically become EU citizens and, as such, benefit from the privileges attached thereto, decisions concerning the award of nationality should also fall within the scope of EU law in a manner akin to situations of revocation and of recognition.[23]

Although this scenario has not yet been addressed by the Court of Justice, it is at the heart of the litigation concerning Malta's investor citizenship framework, which is ongoing at the time of writing.[24] In essence, the Commission suggests that, in deciding who becomes a member of their polity, Member States must have due regard to Union law, and in particular to the principle of sincere cooperation set out in Article 4(3) TEU. National frameworks which are contrary to this principle – for example, because they 'commodify' EU citizenship

[19] ibid, para 10.
[20] *Nottebohm* (Liechtenstein v Guatemala) [1955] ICJ Rep 4.
[21] On *Nottebohm*, see Spiro's chapter in this volume.
[22] Opinion of AG Collins, Case C-181/23 *Commission v Malta* ECLI:EU:C:2024:849, paras 47–48 and 57.
[23] See generally Commission Recommendation of 28 March 2022 on immediate steps in the context of the Russian invasion of Ukraine in relation to investor citizenship schemes and investor residence schemes C(2022) 2028 final.
[24] Case C-181/23 *Commission v Malta* OJ C173/27 (pending).

by making it available in exchange for a financial investment, or because they award citizenship to individuals who lack a 'genuine link' with the Member State – ought to be reviewable by the Court of Justice, which could deem them contrary to Union law.[25]

In situations of *acquisition*, Member States may also be required to have due regard to Union law. However, contrary to those situations of revocation and recognition, the scope for the Union to step in will be more limited. As will be discussed below, the EU legislator will be able to legislate on questions of nationality where the Treaties provide an adequate legal basis: for example, where such rules are targeted at preventing a specific risk which falls within the Union's sphere of competence. Likewise, the Court of Justice will be able to review national rules which constitute a significant breach of Union law, including the values set out in Article 2 TEU.[26] Beyond this limited set of circumstances, the competence remains squarely with the Member States, who, in accordance with Articles 9 TEU and 20 TFEU, are tasked with deciding who becomes a member of their polity. To what extent this reasoning can also apply to cases of investor citizenship is at the heart of the recent legislative developments which will be addressed below. However, it has unambiguously been echoed, in this very context, by AG Collins in his Opinion in *Commission v Malta*.[27] According to the Advocate General,

> Because the enjoyment of EU citizenship is entirely dependent upon the existence of Member State nationality, it is settled case-law that *it is for each Member State, acting within its exclusive competence* and having due regard to international law, *to lay down the conditions under which its nationality may be acquired*.[28]

IV. INVESTOR CITIZENSHIP IN THE EUROPEAN UNION

For centuries, states across the world have competed to attract the world's most talented individuals, including leading artists, scientists, athletes and businesspeople.[29] Indeed, the award of citizenship in exchange for an investment is as old as citizenship law itself, dating as far back as the Middle Ages.[30] Since the mid-twentieth century, the rise of globalisation has led to a revival of investor citizenship, with several countries – including some EU Member States – incorporating such programmes into their national legislation in order to attract the world's biggest fortunes. At the same time, concerns about tax evasion and money laundering,[31] and indeed about the very meaning of citizenship in a fast-changing world, have increased their political salience.

In the past decades, three EU Member States – Malta, Cyprus and Bulgaria – established frameworks which enabled the acquisition of citizenship in exchange for an investment.[32]

[25] 'Investor citizenship scheme: Commission refers MALTA to the Court of Justice' (*European Commission*, 29 September 2022) https://ec.europa.eu/commission/presscorner/detail/en/ip_22_5422.

[26] The academic literature has identified numerous examples of national practices which may fall foul of Union law. See eg de Groot, 'Towards a European Nationality Law' (2004) 8 *Electronic Journal of Comparative Law* 1; Kochenov, '*Ius Tractum* of Many Faces: European Citizenship and the Difficult Relationship between Status and Rights' (2009) 15 *CJEL* 169.

[27] Opinion of AG Collins, *Commission v Malta*.

[28] ibid, para 44 (emphasis added).

[29] Džankić, *The Global Market for Investor Citizenship* (Palgrave Macmillan 2019); Shachar, 'Picking Winners' (2011) 120 YLJ 2088; Surak, *The Golden Passport* (Harvard 2023).

[30] Prak, 'Citizenship for Sale in Pre-modern Europe', in Kochenov and Surak (eds), *Citizenship and Residence Sales* (Cambridge University Press 2023).

[31] For a discussion of some of these risks, see the chapters by Surak and by Veraldi and Gstrein in this volume.

[32] European Commission, 'Investor Citizenship and Residence Schemes in the European Union' COM(2019)12 final

Other Member States have engaged in such practices in a more subtle manner, relying on their discretionary naturalisation procedures or on other legal avenues – such as those rewarding 'extraordinary contributions' to the country – to award citizenship in exchange for investments.[33] Yet others award *residence* by investment, which often enables individuals to obtain citizenship without undergoing the ordinary naturalisation procedure required by a country's legislation.[34]

At first, the EU institutions – and more particularly, the Commission – were reluctant to intervene in such matters. In a press conference delivered in November 2013, after being repeatedly pressed by a journalist on Malta's Individual Investor Program (IIP), a Commission spokesperson highlighted it was 'for each Member State to lay down the conditions for the acquisition of its nationality', a 'clear' competence which the Court of Justice had acknowledged and which the Union had to respect.[35]

It was precisely in response to Malta's IIP, however, that the EU institutions became increasingly vocal.[36] In 2014, the European Parliament adopted a resolution 'on EU citizenship for sale'.[37] Although the resolution noted that the award of citizenship was an 'exclusive competence of the Member States',[38] it argued that the 'outright sale of EU citizenship undermines the mutual trust upon which the Union is built' and called for Member States to bring their citizenship schemes 'into line with the EU's values'.[39] In 2019, the Commission published a report which called for Member States to terminate such programmes.[40] Two main arguments were advanced by the Commission. First, that investor citizenship schemes were unlawful under Union law, which requires 'the existence of a genuine link' between the awarding Member State and its citizens. Absent this 'genuine link', Member States would incur a breach of Article 20 TFEU and of the principle of sincere cooperation.[41] Second, that such schemes gave rise to four areas of concern – security risks, money laundering, tax evasion and the circumvention of EU rules – which warranted their scrutiny under Union law.[42] In her first State of the Union address, President von der Leyen tied investor citizenship schemes to the Union's broader rule of law crisis, declaring that, 'Be it about the primacy of European law, the freedom of the press, the independence of the judiciary or the sale of golden passports, European values are not for sale.'[43]

Following Russia's invasion of Ukraine, the Commission stepped up its fight against investor citizenship.[44] On 28 March 2022, it issued a recommendation requesting that Member States shut down their programmes, citing 'concerns regarding security, money laundering,

[33] ibid 2–3.

[34] ibid 6–9.

[35] 'Midday press briefing from 13/11/2013' (*European Commission*, 13 November 2013) https://audiovisual.ec.europa.eu/en/video/I-082638.

[36] 'Joint Press Statement by the European Commission and the Maltese Authorities on Malta's Individual Investor Programme (IIP)' (*European Commission*, 29 January 2014) https://ec.europa.eu/commission/presscorner/detail/en/MEMO_14_70.

[37] European Parliament resolution of 16 January 2014 on EU citizenship for sale (2013/2995(RSP)) [2016] OJ C482/117.

[38] ibid, recital M of the preamble.

[39] ibid, recital G of the preamble and para 13.

[40] European Commission Report COM(2019) 12 final.

[41] ibid 6.

[42] ibid 9–21.

[43] von der Leyen, 'Building the world we want to live in: A Union of vitality in a world of fragility' (State of the Union Address, Brussels, 16 September 2020) ttps://ec.europa.eu/commission/presscorner/detail/ov/SPEECH_20_1655.

[44] See Kochenov and Basheska in this volume.

tax evasion and corruption'.[45] Three weeks earlier, a similar resolution had been adopted by the European Parliament.[46] In subsequent weeks, Cyprus and Bulgaria shut down their programmes, whereas Malta ceased to award citizenship to Russian and Belarusian nationals. In 2023, however, the Commission brought an infringement action against Malta, arguing that its CBI programme breached Article 20 TFEU, read in the light of Article 4(3) TEU, due to the absence of a 'genuine link' requirement in its national legislation.[47] At the time of writing, proceedings are still ongoing before the Court of Justice.[48]

V. RECENT MOVES BY THE EU LEGISLATOR

It is against this backdrop that two recent moves by the EU institutions, highlighting the Union's increasing willingness to curtail Member States' adoption of investor citizenship schemes, must be understood. These developments entrench in EU law the arguments which the Union's institutions have advanced since 2014: namely, that Union law precludes the award of nationality absent a 'genuine link' with the awarding State, and that awarding nationality absent this link constitutes a breach of Articles 20 TFEU and 4(3) TEU.

In May 2024, the Commission announced the extension of the temporary suspension of the visa exemptions for nationals of Vanuatu, arguing that the latter's investor citizenship programme breached the bilateral agreement signed in 2015.[49] The Delegated Regulation implementing this extension replicates the reasoning advanced in the 2022 recommendation, noting that Vanuatu's investor citizenship scheme poses a 'risk to the internal security and public policy of the Member States' and highlighting that it does not contain 'any requirement of effective residence or physical presence in Vanuatu for the applicants'.[50] This argument is advanced one step further in the recently adopted Anti-Money Laundering Regulation (AML Regulation),[51] in which the EU legislator expressly declares that investor citizenship schemes 'must be considered as undermining the fundamental status of Union citizenship and sincere cooperation among Member States'.[52]

However, the reasoning underlying both such schemes is premised upon two questionable assertions. First, that the Treaties can be relied on to restrict Member States' competence to award nationality to its citizens; in other words, that it imposes a *negative* duty on Member States. Second, and building on the above, that Union law imposes a further *positive* duty on Member States: namely, that they award nationality only where there exists a 'genuine link' between the Member State and the individual in question. As this chapter has illustrated,

[45] European Commission, 'Recommendation on immediate steps in the context of the Russian invasion of Ukraine in relation to investor citizenship schemes and investor residence schemes' C (2022)2028 final, recital 1 of the preamble.

[46] European Parliament resolution of with proposals to the Commission on citizenship and residence by investment schemes (2021/2026(INL)) [2022] OJ C347/97.

[47] 'Investor citizenship scheme: Commission refers MALTA to the Court of Justice' (*European Commission*, 29 September 2022) as well as Tratnik and Weingerl in this volume.

[48] On the Commission's action against Malta, see Weiler's contribution in this volume.

[49] On which, see Kochenov and Worster, 'EU's Neocolonialism: Safeguarding the Purity of Ni-Vanuatu Blood through Blackmail' (EU Law Live, 8 March 2022) https://eulawlive.com/op-ed-eus-neocolonialism-safeguarding-the-purity-of-ni-vanuatu-blood-through-blackmailby-dimitry-v-kochenov-william-thomas-worster/.

[50] Commission Delegated Regulation 2024/2059 amending Regulation 2018/1806 of the European Parliament and of the Council as regards the extension of the temporary suspension of the visa exemption for nationals of Vanuatu [2024] OJ L2024/2059, recitals 3 and 7 of the preamble.

[51] Regulation 2024/1624 on the prevention of the use of the financial system for the purposes of money laundering or terrorist financing [2024] OJ L2024/1624.

[52] ibid, recital 21 of the preamble.

absent specific legislation setting out common rules for the acquisition of nationality, the EU treaties are unequivocal in rebutting the first such assertion, and hence in dismissing the latter. Instead, the TFEU makes it clear that EU citizenship follows from national citizenship, and that the question of who is a national of an EU Member State is 'solely' for the latter to decide.[53] Nor does EU law codify the 'genuine link' criterion set out in *Nottebohm*, a decision which has been heavily criticised by the international law community and which does not transplant well to the Union's legal architecture.[54]

These legislative developments therefore raise serious questions about the limits of the EU's competence to shape Member States' nationality rules. In fact, these concerns have been echoed within the Council, both in relation to the Vanuatu scheme and to the AML Regulation. In relation to the former, the Republic of Malta endorsed the Commission's efforts to strengthen Vanuatu's visa scheme but questioned the inclusion of a 'genuine link' requirement, arguing that it lacked a clear definition under EU or international law and pointing towards the sovereignty of the State in questions of citizenship.[55] Similar concerns were raised in relation to the AML Regulation, with Malta criticising the reference to investor citizenship schemes and pointing towards the pending proceedings before the Court of Justice.

VI. WHEN CAN THE UNION LEGISLATE?

Given the growing prevalence of debates concerning investor citizenship, it is worth addressing two related questions of profound constitutional relevance for Union law: first, when, if at all, the EU can enact legislation concerning the award of citizenship by the Member States; second, when the Court of Justice can review such decisions. Both issues will be addressed in turn.

In relation to the first such question, it is suggested that the Union will be competent to legislate on matters pertaining to the award of nationality where such rules are targeted at preventing a specific risk which falls within its sphere of competence: for example, to combat the financing of terrorism,[56] anti-money laundering[57] or tax evasion.[58] The same applies in relation to the Area of Freedom, Security and Justice (AFSJ), where treaty provisions on matters such as asylum, immigration, external border control or the combatting of crime[59] can serve as the legal bases beyond which the Union will not be able to operate.

Beyond the above, the Union could also make use of legislative tools to cover subject matters which are not within its competence, but which contribute to attain the objectives provided in the Treaties. One possible avenue is Article 352 TFEU, which allows the Union to legislate where such action 'should prove necessary, within the framework of the policies defined in the Treaties, to attain one of the objectives set out in the Treaties'.[60] Article 352 TFEU is designed

[53] Declaration on nationality of a Member State [1992] OJ C191/98.

[54] van der Brink, 'Revising Citizenship within the European Union' (2022) 23 *GLJ* 79; Weingerl and Tratnik, 'Relevant Links' in Kochenov and Surak (eds), *Citizenship and Residence Sales*.

[55] On the latter, see Council Decision on the partial suspension of the application of the Agreement between the European Union and the Republic of Vanuatu on the short-stay visa waiver – Statement by Malta 2022/0001(NLE) https://eur-lex.europa.eu/legal-content/EN/TXT/PDF/?uri=CONSIL:ST_6254_2022_ADD_1.

[56] As mandated, inter alia, by Directive 2015/849 on the prevention of the use of the financial system for the purposes of money laundering or terrorist financing [2015] OJ L141/73.

[57] Regulation 2024/1624 [2024] OJ L2024/1624.

[58] Council Directive 2011/16/EU on administrative cooperation in the field of taxation [2011] OJ L64/1.

[59] Art 67(2) and (3) TFEU.

[60] Art 352(1) TFEU.

to safeguard both the horizontal and the vertical allocation of power in the treaties: horizontally, by requiring both the Council and the Parliament to approve any such measure; vertically, by requiring the consent of *all* Member States.[61]

Notwithstanding the above, Article 352 TFEU cannot be used to expand the Union's competences, nor can it entail 'harmonisation of Member States' laws or regulations in cases where the Treaties exclude such harmonisation'.[62] In other words, although it can enhance the tools at the EU's disposal, it cannot be used to overcome the limits set out in Article 20 TFEU. In relation to investor citizenship schemes, it is therefore unlikely that the EU legislator could rely on this provision to regulate a matter – the award of nationality – over which it expressly lacks competence.[63] Nor does Article 114 TFEU, which allows for the harmonisation of national rules which have as their object the establishment and functioning of the internal market, offer a promising avenue. As the Court of Justice has held, legislative acts adopted under Article 114(1) TFEU must 'genuinely' have as their object the advancement of the internal market.[64] Whether EU legislation governing the award of investor citizenship would 'genuinely' serve this purpose is questionable.

This analysis points towards a more nuanced picture than that which the Commission advances in its 2022 recommendation. In matters of investor citizenship, the Union may indeed be able to legislate in specific contexts. It can do so, for example, by taking limited action, in accordance with the competences set out in the treaties, to respond to well-evidenced threats to interests protected by Union law. This, however, is not the same as enacting general legislation on investor citizenship, a matter which falls within the scope of the Member States' competence.

VII. THE ROLE OF THE COURT OF JUSTICE

The above raises a second, related question: when can the Court of Justice review national decisions on the award of nationality? In other words, following the taxonomy set out in Section III, can the Court of Justice ever scrutinise situations of acquisition, rather than of recognition or revocation?

Building on the analysis carried out throughout this chapter, it is suggested that the Court of Justice will be able to scrutinise 'acquisition' situations only where these are in clear breach of specific obligations imposed by Union law. This can encompass the obligations set out above – for example, on tax evasion, terrorist financing, money laundering or the AFSJ. It could also encompass breaches of restrictive measures imposed by the Union under the Common Foreign and Security Policy, as the Commission suggested in its 2022 recommendation.

However, beyond these limited instances, the judicial review of Member States' naturalisation rules could only be undertaken in exceptional circumstances: namely, where the rules in question constituted a *significant* breach of a general principle of Union law or, more broadly, of the values enshrined in Article 2 TEU. This could arise, for example, where a Member State's naturalisation policy entailed a clear breach of the Union's non-discrimination rules – for example, by discriminating in its decisions on the basis of sex, race, or religion. Likewise, it

[61] Sarmiento, 'EU Competence and the Attribution of Nationality in the Member States' (2019) Investment Migration Working Papers IMC-RP 2019/2.

[62] Art 352(3) TFEU.

[63] Sarmiento and van den Brink, 'EU Competence and Investor Migration' in Kochenov and Surak (eds), *Citizenship and Residence Sales*, 202.

[64] Case C-376/98 *Germany v European Parliament and Council* ECLI:EU:C:2000:544, para 84.

could arise where a Member State awarded nationality in clear breach of international law, for example by engaging in mass naturalisation or by unilaterally naturalising a certain section of the population.[65] Absent such significant risks, however, there will be no grounds for the Court of Justice to review Member States' naturalisation frameworks, including those on investor citizenship.

Introducing a criterion of 'significance', thereby limiting the Union's ability to scrutinise Member States' frameworks, would not exclude such matters from the Court's purview, nor would it be unprecedented. Instead, it would be in line with other areas of the Court's case law, such as the review of decisions entailing a high degree of technical discretion[66] or the 'generalised' or 'systemic' deficiencies in the Member States' judiciaries,[67] where it has acknowledged that different policy interests call for a more cautious review. In the context of Member States' naturalisation frameworks, limiting the Court's ability to review Member States' legislation to cases of a sufficient degree of seriousness would protect the division of competences between the Union and its Member States – one which is set out in Articles 2 to 6 TFEU and further developed through Article 20 TFEU and Declaration No. 2 – and hence uphold one of the key tenets of the Union's federal constitution.[68]

VIII. CONCLUSION

In her speech at the 2016 Conservative Party conference, former British prime minister Theresa May famously declared that 'if you believe you're a citizen of the world, you're a citizen of nowhere. You don't understand what the very word "citizenship" means.'[69] May's statement perfectly encapsulates the tension which underlies ongoing debates concerning citizenship laws: one between traditional understandings of citizenship, which perceive it as a sacrosanct bond between a State and an individual, and more contemporary conceptions thereof, which understand that as the world becomes increasingly globalised and complex, so too do individuals' attachments to countries. In the European Union, the rise of investor citizenship has given rise to a particular set of legal difficulties, deriving from the peculiarities of the Union's legal order and from the division of competences between the Union and its Member States.

This chapter has argued that the Treaties, as they stand, confer no competence upon the Union to regulate Member States' award of citizenship by investment. This follows from the principle of conferral, which upholds the federal allocation of power between the Union and its Member States, and from the latter's Declaration attached to the Maastricht Treaty, which makes it clear that the question of who becomes a Member State national is 'solely' for the Member States themselves to decide.[70] The above does not mean that the Union will never be able to have a say in such cases. Where a Member State's naturalisation policies pose a significant threat to the Union's values – for example, by unequivocally breaching international law or by gravely contravening the values set out in Article 2 TEU – the Court of Justice may be

[65] As suggested in Opinion of AG Poiares Maduro, *Rottmann* ECLI:EU:C:2009:588, para 30.

[66] Case C-13/99 *Pfizer* ECLI:EU:T:2002:209, paras 166–69; Case C-343/09 *Afton Chemical* ECLI:EU:C:2010:419, para 28; and C-62/14 *Gauweiler* ECLI:EU:C:2015:400, para 68.

[67] Case C-216/18 PPU *LM* ECLI:EU:C:2018:586, paras 68–73; Case C-562&563/21 PPU *Openbaar Ministerie* ECLI:EU:C:2022:100.

[68] Lenaerts, 'Federalism: Essential Concepts in Evolution' (1997) 21 *Fordham Int'l LJ* 746.

[69] 'Full text: Theresa May's conference speech' (*The Spectator*, 5 October 2016) www.spectator.co.uk/article/full-text-theresa-may-s-conference-speech/.

[70] Opinion of AG Collins, *Commission v Malta*, paras 45–46.

able to declare such policies in breach of Union law. Likewise, the EU legislator may be competent to legislate in specific instances: for example, to ensure that Member States' naturalisation policies comply with the Union's rules on non-discrimination, anti-money laundering, or the combatting of terrorist financing.

In such cases, however, it will have to rely on an adequate Treaty provision. Most likely, this will require the Union legislator to draw on Article 352 TFEU, which, by requiring the unanimous consent of all Member States and of the European Parliament, protects both the Union's federal allocation of competences and the principle of institutional balance. Beyond these scenarios, it remains for Member States to determine who – and in what circumstances – becomes a member of their polity.

20

It's All about Blood, Baby! The EU's Attack against Investment Migration in the Context of EU Law, International Law and the War in Ukraine

DIMITRY V KOCHENOV AND ELENA BASHESKA*

I. INTRODUCTION AND STRUCTURE

As we learn from the actions of the European Commission[1] and the pronouncements of the European Parliament,[2] millionaires can also be a problem for 'Fortress Europe', especially if they 'buy' the sacred privileges of Europeanness instead of winning them in life's 'birthright lottery'[3] or 'earning' them by cultivating 'genuine links' like the many 'others' who are not fortunate enough to qualify for citizenship by blood connections and whom the European Union (EU) is carefully calibrated to keep at bay.[4] Hans Kundnani seems to be correct in putting an emphasis on the nascent supranational ethno-nationalism in

* A longer early draft of this chapter was released as a COMPAS Working Paper No. 161-2022 (University of Oxford) and an IMC Report (Geneva). The chapter draws on Dimitry Kochenov's London School of Economics LEQS Paper No. 164/2020 'Genuine Purity of Blood'. The authors are particularly grateful to Martijn van den Brink for the helpful criticism of the initial draft.

[1] Including, but not limited to the Case C-181/23 *Commission v Malta* OJ C 173/27 pending; European Commission, 'Investor Citizenship and Residence Schemes in the European Union' COM(2019)12 final and the accompanying Commission Staff Working Document SWD(2019)5 final; European Commission, 'Recommendation on immediate steps in the context of the Russian invasion of Ukraine in relation to investor citizenship schemes and investor residence schemes' C (2022)2028 final, para 13; See also von der Leyen, 'Building the world we want to live in' (State of the Union Address, Brussels, 16 September 2020) https://ec.europa.eu/commission/presscorner/detail/ov/SPEECH_20_1655.

[2] European Parliament resolution on a Comprehensive Union Policy on Preventing Money Laundering and Terrorist Financing – The Commission's Action Plan and Other Recent Developments (2020/2686(RSP)) [2020] OJ C371/92; European Parliament resolution with proposals to the Commission on citizenship and residence by investment schemes (2021/2026(INL)) [2022] OJ C347/97.

[3] Shachar, *The Birthright Lottery* (Harvard University Press 2009).

[4] It is worth bearing in mind that the EU is the only advanced constitutional system in the world where third-country nationals are not entitled to benefit from *any* of the core rights offered to citizens, especially including being part of the EU's internal market. EU law is thus the only law in the world elevating nationality discrimination to an absolute degree: without the 'right' nationality, the EU disappears as a territory of rights and as a horizon of opportunities: Ganty and Kochenov, 'EU Lawlessness Law' (2025) 30 *CJEL* 78, 88–97; Kochenov and van den Brink, 'Pretending There Is No Union' in Thym and Zoetewij-Turhan (eds), *Degrees of Free Movement and Citizenship* (Brill-Nijhoff 2015) 66–100. Cf Balibar, *Nous, citoyens d'Europe ?* (La Découverte 2001) 192.

approaching the EU through 'Eurowhiteness'.[5] The Commission places a special emphasis on the 'genuine links' between the citizen and the Member State of naturalisation, which in its opinion are required by EU law and international law. Naturalisations in the absence of such links are pronounced unlawful and problematic in the EU, although the Union has little to say on the matter, as this work will demonstrate. Only one link is apparently absolute and unquestionable in the eyes of the Commission: that of blood, proving Kundnani's analysis correct.

Millions of putative EU citizens are welcome as 'genuine' Europeans with no questions asked and at no objection from the Commission without any connection with the Union besides having had one of their (usually male and often very remote) ancestors owe allegiance to (the predecessors) of one of the EU Member States, while other individuals who obtain citizenship by investment, thus making significant contributions to the Union of the present day are presented as lacking 'genuine links'. In this chapter we demonstrate that this position is far from being rooted in EU or international law and expresses a purely ethno-nationalist and thus truly problematic understanding of EU citizenship, by a deeply politicised European Commission, where the matters of legality are hijacked by nativist ideology, graduating into blood nationalist interest – quite an unexpected twist, given the history of the Union and the values it aspires to uphold and promote.

It is evident that being ardent about the absoluteness of 'native' superiority, besides being legally obscurantist, is also an extremely costly position. While the marketisation of citizenship and residence can bring billions of Euros to the Member States' crisis-stricken budgets,[6] what is most important is that the law, which the Commission ignores, as well as the principles of legality, Rule of Law and non-discrimination, have an important value in the context of the European integration project, far too important to be dismissed for the politicised nationalist reading of EU citizenship, which gives the concept an increasingly ethnocentric and neo-colonialist understanding.[7]

The Commission has been at the forefront of the attempts to shut down one particular way of conferring citizenship among the many available in the absolute absence of a competence to do so.[8] Professor J.H.H. Weiler is absolutely correct in writing in this volume that 'only in the 1984 world of George Orwell does repeating an untruth 50 times transform it into a truth'.[9] The matter of citizenship conferral is at the core of Member State sovereignty, but the powers that be in Brussels decided to depart from the primary law and to test this clear division of competences using investment migration as a starting point. The Commission was not alone, however. A small but opinionated body of moral panic literature has also mushroomed around the issues of whether citizenship – a randomly allocated status of totalitarian domination[10] – should be

[5] Kundnani, *Eurowhiteness* (Hurst 2023). On the problematic ideology of 'integration', see eg Ganty, *L'intégration des citoyens européens et des ressortissants de pays tiers en droit de l'Union européenne* (Bruylant 2021).

[6] On this complex relationship, see, Lindeboom and Meunier, 'Foreign Direct Investment and Investment Migration Programmes in the European Union' in Kochenov and Surak (eds), *Citizenship and Residence Sales* (Cambridge University Press 2023).

[7] Kochenov, 'Citizenship Apartheid', in Kostakopoulou et al (eds), *Elgar Concise Encyclopaedia of Citizenship* (Elgar 2025); Boatcă, 'Unequal Institutions in the Longue-durée' in Kochenov and Surak (eds), *Citizenship and Residence Sales*; Boatcă, *Global Inequalities beyond Occidentalism* (Ashgate 2016). See also the chapters by Ammann and Ganty in this volume.

[8] Sarmiento and van den Brink, 'EU Competence in Investor Migration' in Kochenov and Surak (eds), *Citizenship and Residence Sales*; Weingerl and Tratnik, 'Relevant Links' in Kochenov and Surak (eds), *Citizenship and Residence Sales*; Jessurun d'Oliveira, 'Union Citizenship and Beyond' in Cambien et al (eds), *European Citizenship under Stress* (Brill-Nijhoff 2020); see also the contributions by Weiler, Sarmiento and Íñiguez and by Jessurun d'Oliveira in this volume.

[9] Weiler in this volume, 400.

[10] Kochenov, *Citizenship* (MIT Press 2019) 1–37.

'for sale'.[11] Naturalisation through investment has even been compared to the 'passport trade',[12] a trade which does not exist, strictly speaking, outside of the clandestine Pacific passport markets[13] and other criminal circles which provide counterfeited official documents.[14] Be that as it may, the European Commission has been at the forefront of branding one particular route to naturalisation as immoral, if not illegal, alongside handful of scholars and politicians, demonstrating what Carl Baudenbacher characterised as '*fragwürdige Aktionismus*'.[15]

In what follows we briefly introduce the complexity of the EU's citizenship and naturalisation landscape, which will enable the Commission's emerging use of a dubious 'genuine links' approach to EU citizenship to be properly contextualised as a flawed ideal in breach of EU law (Section II). We also touch on the actions of the European Parliament (EP), though the latter is of lesser importance as this parliament cannot propose legislation[16] and its resolutions have no binding value on the Member States.[17] In any event, what the EP does on this issue fits entirely within the legally obscurantist propaganda frame that the Commission also adheres to, with the only difference being that the EP is a political institution the members of which (MEPs) could legitimately be expected to seek political gains no matter what the law says. The Commission cannot avail itself of this excuse, and with its role of the 'guardian of the Treaties' – however faulty, as of late[18] – is tasked with upholding the law and providing a reality check when drafting legislative proposals and initiating court cases. Such a reality check in the matters of investment migration is entirely missing from the Commission's political activities, as we will show.[19] Yet, it would be particularly necessary, given the applicable principles and the division of competences in this field as Sarmiento and van den Brink also demonstrate[20] (Section III). Instead, the Commission decided to launch a case against Malta from which it can hardly emerge as a winner in a Court judgment on the merits. Going into further detail, we unpack the false legal claims at the core of the Commission's propaganda, now providing the backbone of its case against Malta in front of the Court of Justice, one by one. By pretending not to know the law and misunderstand the core principles that the EU is built upon (presuming it did not get outright flawed legal advice all along, which would be unlikely),[21] what is at hand is a straightforward and alarmingly large-scale abuse of power by the Commission. As such, this could be yet another facet of a much larger phenomenon, which Sarah Ganty with one of the authors of this chapter branded 'EU lawlessness law',[22] when the institutions attempt to invoke EU law – real and imaginary – in such a way that any rule of law becomes unthinkable,

[11] Shachar, 'Dangerous Liaisons' in Bauböck (ed), *Debating Transformations of National Citizenship* (Springer 2018) 7; Tanasoca, 'Citizenship for Sale' (2016) 57 *EJS* 169. Also Džankić's writings on this matter.

[12] Eg Kochenov, '"Passport Trade"' (VerfBlog, 8 June 2020) https://verfassungsblog.de/passport-trade-a-vicious-cycle-of-nonsense-in-the-netherlands/.

[13] Van Fossen, 'Citizenship for Sale' (2007) 45 *Commonwealth & Comparative Politics* 138.

[14] Gotev, 'Thousands obtained EU citizenship for €5000 in Bulgarian scam' (*Euractiv*, 30 October 2018) www.euractiv.com/section/justice-home-affairs/news/thousands-obtained-eu-citizenship-for-e5000-in-bulgarian-scam/.

[15] Baudenbacher, 'Goldene Pässe' (*NZZ*, 4 December 2020) 19.

[16] Arts 289 and 294 TFEU.

[17] The binding legal instruments of the EU are enumerated and defined in Art 288 TFEU: Regulations, Directives and Decisions. Recommendations and opinions, as well as Resolutions, Declarations and Action programmes are non-binding legal instruments which are also enumerated in Art 288 TFEU.

[18] Scheppele, 'EU Treaties without a Guardian' (2023) 29 *CJEL* 93 (and the literature cited therein); Grześkowiak, 'The "Guardian of the Treaties" Is No More?' (2023) 42 *Refugee Servey Quarterly* 81; Kelemen and Pavone, 'Where Have all the Guardians Gone?' (2023) 75 *World Politics* 779.

[19] See also the divertissement by Shah Guido in this volume.

[20] Sarmiento and van den Brink, 'EU Competence and Investor Migration'.

[21] Flawed legal advice hypothesis also contradicts the insider fable offered by Shah Guido in this volume.

[22] Ganty and Kochenov, 'EU Lawlessness Law'.

as the 'law' as deployed facilitates direct undoing of the most crucial EU and national legal principles and values. To back the abuse of power claim we focus on the core elements of the Commission's narrative regarding investment migration in recent years, dealing specifically with:

- the myth of citizenship by investment (CBI) naturalisations as an example of 'less stringent conditions';
- the lack of EU legislative competence;
- the lack of international law rules to back the Commission's position;
- Commission's reliance on obsolete precedent in breach of EU law;
- practising discrimination on the basis of nationality, ethnicity and the mode of citizenship acquisition;
- residence by investment (RBI) and the critique of minimum presence requirements;
- humiliating and discriminatory rhetoric targeting investment migrants; and
- misrepresentation of the principle of sincere cooperation in EU law.

In full agreement with J.H.H. Weiler we demonstrate that what we are witnessing is a concerted large-scale political campaign by the Commission aiming to mislead the public and befog EU citizenship law.[23] This campaign includes abundant references to the 'law', which are, however, either irrelevant or gravely misrepresented. The European Commission is abusing its authority by waging an attack on a handful of core principles of EU law from non-discrimination to conferral in order to reimagine EU citizenship as a legal status based on 'genuine links' in direct conflict with the key case law of the Court of Justice and the Treaties. Worse still, the most unquestionable links in the eyes of the Commission appear to be those of blood – a somewhat old-fashioned ideology that the Union in Europe was officially created to supersede,[24] rather than boost and glorify (Section IV).

The question 'in the name of what?' arises. We take issue with the abusive use of investment migration as a pretext for the Commission to start forging a new ethno-nationalist understanding of EU citizenship, not rooted in the Treaties and directly contradicting the case law of the Court of Justice of the European Union (CJEU), while at the same time, enlarging the powers of the European Commission to a great degree. Such 'genuine links' EU citizenship risks turning the Union into a platform for repeating nineteenth century-style nationalisms, a U-turn away from a vehicle for establishing an area of freedom, security and justice irrespective of nationality, which the Treaties actually demand.[25] At issue essentially is the core of state sovereignty coupled with the core rationale underpinning the EU as an anti-nationalist liberal project.[26] the Commission aims to deprive the Maltese of the legal tools to determine who is Maltese, and the French of the legal tools to determine who is French. Quite astonishingly, it does not stop here, extending the supranational blood-nationalist tropes also to some former colonies, like Vanuatu.[27] Such moves are in clear contradiction to the EU law in force.

[23] See Weiler in this volume.

[24] For a more complex and nuanced story see Eklund, 'Peoples, Inhabitants and Workers' (2023) 34 *EJIL* 831.

[25] Art 67 TFEU; see eg Acosta Arcarazo and Murphy (eds), *EU Security and Justice Law* (Hart 2014); Walker, *Europe's Area of Freedom, Security, and Justice* (Oxford University Press 2004); Lindahl (ed), *A Right to Inclusion and Exclusion?* (Hart 2009); de Capitani, 'Progress and Failure in the Area of Freedom, Security and Justice' in Bignami (ed), *EU Law in Populist Times* (Cambridge University Press 2020) 375–411.

[26] Cf Wilkinson, *Authoritarian Liberalism and the Transformation of Modern Europe* (Oxford University Press 2021).

[27] Kochenov and Worster, 'EU's Neo-Colonialism' (EU Law Live, March 8, 2022).

II. THE 'GUARDIAN OF THE TREATIES' GONE ASTRAY: BLOOD SUPERIORITY AS AN UNLAWFUL POLITICAL PRIORITY

What is 'citizenship?', or a 'normal' way to acquire it? This is always an interesting question, which is very political, usually turning on the issue of who gets to decide. The absolute majority of citizens are created by *ius sanguinis*: they are the sons and daughters of citizens (de facto this is the case even in all the polities, where *ius soli* is the key vehicle, officially, of the status's distribution). In other words, citizenship is neo-feudal: blood, here, is key.[28] When 'blood' is there, nothing else usually matters: residence, place of birth, income; these factors, although sometimes relevant in truly exceptional circumstances, are of no relevance for citizenship acquisition at birth.[29] The absolute majority of the world population acquired citizenship at birth in this way, without having any say in or enjoying any chance of expressing any preference about it, which is why citizenship is in essence a totalitarian concept.[30] The totality of our rights depends on the status of citizenship we hold, and since these statuses of totalitarian blood distribution of privilege are deeply unequal,[31] the nature of citizenship as one of the core instruments of global inequality is deeply consequential, splitting the population of the world into the global aristocracy – the super-citizens of Western democracies – and the majority of the passport-poor, who are the victims of citizenship.[32] The blood paradigm is only broken by naturalisations, which amount to fewer than 2 per cent of citizenship acquisitions around the world.[33]

The requirements to be satisfied in this latter category vary greatly and are not at all limited to holding a legal residence in a particular state for a certain amount of years[34] coupled with passing 'culture' and language tests:[35] a story, which is often presented in the literature as the dominant mode of citizenship acquisition after birth. While some countries offer CBI to individuals through specially designed naturalisation procedures, others allow for discretionary naturalisation on the grounds of 'special achievements' (or similar notions) – often explicitly including the economic achievements of applicants – enshrined in national legislation. The difference between the specially designed programmes and discretionary naturalisation on the grounds of 'special achievements' is formal rather than substantial – the former are specifically designed to attract foreign investors, set clear criteria for applicants and are marketed by service providers (agents), while the latter is not necessarily exclusively intended for investors, is less transparent in terms of qualification criteria and is not marketed by nor does it involve agents (at least not yet).

[28] Most ironically, some critics, like Tanasoca, take an openly pro-feudal stance, denying the presumption of equal human worth and the principle of dignity, and arguing for the moral superiority of an aristocracy over the 'common' people: Tanasoca, 'Citizenship for Sale'. For a criticism: Roy, 'The "Streetlight Effect" in Commentary on Citizenship by Investment' in Kochenov and Surak (eds), *Citizenship and Residence Sales*. cf Carens, *The Ethics of Immigration* (Oxford University Press 2013); Carens, 'Aliens and Citizens' (1987) 49 *Review of Politics* 251.

[29] One of such circumstances would be the intergenerational transfer of citizenship to children through birth outside of state territory by the parents themselves born outside of the territory of the state of their citizenship.

[30] Kochenov, *Citizenship*.

[31] cf Kochenov and Lindeboom, 'Empirical Assessment of the Quality of Nationalities' (2017) 4 *EJLG* 314; Kochenov and Lindeboom (eds), *Quality of Nationality Index* (Hart 2020).

[32] Kochenov, 'The Victims of Citizenship' in Kochenov and Surak (eds), *Citizenship and Residence Sales*.

[33] cf Kochenov, *Citizenship*.

[34] On the far-reaching differences between holding legal residence, which is usually required for naturalizations and physical presence in the jurisdiction, see the chapter by Kochenov and van den Brink in this volume.

[35] cf eg Ganty, *L'intégration des citoyens européens et des ressortissants de pays tiers en droit de l'Union européenne*, Favell, 'Integration' (2019) 7 *Comp. Migr. Stud.*; Kochenov, '*Mevrouw de Jong gaat eten*' (2011) EUI Working Papers RSCAS 2011/06.

Kin groups are another example of the acquisition of citizenship with no residence in the country of naturalisation: more than a million Italians, more than a million Hungarians and hundreds of thousands of Greeks, Irishmen, Romanians and Bulgarians have been created this way in recent decades. The end result is always the same – the acquisition of citizenship by the qualifying candidate, usually with no residence, language or any other requirements.

EU Member States recognise hundreds of ways of conferring citizenship on foreigners and the requirements always vary depending on the class of persons who wishes to naturalise as well as the jurisdiction in question:[36] a granddaughter of an Italian lady from Argentina only needs her grandparents' birth certificates; a person with Greater-Hungary ancestry needs to demonstrate a minimal knowledge of Hungarian; and someone with a remote Greek family member will have to demonstrate that the relationship is via the male line, as women could not make Greeks, until quite recently. Everywhere in Europe, immigration is also an option: should you be willing to live in Slovakia for several years, you will get a chance to naturalise. Less than 500 people per year were willing to go through this over the last ten years as per Eurostat. If your direct ancestor left the territory of contemporary Slovakia forever after 1918, however, you will get your citizenship just like this, no questions asked.[37] Getting the right spouse can count too: just get together with a Dutch or a French person and the time of living together anywhere in the world, rather than the time spent in the Netherlands or France, will count for naturalisation.

These are the most common ways to naturalise, and the immigration route is not necessarily the main one. Indeed, countries such as Hungary naturalise more individuals (over one tenth of the population) through distant ancestral connections to the territory of a Hungary that does not exist any more, swiftly and without any residence requirements, than they do people through 'immigration' channels, that is, those who have moved to the country and resided there for several years.[38] It goes without saying that anyone who is a citizen can decide if they should relocate to Hungary, stay in native Ukraine or Serbia or, indeed, relocate to any Member State of the EU or Norway, Iceland and Switzerland with their new EU passport: this is what citizenship is about.[39] Residence is a right, not an obligation.[40]

The empirical diversity of the predominant naturalisation modes – whether spousal, ancestral, emigrational or other – raises questions concerning the ideological stakes which underlie the presumption which the European Commission entertains, that the immigrant-to-citizen path is the baseline against which all other forms of naturalisation should be compared. Is boasting the right ancestral pedigree or tracing family origins to a particular area on the map – as opposed to money – a more just way of distributing the most important rights?[41] The focus of any naturalisation discussion turns thus, precisely, on this dilemma and the moral panic it provokes: if EU citizenship is sacred and rooted in the native possession of pure 'Eurowhiteness' blood providing a 'genuine link' to Europe, how come someone can 'buy' it, thus foregoing the

[36] Please consult the EUDO database of the European University Institute in Florence, which provides a reliable snapshot of the numerous ways available to acquire EU citizenship.

[37] 'Slovak Citizenship by Descent' (Consulate General of the Slovak Republic in Sydney) https://mzv.sk/en/web/gksydney-en/slovak-citizenship-by-descent.

[38] Kovács and Nagy, 'In the Hands of a Populist Authoritarian' in Stoyanova and Smet (eds), *Migrants' Rights, Populism and Legal Resilience in Europe* (Cambridge University Press 2021).

[39] Kochenov, 'Interlegality – Citizenship – Intercitizenship', in Klabbers and Palombella (eds), *The Challenge of Interlegality* (Cambridge University Press 2019) 133.

[40] The chapter by Kochenov and van den Brink in this volume.

[41] The two obviously overlap, so the question is necessarily tongue-in-cheek: if an investment visa is annulled, a Russian billionaire may be able to visit London again visa-free on an Israeli or on a Portuguese passport, acquired via an established Sephardic connection – only 'blood' and no money involved: Lesperance, 'Even for The Super-Rich, Citizenship by Descent Is Extremely Useful: Lessons from Abramovich' (IMI, 5 January 2022); Jessurun d'Oliveira, 'Iberian Nationality Legislation and Sephardic Jews' (2015) 11 *EUConst* 13.

necessary humiliation of 'ordinary' naturalisation? The deeply questionable, racist core of this starting point is evident and connects the issue of citizenship conferral to the broader story of the function that citizenship plays in the contemporary world of passport apartheid.[42] Consequently, those who regard citizenship (just like nationalism and blood privilege) as 'just' should think twice.

Indeed, pronouncements about the 'immorality' of citizenship 'sales' do not constitute the only available approach to understanding the issue of investment migration, as the overwhelming popularity of investment migration among the EU Member States testifies. Acquiring residence and/or citizenship in exchange for investment or donation is a historically mainstream practice[43] conducted entirely through the law and in full compliance with it.[44] So although currently, there is but one active formal CBI programme in the EU – in Malta[45] – as of 2022, 23 EU Member States allowed discretionary naturalisation for 'special achievements'.[46] Furthermore, as of 2022 19 EU Member States offered permanent residence statuses for investment, which are often convertible into the citizenships of those Member States.[47] In short, investment migration is legally practised by the absolute majority of the EU's Member States in one form or another.

The presence of investment migration programmes in Europe in general, and in EU Member States in particular, has naturally triggered the interest of EU policymakers. Indeed, EU citizenship and the rights conferred by it are at the heart of what the EU is about. The freedom of movement of people, enjoyed by virtue of EU law, means in practice that the citizens of any EU Member State can settle in EEA[48] or EU Member States and Switzerland, as well as their home country.[49] Non-discrimination on the basis of nationality, which is the core pillar of EU law, assists in the practical use of this right: to make specific Member State nationality matter in any context where EU law applies, is in all likelihood a violation of EU law.[50] Thus a Maltese citizen who obtained his citizenship by investment, just like an Argentinian who has never been to Italy and does not care about that country but found an Italian ancestor and acquired Italian citizenship as a result, can freely relocate to Spain and enjoy most rights that domestic citizens do, including the right to remain, establish or work there. Treating this Maltese and this Italian

[42] See for a more detailed analysis, Kochenov, 'The Victims of Citizenship'; Kochenov, 'Ending the Passport Apartheid' (2020) 18 *I-CON* 1525; Kochenov, 'Citizenship Apartheid'.

[43] Prak, 'Citizenship for Sale in Premodern Europe' in Kochenov and Surak (eds), *Citizenship and Residence Sales*; Prak, *Citizens without Nations* (Cambridge University Press 2018); Jessurun d'Oliveira in this volume.

[44] Weingerl and Tratnik, 'Relevant Links'.

[45] Cyprus repealed its CIP on 1 November 2020, ie after the European Commission initiated an infringement procedure against the country (alongside with Malta), and also after numerous procedural violations and abuses by officials were exposed by an Al Jazeera investigation as well as pointed out by scholars: 'The Cyprus Papers Undercover' (*Al Jazeera*, 12 October 2020) www.youtube.com/watch?v=Oj18cya_gvw; Cyprus stopped processing applications on 15 October 2021, Kudryashova, 'The "Sale" of Conditional Citizenship' in Cambien et al (eds), *European Citizenship under Stress* (Brill-Nijhoff 2020) 413–40. Other formal citizenship programmes around the world, specifically designed to attract foreign investors, are offered by: Antigua and Barbuda, Cambodia, Dominica, Grenada, Jordan, St Kitts and Nevis, St Lucia, Turkey and Vanuatu. For a global analysis, see, especially, Surak, *The Golden Passport* (Harvard University Press, 2023). See also Surak, 'Investment Migration' in Kochenov and Surak (eds), *Citizenship and Residence Sales*.

[46] These include Austria, Belgium, Bulgaria, Croatia, Cyprus, the Czech Republic, Estonia, France, Germany, Greece, Hungary, Ireland, Italy, Latvia, Lithuania, Luxemburg, Malta, the Netherlands, Portugal, Romania, Slovakia, Slovenia and Sweden. See EUI Globalcit database – information under 'Mode A24, Special Achievements' (GLOBALCIT) https://globalcit.eu/modes-acquisition-citizenship/.

[47] These include Bulgaria, Croatia, Cyprus, the Czech Republic, Estonia, France, Greece, Ireland, Italy, Latvia, Lithuania, Luxembourg, Malta, the Netherlands, Poland, Portugal, Romania, Slovakia and Spain.

[48] Liechtenstein remains a notable exception.

[49] For detailed information on the free movement of all nationalities see Kochenov and Lindeboom (eds), *Quality of Nationality Index*.

[50] Davies, *Nationality Discrimination in the European Internal Market* (Kluwer 2013).

in Spain as a 'foreigner' in any key respect pertaining to EU citizenship-based rights is absolutely illegal, as it would result in nationality discrimination: specific Member State nationality is thus made irrelevant by the successful operation of EU law.[51]

This is precisely why the EU could have a legitimate interest in following developments related to the acquisition and loss of citizenship in EU Member States and beyond: it already has an overwhelming albeit informal impact in the field of the acquisition and loss of citizenship at the national level.[52] The core focus of any supranational intervention has traditionally been the usability of supranational rights: preventing the Member States from obstructing the freedom of movement of EU citizens between the Member States of the Union, as well as protecting such citizens from discrimination on the basis of the possession of their particular Member State nationality, whatever form such discrimination could take. Indeed, the Court of Justice has made it abundantly clear, in the case concerning our Argentinian, that Member States of residence are not entitled to question lawfully acquired citizenship of the EU.[53]

The EU's task has never been the preservation and protection of the Member State-level nationalism. Rather, it consists in making sure that EU citizens can use their rights in the entire territory of the Union no matter what the local government in the Member State of their residence might think about the 'genuineness' of their connection with any other state, be it by thickness of blood, eventful family life, or thickness of wallet. Once EU law is the starting point of analysis, the whole problem of 'genuine links' essentially does not exist: the EU is designed to give the nationals of EU Member States, who are thereby EU citizens, tangible rights across the Union and 'genuine links' is *not* among the applicable criteria to make rights effective: there is no such citizenship requirement in either primary or secondary law, let alone the case law of the Court of Justice. This set up could be presented as problematic from the nationalist standpoint:[54] why is it a clear violation of EU law to make a Romanian learn Estonian, which she might never need upon moving to that country, while a Moldovan who is awaiting the arrival of her blood-based Romanian document[55] can be pushed to learn precisely the language she might never need and take countless tests, if not be subjected to constant harassment and discrimination prevalent in Estonia vis-à-vis non-EU nationals?[56] Obligatory tests of this kind emerge as even more arbitrary and counterproductive in this particular setting,[57] obviously hurting nationalist sentiments of those who wish to send a second-rateness signal to all the foreigners and minorities. It is thus an instance of the EU's main constitutional tactic at play, identified by Gareth Davies as 'humiliation of the state'.[58] Freeing EU citizens from absurd nationalist red-tape is one of EU's main successes, creating a class of particularly free individuals.[59]

[51] Kochenov and Lindeboom, 'Pluralism Through its Denial' in Davies and Avbelj (eds), *Research Handbook on Legal Pluralism and EU Law* (Elgar 2018) 179.

[52] For a detailed overview, see Kochenov, 'Rounding up the Circle' (2010) EUI Working Paper RSCAS 2010/23.

[53] Case C-369/90 *Micheletti* ECLI:EU:C:1992:295.

[54] Kochenov, 'EU Citizenship: Some Systemic Constitutional Implications' in Cambien et al (eds), *European Citizenship under Stress* (Brill-Nijhoff 2020) 11.

[55] Cf Iordachi, 'Country Report: Romania' (2013) EUDO Citizenship Observatory Country Report RSCAS/EUDO-CIT-CR 2013/19.

[56] Kochenov et al, 'Do Professional Linguistic Requirements Discriminate?' (2013) 10 *EYMI* 137.

[57] Schinkel, 'Against "Immigrant Integration"' (2018) 6(30) *CMS* 1; Schinkel, 'The Imagination of "Society" in Measurements of Immigrant Integration' (2013) 36 *Ethn. Racial Stud.* 1142; Favell, 'Integration'; Ganty, *L'intégration des citoyens européens et des ressortissants de pays tiers en droit de l'Union européenne*.

[58] Davies, 'The Humiliation of the State as a Constitutional Tactic' in Amtenbrink and van den Berg (eds), *The Constitutional Integrity of the European Union* (TMC Asser 2010) 147.

[59] Davies, 'How Citizenship Divides' (2019) 4 *European Papers* 675; Davies, 'Dialogues – How Citizenship Divides' (2020) 5 *European Papers* 283.

The very logic of the EU's operation as a supranational organisation tasked with the creation of an internal market between the participating states leads to the contrary result to that promoted by the Commission: the practical application of the principle of non-discrimination leads to a situation where naturalisation in the new Member State of residence is not necessary for EU citizens, since they should not be discriminated against there in any case. Worse still: any case of naturalisation of an EU citizen in a new Member State of residence could be presented as a failure of the Union to deliver on its promise in Article 18 TFEU to make the possession of a particular Union nationality legally irrelevant. Put differently: if EU law functions successfully and non-discrimination is secured, there should be no talk whatsoever of any link between an EU citizen and their Member State of nationality beyond the purely legal attachment that the nationality of the Member State itself secures. This is the principle which enables the whole fabric of EU free movement of persons law to persist. To think otherwise would render the free movement of persons impossible in practice and would turn non-discrimination on the grounds of nationality into an empty promise: the exact opposite of what can be observed in practice.

It is crucially important to realise that EU-level rights are not an exception – it is not that a Maltese 'might' work in Germany. EU-level rights are the rule: from the perspective of EU law it is precisely the act of leaving a Member State of nationality forever – whether visited or not matters little – which is the most significant right of EU citizenship, accompanied by a strict protection against nationality discrimination in the whole territory of the internal market. It is impossible to present the central EU law right in the Treaties since the first years of integration as the discovery of something new: the fact that EU citizens have an EU law-given freedom of movement does not per se create the competence to regulate national citizenship. In fact, in full agreement with Hans Ulrich Jessurun d'Oliveira's analysis[60] we can only state that Member State competence on the matter of granting citizenship reigns supreme unless they start deploying nationalist ideologies of citizenship to humiliate Europeans and deprive them of rights related to EU citizenship status, which are provided by EU law. To repeat – and as Martijn van den Brink has also convincingly argued – EU law cannot be deployed to enforce any 'genuine link' requirements without defeating the purpose of EU citizenship.[61] That purpose is to protect EU citizens exercising free movement rights from dangerous nationalisms – not to recreate dangerous blood nationalisms at the EU level. This background overview of the core meaning of EU citizenship and free movement law in the context of the practical operation of the Member States' nationalities and naturalisation requirements is crucial for the assessment of the Commission's actions, as it ignores the core premises and principles of the legal order it was conceived to defend, turning its back on the rules it is there to uphold.

III. THE COMMISSION AND THE EUROPEAN PARLIAMENT'S PROPAGANDA CAMPAIGN

The European Commission and the European Parliament made a number of wild moves in the area of investment migration. The assault on non-discrimination, EU citizenship and the internal market by the two institutions has intensified, in particular, with the start of the war in Ukraine.[62] Institutions have not wasted time or opportunities, using the crisis to again

[60] Jessurun d'Oliveira, 'Union Citizenship and Beyond', 28–43. See also Jessurun d'Oliveira's chapter in this volume.

[61] van den Brink, 'Revising Citizenship within the European Union (2022) 23 *GLJ* 79.

[62] The war was largely used in the EU as a justification for playing down the enforcement of the Rule of Law: Bárd and Kochenov, 'War as a Pretext to Wave the Rule of Law Goodbye?' (2022) 27 *ELJ* 39. At the same time, a number of moves against the key principles of EU law were made by the Commission in the field of citizenship and naturalisation,

tackle investment migration, and to call for security measures against Russians and Belarusians including the withdrawal of citizenship and residency permits: a frontal call to break the law, which none of the Member States, quite expectedly, followed.[63]

A. Investment Migration in the Light of the War in Ukraine

In its 1 March 2022 Resolution on 'Russian aggression against Ukraine', the European Parliament

> [called] on the Member States and allied countries with residence by investment schemes to review all beneficiaries of such residence status and to revoke those attributed to Russian high-net-worth individuals and their families, in particular those linked to sanctioned individuals and companies.[64]

About a week later, it adopted a Report 'with proposals to the European Commission' on investment migration programmes in which it called for the complete phasing out of such programmes across the Member States and for strict regulation of RBI programmes.[65]

The European Commission equally regarded the start of the war as a pretext to voice its opinion on investment migration, calling for immediate termination of existing CBI programmes and stricter checks of RBI in its Recommendation dedicated to Russian and Belarusian citizens who naturalised or obtained their residence through investment.[66] Furthermore, the European Commission called on the Member States to assess and revoke citizenships or resident permits that they had granted to Russian or Belarusian nationals and their family members based on investor programmes if it is determined that they are or were to become subject to the EU restrictive measures or that they supported the war in Ukraine or other 'related activities of the Russian government or Łukašenka regime breaching international law',[67] thereby adding someone's personal opinions about international law to the list of factors to be taken into account when the status of citizenship or a residence permit is to be withdrawn: a novelty in global law. In both cases, the Member States concerned should take into account the principles of proportionality and the protection of fundamental rights.[68]

Strikingly, the Commission did not make the same recommendation about Russians and Belarusians who obtained or were in a process of acquiring their EU citizenship for 'special achievements', often in an almost identical, yet less transparent way, than their compatriots who 'bought' it. Kin-citizenship in the EU for Russian and Belarusian nationals was not even mentioned. Yet, the Commission has been unable to explain why someone whose

as we will see, under the same justification. The European Commission Recommendation C (2022)2028 final on EU Investment Migration Programmes calling for the annulment of thousands of naturalizations of Russian and Belarusian citizens in the EU, which is both arbitrary and discriminatory as well as lacking a proper legal basis, is a good illustration of this hateful policy. Nationality discrimination also emerged as the main approach to sanctions: cf Kochenov, 'Sanctions for Abramovich, but Schröder Goes Scot-Free' (VerfBlog, 11 March 2022) https://verfassungsblog.de/sanctions-for-abramovich-but-schroder-goes-scot-free/.

[63] Problems arose in a different, yet interconnected domain: several Eastern and Central European States started using the possession of Russian citizenship as a pretext to disqualify people from the right to claim asylum or apply for a visa – all in direct violation of EU law. cf Ganty et al, 'Unlawful Nationality-Based Bans from the Schengen Zone' (2023) 48 *YJIL Online* 1.

[64] European Parliament resolution on the Russian aggression against Ukraine (2022/2564(RSP)) [2022] IO C125/2, para 23.

[65] European Parliament Resolution 2021/2026(INL), paras 21–25.

[66] European Commission Recommendation C (2022)2028 final, para 15.

[67] ibid.

[68] ibid, paras 13 and 15.

great-grandfather was born on what used to be post-First World War Romanian settlement territory or, rather pre-First World War Hungarian territory, is a lesser security threat and is less prone in engaging in money-laundering than someone who bought that privilege. Fetishisation of the nativist understanding of citizenship as a blood connection to the nation, which is not rooted in EU law or international law, significantly undermines the Commission's whole crusade against investment migration.

Furthermore, the fact that other EU Member States do not have formal investment migration programmes does not change the reality that citizenship by investment and numerous other ways to acquire citizenship without any 'thick' connection to a particular Member State – which EU law does not require, as we have seen, but which the Commission purports to expect in its attacks against rich Europeans – is or has been practised by other Member States than Malta. Yet, the Commission has only focused on new or future citizens coming from particular countries and acquiring their EU citizenship through a particular mode of naturalisation – choosing a slippery ground as an institution tasked to uphold EU law, an important part of which is rooted in the protection against discrimination.

Moreover, the Commission did not limit itself to recommending withdrawal or non-issuance of residence permits or citizenships to the sanctioned nationals of Russia and Belarus and their family members but went further to request that Member States also apply restrictions to citizenship and residence through investment programmes to *non-sanctioned* Russians or Belarusians. This recommendation comes in the middle of a war which has generated a mass-scale outflow from Russia of business people and other professionals opposed to the Putin's regime and its actions.[69] It applies guilt by association to the nationals of two particular countries both of which are not known to be democratic states and thus do not depend on the support of the population in their government actions, including the decisions to go to war.[70] The European Commission justified this move with 'the difficulty to conduct the appropriate security checks and due diligence in these particular circumstances and in view of the gravity of the situation'.[71] And again, the Commission did not express similar concerns about Russians and Belarusians who are acquiring their EU residence permits on the basis of other grounds than investment migration programmes, nor did it mention the risk of granting EU residence permits to other nationalities. This seriously calls into question the genuineness of the Commission's reasons underpinning the call for the suspension of investment migration programmes in general and RBI in particular.

Indeed, the Commission's Recommendation, as recognised by the European Commission itself,

> is only one element of the Commission's policy to take determined action on both citizenship and residence investor schemes. It should therefore be seen in the context of this larger effort and is without prejudice to ongoing and future initiatives of the Commission in this respect.[72]

In other words, the war in Ukraine has been used by the European Commission to fight its own war against investment migration – a phenomenon, which benefited Russian and

[69] According to data from Russia's Federal Security Service (FSS), more than 8.3 million Russians have left the country in the first half of 2022, which is an increase of around 1.5 million people compared to the first half of 2021. For more details, see the FSS official records on departures of Russian citizens www.fedstat.ru/indicator/38480#; The flights from the country have intensified significantly following the announcement of the 'partial mobilisation' September 2022. See also 'Rise of Russia Hardliners Sows Fear In Putin's Elite' (*Bloomberg*, 8 November 2022) www.bloomberg.com/news/articles/2022-11-08/rise-of-russia-hardliner-yevgeny-prigozhin-fuels-fear-in-putin-s-elite?leadSource=uverify%20wall.

[70] The Commission is not alone, regrettably, as the drive to close the EU borders for the Russians fleeing the Putin regime demonstrates. Ganty et al, 'Unlawful Nationality-Based Bans', 48.

[71] European Commission Recommendation C (2022)2028 final, para 15.

[72] ibid, para 20.

Ukrainian investors alike,[73] as well as the Member States of the EU.[74] The moment seemed right for the Commission to invoke security risks to tackle a largely invented problem which is hardly related to the current circumstances. It is a clear fact that what the Commission refers to as 'policy to take determined action on both citizenship and residence investor schemes' lacks the legal basis and is thus entirely *ultra vires*, as we will discuss in more detail in the next section.

The European Commission's Recommendation on EU Investment Migration Programmes is only one of the many attempts to tackle investment migration which has attracted strong criticism from EU institutions ever since the launch of the Maltese CBI.[75] Indeed, as the following section demonstrates, investment migration has been continuously problematised by the European institutions and by various means and at different levels.

B. Tackling Investment Migration by All Means

Over the last ten years the Commission and the European Parliament have turned to the issues of investment migration on numerous occasions. While the Parliament has passed a number of (non-binding) resolutions calling on EU Member States to abolish such programmes, the European Commission went further, initiating infringement procedures against Cyprus and Malta in 2020 and eventually bringing Malta in front of the Court of Justice.[76] Such action was preceded by a Report that the European Commission issued on the subject, relying heavily on previous documents from EU institutions and bodies.[77] After Cyprus closed its CBI, Malta is the only EU Member State with an active formal CBI amidst the strong political pressure from the European Commission and the European Parliament to comply with questionable demands made outside the area of EU competence against the smallest EU Member State. The rough chronology of the PR attack is the following:

- On 15 January 2014, the Justice Commissioner, Viviane Reding, initiated a plenary debate in the European Parliament about the Maltese IIP asking that Member States 'only award citizenship to persons where there is a "genuine link" or "genuine connection" to the country in question';[78]
- On 16 January 2014, the European Parliament adopted a Resolution on EU citizenship for sale, following Viviane Reding's approach and emphasising that access to funds should not be the main criterion in conferring EU citizenship on third-country nationals;[79]

[73] The quality of both nationalities in question is at the level of the victims of citizenship making Ukrainians and Russians alike the ideal clients of the investment migration industry: Kochenov and Lindeboom, 'Empirical Assessment of the Quality of Nationalities'; Kochenov, 'The Victims of Citizenship'.

[74] Sumption, 'Can Investor Citizenship Programmes Be a Policy Success?' in Kochenov and Surak (eds), *Citizenship and Residence Sales*.

[75] Amendments made to the Maltese Citizenship Act in 2013 provided the possibility of naturalising individuals 'who contribute to the economic development of Malta' as well as their families and a framework for the enactment of LN 47 of 2014 (MT) 'The Individual Investor Programme of the Republic of Malta Regulations' which introduced further amendments. The 2014 Regulations were issued following negotiations between Malta and the European Commission: see 'Joint Press Statement by the European Commission and the Maltese Authorities' (*European Commission*, 29 January 2014).

[76] *Commission v Malta*, pending. See also the contributions by Tratnik and Weingerl, Sarmiento and Íñiguez and by Weiler in this volume.

[77] European Commission Report COM(2019)12 final. For analyses, see eg Margiotta, '"Ricchi e poveri" alla prova della cittadinanza europea' (2020) 55 *Ragion Pratica* 513; Jessurun d'Oliveira in this volume.

[78] Plenary Session debate of the European Parliament on 'EU citizenship for sale' (Strasbourg, 15 January 2014).

[79] European Parliament resolution on EU citizenship for sale (2013/2995(RSP)) [2014] OJ C 482/117.

- On 29 January 2014, representatives of the European Commission and of the Government of Malta met to discuss the compatibility of the Maltese IIP with EU law, upon which Malta agreed to amend its programme (under political pressure from the European Commission) by including a legal residency requirement (ie possession of a residence permit at the moment of application for naturalization);[80]
- On 15 November 2017, the European Parliament adopted a Resolution on the rule of law in Malta, calling on Malta to publish the names of those who had acquired their citizenship through investment;[81]
- On 26 March 2019, the European Parliament adopted a Resolution on Financial Crimes, Tax Evasion and Tax Avoidance, calling 'on Member States to phase out all existing CBI or RBI schemes as soon as possible';[82]
- On 10 July 2020, the European Parliament adopted a Resolution on a comprehensive Union policy on preventing money laundering and terrorist financing calling on the Member States 'to phase out all existing [CBI] or [RBI] schemes as soon as possible';[83]
- 29 September 2022, the Commission brings Malta to Court rehearsing the same questionable arguments.

Non-legislative organs, such as the TAX3 Special Committee on Financial Crimes, Tax Evasion and Tax Avoidance, and the European Economic and Social Committee (EESC) also had their say on the subject, calling for the phasing out of all investor programmes.[84] The TAX3 Special Committee issued a Report on the basis of which the European Parliament adopted a Resolution.[85] The EESC issued an Opinion urging Member States to follow its recommendation on the phasing out of investor programmes.[86] Yet neither the TAX3 Special Committee nor the EESC are legislative organs and whatever reports or opinions they might issue are incapable, just like Resolutions of the European Parliament, to alter the scope of Union competences.

Enlarging the powers of the Union to deal with investment migration, however strictly defined and even if a valid reason for it was to hand, threatens to open the gates to the EU's legislative interference into issues lying at the heart of the remaining 'stateness' of the Member States:[87] the ability to determine who belongs to the people of a Member State and who does not, and for what reason. Such a valid reason, however, is missing here, since whatever the Commission or the Parliament's TAX3 committee may think about preserving the value of EU citizenship is absolutely irrelevant in a context where not a single argument is brought to the table to explain why the absolute glorification of the blood ties as a way of distributing rights and privileges is the right way forward for the EU, and how the sacrifice of the internal market – which the Union was designed to bring about – at the altar of 'genuine links' between EU citizens and concrete Member States

[80] 'Joint Press Statement by the European Commission and the Maltese Authorities on Malta's Individual Investor Programme (IIP)' (*European Commission*, 29 January 2014) https://ec.europa.eu/commission/presscorner/detail/en/MEMO_14_70.

[81] European Parliament resolution of on the Rule of Law in Malta 2017/2935(RSP) [2017] OJ C356/29, para 13.

[82] European Parliament resolution of on Financial Crimes, Tax Evasion and Tax Avoidance (2018/2121(INI)) [2019] OJ C108/8, para 195.

[83] European Parliament resolution (2020/2686(RSP)).

[84] See, similarly, the stance of FATF/OECD, analysed in detail by Kristin Surak in this volume.

[85] European Parliament Resolution (2018/2121(INI)).

[86] European Economic and Social Committee 'Investor Citizenship and Residence Schemes in the European Union' COM(2019) 12 final, para 11.

[87] Wiener, 'Going Home? "European" Citizenship Practice Twenty Years After' in Kochenov (ed), *EU Citizenship and Federalism* (Cambridge University Press 2017) 243.

is at all justifiable in face of the overwhelming harm that the Commission's unlawful 'genuine links' move is bound to cause to the foundational principle of non-discrimination on the basis of nationality. Quite remarkably, the institution appears to be ready to give up its very *raison d'être* in the name of defending what appears to be the superiority of European blood against corrupting attacks from those less ethnocentric of the EU's governments.[88]

The Commission's court case against Malta needs to be considered in this context.[89] As mentioned above, the Court has already clarified EU law on the matter on a number of occasions and the fact that the Commission politicises the law to the point of misrepresenting what it requires could never help it in Court, even if its press releases would collect plentiful likes on twitter. Pointing in the direction of a Union built on the idea of European blood superiority, the Commission explained that investment programmes under which citizenship is granted in the absence of a genuine link or residence requirement undermine the essence of EU citizenship. Ancestral citizenship and kin naturalisations for the millions of those who have never even visited Europe were never mentioned: blood ties, for the Commission *are* the 'genuine links'[90] – and this would make the founders of the Union, who wrote into its very essence that discrimination on the basis of nationality would outlawed by EU law, very ashamed of Miss von der Leyen and her college.

Quite alarmingly, the Eurowhiteness blood-unity nature of the underlying argument, the Commission's propaganda about the law has been effective enough in the supranational circles, especially if one looks at the results of the European Parliament's vote on the Report of Sophie in 't Veld, which was the quintessential blood purity/passport apartheid vote.[91] All the hopes are now with the law to offer a wholesome push back against this ethno-nationalist agenda, which the Union was created to tame, rather than help push forward.

While AG Collins in his Opinion sides with Malta and orders the Commission to pay the costs, the outcome of *Commission v Malta* is still unknown at the time of writing. Be it as it may, it would certainly influence further developments in the investment migration world. Yet, the global context is bound to remain unchanged no matter what the Court finds, as the centre of citizenship by investment industry measured both as a matter of the numbers of applications and by the scale of investments is in Turkey and the Caribbean, not the EU. The same applies to investment residence, long centred on the US with its EB-5 programme. Losing the case before of the Court would be something deeply embarrassing for the Commission after so much energy went into knowingly misrepresenting what the law actually is to give the

[88] This behaviour, although astonishingly *passé* at its heart, does not seem to contradict von der Leyen Commission's eagerness to defend the 'European way of life' despite numerous critics – as put by Andrew Stroehlein, European media director for Human Rights Watch, 'Putting migration under a portfolio named "protecting our European way of life" is another example of just how much mainstream politicians in Europe are adopting the framing of the far right', and also 'Normalizing their ugly rhetoric is a dangerous step toward normalizing their abusive policies that threaten democracy and human rights': quoted in Stevis-Gridneff, 'Protecting Our European Way of Life'?' (*New York Times*, 12 September 2019) www.nytimes.com/2019/09/12/world/europe/eu-ursula-von-der-leyen-migration.html; in fact 'genuine links' and 'European way of life' seem to be reference to the same brand of nationalism, which is of course at odds with the values, which the EU is purportedly built to defend, but has been failing so far: Auer, *European Disunion* (Hurst 2022); Jakab and Kochenov (eds), *The Enforcement of EU Law and Values* (Oxford University Press 2017); Kochenov, 'EU Law without the Rule of Law' (2015) 34 *YEL* 74–96.

[89] Margiotta, '"Ricchi e poveri"'; Interview with Kochenov, 'Commission Would Likely Be "Humiliated" if CIP-Matter Goes to Court over "Genuine Links"' (IMI, 23 October 2020); Weiler in this volume.

[90] Given the bloodlines' essential role in the Eurowhiteness law today, it is impossible to imagine the Commission attacking the ethno-nationalist version of 'genuine links', which makes its stance against investment migration particularly wanting.

[91] Members of the European Parliament voted overwhelmingly in favour of the text with 595 voting in favour, 12 voting against and 74 abstaining from vote. See 'MEPs demand a ban on "golden passports" and specific rules for

Orwellian Eurowhiteness a boost. The Court is not blind and its members have unquestionably read the Commission's unfortunate scribbles and see the implications of the case for the future of the internal market and the consistency of own critically important case-law on EU citizenship. Moreover, the loss would mean that other Member States would quickly join the smallest ones that the Commission has so far been attacking and establish investment migration programmes without paying attention to the Commission's unlawful 'genuine links' propaganda, should it not stop after the Court has spoken.

Given the behaviour of the Commission on the matter so far, it is difficult for legal experts to comprehend what guides its judgement next to raw ethno-nationalist intuitions: the law has so far never been taken into account on this issue by the 'guardian of the Treaties', offering a clear example of the need for reinforced checks and balances within the institution, which seem to be entirely missing at the moment, showing a threat to the basic elements of the Rule of Law.[92] This is certainly unless the Commission reneges on its position and starts searching ways to exit the trap of its own making.

IV. UNPACKING THE MOST UNFORTUNATE ELEMENTS OF THE COMMISSION'S POSITION

The most problematic aspects of the European Commission's attack on the lawful exercise of national competence by the Member States wishing to establish CBI and RBI programmes can be boiled down to eight key elements:

a) The myth of CBI naturalisations as an example of 'less stringent conditions'
b) A lack of EU legislative competence
c) A lack of international law rules to back the Commission's position
d) Reliance on obsolete precedent in breach of EU law
e) Practising discrimination on the basis of nationality, ethnicity and the mode of citizenship acquisition
f) RBI and the critique of minimum presence requirements
g) Humiliating and discriminatory rhetoric targeting investment migrants
h) Misrepresentation of the principle of sincere cooperation

Notwithstanding the fact that some of these issues have already been touched upon above, it makes sense to look at them in some more detail.

A. The Myth of 'Less Stringent Conditions'

Citizenship,[93] together with territory, is the essential starting point of the concept of the sovereignty of states.[94] The limits of the EU competences are governed by the principle of conferral.

"golden visas"' (*European Parliament,* 9 March 2022) www.europarl.europa.eu/news/en/press-room/20220304IPR24787/meps-demand-a-ban-on-golden-passports-and-specific-rules-for-golden-visas.

[92] Pech, 'The Rule of Law as a Well-Established and Well-Defined Principle of EU Law' (2022) 14 *HJRL* 107.

[93] Since Art 2(a) of the European Convention on Nationality (1997) ETS 166 (ECN) stipulates: 'For the purpose of this Convention: a "nationality" means the legal bond between a person and a State and does not indicate the person's ethnic origin'. These two terms are used interchangeably in the legal literature on the subject, understood simply as a classification of a natural person belonging to a particular State.

[94] On sovereignty of states, see, among many authors, Gross 'The Peace of Westphalia: 1648–1948' (1948) 42 *AJIL* 20; Wheaton, *Wheaton's Elements of International Law*, Coleman Phillipson (ed) 5th edn (Steven & Sons 1916);

This means that the EU acts only within the limits of the competences that EU Member States have conferred upon it in the Treaties, and nationality is not among these competences.[95] As per the case law of the CJEU, the limitations on the principle of conferral are interpreted strictly, and require close involvement of the Member States.[96] So when the Commission claims to have discovered what citizenship is about, writing that citizenship 'is traditionally based on … *ius sanguinis* and … *ius soli*',[97] this is all correct, but the Devil, as is only so frequently the case, is in the detail. In giving its 'golden standard', the Commission fails to acknowledge that the reality is much more complex than what its selective summary purports to demonstrate.

Referring to citizenship by investment, the Commission writes that in essence, such 'citizenship is granted under less stringent conditions than under ordinary naturalization regimes'.[98] What is crucial here is to mention the different ways that the citizenship law of all the Member States rationally accommodate enabling the acquisition of citizenship by different categories of applicants.

Perusal of any citizenship law book makes as much clear: when we speak of the acquisition of citizenship, differentiated treatment of different cases is key. It is an essential and characteristic part of nationality regulation. Member States establish what is desirable and while Italy decided that asking an ailing Japanese Cardinal – stateless upon retirement from Vatican service – to wait the usual 10 years to become Italian is undesirable, replacing it with zero years instead, and the Dutch government decided that asking asylum seekers to wait as long as others to naturalise would be unkind, the Maltese government makes the grant of nationality conditional on a significant donation to drive the economy of the islands. In light of the existing differences in procedure, underpinned by the great disproportion in the numbers, where hundreds of thousands became EU citizens through extremely remote ancestry or other ways having nothing to do with the state or its 'culture' through the laws of Bulgaria, Greece, Ireland, Italy, Romania and other states, stating that investment citizenship is 'less stringent', as the Commission does, is an absurd misrepresentation.

To drive this point home, it is even more absurd than what it first seems to be, for at least two reasons. Most importantly, many other ways to acquire citizenship do not require a significant investment. An American kid, like the son of a Venezuelan friend, searching through archives for any Greek connections so as to avoid paying US-rate tuition fees at Bologna Medical School, is not bringing several millions to Greece. To imply that undying Greekness can persist across six generations, however ethno-nationalist and *passé* a notion this might be, is a decision for the Greek government to take, which fits the general international trends, as Christian Joppke has shown.[99] The absurdity of this is amplified by the strict sexism of classical citizenship regulation: a single Greek grandma in the ancestry chain would have made our Bologna student a foreigner in the EU,[100] in need of residence permits and cultural and language tests. This is the law however and it is up to the Greeks to change this, if their democracy so desires.

Merriam, *History of the Theory of Sovereignty since Rousseau* (Lawbook Exchange 1999); Osiander, 'Sovereignty, International Relations and the Westphalian Myth' (2001) 55 *International Organization* 251.

[95] Art 5 TEU. For historic development of the principle, see Barents, 'The Internal Market Unlimited' (1993) 30 *CMLRev.* 85; Bradley, 'The European Court and the Legal Basis of Community Legislation' (1988) 13 *ELRev.* 379.

[96] See in greater detail Sarmiento, 'EU Competence and the Attribution of Nationality', 3 et seq.

[97] European Commission Report COM(2019)12 final, 2.

[98] ibid, sect 2.1, p 2.

[99] Joppke, 'Citizenship between De- and Re-Ethnicization' (2003) 44 *EJS* 429.

[100] Abrams, 'Examining Entrenched Masculinities in the Republican Government Tradition' (2011) 114 *W. Va. LRev.* 165.

The point is that the Cypriot choice to create citizens through investment is at least as rational (or irrational) as the Greek, but not to a protestor in the 'Macedonia is Greece' crowds of course, which our US kid, thankfully, will never join. The question of what is 'legal' does not arise, since it is not up to the Commission to ask or comment on this, and international law, just like European law, is clear: Member States will decide as they see fit. So for Malta EUR 650,000 was more important than blood nationalism, while for Greece the opposite is true. Some would applaud this choice: 'Greek blood is important!' To suggest, however, that some other choice is somehow 'less legal' in the context where EU citizenship is equated with some mythical superiority of European blood, whatever is implied by it, cannot be correct. And morality has never played a role in citizenship law, especially in the EU, with its colonial past[101] and the essentially race-based exclusion from EU citizenship[102] approved by the ECJ in *Kaur*[103] and the constant fine-tuning of the passport apartheid system at the heart of EU law,[104] which varies in its effects 'from indifference to torture and killing',[105] as the growing research on EU's crimes against humanity testifies.[106] Globally the picture is no different: citizenship is currently the main tool for the preservation of global inequality, as Branko Milanović, among others, explained with clarity.[107]

Second, and equally importantly, 'ordinary conditions' – as opposed to the frowned-upon 'less stringent' ones – imply a level of due diligence which is significantly lower than what investment citizenship promises: the entirety of one's finances and business connections, as well as your entire life history would not normally be dug up by independent due diligence providers, unless you are an investor naturalising on that ground.[108]

This is only right: different applicants require different standards. The absurdity of implying, however, as the Commission does, that investing several millions and going through deep scrutiny is less stringent than finding a 'Greek' man whom you have never met in your ancestry, speaks for itself.

B. The Lack of Legislative EU Competence to Regulate the Issue

Of crucial importance is the sovereignty/competence aspect of this story. The crucial question is how far the Commission can actually enforce its own understanding on Member States' nationalities and EU citizenship, however enlightened such an understanding could be. If there is no Competence to regulate, the Commission's opinions – especially if they contradict the Treaties and the settled case law of the CJEU (as we discuss below), let alone be based on startling European blood-superiority visions (as discussed above) – could and should always simply be ignored by the Member States as outright *ultra vires*.

[101] Hansen and Jonsson, *Eurafrica* (Bloomsbury 2014); Eklund, 'Peoples, Inhabitants and Workers'.

[102] Lord Lester of Herne Hill, 'Thirty Years on: The East African Case Revisited' (2002) 47 *Pub L* 52.

[103] Case C-192/99 *Kaur* ECLI:EU:C:2001:106. Cf D Kochenov, '*Ius Tractum* of Many Faces' (2009) 15 *CJEL* 169.

[104] Kochenov and van den Brink 'As if there was no Union'; Kochenov, 'Ending the Passport *Apartheid*'.

[105] Ganty and Kochenov, 'EU Lawlessness Law'; Kochenov and Ganty, 'The Death Machine', in Barnard et al (eds), *Pursuit of Legal Harmony in a Turbulent Europe* (Hart 2024) 67.

[106] Shatz, 'EU Crimes against Humanity' (Doctoral Thesis, Yale Law School 2023). Cf Shatz and Branco, 'Communication to the Office of the Prosecutor of the International Criminal Court Pursuant to Article 15 of the Rome Statute on EU Migration Policies in the Central Mediterranean and Libya (2014–2019)' (2019): www.statewatch.org/news/2019/jun/eu-icc-case-EU-Migration-Policies.pdf.

[107] B Milanović, *Global Inequality* (Harvard University Press 2016).

[108] Corrado and Marsh, 'Investment Migration and the Importance of Due Diligence' in Kochenov and Surak (eds), *Citizenship and Residence Sales*.

The ABC of global citizenship law is that states are free to confer citizenship on those whom they consider qualified. This is the case the Hague Convention of Nationality[109] and unquestionably under EU law – as Shaw,[110] Kochenov,[111] Jessurun d'Oliveira,[112] Sarmiento and van den Brink[113] and Tratnik and Weingerl[114] have demonstrated. By extension, this applies to EU citizenship, which is a derivative – *ius tractum* – citizenship.[115]

The naturalisations of those who are not 'natural born' citizens including a sub-type of investment naturalisations, falls squarely within the realm of what is legal worldwide, including in the EU. While the academic consensus worldwide is well articulated and undisputed, in the EU it is confirmed unequivocally by the case law of the Court of Justice:[116] from *Micheletti* and *Zhu and Chen*[117] to *Tjebbes*[118] and *JY*.[119]

Furthermore, EU citizenship is complementary to, but does not replace, national citizenship.[120] Put differently, EU citizenship protects the rights of Member State nationals which are not granted by their states but by the Union itself.[121] It is for the EU Member States, however, to regulate who qualifies as a national, having due regard to EU law. The EU case law preserves this competence of Member States,[122] with the only exception being instances where it is necessary to ensure effective and uniform protection of the rights of EU citizens. The EU has, therefore, normally only interfered in nationality matters where Member States have enacted measures that restrict the rights of EU citizens rather than where such rights are to be enjoyed by new citizens.[123]

Given that there is no legal basis in the TEU or TFEU for the pursuit of a 'natural' citizenship myth as it once was – as discussed by Spiro,[124] Joppke[125] and others, it comes as no surprise that the Commission has resorted in the course of its anti-CBI propaganda campaign to obsolete legal authority and abundant, flawed legal reasoning to sell the untenable position that it has no legal basis properly to defend.

[109] See Art 1 of the Hague Convention on Certain Questions Relating to the Conflict of Nationality Laws (1930) 179 UNTS 89 (the Hague Convention).

[110] Shaw, 'Citizenship for Sale' in Bauböck (ed), *Debating Transformations of National Citizenship* (Springer 2018) 61.

[111] Kochenov 'Rounding up the Circle'.

[112] Jessurun d'Oliveira, 'Union Citizenship and beyond' and his chapter in this volume.

[113] Sarmiento and van den Brink, 'EU Competence and Investor Migration'.

[114] Weingerl and Tratnik, 'Relevant Links'.

[115] Kochenov, '*Ius Tractum* of Many Faces'.

[116] See, for the general analyses, Kochenov and Lindeboom, 'Pluralism Through its Denial'; Jessurun d'Oliveira, 'Union Citizenship and beyond'.

[117] Case C-200/02 *Zhu and Chen* ECLI:EU:C:2004:639. Kochenov and Lindeboom, 'Breaking Chinese Law – Making European One' in Davies and Nicola (eds), *EU Law Stories* (Cambridge University Press 2017) 178.

[118] Case C-221/17 *Tjebbes* ECLI:EU:C:2019:189; Kochenov, 'The *Tjebbes* Fail' (2019) 4 *European Papers* 319; Jessurun d'Oliveira, '*Tjebbes* en aanhangend nationaliteit' (2019) 37 *NJb* 2265; Swider, 'Legitimising Precarity of EU Citizenship: *Tjebbes*' (2020) 57 CMLRev. 1163.

[119] Case C-118/20 *JY* ECLI:EU:C:2022:34; Kochenov and de Groot, 'Helpful, Convoluted, and Ignorant in Principle' (2022) 47 *ELRev.* 699.

[120] Art 20(1) TFEU.

[121] As stated by the CJEU many times, citizenship of the Union is intended to be the fundamental status of nationals of the Member: Case C-184/99 *Grzelczyk* ECLI:EU:C:2001:458, para 31; Case C-413/99 *Baumbast* ECLI:EU:C:2002:493, para 82; Case C-148/02 *Garcia Avello* ECLI:EU:C:2003:539 para 22; Case *Zhu and Chen*, para 25; and Case C-135/08 *Rottman* ECLI:EU:C:2010:104, para 43.

[122] The landmark case is *Micheletti*.

[123] See eg *Rottman*, para 60; Case C-34/09 *Ruiz Zambrano* ECLI:EU:C:2011:124, para 45. For the context of the latest case law, see, eg Kochenov and de Groot, 'Helpful, Convoluted, and Ignorant in Principle'.

[124] Spiro, 'Cash-for-Passports and the End of Citizenship' in Bauböck (ed), *Debating Transformations of National Citizenship* (Springer 2018) 17.

[125] Joppke, *Citizenship and Immigration* (Cambridge University Press 2010); Joppke, 'The Instrumental Turn of Citizenship' (2018) 44 *JEMS* 1.

C. The Lack of International Law Rules to Back the Commission's Position

In its analyses of the legal positioning of CBI programmes in the EU the European Commission often tries to justify its approach with references to the principles of international law.[126] However, the situation in international law is rather different to what the Commission has been promoting – in short, states have broad discretion, if not complete exclusivity, in deciding who qualifies as their citizen and under what circumstances. The Hague Convention on Certain Questions Relating to the Conflict of Nationality Laws of 1930 (Hague Convention) clarified this point in Article 1: 'It is for each State to determine under its own law who are its nationals.'[127] It further stipulates, however, that: '[t]his law shall be recognised by other States in so far as it is consistent with international conventions, international custom, and the principles of law generally recognised with regard to nationality'.[128] Article 3 of the European Convention on Nationality (ECN) uses almost identical words to define the nationals of a state and the conditions under which a state's citizenship law should be recognised.[129] As the information provided by the European Commission itself in all the documents it released to attack CBI makes absolutely clear, CBI naturalisations are fully recognised and practised in numerous states around the world. It is thus unquestionable that a CBI programme-based citizenship is a lawfully acquired nationality in the eyes of international law, which is also clear from the *Nottebohm* case concerning the recognition of bought Liechtensteiner nationality, which will be analysed in detail below.

In other words, in a context where international law unquestionably allows states to determine who their citizens are and which has traditionally recognised CBI citizenships as lawfully acquired – and the tradition of 'buying' citizenship here goes back centuries, as the brilliant scholarship of Maarten Prak clearly demonstrates[130] – states' competence in the field of citizenship matters is only limited by binding rules of international law. It is clear that CBI programmes as such are a mainstream application of a states' sovereign ability to decide who their nationals are, rather than a breach of any such rule. Consequently, given that citizenship by investment is entirely kosher in the eyes of international law, the one and only rule that could stand in the way of the states in the course of the implementation of their investment migration programmes as far as international law is concerned, is the element of the voluntariness of the individual acquiring the citizenship, as non-consensual naturalisation is precluded. Non-consensual naturalisations have been consistently ruled out as breaching international law at least since the attempts of the Latin American nations to start regarding European expats born outside of their territory – guys like Mr Nottebohm – as if they were local citizens, as Peter Spiro reports.[131] All the CBI naturalisations in the EU and in its direct vicinity have been unquestionably consensual.[132]

[126] cf, on such principles, de Groot and Vonk, *International Standards on Nationality Law* (Wolf 2016).

[127] Art 1, Hague Convention.

[128] ibid.

[129] Art 3 ECN.

[130] Prak, *Citizens without Nations* (Cambridge University Press 2018); Prak, 'Citizenship for Sale in Pre-modern Europe' in Kochenov and Surak (eds), *Citizenship and Residence Sales*.

[131] Spiro, 'Investment Citizenship and the Long Leash of International Law' in Kochenov and Surak (eds), *Citizenship and Residence Sales* and the literature cited therein.

[132] The only possible examples of a non-consensual CBI programme could be found in the Comoros: the island state used to offer wholesale naturalisation options to the Gulf monarchies seeking to reduce the level of statelessness among the Bidoon population. This CBI programme was subjected to clear criticism in the literature as potentially breaching international law: eg Spiro, 'Investment Citizenship and the Long Leash of International Law'.

Furthermore, different treatment of persons in similar situations is always prohibited under the principles of international law, except where it is reasonably justified and the measures taken are proportionate to a legitimate aim. In line with Article 5 of the UN Convention on the Elimination of All Forms of Racial Discrimination[133] and Article 5 ECN, conferral of citizenship cannot discriminate against citizens on grounds including national or ethnic origin. The Commission's Recommendation suggesting stripping EU citizens of Russian and Belarusian origin who acquired their EU nationality based on CBI naturalisations thus strongly suggests a potential breach of this basic rule of international law by the Commission on top of the disregard of the Union law which it also represents. Lastly, discrimination on the grounds of sex in the conferral of nationality is equally prohibited.[134]

While other requirements have also often been discussed in the context of possible constraints on state sovereignty in the field of citizenship, none of them has developed into binding international law which may affect a states' competence in citizenship matters. One of the most commonly discussed cases, which has been wrongly brought into connection with the acquisition of citizenship, rather rigidly by the European Commission, is the *Nottebohm* case of the International Court of Justice (ICJ).[135] Indeed, the European Commission relied heavily on the doctrine of 'genuine links' discussed in *Nottebohm* to justify its opposition to investment migration programmes, missing however, some very important aspects of that doctrine.

D. Reliance on Obsolete Precedent in Breach of EU Law

In the *Nottebohm* case,[136] the ICJ referred to the limitation on the recognition of nationality enshrined in the Hague Convention (Article 1) and described 'nationality' as a legal bond based on 'a social fact of attachment, a genuine connection of existence, interests and sentiments, together with the existence of reciprocal rights and duties'.[137] In particular, the ICJ discussed the genuine link requirement in the context of diplomatic protection and the recognition of citizenship in the absence of a 'genuine link', while confirming the sovereign right of states to determine who their nationals are.

> It is for Liechtenstein, as it is for every sovereign State, to settle by its own legislation the rules relating to the acquisition of its nationality, and to confer that nationality by naturalization granted by its own organs in accordance with that legislation. It is not necessary to determine whether international law imposes any limitations on its freedom of decision in this domain …

[133] Art 5, the Hague Convention.

[134] ibid.

[135] *Nottebohm* (Liechtenstein v Guatemala) [1955] ICJ Rep. 4.

[136] The citizenship of Lichtenstein held by Mr Nottebohm was not recognised by Guatemala, the latter state treating Mr Nottebohm as a German citizen – a status he did not hold. The ICJ agreed with this restrictive vision, ruling that nationality is a 'legal bond having as its basis a social fact of attachment, a genuine connection of experience, interests and sentiments, together with the existence of reciprocal rights and duties'. The ICJ failed to mention, however, that in the absence of any other nationality but that of Liechtenstein and with a 'genuine link' only to Guatemala, precisely the state attacking him, Mr Nottebohm was deprived of any remedy as a result of the controversial decision, even if limited only to the recognition of nationality for the purposes of diplomatic protection. To see the incoherence of the judgment, see the Dissenting Opinions of Judge Klæstad and of Judge Read. For analyses see the literature recommended in Bleckmann, 'The Personal Jurisdiction of the European Community' (1980) 17 *CMLRev.* 467, 477 and note 16.

[137] *Nottebohm*, 23.

> But the issue which the Court must decide is not one which pertains to the legal system of Liechtenstein … It is international law which determines whether a State is entitled to exercise protection and to seize the Court.
>
> The naturalization of Nottelbohm was an act performed by Liechtenstein in the exercise of its domestic jurisdiction. The question to be decided is whether that act has the international effect here under consideration.
>
> International practice provides many examples of acts performed by States in the exercise of their domestic jurisdiction which do not necessarily or automatically have international effect, which are not necessarily and automatically binding on other States or which are binding on them only subject to certain conditions: this is the case, for instance, of a judgment given by the competent court of a State which it is sought to invoke in another State.[138]

The ICJ further noted:

> in order to be capable of being invoked against another State, nationality must correspond with the factual situation …
>
> The character thus recognized on the international level as pertaining to nationality is in no way inconsistent with the fact that international law leaves it to each State to lay down the rules governing the grant of its own nationality …
>
> It may be said to constitute the juridical expression of the fact that the individual upon whom it is conferred, either directly by the law or as the result of an act of the authorities, is in fact more closely connected with the population of the State conferring nationality than with that of any other State.[139]

Therefore, as confirmed by the ICJ, states do not have to recognise the effects of a citizenship granted by another state in the absence of a genuine link. That said, the power of states to decide who their citizens are remains unaffected under international law. Indeed, even in the case itself, Guatemala had unquestionably recognised the Liechtensteiner nationality of Mr Nottebohm when he established residence in the country as a Liechtensteiner. Consequently, the case of *Nottebohm* has rightly and vigorously been criticised by experts since it was rendered[140] and has rarely been applied by international tribunals, and only in the context of dual nationality.[141]

Accordingly, contrary to the allegations of the European Commission that *Nottebohm* imposes an obligation on states to adhere to the 'genuine link' or residence requirement in cases of naturalisation, such a requirement has never been a binding rule of international law.[142] The reasons why are very clear: it is the legalistic and totalitarian nature of citizenship as a legal status, which frequently fails to correspond to any expected 'thick' links on the ground.[143] Rogers Brubaker famously defines citizenship as an 'object and instrument of closure',[144] in other words a means for selecting those who 'belong' from the available number of bodies and guarding the selected few from those who do not 'belong'. It means that not caring about a country and its purported 'values' will not make you less of a citizen in the eyes of the law, just as caring a lot about some officially endorsed 'culture' or language will *not* make you a citizen, unless you are named as such by law. Pretending that this is not the case – and many

[138] *Nottebohm*, 20–21.
[139] *Nottebohm*, 22–23.
[140] eg Spiro in this volume; Jones, 'The *Nottebohm* Case' (1956) 5 *ICLQ* 230; Kunz, 'The *Nottebohm* Judgment' (1960) 54 *AJIL* 536 and the literature cited therein; Sloane, 'Breaking the Genuine Link' (2009) 50 *Harv. Int'l L.J.* 1.
[141] Macklin, 'Is It Time to Retire *Nottebohm*?' (2017) 111 *AJIL* 492, 494.
[142] See eg Klæstad J., dissenting in *Nottebohm*.
[143] Kochenov, *Citizenship*.
[144] Brubaker, *Citizenship and Nationhood in France and Germany* (Harvard University Press 1992).

countries go to absurd lengths with this, such as the Netherlands – but only applying any of the conditions to dual citizens and leaving the rest alone no matter what,[145] is deeply unhelpful and usually only humiliates minorities, who could be more likely to have more than one citizenship and are often unable to renounce the harmful ones, such as Iran or Morocco-imposed statuses.[146]

When the Commission informs us that 'the study looked at other factors … which might arguably create a link between the applicant for citizenship and the country concerned',[147] a citizenship lawyer reading this might well be puzzled. It is fundamental to realise that only *citizenship* can be such a link. To present citizenship – an abstract legal status – as something that requires more than *itself* in order to be enjoyed is not faithful to the letter and the spirit of global citizenship law as it stands today. The Commission's analysis carries with it a whiff of the totalitarianism of nineteenth century approaches to ethno-nationalist allegiance. Only blood links, most regrettably, are taken as unquestionable and 'genuine' – EU citizenship is being turned by the Commission through its clumsy attacks against the CBI, into a deeply nationalist – read also racist – project, bringing it closer to the framing of nationalities at the time of the founding of the Union[148] – the times one would think that were passé.[149]

This is all the more ironic, given that the poor precedent of *Nottebohm* – which is not even good law at the international level anymore – has actually been expressly outlawed by the EU's own Court. Even more, the ICJ in *Nottebohm* clearly accepted the grant of nationality based on an investment as fully in line with international law and practice.[150] In other words, every reference to 'genuine links' by the European Commission is not only a clear misrepresentation of international law – it is also an attack on the well-articulated core of European one. Indeed, the situation in the EU could not have been clearer. As lucidly explained by the Court of Justice in the case of *Micheletti* – which concerned the Argentinian moving to Spain to establish a business using an Italian passport referred to above – checking 'genuine links' is expressly prohibited by EU law.[151]

'Genuine links' is a requirement which *breaches EU law* – the very rationale of EU citizenship, which comes with a right to move between all the EU Member States, while being protected from the expressions of local thick nationalisms, linguistic, 'cultural' and otherwise[152] is endangered by the 'genuine links' approach. This fact, while well recognised by the European Commission,[153] has been regularly brought into connection with the mode of acquisition of citizenship through investment, with the principle of sincere cooperation enshrined in Article 4(3) TEU and with the status of EU citizenship reflected in Article 20 TFEU – as follows directly from the Commission's framing of the case against Malta. The arguments of the European Commission are far from clear, or at least far from what has been established as EU law so far: amounting to a deliberate misrepresentation of EU law.

[145] Kochenov, '*Mevrouw de Jong gaat eten*'. The situation has become much worse since that contribution was written, as the level of absurdity and humiliation which those willing to get the local documents are subjected to has risen sharply.
[146] Swider, 'Legitimizing Precarity of EU Citizenship'; de Groot, 'Free Movement of Dual EU Citizens' in Cambien et al (eds), *European Citizenship under Stress* (Brill-Nijhoff 2020); Kochenov, 'The *Tjebbes* Fail'; Kochenov and de Groot, 'Helpful, Convoluted, and Ignorant in Principle'.
[147] European Commission Report COM(2019)12 final, sect 2.3.
[148] Eklund, 'Peoples, Inhabitants and Workers'.
[149] But see Kundnani, *Eurowhiteness*.
[150] Cf van den Brink, 'Revisiting Citizenship within the European Union'.
[151] *Micheletti*, paras 10–13.
[152] Kochenov, 'EU Citizenship', 11; Davies, 'The Humiliation of the State as a Constitutional Tactic', 147.
[153] European Commission Report COM(2019)12 final, sect 2.4, p 5.

One wonders what hopes drive the Commission ahead of the necessity to defend such misrepresentation in front of the Court. Was the case designed for Malta to blink in order for lawlessness and propaganda to win? The Commission's purely political and legally obscurantist position, in assuming 'genuine links' between states and citizens, is not only flawed in terms of international law, but it also falls short of the 'market citizenship' standard of the Union itself, however criticised.[154] If conditioned on such 'genuine links', the free movement of EU citizens would be endangered, if not impossible, which is precisely the reason why AG Tesauro laughed at the embarrassing position embraced by the Commission in the ancient *Micheletti* case.[155]

It is impossible, with recourse to the law in force, to justify the Commission's position, since such a justification would require the annihilation of all that the EU stands for: liberal values, non-discrimination on the basis of nationality, human dignity and equality, *inter* many *alia*. Should the Commission be allowed to undo all the value core of EU law on the basis of tired and unambiguously racist and blood-nationalist tropes such as 'links' with states and 'cultures' pre-approved by the powers that be, where blood connection is the only unquestioned 'link'? The whole point of the Commission's engagement with CBI, it appears, is the deep dislike of the idea that thick nationalist blood bonds are bypassed: the Commission's apparent desire to play handmaiden to nationalist totalitarianism: a nineteenth century ideal replicated at the supranational level in breach of EU law and imposed on the often smallest Member States by way of propaganda and outright bullying. Is this Maltese a 'real' Maltese? What if he has never visited the European Union? And what about this Irishwoman?[156] And this Brit?[157] This Dutch?[158] This is where the obsolete case law of the International Court of Justice – expressly *overruled* by the EU's own Court of Justice – comes into play: the Commission refers quite extensively to the *Nottebohm* theory of 'genuine links'.[159]

It could of course be possible that the Commission's desk officers might be unaware of the fact that *Nottebohm* was also opposed immediately after it was decided by Jones, Kunz, Panhuys, Weis – the list of authorities could be continued *ad infinitum* – and later dismissed by René de Groot, Jessurun d'Olivera, Macklin, Sloane, Thwaites, Vermeer-Kunzli and many others, as Spiro has splendidly summarised.[160] What they could not overlook, however, is that 'genuine links' are incompatible with a world which has moved on, at least officially, from perpetual allegiance and the glorious mystifications of blood nationalism, as the Court of Justice confirmed in *Micheletti*.[161] As per Advocate General Tesauro, the 'romantic period of international relations'[162] is over. It is thus quite unacceptable, in the respectful opinion of these authors, to provide a reference to 'genuine links' and *Nottebohm* in an official document of the European Commission in reference to the need to have a nationality acquired by naturalisation recognised in the 'international arena'.[163] The reference is flawed, since the

[154] See, for the best available analysis, O'Brien, *Unity in Adversity* (Hart 2017); see also Kochenov, 'The Oxymoron of "Market Citizenship"' in Amtenbrink et al (eds), *The Internal Market and the Future of European Integration* (Cambridge University Press 2019) 217.
[155] Opinion of AG Tesauro in *Micheletti* ECLI:EU:C:1992:47, para 5.
[156] Case C-434/09 *McCarthy* ECLI:EU:C:2011:277.
[157] *Kaur*.
[158] *Tjebbes*; Kochenov, 'The *Tjebbes* Fail'; Swider, 'Legitimising Precarity of EU Citizenship'.
[159] *Nottebohm*.
[160] Spiro, '*Nottebohm* and "Genuine Link"'.
[161] *Micheletti*.
[162] Opinion of AG Tesauro in *Micheletti*.
[163] European Commission Report COM(2019) 12 final, sects 2.3 and 2.4.

Court of Justice of the European Union has *expressly prohibited* the Member States from relying on *Nottebohm* in dealing with each other's nationals. The Commission's position contradicts itself, on a number of occasions, but one such is the most telling:[164] you cannot have a rule of recognition 'in the international arena' based on *Nottebohm*, which is at the same time expressly prohibited by the highest EU Court, with the immediate effect, of course, of blocking *Nottebohm* in the territory of the EU. This point is absolutely crucial: the Commission's positions knowingly *misrepresent EU law* and constitute an indirect assault against the very nature of EU citizenship as a status of liberating the beneficiaries from suffocating and unnecessary local particularisms through the prohibition of discrimination on the basis of nationality.

E. Practising Discrimination on the Basis of Nationality, Ethnicity and the Mode of Citizenship Acquisition

The Commission's attack against investment migration assumes that it is acceptable to target groups of EU citizens and single them out for differentiated treatment based on the ground on which the nationality of an EU Member State and thus EU citizenship had been acquired. This type of discrimination is squarely prohibited in EU law at least since the *Boukhalfa* case-law.[165] Treating Europeans differently based on the particular rule which made them EU citizens is not what EU law allows and the majority of national constitutions would prohibit this too. The crusade against CBI is an assault on this principle.

The Commission's stance on denaturalisations in the 2022 Recommendations is particularly unlawful and out of place, as it seeks to convince the Member States to breach the law. The Commission proclaims inter alia that EU citizens of Russian and Belarusian origin (whom the Commission calls 'Russians' and 'Belarusians')[166] and their family members should, in accordance with the CJEU principles including proportionality and protection of human rights, be stripped of their EU nationality gained through investment if they become subject to EU restrictive measures or because they significantly support the war in Ukraine or activities of the Russian or Belarusian regimes breaching international law.[167]

Deprivation of citizenship as a security measure has resurged in state practices in recent years, including among European states.[168] A Report of the Institute on Statelessness and Inclusion and the Global Citizenship Observatory has identified four deprivation grounds relating to international security: disloyalty, military service to a foreign country, other service to a foreign country and other (ordinary criminal) offences.[169] In the light of the conflict in Ukraine, all these grounds may serve as basis for deprivation of citizenship including instances of Ukrainians who refuse to remain and fight in Ukraine as well as foreign fighters who come

[164] ibid, p 7.

[165] Case C-214/94 *Boukhalfa* ECLI:EU:C:1996:174. Although the Report recognises the importance of non-discrimination on this ground, it is written based on the presumption of the necessity to discriminate, which follows from its questionable 'genuine links' logic in the context of giving effect to nationalities acquired by naturalisation. Under this approach, outlawed by the Court of Justice, Miss Boukhalfa could have had no genuine links with Germany to allow her to be protected from discrimination.

[166] European Commission Recommendation C(2022)2028 final, para 13, and point 3.

[167] ibid, para 15.

[168] van der Baaren et al, 'Instrumentalising Citizenship' (ISI & GLOBALCIT 2022).

[169] ibid 8–12.

from countries where joining a foreign army is considered an offence. EU citizens of Russian and Belarusian origin, as well as any other EU citizens, can be also deprived of their EU citizenship on the grounds established in the national laws of EU Member States.[170] Such grounds are equally applicable to all naturalised citizens notwithstanding their previous (or other) nationality or method of naturalisation. Targeting only Russians and Belarusians who have naturalised through investment, as proposed by the European Commission, is discriminatory on various grounds including ethnicity, national origin and the ground of citizenship acquisition.[171]

In accordance with the Principles on Deprivation of Nationality as a National Security Measure, which were developed by more than 60 international experts, 'States shall not deprive persons of nationality for the purpose of safeguarding national security',[172] and if that happens,

> the exercise of this exception should be interpreted and applied narrowly, only in situations in which it has been determined by a lawful conviction that meets international fair trial standards, that the person has conducted themselves in a manner seriously prejudicial to the vital interests of the state.[173]

This exception is further limited by the international law standards for the avoidance of statelessness; the prohibition of discrimination; the prohibition of arbitrary deprivation of nationality; the right to a fair trial, remedy and reparation; and other obligations and standards set out in international human rights law, international humanitarian law and international refugee law.[174]

The Principles clarify that

> the deprivation of nationality of citizens on national security grounds is presumptively arbitrary. This presumption may only be overridden in circumstances where such deprivation is, at a minimum: … Carried out in pursuance of a legitimate purpose; … Provided for by law; … Necessary; … Proportionate; and … In accordance with procedural safeguards'.[175]

Proportionality requires that

> [t]he immediate and long-term impact of deprivation of nationality on the rights of the individual, their family, and on society is proportionate to the legitimate purpose being pursued; The deprivation of nationality is the least intrusive means of achieving the stated legitimate purpose; and The deprivation of nationality is an effective means of achieving the stated legitimate purpose.[176]

Yet, as noted by some experts in the field, 'the exercise of (certain) functions and powers may never violate peremptory or non-derogable norms of international law, nor impair the essence of any human right'[177] – such as the principles of non-discrimination and equality.[178]

[170] eg Part VI ('Renunciation and deprivation of citizenship'), CAP. 188 of Citizenship Act 1964 (MT) as amended.

[171] Sect 4.1, Principle 4 of 'Principles on Deprivation of Nationality as a National Security Measure' (Institute on Statelessness and Inclusion 2020) [Principles on Deprivation of Nationality]; see also The UN Special Rapporteur on the promotion and protection of human rights and fundamental freedoms while countering terrorism, Position on the human rights consequences of citizenship stripping in the context of counter-terrorism with a particular application to North-East Syria (2022).

[172] Cf Sect 4.1, Principle 4 of Principles on Deprivation of Nationality.

[173] Sect 4.2 of Principles on Deprivation of Nationality.

[174] ibid, sect 4.3.

[175] ibid, sect 7.1.

[176] ibid, sect 7.5.

[177] Scheinin (Special Rapporteur on the Promotion and Protection of Human Rights and Fundamental Freedoms While Countering Terrorism), Ten Areas of Best Practices in Countering Terrorism (2010) A/HRC/16/51, para 16.

[178] Paulussen, 'Stripping Foreign Fighters of Their Citizenship' (2021) 103 *International Review of the Red Cross* 605.

F. RBI and the Critique of Minimum Presence Requirements

The Commission's documents went into great length to establish a connection between legal residence and physical presence, which is not a requirement of EU law. Some residence can even be proclaimed almost fake on this count, should the recipient of the residence permit not give up the usual life of global ambition in favour of a sedentary lifestyle in one EU Member State, which dull Brussels mandarins have so unimaginatively intended. This view is deeply problematic and legally incorrect.

The Long-Term Residence Directive (Directive 2003/109) states unequivocally in Article 13 that: 'Member States may issue residence permits of permanent or unlimited validity on terms that are *more favourable* than those laid down by this Directive' (emphasis added). To imply that the Directive establishes a minimum threshold for defining permanent residence in the EU as some scholars have done[179] is outright incorrect, since the text of the provision above is quite clear. It is of course true that national requirements, which are more lenient than those set out in Directive 2003/109, will not produce EU-level rights for the holders of these permits,[180] but this is not the general point the Commission seems to be making. Instead, it is taking issue, erroneously, with the low physical presence thresholds under national legislation in Member States with RBI programmes. Any criticism of more favourable definitions of residence in national law compared with what can be found in supranational regulation, which we find in the Commission's documents, is entirely moot, since the Directive expressly allows the Member States to set the presence requirement at zero days. Furthermore, the concern of the Commission that a residence permit obtained through investment can be used to naturalise in the host Member State under traditional naturalisation procedures enters again the domain of the acquisition of nationality, which falls outside the scope of EU competences.[181]

Clarifying this point is of crucial importance, since even if residence based on investment, comes to be regulated supranationally as the EP suggests[182] (and here the Commission would have clear competence to propose legislation, of course),[183] such regulation will most certainly contain similar clauses, allowing the Member States to depart from the harmonised regulation in order to meet the needs of specific categories of residents, who would receive better treatment in national law. Not to do this would turn the very rationale behind supranational regulation on its head, since the starting point for thinking about supranational regulation is that it provides a minimum threshold of rights of individuals to be safeguarded no matter what, rather than creating obstacles to rights. Should states be willing to offer more rights in their territory, this is to be allowed, rather than prohibited. Again, the opposite view would imply that supranational regulation is about setting the maximum standard for rights that the Member States can possibly offer and this contradicts the underpinnings of European integration to date pretty much in all the spheres of residency regulation: the Union as such has traditionally been too hostile to non-EU citizen residents to wholeheartedly present itself as the maximum denominator of rights.[184]

[179] See eg Carrera, 'The Price of EU Citizenship' (2015) CEPS Policy Brief.

[180] van den Brink, 'Investment Residence and the Concept of Residence in EU Law'.

[181] This is if we move beyond the simple fact that legal residence does not necessarily imply (any) physical presence, as explained in a comparative study included in this volume: Kochenov and van den Brink.

[182] European Parliament Resolution 2021/2026(INL), paras 21–25.

[183] van den Brink, 'Investment Residence and the Concept of Residence in EU Law'.

[184] Kochenov and van den Brink, 'Pretending There is No Union'; Ganty and Kochenov, 'EU Lawlessness Law'.

G. Humiliating and Discriminatory Rhetoric Targeting Investment Migrants

The Commission routinely demonises investment migrants – an approach which is questionable at best. Its core argument in numerous documents could be boiled down to the following: third-country nationals who invest in Member States may be criminals and therefore, investment migration programmes create security risks; the fact that EU citizenship provides for cross-border rights increases such risks further.[185]

The Commission seems to make assumptions about investors largely on the basis of their status of beneficiaries of RBI and CBI programmes. The Commission is open about its assumption – without explaining its reasons – that rich people who wish to invest and become EU citizens are probably criminals, and the chances of this are even higher because of the qualities of EU citizenship allowing for free movement. The same assumptions are notably missing concerning EU citizens who naturalise, because of kin blood connection, family links (even in cases where such naturalisations does not require any presence in the EU, as French or Dutch law would allow, for instance), or those who naturalise based on the discretion of the Member States. Only CBI clients are criminals in the Commission's mind – and the presumption of innocence apparently does not enter the picture. This is absolutely contrary to the EU Charter and wider EU law, especially given that discrimination on the basis of the particular mode of citizenship acquisition is prohibited. Based on the Commission's abundantly expressed views, its approach to CBI seems to be driven uniquely by discrimination based on the mode of the acquisition of EU citizenship.

To complicate matters further, the Commission continuously underlines the risks related to the freedom of movement between the Member States of these new citizens after their naturalisation.[186] Such purported risks underpin its case against Malta in front of the Court. Yet all the individuals naturalised through citizenship by investment are in fact not only full, but also ideal EU citizens in the light of Part II TFEU and Directive 2004/38, as they will never be a burden on the social security systems of the host Member States and will obviously have comprehensive health insurance – the two core requirements to be met in order to benefit from the free movement right under Article 21 TFEU.

That said, when practised in non-transparent and corrupt ways, investment migration – like any other enterprise – will certainly generate problems that have to be tackled. These precisely involve corruption, money laundering and tax evasion rather than naturalisation as such. Indeed, money laundering, tax evasion, corruption and other illegal activities are one thing, and the acquisition of citizenship through investment quite another. The Commission's attack on CBI and RBI fails to make this distinction. From this perspective, banking, mining or gambling – to name but a few corruptible enterprises – could be frowned upon – yet when banks, casinos or mines are regulated, it is not presumed that these activities should be outlawed. It follows that the Commission is not at all driven in its attacks by the possible negative externalities of CBI and RBI, but indeed by a set of fundamental considerations about the essence of EU citizenship in the light of its questionable 'genuine links' theory, if one can call this approach a theory. So not the risks posed by CBI programmes, but the fact that the very existence of such naturalisations contradicts the Commission's nationalistic view of EU citizenship based on blood privilege and 'thick' links with the nation seems to be the reason for

[185] eg European Commission Report COM(2019)12 final, sect 4, pp 9–10.
[186] ibid.

approaching millionaires willing to naturalise in the EU as criminals: wrong blood cannot be remedied by money on this purely nationalistic view of European integration in the best traditions of passport apartheid[187] and the victimisation of those receiving the worst citizenships by birth.[188] This is why in the context of the shrinking numbers of infringements as per Kelemen and Pavone[189] and the overall failure of the Commission to deliver leadership as the 'Guardian of the Treaties' even across the most crucial domains, from judicial independence and the rule of law[190] to migration governance,[191] the Commission's case against Malta and not against FRONTEX, for instance, busy humiliating and sometimes killing racialised former colonials either directly or by proxy[192] is deeply puzzling from the point of view of EU values. Be that as it may, this approach is absolutely unacceptable and the mere fact that the Commission needs to be reminded of this already sets alarm bells ringing about the state of the rule of law in the Union.

H. Misrepresentation of the Principle of Sincere Cooperation

The Commission's attack on CBI programmes including its court case against Malta makes frequent references to the principle of sincere cooperation. These are embarrassingly misplaced. The reasoning goes as follows: the grant of EU citizenship on the basis of payment or investment and without a 'genuine link' (for instance a blood link) is incompatible with the principle of sincere cooperation enshrined in Article 4(3) TEU and undermines the integrity of the status of EU citizenship provided in Article 20 TFEU.[193] This much-repeated reasoning was rehearsed in the case that the Commission brought against Malta:

> The Commission considers that the Maltese Citizenship by Naturalisation for Exceptional Services by Direct Investment scheme (2020) constitutes such an unlawful citizenship investor scheme. By establishing and maintaining such a scheme, Malta compromises and undermines the essence and integrity of Union citizenship in breach of Article 20 TFEU and in violation of the principle of sincere cooperation enshrined in Article 4(3) TEU.[194]

It remains entirely unclear how investment programmes infringe Article 4(3) TEU, especially in light of the analysis above. For now one can only wonder which Treaty duty, precisely, a Member State breaches when exercising its own competences fully in line with *Tjebbes*, *Micheletti*, *Zhu and Chen*, *JY* and all the other known EU citizenship case law. Since there is no duty to back down in the face of the Commission's propaganda and misrepresentation of the law, the Commission's argument related to sincere cooperation is very weak.[195] It is particularly unclear how precisely EU citizenship status could be undermined by investment programmes. Do, by analogy, other naturalisation modes that do not require genuine links with Member States infringe Article 4(3) TEU and Article 20 TFEU in the opinion of the

[187] Kochenov, 'Ending the Passport Apartheid'.
[188] Kochenov, 'The Victims of Citizenship'.
[189] Kelemen and Pavone, 'Where Have all the Guardians Gone?'.
[190] Scheppele, 'EU Treaties without a Guardian'.
[191] Grześkowiak, 'The "Guardian of the Treaties" Is No More?'; Ganty and Kochenov, 'EU Lawlessness Law'; Shatz, *EU Crimes against Humanity*.
[192] Shatz, *EU Crimes against Humanity*; Urbina, 'The Secretive Prisons that Keep Migrants out of Europe' (*The New Yorker*, 28 November 2021) www.newyorker.com/magazine/2021/12/06/the-secretive-libyan-prisons-that-keep-migrants-out-of-europe; Kochenov and Ganty, 'The Death Machine'.
[193] *Commission v Malta*, pending.
[194] ibid.
[195] See also Weiler's contribution to this volume.

Commission? Or is blood the only true genuine link? The Treaties are silent on all these issues. Given that the Commission has not launched any court actions in relation to a huge variety of other naturalisation modes in the Member States and has selected CBI uniquely as the test ground for attempting to increase the ambit of the Union's powers in this domain, the answer seems quite clear: the reference to sincere cooperation stands for an unlawful attempt of the Commission to usurp the liberating essence of EU citizenship as a supranational legal status by pushing it in the direction of the blood-based nationalist dream that the *Nottebohm* ICJ had in mind in the 'romantic times' of international law, to quote the mocking reference to Commission's key 'principle' by the learned AG Tesauro. Commission's version of 'sincere cooperation' thus seems to be about the enforcement of Eurowhiteness and thus unrelated to any of the values mentioned in Article 2 TEU.

Contrary to the Commission's arguments and as already clarified above, the 'genuine link' theory has not developed into obligatory rules or principles of international law, let alone in EU law, which provides instead for non-discrimination on the basis of nationality, which finds itself in direct and irreconcilable opposition to the Commission's spirited approach to blood-nationalism. Trying to impose a 'genuine link' requirement on Member States with regard to their criteria for the acquisition of citizenship would not only be incompatible with EU law, but would also almost certainly spark ethnic nationalism, undermining the values of the Union itself.[196]

Moreover, it is difficult to imagine that the principle of sincere cooperation could be successfully invoked in the context of investment migration. Article 4(3) TEU concerns the achievement of EU objectives and genuine compliance with EU law, none of which seems to be related with investment migration.[197] Furthermore, the CJEU more recently mapped out the principle of sincere cooperation as a general principle which may be invoked in infringement procedures only when there is first a violation of a more specific obligation under EU law.[198] A possible infringement of that provision could be imagined in the case of mass naturalisation which may have a significant negative impact on the internal market.[199] This is where a Member State confers its citizenship to a large, disproportionate number of third-country nationals. However, this does not seem to be the case with the investment migration programmes in EU (former and current) because the number of citizenships granted through these investment programmes remained low in general and compared to the number of other naturalisations in the EU in particular.[200]

While the European Commission has not clarified the basis for its argument in *Commission v Malta* that CBI could undermine the essence of EU citizenship, the above suggests that 'genuine links' are the essence of EU citizenship, which cannot be further from the truth. The core principle of EU law of persons is non-discrimination on the basis of nationality. It states, to put it very roughly, in simple language that any links – however 'genuine' – with a particular Member State cannot matter: only the legal status of citizenship does. This is the law the Commission is there to respect, uphold and promote. Any action of the Commission contrary to this is therefore, unquestionably *ultra vires* and absolutely unacceptable since it goes against the very rationale of the operation of EU citizenship law and essentially seeks to annul all its added value.

[196] See in greater detail Basheska, 'Why the EU's Top Court Should Clarify EU Law'. See also Interview with Kochenov, 'Commission Would Likely Be "Humiliated"'.

[197] Basheska, 'Why the EU's Top Court Should Clarify EU Law'.

[198] Case T-626/17, *Slovenia v Commission* ECLI:EU:T:2020:402; see also McGarry, '*Republic of Slovenia v. Republic of Croatia*' (2021) 115 *AJIL* 101.

[199] See eg *Bolzano/Bozen Recommendations on National Minorities in Inter-State Relations* (OSCE HCNM 2008).

[200] Basheska, 'Why the EU's Top Court Should Clarify EU Law'.

V. CONCLUSION: BY FORCING 'GENUINE LINKS' ONTO EU CITIZENSHIP, THE EUROPEAN COMMISSION PUTS THE CORE ACHIEVEMENTS OF EU INTEGRATION IN DANGER

Investment migration unquestionably underlines citizenship's absurdity,[201] by allowing those who emerged as losers in the global 'birthright lottery'[202] – members of the absolute majority of the world's population[203] – to 'buy' what others got assigned to them for free by blood, but at once also to be singled out as having uniquely undeservedly acquired this status. When the '(high) price' of citizenship for the randomly unlucky is made clear, the hypocrisy of citizenship's essence is instantly laid bare.[204] It therefore necessarily challenges the glorificatory nationalist paradigm of contemporary citizenship regulation and citizenship studies long noted by Linda Bosniak and other scholars.[205]

Investment migration is legally practised by the absolute majority of the EU's Member States. While only Malta facing the Commission in Court has an official CBI programme in the EU, over 20 other Member States allow for discretionary naturalisation for 'special achievements', including in most instances economic contribution. The differences between the Maltese CBI programme and discretionary naturalisation for economic contributions in other countries are formal rather than substantial. These differences are of principled nature, as limiting the lack of transparency and absolute discretion is at the core of the Rule of Law.[206] Yet the European Commission decided that unlike other countless co-existing types of naturalisations, investment migration programmes infringe the principle of sincere cooperation and undermine the essence of EU citizenship. This approach by the European Commission is inconsistent with the law and directly attacks the anti-nationalist *raison d'être* of the EU.

The attempts of the European Parliament and the European Commission to delegitimise investment migration programmes and interfere in a sphere of exclusive competence of Member States started with the launch of Malta's Individual Investor Programme in 2014 and have continued and intensified ever since then. The European Parliament has been constantly calling for the phasing out of the citizenship by investment programmes and has invited the European Commission to propose legislation on that matter. If a Member State wants an investment migration programme, it can have one: the division of competences as the law stands is crystal clear.

The first problematic aspect underpinning the Commission's stance is thus the lack of EU competence in citizenship matters. The EU can only interfere in cases where rights of EU citizens need to be protected from the actions of the Member States, rather than to determine the conditions for the acquisition of citizenship in EU Member States. The CJEU has been clear on the subject, clarifying in *Micheletti* that Member States may not impose conditions or check 'genuine links' for recognising the effect of citizenship of other Member States. In other words, the 'genuine links' requirement for recognition of citizenship which is applicable in certain instances under international law is strictly prohibited under EU law. The attempts of the European Commission to reverse that prohibition into an obligation for Member States to introduce this excluded 'genuine link' doctrine is self-contradictory, as well as being

[201] Kochenov, 'Citizenship for Real: Its Hypocrisy, Its Randomness, Its Price' in Bauböck (ed), *Debating Transformations of National Citizenship* (Springer 2018) 51; Spiro, 'Cash-for-Passports and the End of Citizenship', 17.

[202] Shachar, *The Birthright Lottery*.

[203] Kochenov, *Citizenship*; Kochenov and Lindeboom (eds), *Quality of Nationality Index*.

[204] Kochenov, 'Citizenship for Real', 51.

[205] Bosniak, *The Citizen and the Alien* (Princeton University Press 2006) 5–9; and further Tully, *On Global Citizenship* (Bloomsbury 2014). See also crucially Joppke's work, virtually all of which could stand as an illustration of this point.

[206] See also Veraldi and Gstrein in this volume.

discriminatory to investment migration as one of the modes of acquisition of citizenship. So is the Commission's impossible expectation that citizenship and permanent residency permits are tied to continuous long-term presence in the host Member State, besides being legally and practically untenable, is also a matter on which Member States decide.

Furthermore, the Commission's arguments that CBI programmes infringe the principle of sincere cooperation and undermine the essence of EU citizenship are not based on a single piece of evidence of any negative impact of investment programmes on the internal market. The European Commission has not clarified which specific Treaty obligation Malta, for instance, violated to infringe the principle of sincere cooperation. Infringement of the principle of sincere cooperation itself – that is, without violation of a more specific Treaty obligation – cannot be successfully invoked and Article 20 TFEU, which is often argued by the Commission in the same context as the principle of sincere cooperation, does not impose such a specific obligation on Member States.

Finally, stripping EU citizens of Russian and Belarusian origin of their EU citizenship acquired through investment may be problematic even if that is conducted for justified security reasons. EU Member States have conditions for the withdrawal of citizenship, including for security reasons, and such rules are equally applicable to naturalised citizens of all nationalities and notwithstanding their grounds for naturalisation. Applying such rules to the naturalised Russians and Belarusians specifically, including individuals not on any sanctioning lists, as apparently suggested by the European Commission, is arbitrary and discriminatory. Moreover, according to experts in the field, the deprivation of nationality of citizens on national security grounds is presumptively arbitrary and exceptions to that are very limited.

In summary, the 'war' of the European Parliament and the European Commission against investment migration programmes has not contributed to the development of EU law in any useful way. It has rather brought confusion and uncertainty to otherwise well-established concepts in EU law, to say nothing of its direct confrontation with EU values[207] by flirting with the ethno-nationalists out there, whose project of Eurowhiteness Europe is something different from what the Treaties intended. The institutions' behaviour so far thus degrades the rationale for the Union, and undermines the promise of an anti-nationalist EU citizenship based on rights in the process.

[207] Klamert and Kochenov, 'Article 2 TEU' in Kellerbauer et al (eds), *The Treaties and the Charter of Fundamental Rights – A Commentary* 2nd edn (Oxford University Press 2024); Spieker, *EU Values before the Court of Justice* (Oxford University Press 2023); Wouters, 'Revisiting Art. 2 TEU' (2020) 5 *European Papers* 255.

Postscriptum

Commission v Malta *(Citizenship for Sale)* Who of the Two is Selling European Values?

JHH WEILER

I.

SO, MALTA OFFERS passports for sale. *Quelle Horreur*! I hear you sniffing with disgust and indignation. They sell their citizenship, and hoopla – automatically these new citizens, *ipso facto* and *ipso jure* are European Citizens enjoying all the rights and duties which attach to such.

And you are probably thinking: 'Three Cheers' to the Commission for prosecuting Malta before the CJEU and hoping that the Court will bring this aberrational practice to an end.

So, it's time to think again. No, I am not about to defend the Maltese Passport for Sale scheme. In this piece I take no position on the rights and wrongs of Golden Passports and Golden Residence. My interest is different. Below the surface of the Commission case lurk far more important issues besides which the Maltese aberration pales into insignificance.

So now, suspend your disbelief, fasten your seatbelts, and patiently read through my text. Then, make up your mind.

II.

Malta is not unique in offering Golden Passports (Investment Citizenship). But the club of similar states is not large and not particularly edifying, comprising such world powers as Granada, St Kitts and Nevis, but also Turkey – even more reason to turn our noses up.

But if we turn to Golden Visa programmes (Investor Residence) the list is much larger and more respectable: According to a 2019 Commission Report,[1] which set the whole saga in motion (hereinafter the Report), no less than 20 Member States have such schemes, where the investment threshold may be as low as 100,000 Euro. In this case, the global club, too, is far more respectable including, inter alia, the United Kingdom, the United States, Canada, Australia and New Zealand.

[1] European Commission, 'Report from the Commission to The European Parliament, The Council, The European Economic and Social Committee and The Committee of The Regions Investor: Citizenship and Residence Schemes in the European Union' COM(2019)12 final.

It is not the same, I hear my readers saying. No, it is not the same. But as a matter of functional interest to fellow Member States, rather than the emotive gut reaction to the notion of 'citizenship for sale', the differences are wafer thin.

Don't take my word for it. Download the Commission Report and see for yourself. It is a sober report, the result of a specific study[2] exploring the policy concerns resulting from the practice of Golden Passports and Golden Visas. As you will shortly see, the Report is interesting and revealing for both what is in it, and what is left out.

Most notable, already in the introduction to the Report the point is made:

> Investor citizenship schemes [Golden Passport] differ from investor residence ('golden visa') schemes … However, the risks inherent to such schemes are similar to those raised by investor citizenship schemes.

And one may add that Golden Visas are often times a prelude to, at times FastTrack, naturalisation and citizenship.

What are these risks? The Commission lists four such risks which result equally from both Golden Passport and Golden Visa schemes:

> Security – concluding that '… [i]t is therefore important that any investor citizenship and residence schemes are organized in such a way as to prevent such security risks'.
>
> Money Laundering – here, too, the Commission concludes that 'Member States should also take into account the potential risks of money laundering linked to investor citizenship and residence schemes in their national risk assessments carried out according to the EU anti-money laundering rules and take the necessary mitigating measures'.
>
> Circumvention of EU rules – notably where licensing requirements include a nationality requirement
>
> Tax Evasion – also linking the risks from both schemes.

These are real and serious concerns, well documented (except for tax) in the Report and its underlying study. I characterised the Report as 'sober' since, with one exception (which I will discuss below), it is bereft from emotive rhetoric and is focused on the real tangible risks that result from both types of schemes. An objective reader of the Report would easily conclude that

> Quantitatively speaking, the major risk surely would emerge from the 20 Member States operating Golden Visa schemes rather than the single Member State which operates a Golden Passport scheme.

The way to tackle these real risks would be to put in place, either under Union law or under mutually agreed Member State law and policy, specific provisions, which the Report suggests, to deal with these risks.

And if these measures – such as securing adequate security and fiscal checks before granting either residence or citizenship – were effective for Golden Visas they would be equally effective for Golden passports. The current new EU migration law which is making its way through the appropriate process is a good example of that. It provides inter alia for agreed security checks which, for example, could in principle be applied also to Golden Visa and Golden passport migrants.

And yet, when one tracks the follow-up (from publicly available Commission Press Releases[3]) resulting in the case against Malta, one notes with some astonishment that practically all references to the various risks mentioned in the Report have disappeared.

[2] ibid, fn 4.
[3] I have no access to the official case documents.

Constitutionally this is important. Because it is the practical consequences of these schemes which bring certain aspects of Golden Passports and Golden Visas into the sphere of application of Union Law.

In the Commission Press Release accompanying the decision to send a Reasoned Opinion to Malta, a first step for bringing the case, there is a change of tonal register: The case against Malta is now framed as follows:

> European Values are Not for Sale [emphasis in the original] which is the title under which the Reasoned Opinion is explained in the Press Release.

One can regard this as a mere rhetorical device designed to whip up public support for the prospective law suit. But given the disappearance of practically all the functional considerations elaborated in the Report, and the single focus on Golden Passports to the exclusion of Golden Visas which raise similar risks and, quantitatively, would appear to be far more serious, one might suspect a much more profound agenda lurking below the surface. One smells a rat.

To put it bluntly, it appears (to me) as I shall argue below that this is but

a. a crass attempt by the Commission to circumvent proper constitutional and decisional procedures required under the Treaties; and
b. a no less crass attempt redefine European citizenship and its relationship to national citizenship,

in the hope that the CJEU will become complicit in these attempts.

III.

The logic of the Single Market is unassailable when it comes to goods. Once they enter the Union, they enjoy free circulation among all Member States. Consequently regimes such as the Common External Tariff are in place. Given free circulation of goods, the Member States are subject, albeit not perfectly, to a common set of disciplines.

In principle, the same single market logic should apply to persons (as 'factors of production') when it comes to citizenship and permanent and long-term residence entries. Accordingly, the conclusion would be easy enough. It would surely be an (ever) 'closer Union' if the Union had for example a Common Migration Policy, common rules for the granting of citizenship and residence, and the like.

And yet, like it or not, the Member States in successive Treaty revision have refrained from going 'all in' in this direction. And why so? Humans are not merely or even principally factors of production which underly the single market philosophy. And the question of granting nationality and long-term residence involves profound social, political, economic, moral and identitarian issues, issues in relation to which the Member States may understandably and legitimately hold very distinct views and consequently want to reserve these decisions to themselves or, at a minimum, seek to reach a deliberative European wide consensus in accordance with established decisional procedures.

But, in the same Press Release of 29 September 2022 we find, too, the following:

> EU citizenship and the rights it confers lie at the heart of the EU.

Maybe it would be a bit more forthcoming to acknowledge that national citizenship lies, too, at the heart of Member State identity and in this way demonstrate cognisance that one is dealing here with the fundamental tension concerning the delicate balance between Unity and

Diversity. Given this tension of fundamentals (this is not, after all, about conflicting customs valuations), extra caution is required as regards, yes, the values of our Europe and the procedures which are designed to protect these values.

Here is a striking example which illustrates the non-'factor of production' sensitivity as regards who would be invited to live with us, whether as citizens or residents.

In a previous piece I heaped praise on Germany and the formidable Ms Merkel, for saving the honour of Europe in the face of the humanitarian crisis resulting from the intra-Syrian conflict. Germany admitted around one million refugees. Not all Member States were happy (some, I imagine, were happy that it was Germany and not themselves). Not everyone within Germany was happy either.

All these new legal residents would immediately enjoy Schengen rights and progressively enjoy all rights under Union law as explained in the Commission Report. They would all present the very risks which the Commission outlines. By comparison, the Maltese scheme is numerically trivial. It is certain that if the German move were to be governed by the Union, it would not have happened. And yet for Germany, this was a profound identitarian issue, part of its self-understanding as a post-World War II democratic republic. It was a policy which put, at least in some ways, values above direct utilitarian considerations.

So how about *Commission v Germany*? One might not be happy with the structural architectural anomaly outlined above. As a 'dyed-in-the-wool' Europhile I would favour a common EU migration policy; I would equally favour a mutually agreed harmonisation of the conditions for granting national citizenship and long-term residence. The structural anomaly I highlighted above is in many ways untenable in the long run. And my rationale is not just a Single Market one. *Nous ne coalisons pas des États, nous unissons des hommes* is a telos not driven by market considerations.

But I am an equally 'dyed-in-the-wool' believer in respecting correct constitutional procedures when translating desirable outcomes to binding Union law. And this is not driven solely by mechanical 'Rule of Law' considerations: The Law is the Law is the Law. It is driven, too, by consideration of the current circumstance of our Union and by my long-held belief that in 'healthy' federal type polities (of which the Union is one) respecting 'fundamental jurisdictional boundaries' and decisional procedures, even if they are 'inconvenient', is as important as respecting fundamental human rights.[4] Undoubtedly the new Migration Law (to come into effect, once it clears the final stages of the process, in 2026) is an example of how these issues should be dealt with.

I use this comparison of jurisdictional and procedural limits to human rights with a particular purpose in mind. We are all in favour of human rights, are we not? But the real test of commitment to human rights, say freedom of expression, is not when we are outraged and protest against the curtailment of expressions with which we agree. The test of our commitment is when we strongly disagree or even hate the expression in question, but defend the right in question.

This is particularly true in the case of fundamental boundaries and procedures in a system of attributed and delegated powers such as the Union. It is also true when the decisional procedures are not to our liking especially when they require unanimity. We might ardently favour this or that policy, but respecting fundamental boundaries and fundamental procedural guarantees must discipline us not to yield to the temptation of achieving such in a manner which

[4] Weiler, 'Fundamental Rights and Fundamental Boundaries: On Standards and Values in the Protection of Human Rights' in Neuwahl and Rosas (eds), *The European Union and Human Rights* (Brill–Nijhoff 1995).

does not respect correct procedures and a solid legal basis. If we allow the end to justify the means, we may win the short-term battle but lose the long-term war and make a mockery of our solemn commitment to our civic Holy Trinity – democracy, human rights and the rule of law.

One must resist the functional institutional ethos, still detectable often times in Commission practice, when a policy desideratum is articulated and then the Legal Service is charged with finding a way of achieving such – 'if there is a political will, there will also be a legal way'.

In my view, odious as one may (or may not) find the idea of 'selling citizenship', the case against Malta is, as mentioned above, an egregious exercise of jurisdictional creep and circumvention of constitutionally correct procedures. And the Commission is hoping that the Court will become complicit in such. I find selling these constitutional values no less odious than selling citizenship. And I should add that it is a perverse notion to consider this position as 'Euroscepticism'.

It is also reasonably clear (more of this below) why the functional considerations (security and all the rest) disappeared. For if these concerns were the true motivation behind the case, the correct route would be to put in place a variety of procedural safeguards rooted in appropriate decisional procedures. And that this would apply both to Golden Passports and Golden Visas which, as the Commission Report explicates, pose similar risks and quantitatively are more serious.

IV.

The key to the case can be found in one anomalous section buried in the Report. I say anomalous since it is the one section that on careful reading departs from the sober functional tenor of the rest. It is worth reading with care.

Section 2.4 of the Report on Investor Citizenship Schemes and EU Law, commences thus:

> In line with the Treaties, every person who becomes a national of a Member State shall be a citizen of the Union. Citizenship of the Union is destined to be the fundamental status of nationals of the Member States.

The logic of this statement seems to be the following: If we have a tension, or even a conflict between Member State constitutional prerogatives when it comes to the issue of nationality and citizenship and European Union citizenship prerogatives, since, 'in line with the Treaties' 'citizenship of the Union is destined to be the fundamental status of nationals of the Member States' the European interest should prevail over Member State prerogatives.

And, relying in the Report on what I consider a tendentious reading of *Nottebohm*,[5] granting naturalisation without a genuine link to the country in question, (assuming that is what the Malta scheme allows) constitutes, in and of itself, a violation of the Treaties – the constitution of Europe.[6]

Yes, except no.

'*In line with the Treaties*' the Commission statement begins. Given the solemnity and gravity of the statement (our destiny, no less!) the innocent reader would be forgiven if he or she thought that 'citizenship of the Union is destined to be the fundamental status of nationals

[5] But this is for a separate post.

[6] It would, of course, be up to the Commission and the Court (if it follows the Commission) to decide what is a genuine link rather than to the Member States.

of the Member States' is actually to be found in the Treaties as the Commission statement implies. It is not.

This formula must count as one of the most unfortunate *dicta* of the Court starting with *Grzelczyk*[7] and followed in all other citizenship cases.[8] No matter how often it has been repeated, this does not give it any epistemic credibility. Only in the Orwellian 1984 universe does repeating an untruth 50 times make it true. The Court never explained how it reached that conclusion. In fact it was and remains pure judicial invention arising *ex nihilo*.

As a matter of text, legislative history and Telos of the integration project the best one can say is that it is an untenable reading of the Treaties.

Text: Although the Commission, citing Article 20(1) says '[i]n line with the Treaties', it conveniently, or dishonestly (take your pick) left out the second sentence of Article 20(1) TFEU.

> Citizenship of the Union shall be additional to and not replace national citizenship.

To put it mildly, this gives the clause a somewhat different flavour to the way the Commission would have us believe, and, to my reading, contradicts the 'fundamental status' rhetoric.

Legislative history: Destined by whom? Certainly not by the Member States who drafted the citizenship clause in the Treaties. In fact, their intention would appear to be quite the opposite. In the original Maastricht Treaty one simply found: 'Every person holding the nationality of a Member State shall be a citizen of the Union.' The Member States were clearly unhappy with this formulation and in Amsterdam and Nice introduced a significant amendment: Citizenship of the Union shall complement and not replace national citizenship.

And, as seen, Article 20 of the TFEU finally settled on Union citizenship being additional. The introduction of these limiting clauses amending the original Maastricht formulation surely points towards a restrictive rather than expansive reading of the clause. Could you imagine the famous 'destined to be the fundamental status' formula being approved by the IGC if anyone dared put it on the table?

So, if you cannot get what you want written into the Treaties, you just pretend it is Treaty law?

If anything, this history indicates, that a respectable hermeneutic reading would suggest that *national citizenship* is destined to remain the fundamental status of nationals of the Union.

Telos: The idea that European citizenship should become the fundamental status is a European version of the American telos – *e pluribus unum* – and harks back to those who dreamt and some who still dream of a United States of Europe. The originality of the European construct, its distinctive character and genius are reflected in the rejection of that telos and its replacement with the Ever Closer Union among the *Peoples* of Europe. Peoples, not destined to be one people. This is a much more original, albeit challenging telos. Granting European citizenship (with its rather limited set of rights enumerated in the clause, some of which predated the citizenship clause) is welcome so long as one does not disturb the delicate balance between the two without clear Member State authority.

Given the above, a correct and hermeneutically respectable approach would be one which gave a restrictive rather than expansive reading of the Citizenship clause in the Treaties. Uncomfortable for some, but on occasion the law is uncomfortable.

[7] Case C-184/99 *Grzelczyk* ECLI:EU:C:2001:458.

[8] I say *dictum* because it was not actually strictly needed to decide the cases. Formally, I would argue, it retains its status as an *obiter dictum*.

The Commission goes further. On the shaky legal basis of the tendentiously cited Article 20 it shores up its case by reference to Article 4(3) TEU, the principle of Sincere Cooperation. This is truly scraping the bottom of the legal barrel. Here, too, conveniently the Commission fails to mention the clause of Article 4TEU which precedes 4.3:

> 4.2. The Union shall respect the equality of Member States before the Treaties as well as their national identities, inherent in their fundamental structures, political and constitutional, inclusive of regional and local self-government. It shall respect their essential State functions, including ensuring the territorial integrity of the State, maintaining law and order and safeguarding national security. In particular, national security remains the sole responsibility of each Member State.
>
> 4.3. Pursuant to the principle of sincere cooperation, the Union and the Member States shall, in full mutual respect, assist each other in carrying out tasks which flow from the Treaties.

Surely Article 4.3 should be read in the light of Article 4.2. As mentioned, the Commission, this time with integrity, mentioned as its first concern with the Golden Passports and Visas, the issue of security. No wonder it disappeared between the Report and the Case, seeing that the Treaty is so emphatic regarding the sole responsibility for security.

Compare the language of 4.2 with its reference to national identities, fundamental structures – political and constitutional –with the language of 4.3 which speaks of the Member States *assisting* the Union and each other, in full mutual respect in carrying out tasks which flow from the Treaty. The Commission, it may be worth reminding some European mandarins, is not synonymous with 'the Union'. *Res Ipsa Loquitur*.

Not only, it would seem, is the Commission, in setting down itself norms for the grant of nationality by Member States using Article 4.3 as a way to circumvent appropriate decisional procedures, but they are at the same time perverting what I would regard as the true meaning of Article 4.3 itself.

Make no mistake. There is every reason for the Union to be concerned with the various dangers which the Report spells out and which result from the underlying structural anomaly in the constitutional architecture mentioned above. But the only way correctly to address the consequences of this anomaly if not by Treaty amendment, would be through appropriate Union legislative and administrative procedures or by a procedure properly agreed among the Member States in the spirit of sincere cooperation ex Article 4.3.

This is not the case here and the Court should not be invited to act as if it were. If Article 4.3 is interpreted in the way the Commission is arguing in this case, it would give them a Golden Visa to avoid the values enshrined in constitutional procedures and achieve results through judicial fiat in endless areas of Union action.

V.

It is also worth considering with a little bit more depth the issue of 'genuine connection'. This is not to deny that these issues could potentially be a matter of concern and even a common European norm. But they are far more complex than meets the eye and should not be resolved by a simplistic categorical black and white rule as the Commission invites the Court to do.

First if you care to take a look, many of our Member States have provisions for granting nationality for example to distinguished artists, or footballers (!), which are quite lax on genuine connection, something barely mentioned in the Report. Why complicate the dossier? In the case of sport it is oftentimes investment residence or nationality by a different name.

One might perhaps dismiss these instances as *de minims*. So consider then the tens of thousands, if not hundreds of thousands of Union nationals who have migrated and have made their life in other countries – Canada, Australia, the United States and elsewhere. There are, thus, a very large number of sons and daughters born in those countries who by virtue of the prevalent *jus sanguinis* provisions in most constitutions, are nationals of Member States. Sometimes the original Member State has quite liberal nationality rules which might go even beyond sons and daughters. A country like Ireland, and there are more, legitimately values this important understanding of itself. And yet, these sons and daughters or grandsons and granddaughters, or great grandsons and granddaughters, have automatically all the rights mentioned in the Report and the Reasoned Opinion (and pose the same risks) even if they have never set foot in the territory of the Union and do not speak its language of their European nationality. Not convinced? Reread the *Collins* case, a sharp reminder of such.[9] By no sense of imagination can one consider the Collins' of the world as having a 'genuine connection' in the sense outlined in the Report to the nation of their ancestors.

Our gut reaction is, correctly perhaps, that it's not quite the same. It is not. But from the perspective of the policy concerns (security, money laundering, etc) it is not all that different. And, after all, it is the functional dimension which would be the justification for the Union to interfere in a domain traditionally reserved to the Member States. So, *Commission v Ireland* next? Or *Commission v Germany* (with its nationality rules concerning historical minorities)?

And here is another issue. Imagine the Court sides with the Commission. How is Malta to comply. Is one year of residence enough to establish a genuine link? Two years? Three years? And what does residence mean: at least 180 days of presence? Maybe more? Maybe less? The tax practice and citizenship practice of the Member States differ in this respect. So who is to guide Malta in the absence of controlling European legislation approved by correct decisional procedures? Even more power to the Commission?

Don't read more into these two examples than I am trying to argue. I am simply saying that the issues are complex and involve a wide range of details which would require serious deliberation and should not be whitewashed by a judicial procedure which avoids all these complexities. It is not for the Commission on its own to address these complexities and, respectfully, neither is it for the Court. If there are to be Union norms setting out conditions for granting citizenship or residence, these delicate political issues should be thrashed out and decided by the appropriate democratic political procedures inconvenient as this might be.

VI.

So, what's behind this Commission gambit? One can only speculate. Here then are some speculations.

We tend to speak of 'The Commission', 'The Court', 'The Parliament', etc. We reify these institutions and forget that they are made of humans, flesh and blood, like you and me, with all the virtues and vices that come with the human condition.[10] Once we de-reify them, the explanation might come down to personal pride, to embarrassment at the failure to have any meaningful action plan to deal with the real problem resulting from the structural anomaly or,

[9] Case C-132/02 *Colins v Secretary of State for Work and Pensions* ECLI:EU:C:2003:409.

[10] Eppink, *Life of a European Mandarin: Inside the Commission* (Lannoo Publishers 2008) is worth reading in this context.

perhaps, frustration with the 10-year process of the Migration Law? All forgivable sins but not a licence for such a constitutional grab.

But there might be more to it. In its September 22 decision to refer Malta to the Court we find in the Press Release the following enigmatic statement. On the one hand they write (referring to Golden Passports):

> These schemes are different from investor residence schemes (or 'golden visas') …

But the Press Release *immediately* adds:

> Both types of schemes pose serious risks, in particular as regards security, money laundering, tax evasion and corruption.

So why pick just on Malta and not go after the 20 or so Member States, where quantitatively, the real serious risks lie? Well, taking on 20 Member States which have different versions of Golden Visas posing such risks is a tad more difficult than taking on Super Power Malta.

There is also an issue of proportionality. If the Commission concern was truly with the four risks, would it not be sufficient, for example, to subject Golden Visa and Golden Passport recipients to the same kind of checks which, under the new Migration Law, are provided for other forms of migration? Would this more restrictive approach not be more respectful of the appropriately narrow interpretation of the Treaty in this constitutionally sensitive area? Do what is strictly necessary to deal with the functional problems and no more?

Taking the appropriate legislative route, with its institutional and democratic safeguards is not easy. It would probably involve Article 308 with its unanimity requirement and possibly an agreement of the Member States outside the framework of the Treaties as has happened in other instances. That's daunting and the Commission is less likely to get all it wants. The new Migration law has been 10 years in the making. Would it not be wonderful, then, if one could get a ruling from the Court that would blow open Article 4.3 TEU and thus allow the Commission to impose its views of what is acceptable and non-acceptable without the headache of Article 352 and all the rest? If one wanted to stretch the meaning of Article 4.3 one could not have chosen a better case because of the emotive appeal which is no more about the various real risks but about 'European Values are not for sale'.

The Commission officials should put back on the shelf their copy of Plato's *Republic*. Constitutional democracy is not about philosopher kings who know best what is good for us. Constitutional democracy is never easy, it requires patience, it requires compromises but it, too, 'lies at the heart of the EU'.

We are all aware that the issue of jurisdictional limits and appropriate procedures – intra vires-ultra vires – has become a lightning rod in the current socio-political circumstance of the Union and quite a few national jurisdictions have been sending signals of such in recent years. I suspect it is too late for the Commission to withdraw from this gambit. In fact I expect they will dig in. But here is a golden opportunity for the Court, in a high visibility case, to assert its authority, and to be seen as asserting such authority, as an effective guardian of the profound values inherent in jurisdictional limits and constitutional procedures.

Divertissement

Investment Citizenship
A Berlaymont Fantasia

SHAH GUIDO

INDULGE ME IF you will, in a fantasy. Imagine a meeting room in the Berlaymont, the triangular sprocket around which the European Commission revolves. Not at the top floor, mind you: this is not a tale of high politics and statecraft. Quite the opposite. This is a tale of low politics and craftlessness.

Ranged round a large table, made of a rare and costly wood strongly reminiscent of formica, are a conspiracy of officials, policy officers, lawyers and the servants of Commissioners, and they are discussing the notion of citizenship, and particularly its sale by Member States of the EU. Scratch that again – conspiracy is too grand a collective noun, redolent as it is of crows and clandestine organisation and malice aforethought. This is a conmisery, a group of anxious, diligent, unimaginative and wholly unwilling bureaucrats, thrust into the role of pioneers and creators; not conspiring together, but desperately trying to escape their part in a shared calamity. Their masters had made grand promises to media-friendly personalities to achieve a thing, and these wretched executive functionaries, at first too optimistic to reflect too deeply on the promises being made, and later too timid to challenge and reverse their masters' incautious language, were now glumly bound to execute an impossible task.

And what a task. The froth of Brussels-based civil society within which Commissioners and Parliamentarians swim had noticed and taken exception to the idea that the intended fundamental status of the nationals of EU Member States was being hawked to all comers for mere huge sums of money. Worse still, this EU citizenship status was being used as an inducement for the purchase of some otherwise truly third-rate nationalities – rich foreigners were being lured not to become Belgian or French, but Cypriot and Maltese. Something had to be done to stop this misuse of money, this insult to every natural born Dutchman and Italian, and to every long-suffering former colonial who had had to endure a proper, full-blooded non-pecuniary naturalisation by ordeal. It was crass, it was an outrage, but it was also an impossible bind, as the lowliest of the functionaries was trying to explain. She explained, glumly,

> The problem we have stems from the fact that the Treaties are quite explicit about our role in the question of Member State citizenships, and it is sadly misaligned to the expectation already created among our stakeholders that we could, at the European level, prevent Member State citizenships from being granted.

A half-dozen pairs of blank eyes followed her. Simplify.

'We don't have the power to stop Member States granting national citizenships. We are not allowed to review their administrative decisions in this area.' 'A decision to grant national citizenship confers EU citizenship', interjected a more senior and therefore (and only therefore) more certain voice, 'surely that means something?' 'Well, that seems to be very much the core of the problem we face', resumed the first voice.

> Member State naturalisation decisions are being exploited to obtain EU citizenship, which happens to be the only way that EU citizenship can be obtained. But the decisions are exclusively national, even if they have a European effect. The courts have been quite clear – it is for each Member State to lay down the conditions for the acquisition and loss of nationality, though they must do so having due regard to Union law.

Our hapless functionary trailed off, realising her mistake. Introducing a little information into an information-starved room so full of desperate straining for a straw to grasp was fraught with risk. A hiding to nowhere.

The straw was grasped as the senior voice returned, triumphantly.

> Then we have a hook! Due regard to EU law must surely mean taking into account all rules forming part of the Union legal order. It means making sure that administration of nationality does is not opened to abuse or criminality. It means awarding Member State citizenship in such as way as to ensure that the benefits of EU citizenship are not obtained and exploited by individuals who have no business to enjoy them. It means above all preventing a situation where Member States examine each others' naturalisation decisions with mistrust and challenge the possibility that EU citizenship should be obtained in this way. You can build a case on that.

The owner of the senior voice glared defiantly at his subordinate, daring her to speak. She weighed her options briefly – speak up now and be damned directly, or let this run its course and be damned later. Ever the able bureaucrat, she instinctively deferred to hierarchy, but her conscience insisted that she provide at least a minimum of advice. For honour – and to spread the blame.

She would not disagree that the Court's intention was to recall that when naturalising new citizens, the Member States would be expected to act lawfully. Of course this would mean that they should refrain from violating EU law, and indeed any other relevant international law and standards. The recognition that the Member States were exclusively entitled to make new citizens in the Union did not mean that they could for instance impose naturalisation on an individual without consent, or naturalise a person but attempt to withhold the status of citizenship of the Union. This imperative to act lawfully does not automatically or generally enable the Union authorities to intervene, however. It is the responsibility of the national courts to make sure that their authorities comply with national law and their constitutional and international obligations, and these national courts will only, if at times unwittingly, be transformed into Union courts if their examination concerns a matter of Union law.

But when examining naturalisation decisions from this perspective we must understand the distinction the Court made between the conditions which permit one to cross the liminal space between the planes of national and European competence, a distinction almost spiritual in nature. Since a national naturalisation decision is not an act of EU law but one which has EU law consequences, defects affecting it must concern the Union plane to attract a Union response. In other words it would not be enough or even relevant for naturalisation decisions to be bad in their own terms – they would have to disrupt Union rights.

'If its Union planes that we are talking about, then we have a grievance right there', a new voice intervened.

> Only airlines owned by Union citizens may benefit from the Union's internal aviation market. Let's not mince words here – if a Russian naturalised for money in Malta owned an airline, that rule would

> be circumvented as the airline would be naturalised along with the person. We have anticircumvention clauses to prevent artificial company structures being used to avoid such rules, surely we can do something similar for natural persons.

Our fonctionnaire stared at this new speaker in wonder. Another senior voice. Her team was nowhere to be seen, and her mind was regressing into her student days as it tried to dig her way out of a hole.

> That is a very pertinent intervention, and we will certainly analyse that further. So that I am sure we are all on the same page: we would be arguing that a Russian – no, a third country national – who owned an airline and who became Maltese by paying for it would by virtue of this also render his airline Maltese, and this would render the naturalisation decision problematic because it would have the effect of allowing an airline unfairly to benefit from the internal market and thus circumvent the applicable nationality requirements, though not actually circumvent them because the owner of this airline would in fact be a national of a Member State?

'In fact a national, but by misbegotten means.'

> That is a very interesting view, which among other things highlights to me that I may not have made myself sufficiently clear. To intervene in a naturalisation decision, when we look at the EU law impact, it is not sufficient to identify that it has an EU law effect. Every naturalisation will have an EU law effect, because it creates an EU citizen who will be able move and reside freely within the Union, own an airline or even vote in the European parliamentary elections in the state of residence. While helpful, our argument might be stronger if we could identify a violation of EU law.
>
> But it is a violation of the law. You become an EU citizen by paying for it. That's not normal. That's not the way people become EU citizens. It's a circumvention of the rules and it cannot be trusted. You cannot trust that a person who bought his passport is as much a citizen as you or me. How can payment give you the right to own a European airline or vote?

She reflected for a moment. Payment was not an unusual way to acquire an airline, and a Russian – no, third country national – who wanted to bring his airline into the internal market could just as easily establish it here, but these were not reflections that were going to save her in the immediate present, as a murmuration of support picked up within the room. She tacked to the right in the hope of escaping from this spiral.

The question of trust is a potentially important element in this discussion. There is precedent for the Court to allow the review of national decisions with an EU law dimension from the perspective of whether they may be trusted. It is important to be clear that this has not typically extended to allowing a decision to be reviewed individually on the basis of the national rules and principles it must comply with; rather, it has enabled a principled assessment of the jurisdiction within which the decision is taken on the basis of EU law principles, including sincere cooperation. Since the decision to allocate a nationality also allocates Union citizenship – a task which flows from the Treaties – it is one in which Member States must assist each other in full mutual respect and trust. Bear in mind, however, that while sincere cooperation has been used to allow some review of national decision-making, the principle effect of this principle is to oblige Member States to trust each other – the idea behind sincere cooperation is to prevent the instrumentalisation of suspicion, not to formalise its use.

To argue by analogy to cases where sincere cooperation was applied, for instance where the Court approved the refusal to execute a European arrest warrant, the Court did not allow the national courts considering the warrant to examine whether there was a problem with the jurisdiction of the issuing courts as a matter of national law, but it was open to their finding on the basis of a deep and substantiated examination of the constitution and functioning of the courts in question and their ability to take decisions independently that there was such a systemic and generalised deficiency in the judicial system of the Member State in question that their decisions could not be fully trusted. It further explained that these defects in the national system must mean a violation of EU law or the infringement of a fundamental right enshrined in EU law. In other words, sincere cooperation first obliges Member States to honour each others' naturalisation decisions, and only where they are taken within a system or by bodies which would systematically violate other EU law, may elements of this rule be relied on to achieve the opposite outcome.

This is all well and good, but to return to the question to hand, what fundamental right or other EU law is being systematically violated here? Misinterpreting the silence for rapt adulation, she had perhaps been a touch too robust.

The second senior voice returned impatiently.

> Showing a systematic violation of EU law is simple enough. In fact it is precisely what brought us together today. These non-nationals who are buying EU passports are investing in the Union. Now, they may be investing in a Member State for legitimate reasons, but may also be pursuing illegitimate ends, such as evading law enforcement investigation and prosecution in their home country and protecting their assets from the related freezing and confiscation measures. These dangerous nationality schemes create a range of risks for Member States and for the Union as a whole: in particular, risks to security, including the possibility of infiltration of non-EU organised crime groups, as well as risks of money laundering, corruption and tax evasion. It is precisely for the protections and rights linked to EU citizenship and the ability that it gives them to break and circumvent the law that these … no, third country nationals, come here to buy an EU nationality in the first place.

They were spiralling inexorably back to votes and airlines. She tried to recover. 'These criminal and security risks are important and should of course be investigated', she replied.

> But we cannot build a position on suspicions alone: we need to show that selling a person a passport is specifically problematic. We need to show, for instance, that the way these passports are granted allows our money-laundering laws to be avoided in ways that they are not when a person naturalises by other means – for instance by having avoided personal checks that are normally applied. But is this the case? We do not know. Simply put, we would need to have some substantiated reasons for the belief that naturalisation for money is specifically differently bad compared to other naturalisations.

'Well if that is the task', said the first senior voice,

> I would have to say that in the first place, it is very much one for you and your service to uncover this systematic violation of EU law wherever it might be found, whether in the market rights, fundamental rights or something else whatever that might be, because it is clear to all of us here that there is one, and it merely matter of putting in the work to make sure that the analysis is performed adequately and in time so that the details can be filled in.

He looked meaningfully as his servant, who shrank. But he continued, in a display of magnanimity.

> If you asked me, the best place to start would be to examine and map how these decisions are normally taken, and to identify how these golden passports meaningfully depart from the norm and from recognised international standards. For instance, if I recall correctly, for nationality acquired through naturalisation to be recognised in the international arena, it should be granted on the basis of a genuine connection between the individual and the State in question. Each Member State needs to ensure that nationality is not awarded absent any genuine link to the country or its citizens. A genuine connection should come from work, from cultural awareness, from speaking the language and living among a country's people. It seems obvious that there can be no genuine connection when you only pay for a passport. As in love, so is it in nationality.

The group smirked and our fonctionnaire blushed. She reflected on genuine links and the origins of the idea in nationality lore: a judgment of the International Court of Justice which provided a means for one country to decide to ignore a documented nationality granted by another if it decided that it had not been obtained with sufficient personal commitment. You could call it an obligation for voluntary naturalisation by the Stanislavski system, on pain of being reverted to whatever other nationality you might have, or nothing in those not uncommon situations where your alternatives had been snatched away, not least as a punishment for having obtained a new nationality. It had some appeal from the perspective of dumb common sense, but on closer examination as a standard for evaluating whether there are systematic and generalised violations of EU rights in a national naturalisation law, it was neither relevant nor safe. The problem, as always, was with the detail. It is easy to say that a genuine connection with a place should be shown in order to obtain its nationality, but how is that to be done in practice for individuals who are by definition not from the place they wish to obtain the nationality of?[1] How do you show that a person is genuinely connected to concepts that defy definition, beyond trivial generalities (proper English people instinctively enjoy a good queue) or characteristics which require endless exceptions? Which signifiers should you use – language skills (are all French speakers entitled to be French? Should a person seeking to remain in Catalonia speak Castilian to prove her attachment to place?), possession of a grandmother from the place in question, awareness of and affection for national quirks such as royal families or culinary preferences, knowledge of specific bureaucratically established milestones in national history and art? Reducing a nationality to an essence solid enough for a stranger to prove a genuine connection with reveals the absence of such an irreducible substance – it all boils away with the liquid. And then, even if we were to cheat and establish some arbitrary set of acceptable links that Member States should use, which set would hold up within a community as diverse in its nationalities and the means by which they are obtained and denied as the Union? On what basis would we ground genuine connection which would accommodate also the diasporas of Ireland, Italy and Greece, the Russian Germans, the penitent approach to Spanish and Portuguese Jews? And would that system survive being tested against the Baltic Russophones, the Roma and Sinti? Would we even want to establish such a set, at the same time as a few million Britons, blissfully unaware of anything about their countries of residence, hurried to obtain new passports before the Brexit trap snapped shut.

Our fonctionnaire opened her mouth, and closed it. She sighed. 'Thank you. It is clear that more work is needed. We must map, and we must analyse. As you say, there is clearly a way forward here, and we must do our homework to find it.' She looked at her feet and felt the eyes of her team boring into her back with sincere and well-earned amazement.

A third and most senior voice spread its rhetorical arms around the room.

> I must thank you all for this rich and very useful debate. I believe that we have found our way forward and I must thank colleagues for their invaluable input. I trust that you have been taking notes, as we will publish the Commission's position as the new season begins, condemning this practice for the reasons you have all described. I trust the relevant services to take this work forward, and to allow us to move to the next point on the agenda.

The fantasy took flight.

[1] Though even this simple thing is not a consistent fact, as the people born in countries which do not grant automatically provide resident births with nationality discover.

Index

NB–page locators in **bold** indicate information in tables and those in *italics* indicate information in figures

www.ingramcontent.com/pod-product-compliance
Ingram Content Group UK Ltd.
Pitfield, Milton Keynes, MK11 3LW, UK
UKHW051029041026
15470UKWH00016B/1815

9 781509 955220